IN SEARCH OF REVOLUTION

D0146100

In Search of Revolution
International Communist Parties
in the Third Period

Edited by

MATTHEW WORLEY

I.B. TAURIS
LONDON · NEW YORK

Published in 2004 by I.B. Tauris & Co Ltd
6 Salem Road, London W2 4BU
175 Fifth Avenue, New York NY 10010
www.ibtauris.com

In the United States of America and in Canada distributed by Palgrave Macmillan,
a division of St Martins Press, 175 Fifth Avenue, New York NY 10010

ISBN 1 85043 407 7

A full CIP record for this book is available from the British Library
A full CIP record for this book is available from the Library of Congress

Library of Congress catalog card: available

Printed and bound in Great Britain by MPG Books Ltd, Bodmin from
camera-ready copy supplied by the author

For Amelia –

Don't Ever Fade Away

Contents

CONTENTS

Contributors

Aldo Agosti is Professor of Contemporary History at the University of Turin and has published several books concerning the history of the Italian socialist and communist movements. These include *Togliatti* (1996), *Bandiere Rosse: Un Profilo Storico dei Comunismi Europei* (1999), *Storia del PCI* (2000), as well as *Enciclopedia della sinistra europea nel XX secolo* (2000). He is also a member of the editorial board of *Passato e Presente*.

John Callaghan is Professor of Politics at the University of Wolverhampton. His books include *Socialism in Britain* (1990), *The Retreat of Social Democracy* (2000), *Cold War, Crisis and Conflict: History of the CPGB 1951–68* (2003), and *Understanding Labour: Approaches to the Labour Party and Labour History* (2003) edited with Steve Fielding and Steve Ludlam.

Carlos A. Cunha is Professor and Chair of the Division of Social Sciences at Dowling College, Oakdale, New York. He is the author of *The Portuguese Communist Party's Strategy for Power, 1921–86* (1992), and numerous articles and chapters on Portuguese politics. He is currently working on a book on the Portuguese Communist Party and International Communism to be published by Edeline Multimedia.

Allison Drew lectures on social and political movements with particular reference to Africa at the University of York. Dr. Drew is the author of *Discordant Comrades: Identities and Loyalties on the South African Left* (2000) and editor of the two-volume *South Africa's Radical Tradition: A Documentary History* (1996–97). She is currently researching the Algerian Communist Party.

Stephen Hopkins is a Lecturer in Politics at the University of Leicester. He has published articles on the French Communist Party for the *Journal of Communist Studies*, as well as several articles on wider aspects of French politics.

Norman LaPorte is a research fellow at the University of Glamorgan. He has recently published a regional study of the German Communist Party (KPD) in Saxony, *The German Communist Party in Saxony, 1924–33: Factionalism, Fratricide and Political Failure* (Bern, 2003). He is currently working with Stefan Berger on a jointly authored book on Anglo-East German relations, *Friendly Enemies: Britain and the German Democratic Republic, 1949–90*, to be published in 2004.

Stuart Macintyre is Professor of History at the University of Melbourne. His earlier work on the British left resulted in *A Proletarian Science* (1980) and *Little Moscows* (1980). Since returning to Australia, he has worked primarily on the history of that country. In 1998, he published *The Reds*, a history of the first two decades of the Communist Party of Australia. He is currently working on a sequel.

John Manley is a Senior Lecturer at the University of Central Lancashire. He has published a number of articles on the Communist Party of Canada and is currently researching 'red' trade unionism in Britain, Canada and the United States.

Tim Rees is a Lecturer in Modern History at the University of Exeter. He is a specialist on Modern Spain, and has published work on the Franco regime, Spanish communism, the Republic, rural and women's history.

James G. Ryan is Associate Professor at Texas A&M University at Galveston. His books include *Earl Browder: The Failure of American Communism* (1997) and (with Leonard Schlup) *The Historical Dictionary of the Gilded Age* (forthcoming). He is currently working on a monograph about Earl Browder and Soviet espionage.

Marco Aurélio Santana is a Lecturer in Sociology in the Department of Philosophy and Social Science, University of Rio de Janeiro. He is the author of *Communists and Trade Unions in Brazil, 1945–92* (2000), and of several articles about communist political action in Brazil.

Patricia Stranahan holds a Ph.D. from the University of Pennsylvania. She has taught at Texas A&M University and the University of Pittsburgh where she was director of the Asian Studies Program. Currently, she is Dean of Faculty and Provost of Hobart and William Smith Colleges. Her publications include *Yan'an Women and the Communist Party* (1983), *Molding the Medium: The Chinese Communist Party and the "Liberation Daily"* (1990), and *Underground: The Shanghai Communist Party and the Politics of Survival, 1927–37* (1998).

Geoffrey Swain is Professor of Modern History at the University of the West of England, Bristol. His publications include *Russian Social Democracy and the Legal Labour Movement* (1983), *The Origins of the Russian Civil War* (1996), *Russia's Civil War* (2000), *Eastern Europe Since 1945* (with Nigel Swain, 3rd edition, 2003), and several articles on Tito and the Yugoslavian Communist Party. He is currently undertaking research into Latvia during the Second World War.

Kerry Taylor is a Senior Lecturer in History at Massey University, Palmerston North New Zealand. He has published a number of articles on the CPNZ and co-edited *Culture and the Labour Movement: Essays on New Zealand Labour History* (1991) and *On the Left: Essays on Socialism in New Zealand* (2002).

Matthew Worley is a Lecturer in History at the University of Reading. He is the author of *Class Against Class: The Communist Party in Britain between the Wars* (2002) and several articles on the CPGB. He is currently writing a history of the British Labour Party between the wars, and undertaking research into Labour, Liberal and Conservative constituency party branches in the period 1918–40.

Acknowledgements

Many thanks to everybody who has helped create this book, particularly to all the contributors and Lester Crook at I. B. Tauris. My appreciation must also go to the Barry Amiel and Norman Melburn Trust for the allocation of funding for translation. Special mention should be made to Dominic Shryane for his expert help in preparing the text, to David Laven for his translation of Aldo Agosti's chapter, and to Kevin Morgan for his welcome comments on the various chapters. Thanks, too, to Andrew Thorpe, Chris Wrigley, Nina Fishman, Kevin McDermott, Stefan Berger and Steve Smith for guidance over the course of the project. Closer to home, my gratitude and love goes to Amelia for putting up with my worrying, and to all my friends for simply being my friends. Thanks, therefore, to Chris, Pete, Emma, Sue, Stan, Scott (too-rye-ay comrade), Tess, Ed, Eileen, Simon N., Tizzy, Terry and Bob, Rachel, Alex, Nick, Jamie and Earl Brutus, Steph, Katie, Melvin, Abi and Becks, Jon M., Cally, Tom, Jo B., Andy, Dom W., Pete C., Katie and Emily, Joel, Hannah, Ben, Mark B., Anne, Dom, Andrea, Pete B., Kath, Louise, John J., Mike, Stu, Mel, Dan, Simon W., Aileen, Mick, Thomas, Jane N., Patrick, B and Emma, Neil, Sarah, Steve the print, Toby Wolfe, Roger and Vin. Due mention should be made to Dave and Sally Smith, to Alison and John Newland (you taught me all I know), to Guinevere Lohneis, and to my friends and colleagues at the University of Reading. Finally, thanks again to my family for continuing to lend their invaluable support, with a necessary mention to Jo and Chris for providing welcome breaks in God's own country and helping with the move – it's good to be back. On the ball, City!

Courting Disaster? The Communist International in the Third Period

MATTHEW WORLEY

Despite the prophecies made by the social democrats and echoed by the right-wing and conciliatory elements, the stabilisation of capitalism has not only become no firmer, but on the contrary, is becoming more and more undermined. The correctness of the estimation made by the sixth congress of the present third period of post war capitalism is being ever more obviously demonstrated as a period of the increasing growth of the general crisis of capitalism and of the accelerated accentuation of the fundamental external and internal contradictions of imperialism leading inevitably to imperialist wars, to great class conflicts, to an era of development of a new upward swing in the revolutionary movement in the principal capitalist countries, to great anti-imperialist revolutions in colonial countries.[1]

Tenth Plenum ECCI, July 1929

Men make their own history, but they do not make it just as they please; they do not make it under circumstances chosen by themselves, but under circumstances directly encountered, given and transmitted from the past.[2]

Karl Marx

The Third Period formed a part of what the Communist International (Comintern) recognised as a 'series of historical phases of development' passed through by the international labour movement in the wake of the Great War (1914–18).[3] Each phase encapsulated a different stage in the 'general crisis of the capitalist system', the third of which was officially proclaimed at the Comintern's sixth world congress in July–August 1928. What this meant, when looked at through Bolshevik spectacles, was a capitalist world poised to enter an era of crisis. In such circumstances, the 'contradictions of world capitalism' were seen to have paved the way for sharpening class divisions, imperialist war, colonial unrest, and growing antagonism on the part of the 'capitalist states' towards the USSR. 'Gigantic class battles' were predicted, into which the fraternal parties of the Comintern were to lead the workers under a banner of 'class against class'. To this effect, communists were to draw on the lessons of the Bolshevik revolution and reject any compromise with 'reformist' social democracy. By 1929, those on the non-communist left were accused of 'assuming' the guise

1

of 'social fascism'; a spiteful piece of communist terminology designed to delineate the polices of organisations and people deemed to 'serve the bourgeoisie as an instrument for the paralysing of the activity of the masses'. Henceforth, communists were to forge an 'independent leadership' of the working class whilst, at the same time, 'unmasking' social democracy – especially its 'so-called left-wing' – as the most dangerous enemy of the revolution.[4] Such reasoning continued to form the basis of Comintern policy through to early 1933, from which point on it was slowly, unevenly and uncertainly phased out in the months leading up to the seventh world congress of July–August 1935.[5]

More often than not, historical references to the theories and policies of the Third Period are closely followed by a variation on the term 'disaster'.[6] This is not necessarily surprising. As outlined above, the years from 1928 were supposed to herald the final crisis of capitalism and a further round of proletarian revolution. Instead, the period occasioned the rise of Nazism and a capitalist depression that only weakened working class organisation. Equally, the overhaul of the communist movement that accompanied the changes imposed by the sixth world congress have traditionally been seen to herald the final victory of Stalin and the complete subordination of international communism to the whims of the Soviet leader. As communist party organisations were purged and realigned under the watchful eye of Vyacheslav Mikhailovich Molotov, so committed comrades were ousted and loyal Stalinist apparatchiks were promoted in their place. Far from advancing the communist cause, it has been argued that the policies of the Third Period threw the movement into disrepair, with national parties being driven underground, marginalised within their respective labour movements, or shattered by a mixture of internal dispute, worker disinterest and often bloody repression.[7] For many historians, such intrigues, in combination with the sectarianism that characterised communist policy from 1928, served only to weaken the left and thereby make the fascist rise to power possible. In the words of Robert Tucker, it was the 'uncompromising belligerence against social democracy (social fascism)' forced on the Kommunistische Partei Deutschlands (German Communist Party; KPD) by Stalin that 'abetted the Nazi victory'.[8]

Unfortunately, such tidy assumptions tend to oversimplify matters. First, the correlation between Stalin's ascendancy and the onset of the Third Period overlooks the long drawn out origins of what was sometimes called the New Line. Second, the period is generally referred to en bloc, when in fact both the theories and strategies of the Third Period passed through a number of different phases. Third, the apparent desire to fit communist history into the 'totalitarian paradigm' of the Cold War has meant that differences, contradictions and fluctuations in policy and action have been ignored in the pursuit of proving that Stalinism was either a despotic dictatorship or a degenerate form of Marxism—Leninism. Hence, Stalin and by extension the Comintern are often portrayed as the cunning architects of history, as if the movement, its leader and the working class in general remained immune from wider factors that may have had a reciprocal impact on communist perspectives, objectives and actions. Historians have too often failed to put the communist experience into a broad context. This period of 'capitalist crisis', for instance, had a detrimental affect on the labour movement beyond communist party circles: Socialist and Labour parties, not to mention trade unions, also faced severe difficulties and suffered (sometimes devastating) setbacks between 1928 and 1933. To what extent, therefore, were the myriad problems faced by communists in the Third Period due to forces beyond the intricacies of specific Comintern policy?

Finally, portrayals of the Third Period have tended to neglect continuities in communist thinking before and after 1928, not least the deep-rooted mistrust of social democracy central to revolutionary socialism since at least 1914, the ambivalent debate surrounding 'capitalist stabilisation' evident from 1921, and the more instinctive desire within a revolutionary movement for an overtly revolutionary policy. As should be well known, theories of 'capitalist stabilisation' and temporary alliances with 'treacherous' social democrats were not popular among large sections of the Comintern during the 1920s, nor were they particularly effective.[9]

Partly in response to such shortcomings, historians have begun to look more closely at communist activity during the Third Period. In particular, they have reassessed the reasons for the change of line sanctioned in 1928–29, placing it in a context beyond but not without reference to the Machiavellian goings-on inside the Kremlin walls. Similarly, recent research has focused on varied interpretations of the New Line in an attempt to explore just how the policies of the Third Period related to the activities and experiences of communists active within their local communities and workplaces. This, in turn, has led historians to consider communist activity in the years *after* the immediate introduction of 'class against class', pointing to shifts in emphasis and the importance of indigenous influence on the fortunes and development of the communist movement during these years.[10] Although we can broadly concur that the Third Period was misguided in its premonition of revolution, that its conception of 'social fascism' was negative and divisive, that the New Line was utilised in the struggle between Stalin and Bukharin over Soviet domestic policy, that its policy and theory with regard to the colonial world often appeared contradictory, and that the various national communist parties suffered as a result of the intra-party purges that accompanied the 'left turn', we must also join with Dick Geary to ask just why the KPD reached its membership and electoral peak 'when it spoke the language of social fascism'.[11] Likewise, we must consider the fact that although certain western communist parties experienced a loss of influence within the factories and the trade union movement during the Third Period, they proved able to mobilise large demonstrations of the unemployed. Amongst the upheaval of the Third Period, communist party memberships increased as well as decreased in the years between 1928 and 1934. Of course, the numerous unpalatable aspects of the Third Period – including the KPD's flirtations (at Stalin's behest) with the Nazi Party, the bloody ramifications of the Chinese Communist Party's (CCP) changing relationship with the Guomindang, rampant ultra-leftism, and the Comintern's ruthless crushing of divergent opinion within its own ranks – remain integral to communist history. But so too do the establishment of Soviet areas in China, the apparent changes in the scope of the New Line over the early 1930s (particularly with regard to work in the 'reformist' trade unions), the aforementioned unemployed demonstrations, and the KPD's street-level battles against Nazism.

The following collection of essays does not seek to find definitive answers to the debates surrounding the Third Period – indeed, it includes a variety of interpretations and perspectives. Moreover, it does not claim to be a comprehensive overview of the international communist movement; to the parties here examined, many other important studies could be added. Rather, *In Search of Revolution* offers a broad range of case studies from which comparisons and information can be drawn. Before turning to the experiences of individual parties, however, we must first outline the origins and development of the Comintern's self-proclaimed Third Period. The following section will concentrate primarily on communist theory and practice in Europe and the West. For the East, see John Callaghan's introductory chapter 'Storm Over Asia'.

The Origins and Development of the Third Period

It was in November 1926 that Nikolai Bukharin, first member to the political secretariat of the Executive Committee of the Communist International (ECCI) and part of a duumvirate with Stalin that dominated the Soviet politburo, announced the emergence of a 'third period' of historical development since the Russian revolutions of 1917. According to Bukharin, a 'first period' of revolutionary struggle had formed in the wake of the Bolshevik's success, giving way to a 'second period' of 'relative capitalist stabilisation' from 1921–23. This in turn, Bukharin announced to the seventh ECCI plenum, was transforming into a 'third period' of crisis characterised by a radicalised working class and intensifying class struggle.

> The first period was the period of storm and stress. The communists arose to the storm. That was the time of the immediately revolutionary situation ... Commencing from the first steps towards the stabilisation of capitalism, we

had a new phase. A certain shifting in the balance of forces took place. This shifting consisted in that the communists had to make a slight retreat, while the social democrats experienced a certain renaissance; a certain growth and they consolidated themselves to some extent. This proceeded along with the stabilisation of capitalism. Now I believe we have a new phase – a phase in which the process of the stabilisation of capitalism brings forward its contradictions in ever sharper form. The relations between the classes are sharpening ... capitalism is attacking. The working class is daily becoming more convinced of the necessity of active and determined struggle. The leftward trend within the working class is an eloquent expression of this process.

Given such circumstances, Bukharin predicted that 'an immediate revolutionary situation' would soon appear in Europe, provided, of course, that the various communist parties followed the correct Marxist–Leninist line.[12]

The rationale behind such thinking came from a variety of sources, many of which were detailed by Bukharin at the fifteenth congress of the All-Union Communist Party in October 1926.[13] As Nicholas Kozlov and Eric Weitz have demonstrated, the continued growth of capitalism inside Weimar Germany and the United States was given primary importance, lending credence to a theoretical conception of capitalism cultivated by Bukharin from at least 1915. In Bukharin's mind, the advances of the capitalist system led dialectically to its 'inevitable' downfall. In other words, technological innovation, increased production and capitalist competition led to crises of productivity, the extension of the bourgeois state, structural unemployment, worker regulation, depressed working class living standards, and intensified class struggle.[14] Equally, the Weimar Republic was recognised as the site of deep-rooted antagonisms between communists and the German Social Democratic Party (SPD), wherein the SPD's leading role in the Weimar system meant that communists regularly came into conflict with authorities that functioned under social democratic jurisdiction.[15] In line with its reformist nature, social democracy was seen to be revealing itself to be objectively and subjectively on the side of the bourgeoisie. Elsewhere, Bukharin looked to Britain's declining economic prowess and the events surrounding the 1926 general strike and miners' lockout to bolster his theoretical reasoning. In response, Bukharin talked of the 'English' [sic] working class moving onto the 'next stage of progress', from where the Communist Party of Great Britain (CPGB) was to ruthlessly expose 'reformist treachery' in preparation for British capitalism's 'imminent collapse'.[16] In China, meanwhile, the CCP's united front with the Nationalist Guomindang was slowly unravelling; and although the Comintern's reply was to prove inadequate and fatally slow, the mounting tensions in the East helped convince Bukharin that the 'Chinese revolution is one of the most important and powerful factors disrupting capitalist stabilisation'. The disproportionate and competitive development of capitalist national economies encouraged global rivalry, Bukharin insisted, so paving the way for imperialist war and revolution.[17]

Of course, Soviet determinants were also fundamental to Bukharin's thesis. On the one hand, the 'achievements' of the revolution had to be set alongside the continued existence of capitalism and the relatively moderate, concessionary polices of the New Economic Policy (NEP). Simultaneously, the on-going struggle with Trotsky and Zinoviev, whose leftist criticism of both Moscow and Comintern policy needed to be deflected by the Soviet leadership, undoubtedly impinged on the tenor of Bukharin's reasoning. For a movement that believed Marxism–Leninism to constitute a scientific analysis, there could be only one irrefutable 'line' of theory and practice. Even so, historians are divided as to the extent to which such schism shaped communist (and world) history. In the current writer's opinion, the reduction of communist policy to simple factionalism just will not do. The debates surrounding capitalist development and the building of socialism in Soviet Russia drew from a far wider range of sources than the battle between Stalin and Trotsky. In relation to the Third Period, many of its conceptions pre-dated the Bolshevik revolution, and much of its rhetoric – particularly the hostility to social democracy – remained synonymous with the early resolutions of the fledgling Comintern and fundamental to its formation.[18] For better or worse, the leftism associated with the Third Period came easily to many comrades baying for revolution and bitterly opposed to a social democratic reformism that helped shackle the workers to capitalism.

What did all this mean in terms of Comintern policy? During the 'first period' of 1917–21, communists were encouraged to follow the Bolsheviks to the barricades and build the revolution. Yet, with the collapse of the Hungarian, Bavarian and Slovakian Soviets and the introduction of the NEP in Russia, a change of Comintern line was steadily introduced. Thus, in July 1921, following another failed German insurrection in March, Trotsky announced to the third world congress that 'the first period of the revolutionary movement after the war ... may be regarded by and large as terminated'.[19] Henceforth, capitalism was seen to be stabilising and the workers' movement pushed back onto the defensive. In response, communists were instructed to build 'united fronts from below' with workers and members of other working class organisations and, in specific instances, to form 'united fronts from above' with social democratic parties and trade unions in defence of workers' interests. That this was a temporary state of affairs was oft repeated within the Comintern. From 1926, therefore, it was again deemed that the 'internal contradictions' of capitalism were set to herald a new round of revolution and imperialist war. But although Comintern rhetoric towards social democracy hardened noticeably in late

1926, only minor alterations in communist strategy were sanctioned. With regard to the principal concerns of the time, the Comintern remained committed to its united front with the Guomindang in China (albeit with a focus on the left-wing), and to the Anglo-Russian Joint Advisory Council (ARJAC) established with the General Council of British Trades Union Congress (TUC). More generally, the Comintern continued to advocate critical support of non-communist working class organisation elsewhere. Debates regarding communist strategy took place within the ECCI and with certain national parties throughout 1927, but it was not until the ninth ECCI plenum in February 1928 that the prevailing Comintern line was fundamentally altered. Not only was the CCP's protracted disengagement from the Guomindang finally elaborated, but both the French and the British communist parties were instructed to come out in direct opposition to their respective Socialist and Labour parties.[20] The slogan of 'class against class' was from here on raised.

This slow drift towards the Third Period was the culmination of a number of factors. First, the disintegrating united front in China that led eventually to Chiang Kai-shek's repression of the CCP necessitated a change of line. Second, the British government's severance of diplomatic relations with Russia in May 1927 exacerbated renewed fears of an imperialist offensive against the USSR. Third, for those who wished to see such things, evidence of an intensified class struggle was discerned in the wake of the British general strike and the disastrous workers' uprising in Vienna in July 1927. In both instances, the non-communist left was perceived to have played a 'treacherous' role in the failure of the workers' protest. Fourth, the dissolution of ARJAC endorsed at the TUC in September 1927 confirmed the ECCI's suspicions of the British trade union leadership and allowed the Comintern to raise the charge of 'splitting'. Fifth, the struggle against Trotsky and Zinoviev continued apace, culminating in their expulsion from the Russian party in December 1927. While the specifics of their leftist critique of ECCI policy found little support in the Comintern, it was perhaps indicative of a general feeling within the wider communist movement that a more combative policy was required. Finally, problems afflicting the NEP in Russia caused consternation in the Soviet party, leading eventually to Stalin's break with Bukharin in early 1928. Consequently, by the onset of the sixth world congress held to launch the New Line in the summer of 1928, the political and theoretical basis of the Third Period was already becoming open to interpretation.[21]

In many ways, the sixth world congress marked the culmination of the Bukharinist Third Period. The adopted thesis on the international situation endorsed Bukharin's theories of capitalist development, pointing to 'technological revolutions' in Germany and the United States, the expansion of foreign trade and the growth of capitalist monopoly in order to demonstrate 'contradictions' arising from structural changes to the capitalist system. Accordingly, tensions between rival capitalist states (and between Europe and the United States), unemployment, restricted internal markets, intensified working practices and the growth of state capitalism, were all listed to explain a perceived increase in class conflict. A 'working class swing to the left' was registered, alongside the co-option of social democracy by the bourgeoisie. Social democracy had now 'passed from shame-faced defence of capitalism to open support of capitalist construction', the Comintern resolved, as demonstrated by reformist support for 'industrial peace', colonialism, rationalisation and capitalist hostility towards the USSR. The 'treachery' of the social democratic leaders had already 'paved the way for the stabilisation of capitalism'; now it helped pave the way for fascism, or the 'open repression of labour organisation and the peasant poor' by the bourgeois state. To the East, colonial and semi-colonial rebellions were noted, most significantly in China and India.[22]

Tactically, the onset of the Third Period meant re-emphasising the 'united front from below' so as to mobilise workers against imperialism, in defence of the USSR, and in opposition to both the bourgeoisie and social democracy. Communists were to 'Fight for the Masses', distinguishing between 'the sincere, but mistaken, social democratic men [sic], and the obsequious social democratic leadership cringing at the feet of imperialism'. The 'everyday needs of the masses', including the unemployed, the non-unionised, women and 'the youth' were to be supported; work inside social democratic parties and trade unions was to be carried out with 'greater energy' so as to convert workers to communism; and party positions within the factories were to be strengthened. More controversially, communists were to 'win over the reformist trade unions, to organise the expelled ... to break away local organisations we have captured and get them to affiliate to revolutionary industrial organisations'.[23] In short, communist parties were to come out openly against the wider labour movement apparatus and present themselves as the only party able to lead the working class to revolution.

Behind the scenes at the sixth world congress, however, it soon became clear that Bukharin had had to fight to protect his relatively sophisticated theory of capitalist development from the mounting criticisms of those – many of whom were KPD delegates – keen to push for a more immediately catastrophic revolutionary thesis. In so doing, he was fighting a losing battle. With Stalin's blessing, rumours spread through the congress corridors of divisions between Bukharin and the Soviet leader, as a concerted campaign was launched to discredit the man who Lenin had once called the 'favourite of the whole party'.[24] Although the official resolutions remained close to the theses expounded by Bukharin since at least 1926, he was forced to concede some ground to his critics, particularly with regard to internal party discipline. At a time when social democracy was seen as a 'most dangerous' enemy of the working class, deviation to the 'right' of the Comintern line, in conciliation towards social democracy, was to be combated ruthlessly by all parties within the International. The fact that Bukharin was to be associated with such a 'deviation', chiefly in relation to his attitude towards internal Soviet policy, was obviously significant. By agreeing to the 'tightening up of internal, iron discipline', he effectively facilitated his own downfall and the future realignment of Third Period theory. From here on, Bukharin was marginalised within the Comintern, criticised openly in the Soviet and communist press, and soon removed from the Soviet leadership in the wake of the congress. In similar fashion, communist party hierarchies throughout the Comintern were purged of their 'conciliatory elements' in accordance with an organisational overhaul that was directed largely by Stalin's close ally Molotov throughout late 1928–29 and into 1930.[25]

The impact of all this was to prompt a further 'left turn' in communist activity over the course of 1929. Most clearly, the theses presented to the tenth ECCI plenum in July 1929 portrayed an exaggerated and somewhat distorted version of Bukharin's original conception of the Third Period. By such reasoning, revolution no longer appeared to be emerging from capitalism's advance but from its decay – a change of emphasis that would gain greater credence following the Wall Street crash of October 1929.[26] The immanency of capitalism's final crisis, evident in Bukharin's thesis, was brought even more to the fore, while the ECCI now denoted clear confirmation of the 'fascist transformation of the state apparatus of the bourgeoisie' and the 'intensification of repression and white terror' in countries such as Yugoslavia, Germany, Poland, Italy and India. 'In the situation of growing imperialist contradictions and sharpening class struggle,' the ECCI reasoned, 'fascism becomes more and more the dominant method of bourgeois rule.'[27]

Significantly, too, the theory of 'social fascism' was endorsed at the tenth plenum, a concept that Bukharin had successfully refuted the previous summer. The origins of the Comintern's social fascist terminology have now been well documented.[28] Essentially, the term related closely to such Leninist labels as 'social patriotism' and 'social chauvinism' applied to denounce leading social democrats following the outbreak of the Great War. The term 'social fascism' was itself first used in the Soviet newspaper, *Izvestiia,* in 1922 to denote the role of Italian social democracy in Mussolini's rise to power.[29] In 1924, speeches by Zinoviev and Stalin were followed by the fifth Comintern congress' assertion that social democracy had transformed from the right-wing of the working class movement to a wing of the bourgeoisie, and even fascism, before Bukharin's allusion to the rapprochement of social democracy and capitalism from 1926 laid the basis for the Third Period's reintroduction of the social fascist label. Even so, Bukharin retained a relatively nuanced approach to the relationship between social democracy, capitalism and fascism. As such, the introduction of the theory of 'social fascism' at the tenth plenum related closely to the hardening New Line evident within the Comintern and the KPD. Indeed, it was the chairman of the KPD's programming commission, Josef Lenz, who has been credited with first beginning to reintroduce the term in mid-1928.[30] With the SPD joining the government coalition in Germany, and with the Labour Party in Britain forming its second minority government, social democracy was seen to be openly assisting the bourgeoisie in its suppression of the working class – a notion reaffirmed following the shooting of German May Day marchers on the orders of the SPD police chief Zörgiebel in 1929. Hence, communists were to 'intensify the fight against international social democracy' in order to win over 'the rising tide of revolutionary workers' moving to the left in the face of mounting class tensions. Not disconnectedly, the tenth plenum reaffirmed the struggle against the 'right danger' inside the communist movement.

At the same time, Comintern policy became somewhat ill-defined amidst these changing circumstances, as the more radical aspects of the New Line were emphasised at the expense of the various caveats introduced by the ECCI to prevent communist policy lurching into ultra-leftism. The distinction between social democratic leaders and 'honest' workers soon became blurred, with sectarianism emerging as an overriding characteristic of the Third Period. This was, perhaps, most apparent with regard to communist policy towards trade union activity. Encouraged by Lozovsky, general secretary of the Red International of Labour Unions (RILU; Profintern), the tenth plenum instructed communists to organise the working class independently of the reformist trade unions; to expose the social fascist nature of the 'official' trade union leadership; and to establish 'red' communist led trade unions and councils of action where circumstances allowed. A focus was placed on the 'unorganised' workforce and the growing ranks of the unemployed, all of whom the ECCI and the RILU insisted could be mobilised by communists in opposition to the ongoing 'capitalist offensive'. As the reformist trade union apparatus fused with the bourgeois state and the 'capitalistic enterprises', so communists were instructed to take the initiative in harnessing the growing dissatisfaction of the workers and channel it into organised revolutionary action. It was soon obvious, however, that although the ECCI had outlined numerous constraints on the formation of 'red' trade unions and emphasised the need for continued work inside the existing union organisations, the prevailing mood within the Comintern encouraged a proactive, rather than attentive, interpretation of the line.[31] With an emphasis on the 'right danger' inside the Comintern, loyal communists endeavoured to display their militant credentials by adopting the revolutionary tempo of the Third Period; the ramifications of which will be demonstrated in the various contributions that follow.

By early 1930, the excesses of 'class against class' were clear to see. The vast majority of communist parties were continuing to lose membership and influence in the wake of the Comintern's change of line, and the purge of the 'right danger' had led to widescale communist in-fighting. But although the basic tenets of the Third Period remained beyond reproach, there was room to re-emphasise certain aspects of the New Line. At the Enlarged ECCI Presidium meeting in February, Dmitri Manuilsky (the foremost ECCI figure from late 1929 until 1934) warned against overestimating the revolutionary situation and called attention to the 'left deviation' of 'rushing ahead' of the masses. Where the 'right danger' of 'lagging behind' the radicalised working class and failing to recognise the treacherous role of social democracy remained the 'main danger', the leftist tendency to exaggerate the potential for revolutionary advance had led communists to ignore the prepatory work needed to build worker support. For this reason, communists were instructed to retain a focus on the 'partial demands' of the workers (wages, conditions, etc.), while the blanket usage of the term 'social fascism' was condemned. More practically, the importance of working within the existing trade unions was pointedly reaffirmed.[32] Not by accident, this coincided with Stalin's notorious 'dizzy with success' letter published in March 1930, warning against the excesses of Soviet collectivisation policy and calling for a 'struggle on two fronts' in response to both 'right' and 'left' deviations. In so doing, Stalin necessarily sanctioned a subsequent realignment in Comintern policy.[33] The spring of 1930, therefore, marked the beginning of a third phase of the Third Period, as the ECCI moved to rein in the ultra-leftism that had come to define 'class against class'.

The eleventh ECCI plenum was held in March–April 1931. In the months that had followed its predecessor, Stalin's policies of industrialisation and collectivisation had begun to transform the Soviet Union, the Nazi Party had emerged as a leading force in German politics, international capitalism had entered into a protracted period of severe crisis that wrecked havoc in economies across the world, and the international communist movement had passed through a series of leadership overhauls and political commissions called by the ECCI to examine communist policy throughout the Comintern. In Manuilsky's words, speaking at a meeting of the ECCI political secretariat in August 1930, 'there are always excesses in the communist movement when sharp changes are made', and the various national commissions were designed to realign indigenous communist policy with international communist theory.[34] But although moves were made to enact a less sectarian interpretation of Third Period strategy over the course of 1930–32, the extent of any theoretical realignment should not be overstated. In 1931, the concept of 'social fascism' remained integral to a Comintern worldview in which social democracy was seen to be contributing to a 'process of evolution towards fascism'. Moreover, there were many in the ECCI, including Lozovsky and Knorin, who remained committed to a hard line interpretation of 'class against class'. Very evidently, the alterations to communist policy made over the early 1930s failed either to forge the revolution or counter the fascist threat.[35]

The theses adopted by the eleventh plenum made much of the contrast between 'decaying capitalism' and the 'building up of socialism' in the USSR. Increases in unemployment, decreases in productivity and the wider capitalist 'offensive' against the working class were each contrasted with the USSR's purported abolition of unemployment, rapid industrial development and improved living standards. Soviet proletarian democracy was likewise contrasted with the rise of fascism. Consequently, the ECCI resolved that 'antagonisms between the capitalistic and the socialist system [had] never been revealed so strikingly', a situation that served supposedly to increase the possibility of military intervention into Soviet Russia. Simultaneously, the class struggle was still seen to be intensifying, fascism was deemed to be 'growing organically' out of bourgeois democracy, and social democracy was accused of lending its 'direct and indirect support' to capitalist attacks on worker living standards and to the 'fascisation of the bourgeois state'. For this reason, the offensive against social democracy was to be maintained, while any notion of its representing a 'lesser evil' to fascism rejected. Conversely, the moment of revolutionary crisis was not seen to have arrived, a state of affairs that the Comintern attributed to communists' underestimation of working class militancy on the one hand (the 'right danger'), and to their mechanical application of the New Line and overestimation of the immediate revolutionary situation on the other. Again, if Comintern policy had been forged from a scientific analysis of the 'objective situation', then only the misapplication of 'the line' could account for its evident shortcomings. Accordingly, communists were instructed to maintain their offensive against 'all forms of bourgeois dictatorship', while the ECCI once more insisted on the need to work inside the reformist trade unions, to focus on the 'daily demands' of the workers, and to apply the 'united front from below' to the 'broad masses of working men and women'. In particular, renewed efforts were made to encourage communists to mobilise and agitate amongst the growing ranks of the unemployed.[36]

As for the emergent fascist threat, the Comintern found it difficult to incorporate the advance of Nazism into its Third Period analysis. Previous studies of Italian fascism had been rejected during the transition to 'class against class'. By 1930, in the midst of 'capitalist crisis', fascism was regarded as the final attempt of the bourgeoisie to retain its economic and political power over an increasingly militant working class. Although different stages of 'fascisation' were recognised by the ECCI in 1931, and the tendency within the KPD to label the existing Brüning government as 'fascist' was criticised, it remained unable to place convincingly the mass basis of Nazism within its own preconception of 'decaying capitalism'. Reference to Nazism was made during the plenum speeches, but it received scant attention in the official resolutions. Even so, the ECCI did warn its delegates not to see fascism as a 'historical necessity' or a prelude to the proletarian revolution – a conception that came easily to many communists in the context of 1930–33.[37] By 1932, the ECCI further recognised 'divergencies [sic] of social democracy from fascism', but maintained that this was due more to socialist fears that open fascist dictatorship hindered their 'special function' of deceiving the working class than it did to committed opposition.[38] 'The social fascists prefer a [more] moderate and [more] "lawful" application of bourgeois class coercion,' the ECCI resolved, though they continued to help 'clear the road for the fascist dictatorship'.[39] All in all, the Comintern's policy towards fascism – and Nazism in particular – remained confused and uncertain. Communists were not alone in this, but the Comintern's primary focus on social democracy as the main prop of the bourgeoisie clearly underestimated the fascist danger. It was not until Hitler's actual ascendance to power in January 1933 that the Comintern began slowly to come to terms with the Nazi threat.

By the time that the twelfth ECCI plenum met in August–September 1932, the crisis in Germany had cast its long shadow over the Comintern's agenda. Once again, the main themes of the Third Period – the end of capitalist stabilisation, the danger of imperialist war, the war danger in the USSR and the growing revolutionary 'upsurge' of the masses – were reiterated, while the associated offensive against social democracy remained in place. Similarly, both the 'right danger' and the 'obstacle' of 'the isolation of party workers from non-communist, reformist and other workers, and the sectarian way of approaching these workers and their organisations', was recognised and much repeated.[40] Clearly, however, as E. H. Carr's overview of the plenum demonstrates, there were divergent opinions in the Comintern hierarchy as to the specific nature of the fascist threat and the 'correct' tactics of the respective communist parties.[41] Within certain parties, too, there was by 1932 evidence of comrades struggling to push at the limits of Third Period policy – not least in the CPGB, the Komunisticka Strana Československa (Communist Party of Czechoslovakia; KSČ), the Komunistièka Partija Jugoslavije (Communist Party of Yugoslavia; KPJ) and, to an evidently inadequate extent, the KPD.[42] These were limited in scope and not always successful. Nevertheless, following Hitler's appointment as German chancellor on 30 January 1933, changes of emphasis within the New Line would become more apparent. The fourth and final phase of the Third Period, therefore, was also the first phase of the united front against fascism and war.

Ostensibly, the thirteenth ECCI plenum held in November–December 1933 revealed little change in Comintern thinking, despite the violent triumph of Nazism in Germany. Impending revolution and 'social fascism' remained firmly entrenched on the Comintern's agenda, although the fight against 'fascisation' and 'fascist ideology' now accompanied the familiar struggle against social democracy. Prior to the plenum, in March, the Comintern had reiterated the need to form a united front with social democratic workers in response to an appeal by the Second International. This critical (social democratic collaboration with the bourgeoisie remained the 'chief obstacle' to the united front) but affirmative reply 'recommended' that fraternal parties approach social democratic parties to organise jointly against the fascist threat. Beyond this, no direct negotiations between the two Internationals were countenanced.[43] More broadly, the Comintern began slowly to move towards what would eventually become the Popular Front policies of 1935–39.

As Kevin McDermott and Jeremy Agnew have suggested, drawing on the work of Julian Jackson, a 'triple interaction' of national, Comintern and Soviet forces facilitated this.[44] At a local and national level, certain communist parties began to advocate a broader interpretation of the united front and initiate anti-fascist actions with non-communist and social democratic workers. Although initial tentative appeals to the Comintern – by Georgi Dimitrov in 1932, and by Klement Gottwald (KSČ) and even Maurice Thorez (Parti Communiste Français; PCF) in 1933 – were firmly rejected, the reality of the fascist threat encompassed in the Nazi's crushing of the KPD led to a formal change in communist thinking over the course of 1934. In particular, the joint response of communist and socialist workers in France on 12 February 1934 to fascist demonstrations held a week earlier helped push the Comintern towards a more collaborative policy. This, in turn, was assisted by the rise of Dimitrov inside the Comintern following his successful defence against Nazi charges that he was responsible for the burning of the Reichstag on 27 February 1933. Once acquitted, the Bulgarian comrade was warmly received in Moscow in February 1934 and promoted to general secretary of the Comintern at Stalin's bequest, from which position he set about convincing the reluctant Soviet leader of the need to radically overhaul existing ECCI policy.[45] This would take time, but Dimitrov's move to 'break down the walls' between communist and social democratic workers was no doubt assisted be the experiences of communists 'on the ground' and the support Dimitrov eventually received from the likes of Manuilsky and the Italian leader, Palmiro Togliatti. Ultimately, of course, Stalin's approval was essential to any change of line, and Soviet determinants were again integral to the Comintern's adoption of the Popular Front at its seventh world congress in 1935. The potential threat of an aggressive Nazi Germany, combined with Soviet calls for collective security, underlay the realignment of Comintern policy in 1934–35.

The responses of sixteen communist parties to the Comintern's Third Period will be analysed in the following chapters. From this, one thing becomes abundantly clear: a Moscow-centric view is not by itself adequate to explain the appeals, limits, achievements and failures of a movement that provoked both hope and fear amongst peoples throughout the world. Evidently, the application of the New Line and the development of the respective parties encompassed both similarities and differences across the International. Thus, while all of the following contributions recognise the significance of Moscow, the USSR and Stalin in determining communist history, they also demonstrate how different people in different countries interpreted and applied the New Line in different ways amid different circumstances. Most obviously, the communist experience diverged notably once the initial overhaul of the 'right danger' had been undertaken in 1928–30. From approximately 1930–31 onwards, the national parties refocused their attentions on applying practical politics in an array of different contexts, and the results varied accordingly. The challenge now for historians, it would seem, is to construct more overtly comparative studies of international communism, to understand the dynamics of communist politics within varied social, political, cultural and economic conditions. By so doing, the tired tribulations of the old cold war debates will surely give way to a more constructive understanding of a movement that helped define the twentieth century. On with the struggle ...

Notes

1. ECCI, *The World Situation and the Economic Struggle: Theses of the Tenth Plenum ECCI* (London, 1929), p. 1.

2. K. Marx, 'The Eighteenth Brumaire of Louis Bonaparte' (1852), quoted in D. McLellan, *The Thought of Karl Marx* (London, 1995 edition), p. 57.

3. The Bolsheviks established the Communist (Third) International in 1919. According to the 'Letter of Invitation to the Congress' written by Trotsky and published on 24 January 1919, this was due to the 'complete bankruptcy of the old social democratic parties, and with them the old Second International ...' revealed during the Great War and the Bolshevik revolution. See A. Adler (Ed.), *Theses, Resolutions and Manifestos of the First Four Congresses of the Third International* (London, 1983), pp. 1–6.

4. See ECCI, *Communism and the World Situation: Thesis on the International Situation and the Tasks of the Communist International, Adopted at the Sixth World Congress of the Communist International, 1928* (London, 1929); ECCI, *The World Situation and the Economic Struggle*, op., cit.

5. 'Activity of the Executive Committee of the Communist International', in ECCI, *Report of the Seventh World Congress* (London, 1936) p. 37.

6. See, for just four examples, F. Claudin, *The Communist Movement: From Comintern to Cominform* (London, 1975), p. 127; D. Hallas, *The Comintern* (London, 1985), p. 107; M. Adereth, *The French Communist Party: A Critical History, 1920–84* (Manchester, 1984), p. 48; N. Branson, *History of the Communist Party of Great Britain, 1927–41* (London, 1985), p. 17.

7. F. Borkenau, *World Communism: A History of the Communist International* (Michigan, 1962), pp. 332–56; M. M. Drachkovitch and B. Lazitch, 'The Communist International', in M. M. Drachkovitch (Ed.), *The Revolutionary Internationals, 1864–1943* (Stanford, 1966), pp. 184–89; F. Claudin, *The Communist Movement*, pp. 191–92; D. Hallas, *The Comintern*, pp. 126–31. Such views also underpin several national party histories.

8. Quoted in K. McDermott and J. Agnew, *The Comintern: A History of International Communism from Lenin to Stalin* (Basingstoke, 1996), p. 116. Ironically, perhaps, the Trotskyist left share this rigid interpretation of communist history with 'traditionalist' right-wing historians.

9. M. Majander, 'The Soviet View on Social Democracy: From Lenin to the End of the Stalin Era' in T. Saarela and K. Rentola (eds), *Communism: National and International* (Helsinki, 1998), p. 78. We should note also that social democratic hostility towards communism was often equal to the hostility shown by communists towards social democracy.

10. For some examples, in English, see E. D. Weitz, *Creating German Communism, 1890–1990: From Popular Protests to Socialist State* (Princeton, 1997); N. N. Kozlov and E. D. Weitz, 'Reflections on the Origins of the Third Period: Bukharin, the Comintern and the Political Economy of Weimar Germany', *Journal of Contemporary History*, Vol. 24 No. 3 (1989); A. Thorpe, *The British Communist Party and Moscow, 1920–43* (Manchester, 2000); K. McDermott and Jeremy Agnew, *The Comintern* op., cit.; M. Worley, *Class Against Class: The Communist Party in Britain between the Wars* (London, 2002); S. Macintyre, *The Reds: The Communist Party in Australia: From Origins to Illegality* (St. Leonards, 1998); E. P. Johanningsmeier, *Forging American Communism: The Life of William Z. Foster* (Princeton, 1994); A. Drew, *Discordant Comrades: Identities and Loyalties on the South African Left* (Aldershot, 2000); T. Kampen, *Mao Zedong, Zhou Enlai and the Evolution of the Chinese Communist Leadership* (Copenhagen, 2000). These histories do not by any means constitute a 'school of thought'. Rather, they are notable for their wider approaches to communist history. The views, conclusions and perspectives of each vary depending on their subject. For an earlier re-evaluation of the Third Period's origins, see T. Draper, 'The Strange Case of the Comintern', *Survey*, Vol. 18 No. 3 (1972).

11. D. Geary, *European Labour Politics from 1900 to the Depression* (Basingstoke, 1991), p. 69; also quoted in K. McDermott and J. Agnew, *The Comintern*, p. 110.

12. *International Press Correspondence (Inprecorr)*, 20 December 1926.

13. *Inprecorr*, 4 November 1926

14. N. N. Kozlov and E. D. Weitz, 'Reflections' op., cit.

15. E. D. Weitz, *Creating German Communism*, p. 187.

16. *Inprecorr*, 4 November 1926 and 3 December 1926.

17. 'Resolution of the Seventh ECCI Plenum on the Chinese Situation', J. Degras, *The Communist International, 1919–43: Documents Vol. II* (London, 1971), p. 336.

18. N. N. Kozlov and E. D. Weitz, 'Reflections' p. 389.

19. 'Theses of the Third World Congress on the International Situation and the Tasks of the Comintern', in A. Adler (Ed.), *Theses, Resolutions and Manifestos*, pp. 184–202.

20. Prior to the ninth plenum, the Parti Communiste Français (French Communist Party; PCF) and the CPGB had offered critical support to the French Socialist Party and the British Labour Party. Now, following terse discussions between the French party and the Comintern from early 1927, they were to rally the working class under an explicitly communist leadership and stand as an alternative to reformist social democracy. The CPGB was first instructed to change its line in October 1927.

21. K. McDermott and J. Agnew, *The Comintern*, pp. 68–78.

22. ECCI, *Communism and the World Situation*, pp. 5–24.

23. Ibid. pp. 25–43.

24. S. Cohen, *Bukharin and the Bolshevik Revolution: A Political Biography, 1888–1938* (Oxford, 1980 edition), p. 152.

25. The impact of such a policy will be explored within the various chapters of this book.

26. N. N. Kozlov and E. D. Weitz, 'Reflections' p. 403.

27. ECCI, *The World Situation and the Economic Struggle*, pp. 1–15.

28. K. McDermott and J. Agnew, *The Comintern*, pp. 98–100; N. N. Kozlov and E. D. Weitz, 'Reflections' p. 391; T. Draper, 'The Strange Case', p. 119.

29. K. McDermott and J. Agnew, *The Comintern*, p. 98.

30. T. Draper, 'The Strange Case', p. 125.

31. M. Worley, 'The Communist International, The Communist Party of Great Britain, and the 'Third Period', 1928–32', *European History Quarterly*, Vol. 30 No. 2 (2000), pp. 194–97; ECCI, *The World Situation and the Economic Struggle*, pp. 41–42.

32. *Inprecorr*, 28 March 1930; *The Communist International*, Nos. 13–14 and 16–17, 1930.

33. We should note that the ECCI had raised concerns about comrades moving too far to the left prior to Stalin's intervention. See E. H. Carr, *Twilight of the Comintern, 1930–35* (London, 1982), p. 12; *Instructions for the Comintern Delegate to the Conference of the Communist Party of Great Britain*, January 1929 (Communist Archive, National Museum of Labour History, Manchester). Needless to say, there was no possibility of a change of line without Stalin's go ahead.

34. *Meeting of the Political Secretariat of the ECCI*, 16 August 1930 (Communist Archive).

35. ECCI, *Theses, Resolutions, Decisions: XIth Plenum of the Executive Committee of the Communist International* (Moscow, 1931), pp. 1–13.

36. Ibid. pp. 1–20.

37. Ibid.

38. 'The Dictatorship of the Bourgeoisie, Nationalism, Fascism and Social Fascism', in ECCI, *Guide to the XII Plenum ECCI* (London, 1932), pp. 59–71.

39. 'Extracts from the Theses of the Twelfth ECCI Plenum on the International Situation and the Tasks of the Comintern Sections', J. Degras, *The Communist International, 1919–43: Documents Vol. III* (London, 1971), p. 225.

40. ECCI, *Guide to the XII Plenum ECCI* (London, 1933), p. 106; 'Extracts from the Theses of the Twelfth ECCI Plenum on the International Situation and the Tasks of the Comintern Sections', J. Degras, *The Communist International*, pp. 221–30.

41. E. H. Carr, *Twilight*, pp. 64–82.

42. K. McDermott and J. Agnew, *The Comintern*, pp. 108–09 and pp. 113–14; G. Swain, 'Tito and the Twilight of the Comintern', A. Thorpe and T. Rees (eds), *International Communism and the Communist International, 1919–43* (Manchester, 1998), pp. 207–08; E. H. Carr, *Twilight*, pp. 57–61.

43. J. Degras, *The Communist International*, pp. 252–54; E. H. Carr, *Twilight*, p. 85.

44. K. McDermott and J. Agnew, *The Comintern*, pp. 120–30; J. Jackson, *The Popular Front in France: Defending Democracy, 1934–38* (Cambridge, 1988).

45. A. Dallin and F. I. Firsov (eds), *Dimitrov and Stalin, 1934–43: Letters from the Soviet Archives* (New Haven, 2000), pp. 7–43.

Storm Over Asia: Comintern Colonial Policy in the Third Period

JOHN CALLAGHAN

The Soviet Union was still largely an isolated state in 1928. In Europe, Spain, Portugal, Belgium, Holland, Switzerland, Luxemburg and much of the eastern half of the continent withheld recognition. Relations with Britain and China were broken in 1927 and did not exist in any formal sense with most of the Americas; Mexico and Uruguay excepted. Neighbouring states such as Poland, Latvia, Estonia and Finland were deeply suspicious of Russia's *revanchist* ambitions, while almost all states continued to regard it as subversive in intent. The Soviet constitution of July 1923 depicted a bipolar world and provided evidence for this perception. The camps of socialism and capitalism were portrayed as fundamentally antagonistic; it was only a matter of time before renewed attempts would be made by the capitalist powers to crush socialism. Soviet diplomacy was designed to delay this for as long as possible and to play off one capitalist state against another by exploiting everything that divided them (the war settlement, the colonial division of the world, economic rivalries and so on). The USSR imagined itself, in this same constitution, if it survived for long enough, as the nucleus of a future world federation of soviet republics as these emerged around the globe. The Communist International (Comintern) was perceived by the foreign powers as the principal device that Russia had designed to achieve this ambition. The Comintern's failures in Europe by 1924 simply drew attention to the growing importance of the colonial possessions of the capitalist powers in Asia in the Comintern's calculations – particularly when Moscow concluded a treaty with China in that year. Just as the Soviet Union expected to benefit from the antagonisms of the Great Powers and from the class struggle that divided each of them, so did it expect to gain from the conflict between imperialism and the colonial peoples. In this most ideological of states, it was important that the founding genius of communism had made these connections long before 1917.

Lenin saw the appearance of national struggles in the colonies as evidence of the emergence of an ally in the struggle of the western working class to overthrow capitalism. He was one of the first members of the Second International to speak of this 'mounting revolutionary struggle'.[1] He was dismissive of those who complained that the national struggle – whether among the subordinate nationalities of central and eastern Europe or those of Africa and Asia – was either irrelevant to the fight for socialism or actually obstructed its growth. When the Great War provided him with the raw material for a theory of systemic imperialist crisis, Lenin became even more convinced of the inevitability of colonial revolts and of their utility in the overthrow of capitalism. Thus, the Easter Rising in Dublin in 1916 – belittled as a *putsch* by the purists – was the first sign of the social revolution in Europe according to Lenin. His judgement on this was informed by the conviction that revolutionaries must welcome anything that weakened their principal enemies. Unlike most of the orthodox Marxists, he saw that the course of the social revolution would be messy, complex and spontaneous. Those waiting for the pure social revolution would never live to see it. Such people, he believed, did not understand the nature of revolutions. Real revolutionaries were perforce tactically supple in relation to the complex revolutionary process:

> We would be very poor revolutionaries if, in the proletariat's great war of liberation for socialism, we did not know how to utilise every popular movement against every single disaster imperialism brings in order to intensify the crisis.[2]

In the dialectics of history, small nations would play a part in intensifying the imperialist crisis. Powerless as an independent factor, they would contribute to the unfolding crisis as 'bacilli' and enable the real anti-imperialist army – the socialist proletariat – to make its appearance on the scene. Whereas most Marxists of the period were content to argue that the socialist revolution depended on the working class movement in the advanced capitalist countries and – to a much smaller extent – the export of these European conditions abroad, Lenin emphasised that the European working class movement must champion the anti-imperialist struggles of oppressed nationalities and see their cause as a contributing factor in the battles against metropolitan capitalism. Once the proletarian revolution succeeded in the West, he believed, the anti-imperialist masses would gravitate irresistibly towards the new proletarian state.[3]

The Comintern

After the Bolsheviks seized power in Russia in October 1917, they made efforts to enlist the support of the many nationalities of the economically backward territories of the Caucasus and Central Asia in their attempt to consolidate the Bolshevik state and undermine the hostile imperialist powers surrounding it, particularly the British Empire. The Bolsheviks demanded self-determination both for the subaltern nationalities of the Tsarist Empire and the colonies of the European powers. They promoted October 1917 as an anti-imperialist revolution as well as an anti-capitalist revolution. The colonies, they maintained, were 'the Achilles heel of British imperialism' and, by extension, of every other imperialism.[4]

But the foundation conference of the Comintern deliberated in 1919 with scant regard to the colonies because it met when an imminent revolutionary breakthrough seemed possible in Europe. In the months that followed, this prospect became more remote. At the same time, it became clear that very serious anti-colonial disturbances had developed in India, the Middle East, North Africa and China. The national and colonial dimensions of the Tsarist legacy which the Bolsheviks had to grapple with within Soviet Russia also gave the appearance of opportunity, rather than obstacle, in the fight for the preservation of the Bolshevik state at this time. Internally and externally, then, the survival of the revolution in 1920 and 1921 seemed to depend on mobilising the sympathies of 'the backward peoples'. Thus, in 1920, the Comintern was ready to discuss the national liberation movements and the socialist revolution in conjunction and to derive tactical and organisational guidance from this analysis. At the opening session of the second world congress of the Comintern in July 1920, Lenin explained how the Great War had dragged the dependent peoples into world history. A small number of oppressor states were now opposed by a large number of oppressed peoples. In these largely peasant nations, he argued, nationalist movements would necessarily fall under the leadership of the local bourgeoisie. The communists would support such national movements in their collision with the imperialist state.

Criticism of this position came from the former terrorist M. N. Roy, whose knowledge of British India gave him a certain authority at the congress. Roy believed that the prospects for revolution in Europe actually depended on the progress of the revolution in the East. As long as imperialism survived, he argued, it would generate the funds to make economic concessions to the Western proletariat possible and thus sustain the conviction that the reform of capitalism was possible – an ideology preached by the Comintern's enemies. The imperialist system would thus have to be undermined in order to demolish these props of reformism and bring the workers over to a revolutionary position. This, Roy believed, was an eminently feasible objective because the colonies themselves were undergoing capitalist change. India, in illustration of the point, was according to Roy subject to a process of rapid industrialisation and this was producing a militant proletariat which, supplemented by the growing army of landless labourers, formed the basis for a revolutionary movement independent of the bourgeoisie.[5] Roy knew from experience that the existing national leadership in India was decidedly modest in its ambitions. The confirmed constitutionalists of the Indian National Congress would never, in his view, drive out British imperialism. But real revolutionaries, organised in communist parties, could force the national struggle forward; capitalist economic developments had made this a realistic goal. It was to be expected, in this analysis, that the real revolutionaries would inevitably clash with the national bourgeoisie whenever the latter's interests were threatened; on these occasions the national bourgeoisie would align itself with the imperialist state. Lenin acknowledged this point, while doubting Roy's grasp of imperialist political economy. The compromise formula, which the congress adopted, said that 'as communists we will only support the bourgeois freedom movements in the colonial countries if these movements are really revolutionary and if their representatives are not opposed to us training and organising the peasantry in a revolutionary way'.[6]

On paper at least, the second congress had promoted the national liberation struggle in the colonies to a position of importance it had never before attained. The discussion was continued at Baku in September 1920, where the Comintern convened a Congress of Peoples of the East. Many ambiguities were left unresolved by these early discussions. The most obvious was the question of who were the real revolutionaries? Communists could be counted only in hundreds in the whole of Africa and India in 1920, and Latin America and Asia were little better off from the Comintern's perspective. Real revolutionaries existed among the nationalists but many of them were doubtful allies. They often preached ideologies hostile to communism – not just religious obscurantisms but also militantly secular ideas such as those of the Kemalists in Turkey. It was unclear how the Comintern would deal with this problem. The second congress expressed hostility to Pan-Islamism, contradicting an earlier Bolshevik tactic of seeking to make use of it in the Russian colonies of Central Asia. Complaints were later voiced at the Comintern's fourth world congress that this belated hostility had damaged opportunities for building communist influence within the Indonesian national movement Sarekat Islam.[7] But such complications were inevitable. The abstractions of the Comintern's colonial theses offered very little guidance when set against the sheer range and complexity of the conditions found in the colonies. The very social categories employed by the Comintern – drawn exclusively from European experience – were often only rough approximations to the socio-economic realities it set out to comprehend, and sometimes not even that. Where was the proletariat, the bourgeoisie, or the feudal landowner in sub-Saharan Africa, for example? What constituted the nation? How were the communists to cope with the reality of numerous ethnic, religious and linguistic identities and the possible rivalries between them? Appeals to a class-consciousness that did not exist would have limited value. Where would the communists stand if there were two or three or more competing national voices – a likely outcome given the arbitrariness of colonial boundaries? How were the small groups of communists – drawn disproportionately from the educated urban minority – to penetrate the villages, 500,000 of them in India alone?

Many of these questions were not even asked at the second congress. But the discussion highlighted a further complication in that considerations of Soviet state interests were identified as an element in the Comintern's calculations:

>...[All] events in world politics are necessarily concentrated on one central point, the struggle of the world bourgeoisie against the Russian Soviet Republic, which is rallying round itself both the soviet movements among the advanced workers in all countries and all the national liberation movements in the colonies and among oppressed peoples ... [Our] policy must be to bring into being a close alliance of all national and colonial liberation movements with Soviet Russia; the forms taken by this alliance will be determined by the stage of development reached by the communist movement among the proletariat of each country or by the revolutionary liberation movement in the underdeveloped countries and among backward nationalities.[8]

Though Lenin in 1920 was insistent that proletarian internationalism demanded that the Soviet state shall 'make the greatest national sacrifices in order to overthrow international capitalism',[9] the opposite was also true; proletarian internationalism demanded 'subordination of the proletarian struggle in one country to the interests of the struggle on a world scale'.[10] Since Lenin himself had characterised world politics as being concentrated on the central point of struggle between the world bourgeoisie and the Soviet Republic, it would be an easy matter to convince communists to support policies which the Russians demanded – on the grounds that these represented the central 'contradiction' of the world struggle – even if they were of dubious value to national 'sections' of the Comintern, or actually destructive of local political opportunities. This was no hypothetical problem.

After the second congress, the Russians supplied military and economic aid to Mustafa Kemal's Turkey and, in March 1921, concluded a treaty of friendship with that country which was fighting a defensive war against members of the Entente spearheaded by Greece. The fact that the Turkish state was engaged in the ruthless elimination of the Türkiye Komünist Partisi (TKP) was not allowed to spoil this policy. Lenin's state had thus assisted 'bourgeois nationalists' despite their suppression of the communists and the peasant movement in Turkey, not to mention their treatment of oppressed nationalities under Turkish domination such as the Kurds. Claudin suggests that the colonial question was not discussed at the third world congress of the Comintern in 1921 because these facts would come to light and perhaps jeopardize Soviet Russia's relations with Turkey. Russia's newly concluded trade agreement with Britain, which involved an understanding that both states would refrain from hostile propaganda against one another, might also have been jeopardized if the Comintern had immediately discussed ways of stepping up the campaign in Britain's colonies.[11] Furthermore, the right of national self-determination, which the Bolsheviks had used to rally the anti-Tsarist forces within the Russian Empire, had now been taken up by their domestic opponents, including Muslim reactionaries in Central Asia. When the Union of Soviet Socialist Republics was declared in the summer of 1922, the right of self-determination became a dead letter for all of these would-be independent states. Though the fiction of national self-determination for the non-Russian minorities was maintained among communists for years to come, the reality of Russian domination was understood elsewhere. The various elites of the Muslim world were quick to use it in the propaganda war against the spread of communism in North Africa, the Middle East, India and Indonesia.

When the Comintern, at its fourth world congress in 1922, debated the colonial question again, there was acknowledgement that different countries required different tactics.[12] But since the rationale of the Comintern was precisely that capitalist development produced sufficient homogeneity on a world scale to make an international army of communists under central direction both feasible and useful, the admission of complexity did not prevent sweeping generalisations on what should be done – and this at a time when the strength of communist parties in the colonies was negligible, where they existed at all. What remained coherent from the Comintern's earlier discussions was Lenin's original conception of the fundamental conflict of interests between the national movement in the colonies and the metropolitan power. Here was the basis for an alliance of these national liberation movements and Soviet Russia. Given the extreme weakness of the working class in the colonies, communists could only play a role in supporting the national struggle. Whether they would do so in communist parties of the western type, even Lenin occasionally doubted.[13] Whether they would be allowed to organise the peasants for an agrarian revolution against the interests of landowners and others who might form the leadership of the national struggle was logically even more doubtful. And yet, the Comintern had seduced itself into thinking that with the aid of the communist parties of the West, backward countries could skip the capitalist stage of development altogether and 'go over to the Soviet system'. The fourth congress thus went further in the direction of magnifying the communist role in the colonies than even its predecessors had.

It persuaded itself that the national bourgeoisie would seek compromise with imperialism unless the peasant masses were unleashed by the agrarian revolution. Without the agrarian revolution, the national bourgeoisie would be too weak to take on imperialism. But since the agrarian revolution would harm the big landowners, the national bourgeoisie would do nothing to encourage it.[14] It would therefore fall upon the nascent communist parties, based in the working class, to provide the necessary leadership within an anti-imperialist united front. The 'Theses on the Eastern Question' acknowledged that capitalist development in the colonies had taken place since the Great War, but warned that it was 'only poorly developed and confined to a few centres' and was unable to absorb the surplus landless workers. Logically, a poorly developed capitalism meant a small and poorly organised urban working class. But while the colonial proletariat was acknowledged to be weak and capitalist development in the colonies was seen to be confined to certain pockets and subject to metropolitan forces that retarded its development, 'the objective tasks of the colonial revolution' were declared to 'go beyond the limits of bourgeois democracy'. The communists in the colonies, it was argued, would act to bring about the most radical outcome of a bourgeois-democratic revolution while organising the workers and peasants to achieve their specific class interests. They would, in short, seek to work for the goals of the national movement while pursuing policies guaranteed to undermine the economic and political interests of its bourgeois and feudal leadership. And they would do this by seeking alliances within the broad national movement while all the while cultivating an independent base within an exceptionally weak proletariat.

This was a policy riddled with inconsistencies and contradictions. But it was made worse when the Soviet factor was added to the mix. The myth of 'Soviet' development in the backward territories of the former Tsarist Empire – that is, social, political and economic progress unheard of in the colonies of western imperialism – entered the picture to further befuddle the Comintern's analysis in 1922. Russian experience, argued the fourth congress, indicated another way forward for the colonies:

> Under capitalist rule the backward countries cannot share in the achievements of modern technology and culture without paying, by savage exploitation and oppression, enormous tribute to great power capital ... For backward countries the Soviet system represents the most painless transitional form from primitive conditions of existence to the advanced communist culture ... This is proved by the experience of the Soviet structure in the liberated colonies of the Russian empire.[15]

The many facets of the Comintern's colonial theses thus offered numerous opportunities for changes of emphasis as circumstances dictated, and we have already seen that the changing requirements of Soviet foreign policy provided one of the main motivations for so doing. This factor – what was good for Soviet Russia – grew in importance as the Soviet state survived in isolation and the European communist parties failed to meet the Comintern's original expectations. The Russian state needed allies in the world and sometimes nationalists – particularly those with a real prospect of power – were attractive candidates for this position. By the Comintern's fifth world congress in 1924, the dominant view in Moscow was that the national bourgeoisie was the best hope the Russian state had for finding such useful friends. The colonial national bourgeoisie was, once again, also perceived as the main thorn in the side of Russia's principal enemies – Britain and France – at a time when Russian foreign policy was also cultivating links with Germany, the other principal 'revisionist' power in Europe, which had lost its colonies under the terms of the Treaty of Versailles. Changing circumstances clearly influenced this political arithmetic and one of the most compelling was the emergence of a friendly national movement in crisis-torn China, which the Bolshevik leaders under Stalin perceived as a serious contender for power in that country. While the number of communists in the whole of Asia amounted to a paltry 5,000 or so, an alliance with the nationalists could move millions.[16]

In China, Soviet aid had helped the nationalist Sun Yat-sen to establish an armed power base around Canton in 1924. At this time, the Comintern believed that Sun Yat-sen's Guomindang organisation was capable of fulfilling the goals of the bourgeois national struggle. The Chinese communists, accordingly, had been required to join the Guomindang as members in 1923. The Comintern and the Soviet leadership around Stalin monitored their progress – using such field agents as Borodin and Roy – making sure that the communists submitted themselves entirely to the preferred policy, even to the point where they agreed to submit to Guomindang discipline and forbore from any agitation in favour of communism, of the Soviet system, or of the social revolution. By March 1926, the Guomindang was admitted to the Comintern as a 'sympathising' party, and Sun Yat-sen's successor, Chiang Kai-shek, was made an honorary member of the Comintern Presidium. Yet, the Guomindang was led by men of landed property who made no disguise of their social conservatism. Stalin and those like him who strongly advocated Comintern tactics in China were perfectly well aware of this fact. It was their intention, as Stalin told a gathering of Moscow party workers in the spring of 1927, to use the Guomindang so that 'squeezed out like a lemon' it could then be 'thrown away'.[17] One of the uses of the Guomindang, Moscow calculated, was to fill the dangerous spaces of neighbouring China with a power that was less hostile to the Soviet Union than the other contenders for this title – Japan and Britain in particular. Soviet state interests had to be considered. Trotsky himself – Stalin's principal opponent in the internal power struggle within the CPSU – expressed concern in early 1927 that the Chinese communists should avoid actions that could worsen Soviet diplomatic relations with Japan and France given the already hostile attitude of Britain.[18]

It should not have been a surprise to find that when Nanking and Shanghai fell under nationalist control in March 1927, the national bourgeoisie became alarmed by manifestations of communist influence in the workers' militias and strikes, not to speak of evidence of the unwanted social revolution in the form of peasant seizures of land in the surrounding countryside. Trotsky now argued that the communists should leave the Guomindang while maintaining their alliance with it. But the old policy remained in force. Chiang Kai-shek, anxious to avoid the fate allotted to him by the Comintern and determined to placate the fears of his wealthy supporters in China, now turned on the communists. Chiang had not only benefited from Soviet arms and military advice, but had also learned Bolshevik organisational techniques. His power was growing and he no longer needed Soviet help. The Shanghai communists were massacred on 12 April and all the forces of the social revolution were ruthlessly hunted down, murdered or suppressed. The Comintern now instructed the communists to consolidate their position within the left Guomindang government in Wuhan, but this disintegrated when most of its forces defected to Chiang. Only now, when the battle was lost, did the Chinese communists receive instructions to rise in armed revolt against the Guomindang. Their suppression was virtually complete by the end of June. In July, communists were expelled from the Guomindang party and army, and those who survived the bloody purge were forced to regroup in the countryside. Stalin was one of the Soviet leaders most closely involved in the policies which had led to this disaster – and his arch-enemy Trotsky had been one of their leading critics – but it was the Chinese communist leaders who took the blame, together with such Comintern agents as Stalin no longer had any use for.[19] Critics of Stalin's policy inside Russia were expelled from the party and sent to Siberian exile as part of the cover up.

The Sixth World Congress

This was the immediate backdrop to the sixth world congress of the Comintern. Thus, at the beginning of 1928, there was no foreseeable prospect of success for the Comintern either in Europe or in Asia. Despite the shambles in China there was, however, no prospect of war against the Soviet Union by any combination of the capitalist powers. The Soviet Union was isolated but faced with no immediate external threat. Stalin nevertheless insisted that Europe was entering upon a new revolutionary phase and that the capitalists were preparing for war against the Soviet Union. The lie was exposed by his decision to inaugurate a massive and catastrophic social and economic upheaval in the form of forced industrialisation and the collectivisation of peasant agriculture. This weakened the country for years and would not have been countenanced in circumstances of imminent war. The drive for 'socialism' was a policy driven by internal considerations and by the consolidation of Stalin's personal dictatorship. By 1930, all opposition had been eliminated. Similarly, the national sections of the Comintern were rendered instruments of this totalitarianism, each one headed by a loyal

Stalinist tolerating only Stalinists.

When the congress opened, none of the delegates – all appointed by their respective political bureaus rather than elected – had seen the report on the colonies which Otto Kuusinen was to present to them. The report opened with the assertion that Lenin's position on the colonial question at the second congress retained 'full validity'. Kuusinen emphasised the role of the 'the labouring masses in the colonies' as a 'most powerful auxiliary force of the socialist world revolution'. The central global contradiction – imperialism versus the Soviet Union and the revolutionary workers of the capitalist countries – would become increasingly a 'fighting front' connected to the struggle in the colonies; 'the most dangerous sector of the imperialist front'. Here, 'the revolutionary liberation movements' were said to be 'rallying to the banner of the Soviet Union'. Kuusinen declared that alliance with the Soviet Union and the Comintern – apart from offering the only road to political independence – 'opens for the masses of China, India, and all other colonial and semi-colonial countries the prospect of independent economic and cultural development, avoiding the stage of capitalist domination, perhaps even the development of capitalist relations in general'.[20]

Kuusinen was adamant that the 'ruling imperialism is related to the colonial country primarily as a parasite', and that the forms of capitalist exploitation 'hinder the development of the productive forces of the colonies'.[21] Such economic development as did occur – ports, railways, harbours – merely reinforced dependence on the imperialist metropolis. 'Real industrialisation' was held back. Kuusinen acknowledged that this 'retarded industrial development puts narrow limits on the process of proletarianisation' while the destruction of 'the old forms of economy' gave rise to extreme 'land hunger' in the countryside and a surplus and pauperised population which the urban centres were unable to absorb into production. It was a line of reasoning at loggerheads with his political conclusions.

In turning to strategy and tactics, Kuusinen began by acknowledging that the colonial revolutionary movement was 'at the stage of the bourgeois-democratic revolution' – immediately adding that this was 'when the prerequisites for proletarian dictatorship and socialist revolution are being prepared'.[22] But he had already explained that both the bourgeoisie and the proletariat in the colonies were not allowed to develop and grow because of the imperialist parasite. The logical conclusion to draw from this, as some delegates to the congress pointed out, was that these social forces had to be as retarded as much as capitalist development itself was retarded in the colonies. But there could be no great leap forward to socialism if that was true. A way out of this impasse might have been offered – superficially at least – by the argument that the development of the socialist revolution in the capitalist world would 'facilitate' the emancipation of the colonies and draw them into the socialist world. But the report insisted that the communists were to operate immediately in 'a consciously revolutionary direction' among the colonial workers and 'incipient peasant movement'.[23] The foreseeable future of the colonies, for all practical purposes, depended on actions taken within them and not on the socialist revolution in Europe.

The colonial peasantry, by far the biggest proportion of the colonial peoples, might have supplied the revolutionary agency that the report needed. Kuusinen maintained that 'the unbearable exploitation of the colonial peasantry' could only be ended 'by the agrarian revolution', but the bourgeoisie of China, India and Egypt were 'so closely bound up with landlordism, usury capital and the exploitation of the peasant masses in general, that they oppose[d] not only the agrarian revolution but every decisive agrarian reform'.[24] In China and India, events had demonstrated the fear of the national bourgeoisie when faced with 'the independent activity of the workers in the struggle for power and above all the growth of the peasant movement into agrarian revolution'.[25] Kuusinen thus identified the peasantry as 'a driving force of the revolution' and the national bourgeoisie as a block on the agrarian revolution.

But he insisted, in accordance with Bolshevik orthodoxy, that the peasantry could 'only achieve its emancipation under the leadership of the proletariat'.[26] This was to be accomplished by the party fighting for the agrarian revolution. The Comintern thus now expected the proletariat to lead the bourgeois-democratic revolution and declared that the national bourgeoisie was 'not significant as a force in the struggle against imperialism'. But who were the proletariat in the colonies according to Kuusinen? Most, he said, derived from the 'pauperised villages' – presumably with little or no experience of organised struggle. He admitted that in most colonies only the first generation of the industrial proletariat existed, the rest were ruined artisans driven from the decaying handicrafts and these were ideologically unreliable because of their 'narrow craft sentiments'. Big city proletariats such as those of Shanghai, Bombay and Calcutta were the exception.

Yet, the communists were expected to fashion this material into parties that could lead the peasants and expose the duplicity of the bourgeois national-reformist leadership. Like the Guomindang, the Swarajists of India (Indian National Congress) and Wafdists of Egypt were expected to join the counter-revolution at some point in the foreseeable future. 'The formation of any kind of bloc between the communist party and the national-reformist opposition must be rejected', Kuusinen declared, though temporary agreements were possible as long as these did not restrict the communists' own agitations.[27] The communists were enjoined to 'demarcate themselves in the most clear-cut fashion', politically and organisationally, from all petty-bourgeois groups and parties. The main priority was to build the party in the trade unions and 'in the factories and the mines, among transport workers, and among the semi-slaves in the plantations'. The party was to penetrate the peasant organisations and organise 'new revolutionary peasant unions'. In China, 'the immediate practical task' was to prepare for and carry through armed insurrection 'as the only way to complete the bourgeois-democratic revolution' and establish a Soviet regime.[28] Even in India, once a single, centralised communist party had been founded, the task was described as 'the agrarian revolution and the establishment of the dictatorship of the proletariat and peasantry in the form of a Soviet republic'. Against Gandhian talk of passive resistance, the communists were told to 'advance the irreconcilable slogan of armed struggle'. Now the duty of communists was to wage war against Gandhism, Sun Yat-senism, Wafdism, and all the other non-communist expressions of colonial nationalism.

The debate on Kuusinen's report was real but extremely limited. China – the great hope of the Comintern's colonial policy for most of its existence – was skirted around, and there was no real attempt to understand the recent disasters of the Comintern's policy there. The discussion on Kuusinen's report focused on the economic impact of imperialism. The British delegation (with the exception of J. T. Murphy) argued that a policy of industrialisation of the sub-continent held sway. It was a view consistent with Marx's vision of the global spread of capitalism. Such a process would also provide a Marxist rationale for the political line that the Comintern now advocated. Industrialisation would mean urbanisation and proletarianisation – a basis for the growth of the communist party. But this perspective was decisively rejected and Kuusinen's fundamentally incoherent analysis was accepted by the congress (against 12 British votes and one abstention). Though it was acknowledged that most communist parties in the colonies were leaders without followers, deprived of trade union fractions, and ideologically 'very weak' – and though imperialism was held to retard the development of capitalism and the working class – the communists were required to strike out on an independent path on the basis of the working class, lead the peasantry, foment the agrarian revolution, steer the bourgeois-democratic revolution, and establish a Soviet regime. The militant voluntarism that the sixth congress promoted thus set impossible targets.

It also demanded that the metropolitan parties did everything in their power to champion anti-imperialism in words and deeds. It declared a war on racist prejudices within these organisations and took steps to promote black party members for leadership within their national sections and the Comintern itself. The sixth congress line demanded a 'Negro Republic in America' and an independent South African Native Republic. It set up a Negro Bureau to oversee this work and to organise the black workers of the globe in trade unions, anti-colonial struggles and communist parties. The Communist Party of South Africa (CPSA) was one of the beneficiaries of this new emphasis, recruiting black activists, reviving its organisation and effectively intervening in strikes despite severe repression. The communists were required to look more critically at racism and prejudice within their own ranks and to take appropriate action. But the more militant and uncompromising temper – and often courageous actions – which the sixth congress encouraged, was accompanied by an extreme sectarianism.

After the Sixth Congress

One of the first effects of the sixth congress was thus to weaken all those communist front organisations whose rationale had been to widen the range of allies drawn into the Comintern milieu. The League Against Imperialism (LAI) was one such victim of the sixth congress. It had been created by communists in 1927 at the Congress of Oppressed Nationalities held at Brussels (10–15 February).[29] It was set up to channel the anti-imperialist sentiments of trade unionists and social democrats in the capitalist countries so that they were brought into contact with nationalists and leftists from the colonial world. It was the first initiative of its kind and achieved a great propaganda success, as well as real potential for future organisational growth on several continents. Unfortunately for its architects like Willi Münzenberg, the application of the sixth congress theses rapidly drove nearly all of the non-communists out of the organisation. Prominent nationalists such as Nehru, together with leading left-wing social democrats such as Fenner Brockway, were identified either as traitors or social fascists. By the end of 1929, the LAI had been reduced to its communist and fellow-travelling members.

The second congress of the LAI, held in Frankfurt in July 1929, was wholly dominated by the communists and revealed the Comintern's new emphasis on organising black workers, both in the colonies and in the metropolitan centres. Africa and the 'Negro Question' had been discussed at Brussels, but they were given new prominence and vigorously discussed at Frankfurt by black members of the CPUSA, representatives of French communist colonial organisations and a handful of African delegates. The Comintern's trade union offshoot, the Profintern, launched an International Trade Union Committee-Negro Workers and a journal *Negro Worker* (established July 1928), edited by George Padmore, with the intention of bringing more black workers into the unions. Under its auspices, an International Congress of Negro Workers was held in Hamburg in 1930, dominated by black Americans and delegates from communist organisations such as the Paris-based *Ligue universelle pour la defense de la race noir*. Jomo Kenyatta (Kenya), Frank Macauley (Nigeria), I. T. A. Wallace-Johnston (Sierra Leone) and E. F. Small (Gambia) were also in attendance. The new emphasis on Africa – the Third Period indeed marked the 'highpoint in the Comintern's concern for colonial Africa'[30] – was immediately conspicuous in communist journals everywhere in Europe, as was the sixth congress' determination to bring black workers into the metropolitan communist parties. Communist parties were required to combat racism within their own organisations and reach out to black workers.[31] For some prominent black activists, the Third Period was the heroic period of the Comintern's anti-colonialism.[32] *Negro Worker* (December 1928) could not disguise the fact, however, that outside of the Republic of South Africa the Comintern was still at the stage of trying to establish contacts with sympathetic individuals in sub-Saharan Africa. In other words, there were no communist parties beyond South Africa and, more often than not, there were no nationalist movements to latch on to either.

The world economic crisis, which hit primary producing countries exceptionally hard, nevertheless generated discontent in the African colonies that the Comintern did its best to exploit. The LAI publicised the general strike in Nigeria at the end of 1929, which was provoked – like the violence against colonial officials in Kenya the following year – by tax rises. It drew attention to the uprising of workers on the Congo–Ocean railroad in 1928 and the mass redundancies inflicted on colonial workers in Africa during the depths of the recession. The British section of the LAI lobbied on behalf of the Kikuyu Central Association and helped its representative, Jomo Kenyatta, when he visited Britain in the summer of 1929 to demand land reform.[33] The Comintern struggled to gain a foothold in the ports, mines and plantations of the African colonies, using South Africa as its field headquarters while smuggling propaganda and persons through agencies such as the International of Seamen and Harbour Workers' Union which was set up in 1931. It succeeded to the extent that it attracted individuals like I. T. A. Wallace-Johnson, who did pioneering work in West African trade unionism, especially in Sierra Leone and the Gold Coast. But the sixth congress line of building independent communist parties had no application in the sub-Saharan colonies, where the Comintern's very concepts – proletariat, bourgeois, feudal, class and so on – bore little relation to reality.

The tenth plenum of the ECCI (3–19 July 1929) sharpened the 'class against class' stance adopted by the sixth congress, leaving less room for doubt about the real meaning of its verbose reports and theses that had evidently produced consternation and confusion in virtually all the national sections. The agrarian revolution in China and India, it was emphatically repeated, was dependent on the leadership of the working class, that is the communist party, which would establish Soviets 'as the organs of the revolutionary dictatorship of the proletariat and peasantry'.[34] Social conflict in all colonial and semi-colonial countries was said to bear a 'profound revolutionary character' favourable for the growth of the communist party, of revolutionary trade unions, and for the elimination of all reformist and national-bourgeois elements from the leadership of strike committees and other organisations of the economic struggle.[35] It was already apparent that actions that fell short of this revolutionary 'maximalism' were to be anathematised. When, for example, the Partido Comunista Mexicano (Mexican Communist Party; PCM) rallied to the government of Portes Gil, faced with a military rebellion in the spring of 1929, it was condemned for its right-wing stance. The government's acceptance of assistance from the USA was invoked by the Comintern as evidence of the Mexican bourgeoisies' betrayal of the bourgeois-democratic revolution. It had become 'openly fascist' and an agent of US imperialism. The Comintern's theoretical journal *Communist International* had declared in November 1929 that the petty-bourgeoisie and bourgeoisie had moved to the right in all the colonial countries. The line was tirelessly repeated. 'As in India, so in Egypt, the masses will overthrow imperialism only when they have established their own organs of struggle and liberated themselves from nationalist leadership.'[36]

The reformists in the metropolitan countries were not alone in having 'social fascist tendencies', according to the Comintern. The petty-bourgeoisie throughout Latin America was becoming fascist. Only organisations and groups subordinate to the communist party could be trusted. Workers' and peasants' parties only served to dilute and compromise communist influence. In Ecuador and Columbia, an 'immediate revolutionary situation' was said to exist. In Palestine, the Comintern perceived revolutionary Arab masses where there were none – ignoring those members of the Palestinische Kommunistische Partei (Palestinian Communist Party; PKP) who pointed out that the labour movement was almost entirely Jewish. Zionism was regarded as a tool of British imperialism pure and simple, while at the same time, the Comintern denounced Islamic leaders as reactionary obscurantists. Of course, denunciations of Soviet repression of Muslims – as were made by a Pan-Islamic congress held in Jerusalem in the summer of 1931 – were simply taken as proof of these positions. Yet, 'Arabisation' of the PKP was declared the order the day and ruthlessly pursued.

War was declared on all rival ideologies among the 'oppressed peoples'. Among black workers, for example, Pan-Africanism, Garveyism, national reformism and trade union reformism were singled out for special consideration.[37] In July 1930, an international conference of Negro workers – originally intended for London, but banned by the Labour government – was held in Hamburg under the auspices of Padmore's Negro Bureau of the ECCI. The latter complained about white chauvinism in the CPUSA and demanded an internal campaign to combat it. Racism in the USA was treated as a question of class as before the sixth congress, but now also as a feature of the black's condition as an oppressed nation (a legacy of slavery but also of 'the still existing slavery') – a peculiarity absent from the situation of other oppressed peoples, so it was said. The Comintern reasoned that the three-quarters of the Negro population domiciled in compact areas of the south lived in a condition of semi-serfdom, whereas the Negroes of the north constituted a mass of low paid, urban, industrial workers. While the struggle for equality applied to all these people, the right of self-determination was salient for the Negroes of the southern 'Black Belt' who could not hope to acquire equal rights short of self-determination. Segregation and 'Jim Crowism' was thus a special form of national, as well as social, oppression.[38] The communists would fight for the inclusion of Negroes in existing rights and institutions – recognising assimilationist demands in the north – but also for the establishment of their own separate institutions 'wherever the Negro masses put forward such demands of their own accord', as they were expected to in the 'Black Belt'.

China remained the main hope of the communists for all the disastrous setbacks inflicted upon the movement there. The Chinese Communist Party (CCP) was now effectively operating as two distinct organisations – one operating clandestinely in Shanghai; the other, about 10,000 strong, in the countryside, organising a red army and largely isolated from Moscow.[39] The proportion of industrial workers in the CCP had fallen from about two-thirds in 1927 to one-tenth by the end of 1928, and Trotsky, as much a slave to orthodoxy on this matter as the Comintern, warned that it was in danger of becoming a purely peasant party and therefore incapable of communist struggle. A campaign against 'disguised' Trotskyists inside the Chinese party was insisted upon – clear evidence of discontent with the policy of blaming the CCP for policies that the Comintern had insisted upon up to the Shanghai massacres. So was the even more high-pitched struggle against 'the right danger'. The Comintern insisted that spontaneous mass revolutionary discontent characterised the Chinese working class. The ECCI stressed the priority of building the party in the towns, trade unions and factories.[40] The main danger was thus said to be 'right opportunism', notwithstanding the Trotskyite problem. The ECCI warned the Chinese communists against any association with 'kulaks', at a time when Stalin was in the process of having the slightly richer peasants of the USSR murdered or deported to slave labour camps in their hundreds of thousands. The goal in China remained the 'bourgeois-democratic' revolution, but the hegemony of the urban working class over the village poor, exercised in and through the communist party, would inevitably speed up the transition to the 'socialist stage' of the revolution, according to the Comintern.

There was, in fact, little direct contact between the Comintern and the Chinese communists operating in the Soviet areas, and Moscow was largely confined to passing resolutions on China rather than intervening in its affairs as before the Shanghai massacres. A premature obituary for Mao Zedong, published in *Inprecorr* in March 1930, estimating the Red Army at 10,000 strong, is evidence of how poor communications were.[41] China – a theatre of intrigue and intervention for almost all of the Great Powers – remained of vital importance to Soviet foreign policy nevertheless. The Guomindang now looked to support from the USA and Britain, but the Russians had been concerned to re-establish diplomatic relations with the Nanking government from as early as the spring of 1932. Russian operations in China, since the Guomindang massacres, had been confined to former Tsarist interests in Manchuria along the Chinese Eastern Railway. These interests were temporarily expropriated by Chiang in July 1929, after the severance of diplomatic relations. Russian military pressure managed to restore the *status quo ante* at the end of 1930. But less than a year later, the Japanese invaded Manchuria and Soviet commercial interests were under attack again. Comintern propaganda insisted throughout this crisis that the Guomindang would prove useless in the fight against Japanese imperialism. But fear of Japanese expansionism dictated that Soviet diplomacy was more prudent, seeking terms with Chiang Kai-shek if only to prepare the ground for collective security against Japan – or prevent a Chinese–Japanese alliance at Russia's expense[42]. Given that Soviet policy was at all times concerned to weaken the hold of the imperialist powers on China, the apparent debacle of policy in March–July 1927 had not been as bad as it might have been. The consolidation and growth of the power of the Guomindang helped to provoke the Japanese intervention in Manchuria in 1931 and thus entangled one of Russia's main enemies in a prolonged conflict that finally led to the Japanese–American war – an outcome that the Russians could only wish for when the emergency began. In 1931, the Russians had actually denounced the Japanese invasion as an American plot to bring about a Russo-Japanese war to facilitate US domination of the Pacific.

It was the fact of widespread and profound peasant discontent which enabled the Chinese communists to regroup after the Guomindang onslaughts and to establish themselves in the lower Yangtze Valley and, later, in northern Shaanxi, using a core of troops composed of the unemployed and deserters from the Guomindang Fourth Army which had mutinied at Nanchang in August 1927. The first Soviet was proclaimed at Ruijin, in Hunan in November 1928, with others forming at Hubei, Fujian, Jiangsu and Sichuan in the course of 1929–30. Attempts to seize cities failed, however, and the directive to establish an urban, proletarian base was shown to have neither military nor political logic attached to it. A group that included Mao and Zhou Enlai took over the direction of the party in November 1931, and the emphasis of policy became more nationalistic and more overtly peasant based. The Chinese communists declared war against Japan in February 1932. By January 1934, Manuilsky reported that the party had 416,000 members in China and 350,000 troops in the Red Army. But any optimism that this evidence of growth might have encouraged was soon tempered by countervailing forces. A fresh Guomindang offensive in August

1935 forced Mao to retreat on the Long March northwest to Shaanxi with much depleted forces. Its membership in 1935, according to the Comintern, was about 148,000.

The general Comintern message continued to insist that the communists lagged behind the spontaneous movement in the colonies that was full of revolutionary potential. In China, as elsewhere, the opposite was true, especially in the urban trade union centres where the party was invariably ahead of the workers. The consequences were disastrous. The red trade unions were completely eliminated by the end of 1930. Mistakes or setbacks – such as the one suffered when the Chinese communists tried to capture Changsha in July 1930 – were blamed on the national parties 'incorrectly' applying the line, as well as on the inadequate support provided by the communist parties of the imperialist countries. The reality was that the communist parties of the colonial world, where they existed at all, could count their membership in hundreds rather than thousands. Most of them, furthermore, existed in circumstances of illegality and persecution. Throughout South America, South East Asia, Indonesia and the Middle East this was so. The Mexican and Cuban parties were rare exceptions of parties with a significant following (about 30,000 and 20,000 members respectively). In most of Africa no communist groups existed, let alone communist parties.

Where communists were functioning in 1928, the official positions were met with resistance everywhere. A few examples will have to suffice. Darsono (Indonesia), a candidate member of the ECCI, was expelled for wanting co-operation with the national reformists – the Partai Komunis Indonesia (Indonesian Communist Party; PKI), having originally grown in intimate relations with them, was now reduced to a rump.[43] The Chilean communist leadership refused to accept the Comintern's directives and tried to assert its independence from the South American Secretariat. Similar objections were raised in the tiny Brazilian party, fearful of losing its trade union connections because of the new ultra-leftism. 'Arabisation' in Palestine led to splits, the resignation of most of the rank-and-file and the loss of electoral support – but not to significant recruitment of Arabs, among whom the politically minded continued to support the Arab Nationalist Movement or Istiqlal.[44] The histories of the national sections of the Comintern show the trend after 1928: splits, expulsions, loss of membership and influence. Membership of the Comintern outside Russia was given as 913,000 all told in mid-1932, of whom 250,000 were Chinese and 332,000 German. The German section was about to be destroyed completely.

Notes

1. V. I. Lenin, 'Inflammable Material in World Politics', in *The National Liberation Movement in the East* (Moscow, third revised edition, 1969), p. 32.

2. V. I. Lenin, 'The Discussion on Self-Determination Summed Up', ibid, pp. 191–92.

3. Ibid. p. 186.

4. 'Theses on the National and Colonial Question', 28 July 1920, J. Degras (Ed.), *The Communist International 1919–43: Documents Vol.I* (London 1971), pp. 138–39.

5. The argument was given exhaustive treatment in M. N. Roy, *India in Transition* (Bombay, 1971), first published in 1922.

6. J. Degras (Ed.), *The Communist International,* p. 139.

7. 'Theses on the Eastern Question', ibid. p. 382.

8. 'Theses on the National and Colonial Question', 1920, p. 141.

9. Ibid. p. 143.

10. Ibid. p. 143.

11. F. Claudin, *The Communist Movement: From Comintern to Cominform* (London, 1975), pp. 250–52.

12. 'Theses on the Eastern Question', pp. 382–83.

13. F. Claudin, *The Communist Movement*, p. 264.

14. 'Theses on the Eastern Question', pp. 383–84 and pp. 386–87.

15. Ibid. p. 388.

16. F. Claudin, *The Communist Movement*, p. 271.

17. Quoted in A. B. Ulam, *Expansion and Coexistence: The History of Soviet Foreign Policy, 1917–67* (London, 1968), p. 177.

18. Ibid. p. 177.

19. J. Degras (Ed.), *The Communist International 1919–43: Documents Vol. II* (Oxford, 1971), editor's notes, p. 447.

20. Extracts from 'Theses on the Revolutionary Movement in Colonial and Semi-Colonial Countries', adopted by the sixth congress of the Comintern, 1 September 1928, ibid. p. 533.

21. Ibid. p. 534.

22. Ibid. p. 536.

23. Ibid. pp. 537–38.

24. Ibid. p. 538.

25. Ibid. p. 530.

26. Ibid. p. 539.

27. Ibid. p. 541.

28. Ibid. p. 543.

29. The idea for the Congress of Oppressed Nationalities originated in a speech given by Willi Münzenberg in Berlin at a meeting of the League Against Colonial Oppression (born in Berlin on 10 February 1926). The sixth plenum of the ECCI, also meeting in February 1926, resolved to establish 'organisations against colonial atrocities and oppression' and Otto Kuusinen spoke of the need for 'a whole solar system of organisations and smaller committees around the communist party'. See *International Information*, 7 October 1927, bulletin of the Labour and Socialist International.

30. E. T. Wilson, *Russia and Black Africa Before the Second World War,* (New York, 1974), p. 159.

31. J. Callaghan, 'The CPGB and Anti-Imperialism Between the Wars', in G. Andrews et al (eds.), *Opening the Books: Essays on the Cultural History of the British Communist Party* (London, 1994), p. 13; J. Degras, *The Communist International Vol II*, p. 15.

32. G. Padmore, *From Communism to Pan-Africanism* (London, 1956), p. 328; J. Degras, *The Communist International, Vol II*, p. 29.

33. See P. S. Gupta, *Imperialism and the British Labour Movement* (London, 1975), p. 193.

34. 'Theses of the Tenth Plenum on the International Situation', July 1929, J. Degras (Ed.), *The Communist International 1919–43: Documents Vol. III* (Oxford, 1971), p. 44–45.

35. 'Theses of the Tenth Plenum on the Economic Struggle', July 1929; *Inprecorr*, 4 September 1929, p. 979.

36. V. Chattopadhyaya, 'The Anti-Imperialist Movement in Egypt', *Inprecorr*, 25 July 1930, p. 628.

37. V. Chattopadhyaya, 'The First International Conference of Negro Workers', *Inprecorr*, 27 July 1930, p. 635.

38. 'ECCI Resolution on the Negro Question in the United States', 26 October 1930, ibid. p. 127.

39. *Inprecorr*, April 1929.

40. 'Letter from the ECCI to the Central Committee of the Chinese Communist Party', 8 February 1929, and 'Letter from the ECCI to the Central Committee' 26 October 1929, J. Degras (Ed.), *The Communist International Vol. III*, p. 6 and p. 87.

41. 'Obituary: Mau Tze Dung', *Inprecorr*, 20 March 1930, p. 259.

42. See on this M. Beloff, *The Foreign Policy of Soviet Russia, Vol. I 1929–36* (Oxford, 1947), pp. 71–87.

43. R. T. McVey, *The Rise of Indonesian Communism* (New York, 1965).

44. C. Furci, *The Chilean Communist Party and the Road to Socialism* (London, 1984), pp. 29–33; R. H. Chilcote, *The Brazilian Communist Party* (Oxford, 1974), pp. 30–39; D. Nahas, *The Israeli Communist Party* (London, 1976), pp. 19–21.

Presenting a Crisis as an Opportunity: The KPD and the Third Period, 1929–1933[1]

NORMAN LAPORTE

In the course of 1928, the Kommunistische Partei Deutschlands (German Communist Party; KPD) reintroduced an ultra-left policy that identified the Sozialdemokratische Partei Deutschlands (German Social Democratic Party; SPD), above all its left-wing, as the 'main enemy'; to achieve communist objectives, its 'social fascist' influence among the working class would have to be destroyed.[2] During 1924 and 1925, the KPD's ultra-left policies coincided with the Weimar Republic's relative political and economic consolidation. The crisis of 1923 had passed and with it the mass movement which the KPD had mobilised. Under these conditions, the policy led the party into a political blind alley isolating the party from the wider workers' movement. In the course of the 1920s, the KPD had increasingly taken on the political mantel of a vehicle of protest for unemployed workers to express their disappointment with the November Republic and its largest party, the SPD.[3] The return to an ultra-left policy in 1928 took place under very different circumstances: the rise of mass unemployement and, crucially, a crisis of policial legitimacy ending in the collapse of the Republic and the advent of the Third Reich. During the 'great depression', the Nationalsozialistische Deutsche Arbeiterpartei (NSDAP; Nazi Party) further consolidated its position as a mass-based political movement, integrating the former votes of the parties of the 'bourgeois middle' and making in-roads into a section of the working class vote.[4] Unable to modify the policies of the Comintern's 'Third Period', the KPD maintained a strategy of outright opposition to the SPD, while trying to win over the 'misled' social democrats and Nazi workers on the road to revolution. The following chapter addresses why the KPD maintained a set of policies dividing the working class during Hitler's rise to power and what impact these policy had on the party and its membership.

Imposing the Third Period: Communist Tactics and the Comintern

The introduction of the Third Period in the KPD precipitated a further phase in the party's factional feud, culminating in the completion of the party's 'Stalinisation'.[5] Since the foundation of the KPD in 1918–19, the party had been faced with a chronic tactical dilema: how to combine an ideological comittement to the German revolution with the party's everyday existence in the 'bourgeois' Weimar Republic. The KPD's failure to trigger a revolution in the crisis year of 1923 made a difficult situation worse.[6] From 1924 until 1929–30, the main focus of the KPD's activities were drawn inwards in an endless feud over what policy would preciptiate the German revolution. All of the policy options were described in the party's Marxist–Leninist lexicon as variations of the 'united front', a term defined to mean social democratic workers (and later 'Nazi workers') coming under KPD leadership 'without and against' their former party leaders. During the mid-1920s, the KPD had combined the 'united front from below' with conditional offers of co-operation to the leaderships of the SPD and the 'free' (i.e. social democratic) trade union movement (Allgemeiner Deutscher Gewerkschaftsbund; ADGB). These 'united front' offers, however, were contingent on reformist leaders accepting communist-styled demands, which, when rejected, the KPD could use to 'unmask' them as allegedly hostile to workers' interests. There actual aim was to mobilise and organise social democrats and workers without political affiliation in communist-dominated 'front' organsations, campaigning on the basis of the KPD's political objectives. This relatively flexible approach to political campaigning had produced some notable success during the mid-1920s, such as intiating a campaign to expropriate the former German royal families in 1926.[7] The policy's main basis of support in the party membership was among skilled workers whose long-standing tradition of membership of the 'free' trade unions conditioned a worldview which regarded improvements in workers' living and working conditions to be compatable with the revolutionary end goal. The introduction of the policies of the Third Period, however, ended this form of tactical flexibility. From 1928, the KPD abandoned the 'united front from above', replacing it with an outright attack on the SPD as a 'social facsist' party. Instead of proselytising disillusioned social democrats, it reinforced the existing divisions running through the working classes. Within the party membership, this policy found its greatest support among the growing numbers of members recruited from the ranks of the unemployed, semi-skilled and unskilled workers who, since the mid-1920s, had increasingly experienced periods of seasonal unemployment. Many of these party members were not organised in the SPD or the trade union movement, which tended to prioritise the needs of organised, skilled workers. In contrast to the long-term commitment to revolution as an ongoing process exhibited among the former, the latter tended only to become politically active in specific campaigns perceived to be of direct relevance to their own immediate situation.[8]

The situation in Germany was greatly complicated by Soviet domination of the Communist International (Comintern), which set a 'general line' for all member communist parties rather than allowing specific national conditions to previal in policy making. However, in an effort to avert another paralysing factional struggle in the KPD, which was the strongest communist party outside the Soviet Union, the Comintern aimed to implement a rolling 'left turn' which, it was hoped, would minimise resistance at all levels of the party, from the politburo to the local groups and cells. The first stage in the KPD's return to an ultra-left policy was the signing of a secret agreement with the Bolsheviks in Moscow during the sessions of the ninth Executive Committee of the Comintern (ECCI) plenum in February 1928.[9] The policy was then officially announced at the sixth world congress of the Comintern in the summer of 1928.[10] However, the Comintern's hopes that the KPD would accept the introduction of the 'left turn' with a minimum of resistance were disappointed. The intensity of the ensuing factional feud is not least explained by the role of the hard-line Stalinist leader of the KPD, Ernst Thälmann. Rather than gradually implementing the 'left turn' and seeking some form of consensus in the coalition leadership, which spanned a number of party factions, Thälmann actually accelerated the policy's implementation in order to oust his detractors from the leadership.[11] This, in turn, precipitated a bid to oust Thälmann as party leader in order to moderate party policy. A group of party officials known as the 'conciliators' used their position in the leadership to launch a last ditch attempt to tone down the KPD's 'left turn' by removing Thälmann from his position as party chairman. As a pretext for their action, the 'conciliators' seized on the opportunity offered by a financial scandal in Thälmann's home district of Hamburg to stage a 'palace coup'.[12] Through Stalin's personal intervention, Thälmann was promptly restored to his position as party chairman. However, new local level documentation indicates that such a coup was far from an event confined to the upper echelons of the KPD. Thälmann's reputation as a hard-line Stalinist fanned fuel on the flames of the factional struggle that raged throughout the membership.

The 'conciliators' were a grouping of party officials with little support in the wider party. However, there was a strongly organised 'right opposition' centred around Heinrich Brandler, August Thalheimer and Paul Fröhlich, with strongholds in the party's trade union division, in municipal politics, and in a number of party districts including parts of Saxony, Thuringia and the cities of Offenbach, Breslau, Stuttgart and Solingen.[13] The channels of factional communication extended from recognised national leaders through district and, crucially, local level officials. The faction's inner-core of prominent personalities was supplemented by a wider network of rank-and-file members who had experienced the destructive impact of the KPD's previous ultra-left policy during 1924–25 and treated the new 'left turn' with a sense of foreboding.[14] Importantly, the ideology of 'social fascism' made no sense to a significant number of communists who based political conviction on local experience. This applied not only to activists involved in trade union work and communal politics but also to many party members whose localities were not one-sidedly dominated by the SPD, such as in the southwest of Saxony and the Saarland.[15] However, it was the function of the final stage of the KPD's 'Stalinisation' to remove this connection between local party members whose politics were rooted in their communities and their factional leaders.

Initially, the KPD had hoped to avoid convening another party congress to legitimise the 'left turn'. However, with significant resistance to putting the ideology of 'social fascism' into pratice at local level, it became evident that the twelfth (and final) party congress would have to meet. In true Stalinist style, nothing was left to chance. The congress represented the culmination of a process that removed all discenting voices from influencing policy making. The first stage in this process was the KPD's second party conference, held in Berlin on 2–3 November 1928. The conference did not express the full spectrum of opinion in the party but, rather, was an expression of the far-reaching domination of the central leadership over the KPD. In order to filter out voices of dissent, the Zentralkomitee (ZK) removed dissident leaders at district level, replacing them with *kommissars* who supported the Comintern's 'general line'. Delegates to the Reich conference from the party's districts were nominated by 'Comintern-loyal' district leaderships and approved, or rejected, by the central leadership.[16] The Reich conference then provided a platform for the new KPD leadership, comprising an inner secretariat of Hans Neumann, Hermann Remmele and Ernst Thälmann, to proclaim membership 'support' for the policies of the Third Period and hostility to the 'wreckers' of the opposition.[17]

More recent, archival-based studies of the KPD have added interesting details to our knowledge of Moscow's mechanisms of control over the KPD. Not only had the Comintern installed the compliant Thälmann leadership and trained a staff of fulltime functionaries who operated the party machine. From the late 1920s, the Soviet secret police operated in Germany through the channels of the party's secret apparatus (*Nachrichtendienst*). The primary role of the *Nachrichtendienst* was to monitor dissent and assist the party leadership to act against it. In the final stages of the KPD's 'Stalinisation', the *Nachrichtendienst* co-operated with the party's organisational apparatus in order to identify and eliminate organised resistance to official (Comintern) policy. Walter Ulbricht, who had been trained at the International Lenin School in Moscow, had earned the epithet 'Comrade Cell' for his (largely unsuccessful) campaign to break up the large city district organisation and replace it with factory and street cells. More importantly, Ulbricht was responsible for eliminating dissent in the party's base organisations and ensuring that members who attended local, district and national conferences and congresses were loyal supporters of the leadership.[18] At local level, party members who were actively engaged in organising resistance to the 'left turn' at party meetings and in the distribution of literature on the streets and in the factories could be called before 'party courts'. The 'party courts', at which the district leadership acted as judge and jury, had the power to search members houses for literature printed by the opposition and, in persistent cases, to expel those involved. The district leaderships also organised so-called 'party workers' conferences' that were less 'conferences' *per se* than internal party campaigns to mobilise the membership on the basis of official party policy and to remove local leaderships who refused to comply.[19]

Against the weight of Soviet support and central control of the party's organisational apparatus, the 'right opposition' had little prospect of moderating party policy in Germany. When the Comintern's 'open letter' against the 'right danger' was published in *Die Rote Fahne* on 22 December, the death knell sounded for further resistance inside the KPD: its main purpose was to publicly sanction the purge of all party dissidents who would not submit to party discipline.[20] In an attempt to influence communist policy from outside the party, the expelled leaders formed the Kommunistische Partei-Opposition (KPO), which some 6,000 former members of the KPD joined.[21] Although the KPO never became a national political force to rival the KPD, the loss of these activists – and an untold number of others who simply left politics altogether – came at a heavy cost to the party's presence in the factories in local politics.[22] The purge of the 'right opposition' introduced a fundamental change in the dynamics of internal party life. While the party leadership could not eliminate dissent in the membership, it could prevent localised resistance from spreading and organising on a factional platform. The days of the party leadership representing a coalition of communist groupings rooted in the membership were over; from 1929, all party leaders' authority was derived exclusively from Moscow.

In the process of selecting delegates to the Reich party congress, the district party congresses were in a position to handpick their representatives, giving the KPD all the appearances of a Bolshevik-style 'monolithic party of the new type'. In a congress hall solidly packed with supporters of the ultra-left political line, the sole delegate to speak against the policy, a worker for the party district of Halle, was forced to abandon his speech under a barrage of catcalls.[23] In a manner modelled on the cult of leadership being constructed around Stalin, Thälmann was received with an evidently choreographed standing ovation followed by the singing of *Die Internationale*.[24] The Reich congress aimed to mobilise a deeply rooted tradition of antipathy towards the 'betrayals' of the SPD, which had their origins in 1918–19 when the social democrats in the Reich government had collaborated with the military in order to suppress localised experiments in 'council communism'.[25] However, in an effort to revive and intensify this tradition, the KPD staged a confrontation with the SPD on the streets of Berlin's working class suburb 'Red' Wedding. In the course of 1929, the SPD-led government in Prussia decided to ban all outdoor celebrations in Berlin during the traditional May Day celebrations. The newly available protocols of ZK meetings confirm that the party leadership intended to use the SPD's ban on demonstrations to justify the ultra-left policy and to overcome remaining internal party reluctance to put the theory of 'social fascism' into political practice. When the KPD defied the ban, the Berlin police force, headed by the Social Democratic politician Karl Zörgiebel, opened fire on the demonstrators, killing some 33 and injuring a further 160.[26] At the KPD congress, which was moved from Dresden to Berlin–Wedding where these events had taken place, *Blutmai* had already transcended its historical circumstances, becoming a party myth justifying the policy of treating the SPD as a 'social fascist' party. The events of *Blutmai* in Berlin did enflame existing antagonisms dividing the workers' movement, convincing many earlier sceptics that the SPD was indeed showing its 'social fascist' credentials.[27] However, the actual implementation of an ultra-left political course continued to be impeded by two factors. First, the policy's inflexibility continued to be criticised by *left-wing* regional party leaders. For example, in West Saxony members of the district leadership concluded that unless the ZK sanctioned the use of the 'united front from above' tactic at local level, communist campaigning could make little headway.[28] Secondly, and crucially, 1929 witnessed the rise of the Nazi Party as a political force.

The Third Period and Communist Campaigning

Between 1929 and 1933, despite significant shifts in emphasis, a number of central underlying features can be identified in the KPD's political strategy.[29] The KPD leadership did not depart from the Comintern's 'general line', despite a number of far-reaching changes in the German governmental and political system. The KPD remained tied to an ideological analysis stipulating that there was 'no principal difference' between bourgeois democracy and a fascist state: both were instruments of bourgeois class domination. Every change in government, from the SPD-led coalition of 1928–29, through the presidential cabinets of 1930–32, to Hitler's appointment chancellor, was defined as a new and 'higher stage' of 'fascist development'. Even after the rise of the NSDAP as a mass movement, the KPD held to the view that, rather than representing an autonomous movement, it remained only an 'agent' of the bourgeois state apparatus. Despite the Nazi movement's sanction of violence as a means to destroy the organised workers' movement, the KPD held to the interpretation that the principal enemy of communism was the SPD. Further still, the SPD's left-wing was identified as the 'main enemy' within the working class, which allegedly 'held back' the masses from communism and disguised the SPD's leading role in an imperialist war of intervention against the Soviet Union. Thus, the 'general line' precluded co-operation against the Nazi Party with those most likely to break out of the SPD leadership's legalistic, parliamentary-based response to the rise of the Nazism, 'tolerating' the presidential cabinets as a 'lesser evil' to a Nazi-led government.[30] Instead, the KPD held to the 'united front from below' tactic of combining vitriolic propaganda against the SPD leadership with a belief that a radicalisation of the masses would lead them into the KPD. The policy of labelling the SPD a 'social fascist' party was carried into the workers' movement, where the KPD split the SPD-dominated sports and cultural clubs and associations.[31] More importantly, the 'free' trade unions were to be treated as an arm of an increasingly 'fascistic' state apparatus. In order to lead economic struggles, the KPD set up the Revolutionäre Gewerkschafts-Opposition (Revolutionary Trade Union Opposition; RGO), which had the role of politicising economic conflicts and escalating them into confrontations with the state on the road to revolution. In practice, the KPD never resolved the question of whether to leave the reformist trade unions or to use the RGO as a Trojan horse inside them.[32]

In the 'relative stability' of 1929, the KPD's political predictions had taken little account of the role of the Nazi Party.[33] However, by 1929 the NSDAP's rise at regional level was already evident. In a series of regional elections during 1929 in Baden (October, 7 per cent), Lübeck (November, 8.1 per cent) and Thuringia (December, 11.3 per cent), the NSDAP made significant gains. In Thuringia, the Nazi Party held the balance of power and, for the first time, was able to enter a regional government in coalition with the parties of the middle classes. This pattern was confirmed in a series of municipal elections, when Nazis took their places in local councils throughout Germany. In a rerun of the 1929 Saxony state election in June 1930, the Nazis took 18.3 per cent of the vote and, jumping from five to fourteen seats, became the second largest party in the *Landtag*. In the September 1930 Reichstag elections, the NSDAP made its national breakthrough, taking six million votes, 18.3 per cent, before peaking at 37.3 per cent of the vote in the elections of July 1932. At these municipal and regional elections the KPD's vote had, by contrast, risen relatively little beyond the party's support at the 1928 Reichstag election. Similarly, the

KPD's rise at national level was an unspectacular increase of 2.5 per cent, reaching 13.1 per cent of the vote.[34] In a telling reflection of how the membership had responded to the return to the 'left turn', membership fell from 130,000 in 1928 to 114,446 in 1929.[35]

The electoral rise of the Nazi Party from late 1929 was above all given impetus by its high profile role in the Deutschnationale Volkspartei (DNVP) instigated campaign for a referendum against accepting a revision of the Versailles Treaty under the provisions of the Young Plan. For the first time since 1923, Nazi co-operation with the DNVP made the movement a significant political factor in an issue of enormous emotional significance to those German's who rejected the Weimar Republic and resented its birth in the national defeat of 1918. Although sufficient signatures were collected to sanction a national referendum on the so-called DNVP–Nazi 'Freedom Law', the referendum on 12 December 1929 received only 13.8 per cent of the vote. In the longer term, this proved to matter less to the Nazi's electoral fortunes than the party's close identification with the causes and concerns of the nationalistic middle classes in a party system where voters were already gravitating to the right.[36]

The KPD, which had also aimed to prevent the ratification of the Young Plan, remained fixated on the allegedly 'social fascist' role of the SPD and its participation in the Reich coalition government. The minutes of the ZK confirm that, behind the rhetoric of the 'social fascist' thesis, the KPD's primary concern was directly conditioned by the demands of Soviet foreign policy. The SPD-led coalition government signed the Young Plan, which the Soviet Union feared loosened the ties built up between Berlin and Moscow since the Treaty of Rapallo (1922), leaving the Bolsheviks diplomatically isolated in Europe.[37] The KPD's task was to act as a political counterweight in Germany to the SPD-led government's 'western-orientation' in foreign policy by attacking social democracy as an alleged protagonist in a plot by the Western powers to launch an 'imperialist' war of intervention against the Soviet state.[38] At the end of 1929, the KPD still refused to enter into any *de facto* tactical political alliance with the Nazis against the Young Plan. However, the first signs of a return to the type of 'National Bolshevik' propaganda used in 1923 were already evident.[39] The KPD leadership's solution to the issues raised by the Young Plan was:

> [The] complete annulment of all debts, the Bolshevik liquidation of the Versailles Treaty and the Young Plan through the overthrow of the bourgeois [state], the setting up of a socialist, Soviet Germany and an alliance with the Soviet Union and the revolutionary workers of all countries.[40]

In the course of 1930, however, any residual political caution was incrementally abandoned. Militant leftist slogans spliced with highly nationalistic propaganda, in a lexicon plagiarised from the *völkisch* far right, increasingly filled the pages of the communist press and the political pronouncements of party leaders. As the SPD remained the leading government party until March 1930, this allowed the KPD to conflate the social democrats' ratification of the Young Plan with the initial impact of the 'great depression' on the working classes. The confident tones of communist propaganda, however, did not reflect the internal party concerns that its was the Nazi Party which had the political advantage in what, after all, was the classic territory of the far right. With the intention of taking the political initiative, the KPD published its manifesto for the September 1930 Reichstag elections, the 'Programme for the National and Social Liberation of the German People'.[41] The programme stated that should the KPD come to power, a future Soviet Germany would renounce all international obligations based on the Versailles Treaty. Above all, this meant abandoning the payment of reparations to the wartime Allies and the return of the German-speaking territories separated from the Reich in 1918. Although the KPD's electoral gains in September 1930 were owed almost exclusively to the deteriorating economic situation, the party leadership held to its official interpretation that the party's political tactics had been a success and that the elections would prove to be the Nazis ephemeral highpoint.[42] Rather than prioritising the interests of its actual constituency among the rocketing number of unemployed workers, the KPD continued throughout 1931 to identify the SPD as communism's 'main enemy'. Parallel to the campaign against the SPD was an all-out attempt to win over 'misled' supporters of the NSDAP among the 'working people' – a term which the KPD appear to have preferred to the more class conscious 'proletariat'.

The 'People's Revolution'

In the months immediately following the September Reichstag election, the KPD continued to combine the policy of nationalist propaganda with organised efforts to physically remove the Nazis from the factories and working class neighbourhoods. However, the accent of the policy was increasingly placed on converting Nazis into communists through 'ideological discussion'. From the autumn of 1930, leading communists attended Nazi public meetings in the hope of winning over rank-and-file supporters by a mixtures of anti-capitalist and ultra-nationalistic overtures. These exchanges were characterised more by political violence than defections from National Socialism to pro-Soviet communism. However, by early 1931 a small number of former prominent Nazis had switched their allegiances in response to the KPD's nationalist propaganda. Most prominent among these new recruits was the former *Reichswehr* lieutenant Richard Scheringer, who had been converted to Marxism during a prison sentence for his part in an attempt to set up Nazi cells in the army. Encouraged by Scheringer's defection, the KPD devoted a vast amount of political energy to propaganda campaigns to recruit support among the army, student groups and, above all, the Sturmabteilung (SA). It was with the intention of proselytising 'National Bolshevik' circles within these groups that Hans Kippenberger, the head of the KPD's *AM Apparat*, launched the journal *Aufbruch* in July 1931. The journal was edited by the former Nazis Wilhelm Korn and Rudolf Rehm, and subsequently by the notorious former *Freikorps* commander, Joseph 'Beppo' Römer. With the exception of a small and highly unrepresentative number of national-socialist idealists, the policy produced no political breakthrough.[43]

The policy of limiting the rise of the NSDAP by winning over the party's mass basis became the cornerstone of the KPD's 'People's Revolution' policy, announced by Thälmann at a meeting of the ZK in January 1931.[44] Despite qualifying clauses claiming that the policy was a synonym for the 'proletarian revolution', the policy called on rank-and-file communists to win over 'misled' Nazis in a process of 'ideological discussion'. By explaining the national and social components of communism, the so-called 'ideological struggle' was to demonstrate that the only path to national liberation ran through the communist-led social revolution and the smashing of the common capitalist enemy.[45] At a local level, the KPD combined propaganda based on the party's aid proposals to ameliorate the suffering of the German *Mittlestand* with organising meetings among specific social and professional groups. Among the KPD's core target audiences were the urban artisan and clerical lower middle classes and smaller scale farmers and landless labourers in the countryside. At these meetings, the KPD aimed to 'delegate' non-communist representative into communist-led 'Action Committees', which would then spearhead local initiatives from tax and rent strikes and the prevention of evictions in cities to stopping the state-sanctioned eviction of small-scale farmers to clear their tax arrears.[46]

The centrepiece of the KPD's campaign to turn Nazi rural strongholds from 'brown to red' was the 'Peasants' Aid Programme', which Thälmann announced in May 1931 in the strongly rural state of Oldenburg where the NSDAP had joined a bourgeois-led coalition government. The programme, which proposed a series of social and economic palliatives to the peasantry, was above all politically rooted in the KPD's call to the impoverished rural population to unite with the proletariat to set up a Soviet, socialist Germany. The 'delegate movement' culminated in the Reich Peasants' Congress, held in Berlin in January 1931, and addressed by the recently recruited radical farmers' leaders Bruno von Salomon and Johannes Nau, who endorsed the KPD's programme and presented the Soviet Union as a latter day Valhalla.[47] Throughout 1931, the KPD had repeatedly claimed that a 'small war' against the state and large landowners had been unleashed in the countryside under communist leadership.[48] The reality was less impressive. The central party directives were simply ignored by local party members who knew only too well that the peasantry remained overwhelmingly hostile to communism, not least because of the party's support for the Soviet policy of collectivising the rural economy.[49] An almost total absence of communist support in the countryside meant that activists in neighbouring urban centre had to travel into rural areas, where the local population often received them with political abuse rather than open arms. Political tensions were made worse when communist activists trampled over peasants' crops, on occasion playing football in peasants' fields, before asking the hard-pressed peasantry to buy their literature and discuss an 'alliance' with the urban proletariat.[50] In the relatively few cases when peasants did attend communist-sponsored 'peasants' meetings', they often took issue with what was perceived as an intrusion by outsiders in the affairs of country people.[51] An indication of the actual impact of the 'People's Revolution' is provided by official estimates of the numbers of Nazis defecting to the KPD in 1931. In Saxony, where the Nazi vote had rocketed in rural areas, and in the small towns and villages of Erzgebirge–Vogtland, only thirteen of the KPD's 14,112 new recruits of April–December were former Nazis.[52]

Prussian Referendum

In the course of 1931, the policy of treating the SPD as the 'main enemy' culminated in the KPD's participation in the Nazi–DNVP initiated campaign to bring down the SPD-led Prussian government. In January 1931, Thälmann stated that there could be no communist co-operation with the Nazis and the DNVP for these ends.[53] By July, however, KPD's policy had changed and the party dressed up what amounted to a 'united front' with the Nazis and the DNVP against the SPD-led Prussian government as a 'red referendum'.[54] New documentation confirms that intervention by the Comintern's political secretariat overturned the earlier policy, which had had the support of the majority of the ZK, and that the new policy's principal proponents in Germany were Hans Neumann and Hermann Remmele.[55] Although the documentation does not explicitly state that foreign policy concerns were again at issue, the most convincing explanation remains Moscow's intention to break up on-going Franco-German diplomatic discussions by heightening nationalistic sentiments in Germany.[56] There is also some indication that the Comintern's political secretariat did not want to abandon a campaign to bring down the SPD's Prussian stronghold to the Nazis and Nationalists, despite the risks this posed to any pro-communist sympathies among social democratic workers.[57]

While the Comintern praised the KPD's participation in the campaign to unseat the Prussian government as a blow against the 'parliamentary illusions' fostered by the SPD, rank-and-file communists thought differently.[58] The referendum on 16 September failed to bring down the SPD-led Prussian administration, despite receiving some 37 per cent of the vote. Electoral returns in centres of communist support also indicated that the party's supporters failed to take part in the referendum.[59] Local communist opposition to joining forces with the Nazis against the SPD was also evident in the referenda in other *Länder*. For example, in Saxony the KPD did not become involved in a campaign to topple an administration 'tolerated' by the SPD, but in Brunswick were a driving force in the referendum to being down a middle class coalition in which the Nazi Party was represented. [60]

Presenting a Crisis as an Opportunity: Towards the 'Antifascist Action'

The greatest obstacle to maintaining the 'People's Revolution' policy was the experience of rank-and-file communists on the streets. A wave of political violence against the workers' movement had accompanied the Nazis' local rise to power in 1929, to which grass-roots militants spontaneously responded in kind. Initially, the KPD sanctioned a policy of meeting force with force under Hans Neumann's slogan 'Hit the Fascists wherever you meet them!'[61] However, the party leadership quickly repealed this policy insisting that only the 'mass struggle' in the factories, and not 'individual terrorism' on the streets, could defeat the 'Hitler–fascists'. However, as political violence was a policy deliberately pursued by the Nazis, and above all by its paramilitary organisation, the SA, which increasingly recruited in working class districts, local communists had little option but to organise the *Wehrhaftenkampf* ('defensive struggle'). The scale and brutality of political violence surged in the course of 1932, not least as a result of the rapidly rising ranks of the unemployed who were thrown out of the factories and onto the streets which became the location of an acutely polarised political confrontation.[62] In Berlin, the KPD leadership had tried to channel its members and supporters' frustrations and resentments with the political system into a series of communist-led boycotts, rent strikes and mass demonstrations. However, the party's control proved tenuous and, in the late autumn and early winter of 1931, a series of mass shooting and bombing of the taverns used as SA local headquarters took place. Out of concerns that street violence would prove a pretext for the state authorities to ban the KPD, on the 31 November the ZK issued a resolution banning 'individual terror'.[63] This proved highly unpopular with party activists and, importantly, the reactive nature of much of the membership's political violence made it entirely unpractical. For example, during an SA convention in Braunschweig on 17–18 October 1931, a deliberately provocative storm troopers' march into working class neighbourhoods resulted in street fighting. [64] One of the most notorious incidents of political violence was the 'bloodbath of Altona' where, on 17 July 1932, a march by the SA into the town's working class districts, under the protection of the SPD-controlled Prussian police force, ended in a pitched battle in which eighteen people lost their lives.[65]

Although Marxist–Leninist ideology stressed that political action, and ultimately the communist revolution, should be launched from the factories, in practice the party had a long tradition of street demonstration in what amounted to displays of party strength.[66] With the meteoric rise in unemployment during the depression, which was intensified by the deflationary emergency decrees issued by Chancellor Brüning, the streets were filled with political opponents. The KPD's need to respond to the situation of the unemployed at local level was reinforced by the party's social composition: by 1932, 85 per cent of party members were unemployed. The KPD drew on a tactic developed during the mid-1920s whereby communist-led 'Committees of the Unemployed' marched on local town halls demanding the reversal of central government sanctioned cuts in benefits. The demonstrations brought with them a surprising number of successes throughout Germany, and included not only financial concessions to the unemployed but also, on occasion, the supply of food and feul. However, as the KPD leadership's aim was to use the movement among the unemployed as a 'demonstration arm' (Baumgarten), contributing to the party's struggle to dominate working class districts, violent confrontation with political rivals and the police escalated.[67]

A further trigger for political violence (detailed in the situation reports of the Ministry of the Interior as *Zusammenstöße*, political clashes) was during election campaigns, when the propaganda colums of political rivals collided. With the seemingly endless series of municipal, regional, national and presidential elections, which reached a highpoint in the spring and early summer of 1932, the scope for confrontation was explosive. [68] However, it was not only the continued electoral rise of the NSDAP that prompted the KPD to modify its political strategy. Even more influential was the growing collaboration between communists and social democrats at a local level, which contradicted the official policy that any contact with rank-and-file social democrats must only be in KPD-led organisations. In November 1931, a leading figure in the SPD, Rudolf Breitscheid, proposed in the pages of the SPD's central organ *Vorwärts* that the two parties form a united front against the Nazis. The KPD leadership dismissed this as a 'demagogic manoeuvre' and stressed the party's ideological view that the SPD had to be destroyed first before the 'bourgois' (to which, it was claimed, the NSDAP was an integral part) could be destroyed. After the 'Stalin Letter' of November 1931, which restated that social democracy and Nazism were 'twins', the party leadership ended its earlier more moderate pronouncement in a return to a hard-line policy.[69] Many rank-and-file communists, however, thought differently. In local elections in Württemberg and Stuttgart, the SPD and KPD stood for election on joint lists in order not to split the vote of the anti-Nazi left. In a whole series of local party groups, including Nuremberg, Hamburg and Oberhausen, there was tactical grass-roots co-operation between the two parties; this also occurred in the Nazi-run administration in Braunschweig.[70] Recent research indicates that these local initiatives to end the fratricide between the workers' parties and to form a 'united front against Hitler' represented only the tip of a political iceberg.[71]

In the spring of 1932, the impact of these developments led to a tactical shift in emphasis in the KPD's policy, which became known as the 'Anti-Fascist Action'. On 25 April, the party leadership launched its 'Anti-fascist Action' appeal, which, although politically ambiguous, publicly stated that the party was ready to 'struggle together' with any other workers' organisation that would fight the Nazis. The ZK's internal directives to the district party organisations also stressed that the political priority was to 'halt the rising wave of Hitler–fascism and beat it back'.[72] The policy was presented to the membership as a political opportunity to lead the struggle against the Nazis. However, its actual function was a response to a crisis of confidence in the party leadership among its rank-and-file members. Over a prolonged period, local party leaderships had requested that, in the face of escalating Nazi violence, they should be 'spared from ideological discussions' with the SA as attempts to win them over were futile.[73] The objective was to stabilise the KPD by responding to the concerns of its membership. To have done otherwise was to risk the 'united front against Hitler' developing outside the party's control.

The example of Saxony illustrates the extent of the political crisis faced by the KPD in maintaining the Comintern's 'general line' of treating the SPD, especially its left-wing, as it 'main enemy'. As a long-established, highly organised and strongly left-wing centre of the SPD, the political behaviour of the Saxon SPD worked against the communists' presentation of the party as a 'social fascist' movement. The SPD had promoted a policy of forming a 'red majority' with the KPD in the *Landtag* on the basis of a left-wing programme, and had expelled the opponents of co-operation with the KPD to achieve these ends. Those expelled formed the Alte Sozialdemokratische Partei (ASPD), which, despite the party's limited electoral support, held the balance of power in the *Landtag*. In 1926, the ASPD's decision to join a middle class coalition, and its adoption of a nationalistic programme, gave the term 'social fascism' a specific meaning in the Saxon context before the term became a rhetorical device in the party's propaganda tirade against the SPD after 1928.[74] The policy of presenting the SPD as a 'social fascist' movement was further impeded by the Saxon SPD's active policies against Nazi violence on the streets.[75] In Leipzig, the SA attributed its inability to control the streets to the activism of the SPD's 'Iron Front' and its appeal to many younger workers.[76] From its position of control of the streets, the local SPD took the offensive; for example, leading united marches of socialist and communist workers into middle class districts shouting anti-Nazi slogans into megaphones. Police reports indicate that the local SPD and the *Reichsbanner* were also involved in street fighting against Nazis.[77] In Freital, the local branch of the Kommunistischer Jugendverband Deutschlands (KJVD) rejected the party leadership's policy of trying to 'unmask' the SPD as a 'social fascist' movement, preferring its own initiatives to establish a political alliance against the Nazis and the SA.[78] One internal party report details how local party members spontaneously co-operated with the SPD and the left-wing splinter groups against Nazi-organised attack, ignoring party instructions that all 'united front' actions must come under communist leadership.[79] Other anxious reports noted how many party activists took part in SPD-led united actions against the Nazis, lamenting that these 'comrades' tended to regard the SPD as a political 'big brother'.[80] In the cottage-industry region running through Erzgebirge and Vogtland, where the economic collapse of the depression had acted as a catalyst to the NSDAP's vast political rise among impoverished textile and handicrafts workers, *ad hoc* co-operation frequently extended from the KPD and SPD into the ranks of the left-wing splinter groups, the Sozialisitsche Arbeiterpartei (SAP) and the KPO. In a series of towns centred around Plauen, KPD groups enthusiastically attempted to establish a *modus operandi* with the SAP, which dominated street-level politics locally.[81]

Instead of stabilising the KPD and shoring up the Comintern's 'general line', the appeal for a 'united front' against the Nazis had led to a desperate search for a genuine political alliance. A number of local KPD leaders had interpreted the ZK's directives as a call to approach the SPD at local level in order to come to a working agreement against the Nazis. This confusion was deepened by news of the KPD's negotiations with the SPD in the Prussian *Landtag* and calls for joint demonstrations with the 'Iron Front' in Berlin.[82] News and rumours of other genuine united actions with Hitler's opponents circulated among local communists, tapping into a mood of enthusiasm for the formation of a political force to rival the Nazis. For example, in the giant Leuna oil refinery outside Halle, communists, social democrats and Christian factory councillors were reported to have issued a joint proclamation against the Nazis.[83] The degree of enthusiasm for co-operation with other workers' organisations against the common Nazi enemy meant that the KPD leadership spent most of the 'Anti-fascist Action' campaign trying to end the 'united front' actions its original ambiguous appeal appeared to have sanctioned.

'First Hitler, Then our Turn!': 'Social Fascism' as the Main Enemy

The twelfth plenum of the ECCI, held in Moscow during August and September 1932, aimed to reinforce the ultra-left 'general line'. At the meeting, both Thälmann and Manuilsky, Stalin's expert on Germany, lambasted all co-operation which had taken place with the SPD, with 'renegades' (former communists) in the SAP and KPD-Opposition, and with the 'counter-revolutionary' Trotskyists. According to the ECCI's resolutions, the SPD's readiness to co-operate against 'Hitler–fascism' was merely a manoeuvre to give the 'illusion' that the SPD was an anti-fascist party. According to the ECCI, it was the KPD's task to 'combat all tendencies for weakening the principal struggle against social fascism in all of its forms'.[84] The Comintern offered no meaningful analysis of the catastrophic course of political developments in Germany, simply stating that the KPD must struggle against all non-communist parties, movements and state authorities as expressions of 'fascism' or its impending approach. The impact of the Comintern's rigid policy in Germany provoked a crisis within the KPD leadership group. Although Thälmann, Remmele and Neumann were ultra-loyalists, resolute in their support of the cause of Soviet-communism, disagreements over how this could be best served had become acute. Moscow's solution was, as ever, intransigent: Neumann and Remmele were removed from the three-man secretariat for their attempts to balance the 'struggle against social fascism' with the need to respond to Nazi violence.[85] At the KPD's third Reich conference, held to enforce the Comintern's 'general line', Thälmann stressed that: 'Only if the main blow is directed against the SPD, the social mainstay of the bourgeoisie, can the main enemy of the proletariat, the bourgeoisie, be beaten and destroyed'.[86] The political slogan 'First Hitler, them our turn!' encapsulated the damage done to the mentality of the party leaders and sections the wider party.[87]

The RGO-Politik

Nowhere was KPD's isolation and growing alienation from the workers' movement more apparent than in the party's relationship with the trade union movement. The fourth congress of the Red International of Labour Unions (RILU), held in Moscow between mid-March and early April 1928, emphasised the need to organise the 'revolutionary' workforce under a communist leadership in opposition to the 'reformist' policies of the SPD-dominated ADGB.[88] The KPD's first opportunity to implement this policy was during a lockout in the iron and steel industry in the Ruhr in 1928. The KPD instructed its local membership to take on the 'independent leadership' by electing 'strike leaderships' that included all workers under communist leadership, directing the strike 'against the will' of the 'reformist' trade union bureaucracy.[89] Although the KPD's local trade union officials and the wider party membership refused to implement the sectarian policy, leftist party leaders were mobilising developments in the Ruhr to justify party policy. For example, Walter Ulbricht presented the lockout as an 'offensive action' by the working class, illustrating the 'left development' of the workers and the 'right development' of their 'reformist' trade union leaders.[90] The KPD's policy was based on a highly abstract, ideological interpretation of the role of strikes as an expression not merely of economic interest, but against the capitalist state system itself: the larger the strike the stronger its anti-state character.[91] For this reason, the KPD aimed to politicise all strikes, escalating localised disputes into generalised conflicts between KPD-led workers on one side and the 'reformist' trade union leaders, employers and the state on the other. Not only had the KPD's political tactics changed, so too had the sections of the workforce defined as 'revolutionary'. No longer were workers without political affiliation regarded as 'politically backwards' but, as they were 'free' from social democratic traditions, their growing social impoverishment would make them the most 'radicalised and revolutionised' layers of the working class.[92]

Despite a general reluctance to carry out an ultra-left policy in the factories, the KPD's trade union policy was imposed on the membership up to and beyond the Nazis' seizure of power.[93] At the KPD's twelfth congress in 1929, resolutions called for a new organisation to be set up in order to organise communist-led strikes. This led to the formation of the RGO at a Reich congress held in Berlin at the end of 1929. However, the KPD never overcame the tactical dilemma of whether to turn the RGO into an independent organisation or to use it as a vehicle to struggle against 'reformism' within the 'free' trade unions. In practice, 'red' trade unions were only ever organised on a localised basis where communist policy had led to the expulsion of party members, such as in the dock workers' union, metal workers' union (Berlin), cobblers' (Berlin, Stuttgart, Erfurt and Dresden), and among the miners in the Ruhr.[94] Instead, the RGO maintained an ambiguous position, working both within the SPD-dominated trade unions and standing on 'red lists' in factory council elections.[95] Here, too, the RGO only achieved a substantial vote in highly localised settings, where specific factories were targeted for intensive communist campaigning. Where the RGO did well, the workforce tended to comprise a high degree of semi- and unskilled workers who had never belonged to the ADGB and were more attracted to spontaneous solutions to industrial disputes than the SPD-sanctioned state arbitration process permitted. Representative cases of this were in the factory council elections in the mining industry in the Ruhr and Upper Silesia, and in the chemical industry, such as the plants at Leuna in Halle, Bayer in Leverkussen, and BASF in Ludwigshafen.[96] These localised KPD strongholds were, however, unrepresentative. In 1930, the KPD had only been able to field 'red lists' in 1,169 specially targeted factories. In the metal industry, with it high proportion of skilled workers and traditions of organisations in the ADGB-affiliated Deutscher Metallarbeiter-Verband (DMV), the communists gained only 2.6 per cent of factory councillors in 1930; the DMV at this point had 82 per cent of all works councillors in the metal industries. Where the KPD did have strongholds in the metal industry, forcing the *RGO-Politik* from above met with outright resistance. For example, in Solingen only 1,000 out of 13,000 party members in the local metal industries joined the RGO. For the first time during the Weimar Republic, the leadership of the local DMV passed from communist into SPD hands. The *RGO-Politik* served largely to accelerate the removal of the KPD presence in the factories. Thus, in Saxony, by late 1932, only 28 union branches still had communist majorities.[97] Economic conditions as well as political practice ensured this. In 1932, at least six million German workers were unemployed. By the end of 1932, only one in nine of the KPD's 360,000 members were still employed in the factories. Despite the official RGO membership figure of 200,000 in March 1932, almost all of them remained paper soldiers; at least three-quarters were unemployed.

BVG Strike

In line with the general political resolutions of the twelfth ECCI plenum, the KPD's policy in the factories was reoriented from throwing Nazi 'strike breakers' out of the factories to winning them over by engaging them in joint struggle.[98] At the third Reich party conference, the statement on political tactics in the factories stated that 'joint actions must be carried out with working class Nazi supporters in the factories against cuts in pay and unemployment benefits and against the Papen dictatorship'.[99] Although 65.6 per cent of the ADGB membership remained unemployed in the autumn of 1932, the first green shoots of economic recovery were sufficient to motivate workers in a number of factories to resort to strike action in order to defend their standard of living against employers' pay cuts. The KPD's claims that from 800 strikes the RGO led 500 can be dismissed as propaganda. However, the excessive moderation of the trade union leadership, which naively continued to believe that the state arbitration system would act even-handedly, gave the KPD greater influence. The KPD's 'strike strategy' of mobilising the workforce against the SPD-led reformist trade union leadership in 'unity organisations' coincided with the NSDAP's drive to expand its influence among the working classes, which, in the factories, focussed on the role of the party's factory organisation – the Nationalsozialistische Betriebsorganisation (NSBO). The KPD's policy of co-operation with Nazi workers in the factories was sufficient to produce a rash of headlines in the SPD's press lambasting the joint actions of the 'Nazis and Kozis'.[100]

Until November, the movement of 'wild' strikes had been confined to small and medium size factories and primarily located in the provinces. The strike in the Berliner Verkehrsgesellschaft (Berlin Transport Company; BVG), however, took on a completely different dimension.[101] The strike had sufficient support to all but paralyse the bus, tram and underground transport in the capital city from 3–7 November, running through the elections to the Reichstag on 6 November. Picket lines crossed the capital with serious disturbances taking place throughout Berlin. Police actions against the unrest included the shooting of strikers, most notably in the city's Schöneberg district where three were shot dead and a further eight were seriously injured. The mood of worker rebellion, if not revolution, was sufficient to produce a 'red scare' in government circles and middle class opinion.

Again, the trade union leadership's commitment to avoiding confrontation allowed workers' frustrations to be channelled by the KPD. In the summer of 1932, the RGO had been able to set up a 'unity committee' in the BVG, drawing support from not only communists but also dissident social democrats, Nazis and the majority of workers who had no political or union affiliation. When the employers announced their intention to cut wages, the 'unity committee' was able for the first time to realise the central objective of KPD policy: leading a strike against the reformist trade union bureaucracy, the system of state arbitration and the police. If the strike was unable to last beyond the Reichstag elections, the returns for Berlin showed considerable working class support for the KPD's role in the BVG strike: in working class divisions the KPD's vote rose more strongly than in the country generally.

To what extent had the KPD actually co-operated with the Nazis? The KPD leadership presented joint actions of Nazi and communist workers at the picket lines as a great success. There can be little doubt that the KPD's policy had muddied the political waters between 'red and brown'. The growing weight of regional evidence increasingly indicates that the BVG strike was not an isolated incident.[102] In Leipzig, in October 1932, the RGO and the NSBO also stood side-by-side on the picket line outside the Tittel and Kruger textile factory, which employed some 1,000 workers. Importantly, however, the number of activists on both sides was small and, despite the enthusiasm of the KPD's district leadership, only recent recruits to the KPD had entered into a political pact with Nazi workers. It should also be noted that a more typical picture was not RGO–NSBO co-operation from inside the factories, but KPD agitation from outside the factory gates, using 'discussion troops' made up of unemployed activists with placards, leaflets and megaphones parading in front of the factories.[103]

Holding the Party Line

If the scale of strikes led by Nazis and communists was small, then the wider implications of KPD's policy were vast. On the eve of Hitler's 'seizure of power', the KPD continued to impose its policy of winning over Nazi supporters among the 'working people' while rejecting all form of co-operation against the NSDAP with the SPD. Although the pressure of Nazi violence against both socialists and communists ensured that many local party activists simply ignored the directives issued by the central leadership, the KPD began a series of purges to remove dissident party members at local level and impose the Comintern's 'general line'.[104] In January 1933, the Saxon KPD initiated a campaign to re-elect the leaderships of all street and factory cells, local groups and city districts, which was to be completed by 30 January – the day Hitler was appointed chancellor. The district leadership stressed that these were not elections on the model of the SPD, but Bolshevik-styled elections: new officials could only be elected if they unconditionally supported official party policy. This was the ultimate consequence of the KPD's Stalinisation. The KPD leadership could not make party members carry out policies that conflicted with their everyday experience. It could, however, purge dissent when it threatened maintaining the Comintern's 'general line'. In January 1933, this meant removing from the party's ranks those militants whose roots in the workers' movement and experience of Nazi political violence on the streets motivated their decision to oppose official policy.

Conclusion and Interpretations

The debate on why the KPD maintained the policy of treating the SPD as the 'main enemy' during the Nazis' rise to power continues to centre on the extent to which this can be ascribed to exogenous and endogenous factors.[105] Did the policy derive from KPD 'Stalinisation', or was a spectrum of German socio-economic developments and political traditions responsible? A number of domestic German factors did influence why certain sections of the KPD were more susceptible to an all-out attack on social democracy than was the case in most other communist parties. A series of studies interpreted the policy's relatively positive reception – at least in the Berlin KPD – as a response to the actions of the SPD in the Reich and Prussian governments. Above all, these studies emphasise the SPD's role in the suppression of the 'council communist' movement of 1918–19 and, most recently, the events of *Blutmai*. As the KPD represented unemployed workers, the SPD's association with the implementation of welfare cuts deepened these political hostilities, as did the wider culture of violence on the streets between communists and the police, fascist organisations and SPD.[106] Other interpretations have focused on how the sociological division of the working class conditioned its political division. In other words, the process of industrial rationalisation, which was stepped up after 1923–24, divided the German working class into a structurally unemployed component of unskilled workers, who stood predominantly outside of the organised labour movement, and a skilled, politically organised and trade union affiliated component. While the former provided the social basis for the KPD and revolution, the latter gave their support to the SPD and its reformist policies. From this, historians have drawn the conclusion that the sociological divisions and differing material interests between the two workers' parties shaped the KPD's policy of treating the SPD as the 'enemy'.[107] Recent research has also identified the role of personal experience and social factors in determining the political culture of communism. The seminal experience of party members was the brutality of the First World War and the process of 'modernisation' during the Weimar Republic, which brought structural unemployment and the dissolution of old certainties and securities. With the failure to spark a revolution in the early post-war years, the KPD invented a political tradition, including constructing a cult of fallen 'revolutionary' martyrs and various rituals of every day life.[108]

However, the most important contribution of more recent research is to stress the differences in the KPD's response to the Third Period.[109] While traditions of organisation and political socialisation brought a greater understanding of what workers were most disposed to an attack on the SPD, experience at local level was also crucial in determining the interaction between the KPD's leadership and membership, and between rank-and-file communists and social democrats. The KPD's membership in Berlin did not respond to the challenges of the 'great depression' in precisely the same manner as in Saxony. There have also been detailed attempts to place German 'Stalinism' in the context of 'socialism with a Prussian face': ascribing 'German Stalinism' to domestic patterns of social, ideological and political developments with the workers' movement taking on the features of the dominant culture of authoritarianism.[110] To subscribe to a dogmatic worldview was one means of 'liberating' one's self from the dilemmas of 'modernity'.

Even so, no explanation as to why the KPD remained fixated on the SPD as the 'main enemy' during the Nazis' rise to power is complete without accounting for the party's 'Stalinisation' in terms of German communism's subordination to Moscow. The KPD's membership of the Comintern obliged conformity to binding policy directives issued by the ECCI; recalcitrant groups, individuals and, ultimately, entire parties could be expelled for non-compliance.[111] By 1928 at the latest, Comintern policy reflected the Soviet Union's policies of state. The Soviet Union did not want a revolution in Germany because of the incalculable international implications. It did, however, aim to destabilise the Weimar Republic and with it to destroy the influence of the SPD and it ambitions to reintegrate Germany within Western Europe.[112] Extending the KPD's 'united front from below' to winning over 'misled' Nazis fitted into this schema much more than the political perceptions of all but a small minority of the KPD's membership.

Notes

1. The author would like to thank Stefan Berger, Mike Dennis and Ben Fowkes for all their help, encouragement and expert comments over the years.

2. For the origins of the Third Period, see N. N. Kozlov and E. D. Weitz, 'Reflections on the Origins of the "Third Period": Bukharin, the Comintern, and the Political Economy of Weimar Germany', *Journal of Contemporary History*, Vol 24 No. 3 (1989), pp. 387–410. For a summary of Soviet research, see K. McDermott, 'Rethinking the Comintern: Soviet Historiography, 1987–1991', *Labour History Review*, Vol. 57 No. 3 (1992), pp. 37–58.

3. D. Peukert, *The Weimar Republic: The Crisis of Classical Modernity* (London, 1991), p. 151. For the sociology of the KPD and its implication for party policy, see H. A. Winkler, *Schein der Normalität: Arbeiter und Arbeiterbewegung in der Weimarer Republik, 1924–30* (Berlin, 1988), pp. 438–39 and p. 447.

4. For a detailed account, see Jones, *German Liberalism and the Dissolution of the Weimar Party System, 1918–33* (London, 1988). The most comprehensive analysis of the degree of working class support for the NSDAP estimates the figure at 40 per cent in 1932: J. Falter, *Hitler's Wähler* (Munich, 1991), p. 225 and p. 371.

5. The term 'Stalinisation' refers to the KPD's restructuring, taking on the organisational forms and ideology of the Bolshevik 'party of the new type'. The standard work (and unsurpassed masterpiece) remains H. Weber, *Wandlung des deutschen Kommunismus: Die Stalinisierung der KPD in der Weimarer Republic, Vol. 1* (Frankfurt, 1969). Other classic studies subscribing to the Stalinisation thesis include, O. K. Flechtheim, *Die KPD in der Weimarer Republik* (Hanover, 1986, third edition); S. Bahne, *Die KPD und das Ende der Weimarer Republik: Das Scheitern einer Politik, 1932–35* (Frankfurt, 1976). B. Fowkes, *Communism in Germany under the Weimar Republic* (London, 1994).

6. For a summary of the events of 1923 and their impact on the KPD, see N. LaPorte, *The German Communist Party in Saxony, 1924–33: Factionalism, Fratricide and Political Failure* (Bern, 2003), p. 62.

7. H. A. Winkler, *Schein der Normalität*, p. 270.

8. For definitions of the KPD's political tactics, see S. Bahne, *Die KPD*, p. 22; H. Weber, *Hauptfeindsozialdemokratie: Strategie und Taktik der KPD 1929–33* (Düsseldorf, 1982), pp. 13.

9. H. Weber, 'Dokumentation. Zu den Beziehungen zwischen der KPD und der Kommunistischen Internationale', *Vierteljahreshefte für Zeitgeschichte* No. 2 (1968).

10. J. Degras (Ed.) *The Communist International, 1919–43: Documents Vol. II* (London 1971), p. 455.

11. On Thälmann's correspondence with Stalin indicating his drive to purge the party of those opposing Comintern policy, see A. Watlin, *Die Komintern 1919–29* (Mainz, 1993), pp. 180–1.

12. For details of the 'Wittorf Affair', see H. Weber, *Wandlung*, p. 199; B. Fowkes, *Communism in Germany*, p. 149; R. Levine-Meyer, *Inside German Communism: Memoirs of Party Life in the Weimar Republic* (London, 1977) p. 131.

13. Bundesarchiv Koblenz (Ba.K), R 134/42/49–97.

14. K. Mallmann, *Kommunisten in der Weimarer Republik: Sozialgeschichte einer revolutionären Bewegung* (Darmstadt, 1996), p. 356.

15. On Erzgebirge–Vogtland, see N. LaPorte, *The German Communist Party*, p. 133. On the Saarland, see K. Mallmann, 'Sozialgeschichte des Kommunismus', p. 9.

16. H. Weber, *Wandlung*, p. 211; B. Herlemann, *Kommunalpolitik der KPD im Ruhrgebiet 1924–33*, (Wuppertal, 1977), p. 143; N. LaPorte, *The German Communist Party*, p. 245.

17. N. LaPorte, '"Social fascism", "Stalinisation" and the case of the Saxon Communist Party, 1928–9', *Labour History Review*, Vol. 67 No. 1 (2002), pp. 65–81.

18. B. Kaufmann et al., *Der Nachrichtendienst der KPD 1919–37* (Berlin, 1993), p. 94. For an overview and introduction to the autobiographical literature, see H. A. Winkler, *Schein der Normalität*, pp. 443–45. On the role of Ulbricht, see B. Herlemann, 'Der deutschsprachige Bereich an den Kaderschulen der Kommunistischen Internationale', *Internationale Wissenschaftliche Korrespondenz zur Geschichte der deutschen Arbeiterbewegung (IWK)*, Vol. 18 No. 2 (1982), pp. 205–29. For an example of Ulbricht's role in eliminating dissent in the KPD membership during the mid-1920s, see N. LaPorte, '"Stalinisation" and its Limits in the Saxon KPD, 1925–28', *European History Quarterly*, Vol. 31 No. 4 (2001) p. 572.

19. 'Protokoll der engeren Bezirksleitung Ostsachsen vom 10.10.1928', Stiftung Archiv der Parteien und Organisationen der DDR in Bundesarchi (SAPMO) I 3/8/25, Bl. 390; U. Neuhäusser-Wespy, *Die KPD in Nordbayern 1919–33: Ein Beitrag zur Regional und Lokalgeschichte des deutschen Kommunismus* (Nuremberg, 1981) p. 22.

20. *Die Rote Fahne*, 22 December 1928.

21. K. J. Tjaden, *Struktur und Funktion der KPD-Opposition (KPO): Eine organisationssoziologische Untersuchung zur 'Rechts'-Opposition im deutschen Kommunismus zur Zeit der Weimarer Republik* (Meisenheim-am-Glan, 1964), p. 100.

22. K. Mallmann, *Kommunisten*, p. 356.

23. 'Protokoll des 12 Parteitages der KPD' (Berlin, 1929), p. 209.

24. O. K. Flechtheim, *Die KPD*, pp. 203–4.

25. For the origins and development of this tradition in the KPD, see S. Bahne, '"Sozialfaschismus" in Deutschland: Zur Geschichte eines politischen Begriffs', *International Review of Social History* Vol. 10 No. 2 (1965), pp. 211–45.

26. L. Schirmann, *Blutmai Berlin 1929: Dichtung und Wahrheit* (Berlin, 1991), pp. 82–168; T. Kurz, 'Arbeitermörder und Putschisten. Der Berliner "Blutmai" von 1929 als Kristallisationspunkt des Verhältnisses von KPD und SPD vor der Katastrophe', *IWK* Vol. 22 No. 3 (1986), pp. 297–317.

27. V. Wunderlich, *Arbeiterbewegung und Selbstverwaltung: KPD und Kommunalpolitik in der Weimarer Republik: Mit dem Beispiel Solingen* (Wuppertal, 1980), p. 57

28. See, for example, 'Protokoll der Sitzung der erweiterten BL vom 18.10.1928', SAPMO I 3/10/114, Bl.343–44.

29. For a five-point summary of the KPD political strategy, see H. Weber, *Hauptfeind*, pp. 18–19.

30. H. A. Winkler, 'Choosing the Lesser Evil: The German Social Democrats and the Fall of the Weimar Republic', *Journal of Contemporary History*, Vol. 25 Nos. 2–3 (1990), pp. 205–27.

31. H. Wunderlich, *Arbeitervereine und Arbeiterparteien: Kultur und Massenorganisationen in der Arbeiterbewegung, 1890–1933* (Frankfurt, 1980) p. 138 and p. 162; 'Thesen und Materialien zum Niedergang der Arbiterkulturbewegung vor dem Faschismus', in H. Caspar et al (eds.), *Deutsche Arbeiterbewegung vor dem Faschismus* (Berlin, 1981), pp. 157–80.

32. H. A. Winkler, *Schein der Normalität*, p. 690.

33. The KPD's initial response to the electoral rise of the NSDAP was largely to underplay its significance. See, for example, 'Zentral-Komittee-Sitzung vom 25.10.1929', in RY 1 I/2/1/74, Bl.353-54.

34. H. Weber, *Hauptfeind*, p. 25. For the rise of the NSDAP in Saxony, see C. W. Szejnmann *Nazism in Central Germany: The Brownshirts in 'Red' Saxony* (New York, 1999).

35. For all statistical details on the KPD membership and vote, see H. Weber, *Wandlung*, pp. 361–95.

36. E Kolb, *The Weimar Republic* (London, 1988), p. 104.

37. 'Resolution des ZK der KPD zum Kampf gegen den Youngplan. Vorgelegt vom Politbüro. Beschlossen in der Sitzung vom 29.10.1929', SAPMO RY 1 1/2/74 (407–12), esp. 407–8.

38. B. Fowkes, *Communism in Germany*, p. 159; H. Weber, *Hauptfeind*, p. 21

39. For the use of a 'National Bolshevik' policy in 1923 and its return in 1929–30, see L. Depeux, *Nationalbolschewismus in Deutschland 1919–33* (Munich, 1985), p. 178 and p. 437.

40. 'Resolution des ZK der KPD zum Kampf gegen den Youngplan. Vorgelegt vom Politbüro. Beschlossen in der Sitzung vom 29.10.1929', SAPMO RY 1 1/2/74, Bl. 412.

41. *Die Rote Fahne*, 24 August 1930.

42. H. Weber, *Hauptfeind*, p. 31.

43. B. Kaufmann et al, *Nachrichtendienst*, p. 231; L. Depeux, *Nationalbolschewismus*, p. 448; J. J. Ward, '"Smash the Fascists": German Communist Efforts to Counter the Nazis, 1930–31', *Central European History*, Vol. 14 No. 1 (1981), pp. 30–62.

44. C. Fischer, 'Class Enemies or Class Brothers? Communist–Nazi Relations in Germany, 1929–33', *European History Quarterly*, Vol. 15 No. 3 (1985), pp. 259–79.

45. E. Thälmann, *Volksrevolution über Deutschland* (Berlin, 1932), p. 1.

46. 'Reichsminister des Innern. An die Nachrichtenstellen der Länder', Staatshauptarchiv Dresden (St.Ha.D.), MdI. Nr.19086, Bl.162.

47. 'An die Nachrichtenstellen der Länder. Betr. KPD Bauernpropaganda', St.Ha.D., MdI. Nr.19092, Bl.41.

48. *Die Rote Fahne*, 7 January 1932; A. Dorpalen, 'SPD und KPD in der Endphase der Weimarer Republik', *Vierteljahreshefte für Zeitgeschichte*, Vol. 31 No. 1 (1988), pp. 77–103.

49. 'Die Instrukteursystem der KPD', in Ba.K., NS Hauptarchiv NS 26/810.

50. *Der Bolshevik*, No. 1 (1932).

51. For the example of a rural locality in Saxony, see St.Ha.D., MdI. Nr.19092, An das MdI Dresden. Betr. KPD Landarbeit. Kh Bautzen, am 28.11.1931, Bl.110;

52. 'Entwicklung der Mitgliederschaft der KPD 1926 – 1931', in Ba.K. NS 26/810

53. E. Thälmann, *Volksrevolution*, p.57.

54. H. Weber, *Kommunismus in Deutschland, 1918–1945* (Darmstadt, 1983), p. 129.

55. K. Kinner, *Der deutsche Kommunismus. Selbstverständnis und Realität* (Berlin, 1999), p. 187.

56. T. Weingartner, *Stalin und der Aufstieg Hitlers: Die Deutschland-Politik der Sowjetunion und der Kommunistischen Internationale 1929–34* (Berlin, 1970), p. 93.

57. K. Kinner, *Kommunismus*, pp. 188–90.

58. 'Resolution zur Frage über den Volksentscheid in Deutschland', RY 5/I 6/3/224, cited in K. Kinner, *Kommunismus*, p. 193.

59. H. Weber, *Hauptfeind*, pp. 40–41; H Duhnke, *Die KPD von 1933 bis 1945* (Cologne, 1972), p. 24.

60. N. LaPorte, *The German Communist Party*, p. 331; G. Reuter, *KPD–Politik in der Weimarer Republik: Politische Vorstellung und soziale Zusammensetzung der KPD in Hannover zur Zeit der Weimarer Republik* (Hannover, 1982), p. 119 and note 12.

61. 'Resolution des ZK der KPD zum Kampf gegen den Youngplan vom 29.10.1929', SAPMO RY 1 1/2/74 (407-12), Bl.12.

62. E. Weitz, *Creating German Communism*, pp. 160–87.

63. The KPD's preparations for a working as an illegal organisation were intensified during 1931, see B. Kaufmann et. al. (eds.), *Nachrichtendienst*, p. 258; J. Wachtler, *Zwischen Revolutionserwartung und Untergang: Die Vorbereitung der KPD auf die Illegalität in den Jahren 1929–33* (Frankfurt, 1983).

64. E. Rosenhaft, *Beating the Fascists? The German Communists and Political Violence, 1929–33* (Cambridge, 1983), p. 76; E. Carr, *Twilight of the Comintern, 1930–35* (London, 1982), pp. 47–51.

65. B. Fowkes, *Communism in Germany*, p. 166.

66. R. Huber–Koller, 'Die kommunistische Erwerbslosenbewegung in der Endphase der Weimarer Republik', *Gesellschaft: Beiträge zur Marxistischen Theorie* Vol. 10 (1977), pp. 81–140.

67. C. Fischer, *The German Communists and the Rise of Nazism* (London, 1991), p. 138. For a local study, see A. McElligott, 'Mobilising the Unemployed: The KPD and the Unemployed Workers' Movement in Hamburg–Altona during the Weimar Republic', in R. Evans and R. Geary (eds), *The German Unemployed. Experiences and Consequences of Mass Unemployment from the Weimar Republic to the Third Reich* (London, 1987), pp. 228–60.

68. 'Monatsbericht (Dezember 1930–Januar 1931)', St.Ha.D., MdI. Nr.11126/4, Bl.385.

69. H Duhnke, *Die KPD*, p. 31.

70. S. Bahne, *Die KPD*, pp. 22–23; H. Weber, *Hauptfeind*, p. 44; G. Fülberth, 'Die Übereinkunft zwischen SPD und KPD in Braunschweig nach den Kommunalwahlen vom 1 März 1931', in H. Caspar et. al. (eds.), *Deutsche Arbeiterbewegung*, pp. 132–56.

71. K. Mallmann, 'Milieu, Radikalismus und lokale Gesellschaft. Zur Sozialgeschichte des Kommunismus in der Weimarer Republik', in *Geschichte und Gesellschaft* 21 (1) (1995), (5–31), p. 21

72. H. Weber, *Hauptfeind*, p. 49; 'Rundschreiben des ZK am 4.6.1932' in H. Weber (ed.), *Die Generallinie. Rundschreiben des Zentralkommittees der KPD an die Bezirke, 1929–33* (Düsseldorf, 1981), p. 492.

73. See, for example, 'Berichterstattung der UB Sekretariat zur Antifaschistischen Aktion am 9.6.1932 (Bautzen)' in Ba.K, R45 IV/28.

74. N. LaPorte, *The German Communist Party*, pp. 70–71.

75. 'Monatsbericht (November 1930)', in St.Ha.D., MdI. Nr.11126/4, Bl.353; D. Ziegs, 'Die Leipziger SPD im Kampf um die Republik', in H. Grebing, H. Mommsen and K.

Rudolf (eds.), *Demokratie und Emanzipation zwischen Saale und Elbe. Beitrag zur Geschichte der sozialdemokratischen Arbeiterbewegung bis 1933* (Essen, 1993), pp. 318–29.

76. *Freiheitskampf*, 3 March and 23 August 1932.

77. See, for example, 'Bericht des Polizeipresidiums Leipzig Abteilung IV am 20.7.1932', in Stadtarchiv Leipzig, Ah. Leipzig Nr. 1721.

78. 'Instrukteurbericht Freital. Sitzung der erweiterten Ortsgruppeleitung am 13.6.1932', in Ba.K., R45 IV/28.

79. 'An die BL der KPD Sachsens. KPD UB4. Freiberg, den 3.6.1932', in Ba.K., R45 IV/28; 'An die BL (Org.). Bericht über Meissen von Instrukteur Rolf. Meissen, den 2.7.1932', in ibid; 'Aufruf zur Antifa Aktion. Freiberg June 1932' (leaflet), in Ba.K., R45 IV/28.

80. 'Bericht des UB 4 über die Antifaschistische Aktion und Reichstagswahl am 31.7.1931 auf Grund des Frage Bodens der BL (undated)' in Ba.K., R45 IV/28.

81. 'An die BL und UBL. Instrukteurbericht vom UB 9 am 21.7.1932, in Ba.K., R45 IV/28; 'An die BL (Pol.). Bericht über die Antifaschistische Aktion. Plauen, den 23.6.1932', in ibid.

82. 'Rundschreiben der KPD Nr.10. Bezirk Sachsens (undated: July 1932)', SAPMO I 3/8–10/151, Bl. 104–5.

83. *Klassenkampf*, 4 July 1932.

84. J. Degras, *Communist International*, p. 213.

85. H. Weber, *Hauptfeind*, p. 79.

86. H. Weber, *Hauptfeind*, p. 58.

87. S. Bahne, *Die KPD*, p. 13.

88. J. Degras, *Communist International*, pp. 432–36.

89. F. Eisner, *Das Verhältniss der KPD zu den Gewerkschaften in der Weimarer Republik* (Cologne, 1977), p. 222.

90. The Ruhr lockout is dealt with in detail by L. Peterson, 'Labour and the End of Weimar: The Case of the KPD in the November 1928: Lockout in the Rheinish-Westphalian Iron and Steel Industry', *Central European History* Vol. 1 (1982); S Bahne, 'Die KPD im Ruhrgebiet in der Weimarer Republik', in J Reulecke, (Ed.), *Arbeiterbewegung an Rhein und Ruhr: Beiträge zur Geschichte der Arbeiterbewegung in Rheinland–Westfalen* (Wuppertal, 1974), pp. 332–39; A. Watlin, *Die Komintern*, pp. 183–4.

91. J. Weiszt, *KPD-Politik in der Krise, 1928–32*, (Frankfurt, 1976), pp. 58–59.

92. Ibid. pp. 35–36 and pp. 341–42; V. Wunderlich, *Arbeiterbewegung und Selbstverwaltung*, pp. 56–58.

93. W Müller, *Lohnkampf, Massenstreik, Soujetmacht: Zeil und Grenzen der RGO in Deutschland 1929 bis 1933* (Cologne, 1988).

94. B. Fowkes, *Communism in Germany*, pp. 158–59; F. Eisner, *Das Verhältniss*, pp. 232–37.

95. H. Weber, *Hauptfeind*, p. 24.

96. U. Stolle, *Arbeiterpolitik im Betrieb: Frauen und Maenner, Reformisten und Radikale, Fach und Massenarbeiter bei Bayern, BASF, Borsch und in Solingen, 1900–33* (Frankfurt-am-Main, 1980), p. 213 and p. 260; W. Zollitsch, *Arbeiter zwischen Weltwirtschaftkrise und National-sozialismus* (Göttingen, 1990), pp. 190–94; L Heer-Kleinert, *Die Gewerkschaftspolitik der KPD in der Weimarer Republik* (Frankfurt, 1983), p. 376 and p. 381; E. C. Schöck, *Arbeitslosigkeit und Rationalisierung: Die Lage der Arbeiter und die Kommunistische Gewerkschaftspolitik 1920–28* (Frankfurt 1977), p. 245.

97. 'Bericht der 2. Bezirksparteitag am 25–7.3.1932', SAPMO I 3/8–10/144, Bl.9.

98.Compare, 'Sächsischer Betriebspressedienst (August 1932)', SAPMO I 3/8–10/158, Bl.187; H. Weber, *Rundschreiben*, p. 572.

99. Cited in H. Weber, *Hauptfeind*, p. 47.

100. H. A. Winkler, *Der Weg in der Katastrophe Arbeiter und Arbeiterbewegung in der Weimarer Republik 1930–33* (Berlin, 1987), p. 751 and note 97. Winkler attributes a greater influence to the RGO in these strikes. However, the evidence from developments in Saxony point to a different conclusion, see N. LaPorte, *The German Communist Party*, p. 346. On the NSBO and its influence among workers in metal-working, mining, transport and smaller handicrafts factories, see D. W. Daycock, 'The KPD and the NSDAP: A Study in the Relationship between the Political Extremes in Weimar Germany 1923–33' Ph.D. thesis (London School of Economics, 1980), pp. 228–29; V Krazenberg, *Arbeiter auf dem Weg zu Hitler? Die Nationalsozialistische Betriebszellen-Organisation. Ihre Entstehung, ihre Programmatik, ihr Scheitern 1927–34* (Frankfurt, 1987), p. 104.

101. H. A. Winkler, *Der Weg*, pp. 765–73; N. LaPorte, *The German Communist Party*, p. 346.

102. C. Fischer, *German Communists*, p. 186.

103. N. LaPorte, *The German Communist Party*, p. 346.

104. Ibid.

105. S. Baumgarten, 'Eine Wende in der Geschichtsschreibung zur KPD in der Weimarer Republik?', *IWK*, Vol. 34 No. 1 (1998), pp. 82–89.

106. E. Weitz, *Creating German Communism*, p. 18; A. Wirsching, *Vom Weltkrieg zum Bürgerkrieg? Politischer Extremismus in Deutschland und Frankreich 1918–33* (Munich, 1999). Wirsching's analysis confirms the position of earlier studies, such as E. Rosenhaft, *Beating*, p.211; E. Hennig, 'Nachbemerkungen zu einem Aspekt des kommunistischen Tageskampfes gegen die Sozialdemokratie', in *Gesellschaft. Beiträge zur Marxistischen Theorie* Vol. 6 (1976), pp. 292–97.

107. D. Peukert, 'Zur Sozialgeschichte der Kommunistsiche Partei Deutschlands', in *Zur Geschichte der Arbeiterbewegung*, Vol. (1978), pp. 35–37; J Wickham, 'Social Fascism and the Division of the Working Class Movement: Workers and Political Parties in the Frankfurt Area 1929–30', *Capital and Class* No. 7 (1979), pp. 1–34.

108. K. Mallmann, *Kommunisten*, p. 165.

109. For a summary of recent findings and a typology of immediate influences on the KPD at a local level, see K. Mallmann, 'Sozialgeschichte des Kommunismus', p. 26.

110. E. Weitz, *Creating German Communism*, p. 5 and p. 391; M Rudloff, 'Politische "Säuberungen" in der KPD der Weimarer Republic', *Leipziger Hefte* No. 1 (1995), pp. 4–23; A. Aviva, 'The SPD and KPD at the End of the Weimar Republic: Similarity Within Contrast', *IWK*, Vol. 14 No. 2 (1978), pp. 171–86.

111. H. Weber, *Kommunismus in Deutschland*, p. 46.

112. H. A. Winkler, *Der Weg*, p. 734; H. Pogge von Strandmann, 'Industrial Primacy in German Foreign Policy? Myths and Realities in German-Russian Relations at the End of the Weimar Republic', in R. Bessel. and E. J. Feuchtwanger, (eds.), *Social Change and Political Development in Weimar Germany* (London, 1981), pp. 241–67; K. Niclauss, *Die Sowjetunion und Hitlers Machtergreifung. Eine Studie über die deutsch-sowjetischen Beziehungen der Jahre 1929 bis 1935* (Bonn 1966), p. 80.

To the Left and Back Again: The Communist Party of Great Britain in the Third Period

MATTHEW WORLEY

[The New Line] accorded completely with our mood of frustration and despair, with our lack of confidence in the recognised labour leadership, our desire for something short, sharp, and spectacular to end the hopeless stalemate of our existence.[1]

Margaret McCarthy

We had 3,500 dues-paying members, no daily paper, and disagreements on policy that required two party congresses to sort out ... I think the party congress in Leeds in November 1929 was the most difficult congress I have ever attended. I made a political report that was received in stony silence.[2]

Harry Pollitt (CPGB General Secretary)

The Third Period was a difficult and often traumatic time for the Communist Party of Great Britain (CPGB). Most immediately, the introduction of the New Line (labelled 'class against class') in 1927–28, provoked a protracted intra-party dispute that lasted some two years and turned the CPGB in, on and against itself. In the process, the party leadership came into conflict with both the Communist International (Comintern) and much of its own membership, while the party's focus on the intricacies of communist theory did much to alienate and repel those workers that the CPGB wished to recruit. Appropriately, therefore, party membership fell to a low of 2,350 in August 1930, and previously significant bases of communist support within the trade unions and among the miners of South Wales, Scotland and Durham fell into disrepair.[3] A militant sectarianism came to characterise sections of the CPGB, as those on the left of the wider British labour movement were dismissed as 'social fascists', and as party members sought to ensure that workers rallied under an explicitly communist banner. Two general elections, in 1929 and 1931, came and went amidst much communist clamour and a collapsed Labour government; yet they brought mainly lost deposits and humiliating defeat to the intractable CPGB. Frustratingly, too, the party could claim only to have had a marginal influence on the industrial disputes that broke out intermittently over the period, in spite of two 'red' trade unions and the revolutionary rhetoric that flowed freely from party activists, party pamphlets, and the newly launched *Daily Worker*. Although the predicted 'capitalist crisis' cast its shadow over Britain at this time, an accompanying workers' revolution did not follow in its wake.

Yet, this list of frustrated militancy and apparent failure does not tell the entire story. In the face of numerous disappointments, the CPGB also headed the pre-eminent unemployed organisation of the period, the National Unemployed Workers' Movement (NUWM).[4] With Britain's staple industries (mining, shipbuilding, textiles) suffering in response to technological modification, structural change, rationalisation, increased competition and the high rate of sterling, so many communist trade unionists became NUWM activists committed to the struggles of the unemployed during the 'class against class' years.[5] Similarly, as industrial action declined in the aftermath of the 1926 General Strike and the ensuing miners' lockout, so worker protest gradually resurfaced in the form of national hunger marches and demonstrations to the local boards of guardians or public assistance committees responsible for relief. In the wake of the Wall Street crash of October 1929 (and the corresponding rise in unemployment over 1929–32), thousands of workers joined the NUWM, and many hundreds the CPGB. As such, communist party membership also *grew* during the Third Period, reaching some 9,000 by the winter of 1931–32, before settling at 5,400 in November 1932.[6] Indeed, the hunger marches and the apparent successes of the Soviet five-year plan in contrast to capitalist depression did much to win both workers and intellectuals (John Cornford, Margot Heinemann, John Strachey) to communism.[7] Finally, party cadres were inspired to forge a distinct communist culture based upon the theoretical constructs of 'class against class', forming theatre groups, football leagues, film societies and training classes, often to the benefit of many beyond the CPGB itself. Amidst the general and more prominent political frustrations of the Third Period, the CPGB also registered some notable achievements.

Of course, none of this justifies the CPGB's or the Comintern's overestimation (or misreading) of the 'revolutionary situation' in the late 1920s and early 1930s. Throughout the Third Period, the British party endeavoured to align itself within the theoretical and political paradigm established by the Comintern and to apply the appropriate communist policy to the varied situations in which party members found themselves. In such a context, the exaggerated and partisan pronouncements of the CPGB often made a bad situation worse. But even here, we must be careful of producing too uniform or sweeping a conception of communist activity in Britain. Differences with regard to the interpretation and the application of the New

Line were evident within the CPGB, and the line itself changed over the period via a mixture of shifting Comintern objectives and pragmatic interpretation. The CPGB's experience during the Third Period was thus a complex and multifarious one. To this effect, the difficulties that the party faced at this time were a combination of interchangeable factors relating to the material circumstances then prevailing in Britain, to the intricacies and peculiarities of Comintern politics – namely the Marxist–Leninist precept of a binding political line and the consolidation of Stalin's grip on power – and to the evident difficulty of transforming theory into consistent and coherent practice. The CPGB failed to forge the revolution during the Third Period, but the party's efforts must be brought into perspective.

Finding the Line

The political line pursued by the CPGB over the course of the Third Period passed through a number of distinct stages. Although the theoretical basis of 'class against class' remained relatively constant, the emphasis or focus of communist policy often changed between late 1927 and 1933, from which point the 'struggle against fascism' began to preoccupy the Comintern and the CPGB. Initially, the New Line proposed by Bukharin in October 1927 and adopted by the CPGB at the ninth plenum of the Executive Committee of the Communist International (ECCI) in February 1928 was primarily concerned with communist policy in relation to the British Labour Party. Thus, the CPGB was to 'struggle not only against the ruling classes, but also against their lackeys ... against the bourgeois leadership of the Labour Party, against parliamentary cretinism in all its forms, and ... [to participate] in the next general election as an independent party with its own platform and candidates'.[8] This, in effect, marked an end to the CPGB's previous policy of attempting to affiliate to the Labour Party in order to work within the larger working class organisation. From 1928, the CPGB contended that the Labour Party was transforming into the 'third party of the bourgeoisie' (next to the British Conservative and Liberal parties) and, by so doing, sought to reveal the 'treacherous' nature of social democracy to the British working class.[9]

To an extent, such a change of line corresponded with a hardening communist perspective evident from at least late 1926. As outlined in the introductory chapter 'Courting Disaster' (pp. 1–17), Bukharin first noted the emergence of a 'third period' of post-war development at the seventh plenum of the ECCI in November 1926, and it was from there on that many of the key concepts of the Third Period found their way onto the CPGB's agenda.[10] So, for instance, the resolutions relating to Britain adopted by the eighth ECCI plenum in May 1927 included reference to the 'sharpening class struggle', to the 'left lackey' role of the ILP inside the Labour Party, to the 'rapprochement' of the Labour Party and trade union leadership with the capitalist state, and to the 'deceptions' of left-wing trade union leaders.[11] This, in turn, was based on the evident failure of the General Strike, which the party (and the Comintern) regarded as clear evidence of reformist betrayal, along with the gradual unravelling of the 'united front' initiatives pursued by the CPGB from its formation in 1920. From 1926 through to 1928–29, communists were expelled from the Labour Party, marginalised (to varying degrees) in the trade unions, and often 'victimised' in their place of employment.[12] Correspondingly, industrial action fell dramatically following the General Strike, as the TUC entered into negotiations with the employers (the Mond–Turner talks), the Anglo-Russian Joint Advisory Council established between the TUC General Council and the Russian trade unions was terminated, TUC links with the NUWM were curtailed, and the Conservative government legislated against worker organisation (the 1927 Trade Disputes and Trade Union Act) and severed diplomatic relations with the USSR. Even so, the Comintern's decision to overhaul CPGB policy came as a surprise to the British comrades – such a change had not been discussed with the British leadership prior to October 1927 – and the party evidently struggled to both comprehend and apply the concepts of 'class against class'. As is well known, a majority of the CPGB Central Committee (CC), including J. R. Campbell, Andrew Rothstein, Ernest Brown and Arthur Horner, resisted the change of line, only to be overruled by the ECCI at its ninth plenum in February 1928.[13]

Significantly, however, the detail, scope and extent of the New Line remained undetermined for much of 1928. As a result, the second stage of the party's Third Period development stretched from the sixth world congress of the Comintern held in July–August 1928, through the tenth ECCI plenum in July 1929, up until the eleventh CPGB congress in November–December of that year. During this time, the policies of 'class against class' were expanded and realigned in response to various overlapping factors. First, the theoretical bases of the Third Period – the leftward development of the working class, the rapprochement of social democracy and the bourgeoisie, intensifying class struggle and revolutionary 'upsurge' – were applied to all areas of communist activity. For example, talk soon turned to trade union policy following the fourth congress of the Red International of Labour Unions (RILU) in April 1928, thereby raising the concept of communist-led 'red' trade unions in opposition to the 'reformist' unions of the Amsterdam International.[14] Second, both the theoretical and the practical formulations of the Third Period were debated in relation to the Marxist–Leninist principle of an immutable, or 'correct', party line. Third, such a debate was incorporated into the on-going struggle for power inside the Soviet Union. As Stalin moved against Bukharin within the Soviet leadership, so the Comintern leader's initial conditions for the Third Period were challenged and modified. Consequently, the New Line moved further to the left, as communists sought to forge a line devoid of 'right deviation' and wholly distinct from the 'conciliatory' policies of the 'second period'. Within the CPGB, this was characterised by criticism being directed at the existing party leadership for its failure to fully endorse and implement Comintern directives. Thus, the party's dwindling fortunes – the continuing decline in party membership (down to 3,500 by January 1929), a poor showing in the 1929 general election, the party's inability to combat the Labour Party and TUC offensive against communists within their respective ranks, or to mobilise the supposedly 'radicalised' workers – were attributed to the 'right deviation' of leading party members. That such criticism was encouraged and utilised by those close to Stalin in order to defeat Bukharin obviously exacerbated matters, facilitating the overt sectarianism that has often come to define the Third Period. Indeed, with the struggle against the 'right danger' at the top of the ECCI's agenda in late 1928 and throughout 1929, British party members often went beyond the political guidelines issued by the Comintern in order to prove their left credentials. At the CPGB's tenth congress in January 1929, delegates effectively voted to withdraw completely from organised activity inside the Labour Party and came close to endorsing what the Comintern had earlier noted to be 'a hazy desire to abandon the struggle inside the existing [trade unions] and create new red unions without taking into consideration the concrete state of affairs and the correlation of forces'.[15] This extremism would be checked, to a degree, from 1930, but for the remainder of 1929 the CPGB descended into factionalism and round after round of self-criticism. By the end of the year, the party numbered just 3,170 and appeared to have lost contact with all but a tiny minority of the British working class.

In the wake of the tenth ECCI plenum, therefore, at which the concept of 'social fascism' had been adopted and the Comintern had strongly criticised the CPGB leadership's apparent equivocation with regard to 'class against class', the left appeared to be in the ascendancy. The British party hierarchy was subsequently overhauled under Comintern supervision – though not to the extent that many on the left of the CPGB demanded – and a markedly different CC was voted in at the eleventh congress under the watchful eye of Walter Ulbricht, the ECCI representative.[16] Moreover, the resolutions adopted by the congress portrayed both Britain and the capitalist world as being on the very edge of a revolutionary precipice (Wall Street had just 'crashed') in such a tone of militant expectancy that the party secretary, Harry Pollitt, later admitted that the congress reports made him want to 'vomit'.[17] Even Rajani Palme Dutt, a leading British theoretician who boasted close links with the Comintern and encouraged the left offensive against the British leadership, feared that the unbridled militancy of many a young communist 'robbed' the Third Period 'of all seriousness'.[18] As such, while the Comintern continued to encourage the struggle against the 'right danger' inside the CPGB, it was sometimes necessary for the ECCI to check the leftist aspirations of many within the British party. This was, perhaps, best symbolised by the ECCI's support for Harry Pollitt, an Openshaw boilermaker and party leader who had championed the introduction of 'class against class' but registered severe reservations about the direction in which the New Line appeared to be heading in late 1928–29. Pollitt was extremely critical of moves to establish 'red' trade unions in Britain, to the extent that he blocked the formation of a 'red' seaman's union in late 1928 against orders from the RILU, and was accused of 'right deviation' following his participation in the Dawdon miners' struggle of March–June 1929.[19] And yet, the Comintern retained its faith in Pollitt, acknowledging his evident capabilities in preference to those who more closely fitted the stereotype 'Moscow automaton' (such as William Rust), appointing him general secretary in July 1929. If the CPGB lurched to the extreme left in 1929, the ECCI entrusted those such as Pollitt to steer the party along a more balanced course once the 'right danger' had been expunged.[20]

The third stage in the CPGB's development across the Third Period, from approximately the beginning of 1930 through to the autumn of 1931, was characterised by attempts to rebuild a party that had dwindled in size and influence since the termination of the miners' lockout in late 1926. Certainly, the CPGB's introspection over the course of 1928–29 had a deleterious impact on the party's fortunes, leading the London district organiser, R. W. Robson, to report that 'the year of great internal discussion [1929]' had provoked some 400 workers to leave the district party because they were simply 'not interested' in the minutiae of the Comintern line.[21] Similarly, of course, the sectarianism engendered by 'class against class' no doubt repelled many workers who encountered the CPGB at this time. To take one example, the Scottish communist William Allan recalled local comrades 'snubbing' five new recruits because their descriptions of conditions inside their respective workplaces were not peppered with adequate Bolshevik jargon.[22] We should note, however, that the problems facing the CPGB ran deeper than the specifics of the party line, as we shall see below. In such circumstances, the party's priority from 1930 was to reintegrate itself amongst the British working class.

A number of initiatives were embraced by the CPGB in order to revive its apparently waning influence. The first British communist daily paper, the *Daily Worker*, was launched on 1 January 1930 with the help of Comintern funding; a revived emphasis on building a 'united front from below' was soon evident, with the intention of drawing non-party workers towards the CPGB and combating 'left sectarianism'; a Workers' Charter of limited demands (minimum wage etc.) was promoted from September 1930 to rally wider working class support, especially from within the trade unions; and the

Young Communist League (YCL) was overhauled and urged to promote cultural, particularly sporting, events. In addition, a more flexible, or tactical, use of Third Period policy was encouraged by the Comintern in the wake of a British Commission held in Moscow in August 1930, whereat the CPGB was instructed to recognise Harry Pollitt as the 'leader' of the party.[23] Not surprisingly, the effect of all this was not immediately apparent. Party membership had only recovered in part by early 1931, sales of the *Daily Worker* remained disappointing, and the Workers' Charter made but minor in-roads into the trade union movement. Elsewhere, sectarianism continued to afflict sections of the party, particularly in Scotland and on Tyneside (as well as among certain comrades in the party leadership), while the party's impact on the widescale textile disputes of 1930–31 was modest to say the least. More positively, the NUWM – which had begun a 'slow revival' from late 1928 – continued to expand in tandem with rising rates of unemployment, and the party's sports movement, the British Workers' Sports Federation (BWSF), attracted relatively large numbers of workers to its initiatives in 1930–32 (see below).

Quite clearly, tweaking with the party line and merely expressing the objective of becoming a mass party was not enough, although such moves at least helped turn the party's face back towards the British working class and away from its own internal intrigues. Rather, the CPGB's own 'revival' began more readily in response to the heightened political climate provoked by the economic depression of the early 1930s, the collapse of the minority Labour government in August 1931, and the ensuing general election on 27 October. As the dole queues lengthened and international capitalism appeared temporarily unable to cope with the crises that confronted it, so hunger marches and unemployed demonstrations became more widespread, potent and expressive.[24] Not only did communist rhetoric appear to have some substance in such a context, but the perceived success of the Soviet five-year-plan offered a working alternative to capitalism – as the CPGB tirelessly propagated. Accordingly, communist party membership expanded from just 2,711 in February 1931 to approximately 9,000 in January 1932, the majority of whom joined the party's ranks from September–October 1931.[25] The NUWM, meantime, boasted an average of 23,643 members in the last two months of the same year, compared to an average of 5,121 in October 1928.[26] It was partly in order to deal with such an influx of (largely unemployed) members that the CPGB sought, from late 1931, to consolidate its organisational basis and further extend its influence to workers both inside the workplace and the trade unions.

This fourth stage of the New Line was most notable for the CPGB's attempt to reassert its presence in the trade union movement. Although the party was encouraged by its increase in membership over the last months of 1931, the CPGB was also concerned about the predominantly unemployed status of its new cadres. Having gained support from at least a section of the ECCI in late 1931, therefore, Pollitt urged his comrades to get back into the trade unions and fight for the workers' basic day-to-day demands. 'The theory that the old unions are schools of capitalism and we are in them to destroy them is absolutely false', he informed the party leadership in January 1932. It was now time to 'strangle' the 'new union psychology' of 'class against class', Pollitt insisted, before going on to encourage a far more flexible approach towards communist trade union work over the course of the year.[27] Inspired, in part, by the Members' Rights Movement inside the Amalgamated Engineering Union (AEU), Pollitt urged the party to support rank-and-file movements within the 'reformist' trade unions (such as the Builders' Forward Movement), and thereby win support for communist policy and initiative.

The wider party membership's initial response to Pollitt's recommendations was lukewarm, but the party leader's approach gained credence as the year wore on. By the time of the twelfth party congress, held on 12–15 November 1932, the party had registered a greater influence within certain trade unions, an increase in factory groups, and had endorsed Pollitt's line of participating in 'every phase of union life and activity'.[28] Although this remained resolutely within the context of 'class against class', and the party's attacks against the ILP and the Labour Party leadership continued to be as vehement as ever, it marked an important shift in emphasis and a broadening of the party's approach to its organisational work. Without doubt, such a move had been helped by certain structural realignments instigated by the party in January 1932. Having drawn up proposals in late 1931, these were discussed by a party delegation to Moscow in December and introduced to the CPGB membership in January 1932. Essentially, the party reduced its central apparatus, focused itself on the four principal areas of communist activity in Britain (London, South Wales, Scotland, Lancashire), and drew up systematic plans for party agitation in targeted factories, pits and unions.[29] Ultimately, however, the NUWM remained the principal forum for communist protest in 1932, with some 60 per cent of the party membership registered unemployed by the twelfth party congress, and with an impressive national hunger march to London gaining widespread media attention in the autumn. It would take an upturn in the British economy and the continued emergence of 'new' industries to facilitate the re-emergence of a significant communist presence within the trade union movement.

From the moment of Hitler's appointment as German chancellor in January 1933, the focus of the CPGB, the Comintern and the whole world began to turn towards the advance of fascism. Within the CPGB, the move towards the 'united front against fascism' first came in the spring following the Comintern's critical but affirmative reply to the Labour and Socialist

International's call for a joint struggle. Debates ensued within the CPGB as to the connotations of the Comintern's somewhat equivocal signal, but Pollitt's lead ensured that the party began to make overtures to the wider labour movement in response to the fascist threat. As such, talks between communists and the ILP began on 17 March. Not surprisingly, the change of line proceeded slowly over the course of 1933–34. As is well known, Stalin was loath to come round to the new mood emerging in important parts of the Comintern, while many in the labour movement remained suspicious of communist motives. Equally, the struggle against social democracy continued to be at the head of the CPGB's wider agenda. Yet, these years did indeed see the slow evolution of the Third Period into the Popular Front and thereby a new chapter in the CPGB's development.[30]

As the above overview suggests, the New Line passed through a number of stages in which the emphases of 'class against class' were reassessed and realigned. Quite clearly, Soviet determinants were integral to such developments. The nature and extent of the offensive against the 'right danger' was undoubtedly shaped by Kremlin power struggles, and later moves to contain the excesses of the 'left turn' were assisted by Stalin's 'dizzy with success' letter of March 1930 that warned against the (left) danger of comrades 'rushing ahead' with their revolutionary exuberance.[31] However, more objective factors were also important. The risk of 'left sectarianism' was acknowledged throughout the Third Period (although the 'right danger' swamped such concern in 1928–29), and the militancy provoked by the New Line quickly turned attention to the excesses of 'class against class'.[32] With regard to Britain, the party's experiences in the Yorkshire woollen dispute of 1930, in the Scots coalfield, amongst the textile workers of Lancashire, and in its own diminishing party ranks, all revealed the need for a more systematic approach to the beleaguered workers.[33] In response, those such as Pollitt who wished to forge a more balanced and adaptable line were supported by the ECCI in their attempts to curtail 'ultra-leftism' within the British party. While the theoretical foundations of 'class against class' remained beyond reproach, communist debate on tactical issues allowed some (limited) flexibility. Of course, the final word would always lay with the ECCI, but the New Line could be interpreted in a number of different ways, as became increasingly apparent once comrades sought to apply the line 'on the ground'.

Applying the Line

When the CPGB adopted the policy of 'class against class' in February 1928, it was very much a party in retreat. Most demonstrably, the relatively large increase in communist party membership that had accompanied the 1926 General Strike and miners' lockout had fallen away dramatically. Having grown from 4,900 to approximately 12,000 over the course of 1926, CPGB membership fell to 7,909 in February 1927, before dropping to 6,396 in October, to 5,556 by March 1928.[34] Secondly, as noted above, the party was being attacked from within the wider British labour movement. As a result, the small but tenuous footholds that the party had established in certain local Labour parties, trades councils and trade union branches since 1920 were under threat and diminishing. Although communists could be amongst the most dedicated and hard-working members of the British labour movement, the party was always cast in the shadow of a Labour Party based on the support of the mass ranks of British trade unionism, not to mention the Radical traditions and constitutional, 'ethical socialism' of its leaders, forebears and constituents. Finally, material conditions were hardly conducive to communist advancement in the late 1920s. In the wake of the General Strike, unemployment and disillusionment began to impinge on areas where the CPGB had previously developed bases of support, particularly in South Wales and Scotland. Given such circumstances, workers tended initially to withdraw from political and trade union activity, or to seek employment elsewhere.[35] Trade union membership and density continued to decline in the late 1920s, while the failure of the General Strike helped consolidate the more conciliatory outlook of many within the organised labour movement. Not only did the years 1927 and 1928 record the lowest number of days lost to industrial action since detailed records began, but they saw also the commencement of the Mond–Turner talks between employer representatives and the TUC.[36] Consequently, many workers turned instead to the parliamentary Labour Party to protect and advance their interests, as revealed by the 8,370,417 voters who elected a minority Labour government in May 1929. Conversely, of course, such 'offensives' against the CPGB and the working class (along with the increase in Labour Party support) actually encouraged communist hopes of renewed worker militancy. For those who wished to believe, unemployment, conciliation and rationalisation lent credence to the revolutionary predictions of the Third Period – all that was needed was the 'correct' application of Marxist–Leninist theory.

Given the CPGB's limited presence amongst the British working class, the party did not expect to register a quantitative success at the general elections of 1929 and 1931. Writing before the former, Dutt highlighted the *principle* of the CPGB's stand against a Labour Party committed to 'rationalisation, industrial peace, imperialism and the maintenance of the capitalist state'.[37] Even so, the party fared badly, losing its one existing seat – Shapurji Saklatvala's in North Battersea – and gaining just 50,634 votes for its 25 candidates. The party's poll improved slightly in 1931, with 26 candidates securing 74,824 votes, but it remained a great disappointment given the failure of the Labour administration and the heightened political climate occasioned by the depression and the government's collapse. Ultimately, the CPGB was not seen as a credible alternative to the Labour Party. As to why this was the case, the question goes beyond the remit of the current study; but the party's association with the 'foreign' USSR, its revolutionary perspective, and its lack of a solid organisational and financial basis within the wider British labour movement, all did much to limit the CPGB's appeal. We should note, too, that the economic downturn of the period was felt unevenly across Britain, that unemployed British workers were afforded some relief, and that British political structures remained firmly in place. The economic problems surrounding the depression did not match the catastrophic predictions of the CPGB, even though they proved distressing for many workers and their families at the time. Where the party did register a respectable showing in one or both general elections, in Rhondda East (Arthur Horner) or Dundee (Bob Stewart), this owed much to a candidate's familiarity with the local community and to his/her place within local working class politics. Locally, meanwhile, the party recorded scattered successes at a municipal level, although the divisions between Labour and the CPGB consolidated by the Third Period could too often split the 'left', as in the District and County Council elections in the Vale of Leven in late 1932.[38]

More alarming for the CPGB than its general election performance, was the party's withering influence inside the factories, pits and trade union movement. Throughout the mid-1920s, the party had sought to organise a communist presence in the trade unions via the National Minority Movement (NMM), a supposedly broad grouping of communists and left-wingers committed to defending workers' interests and propagating a socialist trade union policy. This had been relatively successful in the build up to the 1926 General Strike, winning eminent trade unionists such as A. J. Cook of the Welsh miners' union and the engineers' leader Jack Tanner to its ranks. Hugely inflated claims of representing nearly a quarter of all trade union members were regularly made by the NMM, but there is no doubt that the 228 affiliated organisations claimed by the NMM in December 1926 gave the movement an influence beyond that of the CPGB.[39] In response, both the TUC and individual trade union leaderships began to take more concerted measures to curtail the NMM in the wake of the General Strike, disaffiliating trades councils linked to the movement and refusing to recognise NMM candidates, memorandums and delegates. The NMM had itself resolved to 'crystallise' its influence inside the trade unions in August 1926, bolstered as it was by an influx of support from those miners still locked out and incensed by the 'betrayal' of the TUC.[40] Yet, such militancy merely reinforced the TUC's anti-communism, and the NMM was privately registering a loss of membership by the end of 1927.[41]

The introduction of 'class against class' did not initially alter the CPGB's or the NMM's general approach to the 'reformist' trade unions. Over the course of 1928, however, communist policy was revised to meet the theoretical formulations of the Third Period, and was pushed towards political extremes by Alexander Lozovsky, the head of the RILU and a member of the ECCI. Although tensions appear to have existed between Lozovsky and others on the ECCI, especially regarding Lozovsky's penchant for promoting 'red' trade unions, communists were eventually instructed to overhaul their existing trade union strategies. Essentially, the Comintern asserted that in a period of 'revolutionary upsurge', the 'reformist' unions would fuse with the capitalist state and actively suppress the militancy of the working class in support of the bourgeoisie. In such circumstances, worker militancy was seen increasingly to exist outside of the union apparatus, amongst unorganised workers and often in opposition to the 'reformist' union bureaucracy. Thus, communists were to mobilise non-union (and union) workers into factory committees, to take an independent lead in industrial disputes, and to raise the perspective of, or to form if conditions allowed, communist-led 'red' trade unions in opposition to existing 'reformist' organisations. In addition, communists were to expose those 'left' trade unionists that tried to 'conceal from the workers the real significance of this process and are forming an active and constituent part in the system of social fascism'. Although disagreements emerged within the CPGB over just what role the NMM was to play in such a strategy (some members even argued for its liquidation), the movement was in theory to show a disregard for trade union 'legalism' and to form a 'revolutionary trade union opposition' both inside and out of the 'reformist' apparatus.[42]

Ultimately, the NMM (and the CPGB) proved incapable of instigating such an ambitious policy. With industrial action at a low, unemployment rising, and the support rendered from the miners' lockout proving transient, the NMM fell into disrepair. The main stoppages that did occur between 1929 and 1932, involving textile workers in Lancashire and Yorkshire, took place in localities and mills where neither the CPGB nor the NMM had an established base of support, and to which those communist cadres drafted into the dispute brought little to no local or occupational knowledge. Too often, the NMM appeared on the periphery of the dispute, accusing union officials of 'social fascism', but making little headway with regard to organising workers inside the mills. Most obviously, the party and the NMM were slow to recognise the predominantly female character of the textile workforce, focusing instead on the minority of skilled male workers. In such a way, Isabel Brown's recollection of one striking woollen worker waving a party leaflet and shouting 'up with the lavatory seat, down with the lavatory chain' is perhaps a fitting testimony to the party's record.[43]

In those industries where the NMM had established some support (mining and transport), a mixture of political sectarianism and circumstance combined to limit the movement's influence. Not only did the NMM headquarters in London's Great Ormond Street become a hotbed of ultra-leftism, but many communists took heed of the militant declarations of the ECCI and RILU whilst ignoring the significant caveats that accompanied Comintern policy. Young NMM leaders, including John Mahon and George Allison, regularly emphasised the need to mobilise unorganised workers around the communist banner, only to ignore those who were already in the trade unions. Similarly, the drive towards 'red' trade unions appeared to be given priority over the more basic task of building initial NMM support in the factories, pits, depots and mills. Erstwhile allies were either lost or alienated, rank-and-file groups inside the unions but opposed to official union policy were condemned unless they bowed to communist dominance, and even non-party trade unionists who remained in the NMM baulked at the militant sectarianism emanating from the movement. So, for instance, Alex Gossip, leader of the National Amalgamated Furniture Trades Association (NAFTA), briefly distanced himself from the NMM following communist insistence that workers outside of Gossip's union had the more 'revolutionary character' during a 1929 furnishing dispute.[44] Even within the CPGB, those who had fought hard inside the trade union movement for much of their political lives, such as Arthur Horner and Harry Pollitt, despaired of the rampant and misguided militancy of the NMM. Both men served as secretary to the NMM during the Third Period, and both were relocated because of their disagreement with aspects of the New Line. Famously, Arthur Horner took his concerns to the RILU following the Welsh miners' dispute of January 1931, describing the NMM's conduct of the strike as 'infantile'. He in turn was criticised by his comrades in South Wales and the party executive, before the ECCI admonished him for his 'tactical errors'. Notably, however, Horner's criticisms were taken on board by the ECCI, and the Welsh strike was later used by Otto Kuusinen as an example of how *not* to employ an independent leadership of the working class.[45] By 1932, Pollitt's campaign to widen the CPGB's approach to trade union work effectively marked the death knell for the NMM. With just 300–500 individual members in late 1930, compared to 3,460 in December 1926, the NMM lacked both the cadres and the administrative machinery to constitute an alternative trade union leadership.[46]

The CPGB's two attempts to establish 'red' trade unions during the Third Period were similarly dispiriting. The first, the United Clothing Workers' Union (UCWU), was launched in March 1929 following an unofficial dispute among workers at Rego Clothiers in London.[47] Led by Sam Elsbury, an executive member of the NMM and the Tailors' Union official who had organised the Rego workers, the UCWU was a classic example of forming a 'red' union without due consideration of the wider circumstances. Certainly, Harry Pollitt, who was in the USA at the time of the UCWU's instigation, later claimed that he would have opposed its formation, and the union had all but disintegrated by the end of its first year. As well as having the support of only a minority of Tailors' Union members, the UCWU confronted official union, wholesaler and employer opposition, and quickly entered into an ill-advised strike that the CPGB promised but proved unable to support financially. Elsbury duly took the blame for the union's failings and was expelled from the party in December 1929. The union subsequently limped on with just a few hundred members until its dissolution 1935.[48]

The second 'red' union, the United Mineworkers of Scotland (UMS), emerged from a protracted intra-union dispute that had its origins pre-'class against class' and may well have formed (though in a different guise) with or without the New Line.[49] As such, the UMS proved somewhat more durable than the UCWU, and did at least offer a challenge to the 'official' miners' union in the Fife coalfield. Even so, the 'red' union was supposed to form the basis for a national alternative to the National Union of Scottish Mine Workers (NUSMW) and, in time, the Miners' Federation of Great Britain (MFGB). Ultimately, however, its perseverance in Fife gave way to frustrated militancy in other areas of the Scots coalfield. Formed in April 1929, the UMS was faced with NUSMW and employer opposition, rising unemployment in the pit villages, financial instability, and internal disagreements relating to both regional and political differences. The first year of the union's existence was marked by a series of hurriedly called strikes that generally ended in damaging defeat, before a change of leadership in 1930 coincided with attempts to combat the sectarian approach of many union members. Following a second leadership overhaul in August 1931, when Abe Moffat became the union general secretary, the UMS worked to consolidate its strongholds in Fife and present a more balanced and systematic approach to the Scottish mineworkers.[50] It too was dissolved in 1935.

Beyond this, the prospect of a 'red' union was occasionally raised but rarely given much consideration within the CPGB. As mentioned above, Pollitt blocked the formation of a 'red' seamen's union in late 1928, and only once did the possibility of extending the UMS beyond the Scots coalfield present itself to the CPGB. In February 1930, the militant Mardy branch of the South Wales Miners' Federation (SWMF) was expelled following its unrepentant support for Arthur Horner's stand against the Labour candidate at the 1929 general election. After some deliberation, and under pressure from the RILU, the party eventually adopted the perspective of a 'new union' in April before seeking confirmation from the Comintern. Essentially, the party line was a compromise that belied many in the CPGB leadership's uncertainty at the prospect of establishing a 'red' union from the largely unemployed rump that made up the Mardy branch. By adopting the perspective a 'red' union, the party remained within the boundaries of

Comintern policy, while simultaneously avoiding any commitment to immediately establish such a breakaway organisation. By the summer of 1930, however, the ECCI had begun to reassess the belligerent aspirations of the RILU, and so ruled that although the CPGB's position was theoretically correct, such a policy was nevertheless 'premature' given the existing circumstances. It was from here onwards that Pollitt began his campaign to revise the party's approach to trade union work.[51]

Overall, the CPGB's declining presence within the trade unions and the workplace represented the party's greatest failing of the Third Period. Without doubt, the excesses of 'class against class' contributed to such a development, but we must also keep in mind the particular circumstances in which the party and the NMM were attempting to function. First, Labour movement hostility to the NMM predated the adoption of 'class against class' and served effectively to marginalize the movement in a number of trade unions. Secondly, a loss of influence and membership characterised trade union organisation beyond the NMM. As mentioned above, trade union membership and density continued to fall over the Third Period, while recourse to 'direct action' diminished.[52] Both the CPGB and the NMM tended to gain ground in the midst of an industrial struggle, and so suffered in a period of relative industrial calm and general trade union weakness. Thirdly, not all communists interpreted the New Line in its most sectarian form. Although we must be wary of generalisation, UMS activists in Fife tended to demonstrate a more pragmatic approach to union activity than their Lanarkshire comrades, while disagreement over communist strategy coloured most of the scattered industrial disputes of the period. With Pollitt's further re-emphasis on communist activity inside the trade unions, moreover, the party began to register some renewed influence, as in the London busmen's strike in August.[53] Fourthly, unemployment and the threat of unemployment had an effect on several former NMM 'strongholds', as Hywel Francis has recognised. First in South Wales, but later in Scotland and beyond, '[erstwhile trade union] militants redirected their energies into the National Unemployed Workers' Movement' over the course of the Third Period.[54] And even when the NMM could claim a rare success, as in the Lucas strike in Birmingham in 1932, after which the party district organiser Tom Roberts was carried on the shoulders of the workers in the name of the NMM, fear of victimisation denied the local party or the NMM reaping any numerical reward for their efforts.[55] Simultaneously, the communist presence shifted during the Third Period – out of the workplace and into the streets.

The main beneficiary of such a shift was the NUWM. As communist influence inside the workplace diminished, so communist activity amongst the unemployed increased, with the NUWM's average membership rising sporadically from 3,831 in early 1928, up to 7,836 in late 1929, to 14,815 by the winter of 1930, to a high of 23,643 by the end of 1931. As Sam Davies has shown, average membership then remained at around the 20,000 mark throughout 1932 and into 1933, and never fell below 13,000 before October 1936.[56] Moreover, NUWM membership turnover was rapid. Many unemployed workers joined the NUWM in the heat of an unemployed march or local protest to the board of guardians/public assistance committee, only to let their membership lapse soon after. Alternatively, some workers joined temporarily in the interim between jobs, or simply to benefit from the advice and legal assistance offered by the NUWM. Equally, some unemployed workers may have joined only to leave because they proved unable to keep up the weekly subscription of 1d per week. As such, the number of workers who passed through the NUWM, or who gathered in support of the movement, was almost certainly higher than the average membership figures suggest. In such a way, the CPGB retained a lively presence amongst a section of the British working class via its heading and directing of the NUWM during the Third Period. Thus, party members such as Wal Hannington, Sid Elias and Emrys Llewellyn led the movement nationally, while communists such as George Middleton (Glasgow), Joe Rawlings (Birkenhead) and Edwin Greening (Aberaman) organised the movement at a local level. As many a communist autobiography reveals, the NUWM offered either a way into the CPGB or became the principal focus of an active communist's agitational work in the late 1920s and early 1930s.[57] Politically, meanwhile, the NUWM officially adopted the theoretical constructs of 'class against class' at its sixth national conference on 14–16 September 1929.[58]

NUWM activity took a variety of different forms. At a general level, the NUWM organised four national hunger marches between 1929 and 1934, along with 'unemployed days' in the spring of each year from 1930. These initiatives varied in terms of size and accomplishment, but they did much to raise attention as to the plight of the unemployed, not least in the eyes of the middle class. It was, for example, during the 1930 hunger march that students in Oxford emerged to hand out walking sticks to the contingent making its way through the university city.[59] The NUWM also did its best to widen its appeal, forming a women's department in 1929, along with a legal department designed to advise workers on their right to benefit. Locally, the NUWM provided legal 'experts' – often CPGB members – such as 'Fatty' Barraclough in Barnsley or Ernie Benson in Leeds to represent workers seeking unemployed relief; sometimes constructing mock courts to prepare workers for their visits to the labour exchange. Also at a local level, the NUWM utilised its resources to rally support to prevent evictions, to organise entertainment for the unemployed (the Bootle NUWM had billiard and football teams), as well as to arrange regular marches to the local authorities. These latter protests gathered pace over the Third Period, culminating in the widespread local demonstrations of late 1931–32. Too often, such a show of discontent would end in violence, but the large numbers involved, ranging from a few hundred to as many as a reported 100,000, brought communist agitation to the heart of most British town and city centres. In the process, of course, communist activists became regular targets for arrest, but the commitment and sacrifice of these dedicated militants did much to win new members and some sympathy to the CPGB.[60]

Not surprisingly, the 'rise' of the NUWM coincided with an increase in unemployment across Britain as a whole. This began in areas based on the old staple industries, particularly South Wales, where an unemployed miners' march to London in November 1927 helped raise the NUWM's profile, before spreading to other areas of Britain over the period of the 'great depression'. By December 1930, some 2,500,000 workers were registered unemployed, and this had risen to 2,783,000 by the summer of 1931. Eighteen months later, in January 1933, some 2,979,000 workers were officially out of work.[61] Yet, the relative achievements of the NUWM related to more than simply the rising number of unemployed. Government intervention, such as the family means test introduced in 1931, caused resentment amongst the ranks of jobless workers, while both the TUC and the Labour Party's apparent unwillingness to develop specifically unemployed organisations gave the NUWM the space to forge a virtual monopoly on unemployed agitation. Furthermore, the NUWM's concentration on local labour exchanges and relief agencies was conducive to the 'grass roots' agitation of the movement, providing a captive audience and a clearly apparent focus for complaint. The fact that relief was decided and distributed at a local level meant NUWM pressure was easily targeted and often effective. As for organisation, Hannington's experience as a member of the AEU informed his approach to the unemployed. In such a way, the systematic and patient building of the NUWM was complemented by a tactical flexibility that proved relatively successful. Although the NUWM never managed to mobilise the majority of the British unemployed, its activities gave a sense of purpose to many who suffered in the face of the economic downturn.

But while the CPGB received a degree of comfort from the achievements of the NUWM, the party did not welcome all of the movement's activities. For a communist party, of course, the priority was to organise a factory-based *working* proletariat, not simply the unemployed, and this gave rise to complaints that the NUWM operated as a 'specialist trade union', detached from the mass of the working class. Significantly, however, Wal Hannington regularly resisted CPGB, Comintern and RILU attempts to intervene into NUWM practice, defending the movement's legal department and commitment to a dues-paying membership (which some comrades construed as 'legalism'), and ignoring attempts to fuse the NUWM with the floundering NMM. Rather pertinently, but understandably, Hannington objected 'to comrades who had made a muddle of other things, now trying to make a muddle of the NUWM'.[62] As a result, the unemployed leader lost his place on the party's central committee in 1932, and became estranged from a number of his comrades in the process. Conversely, Hannington protected the NUWM from the worst excesses of 'class against class'. Although he never publicly criticized the theoretical basis of CPGB policy, he won the argument with regard to methods of NUWM work by dint of the movement's evident achievements. By early 1933, after a national hunger march to London the previous autumn had sent the capital's press into a frenzy of communist scare-mongering, the NUWM claimed 19,597 members gathered in 349 branches, 36 district councils, and 34 women's sections based all over the country.[63]

In similar fashion, the shift from workplace organisation to street-level agitation also gave new life to the CPGB's more cultural activities. These tended to emerge out of relatively broad labour movement organisations, such as the aforementioned BWSF, formed in 1923 following a proposal by the Clarion Cycling Club; the Workers' Theatre Movement (WTM), conceived in the wake of the 1926 General Strike by communist party, ILP and Plebs League members; and the Federation of Workers' Film Societies (FWFS), established in 1929 by the CPGB from the remnants of the non-party aligned London Film Society.[64] Communists had come to dominate such organisations by the beginning of the Third Period, but it was the change in method inspired by 'class against class' that distinguished these marginal attempts at forging a proletarian culture. Frustrated by the limitations of established forms of workers' theatre, and bolstered by the revolutionary rhetoric of the New Line, communists such as Jimmy Miller (Ewan MacColl), Tom Thomas and Phil Poole sought to take their theatre groups into the streets and appeal directly to the working class. A 'propertyless theatre for a propertyless class' was envisaged, as worker theatre groups such as the Manchester Red Megaphones or the Dundee Red Front Troupe set about performing agit-prop skits and songs on street corners, at labour exchanges, or to striking workers outside factory gates. These sketches, in turn, were often written specifically to apply to local disputes or concerns, as well as focusing on the CPGB's priorities of the day (performances included *Rationalisation* and *The PAC Sketch*). The BWSF, too, was injected with a healthy dose of Bolshevik militancy from late 1927, as the federation resolved to 'struggle against the capitalist domination of sport' and to 'direct the instinct for sport on the part of the workers into channels that serve their own interests on the sports field and in the field of industry'.[65] Football teams, cycling groups (Red Wheelers) and rambling clubs were established, sports days were organised, and sports events were utilised to raise money, support and morale during industrial disputes and election contests. Red Wheelers were even called on to rally support for families threatened with eviction, as in Leeds in 1931.[66] By June 1931, the BWSF claimed to represent 6,000 workers in 90 branches across the country, while its campaigns around such local issues as the Tottenham district council's banning of Sunday games proved popular and effectual. Most notoriously, the mass trespass organised by Manchester ramblers around Kinder Scout in Derbyshire in April 1932 was to become one of the most well known communist-inspired protests.[67]

Unsurprisingly, perhaps, the FWFS proved less conducive to such 'direct action', although there were attempts to project films onto the South London streets in 1932. As with the WTM and the BWSF, however, the FWFS committed itself to overtly political activities, dedicating its films, shows and productions (four *workers' newsreels* and two *workers' films*) to the portrayal of workers actively engaged in 'the struggle'. By late 1931, the federation claimed some 3,000 members gathered in societies across a number of British cities. Not dissimilarly, the party's more cerebral pursuits – party education, training groups – had little immediate impact beyond communist circles, despite the fact that the CPGB extended its political curriculum over the course of the Third Period. That said, the party's training classes included a number of non-party members, while the objectives of 'class against class' encouraged worker correspondents to contribute and develop workplace newssheets and pushed the CPGB to widen its appeal beyond the organised labour movement. In such a way, communist attention was focused – albeit to a limited extent – more fixedly on working class women (the UMS, for example, attempted to establish women's guilds) and ethnic minorities (campaigns in defence of the Meerut prisoners and the Scottsboro boys) from at least 1930 onwards.[68] The influence, significance and extent of such initiatives can be queried, but they remained an important part of the communist worldview constructed over the Third Period.

Conclusion

Pointing to the relative achievements of the NUWM and certain communist-led cultural activities is not intended to somehow justify the CPGB's approaches to the British working class over the Third Period. Nor is it an attempt to suggest that the period was in some ways a 'positive' one for the CPGB – it most certainly was not. No doubt, many party members of the time would have concurred with the UMS organiser John McArthur's reference to the 'class against class' years as being 'the most difficult in my whole industrial and political life'.[69] Rather, it is an attempt to produce a balanced overview of the communist experience between 1927–33, and to warn against blanket oversimplifications relating to this, and any other, designated 'period'. Similarly, it is an attempt to place communist activity within the local, regional and national contexts of the time, and to demonstrate that the fortunes of the CPGB were dependent on far more than the specifics of the 'party line'. While ECCI intervention and communist sectarianism contributed to the party's difficulties in these years, they do not adequately explain the varied and distinctive developments that occurred over the Third Period as a whole. Even a focus on party membership figures raises disparities in attempting too general an approach. If certain party 'strongholds' declined over the Third Period (South Wales), others soon revived (Scotland), with the London district party actually registering a larger membership figure in 1931–32 than during the party's previous 'high point' of late 1926.[70] Besides, the New Line was never a fixed entity. While the theoretical basis of 'class against class' retained some consistency both before and after the initial disagreements symbolised by the fall of Bukharin, the priorities or emphases of communist policy changed over time. Again, Soviet and ECCI determinants were integral to this, but so too were problems thrown up by the implementation of the New Line and disagreement as to methods of application. It was in this context that Harry Pollitt was able to win ECCI support in order to re-emphasise the need for a communist presence inside the 'reformist' trade union movement. Interestingly, too, different people interpreted the New Line in different ways at different times in different circumstances. Many on the left of the CPGB went beyond the guidelines laid down by the ECCI, while other communists accepted the ECCI's authority only to despair at the hardheaded sectarianism that it inspired in some of their comrades. The years of 'class against class' were undoubtedly challenging and frustrating for the expectant CPGB. But they also marked a most complex and intriguing period of the British party's history.

Notes

1. M. McCarthy, *Generation in Revolt* (London, 1953), p. 138.

2. H. Pollitt, *Twenty Years' Fight for Socialism* (London, 1940), p. 2.

3. *Minutes of the ECCI Presidium*, 12 December 1930 (Communist Archive). The Communist Archive is located in the National Museum of Labour History (NMLH), Manchester.

4. The NUWM was named the National Unemployed Workers' Committee Movement (NUWCM) until September 1929. By dropping the word 'committee', the NUWM demonstrated its more centralised organisation.

5. For just two examples, see W. Paynter, *My Generation* (London, 1972); E. Benson, *To Struggle is to Live: A Working Class Autobiography, Vols. I and II* (Newcastle 1979–80).

6. *Minutes of the Political Bureau of the CPGB* (PB Mins), 31 December 1931; *PB Mins*, 9 November 1932 (Communist Archive); A. Thorpe, 'The Membership of the Communist Party of Great Britain, 1920–45', *The Historical Journal*, Vol. 43, No. 3 (2000), p. 792.

7. See J. K. Hopkins, *Into the Heart of the Fire: The British in the Spanish Civil War* (Stanford, 1998).

8. *Wire to the Ninth Congress for the Political Secretariat of the CPGB, Decided on 1 October 1927* (Communist Archive).

9. See CPGB, *Communist Policy in Great Britain: The Report of the British Commission of the Ninth Plenum of the Comintern* (London, 1928), for full details of the initial New Line.

10. *International Press Correspondence (Inprecorr)*, 20 December 1926.

11. 'Resolution of the Eighth Plenum of the ECCI on the Situation in Great Britain' in CPGB, *Communist Policy in Great Britain*, pp. 116–26.

12. For more on this, see M. Worley, *Class Against Class: The Communist Party in Britain between the Wars* (London, 2001), pp. 52–79. Measures had been taken to limit communist influence in the Labour Party before 1926, but such efforts became more concerted following the General Strike.

13. A. Thorpe, *The British Communist Party and Moscow, 1920–43* (Manchester, 2000); M. Worley, *Class Against Class*, pp. 90–101.

14. *Minutes of the Central Committee of the CPGB (CC Mins)*, 28–30 April 1928, Klugmann Papers (Communist Archive).

15. *Instructions for the Comintern Delegate to the Tenth Congress of the CPGB* (Communist Archive). See also CPGB, *The New Line: Documents of the Tenth Congress of the Communist Party of Great Britain* (London, 1929).

16. For the protracted leadership debate inside the CPGB, see M. Worley, *Class Against Class*, pp. 137–43.

17. *PB Mins*, 10 October 1932 (Communist Archive).

18. R. P. Dutt, *Letter to the Political Bureau of the CPGB*, 25 September 1929, Dutt Papers (British Library).

19. *PB Mins*, 25 October 1928 (Communist Archive); *Communist Review*, August 1929.

20. The ECCI also retained its 'faith' in those such as J. R. Campbell and Arthur Horner, despite their concerns regarding the New Line, and despite pressure within the CPGB to remove such renown 'right deviationists'. See M. Worley, *Class Against Class*, pp. 140–41.

21. R. W. Robson, *Report of the London District Party*, 9 July 1930, Klugmann Papers (Communist Archive).

22. *Meeting of the Anglo-American Secretariat*, 3 December 1931 (Communist Archive).

23. *Meeting of the Political Secretariat of the ECCI*, 16 August 1930; *CC Mins*, 13–14 September 1930 (Communist Archive).

24. The best overview of the NUWM remains R. Croucher, *We Refuse to Starve in Silence: A History of the National Unemployed Workers' Movement, 1920–46* (London, 1987).

25. A. Thorpe, 'The Membership of the Communist Party of Great Britain', p. 792.

26. S. Davies, 'The Membership of the National Unemployed Workers' Movement, 1923–38', *Labour History Review*, Vol. 57, No. 1 (1992), p. 35.

27. *PB Mins*, 9 January 1932 (Communist Archive).

28. CPGB, *The Revolutionary Way Out: Resolutions Adopted by the Twelfth Congress of the CPGB* (London, 1932), pp. 8–14.

29. *PB Mins*, 9 January 1932 (Communist Archive).

30. A. Thorpe, *The British Communist Party*, pp. 202–219; A. Dallin and F. I. Firsov (eds), *Dimitrov and Stalin, 1934–1943: Letters from the Soviet Archive* (New Haven, 2000), pp. 7–43.

31. E. H. Carr, *Twilight of the Comintern, 1930–35* (London, 1982), p. 12. The article was published in *Pravda* on 2 March 1930.

32. See Manuilsky's speech in *Inprecorr*, 28 March 1930; *Minutes of the Political Secretariat of the ECCI*, 16 August 1930 (Communist Archive).

33. For discussions regarding the problems of sectarianism, see *CC Mins*, 31 May–2 June, 19–21 July, and 13–14 September 1930 (Communist Archive).

34. Very clearly, the New Line did not on its own cause the CPGB's loss of membership: for example, all of the new branches established by the Tyneside district party over the course of the lockout had collapsed by the spring of 1927, long before the implementation of 'class against class'. A. Thorpe, 'The Membership of the Communist Party of Great Britain', p. 792; *Materials for Organisational Report*, April 1928, Klugmann Papers (Communist Archive).

35. H. Makower, J. Marschak and H. W. Robinson, 'Studies in the Mobility of Labour: Analysis for Great Britain', *Oxford Economic Papers*, No. 2 (1939). Migration increased most notably in 1927–29 and 1933–36, and did so in areas centred on the old staple industries.

36. See figures in H. A. Clegg, A. Fox, A. F. Thompson, *A History Of British Trade Unions since 1889, Vols. I and II* (1964 and 1985).

37. R. P. Dutt, 'Notes of the Month', *Labour Monthly*, May 1929.

38. Examples of municipal successes include Jimmy Stewart in Lochgelly, Alex Moffat in Lumphinnans, Annie Cree in Sheffield, and Bob Selkirk in Fife. See S. Macintyre, *Little Moscows: Communism and Working Class Militancy in Inter-war Britain* (London, 1980). In the Vale of Leven, the communists out polled the Labour candidates in both the District Council and County Council elections of late 1932.

39. *Report of the Minority Movement*, 31 December 1926, Klugmann Papers (Communist Archive).

40. NMM, *Report of the Third Annual Conference of the National Minority Movement* (London, 1926).

41. *CC Mins*, 28–29 October 1927, Klugmann Papers (Communist Archive).

42. ECCI, *The World Situation & Economic Struggle: Theses of the Tenth Plenum ECCI* (London, 1929), pp. 22–51; NMM, *On Strike! A Word to all Workers in Dispute* (London, 1929).

43. Quoted in R. A. Leeson, *Strike! A Live History* (London, 1973), p. 122. In August 1929, the NMM annual conference greeted just six delegates from the textile industry. Furthermore, only a sixth of the CPGB's Lancashire membership (approximately 30) in 1929 were textile workers. See NMM, *Now For Action! The Policy of National Minority Movement: A Report of the Sixth Annual Conference* (London, 1929), p. 39; *Communist Review*, September 1929.

44. *Meeting of the Anglo-American Secretariat*, 8 August 1930 (Communist Archive).

45. *Letter from Arthur Horner to the RILU*, 21 August 1931, Klugmann Papers; *Minutes of the Political Bureau of the CPGB*, 23 January 1931 (both Communist Archive); E. H. Carr, *Twilight*, p. 220.

46. *Meeting of the Anglo-American Secretariat*, 8 August 1930 (Communist Archive); *Report of the Minority Movement*, 31 December 1926, Klugmann Papers (Communist Archive).

47. S. L. Lerner, *Breakaway Unions and the Small Trade Union* (London, 1961).

48. Ibid; M. Worley, *Class Against Class*, pp. 167–69.

49. For background, see A. Campbell, *The Scottish Miners, 1879–1939, Volume II: Trade Unions and Politics* (Aldershot, 2000).

50. Ibid; I. MacDougall, (Ed.), *Militant Miners: Recollections of John McArthur, Buckhaven; and Letters, 1924–26, of David Proudfoot, Methil, to G. Allen Hutt* (Edinburgh, 1981); M. Worley, *Class Against Class*, pp. 162–67 and pp. 298–99.

51. See M. Worley, *Class Against Class*, pp. 245–48 for more on this.

52. C. J. Wrigley, 'The Trade Unions Between the Wars' in C. J. Wrigley (Ed.), *A History of British Industrial Relations, 1914–45* (Brighton, 1987), pp. 74–124.

53. N. Fishman, *The British Communist Party and the Trade Unions, 1933–45* (Aldershot, 1995).

54. H. Francis, *Miners Against Fascism: Wales and the Spanish Civil War* (London, 1984), pp. 72–73.

55. *Report on Meeting in Birmingham*, 20 March 1932, Dutt Papers (Working Class Museum Library, Salford).

56. S. Davies, 'The Membership of the National Unemployed Workers' Movement', p. 35.

57. H. Horne, *All the Trees were Bread and Cheese: The Making of a Rebel* (Luton, 1998); H. McShane and J. Smith, *No Mean Fighter* (London, 1978). These are just two of many examples.

58. NUWM, *Report of the Sixth National Conference of the NUWCM*, 14–16 September 1929 (Working Class Museum Library, Salford).

59. J. K. Hopkins, *Into the Heart of the Fire*, pp. 28–29. For example, the author Graham Greene later claimed to have been 'educated by the hunger marchers'.

60. See R. Croucher, *We Refuse To Starve*, pp. 106–46. Also, J. Stevenson, 'The Police and the 1932 Hunger March', *Bulletin of the Society for the Study of Labour History*, No. 38 (1979) for one of several accounts of police–communist interaction.

61. *Ministry of Labour Gazette*, December 1930, 1931 and 1933.

62. *PB Mins*, 21 March 1930 (Communist Archive).

63. R. Croucher, *We Refuse To Starve*, p. 148.

64. See my 'For A Proletarian Culture: Communist Party Culture in the Third Period, 1928–35' *Socialist History*, No. 18 (2000), for a more detailed overview.

65. *Report of the First National Conference of the BWSF*, 28 April 1928; *Report of the Second National Conference of the BWSF*, 6–7 December 1930, Sinfield Papers (Communist Archive).

66. *Sport and Games*, January 1932.

67. B. Rothman, *The 1932 Kinder Trespass: A Personal View of the Kinder Scout Trespass* (Timperly, 1982); D. Cook, 'The Battle for Kinder Scout', *Marxism Today* (August, 1977).

68. See M. Squires, 'Communism and the fight against racism in the 'class against class' period', *Communist Review*, Summer (2000).

69. I. MacDougall, *Militant Miners*, p. 134.

70. *Report on Organisation*, October 1927, Klugmann Papers; *PB Mins*, 20 February 1930, 9 November 1932 (Communist Archive). The London district party registered 1,222 members in June 1925, 1,560 in September 1926, and 1,321 in September 1927. It fell to 1,003 in December 1929, and down to just 916 at the end of 1930. From there on, it increased to 992 in February 1931, 1,461 in September 1931, and up to 2,000 by the end of the year. By November 1932, it numbered 1,800.

The Italian Communist Party and the Third Period[1]

ALDO AGOSTI

The Third Period caught the Partito Comunista Italiano (Italian Communist Party; PCI) in a rather delicate phase of internal reorganisation with regard to its own political line.[2] The 'exceptional laws' passed by the Fascist government in November 1926 had eliminated the narrow legal room for manoeuvre in which the party had managed to survive after Mussolini's advent to power in 1922.[3] With the imprisonment of party secretary Antonio Gramsci and all its important leading figures (of whom only Palmiro Togliatti escaped arrest because he was in Moscow), with its organisations dissolved and its press silenced, and with thousands of its activists denounced to the Tribunale speciale per la difesa dello stato (Special Tribunal for the Defence of the State), a long period of underground activity began for the PCI.

The party leadership was reorganised on a dual basis. On the one hand, a foreign centre was quickly set up in Paris, with Togliatti as secretary; on the other hand, there was an internal centre, initially entrusted to Camilla Ravera, on which clandestine activity inside Italy depended. Although the exceptional laws had surprised the PCI, it was the only party to have prepared its own illegal structure: militants had already gone underground, and it possessed a network of connections and logistic and organisational bases. For several months, the PCI was thus able to engage in feverish propaganda activity, in particular distributing a vast number of newspapers and flysheets. It was an almost over-confident activism, tied both to a faith in the fact that the internal contradictions of fascism rendered its fall imminent, and to a desire to maintain a presence in the country at whatever cost. Without doubt, it contributed to the PCI's emergence as the most combative expression of the struggle against fascism at exactly the time that other opposition parties, reduced to small groups of exiles, disappeared entirely from view on the Italian stage. But the communist effort could not be sustained for long. If, in May 1927, there were still almost 10,000 communists in Italy, for the most part concentrated in the north of the country, by the second half of the year a great many cadres had been imprisoned or sentenced to internal exile. The internal network, while patiently patched up after every arrest, was profoundly infiltrated by agent provocateurs from the fascist police. It has recently emerged that the police even managed to get Ignazio Silone, a member of the highest rank of the party's politburo, to collaborate. Before the end of the 1920s, the Italian network had been reduced to a delicate thread of activists.

For the party, therefore, its solid basis of support among emigrant workers, especially in France, Belgium and Switzerland, became an ever more important source of power. These workers were driven to emigrate by a mixture of economic and political motives. Among them was a substantial percentage who were highly qualified, but had been forced to quit Italy because of ill-treatment by their bosses or on account of police persecution. The communist activists did not have their own autonomous organisation but, from 1923, in accordance with the decisions of the Communist International (Comintern), they joined the party of the country in which they had taken refuge, and gathered in so-called 'Italian language groups' with the specific task of spreading propaganda and recruiting emigrant labour. This inclusion within the structure of the host nation party could give rise to friction, especially with the Parti Communiste Français (French Communist Party; PCF), but for the PCI their support constituted an important resource.

When not actually openly hostile to one another, relations between the PCI and other anti-fascist parties were for a long while dominated by mutual diffidence. The communists not only failed to adhere to, but tenaciously opposed the Concentrazione antifascista (Anti-Fascist Concentration), which had been established in France in 1927 and survived with difficulty until 1934. The Concentrazione united socialist, democratic–republican and radical forces, but never included – bar a few insignificant exceptions – the meagre elements of Catholic and liberal anti-fascism. In Italy itself, collaboration between the underground forces went no further than quickly aborted attempts to establish a 'united front' of communist groups and dissident members of 'Giustizia e Libertà', a democratic movement with considerable influence in intellectual circles, in which vaguely socialist tendencies coexisted with more moderate ones.[4] In such circumstances, the ties with the Comintern exercised an extremely strong influence on the Italian communists. Firstly, because the sense of belonging to an 'army of world revolution' was a factor that gave both moral cohesion and a sense of optimism for the future, so helping them confront a very difficult period. Secondly, because the technical apparatus and financial subsidy offered by the Comintern was indispensable for the very survival of the party.

Yet, the strength of this bond did not prevent relations between the PCI and Moscow from going through intermittent stormy periods. Under the direction of Amadeo Bordiga, the Italian party proved very reluctant to adopt the tactic of the 'united front' launched by the third congress of the Communist International in 1921. And even the leadership of Gramsci, who with the help of the Comintern painstakingly rooted out the influence of

Bordiga, raised many reservations about the Moscow directive to reunite with the Italian Socialist Party (PSI), which in 1922 had expelled the reformist wing from its ranks. There were also instances of serious disagreement between the Executive Committee of the Communist International (ECCI) and the PCI with regard to the tactics adopted after the murder of Giacomo Matteotti (a reformist socialist and staunch critic of Mussolini) and, in particular, with regard to communist disassociation from the other anti-fascist parties' decision to boycott parliamentary business (the so-called Aventine secession).[5] In the face of the furious conflict that flared up within the Bolshevik leadership after the death of Lenin, too, Italian communists displayed a degree of reserve. In October 1926, a few weeks before his arrest, Grasmci had greeted developments in the Soviet party's internal struggle with anxiety, warning the Moscow leadership that they risked losing their function as a reference point for the world proletariat by dissipating their energies in a contest for power. At the opening of the eighth plenum of the ECCI in May 1927, the same Palmiro Togliatti (Ercoli) who, from his position as the PCI's delegate in Moscow had considered such a conflict over power inevitable and had not doubted the necessity of the PCI's aligning itself with the majority, refused to support Stalin's motion condemning Trotsky's criticisms of the Comintern's Chinese policy and proposing the expulsion of the ex-commissar for war from the ECCI. Even so, by November 1927, a few weeks after the expulsion of Trotsky and Zinoviev from the central committee of the All-Union Communist Party, every scruple had vanished. Togliatti himself expressed in the clearest possible manner the unconditional adherence of his party to the doctrine of 'socialism in one country':

> The strategic plan of the Russian Revolution and the strategic plan of the world proletarian revolution are so closely linked that they form a single thing. Take away the possibility of Russian progress towards true socialism, deny the possibility of the victorious building of socialism in Russia, and the entire historical–political idea at the foundations of the Communist International collapses … If we abandon this idea … we are left with only two paths to choose from: either a return to the ideas of social democracy, or a descent into revolutionary romanticism that substitutes infantile babbling for the mastery of reality.[6]

Thus, on the political level, the longstanding antagonism that had set the PCI against the Comintern between 1921 and 1925 seemed to have been substantially overcome. The line affirmed by the third party congress at Lyon in February 1926 was based on a much more nuanced analysis, and was expressed in a way that gave more attention to the relationship between the various social forces and their political expression. It had also received the blessing of the ECCI. After the arrest of Gramsci and the party's going completely underground, it was then further clarified by a leadership centred on Togliatti, who in 1927–28 could now count on the full collaboration of Angelo Tasca, the most authoritative exponent of the 'right' of the party. On 28 January 1927, the ECCI Presidium approved a resolution 'On the economic and political situation of Italy and the duties of the PCI', which affirmed that the fascist regime would only fall 'from the blows delivered by a popular revolution of the workers and peasants in alliance with some strata of the middle classes', and that the development of this 'popular revolution' into a 'proletarian revolution' would not be 'inevitable and automatic', depending instead on the part that the communist party would carry out in the preparation and direction of the struggle, and on its capacity to win over the faith of the worker and peasant masses. The final formulation of this resolution was the fruit of a compromise reached after discussions that lasted for three weeks. The idea that the Italian revolution need not be a proletarian revolution *tout court*, but might experience two stages was initially contested by certain leading figures in the International, such as Manuilsky, Lozovsky and Shatskin, in addition to the representative of the Italian Communist Youth Federation (FGCI), Luigi Longo. Togliatti instead defended this thesis energetically, supported by Grieco, Tasca and Humbert-Droz, stating to the ECCI on 5 January that,

> We cannot today work with the sole prospect of a proletarian revolution, or say that every revolution will inevitably become a proletarian revolution. It would be too simplistic. It will take place to the extent that we manage to mobilise the masses and give the working class the leading role in the revolution through our own work in the vanguard ... We cannot impose a rigid outlook on our party during a period when the masses are passive.[7]

This outlook, however, was by no means unanimously shared within the PCI itself. The analysis made by Togliatti and by Tasca and Grieco, his two closest collaborators within the new party leadership, was rejected by Longo and by the leaders of the FGCI, notably Pietro Secchia and Edoardo D'Onofrio. The 'giovani' essentially contested the conception of the Italian revolution elaborated at the Lyon Congress: they rejected the rallying cry launched on that occasion of the 'Republican assembly based on workers' and peasant committees', and were equivocal about the formula of 'popular revolution'. For them, the disappearance of the liberal and social democrat opposition, following the failure of the Aventine secession from parliament of 1924–25, had radicalised the Italian situation, rendering any intermediate rallying position unrealistic and out of the question. It was necessary to state explicitly the character of the revolution, and to delimit its class basis and its socialist ends. These latter were seen as the creation of a 'worker and peasant government', defined according to the sense given by the fifth Comintern congress as a synonym for the dictatorship of the proletariat.

Togliatti, Grieco and Tasca did not retreat from their position regarding the prospects of the Italian situation. In June of 1928, in an article written for a Comintern review, *La Correspondance Internationale*, the party secretary held probable 'a period in which, in the open struggle of the masses against fascism, non-communist anti-fascist forces (democrats, social democrats) will succeed at being at the head of the masses, or at least of a section of them, and will succeed in seriously hindering the proletarian and communist direction of the movement'.[8]

It was a line that seemed substantially in tune with the more flexible attitude assumed by the Comintern under the direction of Bukharin, with whom Togliatti and Tasca established a particularly close and trusting relationship. However, in the course of 1927, more radical positions – to which Bukharin himself made certain concessions – began to make themselves felt within the International. These were confirmed in the debates and resolutions of the ninth plenum (9–25 February 1928). On this occasion, Togliatti approved without reservation the change in direction imposed on the French and British communist parties, obliging them to abandon the electoral tactics they had hitherto used of supporting candidates from the socialist left or Labour Party. More generally, however, the Italian party could certainly not be counted among those that pressed for a turn 'to the left'. The PCI had already resisted pressure from the Comintern, which following the dissolution of the Confederazione Generale di Lavoro (General Confederation of Labour; CGL) and its clandestine re-establishment in Italy on the part of the communists, had pushed for an official breach from the International Federation of Trade Unions (IFTU) and for open adherence to the Profintern (Red International of Labour Unions; RILU). After the ninth plenum, moreover, Togliatti continued to show his opposition to a policy of splitting from the social democrat unions in order to establish 'independent' organisations controlled by the communists. Arguing with Lozovsky during an ECCI commission on trade unions, he said that it was a mistake 'to create unions everywhere ... to create any old nucleus merely with the goal of being able to say: look, we have another central union, we have extended our sphere of influence'.[9] In his opinion, the same task of organising the non-unionised masses should not come into conflict with the principle of the unity of the unions.

At the Comintern's sixth world congress in the summer of 1928, the PCI appeared, therefore, as a section that was aligned with the ECCI's directives but generally inclined to support a rather prudent interpretation of them. Its leadership welcomed (with some reservations on the part of Tasca) the predictions of the congressional theses regarding the imminent beginning of a 'third period' of development in the class struggle after the October

Revolution, distinguished by the growing threat of war against the USSR, the sharpening of the internal contradictions within capitalist societies, and the consequent radicalisation of revolutionary tensions within the masses. On one important point, however, the position of the PCI kept a certain distance from the tendency winning ground within the Comintern, and especially within the Kommunistische Partei Deutschlands (German Communist Party; KPD): the analysis of fascism. Since May 1926, in an article entitled 'The social bases of fascism' which appeared in the Comintern's theoretical journal, Togliatti had criticised 'the habit of using the term "fascism" in so general a sense that it can be used to designate the most diverse types of bourgeois reactionary movements'.[10] He insisted on the need for 'analysis that drew distinctions'; that any attempt at generalisation should be preceded by the identification of the *particular nature* of individual movements that could approach fascism. While not denying that the bourgeois state was in general becoming markedly more reactionary, he still believed on the eve of the sixth world congress that this process would lead to fascism only under certain precise conditions, namely the existence of a weak economic structure that obliged the bourgeoisie to exercise a more intense pressure in order to maintain 'complete control' of a country's economic and political life, coupled with 'a realignment and mass movement of the petty and middling urban and rural bourgeoisie'. He identified as characteristic traits of the 'fascist type' – that is of Italian fascism – the suppression of the parliamentary regime and the destruction to an extreme level of 'formal democratic freedoms' that led to a complete rejection of any compromise with social democracy.[11] In his speech to the sixth congress, Togliatti explicitly rejected the formal identification of fascism and social democracy, which many portrayed not only as a tendency but as an established fact.

Togliatti also gave voice to anxieties over 'the lack of a genuine internal democratic system' at the heart of the Comintern and its sections. He was thus the only one of those present to take up the allusions along these lines contained within Bukharin's report. All the defects frequently noticed in the activities of the sections of the Communist International – bureaucratisation, the poor level of ideology, the instability of the leadership – could be attributed to the absence of such a system, but little was being done to address these problems. Togliatti complained that in too many cases the practice of open political discussion had been replaced by 'that of a struggle without principles and of compromises between different factions'. Recalling Goethe's deathbed words ('More light!'), he did not hesitate to issue a dramatic warning about the underground struggle that was tearing the Russian party to pieces and which was casting its shadow over the congress. 'The vanguard of the proletariat cannot fight in the dark! The general staff of the revolution cannot take shape in a struggle that is devoid of principles.'[12]

In reality, Togliatti could not make this final appeal in front of the delegates, having lost the floor because he had gone over the available time; but, despite being put under pressure, he included these words in the official edition of the protocol. Without doubt, it was a brave and independent speech given that the prevailing climate of the congress was one of marked radicalism and 'triumphalist unanimity': the Italian communists still seemed reluctant to accept either of these tendencies.

Immediately after the sixth congress, however, the PCI appeared above all to be absorbed by the necessity of overcoming the severe organisational crises in which it had found itself for more than a year, and by the need to re-establish less precarious links with Italy. The analysis made of the country's situation by the party's central committee in October 1928 realistically highlighted the capacity demonstrated by the Fascist regime for maintaining the solidarity and loyalty of the dominant Italian capitalist classes during the economic crisis that had followed revaluation of the lira. In consequence of this, the regime was unlikely to be short-lived. In addition, even if it was held that the very duration of the regime would have eventually brought about an accumulation and deepening of unresolved contradictions, the policy developed over the previous two years was not up for renewed discussion. If anything, the problem of the exploitation of legal means, and particularly that of working within the fascist trade unions, was raised with ever more force.

This line, however, was not destined to survive for long. The relationship between the PCI and the Comintern took a new and abrupt turn at the beginning of 1929. At the sixth congress, the party had decided to appoint Angelo Tasca – without doubt the nearest to Bukharin of any of its leadership – as its representative on the ECCI. Tasca was getting ready to leave for his new destination when the KPD crisis, which had its origins in the 'Wittorf Affair', broke out, culminating in the provisional dismissal of Thälmann from the post of party secretary. Togliatti immediately revealed himself to be very anxious at the turn that such a situation might take: in a 'private and personal' letter of 6 October he invited Tasca 'not to let himself get dragged in any way into the fervent and uncertain terrain of the struggle between one group and another' inside the ECCI, because 'in such territory it is easy to loose one's way'. He went on to say that by staying 'on the terrain of the general principles on which the management of the party is founded, one might perhaps seem provincial or cautious, but one is sure of being able to exercise at least a little influence both today and the day after'.[13]

No doubt, Togliatti recognised that there would be no delay in a straightforward choice being presented to the PCI in a clear and unavoidable fashion: either it could align with the prevalent position in the ECCI, or it could enter into open conflict with it. But once in Moscow, Tasca did not feel like following this moderate advice. In a meeting of the ECCI Presidium on 19 December, he abstained over proposals for a series of disciplinary measures to be taken against certain leaders on the 'right' of the KPD. He was consequently accused of 'mobilising' the Italian party against the Comintern, and was attacked fiercely by Stalin himself, who bracketed him with Humbert-Droz and accused them of 'cowardly opportunism'. Shortly afterwards, as soon as the conflict within the Soviet party moved into the ECCI, Tasca sided with Bukharin, criticising Stalin's support for the dramatic acceleration of industrialisation and forced collectivisation of agriculture, and openly siding against the degeneration of the internal regime of the Comintern in which slavish adherence to the majority line of the Soviet party was becoming the precondition for the political survival of the leadership of the fraternal parties. The PCI summoned Tasca back to Paris and criticised his stance very severely. But, for the moment, it abstained from taking disciplinary measures against him.

When, with Bukharin and the 'right' defeated on all fronts, the tenth ECCI plenum took place, the PCI found itself in the dock. In his first intervention in the plenary session, Togliatti tried to show in vain that he had adapted to the prevailing climate, unreservedly espousing Stalin's positions on Russian issues and anticipating the order of the day for Italy of a 'proletarian revolution'. In the longer term, in the climate of 'settling of accounts' that the Comintern had created with regard to the Italian party, not even this self-critique was considered sufficient. Kuusinen invited Togliatti to jettison 'this sentimentalism, this unpolitical tact' that he had shown to Tasca, and did not miss the chance of reminding Togliatti that the same 'tact' had been shown at the eighth plenum with regard to Trotsky. At this, Ulbricht – one of the new leaders of the KPD – insinuated that 'perhaps they were dealing with something more than tact', while another German, Heinz Neumann, sarcastically pointed out that Serra (Tasca) 'had passed the Pillars of Hercules (Ercoli) in opportunism'.[14]

The retreat affected by Togliatti in the face of this volley of accusations did not take place without his defending certain aspects of his position. For example, on one theme that was particularly familiar to him – that is the issue of trade union tactics – he intervened on 16 July in response to the oral reports of Thälmann and Lozovsky, once more stressing the necessity of an analysis that differentiated between individual countries. He rejected as 'pure and simple anarcho-syndicalism' the idea that only the establishment of small 'red' trade unions opened the prospect of victory in the economic struggle. He also objected to another affirmation by those making the reports, according to whom the conquest of the trade union apparatus was virtually useless in so far as it constituted an irreversible process of fusion between reformist unions and the bourgeois state apparatus. Togliatti argued that, on the contrary, the apparatus of a union did not merely consist of the summit, but of its intermediate and lower levels, and that, through patient work, the communists could successfully establish their hegemony over the latter.[15]

On 19 July, at the end of the plenum's labours, Togliatti was entrusted with the closing speech. It was recognition of his still important role within the Comintern, and perhaps a way of compensating for the criticisms that had been levelled at him. But at the same time, it was also a way of publicly obliging him and his party to adhere unconditionally and completely to the political line that had been ratified by the plenum. Togliatti's dull and lifeless speech did not disappoint in this sense. On the same day, too, the direction taken by the Italian Commission gave a glimpse of another side of the situation.

Togliatti's introductory report to this commission dwelt above all on the organisational aspects of the PCI's illegal operations, and on the difficulties – difficulties that were considered as being in the process of being overcome – confronted in re-establishing the party in Italy. In the discussion that ensued, not only Grieco and Di Vittorio took part. Manuilsky, Ulbricht and two further authoritative officials from the Comintern, Vassiliev and Stepanov, also took part. But it was both closed and at times very tense. The abortive expulsion of Tasca became only a minor charge, while another problem became explicitly stated: that of revising the whole political line of the PCI, such as it had emerged at the outset of Gramsci's leadership. Manuilsky targeted the overestimation and the improper use of short-term slogans, in particular that of a Republican Assembly based on worker and peasant committees, criticising it for the vague way in which it addressed the problem of proletarian hegemony. Vasiliev echoed him, and insisted on the need to apply the label 'social fascism' to Italian social democracy too. The Italian delegates energetically asserted the validity of their own party's experiences. They did not accept an overly simplistic equation between fascism and social democracy: 'We cannot say that Matteotti came to power and fired on workers in the streets,' Togliatti replied to Vasiliev, before going on to predict that if there was a section of Italian social democracy that could reach agreement with fascism, then the remainder would stay stalwart in its anti-fascism. Above all, they did not give up stressing the need of offering different analyses for diverse situations. As far as the character of the Italian revolution was concerned, Togliatti replied to Manuilsky:

Is it right or not to pose these questions with comrades at the centre of the discussion in the party? If the Comintern says it is not right, we shall not pose them again; each of us will think these things but not speak about them again; one will only say that the anti-fascist revolution is a proletarian revolution. But each of us will think that it is not at all certain that we shall lead it from the outset, and that we will think that we can only win the leadership during the course of the struggle.[16]

Shortly afterwards, in answer to Manuilsky's accusation of 'exceptionalism' against the PCI, Togliatti replied:

> We have always said that it was the duty of our party to study Italy's particular circumstances ... If the Comintern asks us to desist, we shall do so ... If doing this is 'exceptional', we shall do so no longer; but since one cannot stop thinking, we shall keep these things for ourselves and limit ourselves to making general statements.[17]

These phrases, often assumed to be demonstrations of a sort of congenital 'Togliattian' duplicity, bore eloquent testimony to the climate that had by now been established within the Comintern, and which clearly set the parameters within which the PCI would be able to develop its policies in years to come. The price paid for international discipline was clearly extremely high. But a small underground party, dependent financially on assistance from the Comintern, really had no other choice but to accept this discipline, and probably believed that it was only by avoiding an open breach in the Lyon leadership that it might be possible somehow to keep alive the continuity of inspiration that had hitherto guided the struggle against fascism. In November 1929, by now expelled from the party, Tasca revealed that he had gathered from 'a comrade member of the secretariat of the PCI' the following important confidence from Togliatti:

> We must back down over Russian and international questions in order to defend our party's Italian policy. Otherwise, Moscow will have no scruples about imposing a leadership from the left, with a few lads from the Lenin School. This would ruin the work we have been doing for years.[18]

In reality, almost nothing was preserved of the policy of 1926–28; even the leadership of the Lyon congress fragmented within the space of a few months. In September 1929, Tasca was expelled and Togliatti's position within the party seemed at that moment distinctly shaky. It was without question to defend his position that he decisively embraced the extreme interpretation of Third Period theory. He maintained that 'the elements of an acute revolutionary crisis' were in the process of ripening in Italy; he extended the theory of 'social fascism' to Italian social democracy and the 'Giustizia e Libertà' movement; and he rejected the hypothesis of an intermediate phase between the collapse of fascism and the proletarian revolution.

A new field of battle was, however, beginning to be marked out: the problem of the Italian party's activity. At the end of December 1929, Luigi Longo ('Gallo') presented a plan to the secretariat. This anticipated that 'the party apparatus [regional committees, labour sections, the politburo] should be decisively geared towards a return to Italy, not only in terms of action [which had always been the case], but also as a seat'.[19] His proposal led to a profound breach with the politburo. Alfonso Leonetti, an ex-journalist form the Turin *Ordine Nuovo* who had been very close to Gramsci, and two other leaders with longstanding experience of trade union work, Pietro Tresso and Paolo Ravazzoli, opposed it vigorously, fiercely attacking Togliatti for having accepted such a line. The 'Three', as they came to be known, considered the decision to re-establish an internal political centre in Italy a dangerous hazard. They countered it with the need of 'not wasting our own forces, not wearing them down or destroying them seeking objectives that can be achieved with fewer losses and by different means', suggesting instead the development of the existing regional committees.

It should be noted that the difference of opinion was not over the issue of the radicalisation of the Italian situation – which everyone recognised – nor was it over the necessity of taking some form of action to fill the organisational gap that the party acknowledged. The possibility of a so-called 'transitional phase' – that is a period of democratic, bourgeois revolution that would precede the proletarian revolution during which it would be possible for the PCI to organise legally or semi-legally – was ruled out. No one denied the Italian party faced 'new tasks' since, however much the situation was 'pushed inexorably forward by a series of objective factors', it was a mistake to believe that the masses would become 'spontaneously' revolutionary without precise and daily political and organisational work. From the outset, disagreement only arose over the means to respond to these needs. Even so, in the climate that had developed after the polemics of late August, this was sufficient to cause a fierce clash.

In the politburo, an alliance formed between Togliatti, Longo and Secchia, the 'giovani', who had fiercely opposed his line in 1927–28. In fact, the party secretary had completely embraced the political theses of his former adversaries, abandoning the Lyon congress's line on 'popular revolution'. Certainly, there was no lack of reasons that could support Togliatti in the choice he had made. In the space of two months, between late October and early December 1929, two processes had begun which it is no exaggeration to say changed the world profoundly and irreversibly: a violent, radical and general crisis of the capitalist system triggered by the Wall Street crash, and the forced collectivisation of the Soviet countryside that together with the intense industrialisation already begun at the start of the year signalled the start of the 'revolution from above' which was destined to promote the USSR to the status of world power within the space of a few years. The almost simultaneous beginning of these two processes opened the door to a motif that would be recurrent in the propaganda of the Comintern: an insistence on the startling contrast between capitalism in ruins and the building of socialism, and the idea underlined by this that history was leading humanity to a decisive juncture. This theme would become an integral part of the mental structure for many generations of communist activists, and it was logical that a small, persecuted, underground party like the PCI would not escape its appeal. The idea of moving with history constituted a psychologically reassuring factor that compensated for the PCI's isolation and its sparse achievements over the short-term.

At the same time, there was no absence of indications that the masses were again becoming more militant. Between the summer of 1929 and the first months of 1930, strikes and demonstrations of discontent took place with a certain frequency. In reality, they were significant but reasonably localised episodes. The part played by the flimsy communist organisational network was virtually negligible, and it was only by stretching the imagination out of a love for ideology that it was possible to represent these events as symptoms of a situation on the edge of insurrection. Leonetti, Tresso and Ravazzoli evaluated them more realistically. However, they were sufficient to legitimate shifting the party's centre of gravity towards Italy and justifying 'la svolta' ('the turn'), as the new political and organisational orientation was termed. Longo's proposal was approved by a narrow majority of the politburo in February 1930 and ratified a month later, having obtained the full support of both the Latin Secretariat of Comintern and the central committee. In June, the 'Three', already excluded from the leading organs, were expelled from the party for having made contact with the international Trotskyist opposition; the same fate awaited Ignazio Silone – whose collaboration with the Fascist police was apparently unknown – in July 1931.

However, the 'svolta' was not imposed without significant resistance. Umberto Terracini and Antonio Gramsci, who were kept abreast of the major lines of debate within the party, showed their opposition from their prison cells both to the party's treatment of the opposition and to a political stance which they considered abstract and wanting in any prospects. Both considered it a mistake to rule out a phase of democratic transition after the fall of fascism, and they believed the equation of social democracy and fascism unjustified. Gramsci did not hesitate to display his disagreement to comrades who were in gaol with him.

The majority of the party's rank-and-file, in other words the few cadres who continued to work underground within Italy and the only slightly more numerous activists among Italian emigrants, never knew anything of this dissent. No mention of it figured in any report or correspondence of the Comintern. Togliatti probably wanted to avoid creating a new 'affair' through circulating criticisms from within prison, and was perhaps anxious to shield the two comrades from possible excommunication by the ECCI. However, it is a fact that for a relatively long period (from June 1931 to December 1933) there was no political–theoretical mention in the Italian communist press of Gramsci. And it is certainly not insignificant that in the 'autobiography' written for the cadres section of the Comintern (dated 21 August 1932), Togliatti did not make any mention of Gramsci's name despite his going back over his political career in enormous detail.[20]

This did not mean – as the individual concerned came to suspect and as some historians have maintained – that the PCI deliberately sought to obstruct plans involving Soviet diplomacy to free Gramsci. No documentary proof exists for such a plot, and all the research that has been done tends to discount such a thesis. But it is important to point out that the level of democracy and debate hitherto existing in the party had been dramatically curtailed. The capacity of the party for political analysis of the Italian situation diminished, being stifled and impoverished by its new orientation.

Despite these negative characteristics and the extremely high human costs in terms of arrested and imprisoned activists that it involved, the 'svolta' initially marked an energetic resumption of the PCI's underground activity in Italy. At least in certain aspects it represented an important re-establishment of Italian communism. It actually signalled the emergence of different viewpoints and a different psychology, even on a cultural and generational level, as well as the affirmation of a type of communist cadre no longer tied to the 1921 climate of schism but to that of daily resistance to fascism. At the same time, this was displayed in a clear change of the party's geographical axis. While in 1927 more than half its membership was located in the northern regions of the country, by 1932 its power base was firmly based in Emilia and Tuscany. This phenomenon can be explained by the fact that it was less difficult to maintain even a flimsy network of clandestine links in the countryside than in the factories of the major cities where control and surveillance were much more rigorous. But it is also important to take account of the fact that by destroying the network of workers' organisations, and by introducing a harsh regime of exploitation and persecution, fascism revitalised the traditional subversiveness of the masses, whose oldest and deepest roots were in what were later to become the 'regioni rosse'.[21] Besides the different geographical distribution of support, what is striking is the relative stability of a communist membership that numbered about 7,000 in 1932, more or less what it had been at the end of 1927. In fact, there was a high level of fluctuation. Following the 'svolta', 5,000 new members joined in only a year-and-a-half. In a situation like that in Italy, where the party was banned, such a fluctuation cannot be simply attributed to the general trend of communist parties in this period. It was also an indication of a capacity for change that could only be sustained by a lively – if ever more problematic – relationship with certain social groups (workers, day labourers, sharecroppers), as well as with small cells of intellectuals who were disillusioned by the passivity of the 'Aventine' parties and critical of the programme advanced by 'Giustizia e Libertà', which they considered to be insufficiently characterised by a clear line on class.

In effect, beyond the 'thin and uniform veneer of ideology'[22] that concealed a variety of different circumstances, it was a pattern of collective behaviour, especially at the level of the proletarian rank-and-file, which nourished this change. Over time, these patterns of behaviour were consolidated, operating through networks of family and friends. The presence of a communist nucleus within the Italian population thus succeeded in confirming itself in a continuous fashion, notwithstanding the fact that relations between rank-and-file and summit became ever more precarious. And this was going on while hundreds of low-level cadres and mid-level leaders were swelling the ranks of political prisoners and internal exiles, creating a real 'parallel' party that, despite its sectarianism, kept alive a force for cultural and political formation and a rigid sense of discipline that were destined to bear fruit later.

Nevertheless, in the short term the consequences of the 'svolta' did not correspond to expectations. Far from approaching a pre-revolutionary situation, Italy witnessed a further strengthening of the fascist dictatorship that managed to perfect its own organisation as a mass, reactionary regime. Indeed, considering the exceptionally difficult circumstances under which it had to operate, the communist party displayed a remarkable vitality, putting the lie to Manuilsky's overly severe assessment that the PCI was just a 'closed circle of friends'. But the beginnings of protest were not channelled into visible or organised mass movements whilst the police maintained surveillance and struck with extreme efficiency. On the 'fall' in July 1930 of the first internal centre, organised according to Longo's plan and under the direction of Camilla Ravera, there followed the systematic arrest of communists throughout Italy, until a severe blow was inflicted on the party with the arrest of Secchia on 2 April 1931.

Secchia fell into the hands of the police on the eve of the fourth congress of the PCI, having made a significant contribution to its organisation, co-ordinating meetings of activists throughout the country and even secretly sending numerous delegates abroad. The congress, held in Cologne and Düsseldorf with the help of the KPD, endorsed the political platform that had been at the basis of the 'svolta' and confirmed Togliatti as secretary. Immediately afterwards, however, a profound change in the working methods of the party began to take place. This could not but have repercussions on the political line as well. Concealed with a certain caution in the report made by Togliatti at the Latin Secretariat in Moscow in July 1931, this change had been authorised by the ECCI, which had already been pouring cold water on the revolutionary enthusiasm of the PCI for more than a year. The nature of the change was illustrated at the meeting of the PCI central committee at the end of the August. In the report that Togliatti gave on this occasion,[23] the central basis of the 'svolta' – namely to make

Italy the centre of gravity for party activity – was reconfirmed, but within a frame of reference that 'assumed as fixed points the observation of the process of consolidation of the organisation of the masses from above effected by the fascists and, in consequence, the prospect of working patiently and of no immediate concrete results'.[24]

Without discussing the general perspectives on which the 'svolta' had been based, the PCI did not refrain from subjecting the new reality of the country's situation to a careful and concrete analysis. In Italy, fascism had refined and perfected its dictatorship, regimenting the middle classes and the proletarian masses themselves within a tight network of organisations. Although bureaucratised and subjected to the oppressive control of a single party, these had now become, after ten years of the regime and the systematic and efficient repression of underground anti-fascist activity, the sole channels through which any form of political discussion could take place. The communists were the first to take note of this, even under the spur of constant criticism from the Comintern, which often rather ungenerously reproached them for 'carbonarism'.[25] From 1931, and especially from 1932, the PCI's almost obsessive policy aim was to establish breaches within the fascist ranks. As such, the PCI sought to highlight the contradictions between the demagogic declarations of the regime and the persistently miserable conditions and exploitation of a substantial section of the Italian population, taking advantage of every legal space to undermine the pro-fascist consensus from within.

From this emerged a painstakingly detailed analysis, which was extended from the trade unions to other mass organisations of the regime ('mutual aid associations' and above all the Dopolavoro[26]), and the conviction began to grow stronger that only a long and determined action conducted legally, exploiting all the opportunities for association offered by fascism's own social demagogy and its tendency to create a mass basis of support, would permit the development of a mass movement ultimately capable of smashing fascist legality. This analysis was to find its most mature expression in the course held by Togliatti for communist cadres in Moscow in January 1935. A text that came to light in the Moscow archives only in 1970 – and which was immediately published with the title *Lessons on Fascism* – appeared at the time totally innovative and 'swimming against the tide' of most interpretations of the reality of the dictatorship. In part, this is really what it was, but even in their rigid schematisation, the attempts to acknowledge Italy's economic and social situation that were published after 1931 in the PCI review *Lo Stato Operaio* already contained several gestures towards this approach.

If the PCI had been one of the last sections of the Comintern to accept, with evident reluctance, the new extreme left course sanctioned by the tenth plenum in 1929, it had subsequently displayed an almost excessive zeal in making the aberrant formulae of 'social fascism' its own, and it was certainly not one of the precursors of the new line that laboriously made headway in the Comintern after Hitler's advent to power. During the early stages of the political transformation that would bloom in the Comintern's seventh congress, attempts to establish some form of collaboration with the two other working class parties – following the directives already issued by the ECCI in March 1933 – failed with regard to the PSI (which had since 1930 been reunited under the leadership of Pietro Nenni), and had only a transitory and rather insignificant success with regard to the surviving rump of the 'maximalists' led by Angelica Balabanoff. The PCI was induced to view the other anti-fascist organisations with distrust. This was probably because of the growing emphasis placed by the party after its fourth congress on the widespread and pervasive structure of the fascist dictatorship, and the awareness that the struggle against it would have to take place first and foremost within its own institutions. Conversely, it was a party that could not but recognise its condition as a persecuted and illegal political organisation, removed from direct comparison with other political bodies. At the same time, it was animated by a fierce patriotism and a sense of its own exclusive nature, something that was felt especially strongly with regard to the traditional socialist forces. Suffice it to say, Togliatti was still labelling 'Giustizia and Libertà' as 'dissident fascism' in an article published in June 1934.[27]

The Comintern's policy change of 1934 came at a moment when the PCI's underground activity in Italy was in severe crisis. Relations with the rank-and-file organisations were at an especially low ebb. Numerous activists and groups of activists still existed, but with no links with one another and, with the executive centre abroad (attempts at establishing centres in Italy had been jettisoned by this stage), they were isolated and had no choice but inaction. Severely criticised by the ECCI for the scant effectiveness of its activities, the PCI remained tied to its old sectarian position in the early months of 1934. Only slowly did this change. The leadership in exile in Paris, which after Togliatti's return to Moscow in September had Ruggiero Grieco at the head of the politburo, could not help but be profoundly influenced by the developments in France after February. The pact made between the PCF and the SFIO for common action was followed a few weeks later on 17 August 1934 by a similar one between Italian communists and socialists. Signed by Longo and Nenni, this marked the renewal of dialogue and collaboration between the two parties after a long period of antipathy.

For the PCI, these developments meant the end of the era of 'class against class' and the equation without distinction of fascism with any other form of 'bourgeois domination'. In its most extreme form it had not lasted for long. The historiography of the PCI has, however, been too ready to stress the particular nature of Italian communism and to see its *leitmotif* of a 'national' and 'democratic' path to socialism as already clearly marked out. In fact, the period of 'class against class' cannot be placed neatly within parentheses. Although imposed by the Comintern, the policy of the Third Period had found fertile ground in certain aspects of the political culture of Italy's communists, and the entire leadership – Gramsci included – had played their role. The attitude of the PCI towards the framework of democratic institutions had from the outset been one of non-involvement, of indifference, even when they had been in mortal danger. As Antonio Graziadei – spokesman of the most 'moderate' of the Italian communists – stated at the Livorno congress which saw the creation of the party, 'democracy like all forms of existence needs to be considered in terms of the class system: there is bourgeois democracy and there is proletarian democracy, and the sad truth is that proletarian democracy must tend towards the suppression of bourgeois democracy that the bourgeoisie employs to exploit the workers'.[28] Statements of this type were certainly not just echoes of the language of the Third International. They drew on older roots, fed by the 'crisis of democracy' that shook Italian society in the first fifteen years of the twentieth century, and which, even for men like Gramsci and Togliatti – as would be expected in the culture of those times – was transformed from a 'crisis of faith and respect for the political class' into 'a crisis of belief in the way in which it was generated', and thus into 'a crisis of the very idea of representation'. Even before 1929, the PCI had experienced 'fascism as the enemy, of course, but also as confirmation of the impossibility of democracy'.[29]

At the same time, the damage inflicted by the PCI's unquestioning alignment with the spirit of the Third Period survived long after the 'class against class' line was abandoned. The acceptance of a dualist and Manichean view of reality based on the juxtaposition of 'capitalism in ruins' and 'building socialism', the impoverishment of the criteria for analysis of capitalist societies, and the virus of conformism that corroded internal freedom of discussion, were all phenomena that did not disappear in 1935: they became hereditary traits of the party. It would take a great deal of hard work to free it from them.

Notes

1. Translated by David Laven, University of Reading. The editor wishes to offer his profound thanks to David for his expert help.

2. This article's reconstruction of the history of the PCI is principally based on Italian sources and, in particular, the following works: P. Spriano, *Storia del Partito comunista italiano*, Vol. 2, *Gli anni della clandestinità* (Turin, 1969); E. Ragionieri, *Palmiro Togliatti: Per una biografia politica e intelletuale* (Rome, 1976); A. Agosti, *Togliatti* (Turin, 1996).

3. Translator's note: In November 1926, Mussolini introduced a second set of laws to bolster those passed during the period from November 1925 to April 1926. The aim of these laws, taken as a whole, was to consolidate the power of the Fascist state by severely curtailing individual freedoms, outlawing anti-fascist activity, and effectively eliminating

opposition. The most significant legislation of November 1926 was the decree of Public Security allowing for extensive police surveillance of anyone suspected of being 'dangerous to the national order of the state', and the law for the Defence of the State which established a Special Tribunal to deal with those charged with political crimes

4. Translator's note: 'Justice and Liberty' was an organisation founded in 1929 by Emilio Lusso, the Rosselli brothers and others. Giustizia e Libertà sought to find common ground between republicans, socialists and democrats.

5. Translator's note: In protest at Fascist vote rigging and the murder of Matteotti, the main opposition parties decided to boycott parliament to deny the Fascist majority legitimacy. Those who joined the protest were said, with reference to an episode of Ancient Roman history, to have 'gone to the Aventine hill'.

6. P. Togliatti, *Rottura necessaria*, in *Opere* Vol. 2 (Rome, 1972), p. 266.

7. 'Speech to the Italian Commission of the ECCI', in *Opere*, Vol. 2, p. 138.

8. *Osservazioni sulla politica della nostro partito*, in *Opere*, Vol. 2, p. 404.

9. Speech to the ninth Enlarged Executive of the Communist International, *Opere*, Vol. 2, pp. 329–37.

10. *Opere*, Vol. 2, pp. 23–38.

11. *A proposito del fascismo*, in *Opere*, Vol. 2, pp. 542–59.

12. *L'orientamento del nostro partito nelle questioni internazionali*, in *Opere*, Vol. 2, p. 440.

13. Istituto Giangiacomo Feltrinelli, *Annali* (1966), p. 515.

14. *La correspondance internationale*, 27 September 1929, pp. 1292–293.

15. P. Togliatti's 'Speech on the trade union question at the Tenth Enlarged ECCI', *Opere*, Vol. 2, pp. 748–59.

16. 'Speech at the tenth expanded ECCI', *Opere*, Vol. 2, p. 794.

17. Ibid. pp. 796–97.

18. Istituto Giangiacomo Feltrinelli, *Annali* (1966), p. 982.

19. M. Salerno (Ed.), *L'opposizione nel PCI alla svolta del 1930* (Milan, 1966), p. 129.

20. Rossiskij centr chranenija izucenija dokumentov noveišei istorii, f. 495. op. 22.1, 11258–261.

21. Translator's note: Literally the 'red regions', the so-called 'red belt' of central Italy.

22. G. De Luna, *Donne in oggetto: L'antifascismo nella società italiana, 1922–39* (Turin, 1995), p. 67.

23. 'Report to the Latin Secretariat of the Communist International', in *Opere*, Vol. 3/i (Rome, 1973), pp. 362–99.

24. G. Santomassimo, 'Introduzione a Rapporto di Torgliatti al comitato centrale dell'agosto 1931', *Studi storici*, Luglio–Settembre (1985), p. 545.

25. Translator's note: This is a reference to the liberal and sometimes nationalist secret societies of the early nineteenth century, often vilified by more radical revolutionaries because of their poor organisation and want of ideological coherence.

26. Translator's note: The Dopolavoro – literally 'after work' – was a national network of clubs and other leisure, recreational and welfare organisations that was established by the Fascist regime in 1925. The membership expanded to around four million by 1939, taking advantage of the bars, libraries, dances, organised holidays, outings, sporting and cultural events that the Dopolavoro provided

27. *Caladra e gli altri*, in *Opere*, Vol. 3/ii, p. 392.

28. Stenographer's Minutes of the Seventeenth National Congress of the Partito Socialista Italiano, Livorno, 15–20 January 1921 (Milan, 1963), p. 41.

29. L. Cafagna, *Il luogo d'origine: Gramsci e la "critica della democrazia"*, in *C'era una volta ... Riflessioni sul communismo italiano* (Venice, 1991), p. 9.

French Communism, The Comintern and Class Against Class: Interpretations and Rationales

STEPHEN HOPKINS

This chapter seeks to reassess the experience of the Parti Communiste Français (French Communist Party; PCF) during the 'class against class' period, analysing the overall evolution of the policy and its subsequent interpretation by historians, whether communist, anti-communist, non-communist or 'professional'. In particular, an important focus shall be the way in which this policy was implemented over time, in respect of electoral strategy conducted by the PCF and its relations with the Section Française de l'Internationale Ouvrière (SFIO). Also, the significance of the 'turn' of 1934 away from 'class against class', and the diverse and complex explanations for this critical development, will be the subject of study.

It is a commonplace that this period cannot be understood properly except in terms of the relationship between national sections of the international communist movement and the headquarters of that movement, the Communist International (Comintern), based in Moscow. In the French case, as in others, this international context for analysing the PCF's development is absolutely crucial, but it is also the case that this context has tended to be elevated above the national (or regional/local) context as the privileged site for understanding French communism in the interwar era. Now, it may well be correct to argue, as many authors have done, that 'foreign communists *did* succumb to the dictates of the Stalinists, and *did* loyally trumpet the glories of the USSR'.[1] However, this chapter also recognises that 'the interwar communist experience should not be reduced to the crude equation "communist party=Comintern=agent of Moscow"'.[2]

The complexity and variegated character of relationships between national sections and the Comintern needs to be understood in greater depth, but it is also true to say that we should avoid the temptation to falsely dichotomise contributions to the study of this relationship according to whether they either *totally* subordinate all aspects of national communist experience to the international context, or whether they deny the Comintern's overarching power. In practice, most recent literature, which has tended to be produced by academics rather than protagonists, recognises the requirement to study both national and international contexts, and the often highly complex and dynamic inter-relationship between them.[3] None of this is intended to deny the real power of the Comintern (and the USSR) within the PCF. Nor is it to deny the asymmetry of power resources during the period under consideration, most obviously at the level of the leadership, but also among party members 'at the base'. Decision-taking and policy-making in the PCF was, undoubtedly, directly and powerfully influenced by Comintern representatives assigned to the French party (whether in the shape of Jules Humbert-Droz from 1921–29 or, later, Eugen Fried and his associates); and PCF officials in Moscow (for example, Albert Vassart or André Ferrat) were also important in transmitting the results of Comintern deliberations back to Paris. But, once again, we can note that these processes did not happen without internal debate, and occasionally vociferous argument. Neither the Comintern nor the PCF were monolithic organisations, and this should be borne in mind more regularly than hitherto in the literature.

The 'orthodox' PCF interpretation of its own history during the Third Period has changed over time. In 1931, while 'class against class' remained the party's touchstone, André Ferrat, a leading figure from the communist youth wing, published his *Histoire du PCF*. The next significant efforts to deal with the PCF's history came at the end of the era marked by the leadership of Maurice Thorez, who died in 1964 after more than thirty unbroken years at the head of the party; in 1960, the dissenting group, UNIR, published a three-volume study, deliberately foreshadowing the leadership's own 'official' history, *Histoire du Parti communiste français: manuel* (1964). This document was designed to show the Thorezian leadership group in a favourable light, and it was only from the 1980s onwards that this prevailing orthodoxy was subjected to criticism from within the PCF itself.[4] The history that communist historians tell about controversial periods in the party's past (and, often, their own personal pasts) is a crucial gauge of the maturity, or otherwise, of communist self-reflection.

In addition, with the revue *Communisme*, which first appeared in the early 1980s, authors like Stéphane Courtois and Marc Lazar (who published their own synthetic account, *Histoire du Parti communiste français* in 1995) have continued to build upon the strong foundations laid by Annie Kriegel, Jacques Fauvet and others, for an 'independent' or more 'professional' historiography of French communism.[5] It is not the place of this chapter to attempt to survey the voluminous literature devoted to the PCF's history, especially between the 1960s and 1990s, but it is intended to use both articles that specifically address 'class against class' as well as more general historical overviews that nevertheless often recognise the central place of the period in the party's overall evolution.

Introducing 'Class Against Class' in France

While the origins of the Third Period or 'class against class' within the international communist movement have been the subject of much controversy, it is sufficient for the purpose of this chapter to note that not all national parties reacted in exactly the same fashion to the 'left turn'. As McDermott and Agnew make plain, 'the origins of the Comintern's Third Period lie in the complex interplay of socio-economic analysis, internal factional struggles in the USSR, Soviet foreign policy concerns and the concrete experiences of the communist parties themselves'.[6] After the years of revolutionary upheaval in the period following on from the October Revolution, an era of relative capitalist stabilisation was discerned, accompanied by serious efforts to 'Bolshevise' the internal organisation of non-ruling communist parties and internationalise their political action, bringing these parties under the predominant influence of the Comintern. Only once these objectives were considered largely achieved was the international communist movement able to discern opportunities to go back on the offensive, as the working class movement allegedly became radicalised, and capitalism's inherent instability supposedly brought revolutionary possibilities to the fore once more.

According to one view, the PCF had been involved in 'repeated clashes' with the Comintern up until 1924,[7] but it is perhaps more accurate to say that the PCF had been deeply divided over the correct attitude to take to the International. At the PCF's fourth congress, at Clichy in January 1925, the party was internally fractious, and although (or because) efforts had been made to develop and transform the party as a centralised and integral part of the international apparatus, the PCF remained nonetheless incompletely 'Bolshevised'. For Courtois and Lazar, the drive to institute factory cells met with little enthusiasm from leaders such as Albert Treint and 'passive resistance' from the base of the party. An indication of the still highly fluid nature of the PCF in the mid-1920s is provided by the same authors: in the space of 18 months, from the summer of 1924 through until the beginning of 1926, there was a 70 per cent turnover in membership, which had grown substantially to approximately 75,000.[8]

Tiersky argues convincingly that for French communism the 1920s was 'above all else a period of homogenising a mixed and contradictory heritage, of resolving fundamental conflicts over organisation, method and purpose...' He distinguishes three 'generic oppositions', which needed to be worked through before the PCF could be said to have gained a stable political character: first, the ideological triumph of Leninism over the social democratic tradition (associated in France with SFIO leader, Jean Jaurès); second, the communist party became the major vehicle for revolutionary politics in interwar France, displacing the anarcho-syndicalist organisational tradition; and third, alongside the ideological and organisational struggles for control of the PCF, the Comintern was searching for a reliable leadership core to lead the 'Bolshevised' and, latterly, 'Stalinised' party.[9] In this venture, Tiersky notes that 'it is not an exaggeration to say that until the final consolidation of power by Maurice Thorez and his allies, culminating with Stalin's anointment of Thorez rather than Jacques Doriot in 1934, the French party did not experience unified and disciplined leadership in the Bolshevik sense … it was not until 1932–34 that the leadership weaknesses were finally resolved in the PCF and the process of Bolshevisation definitively completed'.[10]

During 1925, the PCF was engaged in internal struggle and dispute over the organisational reforms implied in Bolshevisation. In terms of its impact on French society more generally, the PCF was 'largely absent'.[11] The SFIO, through its strategy of alliances with the Radicals, was moving into a prominent position in national life. Treint's famous description of the PCF's 'united front' posture towards the SFIO, that it represented an opportunity to 'pluck the Socialist goose', may have appealed to communist militants, but it did little to make the rhetoric realistic.[12] The Comintern sent Dmitri Manuilsky to Paris in late 1925 in an effort to address some of the perceived weaknesses. Whether his brief was understood more in terms of the coming break between Stalin and Zinoviev, or as a necessity to 'save' the French party from its largely self-imposed isolation, is open to question. His visit was clandestine and, of course, ordinary party members knew nothing of these manoeuvres. The upshot, at any rate, was a politics of greater 'openness', with the PCF indicating its willingness to support the government of the 'Cartel des gauches' and seeking to broaden the united front to include not just reformist trade unionists (from the Confédération générale du travail; CGT) and non-organised workers, but also the Ligue des droits de l'homme.[13] This departure may not have been greeted with universal favour in PCF ranks, where support for the government, however lukewarm, sat uneasily with revolutionary fervour.

Nonetheless, at the sixth plenum of the Executive Committee of the Comintern (ECCI) in February–March 1926, a commission was established to examine the 'French question' comprising the PCF *Bureau Politique* (Political Bureau; PB), Stalin, Zinoviev, Manuilsky and Humbert-Droz. This commission enshrined the new strategy and entrusted its delivery to a new leadership. At the PCF's own fifth congress (in Lille, held on 20–26 June 1926), described by Martelli as 'underestimated in the historiography of the PCF', there was a sometimes disjointed effort to adapt the party more closely to the realities of French political life.[14] Aside from the politics of *ouverture*, this congress also ushered in a new leadership group, many of whom would play central roles in the PCF over lengthy careers, sometimes lifetimes.

According to Courtois and Lazar and Mortimer, this group were sociologically distinct from the previous generation, given that the vast majority had either been workers themselves or were from working class backgrounds: Pierre Sémard, the new general secretary, had been a railwayman; Gaston Monmousseau, Benoît Frachon, Edouard Dudilieux and Julien Racamond were integrated into the PB or Central Committee (CC) as representatives of the communist-led trade union confederation (CGT-*unitaire*); and Thorez, Jean Cremet and Georges Marrane came from mining or metalworking backgrounds.[15] In addition, Jacques Doriot and Henri Barbé came to prominence as leaders of the *Jeunesse communiste*. Of these leaders elected (or promoted) in 1926, it is an indication of the relative success of the attempt to create a stable, proletarian core at the heart of the PCF that five remained on the PB at the beginning of 1934. These were Marcel Cachin, the long-term editor of *L'Humanité*, a great survivor and the only representative of the old, pre-split SFIO generation, Thorez, Doriot, Monmousseau and Sémard.

However, there are competing views regarding the outcome of the fifth PCF congress. For the communist historian Martelli, it represented a qualitative leap forward, with the outcome a 'more dynamic style, "Bolshevised" or "Leninised", but better integrated into the social and political landscape of France'.[16] In this view, the interests of the Comintern and the PCF are understood as coincidental, and the increasing influence of the former on the affairs of the latter is not remarkable. Of course, it is worthwhile to note that leading figures in the PCF often held formal positions within the structures of the Comintern. Sémard, for instance, became a vice-president of ECCI at the fifth world congress. By contrast, for Courtois and Lazar, despite the obvious benefits that accrued to the party through the establishment of a permanent 'core' at the heart of the organisation, the Comintern was in large measure responsible for *imposing* both the individuals concerned and the structure within which they would have to operate.[17] From this perspective, although there were advantages for the PCF in following the political line of the International in the short-term, subsequent abrupt changes in strategy and tactics would be bound to undermine the coherence of the PCF's action and the cohesiveness of its leadership, not to mention the confidence and trust of the party membership and its likely appeal to the French working class.

There is no dispute that 1926 saw the PCF move towards a more 'open' politics and, as outlined above, a renewed and more stable leadership. In social terms, the accent placed upon trade union activity and intermediate demands (*revendications partielles*) chimed more closely with the actual demands of the working class, and there were also efforts to reach out to other sectors (notably, intellectuals). In political terms, the PCF was able to improve its electoral prospects by renewing the practice of 'republican discipline'. The

Seine by-election in March 1926 saw Jacques Duclos elected, after a deal was struck for the second ballot with the SFIO and Radicals; the 'united front from above and below' was starting to appear more than simply a slogan to mask anti-socialist practice.[18] And, in ideological terms, there were tentative steps made to try and reconcile 'proletarian internationalism' and defence of the Soviet Union with 'audacious formulations relating to the [French] communists' attachment to their own country [*pays*]'.[19] The 'ambitious objective' of the Comintern in this regard, was to 'ensure the independence and absolute otherness [*exteriorité*] of the PCF in relation to the French State and political system, while at the same time trying to make the [PCF's] mass audience impact upon political life'.[20]

These tentative openings and debates were brought to an end by the onset of 'class against class' before they could be properly digested within the PCF, particularly at the regional and local levels.

Electoral Strategy and (Self-imposed) Isolation

The influence of Bukharin on the strategic turn to 'class against class', and the machinations within the Comintern made manifest at the seventh and eighth ECCI plenary sessions held in November–December 1926 and May 1927 respectively, form the backdrop to the international communist context facing the PCF during the run-up to the legislative elections of April 1928.[21] In a piecemeal process that continued through 1927, the director of the Comintern's Latin Secretariat, Jules Humbert-Droz, had already been warning of 'opportunistic' behaviour from the PCF leadership, especially in relation to its overtures to the SFIO. Palmiro Togliatti, who spent time in Paris in the summer of 1927 attempting to reorganise the Italian communists in exile, was scathing in his assessment, and related his views to Humbert-Droz: 'The party [PCF] has forgotten and is forgetting that it is a revolutionary party, that it must teach the workers to break by all methods the legality of the bourgeois republic, and that we only appeal to legality when that helps us to cover our revolutionary action and embarrass the enemy.'[22]

While coming under some 'endogenous' (ie. both from 'leftists' in the PCF and Comintern representatives) pressure to modify the party's practice, it should also be remembered that 'exogenous' events impacted upon the party's calculations. The government had yet again reverted to a primarily right-wing posture under Poincaré, and this was the signal for a much more aggressive pursuit of communists through the courts – summed up by Minister of the Interior Sarraut's famous comment, '*Le communisme, voilà l'ennemi!*' It was a concern to Humbert-Droz that the return of the SFIO to an oppositional stance against the government might push the PCF to adopt an 'opportunistic' position with regard to the forthcoming elections.[23] The fluid nature of communist strategy at this point is clear if we consider Humbert-Droz's belief that another Comintern agent, Petrovsky, had been sent to France by Stalin to encourage the possible electoral alliance with the SFIO (and even the left-wing of the Radicals) in a revival of the *Bloc des gauches*.[24] Eventually, in April 1927, the ECCI Presidium despatched a letter to the PCF making it plain that 'the party must envisage an electoral tactic which is not a mechanism for standing down [PCF candidates] in favour of "left" candidates, but a method of mobilising the masses; it must ... condemn the tactic of common electoral lists with the Socialist Party by unmasking the "socialist left"'.[25]

Even before this dispute had been resolved, the notion of a monolithic Comintern or, indeed, PCF position had been exposed by disagreement between Sémard and Bukharin at the seventh ECCI plenum over the PCF's alleged 'opportunism', and the following month (January 1927) Thorez issued a 'strong protest' against an article by Humbert-Droz in the Comintern's journal.[26] Under the new electoral law, introduced in July 1927, a two-ballot majoritarian system replaced the list system and so posed new problems for PCF strategy. Although this system was adopted, at least in part, because it was hoped to restrict potential communist gains,[27] the dilemma it created was plain: according to the tenets of 'republican discipline', parties of the left would stand aside at the second ballot in individual constituencies in favour of the single candidate best placed to defeat (or at any rate, challenge) the 'reactionary' candidate. A failure to take this course could very well lead to the fragmentation of the progressive electorate at the second ballot and permit the victory of the Right. As with the *Front national* during the 1980s and 1990s, an isolated party faced with an electoral system that privileged the ability to forge second ballot alliances, risked winning substantial support in the country but failing to turn that popularity into parliamentary seats.[28] This was a genuine test of the resolve of the PCF to follow the Comintern line, and of the latter's understanding of French conditions.

The April 1927 letter from the ECCI Presidium had caused heartfelt debate within the upper echelons of the PCF, and it was not until the November CC that the bulk of the leadership swung behind the 'class against class' line. An 'Open Letter to the Party' was issued, urging the PCF militants to convince the French working class to appreciate 'the nefarious and anti-working class role of the socialist leaders, who, by their negligence, are objectively the prolongation of the National Union [government]'.[29] According to Brower, the 'open letter' condemned electoral coalitions with the SFIO, and the initiative was not received well in the middle-ranks of the PCF leadership. 'At a stormy meeting of the central committee in January 1928, one speaker warned that the workers would "accuse us of playing the game of the reactionaries."'[30]

For Mortimer, however, the electoral tactic was to offer coalition with the

SFIO and second ballot agreements only if a 'minimum programme' could be engineered and socialists would refrain from *désistement* in favour of 'bourgeois' (ie. Radical) candidates. The programmatic elements put forward by the PCF were 'fairly moderate', and Mortimer argues that at this point it 'was still not entirely clear whether the [communist] party genuinely aimed at a united front *with* the Socialist Party, or whether it proposed this only as a cover for a "united front" *against* it'. [31] Hoisington makes it clear that the letter proposing a joint programme with the SFIO was *intended* to be rejected; indeed, the letter spells out that 'in case the Socialist Party rejects its proposal for a Worker and Peasant Bloc ... it [the PCF] reserves the right to maintain a proletarian candidate against all the Socialist leaders who are performing a counter-revolutionary task and who declare themselves defenders of bourgeois democracy against communism'.[32] Hard-line supporters of the new policy argued, for example in the PCF's theoretical journal *Cahiers du communisme*, that even to make any *proposal* to the 'traitorous' SFIO was antithetic to Comintern policy. Others took the view that this was merely a device, a means to hand the PCF leadership a convenient albeit transparent *casus belli* in order to go it alone. Finally, some who questioned the wisdom of 'class against class', like Jacques Doriot, could go along with the letter in the hope against hope that the SFIO would accept.

If it is acknowledged that this apparent lack of clarity reflected authentic uncertainty – rather than a tactical *démarche* – we may speculate, along with Mortimer, whether this ambiguity was due to continuing division within the PCF leadership or to conflicting signals emanating from Moscow with regard to the exact interpretation of the Comintern line. It ought to be remembered, that the PCF was in a state of some dislocation at this juncture: a large proportion of the CC, PB and secretariat had been imprisoned and, whilst conditions did not make political activity impossible, it is clear nevertheless that normal channels of communication and debate were impeded. For Henri Barbé, at this time leader of the communist youth organisation, the New Line, if faithfully followed to the letter, inevitably entailed the PCF categorically breaking with its past practice: 'It must no longer consider itself a party of the left and of the French republican family.'[33] That the insistence on the new electoral tactic was closely connected to the perception that the PCF remained insufficiently 'Bolshevised' is clear from those figures who are known to have opposed its introduction: Marcel Cachin was the only survivor in the leadership of the pre-1920 generation, and Renaud Jean was aware of the potential effects of the new policy on the PCF's rural support, which was largely 'republican' in outlook. Humbert-Droz certainly seems to have connected the necessity of the New Line with the overwhelming objective of creating a more disciplined, or pliant, leadership group.

The case of Jacques Doriot, mayor of Saint Denis, is also of great interest.

Doriot eventually accepted the new electoral slogan of 'class against class' but, 'isolated in the leading party organs, cut loose from his old base of power in the communist youth, his personal following decimated by resignations and purges, he had apparently decided to lie low until the new tactic had run itself out, and to concentrate on organising a political fief ...'[34] Still, Doriot appears to have sought to undermine the New Line's impact almost from the start. In particular, he argued that in 'exceptional cases' the PCF should stand down its candidates in second ballot constituencies where there were better placed socialists. Barbé reported that he envisaged 580 of these 'exceptions', from a total of 610 constituencies! In view of his subsequent stance within the PCF, particularly in 1934 (see below), it is interesting to note that Doriot, despite his powerful local implantation, decided to go along with the policy. Perhaps this was because at the January 1928 CC and the national conference held a few weeks later, Doriot and other waverers succeeded in their aim to permit some leeway in the interpretation of the new electoral tactic: PCF candidates would maintain their presence 'except in those cases determined by the central committee in agreement with the Comintern'.[35] Whether this represented a significant modification of the tactics remained unclear.

It was only after the ninth ECCI plenum, which devoted much of its energy to discussing the 'French question', had confirmed the new tactic (in February 1928) that Doriot succumbed to the intense pressure. However, 'the chastisement he received embittered him against the Comintern leadership and many of his colleagues in the French party', and this latent hostility was to resurface to spectacular effect subsequently.[36] Thorez, in his autobiography, claims that although Doriot parroted the policy he showed by his 'adventurism and opportunism' that he did not understand it.[37] From a very different perspective, Brower recognises that Doriot 'never accepted the extremist tactics and the wholesale condemnation of the socialist movement'.[38] Allardyce offers another perspective; in his view, Doriot, though he 'increasingly became an alien element within the leadership' and was 'undisciplined', nonetheless believed the 'united front from below' was a correct tactic. What he envisaged – despite 'masking his opposition to the party line behind intermittent proposals that were hostile to its spirit' – was not a wholesale remaking of the policy, but rather 'greater flexibility in the party's traditional sectarian policies'. The problem with the policy of 'class against class' was not its *objective* of luring Socialist Party workers away from their leaders, but that the desire to 'pluck the goose' was 'too transparently deceitful to have success'. For Allardyce, Doriot's hope was that 'revolutionary sincerity would work [in convincing socialists of the PCF's credentials] where sectarian duplicity had failed'.[39] Of course, this laid Doriot open to the charge – gleefully picked up in 1934 by Thorez after the line changed – that Doriot *himself* was guilty of 'a mere manoeuvre', and that he was intent only on 'plucking the goose'. Once the PCF had engaged in a bout of self-criticism of its shortcomings in articulating Comintern policies, and the socialists had duly refused to respond to the 'insulting' PCF letter, the election itself proved a mixed experience.[40]

Courtois and Lazar describe the campaign as 'violently anti-socialist', but the SFIO did not rule out the possibility of standing down in constituencies where the PCF candidate came ahead at the first ballot.[41] Despite the fact that, for SFIO leader Paul Faure, the PCF was guilty of 'suicide and treason', nonetheless most socialists took the line that Blum had formulated: whichever progressive candidate had the best chance of defeating the reactionary would benefit from SFIO support at the second ballot.[42] Blum calculated that 'class against class' was a bluff; the PCF would not jeopardise its parliamentary existence by sticking rigidly to the notion that all other 'left' parties were objectively engaged in the ongoing 'fascisation' of French political life and therefore must be opposed by the only proletarian party. In the event, after predictably failing to win a single seat at the first ballot (where 187 candidates did achieve the required 50 per cent plus one of the valid constituency poll) on 22 April, many in the PCF appeared ready to accept the logic of their position. This was to provoke a large number of 'triangular' contests, which would almost certainly lead to substantial gains for the Right.

The overall vote had improved considerably on the PCF's score in 1924, 11.4 per cent of those voting as against 9.5 per cent (1,063,943 votes versus 875,812), but the risk that the party would have no presence at all in the Assembly, an entirely foreseeable risk for anyone with knowledge of French conditions and electoral behaviour, seems only to have hit home in the corridors of the Comintern after the first round.[43] According to Hoisington, Stalin met with Humbert-Droz, Bukharin and Barbé (whose account he bases his view on) and, after discussion of the likely pattern of second round voting, decided on 'a reversal in tactics'. For Courtois and Lazar, Stalin furiously demanded that the PCF work out a deal with the SFIO for the second ballot, a deal which would fly in the face of the hard-won 'class against class' line. Given the bitter struggle to convince French communists of the correctness of the policy and tactics, a reversal at this point could only have produced deep-seated confusion and resentment at both Comintern interference and incompetence. In the end, Stalin deferred to Humbert-Droz, who assured him that the PCF would not be wiped out altogether.[44]

At the second round, the SFIO and Radicals lost the election, and there is no doubt that some seats were won by the Right as a result of communist voters continuing to back PCF candidates. However, in other seats, communist defections helped SFIO candidates to victory. The PCF ran in 364 of the 422 second round contests, but managed to win just fourteen seats (compared to 26 in 1924). The costs of (self-imposed) isolation were plain: in some constituencies, the majority of PCF voters had followed 'class discipline' and the communist vote almost matched the first round, however deleterious the consequences. In others, communists had deserted their own candidate in favour of a 'useful' vote for a better placed Socialist or Radical, and 'republican discipline' prevailed.[45]

We can conclude that 'class against class' had not, in its own terms, been a disastrous policy as far as the 1928 parliamentary election was concerned. Although the electoral tactics 'aroused bitter hostility and were adopted belatedly and under duress', it could be argued by the proponents of the policy (such as Jules Humbert-Droz) that the PCF had done a great deal to 'promote the independent identity of the communist party as a distinct and separate entity from the social democrats'.[46] The party had managed to establish itself as more different from the other parties than previously, and the idea that the success or failure of the PCF must be measured primarily in terms of its proximity to the Comintern's positions had gained extra currency. Tiersky reinforces the point, arguing that here was 'an unmistakable demonstration of its [PCF's] increasing willingness to weigh gains and losses on an international scale'. To be sure, Tiersky goes on to claim that even if the 1928 election represented 'the first indication that large numbers of electors might vote for the PCF without either joining the party or accepting its strategy and maximum goals', the results revealed nonetheless 'that the PCF was unable to mount sustained electoral pressure against the socialists, [and] ensured the failure of 'class against class' tactics as a whole over the next five years'.[47] One can doubt the direct linkage between the former short-term inadequacy and the longer-term problems associated with the overall tactics, but the essential point is convincing.

Martelli puts forward the argument that the not unhealthy electoral performance was in fact 'the fruit of the Lille Congress [June 1926]', but that it was wrongly interpreted as a sign that 'class against class' was the only possible orientation.[48] However the electoral performance is judged, the lesson drawn both within the Comintern and among some of the leaders of the PCF, was that acrimonious dispute within the leadership must, in future, be avoided, and that the best means to ensure this was to remain four-square behind the International line. At both the Comintern's sixth world congress (17 July–1 September 1928) and the PCF's sixth congress (31 March–7 April 1929), the consolidation of the French leadership around a homogeneous core, which was effectively 'Bolshevised', is the crucial characteristic for an understanding of the party during this era.

Thorez and the Comintern's 'Mysterious Delegate': PCF at 'Low-water Mark'[49]

Replacing the post of general secretary and removing Sémard, the PCF's sixth congress instituted a collective leadership based around four secretaries (Barbé, Thorez, Frachon and Célor) that took over the party's reins. Louis Sellier and Renaud Jean were dropped from the PB and, once Molotov had replaced Bukharin at the head of the Comintern, the writing was on the wall for these 'rightists' in the PCF. Both before and after 1 August 1929, designated an international day of action for the defence of the Soviet Union and against imperialist aggression, the French State's repression of PCF activity continued apace, and the atmosphere within the party became fraught. According to Kemp, the intensity and accuracy of police action led some PCF leaders to suspect a highly placed informer.[50] Whether these fears were genuine or contrived, the possible existence of traitors and spies, allied to fierce State repression, helped to produce a siege mentality and a constant search for scapegoats within the PCF over the coming years.

There may be disagreement among commentators with regard to the indices of decline (membership figures are, of course, notoriously unreliable),[51] but there is little serious dispute that the years 1930–31 represent a 'low-water mark' in the fortunes of communism in France.[52] Arguably, it is only with the pitiful performance of PCF candidate Robert Hue in the 2002 Presidential election contest (3.4 per cent) that the fortunes of the party have definitively reached an even lower ebb. The removal of successive so-called 'dissident' factions, like the group around Sellier (who went on to found the *Parti ouvrier et paysan*)[53] and the so-called 'Barbé–Célor' group in 1931, may have left the leadership in the hands of Thorez and his supporters, but the PCF remained isolated and apparently with few strategic options.[54]

It is worth pointing out that just because the PCF leadership was now committed wholeheartedly to the 'proletarian internationalist' conception of its place within the communist hierarchy, this did not mean that the Comintern was about to relax its scrutiny of the party. If anything, the opposite was the case. In October 1930, the Comintern's political commission considered a damning report on the activities and operation of the PCF. The report concluded that the International needed not simply to provide '*une aide politique profonde*' to the French party, but that Thorez required specific direction and 'political–theoretical training'.[55] Since the removal of Humbert-Droz as the ECCI's eyes and ears in Paris the previous year – over his alleged sympathy for 'Bukharinism' – the Comintern had had no permanent high-level presence in France. To rectify this perceived weakness, and with Thorez as sole general secretary from 1931, an ECCI representative – the Czechoslovak communist Evzen (or Eugen) Fried,

better known to French party members as Comrade Clément or Le Grand –
was despatched to Paris along with a number of lesser functionaries, Anna
Pauker (Romania), Georges Kagan (Poland) and Ernö Gerö (Hungary), and
'exercised a determining influence on Thorez and indeed on the policy of the
French party down to the outbreak of war'.[56] Even before this, at the
eleventh ECCI plenum in March–April 1931, Manuilsky had excoriated the
PCF for its perceived failures and, in July, he travelled clandestinely to Paris
(as in 1925) in order to take a personal hand in the party's restructuring.

There is considerable debate in the literature concerning the character of
the influence exercised by Fried and his group, and specifically the close
professional relationship he enjoyed with Thorez. For Adereth, the two sides
of this question are best represented in the conflicting accounts of Robrieux
– whose biography of Thorez claims that the PCF leader became a 'tool of
the CI's delegate in France' – and Giulio Cerreti, who by contrast argues that
Fried 'was certainly a guide [to Thorez] but above all a friend'. Jackson backs
up this view, and provides details of the two men's interconnected personal
lives. Cerreti was an émigré Italian communist who spent the 1930s in
France and rose to become a member of the PCF CC. His view of the
'mysterious delegate' of the Comintern is instructive; he was clearly
impressed with Fried's political talent, his knowledge of French history and
conditions, and his diplomatic ability. One of Fried's many qualities was his
capacity to 'transmit to others his ideas while leaving the impression that
they were, in fact, their own'. Nevertheless, occasionally, if these opinions
failed to register with the intended receiver, he could react in 'an acid and
extremely polemical fashion'. Still, for Cerreti, the oft-expressed view that
Fried was directly responsible for introducing the Popular Front policy in
1934–35 is erroneous and misunderstands the way in which Fried was
completely *integrated* into the decision-making processes of the PCF
leadership: 'the truth is that all four [Fried, Thorez, Duclos and Frachon]
were perfectly interwoven in order to correctly analyse the French situation'.
In his desire to negate the external perception of undue Comintern control
of the PCF, Cerreti unwittingly demonstrates that this un-elected non-
member nonetheless enjoyed a hugely influential position at the heart of the
party's deliberations. Jackson points out that it is 'impossible to distinguish
between the contributions of Thorez and Fried [to the development of the
Popular Front policy] who worked in total intellectual symbiosis'.[57]

Several other prominent commentators with direct personal experience,
reflecting on this significant question, tend to support the Robrieux line.
Lazitch extensively cites Albert Vassart,[58] who argued that 'Fried did not
simply use Thorez as a front with himself as the actual leader of the French
party; he applied himself to correcting Thorez's inadequacies and faults in
order to make a real leader out of him'. This formulation hints at the
complexity of the relationship, but does nevertheless tend towards the idea

of the hidden and undemocratic 'controlling' presence of the Comintern directing the PCF's affairs. This view is backed up by André Ferrat, also an experienced PCF leader of this period.[59] In a later review essay that is highly critical of Jacques Fauvet's *Histoire du Parti communiste français* (1964), Ferrat takes issue with the essentially benign interpretation of Fried's influence. According to this critique, after the elimination of Bukharin, 'a new era began in the Comintern ... from this moment on, the authority and means accorded to Stalinist [ie. Comintern] delegates [to foreign parties] are incomparably stronger than those of their predecessors'. No longer was the International content with keeping 'the eye of Moscow' upon parties such as the PCF, but rather Fried's function was to 'take in hand the real leadership [of the PCF] on a daily and permanent basis'. Mortimer summarises Ferrat's view as follows. 'The team headed by Fried in fact took over the real leadership of the party during the winter of 1931–32. The official and public leadership became only its "executive agent and legal screen."'[60]

It is of more than passing interest to note that both Vassart and Ferrat subsequently left (or were expelled) from the PCF, the former in 1940 and the latter in 1936, and this information has a bearing when considering their testimony. As Mortimer recognises, Ferrat was not an 'impartial witness'.[61] In an interesting discussion of the use of eyewitnesses, Adereth points out that Brower, who shares the analysis of Lazitch and also interviewed personally Ferrat and P. L. Darnar (assistant editor of *L'Humanité* from 1934–39), 'took their statements at face value, never wondering whether their subsequent careers outside the party may not have coloured their opinions and their recollections. Is an eyewitness reliable only when he has left the CP?'[62] Of course, the reflections of these eyewitnesses may, nonetheless, contain very useful and accurate material.

Certainly, as Mortimer goes on to argue, the existence of Fried and his group's 'shadowing' the PCF leadership 'remained a secret from all but the members of the *Bureau Politique* and a few members of the central committee ...'[63] Rank-and-file communists acted in their cells and sections *as if* the decision making process and implementation of decisions were only conducted by their public leaders. In this sense, the fact of unprecedented Comintern influence within the PCF *leadership* after 1931 – whether we interpret this as closer to 'control' or 'partnership' – and the secrecy surrounding it, did not immediately impact on the lived experience of most French communists. This is not to argue that some of these communists were not disoriented and dismayed by aspects of the party's tactics and strategy during these years, not to mention the unrelenting search for 'left' and 'right' deviations, with concomitant theoretical somersaults and about-turns. Rather, it is logical that for these communists other issues informed their political experience, knowledge and opinions (the regional, departmental or communal fortunes of the party, the strength and presence of opposition parties, trade union and industrial work, electoral preparation, police and State repression, personal socio-economic circumstances in a time of crisis). Again, this does not suggest a necessary parochialism among the rank-and-file, for defence of the Soviet Union and a keen interest in international developments were encouraged. However, the specific role of the Comintern in the PCF was out of bounds to all but a handful of comrades.

By the time of the PCF's seventh congress (11–19 March 1932), there were very few signs of the party either establishing itself as a genuine mass party of the working class or of making any headway with its 'united front from below' strategy. Misreading the German example, the PCF continued to 'pursue the chimera of an imminent revolutionary crisis'.[64] As these authors demonstrate, in contrast to the Anglo-Saxon economies, the French economy had stabilised over the previous two to three years. The party again campaigned vociferously in the run-up to the May 1932 legislative election against the 'social fascism' of the SFIO. The results, however, were certainly more dispiriting than 1928: the PCF won 8.4 per cent (782,147 votes according to Courtois and Lazar, 794,883 for Fauvet), and only ten seats (compared to the SFIO's 131 deputies). Despite the loss of approximately 270,000 first-ballot votes in comparison with 1928, the PCF maintained its candidates in 284 second-round constituencies, refused any *désistement* with the SFIO, and was duly punished at the poll. Thorez and Doriot lost their seats, but even more alarming, the party was reduced to the core regions it had managed to prise away from the SFIO in 1924.

More than two-thirds of the PCF vote was concentrated in only fifteen departments, and almost a half in the two regions that formed the *noyau dur* (hardcore) of French communism: the Paris basin (Seine, Seine-et-Marne, Seine-et-Oise), and the Nord-Pas-de-Calais. Interestingly, these regions corresponded to the fiefdoms of the two major protagonists in the internal party debate concerning the possible transformation of the 'class against class' line over the coming period (1932–34): Doriot was mayor of Saint-Denis in the Paris 'Red Belt', while Thorez was firmly implanted in the coal region of the Nord.

Towards the Popular Front: The PCF and the Demise of Class Against Class

There is insufficient space here to give a lengthy commentary upon the intricacies of the decision to end the 'class against class' policy, but we should consider some of the vital elements of this process. Indeed, there is considerable debate in the literature as to whether this should be described as really a *process* at all, or a decision ('turn' is often the favoured vocabulary)

imposed upon the PCF by the Comintern with the changed demands of
Soviet foreign policy as the sole, or at least predominant, catalyst. The latter
view is clearly expressed by Célie and Albert Vassart and Brower, but more
recent and less obviously partisan scholarship has tended to argue that anti-
fascist unity was the product, at least in part, of pressure from ordinary
communists (and socialists) transmitted upwards to national party
leaderships, which was also reflected in changing views among some
Comintern officials.[65] Santore argues that the prevailing Vassart/Brower
view tends 'to reduce what was a complicated and dynamic process of
change to a mere caricature, to conceal the difficult problem of the flow of
influence within the Comintern behind a sterile facade of authority relations'.
Instead, Santore convincingly demonstrates that the decision 'should be seen
as part of a complex reaction to a long series of events which had come to
threaten the International *as a whole* ...'[66]

Still, there is some evidence to support both interpretations, but Jackson's
opinion that both longer-term structural factors and shorter-term political
considerations played their part has merit. Certainly, the accession of Hitler
to the position of German chancellor, and the shock this administered not
only to the KPD but also to the international communist movement as a
whole, meant that 'the year 1933 was a disaster for the Comintern'.[67] Other
structural factors concern the diplomatic manoeuvring of the USSR as it
struggled to come to terms with the growth of fascism and Nazism, and the
inescapable evidence that the theory of the Third Period was not matched by
the unfolding reality in both the national and international arenas.

For Jackson, the dynamic character of these processes is evident in the
confused and fragmentary responses of communists, whether in the
Comintern, national party leaderships or rank-and-file members/voters. 'By
the end of 1933, the gulf between political reality and Comintern rhetoric
could hardly have been wider.' At the thirteenth ECCI plenum in
November–December 1933, the PCF, with perhaps 30,000 members, was
the third largest party (after the Bolsheviks and the Chinese party) in the
International: a clearer expression of the scale of the crisis affecting the
movement is difficult to imagine. Jackson goes so far as to argue that 'the
international communist movement did not seem far from extinction ...'[68]
There was increasing pressure over the following year to change tack, but
this amounted to a desperate groping towards a new strategy rather than a
Machiavellian master-plan to be foisted upon unwitting and unwilling
national parties by Stalin or Soviet officials. Kemp acknowledges that 'the
old line was rapidly stripped of all credibility but there was indecision about
what was to be put in its place'.[69]

Thorez, on behalf of the PCF, was highly unlikely to *independently* decide
upon the necessity of a change in strategy. As Kemp makes clear, both
Thorez and Doriot, though for different reasons perhaps, 'would dearly have

liked to break out of the straitjacket of the Third Period ... Unless that body [the Comintern] itself changed, however, there was no possibility of the French party being able to do so'.[70] The party leadership had been successfully Bolshevised and, with Fried in close attendance, we know that Thorez saw the Comintern and the USSR as the apex of the international movement. However, 1933–34 can be understood as a period of flux, when there was no linear progression towards a new policy, but political developments within the Comintern (specifically, the rise to prominence of Dimitrov and the increasingly sharp internal debate over 'class against class') provided a changed context for the PCF, which itself faced dynamic socio-economic circumstances in France. As Santore states, 'the transformation of Comintern policy in the spring of 1934 was the result of a long period of fierce and often bitterly partisan internal struggle'.[71]

Not even commentators sympathetic to the PCF have portrayed the movement away from 'class against class' as an inexorable process. Rather, although they point out the significance of movements like the Amsterdam–Pleyel committees of anti-war intellectuals during 1932–33, these authors recognise that the PCF was taken aback by the magnitude of the events of February 1934.[72]

Under pressure from the growing economic crisis in France and the looming threat of fascist 'leagues', a leader like Doriot with his independent base in local government – who has been described as 'the most volatile of the dissenters ... outspoken and unpredictable'[73] – understood the desire for unity expressed by ordinary communist, socialist and non-aligned workers. In the aftermath of fascist rioting on the 6 February, Doriot was quick to call for a softening of the line with regard to the SFIO and joint action; a position he had adopted at the previous month's CC meeting. According to Martelli and Kemp, Doriot wanted to seize the opportunity to affirm his authority and effectively challenge Thorez for the leadership.[74] Already, at the twelfth ECCI plenum in August 1932, 'Doriot left [Moscow] believing he had come out on top [in the internal struggle with Thorez]', but he appears to have misread internal Comintern politics on successive occasions.[75] In 1932, despite his convincing explanation of the PCF's poor electoral performance, Doriot left Moscow before Thorez, and the latter was able to institute a party reorganisation in the Paris region that reduced the former's powers. Now, in the face of Doriot's strongly argued demand for unity, Thorez (presumably supported by Fried and his team) resisted.

Communist historians tend to emphasise the 9 February anti-fascist demonstrations by the PCF and CGTU, but three days later, despite the misgivings and vacillation of Thorez, communists and socialists took part in a huge joint action, pre-empting the 'united front from below'.[76] This demonstration has gone down in the folk mythology of the PCF and the wider working class movement as the moment when 'unity' prevailed and the ground was prepared for the great victory of 1936. In the immediate aftermath, however, Thorez was distinctly worried that 'pressure from below had forced them [PCF leaders] to co-operate with the Socialist leaders, and so contribute to the prestige of the very people whose treachery the Comintern had instructed them to expose'. Fearful of the reaction from Moscow, Thorez 'set out to unsay what had been said and to undo what had been done'.[77] The irony here is that Doriot and his followers (like Ferrat, Barbé, Vassart and quite possibly the bulk of the party at the base) provided 'powerful support for those leaders within the [ECCI] who believed that the formation of a united front was the only real alternative left ...' Against the 'rigid adherents' of 'class against class', Doriot and the 'communist rank-and-file in France had been able to make its influence felt during the critical Comintern debates'.[78] Thorez was slow to react, partly because he had been rebuked the previous year for tentatively postulating talks between the Comintern and the Second International and, when he did, it was to vehemently attack Doriot's position.[79] The national and international debate over the potential for 'renewing' the line was caught up, perhaps inevitably, with a vicious power struggle at the top of the PCF.

In early April 1934, as Doriot vigorously supported a joint anti-fascist committee in Saint-Denis, the Paris region of the PCF only narrowly backed the Thorez leadership, even though 'the sternest disciplinary measures' were in place.[80] In the weeks after 12 February, the battle between 'the loyal functionary' and 'the charismatic mayor' intensified; but, as Thorez knew from experience, this kind of dispute would be resolved only with Moscow's intervention.[81] Interestingly, Doriot also seemed to recognise this reality; he sent an 'open letter' to the ECCI (signed by 600 local party and trade union officers), in which he argued that 'the party's tactics contain certain essential defects ... these tactics are opposed to the true feelings of both socialist and unorganised workers alike [who wanted united action]'.[82]

The intervention came in the form of a telegram from ECCI, 'inviting' both leaders to come to Moscow and explain their differences. In the end, Doriot refused to attend and, whatever the reason for this decision, his fate as a PCF leader was effectively sealed.[83] McDermott and Agnew speculate that 'Doriot, no doubt expecting to perform a ritualistic recantation, refused to attend'. Tartakowsky believes that the hypothesis that Doriot himself was cast aside by the Comintern but that *his* policy was adopted is too simple a formula, given that it was still another month, at least, before the line was definitively changed and overtures to the SFIO leadership were actively followed through.[84] However, the fact that Doriot was given unprecedented leeway, despite his clear insubordination with respect to the PCF leadership and ECCI demands, suggests otherwise.

The *dénouement* came at the PCF's national conference in Ivry on 24–26

June 1934, which accepted the necessity for a non-aggression pact between the SFIO and PCF, and indeed went further and called for a pact of anti-fascist unity. Thorez, according to most accounts, was forced by the arrival of a new telegram from Manuilsky to adapt his speech in an unscheduled extension to the conference, and called for unity 'at any price'.[85] Thorez (and Fried) had finally seen the writing on the wall for 'class against class'. He had come under severe pressure from below, from ordinary party members and workers, as well as from Doriot, but also from above, in the shape of the Comintern's eventual willingness to sanction a new line for the global movement. While he may have been happy to resist pressure from the former (and to engage Doriot in a ferocious personal battle), he certainly was not willing to resist the latter. Doriot was duly expelled and, in an 'illogical conclusion', he was accused of being an obstacle to the introduction of the new line and the abandonment of 'class against class'. Doriot's bitter and wry comment was that 'what was criminal and opportunist in January becomes indispensable and revolutionary in June'.[86]

Of course, although a pact of unity of action with the SFIO was duly signed on 27 July 1934, the PCF presented this new line, and the Popular Front that followed in the autumn, as a *continuation* of its policies. No genuine criticism of the 'class against class' period and its effects on the party's fortunes was forthcoming, at least not until much later. This 'mask of fictitious continuity' was to be repeated on several subsequent occasions in PCF history, and the whole period was subject to a great deal of deliberate mystification.[87] The multiple complexities in the relations within and between the Comintern and the PCF should not blind us to the need for clear-headed critical analysis. Re-examination of this era can certainly be helped by recent access to Soviet and Comintern archives in Moscow, but perhaps as important is the freedom for researchers to operate outside a constricting ideological straitjacket, recognising continuities and discontinuities in communist theory and practice.[88]

Notes

1. K. McDermott and J. Agnew, *The Comintern: A History of International Communism from Lenin to Stalin* (Basingstoke, 1996), p. xxi.

2. Ibid.

3. M. Worley, 'Left Turn: A Reassessment of the Communist Party of Great Britain in the Third Period, 1928–33', *Twentieth Century British History*, Vol. 11, No. 4 (2000), pp. 353–78.

4. R. Bourderon et al., *Le PCF: Etapes et problèmes* (Paris, 1981); D. Tartakowsky, *Un histoire du PCF* (Paris, 1982); R. Martelli, *Communisme français: histoire sincère du PCF* (Paris, 1984).

5. S. Courtois and M. Lazar, *Histoire du Parti communiste français* (Paris, 1995).

6. K. McDermott and J. Agnew, *The Comintern*, p. 68.

7. M. Adereth, *The French Communist Party: A Critical History: From Comintern to 'the Colours of France'* (Manchester, 1984), p. 8.

8. S. Courtois and M. Lazar, *Histoire*, p. 91.

9. R. Tiersky, *French Communism, 1920–72* (New York, 1974), pp. 23–32.

10. Ibid. p. 25 and pp. 29–30.

11. S. Courtois and M. Lazar, *Histoire*, p. 93.

12. Adereth translates *plumer la volaille socialiste* as to 'pluck the socialist goose', while Allardyce refers to it as 'chicken-plucking'. Treint's expression is reminiscent of the threat issued by Tommy Jackson (a leader of the Communist Party of Great Britain in the 1920s), that 'he would happily take the Labour leaders by the hand as a preliminary to taking them by the throat'. See M. Adereth, *The French Communist Party*, p. 40; G. Allardyce, 'The Political Transition of Jacques Doriot', *Journal of Contemporary History*, Vol. 1 No. 1 (1966), pp. 59–60; W. Thompson, *The Good Old Cause: British Communism, 1920–91* (London, 1992) p. 39.

13. S. Courtois and M. Lazar, *Histoire*, p. 96.

14. R. Martelli, *Communisme français*, p. 46

15. S. Courtois and M. Lazar, *Histoire*, p 96; E. Mortimer, *The Rise of the French Communist Party, 1920–47* (London, 1984), pp. 119–20. On the complex question of the proletarianisation of the PCF, and the sociological character and identity of the party, see J. P. Molinari, *Les ouvriers communistes: Sociologie de l'adhésion ouvrière au PCF* (Thonon-les-Bains, 1991).

16. R. Martelli, *Communisme français*, p. 46.

17. S. Courtois and M. Lazar, *Histoire*, p. 96.

18. Ibid. p. 97; R. Martelli, *Communisme français*, p. 46.

19. R. Martelli, *Communisme français*, p. 46.

20. S. Courtois and M. Lazar, *Histoire*, p. 98.

21. K. McDermott and J. Agnew, *The Comintern*, pp. 68–72.

22. E. Mortimer, *The Rise of the French Communist Party*, p. 132; citing J. Humbert-Droz, *L'oeil de Moscou à Paris* (Paris, 1964), pp. 255–56.

23. W. A. Hoisington, 'Class Against Class: The French Communist Party and the Comintern: A Study of Election Tactics in 1928', *International Review of Social History*, Vol. 15, No. 3 (1970), pp. 19–20.

24. E. Mortimer, *The Rise of the French Communist Party*, p. 133; W. A. Hoisington, 'Class Against Class', p. 21.

25. E. Mortimer, *The Rise of the French Communist Party*, p. 134.

26. M. Adereth, *The French Communist Party*, p. 38.

27. W. A. Hoisington, 'Class Against Class', p. 24; P. Campbell, *French Electoral Systems and Elections, 1789–1957* (London, 1958).

28. For example, in 1993, the National Front scored 12.7 per cent in the National Assembly election, compared with 9.2 per cent for the PCF. Due in large measure to the latter's second-ballot arrangement with the Socialists, there were 23 Communist deputies elected, but none from the FN.

29. E. Mortimer, *The Rise of the French Communist Party*, p. 136; R. Martelli, *Communisme français*, p. 49

30. D. R. Brower, *The New Jacobins: The French Communist Party and the Popular Front* (New York, 1968), p. 14.

31. E. Mortimer, *The Rise of the French Communist Party*, p. 138.

32. W. A. Hoisington, 'Class Against Class', p. 28.

33. Ibid. pp. 26–7.

34. G. Allardyce, 'The Political Transition of Jacques Doriot', p. 58.

35. W. A. Hoisington, 'Class Against Class', p. 30.

36. Ibid. p. 38.

37. M. Thorez, *Fils du Peuple* (Paris, 1949), p. 57.

38. D. R. Brower, *The New Jacobins*, pp. 14–15.

39. G. Allardyce, 'The Political Transition of Jacques Doriot', pp. 58–60.

40. E. Mortimer, *The Rise of the French Communist Party*, p. 139.

41. S. Courtois and M. Lazar, *Histoire*, p. 101.

42. W. A. Hoisington, 'Class Against Class', p. 35.

43. J. Fauvet, *Histoire du Parti Communiste Français: De la guerre, à la guerre, 1917*–39 (Paris, 1964), p. 281; S. Courtois and M. Lazar, *Histoire*, p. 101; M. Adereth, *The French Communist Party*, p. 47–48.

44. W. A. Hoisington, 'Class Against Class', p. 36; S. Courtois and M. Lazar, *Histoire*, p. 101.

45. For a detailed assessment, see W. A. Hoisington, 'Class Against Class', p. 39.

46. K. McDermott and J. Agnew, *The Comintern*, p. 73.

47. R. Tiersky, *French Communism*, pp. 47–48.

48. R. Martelli, *Communisme français*, p. 50.

49. The term 'mysterious' to describe Fried was apparently coined by the French contemporary weekly, *Candide*, which also called him Thorez's alter ego. G. Cerreti, *Con Togliatti e Thorez: Quarant'anni di lotte politiche* (Milan, 1973), p. 169. Also published as *A l'Ombre des deux T: 40 ans avec Palmiro Togliatti et Maurice Thorez* (Paris, 1973).

50. T. Kemp, *Stalinism in France, Volume 1: The First Twenty Years of the French Communist Party* (London, 1984), pp. 91–92.

51. According to Courtois and Lazar, PCF membership was 55,213 in 1926 and remained above 50,000 until 1928, but then suffered a sharp decline to 38,477 in 1929. During the 'class against class' period, the decline continued to 31,500 in 1930, and then flattened out at 30,743 in 1931 – and 28,825 in 1933 – before picking up to 42,578 in 1934 and more than doubling to 86,902 in 1935. There are some discrepancies between these figures, cited in the 'Appendices', which are based upon Philippe Buton's study, and those included in the body of the text. See, S. Courtois and M. Lazar, *Histoire*, p. 106 and p. 423; P. Buton, 'Les effectifs du PCF, 1920–84', *Communisme*, No. 7 (1985). For Kemp, there is broad agreement with the 1926 figure, but he puts the 1930 membership at 39,000, though acknowledging that this is a 'high estimate'. See T. Kemp, *Stalinism in France*, p. 90. Adereth puts the 1930 figure at 30,000, and this has risen to 40,000 by 1934. See M. Adereth, *The French Communist Party*, p. 291. Mortimer gives broadly similar figures, and includes detailed sources (the majority of them internal or Comintern based), the only significant variations being 38,000 for 1930 and 25,000 in 1932, the lowest figure of any commentator. See E. Mortimer, *The Rise of the French Communist Party*, p. 113. Fauvet makes the important point that the figures quoted by analysts tend to be based upon party cards sent out at the beginning of the year (*cartes expédiées*) to federations, who estimated their likely needs. Generally, these were overestimations. See, J. Fauvet, *Histoire*, pp. 280–81.

52. S. Courtois and M. Lazar, *Histoire*, pp. 103–11.

53. M. Dreyfus, *PCF: Crises et dissidences de 1920 à nos jours* (Brussels, 1990), pp. 32–35.

54. There is insufficient space to go into detail about the expulsion of the 'Barbé–Célor group', but it is a fascinating example of the search for scapegoats within the PCF and the consolidation of a leadership group favoured by the Comintern. See, for example, ibid, pp. 41–50). Thorez claimed that the 'group' resolved to leave languishing in prison other PCF leaders, including himself, in order to follow through its *'politique néfaste'*. In April 1930,

Thorez, acting against party policy, paid his fine and was released from jail, thus compromising with bourgeois legality in the eyes of the 'group'. Thorez argued that 'the party and the International supported me'. Both Barbé and Célor were eventually expelled and, in the end, joined up with Doriot in the collaborationist *Parti Populaire Français*. They subsequently published an account of the *affaire* in 1957. See M. Thorez, *Fils du Peuple*, p. 69.

55. S. Courtois and M. Lazar, *Histoire*, p. 103.

56. T. Kemp, *Stalinism in France*, p. 96.

57. M. Adereth, *The French Communist Party*, p. 35; P. Robrieux, *Maurice Thorez: vie secrète et vie publique* (Paris, 1975); G. Cerreti, *Con Togliatti e Thorez*, pp. 198–203; J. Jackson, *The Popular Front in France: Defending Democracy, 1934–38* (Cambridge, 1988), p. 65.

58. Vassart was PCF representative to the Comintern in Moscow during 1934–35 and a member of the PCF secretariat.

59. Ferrat became a member of the PB in 1928 and was successively the PCF permanent representative to the ECCI from late 1929 until August 1931, and then responsible for colonial affairs; he also wrote the first attempt at a party history in 1931.

60. B. Lazitch, 'Two Instruments of Control by the Comintern: The Emissaries of the ECCI and the Party Representatives in Moscow', in M. M. Drachkovitch and B. Lazitch (eds), *The Comintern: Historical Highlights, Essays, Recollections, Documents* (New York, 1966), pp. 52–53; A. Ferrat, 'M. Fauvet saisi par la légende', *Preuves*, No. 168 (1965), pp. 53–61; E. Mortimer, *The Rise of the French Communist Party*, p. 149.

61. M. Dreyfus, *PCF*, pp. 60–67 and p. 75. E. Mortimer, *The Rise of the French Communist Party*, p. 150.

62. M. Adereth, *The French Communist Party*, p. 67.

63. E. Mortimer, *The Rise of the French Communist Party*, p. 149.

64. S. Courtois and M. Lazar, *Histoire*, p. 107.

65. D. R. Brower, *The New Jacobins*; C. and A. Vassart, 'The Moscow Origin of the French "Popular Front"', in M. M. Drachkovitch and B. Lazitch (eds.), *The Comintern*; K. McDermott and J. Agnew, *The Comintern*, p. 120; J. Jackson, *The Popular Front*, p. 35.

66. J. Santore, 'The Comintern's United Front Initiative of May 1934: French or Soviet Inspiration?' *Canadian Journal of History*, No. 3 (1981), p. 406 (emphasis in the original).

67. K. McDermott and J. Agnew, *The Comintern*, p. 121.

68. Ibid. p. 122; J. Jackson, *The Popular Front*, p. 35.

69. T. Kemp, *Stalinism in France*, p. 107.

70. Ibid. p. 106.

71. J. Santore, 'The Comintern's United Front Initiative', pp. 406–7.

72. D. Tartakowsky, *Un histoire du PCF*, pp. 28–32; R. Martelli, *Communisme français*, p. 58.

73. J. Santore, 'The Comintern's United Front Initiative', p. 413.

74. R. Martelli, *Communisme français*, p. 62; T. Kemp, *Stalinism in France*, p. 112.

75. A. Kriegel, *The French Communists: Profile of a People* (Chicago, 1972), p. 220.

76. Mortimer and Kemp claim that Thorez and other leaders absented themselves from Paris during this crisis, fearing police repression (six communist demonstrators were killed on 9 February), and 'this enabled Doriot to occupy the limelight'. See, E. Mortimer, *The Rise of the French Communist Party*, pp. 210–11; T. Kemp, *Stalinism in France*, pp. 110–11. Perhaps unsurprisingly, Thorez himself makes no mention of his absence, but is quick to take credit for the demonstration and to blame the SFIO leaders for placing 'objections and obstacles' in the path of the absolute necessity for a vast united front. See, M. Thorez, *Fils du Peuple*, pp. 82–85.

77. E. Mortimer, *The Rise of the French Communist Party*, p. 211.

78. J. Santore, 'The Comintern's United Front Initiative', pp. 416–17.

79. K. McDermott and J. Agnew, *The Comintern*, p. 122; J. Jackson, *The Popular Front*, p. 36.

80. J. Santore, 'The Comintern's United Front Initiative', p. 415.

81. K. McDermott and J. Agnew, *The Comintern*, p. 124.

82. J. Santore, 'The Comintern's United Front Initiative', p 416.

83. According to Santore, Doriot refused to go to Moscow until the 'leaders of the Communist International have disavowed and rectified the slander and lies that have been spread about me for the last three months by the party press and central committee'. See, J. Santore, 'The Comintern's United Front Initiative', p. 418, note 51. Mortimer argues that Doriot resisted two summonses, asserting that he could not leave until after the Saint-Denis municipal election in May. But Doriot had engineered these elections – he had resigned as mayor precisely to force 'a plebiscite [that was] run against his own party'. See E. Mortimer, *The Rise of the French Communist Party*, pp. 215–16. However, even after his triumph in this contest, he still refused to attend. We can only speculate about the possible outcome had Doriot realised then that the ECCI line was soon to be unveiled. See, G. Allardyce, 'The Political Transition of Jacques Doriot', p. 63.

84. K. McDermott and J. Agnew, *The Comintern*, p. 125; D. Tartakowsky, *Un histoire du PCF*, pp. 32–33.

85. E. Mortimer, *The Rise of the French Communist Party*, p 218; M. Thorez, *Fils du Peuple*, p. 85; S. Courtois and M. Lazar, *Histoire*, pp. 121–3.

86. G. Allardyce, 'The Political Transition of Jacques Doriot', p. 63.

87. D. R. Brower, *The New Jacobins*, p. 49.

88. G. Bourgeois, 'French communism and the Communist International', in T. Rees and A. Thorpe (eds), *International Communism and the Communist International, 1919–43* (Manchester, 1998).

Wreckage or Recovery: A Tale of Two Parties

GEOFFREY SWAIN

At the time of the sixth world congress of the Communist International (Comintern) in the summer of 1928, the condition of the Latvian and Yugoslav Communist Parties seemed very similar. Both had once played a significant role in the revolutionary events of 1917–21 and therefore had a strong heritage on which to draw; both were declared illegal at the start of the post revolutionary period and by 1928 had approximately 1,000 members; but both operated in parliamentary democracies, which tolerated trade unions and thus provided many 'legal opportunities' for communists to exploit. By the time of the Comintern's seventh world congress in the summer of 1935, these two parties could no longer be compared. Now operating in authoritarian states, the Komunistièka Partija Jugoslavije (Communist Party of Yugoslavia; KPJ) was about to enter the Tito era when it became for a while the *primus inter pares* of all communist parties[1]; the Latvijas Komunistiskâ Partija (Latvian Communist Party; LKP), on the other hand, was in a state of such decline that it would be, to all intents and purposes, re-founded in the following year.

Why were the fates of these parties so different? Why did the implementation of the decisions reached at the sixth world congress have such different consequences for similar parties when the impact of the decisions was supposed to be the same? There were objective factors. In January 1929, King Alexander of Yugoslavia carried out a coup and established his personal dictatorship; this meant the KPJ had six years before the seventh world congress in which to adapt to the new conditions. Former Premier Kārlis Ulmanis of Latvia staged his authoritarian coup in May 1934, allowing the LKP little time for recovery. However, this chapter will show that subjective factors, in other words personalities, were what made the difference. Although initially the KPJ and the LKP interpreted the guiding principles of the Third Period in the same way, by 1932 they were being interpreted very differently and as a result the KPJ recovered while the LKP was wrecked.

The Wrecking of the Yugoslav Communist Party

The Yugoslav Communist Party was the heir to the Serbian Socialist Party and its first leader, Sima Marković, was loyal to many of the precepts of

129

Austro-Marxism; he had had to be persuaded of the benefits of accepting the Comintern's twenty-one conditions. Although the KPJ was dissolved after the November 1920 constituent assembly elections (when it emerged as the third largest party) and its parliamentary fraction arrested in the summer of 1921, the communist run Independent Trade Unions were allowed to continue their activities. As a result, the Marković wing of the party, based in Belgrade where the headquarters of the Independent Trade Unions was situated, adopted an overtly right-wing stance; it argued that the ban on the KPJ was temporary, that the Independent Trade Unions provided a perfect cover for party work; and that, if the party were too obviously linked to the Independent Trade Unions, they in turn could be closed down. To the KPJ's left-wing, such an attitude was unprincipled capitulationism and opportunism.

For much of the 1920s, this factional in-fighting dogged the KPJ and more than once the Comintern intervened to hold the ring. In May 1926, the Executive Committee of the Communist International (ECCI) lost patience and described the party as 'paralysed and transformed into a permanent debating club'.[2] Determined to foster a new proletarian generation of leaders, it watched with interest the emergence of Tito's 'anti-faction' group. Zagreb had traditionally been the centre of the left. Although the Independent Trade Unions had their headquarters in Belgrade, their biggest branches were in Zagreb, giving a 'proletarian' colouring to the left's assault on the right. From March 1927 onwards, Tito began a campaign among the Zagreb trade unions for a 'workers' front' opposed to both the left and right camps. By March 1928, he had ousted the left leadership in Zagreb at the eighth conference of the Zagreb party organisation and sent a letter to the Comintern appealing for intervention. The Comintern duly obliged. In April 1928, the Balkan Secretariat issued an 'open letter', which appealed for an end to all factionalism and praised Tito's initiative.[3]

Ending factionalism was never going to be easy – when the new KPJ leadership appointed by the ECCI tried to expel the Belgrade party organisation in June 1928, Marković simply brushed aside the threat – but the decisions of the sixth world congress meant that the campaign against factionalism was turned into a one-sided assault on the right. The dominant figure in the leadership appointed in April 1928 was Đuro Đaković. He had a rightist reputation – he had been elected to the constituent assembly when the KPJ was legal in 1920[4] – and the Comintern found it difficult to impose this choice in the new anti-right climate it had created. When the fourth KPJ congress took place in Dresden in November 1928, the Comintern's representative, Palmiro Togliatti, had great difficulty overcoming left foot-dragging and securing a majority for Đaković's election.[5]

Đaković went from Dresden to Moscow to receive further instructions, and by the time he arrived in Yugoslavia, King Alexander had carried out his coup of 6 January 1929, which ended parliamentary democracy and outlawed the Independent Trade Unions. In the new circumstances, the factional struggle within the KPJ intensified. Sima Marković, determined to see if there was any possibility of the Independent Trade Unions surviving even in the most restricted form, was prepared to talk to the socialist leaders of the reformist trade unions. The left were convinced that King Alexander's coup was a desperate measure to save a crumbling regime and that an 'armed uprising' now topped the agenda. From January 1929 until May 1929, the KPJ tried to ignite just such an insurrection, although in reality the armed insurrection petered out in gun duels between communist fanatics and policemen, 'ambushing each other in dark alleys'.[6] Some thirty communists died in these erratic exchanges of fire, the most serious victim being Đaković himself, who died at the hands of the police after being arrested in the middle of April 1929.[7] His loss to the party was enormous, for he was seen by many as one of the few communists with sufficient authority to bring factional strife to an end.[8]

Đaković's death left the left unchallenged. Although the call for an armed uprising was abandoned as the party's immediate slogan in May 1929, it was only a limited downgrading. The politburo's new resolution talked of 'sharpening revolutionary struggles and preparations for an armed uprising'. The Central Committee (CC) plenum held in October 1929 stressed that the time had come 'to go from defence to attack'.[9] This swing to the left had an immediate impact on trade union work. The party concluded that the correct response to the banning of the Independent Trade Unions was to call for the formation of illegal trade unions. However, as Đaković's temporary replacement Filip Filipović told the tenth ECCI plenum in July 1929, the right had refused to take any notice. What particularly angered Filipović was the way in which Moscow had not issued clear guidance on the question of illegal trade unions, thus allowing Marković to take great comfort from the fact that it was five months before the Red International of Trade Unions (RILU; Profintern) endorsed the policy of forming illegal trade unions, even though they were essential, Filipović argued, 'to improve our mass work in regard to the conquest of the majority of the working class'.[10]

The new mood was summed up in the July issue of the newly launched KPJ paper *Proleter*. The lead article, 'For the Party, Against Liquidationism', stressed that ever since its foundation the party had been blighted by rightist errors; but the coup of 6 January had 'torn off their masks' and they now openly refused to undertake illegal work, refused to organise illegal trade unions, and cosied up to the social fascists. That the formation of illegal trade unions was quite possible was stressed in *Proleter*'s following issue which reported that at the end of October 1929 illegal trade unionists gathered clandestinely in Belgrade to hold the first (and purely fictitious) national conference of Revolutionary Independent Trade Unions.[11]

Organising illegal trade unions was only one part of this new strategy. The July 1929 edition of *Proleter* also stressed the importance of a new tactic. 'On Organising Flying Meetings' gave details of how best to protect the speakers at such events from the police, and how important it was to have a regular series of such short meetings outside factory gates. For a while, 'flying meetings' were seen as an effective alternative to mass trade union work, but by their very nature these meetings exposed leading party members to police surveillance. Marković and the right opposed the use of 'flying meetings' on the grounds that such 'adventures' simply encouraged police infiltration.[12]

Left dominance was endorsed at the end of October 1929 at an enlarged CC plenum held in Vienna. The KPJ 'declared the foremost task to be that of a political mobilisation of the proletariat, peasantry and nationalities... for a revolutionary overthrow of the military–fascist dictatorship', and 'recognised the necessity of purging the party of all opportunist renegades'; as a result, Marković was expelled. However, the plenum concluded that it was not sufficient simply to attack the right; alleged 'conciliators' were also put in the firing line. They were confronted with an ultimatum; join the struggle against the right or face expulsion.[13] *Proleter*'s account of the plenum summed up the new state of affairs with two reminders: in the struggle with the right 'he who is not with us is against us', and 'none of the party's demands can be implemented other than through an armed uprising'.[14]

By spring 1930, the KPJ began to recognise the damage that these policies had caused. The first discussion of the growing disorganisation of the party apparatus took place in March 1930 at an expanded meeting of the politburo. At this stage, the explanation given was still the opportunism and passivity of the right, who were duly denounced, but that began to change in May 1930 when *Proleter* carried an article looking forward to the planned fifth congress of the Profintern. Although carefully worded, it was essentially an appeal for the issue of illegal trade unions to be reconsidered in the light of the Yugoslav experience, which was, although this was only implied, that illegal trade unions were leading nowhere.[15]

On 26–27 July 1930, there was a meeting of the KPJ politburo and the CC's foreign bureau which heard Filipović give a sobering report. The party apparatus was now so disorganised that there were no communication channels with regional secretaries through which party literature could be distributed. Literature could be got across the frontier, but there was no apparatus for taking it further. A written report produced on 11 August 1930 made the same point, there was no stable communication network and literature was piling up either side of the frontier.[16] The situation in the communist youth movement was no better. The slogan of the 'armed uprising', the attempt to establish illegal trade unions, and the boycott of all legally sanctioned educational and cultural organisations, had reduced the activity of young communists to attending secret cell meetings which did nothing but produce calls for 'an immediate general strike'.[17]

It was the Comintern, rather than the KPJ, which took the first step. In July 1930, the ECCI produced a statement that helped bring the KPJ back to earth, making clear that the slogan of 'an armed uprising' had been widely misinterpreted in Yugoslavia. This was brought home to party members when one of the leading representatives of the left, Stjepan Cvijić, wrote an article entitled 'Against the Terrorist Tendency in our Movement' for the Moscow based theoretical journal of the party, *Klasna borba*. Then, in August 1930, the ECCI moved to impose a new leader. Đaković's death made Filipović temporary leader, but he had been speedily replaced by J. Martinović. It was now decided that Martinović had not been following the spirit of the Tito inspired 'open letter' of 1928. Instead of 'gathering healthy proletarian elements', he had tried to operate by ignoring the old left and right fractions and built up an alternative 'third group'. By so doing, he had hushed up past mistakes and developed 'a cliquish cadres policy'.[18] He was replaced by Antun Mavrak.

The ECCI's intervention was explained to the broader party membership in the September 1930 edition of *Proleter*. This pulled few punches. It was no good blaming police terror for the current state of affairs, the party leadership had to accept responsibility. Its main fault had been to allow an obsession with 'putschism' to develop at the expense of work in the factories. Thus, the slogan 'an armed uprising' was used in a deliberately vague manner, allowing people to see it as an 'action slogan' rather than an 'agitational slogan'. There was no immediate prospect of an armed uprising, so it could not be an 'action slogan'. It was to be reserved for more general discussion, since there could be no successful revolution without an armed uprising; so, 'the slogan of an armed uprising remains in force as a slogan for mass agitation, but not for immediate action'. Looking to the future, *Proleter* tried to get to grips with what had happened in the trade unions, for the party had lost its ability to head economic unrest.[19]

The November 1930 issue of *Proleter* began to elaborate a more flexible trade union policy: instead of establishing illegal trade unions, the party should concentrate on creating 'militant strike committees in the factories, workers' self-defence groups, Independent Trade Unions and red shop stewards'.[20] This could only be done by working inside the factory gates rather than organising flying meetings outside them. *Proleter*'s editorial in May 1931 duly took up the theme: 'winning the majority of the working class' would be achieved by increased work in the factories, guided by the principle of 'the united front from below'.[21] This was easier said than done. Improving party work in the factories became a regular propaganda theme. In December 1931, *Proleter* published 'The Situation of the Working Class and the Tasks of Revolutionary Trade Unions'. This made clear that the communists were no longer interested in entirely separate revolutionary trade unions, but in establishing 'revolutionary groups in the factories'. These, in turn, were to exercise whatever leadership they could, while, at the same time, undermining the influence of the social fascists.[22]

However, the practical results of this policy were small. A detailed analysis carried out at the end of the year showed that the KPJ had still not outlived its 'narrow sectarian spirit', while Sima Marković, making light of his expulsion, continued to issue propaganda in the name of the communist party, and called on workers to join those reformist trade unions legally permitted after the 1929 coup and to ignore the 'adventurist' calls from Moscow to establish a Red Trade Union Opposition.[23] The Comintern again put this failure down to its choice of leader. Mavrak had soon fallen out with his colleagues. For all the Comintern's efforts, the left–right divide still dogged the leadership. Mavrak's background as Zagreb party secretary in 1925 and Croatia secretary in 1928 had suggested that he would be a left-winger, but if he had been on the left in the past, he no longer was. On 13–14 January 1931, the KPJ leadership debated the future of *Klasna borba*, the theoretical journal of the party which was edited in Vienna but published in Moscow; Mavrak told the meeting that he thought producing *Klasna borba* was a waste of effort and called for it to be scrapped. Filipović and others on the CC condemned this stance as 'liquidationism'.[24] There was a similar incident in Moscow shortly after his appointment. Asked to address the Communist University of Western National Minorities, he launched into a bitter denunciation of the left.[25]

So, the Comintern met with KPJ officials on 7 December 1931 and decided more changes were needed. First, they issued a clear statement that the prerequisites for an armed uprising did not yet exist in Yugoslavia and then they set about the replacement of Mavrak.[26] Filipović was again chosen as an interim figure, but when the ECCI Political Commission met on 3 April 1932, a completely new leadership was established, headed by Milan Gorkić.[27] Gorkić was KPJ leader from April 1932 until his arrest during Stalin's purges in late July or early August 1937, and 'the recovery of the KPJ took place during his relatively long stewardship'.[28]

Isolating the Latvian Communist Party

The LKP had a unique history. In the revolutionary ferment of 1917–18, it won power in elections to both soviet and parliamentary assemblies; it was deprived of power by German Imperialism and the Treaty of Brest-Litovsk; it recovered power by military force in January 1919; and it established such an intolerant sectarian dictatorship that its people rose up in revolt five months later. Driven from power, the party hoped that Red victory in the

Russian Civil War would persuade Lenin to incorporate the Baltic States into Soviet Russia; when he could not be persuaded some 250,000 Latvians preferred brooding in Moscow to returning to their homeland. In January 1920, the party severed its link to the Russian Communist Party and became a section of the Comintern; it was promptly declared illegal. The Latvian communists liked to boast that, unlike the KPJ and most communist parties of the early 1920s, which had had to overcome 'social democratic survivals', their experiences in 1919 had shown them the true face of social democracy.[29]

The sectarian tendency within the LKP continued to be strong. When in 1924–25 the Comintern adopted its 'united front' tactics, the LKP did not respond. Thus, in February 1925 the Riga LKP committee was criticised by the ECCI for sectarianism when it refused to attend the funeral of a member of the socialist Workers' Sports Society who had been killed in a clash with right-wing thugs; the Riga LKP committee argued that since the LKP had established its own 'revolutionary' sports society 'Energy' in November 1924, it should have no contact with the Workers' Sports Society. It was not until June 1926 that the twenty-third LKP conference adopted the 'Theses on the United Front'.[30]

Yet, the prospects for developing a united front tactic in Latvia at this time were good. First, there were signs that the isolation of the Soviet Union was ending: in September 1926, Bruno Kalniņš, the socialist leader of the Workers' Sport Society, took a group of athletes to Moscow and there was much talk of uniting the separate Sport Internationals[31]; a year later a Latvian workers' delegation, including some dissident social democrats, attended the celebrations of the tenth anniversary of the October Revolution.[32] Second, from December 1926 until its collapse in January 1928, the country was ruled by a social democrat led coalition. This embarked on a series of radical reforms, but because of its dependence on coalition allies to the right, actually delivered very little. The powerful Latvian Social Democratic Party, which made much of its left-wing credentials and its adherence to Austro-Marxism, was failing to deliver, and this could have opened up many possibilities for communist agitation.

During 1927, police reports revealed growing communist influence and a steady drift of activists away from the social democrats.[33] To capitalise on this, on 9 February 1927, the ECCI Polish–Baltic Secretariat called on the LKP to explore the possibility of establishing a legal 'socialist' party as a front organisation. It took several attempts, but this was achieved in February 1928 when the Independent Socialist Party was legally registered.[34] The move was well timed, since the collapse of the social democrat government would be followed by both local and national elections in autumn 1928. In the interim, the new right of centre government embarked on a number of anti-labour moves, which could be exploited by communists and social democrats alike.

In spring 1928, the eastern industrial city of Daugavpils became a focus for much labour unrest. The new government, as part of a move to control public expenditure, stopped a local job creation scheme and closed down the local labour exchange, provoking widespread demonstrations in mid-April. The local leader of the Independent Socialist Party, Leonid Ershov, proved a skilled campaigner on this and other issues, and that party's electoral list (List 19) won a majority of working class support when the votes of 11–12 August were counted in the local elections; some accounts gave them twice as many votes as the social democrats. Electoral success was followed by a political strike on 22 August held in protest at continuing government attempts to limit unemployment benefit spending; a quarter of the Daugavpils workforce took part. Elsewhere, government actions continued to inflame labour unrest. In July 1928, the government closed down the Left Trade Unions in Riga, Liepaja and Ventspils. Thus, the prospects for both communists and social democrats in the national elections on 6–7 October 1928 looked good.[35]

For the national elections, the communists tried to register a worker–peasant list (List 22). This was successful in Riga and the regions of Zemgale and Kurzeme, but unsuccessful in the regions of Vidzeme and Latgale. In Vidzeme and Latgale, the communists tried to use List 19, the Independent Socialist Party, but this was only successful in Latgale, whose capital Daugavpils had been the site of so much unrest. The communists interpreted the election results as a triumph: they achieved 10 per cent of the vote,[36] won five seats, and 'for the first time in the history of Latvian "democracy" revolutionary workers would be represented in parliament'. This was achieved despite a police ban on adherents of List 22 organising agitation campaigns and the arrest of the best known candidate and future leader of the 'worker–peasant fraction' Linards Laicens.[37]

No sooner than the elections were over, however, the impact of the decisions taken at the Comintern's sixth world congress began to be felt. In October 1928, some left social democrat leaders tried to make contact with the LKP leadership by approaching the Soviet Commissariat of Foreign Affairs. They wanted to know if the new worker–peasant fraction in parliament might be prepared to support a left government led by the social democrats; the foreign bureau of the central committee replied there would be 'no coalition', and informed the LKP Central Committee (CC) of this decision.[38] The worker–peasant fraction itself was quickly put under close scrutiny. It did much to publicise the cause of labour with its 32 law proposals and 99 parliamentary questions, but on 15 February 1929 the ECCI accused it of 'opportunist errors' and of failing to undertake enough work outside parliament; the LKP CC was instructed to give it greater guidance.[39]

The Comintern's new policies soon had an impact on trade union work. In Daugavpils, one of the biggest trade unions was the General Union, which united many textile, leather and forestry workers. It had several communists amongst its leaders; three of the five delegates sent to the 1926 trade union congress had been communists. In October 1928, the social democratic leadership of the General Union decided to carry out one of its periodic re-registration of members; a device used to filter out communists whose presence in the union could lead to closure. Previously, the communist response had been to tolerate this and then re-infiltrate their members; at meetings of both the LKP Daugavpils city committee and the Latgale regional committee – and against the 'opportunist' protests of the communist fraction in the General Union – it was decided to establish in protest a breakaway communist Latgale General Union, even though this meant losing influence in a union where 80 per cent of the members were believed to be sympathisers. When the Railway Workers' Union in Daugavpils carried out a similar re-registration, those excluded formed a new Revolutionary Railway Workers' Union. When communist activists among the Daugavpils boot-makers protested about party instructions to advance what they saw as inappropriate political slogans, they were branded 'opportunists'.[40]

Unlike in Yugoslavia, where 1929 saw a coup and a brutal clamp down on labour activity, the prospects for labour unrest continued to improve in Latvia in 1929. In March, the LKP Daugavpils city committee planned a hunger march against unemployment with the co-operation of the worker–peasant fraction; police prevented the planned progress to Riga.[41] However, on 25 May 1929 the trial took place in Daugavpils of those who had participated in the demonstration of 22 August 1928. The accused were condemned to periods of imprisonment ranging from three months to seven years and, as the accused were taken from the court to the prison, a furious crowd of about 300 gathered and shouted slogans denouncing bourgeois justice. The condemned men took up the same cry and as a result were sentenced to fifteen days in the punishment cells. In protest, they went on hunger strike and, when the prison governor allegedly assaulted the ringleader of the protest, other prisoners began to riot. A crowd then gathered outside the prison, close to the centre of town, and the army had to be brought in to help restore order.[42]

Demonstrations were even more widespread over the summer of 1929. Latvia operated a social insurance benefit scheme developed from the one which had existed in the Tsarist empire. This involved a degree of self-administration through the election of worker representatives. During 1929, the government decided to limit this worker representation, just at the moment when elections were being held for worker representatives, allowing the communists to score some notable successes. On 18 October, the social democrats called a one-day protest strike against the government's plans and this forced the government to back down. The communists, arguing that the attack on worker representation showed how 'the social democrat leaders had concluded an alliance with the bourgeoisie in order to drive out the revolutionary workers from the sickness insurance funds where they were beginning to get the upper hand', were determined to turn the one-day strike into a general strike.[43] The social democrats wanted no demonstrations on the 18th, but the communists went ahead carrying banners in Riga that read 'Long Live Soviet Latvia!'[44]; in Daugavpils, the local deputy for the worker–peasant fraction Ershov addressed a crowd of 800 strikers, but used the occasion to stress the danger of war with the Soviet Union.[45]

In mid 1929, the LKP Latgale regional committee met in the forest near Daugavpils. It was concerned that those workers who had willingly handed out leaflets during the 1928 elections had now distanced themselves from the party. The correct problem had been identified, but the wrong solution was adopted. The committee recommended 'flying meetings': this was the way to re-engage with the working class; all opponents of the tactic were nothing better than 'opportunists'. Regular 'flying meetings' and small demonstrations were the way ahead.[46] A typical 'flying meeting', held in August 1930, was later recalled by a communist in the Daugavpils Railway Engine Works: 'as the workers set off for home, a group of communists began to hand out leaflets while Isaac Borok, just out of prison, addressed them; he was grabbed by members of the nationalist militia and the workers trying to protect him could not free him'. Borok, like Ershov, had been addressing the workers on the danger of a war against the Soviet Union.[47]

Demonstrations were always to be confrontational: on 16 January 1930, the social democrats organised a demonstration against unemployment in Riga, lobbying the Ministry of the Interior; when he turned the crowd away, it moved on to Riga city council, which was then debating the unemployment plans of the communist labour fraction; and when the city council rejected the communists' proposals, the fraction members walked out and joined the demonstrators, leading to a fracas with the police.[48]

As to the trade unions, any revolutionary trade unions were closed down in a wave of arrests and searches early in 1930.[49] The attempt to re-found the closed left trade unions on an illegal footing came to nothing. Although a membership of 5,000 was claimed by summer 1930, a year later the unions had all collapsed. The popularity of the idea of illegal trade unions among party members, however, is attested by the fact that in 1931 the CC was forced to intervene more than once to prevent their formation.[50] Enthusiasts for underground work could not recognise that the achievements of 1928 were being frittered away as contact with the working class was lost.

When the LKP held a CC plenum in Moscow in February–March 1930 there was no hint of criticism of the new policies. The forty people who attended, most of them émigrés, praised 'the transfer to new forms of mass work, flying meetings, mass demonstrations and the establishment of workplace cells'. The plenum condemned those who in 1928 'got carried away by legal work' and again criticised the work of the worker–peasant parliamentary fraction; it still needed to more improve its work outside parliament.[51] It was only at the eighth LKP congress, held in Moscow from 7 January to 6 February 1931, that there was any recognition of the party's growing isolation from the working class. There were 29 delegates from Latvia, nine from Riga and eight from Latgale, plus one hundred guests from the émigré community. At first sight, the congress endorsed all the developments of the previous two years, condemning 'right opportunism', 'passivity' and 'capitulation before difficulties' in equal measure, while praising clashes with the police as a positive way of mobilising the masses. However, the only party organisations of any size, in Riga and Latgale, were both singled out for criticism. The Riga organisation was accused of failing to develop the 'united front from below': while the word sectarian was not used, the substance of Riga's failing was sectarianism; its members failed to distinguish between the social democrat leaders and the rank-and-file, thus branding all social democrats 'spies'. As to Latgale, the congress heard a special report on the situation there.[52]

Despite there being warnings about sectarianism in the small print of the proceedings of the eighth congress, little changed. In 1931, some 20 local social democrat committees established opposition groups to try and push the party leadership to the left; the communists made no attempt to work with them. [53] When new parliamentary elections were held in October 1931 a new worker–peasant fraction was established; but although it was praised for introducing a law proposal on unemployment, it was again accused of not doing enough outside parliament at the January 1932 expanded CC plenum.[54] It was only six months later that a dramatic step was taken to check sectarianism: in July 1932, Alberts Strautiņš, known as Citrons, who had served as both CC secretary and secretary of the foreign bureau, was expelled from the party.

The Recovery of the KPJ

Gorkić had first been approached about taking over the party leadership at the moment of Mavrak's dismissal in December 1931. He had been a socialist in Sarajevo before 1914 and was extremely active as both a trade unionist and a communist in the immediate post war years, being a delegate to the first two congresses of the communist party. By 1923, he had been forced to flee to Moscow. From then on his life revolved around the Comintern. From 1924–27 he worked in the Sport International in Moscow, but was not completely divorced from the KPJ, helping to organise the third KPJ congress in Vienna in 1926 and attending the Balkan Secretariat meeting of April 1928 which produced the 'open letter'. Đaković had wanted him to return to Yugoslavia to help enforce the 'open letter', but the Comintern refused to release him. His subsequent activities in Moscow were not well received, for on 10 August 1928 the Balkan Secretariat heard complaints that he had 'flirted with Marković' and had tried to construct a 'third group' loyal to the 'open letter'. There would be many other accusations about Gorkić's secret rightist sympathies but, in public, he was always loyal; his lectures to the Communist University of the Western National Minorities given in spring 1929 stressed the imminence of an armed uprising and he helped organise the October 1929 plenum which denounced the right. Nevertheless, during 1930 he was distant from Yugoslav affairs, working solely for the Comintern on whose behalf he visited Austria, Germany, France, Bulgaria, Greece, Czechoslovakia and Britain, where for a while he was 'a Comintern instructor'.[55]

His visit to Britain was to have enormous impact on his subsequent career. He was there in early or late spring 1930, at a time when the future of the National Minority Movement, the Revolutionary Trade Union Opposition in Britain, was under urgent discussion. Gorkić can therefore scarcely have been unaware of the subsequent row between the British communist leader Harry Pollitt and the Profintern leader Solomon Lozovsky over whether the time was right formally to split the trade unions by announcing the establishment in Britain of a communist mineworkers' union. For a while the Comintern and the Profintern faced different ways on this issue, before a commission agreed in the first half of August 1930 that there were to be no communist trade unions in Britain where the immediate task would be to work within the reformist trade unions. The settling of this dispute brought to the fore a new *de facto* leader of the Comintern, Dmitri Manuilsky, with whom Gorkić was particularly close.[56]

The decisions of this British Commission were quite at odds with the public pronouncements adopted at the fifth Profintern congress held in the second half of August. Here, Lozovsky could describe 'as a turning point in the strategy and tactics of the RILU in western Europe' the decision to establish revolutionary trade unions in Germany and Poland; similar unions were to be set up 'wherever possible'. Although it was conceded that not every country could move quite as fast as the Germans and Poles, the clear public message of the congress was that the future belonged to revolutionary trade unions.[57] And, although Pollitt and Lozovsky disputed who was responsible, the special dispensation given to the British to continue working in the reformist trade unions took several months to communicate to London and the British rank-and-file.[58]

Trade union policy remained confused for most of 1931. The tone of the eleventh plenum, 25 March–13 April 1931, continued to stress the importance of independent revolutionary trade unions, yet at the same time Manuilsky was keen to put this in the context of what now became the 'chief task, winning the majority of the working class'.[59] It would not be until the Profintern's central council met in December 1931 that Lozovsky was prepared to clarify that the British dispensation was available to all and that 'work within the reformist trade unions remains of the greatest importance'.[60] Gorkić, however, privy through Manuilsky to the emerging new line, was determined to use trade union work to engineer a recovery in the fortunes of the KPJ. Even before the Profintern's public change of line, from the very end of 1930 and throughout 1931, *Proleter* had been developing its own line on the trade unions; the paper had first hinted at the need for change immediately after Gorkić returned from Britain.

Yugoslav labour legislation allowed for the election of 'trusted men', a sort of shop steward with limited rights. Elections were scheduled for these posts in early 1932 and, instead of boycotting them, the KPJ decided to take part. Thus, in February 1932, *Proleter* called for active participation and the elaboration of 'day-to-day transitional demands' that would help establish 'a united front from below'. The same issue of *Proleter*, after discussing the ECCI's criticism of party operations during 1929 and 1930, stressed that the biggest single failing was the party's poor links to the country's biggest industrial plants; the party had to take seriously the task of moving the centre of gravity of its work into the factories.[61] The process took time. In autumn 1932, *Proleter* was still arguing that salvation would only come through reviving the party in industrial centres. The slogan 'Communists to the Trade Unions' was elaborated in the September issue of *Proleter*, which stressed that militant revolutionaries not only could join reformist trade unions but should do so. The October issue reminded members that this did not mean 'going soft' on socialists or even renegades like Marković; but Marković's claim that his expulsion from the party had been a mistake and that only his communist organisation operated in Belgrade had to be countered effectively.[62]

Contemporaries noted that Gorkić devoted a lot of time to evolving a strategy that would protect the KPJ organisation from police infiltration as it recovered.[63] He certainly used the December issue of *Proleter* to explain in detail how cells, factory committees and regional committees should intersect. The most original aspect of Gorkić's schema was the stress given to 'initiative from below'. He argued that the way to revive moribund cells was to get them involved in action, and action would be provided by issues which arose in day-to-day factory life and which could not be predicted in advance. Gorkić also argued that, to revive the party, the tactics used against 'liquidators' like Marković needed to change. In 'Struggle Against the

Liquidators', published in the same issue, the party was urged as ever to combat 'open liquidators', but a distinction was drawn between them and 'hidden liquidators', ie. those who were simply passive and appeared to accept the line that nothing could be done until the organisation was strong; these people would respond to clear leadership.[64] Gorkić's view was clear: there was more to combating liquidationism than vitriolic headlines; liquidationism could be countered by giving a lead; the era of 'who is not for us is against us' had passed. The success of this tactic was shown over the summer of 1933, when the KPJ was able to restore its organisation in Belgrade.[65]

It is clear that Gorkić's policies met with some resistance from within Yugoslavia. In spring 1933, *Proleter* again took up the cause of KPJ participation in shop steward elections, but the March edition had to make clear that this did not mean organising 'flying meetings' which ended with the cry 'Long Live the Armed Uprising!' To rub the point home, the June edition of *Proleter* published and article 'Sectarianism as the Aid and Support of the Police' which took a vitriolic swipe at the policies pursued by the left over the years 1929–31 when party activity had been limited to nothing more than the distribution of leaflets.[66] However, more troubling for Gorkić than the tardiness of the rank-and-file at home in adopting his new policies was the opposition that welled up in the CC in emigration. Although Gorkić was clearly the head of the leadership appointed in April 1932, two others joined him on the executive troika, Vladimir Ćopić and Blagoje Parović. By August 1933, Ćopić had become very critical of Gorkić, pointing to a number of 'right errors'. Although Ćopić got rather carried away in his denunciation, calling Gorkić at one point 'a Bukharinite, a conciliator and a rightist', there were three substantive issues: first, he was not sufficiently critical of Sima Marković; second, he had pushed through the slogan 'Communists into the Trade Unions' in the face of opposition from Miloš Marković, who had been co-opted to the CC in the course of 1933; and third, that in all the criticism of the years 1929–31 he never owned up to his own association with the so-called 'third group'.

If Ćopić hoped to unseat Gorkić, he was out of luck; the Comintern informed him that denunciations like this risked a new bout of factionalism, and that Gorkić was well aware of his past errors.[67] The KPJ leadership did agree on 20 September, however, that the former leaders of all fractions should write self-critical articles in the party press.[68] That Gorkić overcame this hiccup fairly easily is clear from the October 1933 issue of *Proleter*, which analysed six months work in the trade unions since the slogan 'Communists into the Trade Unions' had been launched. The article reminded members that this had been done with the approval of the Comintern and yet far from all party members had responded; nor had all of those who had responded done so correctly. Working in the trade unions meant just that, working with everybody other than the trade union bosses; it did not mean simply forming a cell and waiting. Forming a Revolutionary Trade Union Opposition meant uniting with anyone prepared to struggle, and that included 'hidden liquidators'. Above all, it meant acting self-critically and asking whether some KPJ actions did not drive people away rather than attract them.[69]

Gorkić was slightly more cautious when he addressed the thirteenth ECCI plenum in December 1933. He could report a five-fold increase in membership since 'most communist party organisations were smashed during the period 1929–30', as well as a steady increase in the number of strikes and strikers. But not everything was rosy. To this audience he found it necessary to recall that the right danger still existed. He conceded that in the KPJ's recent struggle against 'phrase-mongering about an armed insurrection' the CC had not done enough to counter the right. This had led to rightist errors in trade union work as well as leftist ones. When discussing the leftist errors, he merely repeated the concerns raised in the October issue of *Proleter*; as to the rightist errors, he singled out an unwillingness to struggle against the trade union bosses and a willingness 'to smuggle through communists on social democratic lists' in trade union elections rather than putting up a communist list of candidates.[70]

Basking in what appeared to be an unassailable position, Gorkić could afford to write the self-critical article demanded of all former fraction leaders. Technically he had not been a fraction leader, but there were sins he could confess. Thus, in *Proleter*'s September–October issue of 1934, there appeared 'A Statement by Comrade Gorkić'. He accepted that, even though for most of the period 1929–32 he had been distanced form the party, he was ultimately responsible for the misuse of the slogan 'an armed insurrection'; by a tortuous piece of logic he argued that this was a right error as much as a left error, since it related to allowing too much spontaneity to the masses. He then confessed that, although he had always acknowledged the 'open letter' of 1928 and the decisions of the sixth congress and the October 1929 plenum – and had written in a similar vein to the politburo in 1929 and 1930 – the reality of his activity at this time had been to encourage the formation of 'an anti-party third group'. He concluded his confession by assuring members that all these sins, committed by himself and other leaders from 1929–31, were in the past and that the party had renewed and consolidated itself.[71] On 25 September 1934, the CC drafted the resolution 'On the Years 1929–31' which would be adopted at the fourth KPJ conference.[72]

By summer 1934, it was clear that Gorkić had got the KPJ back into the trade unions; only the rural areas of Bosnia, Montenegro and Vovjvodina had made no progress.[73] However, the nature of party work in the trade unions was still causing confusion. For this reason, Gorkić, accompanied by Parović, visited Yugoslavia in November and early December 1934 to assess the state of trade union work.[74] Their trip was made against a back drop of tensions among leading party figures as preparations were made for the fourth KPJ conference held in Ljubljana on 24–25 December 1934. Writing in *Proleter*, Gorkić had argued that trade union work 'should be as legal as possible',[75] but such guidance was vague. In his report to the thirteenth ECCI plenum, Gorkić had criticised some party members who 'set up the Revolutionary Opposition only in the trade unions and not in the factories'.[76] The implication of this was that it was wrong to make the centre of gravity of trade union work an assault on the trade union bosses rather than practical work in the factories. But when the resolution on the trade unions was being discussed in the CC for adoption at the fourth KPJ conference, Gorkić had not been able to force this through. So, Parović, who had worked closely with Gorkić on trade union affairs, supported by Tito, who had just been released from prison and co-opted to the CC, voted against the initial draft resolution because the two of them opposed the idea of party cells within the trade unions.[77] As a result, Gorkić and Parović were entrusted by the CC to finalise the resolution.[78]

When adopted, that resolution endorsed the notion that the greatest danger was no longer that communists might ignore the trade unions, but that they would follow the wrong policies within them. The resolution made clear that the Revolutionary Trade Union Opposition 'was no longer to be seen as the beginnings of an independent revolutionary trade union movement' but a means of converting reformist trade union to the concept of class struggle. The point made by Parović and Tito was incorporated into points four and five of the resolution, which identified the factories as the basic units for the Revolutionary Trade Union Opposition and stressed that its groups should not have 'a narrow, rigid organisational form' but a wide variety of forms depending on circumstances with the aim of uniting as many workers as possible.[79]

The measure of Gorkić's triumph can be seen in the increasing success the KPJ had in organising and leading strikes. In 1932, of the 17 strikes that took place, the communists led only three. By the end of 1933, the communists claimed to be leading half the strikes. By the end of 1934, two thirds of all strikes were led by communists.[80] Gorkić may well have been a secret 'Bukharinite'; his later disagreements with Tito certainly centred on his gushing enthusiasm for popular front style co-operation with the socialists.[81] However, as a Comintern professional he knew both how to keep quiet and how to make the best use of the current political line. By persuading the Yugoslav communists to return to the trade unions, he paved the way for Tito's future triumph.

The Wrecking of the Latvian Communist Party

There was to be no salvation of the LKP through trade union work for there was to be no Latvian Gorkić. At the same time that Gorkić was taking over the KPJ, Citrons and his supporters were being excluded from the LKP in a messy affair which lasted for the best part of a year and virtually paralysed the party at a time when former Premier Ulmanis's preparations for his coup were all too evident.

Citrons was born in 1896, fought in the Red Army during the Russian Civil War, stayed in Soviet Russia after 1920 and on demobilisation in 1922 entered Moscow's Communist University for Western National Minorities. After graduation in 1927 he was sent into Latvia in 1928, and from the end of 1929 until 1931 he was CC secretary; then in February 1931 he joined the CC foreign bureau and was its secretary from January until June 1932, when his sudden expulsion from the party took place. He had a deserved reputation for plain speaking: in 1928, the CC debated the decisions adopted at the sixth world congress and Citrons pointed out bluntly that, with under 1,000 members, the party was simply too small to influence events in Latvia in any meaningful way. As time passed, he developed a critique of party policy that echoed issues raised by Gorkić. He argued that the party often put forward slogans that workers simply did not believe. He argued that not enough was made of the work of the worker–peasant fraction and that their legal position was being constantly jeopardised by asking them to address the unemployed, thus blurring the boundaries between legal and illegal work. He repeatedly stressed that the right danger was being exaggerated in order to avoid a serious analysis of the party's failings. Yet, although this sounded like a right critique, Citrons was the very opposite of being a rightist; he was an ultra-leftist who, before joining the foreign bureau, had accused it of 'idealising bourgeois democracy'.[82]

Citrons made his mark by campaigning against the right and once he had been elected CC secretary, that struggle continued. For all his desire to protect the worker–peasant fraction from arrest, he was determined to stop any of their actions which smacked of opportunism and demanded in 1930 and 1931 that certain of the deputies be sent to the CC in Soviet Russia to receive guidance.[83] Not surprisingly, given the work of Manuilsky and the success of leaders like Gorkić, what brought matters to a head in 1932 was a dispute over work in the trade unions. Although Citrons always insisted that he had called for a flexible approach to be adopted towards the social democrats, he was deeply hostile to the trade unions. In the charge and counter-charge surrounding his expulsion, he agreed that he had called the reformist trade unions 'counter-revolutionary organisations of fascism', but denied that he had stated 'do not work in the trade unions'; his critics were sure he had made just such a statement.[84] The official account of his expulsion made clear that he had denied the need to work in trade unions and any other legal areas of work and, as such, he was a sectarian.[85]

What made the expulsion of Citrons doubly dramatic was the second charge brought against him, that he had tried to exploit the antagonism between the younger party members and the older generation, thus disorganising both the CC and its foreign bureau. The generational issue was real. The majority of the one hundred guests at the eighth LKP congress were veterans of 1919, while the majority of the delegates from Latvia had joined the party since 1921.[86] Citrons certainly seems to have been plain spoken enough to have been able to draw unflattering comparisons between the dangers faced by illegal professional revolutionaries in Latvia and the comfortable retirement enjoyed by the veterans in Moscow. Yet, his pre-eminence in the party was largely a result of his association with the émigré leader Pēteris Stučka. Stučka wanted the eighth LKP congress to give retrospective blessing to the ultra-left land policy he had imposed on Soviet Latvia in 1919, and Citrons seems to have seen the benefits such an alliance could bring him. Thus, Citrons was ready to co-operate in the dubious deal that resulted in Stučka's greatest critic, Kārlis Krastiņš, being denounced as a provocateur.[87]

It was no coincidence that as soon as Stučka died, Citrons' power began to wane. The expanded CC plenum of 23–24 January 1932 was the first held after Stučka's death and in the following six months Citrons influence faded as his colleagues on the plenum presidium, Fricis Deglavs and Jānis Krumiņš, both turned against him, believing he was 'disorganising the work of the central committee'. Although the Deglavs–Krumiņš alliance would scarcely see out the year, it was enough to unseat Citrons; on 9 April 1932, he was defeated in a vote on the CC foreign bureau for the first time.[88] But Citrons did not go quietly: he appealed to the Comintern against his expulsion in January 1933, while his supporters tried to publish a memorandum he had sent to the ECCI in 1931 entitled 'On the Right Wing in the LKP'. The response of the foreign bureau was to pass a resolution in April 1933 'On the Anti-Party Bloc of Left and Right Deviations in the LKP'. This was endorsed by the Comintern's Poland–Baltic Secretariat in May 1933, and by the ECCI in June, which not only found Citrons guilty of 'sectarianism' and misinterpreting the decisions of the twelfth ECCI plenum, but also spelled out in some detail the harm sectarianism could do and called for a determined struggle against it. On 18 June, the LKP CC passed a resolution 'On the Advance of Fascism and the Tasks of the LKP' which not only condemned Citrons but also identified a Citrons group, which included the former leader of the Latgale region and demanded the most determined struggle against sectarianism. Finally, the CC summoned a conference to address the dangers posed by 'left and right opportunism'.[89]

With this dispute raging in Moscow, it is not surprising that the struggle against sectarianism had little impact in Latvia. Unlike in the past, the new CC secretary Deglavs used his reports of late 1932 and early 1933 to praise the work of the worker–peasant fraction and its contacts with 36 legal organisations, but this comment was made in the context of improvements after three of the deputies had been damned as opportunist in October and November 1932.[90] Despite all the debate about work in the trade unions and the official directives that the communists should participate in the reformist trade unions, early in 1933 the party refused to support a strike by Riga port labourers simply because it was led by the social democrats.[91] In March 1933, the LKP, along with all other west European communist parties, proposed to the social democrats that there should be united action against the fascist threat in view of the situation in Germany. The invitation was rejected and the LKP CC conceded that the proposal had not been helped by the Latgale regional committee putting out a leaflet that described the social democrat leaders as 'heading the fascist onslaught'.[92]

There were moments of co-operation between communists and social democrats. In February 1933, the worker–peasant fraction agreed to support the social democrats in putting to a national referendum the social insurance bill presented to parliament by the social democrats but voted down by the conservative majority; this joint action, which included the worker–peasant fraction being permitted to address a social democrat rally, resulted in 400,000 votes being cast for the bill, twice the vote achieved by the social democrats in the 1931 national election.[93] In July 1933, Fricis Bergs, a leading member of the worker–peasant fraction, organised an anti-fascist conference attended by some 400 delegates including twelve prominent social democrats.[94] Yet, in autumn 1933, Bergs was sent by the CC to disrupt a meeting of the Workers' Sports Society. Bergs asked to be allowed to speak 'on the worker's united front against the bourgeois assault' and his request was refused; he then delivered an impromptu harangue before being forcibly removed from the building. The purpose of this provocation was to embarrass the social democrat leader Bruno Kalniņš who was chairing the meeting. Bergs' clash with Kalniņš came on the eve of the banning of the Workers' Sports Society in September 1933, and shortly before the arrest of the worker–peasant fraction on the night of 21–22 November 1933; indeed, it must have occurred just at the moment when the communists were calling on the social democrats to support them in joint action to defend the worker–peasant fraction.[95]

Deglav's report to the thirteenth ECCI plenum in December 1933 could not hide the situation. It was the antithesis of the report presented by Gorkić. 'The broad strata of social democratic workers are dissatisfied with the policy of their leaders,' he argued, but in spite of this, 'they still do not come to us.' This could only be put down to the disastrous state of the party. There were over 25,000 workers in reformist trade unions, yet the continuing sectarian attitude of refusing to work in the unions or setting up illegal trade union groups presented 'a serious hindrance towards overcoming the mass influence of the social fascists'. What was particularly alarming was evidence from recent social insurance elections that suggested disillusioned social democrats were going over to openly fascist groups. With Comintern help, Citrons' right–left opportunist bloc had been defeated, but its influence was still felt in Latvia where some were now urging 'organisational passivity' and arguing that the masses should be organised 'without the direct help of the party'.[96] Although this was not dealt with by Deglavs, the LKP's second biggest organisation was in chaos. At the end of autumn 1933, a purge began of the Latgale regional committee, which lasted well into 1934, while in that region's capital, Daugavpils, local activists had tried to set up a rival communist organisation.[97] This was a dramatic turnaround from 1928 when Latgale was at the very forefront of communist activity.

On 15–16 May 1934, Kārlis Ulmanis carried out his coup and established his personal authoritarian regime. When two years later the ECCI considered the fate of the LKP at its session on 21 June 1936, it stressed that Ulmanis' action had been the *coup de grace* for a party whose condition was already terminal; if in 1932 membership stood at 1,070 members (255 in Riga and 334 in Latgale), by 1936 there were less than 500 members, with significant numbers only in Riga and Latgale.[98] The real cause of this collapse of membership and paralysis of organisation was that 'the party leadership followed a typically sectarian line, isolating itself from the masses'.[99] As late as May 1934, the Riga party secretary had simply been hiding Comintern directives critical of sectarianism, and after the coup, in August 1934, the Riga party organisation refused to sign a united front pact with the illegal Socialist Workers' and Peasants' Party, formed by left-wing social democrats when Ulmanis banned the Social Democratic Party. The ECCI meeting noted that a serious struggle against sectarianism had only begun in autumn 1934, and that since then the party had been destroyed by a wave of arrests in March, November and December 1935. The ECCI felt it had no choice but to dissolve the Riga committee, dissolve the foreign bureau, and start rebuilding the party from scratch.[100]

Conclusion

What does this tale of two parties tell us about the fate of Europe's small illegal communist parties during the Third Period? First, it shows that the policies of the Third Period were not monolithic but evolved over time. For eighteen months, from the fifth Profintern congress of August 1930 until its central council plenum in December 1931, confused signals were given about the possibility of working in the reformist trade unions, although the eleventh ECCI plenum of April 1931 had given clear hint of the way things were going with its talk of 'wining a majority of the working class'. Second, the speed with which individual parties responded to this evolution in the Comintern line depended on the political views of individual communist leaders. Gorkić jumped to implement them; Citrons refused to implement them; and the consequence for the two parties were completely different.

Notes

1. See this author's 'Tito and the Twilight of the Comintern' in T. Rees and A. Thorpe (eds), *International Communism and the Communist International, 1919–43* (Manchester, 1998), pp. 205–21.

2. I. Avakumovic, *History of the Communist Party of Yugoslavia* (Aberdeen, 1964), p. 79.

3. Ibid. p. 89.

4. *International Press Correspondence (Inprecorr)*, No. 22, 1929.

5. I. Avakumovic, *History*, p. 91.

6. Ibid. p. 95.

7. Ibid. p. 97; *Inprecorr*, No. 22, 1929.

8. S. Belić, 'O Komunističkog Internacionali', *Prilozi za istoriju socializma*, Vol. 7, (Belgrade, 1970).

9. I. Avakumovic, *History*, p. 94.

10. *Inprecorr*, No. 57, 1929.

11. *Proleter*, No. 4, 1929; No. 6, 1929.

12. *Proleter*, No. 26, 1932.

13. *Inprecorr*, No. 63, 1929.

14. *Proleter*, No. 6, 1929.

15. *Proleter*, No. 13, 1930.

16. N. Jovanović, '*Klasna borba*: Teorijski časopis KPJ (1926–34, 1937)', *Prilozi za istoriju socijalizma*, Vol. 7, (Belgrade, 1970).

17. M. Vasić, 'Prilog izučavanju razvitka SKOJ-a i naprednog omladinskog pokreta u Jugoslaviji, 1933–34', *Istorija Radničkog Pokreta: Zbornik Radova*, Vol. 2, (Belgrade, 1965).

18. I. Avakumovic, *History*, p. 97; N. Jovanović, '*Klasna borba*', p. 511.

19. *Proleter*, No. 14, 1930.

20. *Proleter*, No. 16, 1930.

21. *Proleter*, No. 19, 1931.

22. *Proleter*, No. 22, 1931.

23. Ibid.

24. N. Jovanović, '*Klasna borba*', p. 502.

25. S. Belić, 'O Komunističkog Internacionali', p. 418.

26. I. Avakumovic, *History*, p. 94.

27. N. Jovanović, 'Milan Gorkić', *Istorija 20 veka*, No. 1 (Belgrade, 1983), p. 36.

28. I. Avakomovic, *History*, p. 99.

29. I. A. Shteiman, 'Velikaya oktyabrskaya sotsialisticheskaya revolyutsiya i rabochee dvizhenie v Latvii v 1920–40 gg.', *Izvestiya Akademii Nauk LSSR*, No. 12 (1966), p. 5.

30. A. Ya. Arnte, 'O taktike LKP v bor'be protiv sotsial-reformizma v rabochem sportivnom dvizhenii 1920–34 gg.', *Izvestiya Akademii Nauk LSSR*, No. 3 (1977), p. 65.

31. A. Ya. Arnte, 'O taktike', p. 67.

32. I. A. Shteiman, 'Velikaya', p. 7.

33. I. A. Shteiman (et al.), *Daugavpils v proshlom i nastoyashchem* (Riga, 1959), p. 25.

34. 'Ocherki po istorii LKP', *Kommunist Sovetskoi Latvii*, No. 1 (1964), p. 42. Hereafter 'Ocherki' followed by the issue number and year.

35. 'Ocherki', No. 1 (1964), p. 41. These events are recalled by many of those who recorded their memoirs in *Kommunisty Latgalii v gody podpolya*, (Riga, 1960), p. 102, p. 108, p. 124 and pp. 201–5.

36. 'Ocherki', No. 1 (1964), p. 45.

37. *Inprecorr*, No. 73, 1928.

38. O. Niedre & V. Daugmalis, *Slepenais karš pret Latvija* (Riga, 1999), p. 66.

39. 'Ocherki', No. 2 (1964), p. 49.

40. *Kommunisty Latgalii*, pp. 93–4, pp. 110–14 and p. 130.

41. Ibid. p. 137.

42. *Inprecorr*, No. 32, 1929.

43. *Kommunisty Latgalii*, p. 134.

44. *Inprecorr*, No. 62, 1929.

45. *Kommunisty Latgalii*, p. 133.

46. *Kommunisty Latgalii*, pp. 136–37.

47. *Kommunisty Latgalii*, p. 216.

48. *Inprecorr*, No. 4, 1930.

49. *Inprecorr*, No. 9, 1930.

50. 'Ocherki', No. 7 (1964), p. 63.

51. 'Ocherki', No. 2 (1964), p. 53; I. Kapeniece, 'Leninskie printsipy parlamentskoi taktki LKP', *Kommunist Sovetskoi Latvii*, No. 1 (1970), p. 50.

52. 'Ocherki', No. 4 (1964), p. 48; for the attendance figurers, see S. Ziemelis, 'Vazhnaya vekha na puti razvitiya LKP', *Kommunist Sovetskoi Latvii*, No. 2 (1961), p. 21.

53. I. A. Shteiman, 'Velikaya', p. 7.

54. I. Kapeniece, 'Leninskie', p. 50; 'Ocherki', No. 7 (1964), p. 66.

55. N. Jovanović, 'Gorkić', pp. 27–36.

56. Jovanović is clear that Gorkić visited Britain in 1930, but it has never been possible to determine with absolute clarity whether Gorkić was 'Jakob', who Andrew Thorpe records as having visited Britain from mid-February to mid-March 1930 – A. Thorpe, *The British Communist Party and Moscow, 1920–43* (Manchester, 2000), pp. 158–63 – or 'Butler', as discussed in M. Worley, *Class Against Class: The Communist Party in Britain between the Wars* (London, 2002). For Gorkić's relationship with Manuilsky, see S. Belić, 'O Komunističkoj Internacionali', p. 420.

57. J. Degras (Ed.), *The Communist International 1919–43: Documents Vol. III* (London, 1971), p. 142.

58. *Inprecorr*, No. 2, 1932.

59. J. Degras, *Documents*, p. 153.

60. *Inprecorr*, No. 2, 1932.

61. *Proleter*, No. 23, 1932.

62. *Proleter*, Nos. 26 and 27, 1932.

63. N. Jovanović, 'Gorkić', p. 37.

64. *Proleter*, No. 28, 1932.

65. M. Vasić, 'Prilog', p. 209.

66. *Proleter*, Nos. 2, 3 and 6, 1933.

67. N. Jovanović, 'Gorkić', pp. 37–38.

68. N. Jovanović, 'Klasna borba', p. 507.

69. *Proleter*, No. 10, 1933.

70. *Inprecorr*, No. 15, 1934.

71. *Proleter*, No. 8–9, 1934.

72. J. B. Tito, *Collected Works*, Vol. 2 (Ljubljana, 1978), p. 213.

73. *Proleter*, No. 4–5, 1934.

74. N. Jovanović, 'Gorkić', p. 43.

75. Ibid.

76. *Inprecorr*, No. 15, 1934.

77. J. B. Tito, *Works*, p. 214.

78. N. Jovanović, 'Gorkić', p. 43.

79. *Proleter*, No. 2–3, 1935.

80. I. Avakumovic, *History*, pp. 102–3.

81. For Gorkić's subsequent relationship with Tito see this author's 'Tito: The Formation of a Disloyal Bolshevik', *International Review of Social History*, Vol. 34 No. 2 (1989), pp. 248–71.

82. A. Paeglis, '"Citronism" – Beloe pyatno?', *Kommunist Sovetskoi Latvii*, No. 5 (1990), pp. 94–96. For his demobilisation and time at the Communist University, see O. Niedre & V. Daugmalis, *Slepenais*, p. 45.

83. O. Niedre & V. Daugmalis, *Slepenais*, p. 69.

84. A. Paelgis, '"Citronism"', p. 97.

85. 'Ocherki', No. 5 (1964), p. 46.

86. I. A. Shteiman, 'Velikaya', p. 5.

87. O. Niedre & V. Daugmalis, *Slepenais*, p. 50.

88. Ibid. p. 78 and p. 80.

89. Ibid; A. Paeglis, '"Citronism"', p. 96.

90. I. Kapeniece, 'Leninskie', p. 50; O. Niedre & V. Daugmalis, *Slepenais*, pp. 69–71.

91. 'Ocherki', No. 6 (1964), p. 47.

92. 'Ocherki', No. 9 (1964), p. 42.

93. 'Ocherki', No. 6 (1964), p. 50.

94. 'Ocherki', No. 8 (1964), p. 46.

95. A. Ya. Arnte, 'O taktike', p. 61; 'Ocherki', No. 9 (1964), p. 42.

96. *Inprecorr*, No. 15, 1934.

97. 'Ocherki', No. 11 (1964), p. 50; *Kommunisty Latgalii*, p. 50. The party's previous support for independence for the Latgale region seems to have been part of the problem, with some people interpreting this as favouring separate organisational rights for the large local Russian population.

98. O. Niedre & V. Daugmalis, *Slepenais*, p. 82 and p. 86.

99. A. Stranga, 'Kommunisticheskii Internatsional i LKP, 1936–39', *Kommunist Sovetskoi Latvii*, No. 4 (1989), p. 49.

100. Ibid; 'Ocherki', No. 12 (1964), p. 32.

The Portuguese Communist Party, Its Ancillary Organisations, and the Communist International's Third Period[1]

Carlos A. Cunha

The Partido Comunista Português (Portuguese Communist Party; PCP) has played an interesting role in the international communist movement.[2] This chapter examines the PCP and its members' evolution during the Communist International's (Comintern) Third Period. The focus is on those events, personalities, national characteristics and social composition which, when poured into the mould provided by the Comintern, left the PCP and its ancillary organisations with a unique 'mask' (party character) distinguishing it from its namesakes in Europe and the rest of the world. It will also address the extent to which the PCP retained an independence vis-à-vis the Comintern.

The link between Comintern and PCP history is very close. The PCP, similar to other communist parties, had its own national characteristics and peculiarities. But it also dealt with many recurring themes similar to those that plagued the Comintern.[3] These included:

- Continuities and discontinuities between anarcho-syndicalist, republican, Leninist and Stalinist factions
- The relationship between central Comintern authorities in Moscow and the national communist parties in terms of the degree of autonomy retained by the PCP
- The impact of Comintern and official Soviet foreign policy on PCP national interests
- Attitudes adopted by communists toward social democrats and other political rivals

As in other nations, in addition to fomenting and organising a national revolution (its contribution toward Lenin's world revolution), domestic and international concerns were often knowingly or unknowingly subverted by a Stalinist desire to place Soviet national interests above all others. While the Comintern expected a one-way flow from its Moscow-based central authorities to the various national parties, there always existed some room for manoeuvre, the extent to which depended on the importance of the issue to the Comintern or the Soviet Communist Party (CPSU). It is clear that the PCP did not always faithfully carry out Moscow's directives. When it chose to do so, the edicts were regularly reinterpreted, adapted or subverted to suit local conditions.

McDermott and Agnew offer the following periodisation in their analysis of Comintern–national relations: The Lenin era (1919–23), Bolshevisation (1924–28), Stalin and the Third Period (1928–34), Popular Front and Stalinist Terror (1934–39), War and Dissolution (1939–43). This analysis of the PCP will juxtapose the Third Period with a Portuguese time framework to establish historical similarities and differences. Does the McDermott/Agnew argument, that the main motivation for change came from Moscow but the national parties had some latitude to adapt to local conditions, hold true in the Portuguese case? They contend that strategies were defined in Moscow, but tactics, to a certain extent, were left to the periphery.

Bolshevisation

For the Comintern, 1924 to 1928 saw a shift towards 'united front' tactics and the 'Bolshevisation' of both the International and its 'fraternal parties'. The Comintern was increasingly 'Russified' as it sought to impose Moscow's will, in terms of ideology and organisational structure, on its various sections. To this effect, the fifth Comintern congress (July 1924) directed the national parties to adhere to democratic centralism and to transform themselves into non-sectarian Marxist revolutionary organisations.[4] Given the turmoil experienced by the PCP in the 1920s, it is not surprising that it was only negligibly Bolshevised in this period; the process did not seriously begin to take hold until the 1929 reorganisation discussed below.[5] Indeed, the party would not be truly 'Stalinized' until the dramatic reorganisation of 1940–41.[6]

An emphasis on doctrinal purity and organisational unity did, in the Portuguese case, contribute towards sustaining the PCP during the state repression that followed the military coup of 28 May 1926, which overthrew the First Republic (1910–26) and replaced it with a right-wing dictatorship. Prior to this, and like many other communist parties during their infancies, the PCP was a weak, minor organisation with a fluctuating membership and leadership. In its early years, the PCP also shared with other communist parties the experience of inconsistent political directives, poor leadership discipline, poor communication with the Comintern, and rivalry among party factions. Nevertheless, it had, from 1921, adhered to the Comintern's policy of a united workers' front, a political line that attempted to revolutionise workers indirectly. The argument was that joint defensive struggles with socialists against a capitalist offensive would popularise communist methods and expose the hypocrisy of reformist leaders. These innovations, despite intense opposition from some Comintern sections, formed the basis of official Comintern practice through until 1928.

Over the 1920s, PCP membership fell dramatically. Even so, the main reasons for the party's decline from 3,000 members in 1923 to only 49 members in 1929, cannot be blamed solely on early leaders such as Carlos Rates, as the PCP officially claims.[7] It is true that Rates' turn to 'putschist' tactics in 1927 led to a decline in party numbers, but so too did the Comintern's policies. Moreover, as a fractious party, each reorganisation of the PCP led it to haemorrhage members through voluntary disassociation or expulsion.[8] As such, the PCP was weak in terms of 'grass roots' membership over the 1920s. It was a predominantly male organisation with little female participation. It was also primarily urban, concentrated in Lisbon, and not yet strong, as it would be later, in either the Alentejo or Setúbal.

PCP Membership Surrounding the Third Period

1921	400–1,000 PCP members and 260 Young Communists
1922	2,900 members (1,702 paying dues)
1923	3,000 (early)
	500 (November)
1924	700
1926	70 (50 in Lisbon and 20 in Porto)
1928	70
1929	49 (the PCP claimed 40 members; the secret police claimed 28 members)
1932	700 (100 in the military)
1933	700 (100 in the military)
1934	700 (150 in the military)
1935	1,200 (250 in the military)
1936	500 (230 in the military)

Source: J. Pacheco Pereira, *Problémas da História do PCP, Colóquio Sobre o Fascismo em Portugal, Faculdade de Letras de Lisboa, March 1980* (Lisbon, 1982), p. 12; Torre do Tombo National Archives (Lisbon) PIDE/DGS SC GT 387; and Russian Centre for the Conservation and Study of Documents on Contemporary History [RCEDHC] Moscow, f.493, op.1, d.20 and f.495, op.12, d.106.

Third Period

The Comintern's Third Period of capitalist crisis was characterised by working class radicalisation ('class against class'), ultra-leftist attacks on social democracy ('social fascism'), and the emergence of Stalinisation.[9] The

Comintern continued to intervene in PCP affairs throughout this period and into the 1930s, until the party was finally expelled from the organisation in 1938–39. Indeed, the sectarianism of the PCP in 1928, and its reorganisation of 1929, was undoubtedly influenced by Comintern policy. The minutes of the PCP executive committee, composed of Augusto Machado, João Lucas (secretary) and Júlio Diniz, clearly demonstrate the influence of the Comintern. Not only did the party receive a regular subsidy of $300 quarterly, but it also consulted the Comintern when it encountered difficulties.[10] There was, for example, an evident rift between Lucas (who preferred a more active implementation of the latest Comintern directives) and Machado (who was much more cautious and focused on publications), which intensified with each meeting to the point where an appeal was made to the Comintern to send a delegate to reconcile the dispute. A 1932 PCP analysis of the reorganisation claimed that Machado had fallen in line with the 'capitulation policy' of anarchist leaders; he adhered to the 'liquidationist' theory of the impossibility of labour struggle or communist political activity under the existing regime, advocating instead the reduction of party work to a mere publishing and propaganda office.[11]

The overhaul of 1929 was initiated in response to demands made by a cell of naval arsenal workers who insisted that the party either renew its trade union activities or face reorganisation. When the PCP executive did not respond, the cell moved to take over the PCP. The list of major characters leading the party's reorganisation varies depending on the historical sources used, but all include Bento Gonçalves as a key player.[12] Gonçalves, a naval arsenal worker, had been selected to travel to Moscow as a worker delegate in November 1927, even though he was not then a communist party member. He was obviously influenced by the changes occurring in Moscow and quickly joined the PCP, becoming secretary of his cell in November 1928.[13] Consequently, a plenum was held in April 1929 (known as the 'conference of 1929') to refound the PCP with Gonçalves as the main party leader. His many travels to Moscow, Paris and Madrid made him the first Portuguese leader to have regular Comintern contacts. Although he was arrested in September 1930 and sent to the Azores penitentiary the following month, he was released in 1932 and returned to the arsenal. In the fall of 1933, he went underground to devote his energies full time to the PCP.[14]

The phase that began under Gonçalves' leadership focused necessarily on defensive tactics because of the repressive atmosphere under which the party worked. At the same time, the new leaders were more determined on adhering to a Leninist strategy for power. They struggled against the persistent anarchist tendencies within the PCP, endeavoured to connect the party with the working class, and sought to Bolshevise the organisation, forming directive organs, ancillary mass organisations, and the clandestine press necessary to implement the party's covert strategies. This transition to an underground party eventually attracted working class confidence and catapulted the PCP to the position of workers' vanguard.[15] Yet, the turbulence that surrounded the reorganisation helps explain why the Comintern wrote to the party in April 1929 requesting information on its activities; it had not received reports for some time.[16]

'Official' party historians claim that the reorganisation found the PCP in dire straits in terms of its clandestine experience, its ability to combat repression, its ideological preparation, and its finances. The few members that remained in the reorganised party were mainly militant workers with long years of experience within the trade union movement. When it became evident that the 'fascist' regime could only be overthrown by an invigorated popular movement led by strong, well-organised and combative political organisations, the leaders worked in that direction, establishing unitary or partisan organisations. The PCP attempted to create an agricultural workers' political organisation in 1931, Bloco Operário Camponês, to run in future elections. The Bloco did not have an autonomous organisation and was an attempt by the party to ensure that both classes, worker and peasant, could run for elections under PCP control if the government decided to hold them. The party also formed such organisations as the Organização Revolucionário de Armada (Revolutionary Organisation of the Armada; ORA), Liga dos Amigos da URSS (Friends of the USSR), and the League Against War and Fascism.[17] The Friends of the USSR was mainly composed of students and sought to inform the nation of Russia's economic and cultural progress.

By the fall of 1931, the PCP secretariat comprised Bernard Freund, José de Sousa, Manuel Alpedrinha and Francisco Rodrigues Loureiro. The minutes of 24 August offer a snapshot of the party's concerns at this time. Significantly, there was considerable discussion of the imminent bourgeois upheaval against the government. In particular, the republican opposition had sought out the PCP's participation in a revolutionary situation that was portrayed as ready to burst. The secretariat rejected any involvement in a bourgeois revolution, and emphasised its position to the rank-and-file. However, the PCP leaders were also aware that, given the great unrest among the working class, workers would most likely join the struggle despite the secretariat's directives, thereby demonstrating the incomplete process of Bolshevisation within the party. The secretariat contemplated how they could organise the masses and channel the revolution away from the bourgeoisie and towards their own interests. In the end, a number of militants were involved in the revolutionary attempt of 26 August, which led to a dictatorial backlash against the party.

The minutes also portray a lively debate between Freund, who headed the communist youth organisation (see below), and the PCP concerning who should have control of organising the schools. Some PCP leaders felt that they should control the technical schools. In addition, there was a report on the Porto organisation, which was weak with only 40 members and two functioning zones. It was especially frail in terms of propaganda and was sent money from Lisbon to help purchase publishing equipment.

By this time, it is clear that the PCP was under attack by the Portuguese secret police, which helps explain its leadership turnover. Manuel Alpedrinha, for example, had a meteoric rise to the party's highest levels. He tried to expand the PCP in the countryside by forming a cell in Tomar. When he suspected that he was being pursued, he left Portugal with José de Sousa and lived in Moscow for three months with a Comintern subsidy. Both took a course on 'revolutionary organisation' while there. When Alpedrinha returned from Russia in November 1932, he found the PCP without a clear orientation, and moved to increase its vitality. Thus, he took charge of the organisational commission, Júlio dos Santos headed the Lisbon regional committee, Quirino the trade union commission, João Vidal the publications commission, and Francisco Paula de Oliveira Júnior ('Pavel') represented the communist youth.[18]

A further snapshot of the PCP can be gleaned from a report on the party's position given at the end of 1932, which presented a 'class against class' analysis of the situation in Portugal, berating the tactics of the socialists, republicans and anarchists.[19] The analysis argued that the PCP had increased its membership tenfold since the 1929 reorganisation, improved its influence among the masses, organised street demonstrations, and led strikes. It recommended that the party should study the development of the Spanish Revolution, due to its similar conditions, but to avoid the sectarian and semi-anarchistic errors committed before and during the revolution that had hindered the mobilisation of Spanish revolutionary forces. The essential revolutionary role of the peasant masses in the context of a *latifundio* and semi-feudal system of exploitation of the villages had to be considered. As such, the PCP's slogan 'Down with the Dictatorship, Long Live the Workers' Government', was not deemed to correspond to the actual situation in Portugal. Despite republican governments from 1910 to 1926, bourgeois democratic changes had not abolished feudal religion, nor had they provided a solution to the agrarian problem or eradicated British capital's domination of the Portuguese economy. Thus, revolutionary change could only be brought about by breaking the resistance of *latifundistas*, clergy, elite military officials and the bourgeoisie (the main counter-revolutionary force). The military dictatorship had increased the power of the church by restoring some of their lands, subsidies and privileges. A goal of the bourgeois democratic revolution, therefore, would be to destroy the power of the church. As such, the revolution being prepared was bourgeois democratic, but the proletariat had to be the main motivational force because it was the only class with a true revolutionary end. The proletariat could, and had to, lead the democratic revolution, ensure its victory, and install the revolutionary democratic dictatorship of the proletariat and peasants while breaking the resistance of the counter-revolutionary bourgeoisie which would halt transformations mid-way without proceeding from the democratic revolution to the socialist revolution. The agrarian revolution would play a major role in the democratic revolution, with the peasant masses acting as one of the most important driving forces. Accordingly, the PCP had to have a decisive influence with the proletariat, peasants and even poor sections of the urban petty-bourgeoisie.

The PCP's former position on this issue showed a misconception of the tasks of the proletariat in the democratic revolution. It had underestimated the aspirations and will to fight of the peasant masses and petty-bourgeoisie – that were also oppressed – as well as the colonial populations that were allies of the Portuguese proletariat in the struggle against the dictatorship of the big *latifundistas* and counter-revolutionary bourgeoisie. The proof that the party misunderstood the importance of the proletarian allies in the revolutionary struggle was shown in the passive attitude of party organisations in the coup attempts that had been organised by leaders of the petty-bourgeois parties deported to Funchal (Madeira) in the summer of 1931. While continuing to expose the leaders and criticise their methods and putschist attempts, the party should have emphasised the Leninist concept of armed insurrection based on his views with regard to the difference between Marxism and Blanquism. At the same time, the party should have supported all those revolutionary actions that had already begun in which the masses were involved in order to lead them away from a coup and towards mass struggle.

The sectarianism of the PCP was reflected in other areas of activity. In the trade union sphere, this weakness had led to the tendency of mechanically separating party tasks from those of the trade unions, of underestimating the struggle for the partial demands of the workers, of leading to the absence of serious mass work in the chief branches of industry, and of leading the Red Trade Union to abandon local and partial struggles under the pretext of appeals for a national general strike. In the villages, the party was weak with an almost complete absence of activity among the peasants. In the organisational sphere, the party suffered from weaknesses expressed in the mechanical habits of inner party life and the system of routinely appointing party cadres from above, which increased consolidation and hindered the regular promotion of cadres. To overcome all this, a determined struggle was to be carried out against the influence of petty-bourgeois and anarchist traditions within the Portuguese workers' movement and the PCP in an attempt to raise its members' ideological level. The party was to lead the masses against the dictatorial policies that were robbing citizens of their human rights, were leading to the 'fascisisation' of the trade unions, and were negatively conducting social and economic policy. In so doing, it was not to abandon the fascist organisations, but to infiltrate those that already existed while it rallied to oppose new ones. Furthermore, the PCP was to formulate a military policy, attract discontented soldiers and sailors, and infiltrate the military branches. In the process, the party was to expose the collaborationist policies of the socialists, the passivity of the anarchists, and the false and ineffectual policies of the illegal petty-bourgeois parties by isolating their leaders. It was to increase its struggle against Portuguese dependence on British imperialism, which was dragging the nation into an imperialist war and draining millions from the workers and peasants to pay dividends. Against the regime itself, the PCP was to make political demands regarding the struggle against the eradication of the right to strike, the torture of prisoners, press censorship, and the right of assembly. It was to insist on the complete liberation of the Portuguese colonies, and contact colonial revolutionary elements to assist them in organising their struggle for independence.

Within the PCP, the party was recommended to work closely with the Portuguese Communist Youth Federation (FJCP) to guide it in overcoming the organisational weaknesses and sectarian mistakes noted by the Communist Youth International (YCI). Those young communists who had proved their loyalty and class-consciousness were to be drawn into the PCP. In the meantime, the party was to introduce the consistent operation of democratic centralism, develop initiatives at all levels of party organisation, educate new cadres, create new factory nuclei, improve internal functions, and increase contacts with the toiling masses. In particular, the PCP was to focus on the most important industrial sectors, especially in Porto, which were anarchist dominated. All legal possibilities open to the party had to be utilised. To do all this, the decisions of the Comintern's twelfth plenum had to be clearly related to the party membership. Once done, the party would strengthen itself so that it could progress towards becoming a real mass party in the revolutionary struggle for the liberty of the broad working masses from the fascist military dictatorship.

The experience of the FJCP between 1929 and 1933 is, perhaps, instructive. [20] The reorganised PCP had developed quickly from April 1929, so that in November Gonçalves felt that the party was ready to establish a youth organisation and approached Freund – a Czech citizen and communist sympathiser working in Lisbon – to join the organisational commission. In May 1930, Freund became a member of the PCP, and the commission was transformed into the secretariat of the FJCP. In addition to creating cells, a preliminary task was to publish its official bulletin, *O Jovem* (*The Youth*), which it did in April with an initial press run of 250 copies. Gonçalves then invited Freund onto the PCP secretariat as the connecting agent between the two organisations. Next, in October 1930, the secretariat suggested that the FJCP officially affiliate to the YCI. Freund was able to do this via the German publishing house Verlag der Jugendinternationale in Berlin, which acted as intermediary. Two months later, the FJCP was officially welcomed by the YCI executive, from which point on it began receiving circulars with general directives on tasks that it was expected to carry out. However, the FJCP largely ignored these directives – which included anti-clerical propaganda for the Christmas festivities, various propaganda and agitation campaigns, paying homage to Lenin on the date of his death, and organising among the working class youth – primarily because they required a level of organisation that had not yet been reached.

Despite this, in January 1931, the FJCP received details of a Comintern representative in Paris, 'José', who became the party's new correspondence link with Moscow. During a trip to Paris, Freund also met with 'Paul'. At the time, the FJCP requested a subsidy to purchase a typewriter that was granted by the YCI at the end of the year, and FJCP was authorised to send one member to the International Lenin School (ILS) in Moscow. Fernando Quirino ('Santos') was chosen as their envoy, leaving for Moscow in August 1931. Given the Comintern norm of sending half of a student's stipend to support the enrolee's family, in Quirino's case it went to his mother in Portugal. Unfortunately for the FJCP, things did not proceed smoothly.

A report of FJCP development in March 1931 found the leadership to be primarily intellectual and functionary. It also found its activities and publications to lack a youthful orientation, focusing instead on general communist issues that were often applied as mere translation of YCI directives without adaptation to local conditions. There was, too, a considerable amount of sectarianism noted amongst the young members. As a result, the FJCP was encouraged to study the working conditions of young workers, and to focus on worker demands and unemployment. Its activities were to then revolve around addressing related issues, including appeals to soldiers and sailors. *O Jovem* was to be transformed into a newspaper of 'mass appeal' and adapted, in terms of content, to young workers and distributed in factories. Specialist bulletins were to be published for factories, schools, neighbourhoods and ships. Organisational development was to be broadened beyond Lisbon to other industrialised areas, such as the neglected Porto region. Furthermore, the FJCP leadership was to be 'proletarianised'.[21]

A month later, in April 1931, as the FJCP's connection to Paris was transferred to Berlin, the communist youth had expanded to four zone committees and one regional committee. Attempts were also made to extend the FJCP's influence into the countryside. According to José Ribeiro, the FJCP at this time advocated the use of literature, movies and sports to awaken the Portuguese youth, believing that the dictatorship was 'lulling the proletariat to sleep'. Among its many activities was the distribution of *Avante!*, *O Jovem*, communist leaflets and Spanish communist publications.

Demonstrations were also organised, including an unemployed protest on 25 February 1931, and a May Day celebration of that year.

In its early years under Freund, the FJCP used deceptive and often intimidating methods to increase and retain its members, a dangerous practice for an illegal organisation existing under dictatorial rule. For example, Freund impressed upon Ribeiro that party discipline included death for those either betraying or leaving the party, a threat that Ribeiro claimed prevented him from breaking openly with the FJCP until August 1931. Similarly, Francisco Fernandes Mendonça told the secret police that he was not aware that he was a member of the FJCP until he attended his fourth cell meeting. He thought he was only a member of International Red Aid. This helps, perhaps, to explain the organisation's interest in expanding quantitatively rather than qualitatively.

In terms of organisational structure, Armando José de Sousa Soares' account suggests that the FJCP was headed by an executive central committee and secretariat, which in turn comprised links with a national and international commission, an organisational commission, a publication commission, a trade union commission, a women's commission, and a military commission. *O Jovem Militante* was its theoretical and practical journal. As the organisation evolved, numbers were used in place of members' names, later replaced by pseudonyms. The organisational commission sent a delegate to the regional committee, which was composed of delegates from the four zone committees. More widely, the FJCP spread to Coimbra, Porto and Viseu, while the party as a whole was instructed to conform to the Comintern's directives on work among women.

The further strengthening and expansion of the FJCP was an on-going task that often had its difficulties during the Third Period. Thus, António dos Santos Figueiredo stopped attending cell meetings when he was asked to leave the FJCP upon criticising what he viewed as poor organisation. João dos Santos Barros, meanwhile, has recounted how cell No. 4 fell apart because of disagreements among its members; for two months he found himself inactive within the FJCP. And while Henrique Chaves Lopes had to await a delegate of the FJCP to create a military cell of Amadora cadets and soldiers, Manuel Francisco Roque Júnior later explained that when he first became interested in communism the FJCP did not yet exist. He therefore participated in the PCP as a 'sympathiser' until mid-1929, when the PCP executive finally decided to create its separate youth organisation. All communist youths then moved to the FJCP. The attentions of the military dictatorship also caused problems. It is clear that much of the information gathered by the secret police came from within the communist organisations. Hence, party cells were limited to a maximum size of eight members, and meetings were held in public places such as gardens and parks.

FJCP communication with the Comintern did not always proceed smoothly. On 27 July 1931, a letter was sent to the Parisian contact 'Jules' regarding promises made by the Comintern to support the FJCP that had not been fulfilled. The budgetary allocation for the organisation had not been delivered, and funds were evidently required to carry out important work in Portugal. In addition, the party had not received the 1,000 francs needed for Quirino to go to Moscow to study Marxist theory, and a lack of funds prevented their sending a delegate to Russia for the seventeenth International Youth Day. In fact, Freund claimed that the PCP and the FJCP had been completely abandoned by the Comintern for almost two years because of 'the famous battle against bureaucratisation, etc ...' The International seemed only to send directives, he complained, but never answered the questions posed by the FJCP.

Freund's frustration was evident in a letter sent to 'Jules' dated 28 September 1931.

> Despite our great desire to send you a thick letter detailing all of the negligence and lack of interest that you (Paris??? Berlin??? M.??? – we don't know who) [have] for our Portuguese Federation, we cannot do so. We have so much work that we cannot lose more time after so many requests, letters, and even reports and materials addressed to you.

Freund insisted that the FJCP had actually accomplished more than even they thought possible. It had made progress on women's issues, which he argued was difficult to do in Latin nations, as well as on trade union work among young workers, the reinforcement of anti-military work (penetration of the navy, cruisers, naval aviation, artillery, machine gunners), publications, and the preparation of large movements in schools; and all despite the deportation and imprisonment of about 40 PCP and FJCP militants. If the Comintern constantly alluded to reinforcing the FJCP's work, then the reality was somewhat different. The result was that the FJCP (and the PCP) was impeded from achieving maximum activity and becoming an integral part of the Comintern. The PCP had experienced the same neglect for two-and-a-half years. 'From everywhere all we get are "promises" and "circulars", and that is what we should use to prepare the PROLETARIAN REVOLUTION!!!'

Two days later, in another letter to 'Jules' regarding a 1930 memo informing the FJCP that its budget was to be cut in half, Freund again lambasted the Comintern.

> We now have received another 'directive' asking FJCP to *submit a summary of our budget and its application during 1931*. The FJCP has now existed for 1.75 years, and has been the 'official' link to the Comintern for more than one year. Yet, all it receives are 'directives' and 'promises'. It is ironic that three days ago the PCP gave us a copy of the Comintern Presidium's resolution on the need

to struggle against BUREAUCRATISM AND OPPORTUNISM IN THE
ORGANISATION.

By the end of November 1931, the FJCP secretariat was composed of
Freund (in charge of international issues and as the delegate to the PCP
secretariat), Eliseu Monteiro (trade union organisation), Pavel (publications),
Armando José de Sousa Soares (military propaganda and recruitment), and
Carolina Loff da Fonseca (work among women). At the time, the FJCP had
approximately 20 cells. By this time, the FJCP was also complaining of a lack
of support from the PCP, as revealed in another letter sent by Freund to
'Jules' in August 1931. The organisation, he reported, was in a perilous state.
O Jovem had ceased publication, and a number of cells, from a total of about
two dozen, had been neglected or abandoned by members. To deal with
these problems, the zone committees and Lisbon regional committee were
reorganised. Progress was slow, however, primarily because more members
were required. Meanwhile, the flight of indecisive, as well as some of the
most experienced communist youths, continued. The FJCP was still in the
process of transforming street (neighbourhood) cells into factory cells, but
they were mostly weak, with three to ten comrades, and illegal. Lisbon had
about eighteen to 20 FJCP cells that functioned regularly. Two were in
military arsenals (navy and army), four were among metal workers, one
among railroad workers, one in the British telephone concession, one among
the bakers, and one among the dock workers. The remainder were street
cells. But logistical problems still hampered the FJCP. Although a print run
of 600 copies of *O Jovem* (issue ten) sold out in only a few days, producing
more was laborious because they were printed by hand on apparatus which
belonged to the International Red Syndicate. Moreover, trade union activity
was something in which the FJCP was clearly lacking, although it was an area
that the PCP had developed well. The work of the FJCP military section also
needed developing, while its sports division had begun but lacked both a
programme and political direction.

Many of the problems afflicting the relationship between the PCP and
FJCP were due to sectarianism, as revealed in Freund's letters to the YCI.[22]
It was also due to simple lack of numbers. According to Freund, the PCP
claimed to have seventeen cells in Lisbon, but only seven functioned. While
the FJCP could create communist cells in almost all the factories in which it
had members, it could not do so because the party did not have sufficient
members to send to direct the new cells. Freund also felt that the party
treated the FJCP with less value than it deserved. Instead of helping, it often
did the reverse. The secretariat, for example, complained that the PCP often
recruited youths directly as members, thereby weakening the FJCP.

Perhaps the stress of surviving within a dictatorial regime was partially
responsible for Freund's concerns, and for the detailed information

regarding the organisation that he provided to the secret police. In an earlier letter dated 27 August 1931, Freund informed 'Jules' that the secretary of the PCP's Lisbon regional committee had been arrested at his home the previous dawn, and the addresses of all party members and sympathisers in the Lisbon region seized (including Freund's). Perhaps a dozen comrades had already been arrested; others were sought by the police. 'Roberto's' address, the PCP's Parisian liaison, was also captured. Worse was to follow. Following republican attempts to overthrow the regime in August 1931, the PCP secretary was arrested, along with approximately fifteen PCP members and about 50 party sympathisers who had tried to take part in the coup. Consequently, the entire city had been under a state-of-siege, forcing the FJCP to abandon its preparations for the seventeenth International Youth Day, which had included self-defence brigades, a defence plan to fight against police attacks, and even the procurement of bombs and revolvers. The PCP secretariat supported this decision, fearing the loss of the FJCP's best militants. Despite such a blow, however, the FJCP organisation remained intact, although Freund would himself be arrested in January 1932 at the same time as both the PCP and FJCP headquarters were raided. Yet, the FJCP's activities continued, with 'lightening rallies' firing shots in the air for emphasis, pamphlet distribution, poster plastering, fund raising sweepstakes and sales of other items, the creation of 'shock brigades', bomb making activity, and armed actions which at times led to shoot-outs with the police. In 1932, the PCP and FJCP collaborated in their commemoration of the eighteenth International Youth Day. In January, English language pamphlets were distributed to British sailors docked at Alcántara, and agitation was planned for 29 February at Santo Amaro, before a large police presence prevented its occurrence.

The pressures imposed by the dictatorial regime were still clear, however, with widespread arrests constanly frustrating the party's development. Following Freund's arrest in early 1932, Pavel became the leading figure in the FJCP. At the time of his own first arrest in February 1932, Pavel was the secretariat member in charge of the publications commission and author of many articles for O Jovem. Given his poor health, however, he was released the next day with the secret police seemingly unaware of his importance within the PCP. Even so, the police had smashed the youth organisation when they had arrested Freund several days earlier, so Pavel's immediate task was to reorganise the FJCP with the assistance of the PCP's Roque, who gave Pavel 3,300 francs sent from the Comintern via José de Sousa in Paris. Pavel and Roque then met with Álvaro Duque da Fonseca and Silvino Leitão Fernandes Costa, sending despatches to the provinces and the Lisbon organisation regarding the arrests, their impact, and calling for a meeting of all secretaries of cells of the regional organisation to vote on filling the vacant positions. Pavel also reported to the YCI with regard to the arrests and the impact of the captured FJCP archive. Virgínio de Jesus Luis, a barber, was chosen to head the 'reorganisation commission' of the FJCP secretariat, along with Júlio dos Santos Pinto, Fonseca, Loff, Tôgo da Silva Batalha, and José Pedro da Rocha.

Following his nomination by the FJCP secretariat in April to attend the congress of the Spanish Communist Youth (JCE) in Bilbao, Pavel returned to Portugal to squash a faction of 'avant-guardist tendencies' (Trotskyists) within the organisation.[23] The FJCP executive central committee was then reformed, with Luis in charge of the adversarial [sic] organisation commission, Pavel the agitation and propaganda commission, Fonseca the organisational commission, Loff the women's commission, 'Caralinda' the pioneers commission, Pinto the trade union commission, Rocha the International Red Aid commission, and Eliseu Monteiro as general secretary of the Lisbon regional committee.[24] Very soon, however, following a major demonstration in Alcántara on 4 September 1932, at which a policeman was shot and killed, further arrests meant that the FJCP secretariat was again restructured.[25] This time, Luis became the general secretary of the Lisbon regional committee, Pavel continued to control the agitation and propaganda commission, João Ferreira de Abreu led the agrarian and peasant commission, António da Piedade Cipriano the pioneers commission, 'Caralinda' the trade union commission, Quirino the organisational commission, while Rocha remained head of the International Red Aid commission. Loff and Fonseca moved party organisation material to a different location after the arrest of Costa and Carlos Luís Correia Matoso, fearing that they would give away the headquarters' address. A meeting was then called for Costa da Caparica on 11 September, with Pavel given the task of sending the Comintern a report on the events.

A few days later Fonseca and Roque were arrested at the FJCP's headquarters, with the capture of the active Roque being a big blow to the PCP. Pavel convened the remaining members of the secretariat, reorganising it once again. (Pavel was charged with politics, propaganda and agitation, Rodrigo Ollero das Neves with International Red Aid, João Vidal with the Lisbon regional committee), and it was resolved to print a joint PCP/FJCP official organ, given the obvious difficulties in publishing both *Avante!* and *O Jovem*. In October, Pavel met with Grilo, who escaped the police search, and discussed writing *Frente Vermelha* as the joint edition. This time, however, problems within the party itself led to the paper's suspension after just two editions. Not surprisingly, perhaps, given the upheaval of the early 1930s, controversy was frequent in the party. In this instance, Pavel denounced Grilo's fractional work. Both were suspended, with Pavel restrained from activity in the secretariat's publishing central commission, and Grilo from party activity until blame could be placed. Yet, the arrests continued. Pavel was again arrested for being a communist leader on 13 March 1933. He was diagnosed with tuberculoses while in prison in May, and the penitentiary officials requested his transfer to a sanatorium for treatment. He then escaped from the Ajuda sanatorium in September and, by October, had returned to active membership, but now within the PCP central commission. That month he was sentenced to two years of prison in absentia.[26]

By 1933, following the twelfth plenum of the Executive Committee of the Communist International (ECCI) held the previous year, the PCP's principal tasks were listed as:

To purge the anarchist tendencies that remained within the party

To strengthen the bonds between the agricultural labourers and the industrial workers by creating a strong unitary organisation

To shift the basic organisational unit from the neighbourhood cell to the factory cell

To continue strengthening its activity in the trade union movement

To devote more time to the problems of the agrarian poor

The main reasons given for the difficulties faced by the party were that its organisational strength was much weaker than its actual influence. The party's cadres were primarily young, inexperienced individuals who still harboured anarchist tendencies and occasionally resorted to terrorist activity.[27]

According to the Comintern, it was essential that the PCP entrench itself in Portuguese society as a clandestine organisation designed to enlighten and prepare the masses for the inevitable revolution.[28] Social democracy, a label that was also applied to 'bourgeois collaborators' (anarchists), was considered the primary obstacle to developing a revolutionary movement, especially during 1929–33. It was 'social fascism' that was to be combated through the workers' unitary front,[29] an attempt to wean socialist workers away from their social fascist leaders. Yet, while the party leaders' interpretation of the Comintern's 'class against class' tactics theoretically dominated PCP strategy from 1928 to 1935, in reality the Portuguese proletarian base was small, and the party often worked alongside the bourgeois elements. Although PCP leaders officially opposed participation in bourgeois putsch movements, which they labelled 'reviralhista', militants continued to take part, as is evident from the number of communists imprisoned after the 1931 putsch.[30] Following the increased repression of 1932 (which hindered distribution of the party press), and with Gonçalves' return from prison in 1933, the PCP intensified its shift from mere agitation and theoretical discussion to mass political action (such as strikes) through the organised class movements that were designed to fulfil workers' economic and political demands and end repression.[31]

A comparison of such a tactical shift with the decisions made at the twelfth Comintern plenum shows a close correlation and will help reveal why the change occurred when it did. Throughout Europe, class struggles for economic and political reasons were numerous as the great depression approached its most difficult years. The grave crisis was reflected in the polarisation of the classes, which was paralleled by the increasing strength of fascist and communist parties. The ECCI analysed the increasing turmoil throughout Europe and concluded that the communist parties needed to organise the workers, strengthen the unity of the working classes (especially between the employed and the unemployed), and fight for the fulfilment of workers' demands even if it meant the expulsion of sectarian tendencies from within the party.[32] This helps explain the PCP's increased involvement in strikes and insurrectional activity that sought to block the dictatorship's efforts to replace free unions with state dominated ones. According to Pavel, after such an attempt in June 1933, the Inter-Syndical Commission (ISC) set up the first unitary front to combat the government's moves, bringing together the central anarchist, communist, reformist and independent organisations.[33] By 1934, the leaders praised the party's successful strategy by declaring that the membership in ISC had increased to 25,000, as compared to 15,000 in the anarcho-syndicalist CGT, and 5,000 in the socialist FAO.[34] Given that at the twelfth ECCI plenum the PCP claimed to have only 15,000 ISC members, this meant that the PCP had actually increased inter-syndicalist membership by 67 per cent in only one year.[35]

Bento Gonçalves had not been a member of the PCP secretariat while imprisoned and deported from 28 September 1930 to March 1933. He did, however, take an active role in the PCP's preparation for the partial strikes of 18 January 1934 directed against a series of decrees promulgated by the dictatorship in September 1933 in order to disband the independent trade unions. Gonçalves did everything he could to prevent the general strike of January 1934, which he foresaw as damaging the Portuguese workers' movement, and did not accept its characterisation as a 'general revolutionary strike' but, instead, a movement of 'partial strikes and mass demonstrations' to maintain the freedom to democratically organise trade unions. Even before the emergence of the movement, he had written a manifesto that expressed the fundamental PCP position concerning the efforts that were then in preparation; the party always struggled against isolated acts of terrorism.[36]

The government's substitution of fascist trade unions for ISC dominated ones was a major blow to José de Sousa's years of hard work converting the unions to PCP dominance. Ever since the 1929 reorganisation, Sousa had been the party's main trade union organiser. Indeed, he continued his work within the illegal unions, which later led to a major conflict when Comintern directives pushed for 'united front' tactics and the infiltration of official unions at the expense of the underground network. As general secretary of the ISC connected to Red International of Labour Unions; RILU or Profintern), he addressed an invitation to central workers' organisations to establish a 'united front' against the 1933 fascist labour decrees disbanding independent trade unions. It was from this that the workers' movement of 18 January 1934 emerged. Sousa accepted full responsibility for the organisation of the movement, including the ISC clandestine publications and its newspaper, *O Proletario*, except for its terrorist activities. As such, the unitary front's call for a general strike and demonstrations in the nation's industrial centres led to the 18 January 1934 protests against the dictatorship. In Marinha Grande, a two-day general strike evolved from demonstrations to insurrectional attempts. With the support of the populace, the insurrectionists were able to seize control of the city and overpower the police forces for a few hours. These 'errors', which the PCP leaders claimed were committed by the anarchists as well as by those with 'anarchist tendencies' within the PCP, undermined the front's policies and destroyed the campaign to stop the fascisisation of the unions. However, it did display to the masses that they could demonstrate against fascism so long as they maintained unity.[37] The PCP leaders also concluded that the party should focus on organising partial strikes because total strikes and insurrectional attempts could lead to backlashes from the government.[38] Indeed, one result of the repression that followed the January demonstrations was that all PCP activities became clandestine. Prior to 1934, the party had been able to continue legal, quasi-legal and illegal activities, partly as a result of disorganised censors and police.[39]

Such events seem to have increased the PCP's importance in the eyes of the ECCI. In late 1934, the Comintern considered Pavel's request that the PCP be, a) guaranteed the possibility of participating in the Comintern congresses and ECCI plenums, b) authorised to have a permanent representative on the ECCI, c) given material aid in the value of $100 per month (as was given in 1932), d) authorised to organise a party conference in Spain and provided material aid to do so, e) authorised to send three students to the ILS, f) aided via a charge to the delegation of the ECCI attached to the Partido Comunista de España (PCE) to give political assistance to the PCP's leadership, and g) given the possibility of sending its representative to Spain to reach an accord with the PCE's central committee on the establishment of regular relations, technical assistance and publication transportation.[40] Pavel then assumed the role of the PCP's permanent representative to the ECCI in Moscow.

Even so, the PCP's experiences during the Third Period continued to impinge on the party following the Comintern's adoption of the new Popular Front policy at the seventh world congress in 1935. Most obviously, it has been claimed by a very knowledgeable secret police informant (the name of the individual was purged by archival personnel to protect their identity) that the PCP was considered among the worst communist parties in the world in terms of its infiltration by provocateurs at its highest levels (secretariat and central committee), to the extent that the police eventually avoided ad hoc arrests in favour of well-planned strikes. Pavel had similarly developed a reputation within the Comintern of not knowing how to struggle against such informants; without provocateurs inside, how was it that every party press could be captured and Gonçalves arrested upon his arrival in Portugal from Russia in November 1935. An example was the Comintern control commission's dealing with Roque's case on 19 June 1936. Roque had been arrested many times and, in 1932 – after being tortured by the secret police – provided the location of a clandestine party press. Despite knowledge of these lapses by some individuals, including Pavel, Roque was reintegrated into leadership positions within the PCP, representing the party at the Comintern's seventh congress in 1935, and then working for the Profintern. The control commission emphasised:

> [In] the PCP, as this case shows, there is an inadmissible conciliatory attitude with the declarations [to the police]. The PCP central committee should [enlighten] members of the party on the enormous costs of revealing conspiracy to the enemy and of treason, and dedicate itself seriously to uncovering provocateurs, calling for a harsh party response not only to those who reveal information, but also to those who mask similar communists and traitors, getting from all party members avowed fidelity to the party.[41]

A PCP report of 27 April 1936 on cadre development, based primarily on Pavel's knowledge of the party, although he was not aware of the situation in 1936, portrayed the organisational difficulties evident in Portugal during the Third Period.[42] Since 1929, the Portuguese communist leadership had changed almost annually at all levels of the organisation, before the arrest of Gonçalves and Sousa in November 1935 decapitated the party. Throughout these years, a central committee did not exist, and the secretariat was formed only by the constant co-optations of members who were themselves frequently imprisoned. Thus:

1930–31	seven members:	1 jailed, 5 purged
1932	six members:	3 jailed, 2 purged
1933	five members:	3 jailed, 0 purged
1934	five members:	1 jailed, 0 purged
1935	nine members:	7 jailed, 0 purged

It was assumed that these systematic annual collapses, following each reformation of leading organisations, resulted from systematic police work after infiltrating the party. Each serious collapse was accompanied by entry into the secretariat of unverified comrades, promoted casually to one of the secretariat's ancillary commissions; policies and practical support was absent in the promotion of the party members. Moreover, the PCP leadership did not attend to educating substitutes as reserves. For example, in 1932, a student who had previously been purged from a leadership position was included in the secretariat. In 1935, a student from a 'bourgeois fascist party' joined the secretariat as secretary of the party and leader of the military commission. Similar problems existed at lower levels of the party. In addition to the Lisbon committee of five individuals, the party also had neighbourhood cells of five individuals each. However, meetings were often too large, with fifteen to eighteen individuals present, and needlessly included secretariat members. Furthermore, the party leaders constantly violated the elementary rules of secrecy. The addresses and biographical information of all party members were kept by the most responsible functionaries or by active members of the party directly connected to them. Meetings and encounters were held in the streets, frequently in the centre of the city, often on the same street. The illegal technical information was generally entrusted only to the party secretary, but at times had been in the hands of a mere member. There was often a frivolous attitude regarding the norms of conspiracy. Thus, at one point a secretary of the organisation, Vilaça, lived in an apartment that simultaneously contained the underground press. And Gonçalves, having returned from the seventh Comintern congress, had conversations with republicans and Portuguese emigrants in Madrid. He crossed the Portuguese border with two other people, carrying a suitcase of illegal material. One of these individuals was an unverified 'comrade', 'Lino', who attended all subsequent meetings except the last one, when Gonçalves, Sousa and Júlio Fogaça were arrested. It appeared that the party had not taken necessary steps to struggle against arrests and their repercussions. There appeared to be an almost liberal attitude within the party toward chatter and treason at the hands of the police. Quirino and Roque, both secretariat members, had given the police addresses that led to further arrests. Given police torture, these lapses were considered justifiable treason, and the leadership rehabilitated them into governing positions within the party after their release.

Following such a damning report, the ECCI concluded that a PCP conference had to be held immediately. A special Comintern delegation made up of comrades was to direct the conference and canvass the party cadres, selecting strong elements for possible inclusion in the leadership. PCP members from the ILS were to also return to Portugal for placement in the most important areas of the party so as to strengthen the organisation and implement the 'new policies'. Finally, a school was to be created in Spain in 1936, with the specific objective of training ten PCP members in three-month sessions. The party leaders were to immediately and completely change and decentralise their organisational methods to conform to the exigencies of conspiratorial, clandestine work. They also had to begin a systematic struggle to unmask police methods and portray them as enemies of the masses.

Conclusion

At the beginning of 1936, a united front was formed. Active work began inside the fascist trade unions, and steps were taken to initiate joint work between the red and anarchist trade unions. The united front included the illegal organisations of the PCP, FJCP, International Red Aid, Republican Alliance, Anti-Fascist League, Autonomous Syndicates, Students' Anti-Fascist Bloc, and the Anti-Fascist Anti-Military Anti-Clericals, but excluded the anarchist General Confederation of Workers and Ribeiro de Carvalho's military organisation. The weakness of all Portuguese anti-fascist organisations and the increasing influence of the PCP meant that it was increasingly considered the centre of the anti-fascist movement. Party influence was now mainly among military arsenal, trolley and railroad workers in the Lisbon area. In 1935, however, the PCP had begun to make inroads into the Alentejo, the Algarve and Marinha Grande, so that by June 1936 the PCP was organised in every region of the nation.

As has been shown, the links between Comintern and PCP history are very close. Indeed, the impact on the party continued into the 1970s and beyond; the PCP remains a Marxist–Leninist party even after its latest party congress (the sixteenth, held in December 2000).[43] Events that may at first seem to be part of the PCP's historical evolution take on an extra dimension given the parallels with Comintern internal politics in the 1920s and throughout the Third Period. As in other national sections, the Comintern regularly influenced and intervened in PCP policies until 1943. The influence from Moscow then continued via the Cominform and other organisations. It is clear that while each national section developed its own 'uniqueness', political engineers inserted a Comintern gene into each party so that national sections shared a common historical experience.

Notes

1. Research for this article was partially supported by grants from the International Research and Exchange Board, with funds provided by the US Department of State (Title VIII) and the National Endowment for the Humanities, the Dowling College Travel Funds and Released Time Programs, and the Luso-American Development Foundation (FLAD) and Portuguese National Archives/Torre de Tombo (Lisbon). The research was conducted at the Russian Centre for the Conservation and Study of Documents on Contemporary History (RC) in the summers of 1993 and 1994. It is complemented with work in the Jules Humbert-Droz collection at the International Institute for Social History (Amsterdam), with diplomatic and

secret police documents held in Lisbon's National Archives (PT/TT), and with Comintern documents from the University of Lisbon's Institute of the Social Sciences.

2. Some of the themes in this chapter were covered much more extensively in C. Cunha, *The Portuguese Communist Party's Strategy For Power, 1921–86* (New York, 1992).

3. See, K. McDermott and J. Agnew, *The Comintern: A History of International Communism from Lenin to Stalin* (New York, 1997), pp. xx.

4. For more discussion on this period, see ibid. pp. 41–80.

5. For more on the 1920s, see C. Cunha, *The Portuguese Communist Party's Strategy For Power*, pp. 106–36.

6. J. Pacheco Pereira, 'Contribuição para a História do Partido Comunista Português na I República (1921–26)', *Análise Social*, Vol. XVII, Nos. 67–68 (1981), pp. 695–713; *Problemas da História do PCP, Colóquio Sobre o Fascismo em Portugal, Faculdade de Letras de Lisboa, March 1980* (Lisbon, 1982), pp. 12.

7. Ibid.

8. See C. Cunha, *The Portuguese Communist Party's Strategy For Power*, pp. 152–59.

9. For more discussion on this period, see M. Worley's introduction to this book, and K. McDermott and J. Agnew, *The Comintern*, pp. 67–119.

10. RC 495/179/4.

11. RC 495/3/342.

12. For information on Bento Gonçalves, see the following PIDE (Secret Police) files held in the Torre do Tombo National Archive: PIDE/DGS SC PSE 4695, PIDE/DGS SC PC 2290/35, PIDE/DGS SC SPS 1664, PIDE/DGS SC GT 387, and PIDE/DGS SC RGP 2075. See also *60 Anos de Luta* (Lisbon, 1982), p. 43, for the official biography, and J. Pacheco Pereira, 'Bento Gonçalves Revisitado', *Diário de Notícias* (December 1979), for a more critical and realistic biography.

13. J. Pacheco Pereira, *Alvaro Cunhal: Uma Biografia Política: 'Daniel', o Jovem Revolucionario Vol. I* (Lisbon, 1999), p. 68.

14. PT/TT AC PIDE/DGS SC GT 387.

15. *60 Anos de Luta*, p. 40.

16. RC 495/18/745.

17. *60 Anos de Luta*. p. 44.

18. PT/TT AC PIDE/DGS SC SPS 713.

19. Unless noted, the following paragraphs are based on RC 495/3/342.

20. Unless noted, the following paragraphs are based on PT/TT AC PIDE/DGS SC Cad 3523.

21. RC 533/8/239.

22. PT/TT AC PIDE/DGS SC SPS 128 has good examples of the sectarianism rampant in these organisations.

23. RC 495/253/50.

24. PT/TT AC PIDE/DGS SC SPS 626.

25. Unless noted otherwise, this historical analysis is based on PT/TT AC PIDE/DGS SC Cad 4266.

26. After being rearrested in 1938, Pavel escaped the Aljube prison and eventually ended up in Mexico. After the escape, he went to Spain and then to Russia to a sanatorium in the Caucuses for two years for TB treatment.

27. 'Intervenção de 'António' na XII Reunião Plenária da Internacional Comunista', *Estudos Sobre o Comunismo*, No. 0 (1983), p. 31.

28. 'Apontamentos duma Entrevista com Firminiano Cansado Gonçalves', *Estudos Sobre o Comunismo*, No. 0 (1983), pp. 37–38.

29. The emphasis here is on 'unitary front' to distinguish it from 'united front'. While the latter would imply an electoral or formal unity for participation in 'bourgeois' democratic politics, the former would focus on a unity of workers for trade union and revolutionary activity.

30. J. Arsénio Nunes, 'Sobre Algúns Aspectos da Evolução Política do Partido Comunista Português após a Reorganização de 1929 (1931–33)', *Análise Social*, Vol. XVII, Nos. 67–68 (1981), pp. 720–24.

31. 'Intervenção de "António"', pp. 29–30.

32. J. Arsénio Nunes, 'Sobre Algúns Aspectos', pp. 729–30.

33. 'Intervenção de "António"', pp. 29–30.

34. *60 Anos de Luta*, pp. 45–47.

35. 'Intervenção de "António"', pp. 29–30.

36. Unless noted otherwise, this historical analysis is based on PT/TT AC PIDE/DGS SC SPS 1664.

37. *60 Anos de Luta*, pp. 47–49.

38. 'A Reorganização do PCP em 1929', *Bandeira Vermelha*, 25 April 1974.

39. J. Arsénio Nunes, 'Da Política "Classe Contra Classe" ás Origens da Estratégia Antifascista: Aspectos da Internacional Comunista Entre o VI e o VII Congressos (1928–35)', in *O Fascismo em Portugal* (Lisbon, 1982), pp. 69–70.

40. RC 495/4/313.

41. RC 495/18/1099.

42. This analysis is based on RC 495/12/4.

43. See Portuguese press throughout November and December 2000 for coverage of the sixteenth PCP congress. For analysis, see C. Cunha, '"Mais CDU! Mais Portugal!" … Mais PCP? The Portuguese Communist Party at the turn of the 21st Century', in J. Botella and L. Ramiro, *The Evolution of Communist and Post–Communist Parties in Western Europe* (Barcelona, forthcoming).

The 'Good Bolsheviks':

The Spanish Communist Party

and the Third Period

TIM REES

Even when judged against the persistent failure of the Communist International (Comintern) to fulfil its mandate to spread the Bolshevik Revolution beyond the borders of the USSR, there is no doubting that the strategies adopted at its sixth world congress in August 1928 were the most controversial in the history of the organisation. Declaring that capitalism had entered into a 'third period' of crisis and imperialist war, the national sections of Comintern were urged to adopt the infamously sectarian strategy of 'class against class' and the tactics of 'the united front from below' in pursuit of a renewed revolutionary offensive against supposedly weakened capitalist forces. This led individual parties to attack any other organisations that claimed to speak on behalf of the working classes, particularly social democrats, as traitors to the revolutionary cause. McDermott and Agnew have accurately summarised the retrospective judgment on this era: '[There] is a near universal consensus that the "ultra-leftist" tactics of these years proved disastrous, in some cases suicidal.'[1] That a particular nadir had been reached at this time was apparently confirmed when, after a preceding period of uncertainty and realignment, the Comintern itself adopted the more defensive Popular Front policy in 1935. Within this overarching narrative, the emphasis is upon explaining the illusions that launched the policy of 'class against class' and the apparent madness that sustained it until the growing pressures of 'reality' led to a return to sanity. It is not surprising, therefore, that historians have tended to characterise the Third Period as one in which malign and irrational impulses emanating from a 'Stalinized' Comintern were visited upon national parties by compliant leaderships and for which their ordinary members suffered. In the official communist view, it became represented as an aberration, while for others it was a strategic error in the face of a rising threat from fascist and right-wing authoritarianism; or, more simply, as yet another episode in the tragic story of communism.

Class against Class as a Failed Dogma

It is the fate of German and Austrian communists that has most particularly epitomised the consequences of 'class against class' for individual parties and their members. However, from a different perspective, the Spanish party, the Partido Comunista de España (PCE) would also seem to lend credence to the conventional picture of failure and division associated with the Comintern during the Third Period.[2] In fact, the PCE was unique among European communist parties in that it operated in a country that moved in 1931 from a military dictatorship to a liberal democracy under the Second Republic. Thereafter, the party joined the relatively privileged group of communist parties that was able to operate virtually openly. Nevertheless, this did not lead it to thrive. Looking back with no little bitterness, José Bullejos – party leader until 1932 when he was replaced by Comintern – commented on the development of the PCE that: 'The new party, the communist party, was born into political life as a minority group of little importance and without trade union forces, a situation that was conserved until 1936.'[3] 'Class against class' placed the PCE in opposition to the Republic and in direct conflict with the regime's principal base of support in the Socialist Party, the Partido Socialista Obrero Español (PSOE), and its trade union federation, the Unión General de Trabajadores (UGT). The PCE was further marginalised by the existence of Spain's powerful Anarco-syndicalist movement, the Confederación Nacional del Trabajo (CNT), which represented a well-established revolutionary alternative to conventional politics and to any kind of state. Even within the communist camp, internal divisions fed into the development of dissenting alternatives to the PCE in the form of breakaway movements and rivals. The most significant of these were the Bloque Obrero y Campesino (BOC), formed in 1930 by Joaquín Maurín from the PCE's own Catalan Federation, and the Izquierda Comunista de España (ICE) created by Andreu Nin in 1932.[4]

Under the strictures of Comintern discipline, which was enhanced by the change of party leadership, the PCE was confined to the sidelines of working class politics. The prevailing tactic of the 'united front from below' apparently gained the party neither greatly increased membership and influence, nor did it seriously weaken its anarchist and socialist rivals. When a reforming coalition of republicans and socialists took power in 1931, the Spanish communists vainly campaigned for 'A Workers and Peasants Government' and a 'Soviet Spain'. This position was essentially unmodified by the rapid rise of conservative opposition to the reforming governments of the first two years of the Republic and the shift to centre-right rule after the general elections of November 1933.[5] For the PCE, this was only a tactical alteration on the part of the bourgeoisie and actually a sign of their desperation. In his memoirs, one of the leading party figures of the time, Enrique Castro Delgado, sarcastically explained the reasoning: 'The communist party was content. It was content because the rise of counter-revolution would precipitate the revolution. Dialectics.'[6] By continuing to attack vociferously its working class rivals after this alteration in government, the PCE seemed to fall into a familiar pattern of ignoring the real threat from the right in favour of the sectarian struggle on the left. Party propaganda continued to proclaim that a 'revolutionary situation' existed, and that 'the social fascists and traitors were diverting the revolutionary energies of the proletariat and peasantry towards the defence of the bourgeoisie'.[7] Doubters within the party were silenced or forced out, as in the prominent example of the political gadfly José Antonio Balbontín, who questioned the party's dismissal of co-operation with other political forces and who rejected what he saw as the 'austere discipline and blind obedience' that characterised the PCE. A member of the Communist Youth, Manuel Tagüeña Lacorte, also recalled meetings in Madrid where he 'assisted in painful "self -criticisms" of some second ranking *bullejistas*. I was also present at some expulsions, like that of one of the Granell brothers who, on being "unmasked", had the courage to declare himself a Trotskyist'.[8] Typically, the public announcement of Balbontín's exclusion from the party, 'for desertion in the decisive moments of combat, for his double-dealings in his relations with the party', ended with the strident assertion that: 'The communist party NEVER PACTS with counter-revolutionary parties'.[9]

Though there were some qualms within the party leadership at the cost of maintaining this hard line, real doubts surfaced tentatively and only became openly expressed when conditions within the Comintern, under the direction of Georgi Dimitrov, made this both acceptable and desirable.[10] Accordingly, reports to Moscow in the spring and summer of 1934 by party leaders and the Comintern's wily delegate in Spain, Vittorio Codovilla ('Luis' or 'Moreno'), continued to give an optimistic view of developments – though this was, of course, always a sensible response to enquires from ECCI (Executive Committee of the Communist International) officials. What did give cause for concern was evidence that the membership of the party was stagnating following modest growth from a very low base.[11] Clearly, appeals to the rank-and-file of the socialists and anarchists to abandon their leaderships in order to join 'united fronts' led by communists were falling on deaf ears.

It has always appeared significant that an improvement in the fortunes of the PCE coincided with the relaxation of the party's sectarianism, and that this trend accelerated following the Comintern's abandonment of 'class against class'. That some sort of *viraje* (about turn) was getting underway was already detectable when a delegation from the PCE was in Moscow for extensive consultations in July and August 1934. From these discussions, and via resolutions and letters from the ECCI directed at the PCE, came the clearest signs that the days of rigidly applying the 'line' were over. There was a growing sense that Spain was another country where the divisions between working class organisations were proving counter-productive, if not fatal. By July, the PCE was producing 'open letters' to the PSOE calling for joint action and, in September 1934, the party endorsed membership of the *Alianzas Obreras* (Workers' Alliances) which aimed, in theory at least, to co-ordinate the efforts of the various working class movements.[12]

Though eventually crushed by army and police forces, the relative effectiveness of the Asturian uprising in October 1934 suggested the importance of such co-operation, though efforts by the PCE to find a rapprochement with the socialists were still largely rebuffed. Guided by Codovilla, who carefully made sure the party was neither too far in advance or too far behind Comintern thinking, a further drift away from the main tenants of 'class against class' occurred. A decisive step in this direction was signalled by the famous speech calling for anti-fascist unity delivered by the party leader, José Díaz, on 2 June 1935 to an invited audience in the Monumental cinema in Madrid.[13] Not surprisingly, the victims and critics of 'class against class', such as Bullejos and Balbontín, judged favourably the 'moderate and collaborationist' path represented by the new Popular Front policy adopted by Comintern.[14] But the change also seemed to produce more concrete gains. As a junior partner in the broad electoral alliance that successfully fought the February 1936 general elections, the PCE found its first real electoral success and gained fourteen deputies. Negotiation rather than confrontation also began to produce results in terms of membership and influence, particularly in relation to the socialists. In April, the communist and socialist youth movements merged to form the Juventud Socialista Unificada (JSU) and, in July, a similar move in Catalonia produced the Partit Socialista Unificat de Catalunya (PSUC). Finally, the view that ultra-leftism had been, at very best, a blind alley was decisively reinforced by the fact that the PCE found its greatest level of support and influence during the Civil War, when it was most closely identified with the Popular Front.[15] Belated success naturally fed into retrospective feelings of relief within the PCE. Symptomatic was the opinion of Santiago Carrillo, a future leader of the party, who stated in his memoirs that, '... firmness and strategic intelligence had been introduced into the project of change of that period, which contributed to overcoming, at least in part, the closed precepts of "class against class".'[16]

Carrillo was not actually a member of the PCE during the period upon which he was passing negative judgement. Like many others, he was also commenting with the benefit of hindsight. Spanish communists, like everyone else, were very adept at putting an inconvenient past behind them. This is not to say that the demise of 'class against class' was not supported by many at the time, as it clearly was, but rather to suggest that the driving force for change was essentially pragmatic. What is even more glossed over by hindsight is the mixed reactions to the *viraje* and the extent to which many of the new enthusiasts for the Popular Front had been equally vocal in their support for 'class against class'. There is also, of course, the well-established view that communists everywhere simply jumped to the orders of Stalin, no matter how illogical or contradictory those orders might be. And certainly, for shrewd, cynical operators like Codovilla – one of the great survivors of inter-war communism – the ability to pass seamlessly from one position to an opposite one was practiced as an art form.[17] However, on a wider scale, it would have to be assumed that enthusiasm for the Popular Front was essentially as feigned as that for the preceding 'line'.

This suggests that we need to look at the Third Period, and particularly 'class against class', in at least a more ambiguous light. In the case of the PCE, as with other parties, the strongly perceived negative effects of the Comintern's line have dominated our understanding and analysis. What needs greater consideration is why the tenets of the time were so widely accepted and what accounted for their endurance. Again, the PCE is an intriguing case to follow in this regard, particularly because of the tests that the party and Comintern faced in terms of the change of regime in Spain, the replacement of the leadership, the growing ascendancy of the political right, and the descent into violence that occurred. In fact, the thinking behind the Third Period found a positive echo in Spain, which appealed to a deep sense of what it meant to be a communist – or a 'good Bolshevik', the term that was much more widely used. Moreover, while 'class against class' clearly had its costs, it was also perceived as bringing benefits even after diminishing returns had set in and the turn towards the Popular Front began.

Spain and the New Faith

When the Comintern adopted the Third Period at the ninth ECCI plenum in February 1928 and sixth world congress in August–September, the PCE played no real part in the proceedings. Nor did Spain figure much at all in the political analysis that underpinned them. The basic reasons for this were simple: the PCE led a precarious and fractious existence at the time and Spain was, at best, on the margins of Comintern interests.

Disarray and weakness had been features of the Spanish party since its inception, but it was dealt a severe blow by the military coup of General Primo de Rivera.[18] In the crackdown on opposition, which followed the regime's seizure of power in 1923, almost all the leading figures – including the general secretary, César Rodríguez González – and a good part of the small PCE membership were arrested, driven into exile or clandestinity. A vacuum of leadership was matched by the disintegration of the party into small grouplets with distinct regional bases and political backgrounds, which made reconstructing the central party apparatus and extending its authority no easy matter. The original heartland of the PCE was in the northern mining and industrial regions of Vizcaya and Asturias, with a lesser number of adherents in Madrid and the southern area of Andalucia, almost all drawn from the ranks of the PSOE and its unions.[19] As well as César Rodríguez, the north also produced the next leading figure of the PCE, Oscar Pérez Solís, who briefly and disastrously became general secretary in 1925, before being arrested, renouncing the party, and converting to Catholicism. The fragmentation of the party was exacerbated further by a group of dissident syndicalists, led by Joaquín Maurín and based in Catalonia and Valencia, who incorporated themselves into the PCE in 1924 as the Catalan–Balearic Federation, the Federación Comunista Catalano-Balear (FCC-B), instantly becoming the largest section of the party – though this was measured in dozens rather than hundreds of militants. This made Barcelona an important alternative centre of power in the party. A short-lived attempt following the resignation of César Rodríguez to bring Maurín into a unified national central committee based in Barcelona failed, leaving the party once again without leadership and even more a set of quasi-independent regional federations.[20]

With the PCE unable to sort out its own internal affairs, ECCI officials intervened with a symptomatic sense of exasperation. A Spanish Commission was formed, which nominated José Bullejos – a Vizcayan miner's leader with a socialist background – as general secretary. The main reason for choosing him was simply that he was available: present in Moscow as representative of the PCE to the Comintern following a period of imprisonment by the dictatorship. And the chalice he was being passed was a decidedly poisoned one: 'to reorganise the party and reconstruct the central committee'. Bullejos was dispatched to Paris, where the PCE was based in exile and effectively functioning as a section of the Parti Communiste Français (PCF). The party organisation in France was scanty and essentially consisted of three individuals, Luis Portela, Juan Andrade (director of *La Antorcha*, the main party newspaper) and Gabriel León Trilla. Initial attempts to rebuild the party swiftly established the pattern that was to prevail. Bullejos adopted a hard-line interpretation of the Comintern's mandate of 'wide powers' with which to fulfil his most basic task, trying to browbeat rivals and corral the federations under his control. Anyone who was not prepared to accept his discipline was denounced as a wrecker and part of an 'anti-Bolshevik opposition', chief amongst whom were Maurín and the FCC-B. Not surprisingly, most of the federations, including those of Asturias and Vizcaya, baulked at the threatened loss of their autonomy.

Bullejos's stance as a centraliser was theoretically in perfect alignment with the ECCI's stated aim of 'Bolshevising' its national sections –

introducing greater control and discipline in order to create model images of the Bolshevik Party. Nor was there anything unusual about the method of expulsion from the party that he and his supporters sought to use against those declared to be non-conformists. As such, it might have been anticipated – and Bullejos clearly expected – that the ECCI would wholeheartedly back this process. However, in practice, the Comintern was ambiguous towards dissent in PCE ranks, frequently urging conciliation and attacking the party leaders as much as their opponents during the complex power struggle that unfolded over the next few years.[21]

The ECCI's toleration of the chronic problems within the PCE seemingly ran counter to the 'Stalinisation' of international communism that was occurring. The Comintern's weak response was clearly not a sign of contentment but instead was the product of a number of considerations. The lack of any sense of urgency was one important factor: Spain and its small party were simply not at the centre of Comintern's concerns. Indeed, an ECCI resolution of May 1928 made it clear that in the Comintern's view, the dictatorship had become 'normalised' and no revolutionary situation was likely to emerge in Spain for some time.[22] In these circumstances, the lack of Spanish participation in the deliberations that led to the adoption of the Third Period theses was barely noticed and no mention of Spain was made during them. Another problem was the paucity of hard information from Spain and a concomitant difficulty in acting decisively. The ECCI had no permanent delegate in Spain, and therefore no means to acquire reliable independent knowledge or to enforce decisions on a fractious PCE. Even when ECCI representatives were sent to Spain on one-off visits, they were frequently intercepted and deported. Even so, when a ECCI official, Walecki, managed to attend a party conference in Durango in August 1927, he simply reiterated the Comintern's conciliatory line.

The very weakness and division of the PCE was also, paradoxically, another primary reason why the ECCI trod carefully, for fear of making a bad situation only worse. This was particularly evident in relation to the FCC-B which, in the event of a schism, would have represented the loss of one of the most significant sections of the party in one of the truly working class parts of the country. Moreover, Maurín was recognised as one of the most energetic and talented, if independent figures, to emerge from Spanish communism. It made sense that the Comintern preferred if possible to have him inside the tent and, therefore, urged the party leadership towards accommodation rather than confrontation.[23] This then raises the question of why the party leaders were left in place when they so singularly refused to follow this advice. Though centralisers within the PCE, both Bullejos and Trilla were quite the opposite when it came to Comintern authority over the party. Nor was their attitude to party organisation and discipline their only failure in the eyes of Moscow, where the 'passivity' of the PCE in the face of the dictatorship had been a further source of irritation. Almost all initiatives had proved fruitless, from a farcical attempt to plot a putsch with the Catalan Nationalists to an equally stillborn plan for a trade union united front with the anarchists. The leadership's refusal to follow the Comintern's advice to adopt 'entryist' tactics when the dictatorship proposed the creation of a consultative assembly seemed about to become the proverbial last straw.[24] What saved them were some belated signs of success. In September 1927, a significant group of erstwhile anarchists from Seville, including José Díaz, Manuel Adame, Antonio Mije and Manuel Delicado, joined the PCE, shifting the balance of power away from Catalonia. At the same time, the party claimed a leading role in the strikes that suddenly erupted in Vizcaya and Asturias, prompting another round of repression but also highlighting the inertia of the FCC-B, which had no counterclaim to be able to 'rouse the masses'.[25] At a crucial moment, Bullejos' position as leader was strengthened in relation to the 'opposition', forestalling any serious attempt to oust him. Unable to choose, for the time being ECCI opted to keep the devils it knew.

The Comintern's Spanish dilemma was eased by the realisation that these conflicts involved little in the way of ideological divergence, nor did they present a direct challenge to its authority. Indeed all the factions continued to profess their higher loyalty to the Comintern, appealing to it for support even as they avoided or subverted its orders. Thus, Maurín's threat to break away from the PCE contained no suggestion that he wanted to reject the Comintern, and all his writings and public pronouncements at this time were protestations of 'Leninist orthodoxy'. In fact, it was actually Gabriel León Trilla who was considered closest to being a 'Trotskyist' in ideological terms.[26] In his memoirs, Bullejos criticised the 'constant diminution in the margins of political independence and national autonomy' of individual parties in the late 1920s, reflecting the contemporary frustration of the party leadership that they did not receive unqualified Comintern backing in their struggle to subdue the 'opposition'.[27] Such concerns focussed essentially on the patterns of control and decision-making within the PCE and in its relations with the Comintern. Within the PCE, all the factions were careful to stress that they were 'good Bolsheviks' and firm adherents to the values of the International.

Remarkably, this underlying loyalty to the Comintern extended into a broad acceptance within the PCE of the basic principles of the Third Period, though this was not due to any unexpected outbreak of peace inside the party. If anything the situation worsened considerably after 1928, making the reluctance of the different factions to criticise openly the International even more remarkable. Internal resistance to the Bullejos' leadership widened to include the Asturian and Levante federations, a tiny Agrupación Comunista de Madrid formed by Luis Portela, as well as the FCC-B. The third party congress, held in Paris in August 1929, and the so-called 'conference of

Pamplona' (actually held clandestinely near Bilbao) in March 1930, became the set-piece battles in the renewed factional struggle. As before, the party executive was determined to assert its authority by almost any means available and in defiance of the Comintern's continued calls for unity. So, Maurín was prevented from attending the Paris congress on the grounds that he was now actually a member of the French party rather than of the PCE. Similarly, dissidents were largely excluded from the election of a new party executive at the Pamplona conference, while the so-called 'troika' of Bullejos, Trilla and Manuel Adame (joined by Etelvino Vega) placed themselves in control. In July 1930, this new executive publicly announced its decision – taken privately two months earlier – to expel the leadership of the FCC-B, though final victory for Bullejos was not confirmed by the Comintern until July 1931, when the expulsions were reluctantly ratified. This, in turn, followed the PCE's rejection of a call for a unity conference made by a number of 'opposition' groups, and the failure of the FCC-B to respond to a final offer from the ECCI to come to Moscow to discuss the issue. After expulsion, Maurín reacted by denouncing the bureaucratic centralism of the Comintern and the 'dictatorship' within the PCE.[28] Nevertheless, as Humbert-Droz discovered after he was sent by the ECCI to Barcelona in January 1931, most FCC-B members that he spoke to continued to profess their adherence to Comintern.[29] More extraordinarily still, the Federation leadership reacted by declaring its 'complete agreement with the line of the Communist International'.[30] Whatever his private thoughts, Maurín continued to express his general support for the basic rationale of the International, even as the steps to build an alternative communist organisation to the PCE were being taken. Indeed, it was not until 1932 that he definitively declared the Comintern a failure and denounced the 'Stalinisation' of the USSR. Thus, when the rupture within the PCE finally came – and even afterwards – it was not the turn towards the New Line that was the central issue of dispute.

This underlying acceptance, and reluctance to break with it, was evidence of the positive attractions that the Third Period strategy held for many convinced communists in Spain. It was also a sign, of course, of the extent to which the Comintern remained the Mecca of the communist world, and of the fear of being consigned to the outer darkness that too much dissent implied. But after a period of inertia in the mid-1920s, the unique identity, and the special mission and methods of communists, were reasserted in a manner whose force few adherents could deny. Many of the ideas and language invoked were actually drawn from across the range of communist thinking and were quite inclusive as a result; as within the USSR itself, the 'Stalinist' authorities shamelessly repackaged much of the thinking of the supporters of Trotsky and Bukharin once they had been organisationally defeated. For example, the notion that revolution was once again possible and that only a disciplined Bolshevik party could lead an authentic revolution, signified a return to fundamental principles rather than being simply knee-jerk 'leftism' or Stalinist device.

The unexpected fall of Primo de Rivera from power in 1930 also made the idea of revolution seem more probable, reversing to some extent the pessimism of the ECCI and the PCE about the situation in Spain. Some conviction was placed behind the kind of populist rhetoric that continually asserted that the PCE was 'the only hope of the working classes' and 'the one true hope of mankind', which gave José Balbontín the sense of 'having entered the heart of the Marxist Church' when he joined the party.[31] A certain reformation zeal also underpinned the 'social-fascist' and 'class against class' formulations that invited communists to see rivals for working class support as heretics from the path of true Bolshevism. The fact that the Spanish socialists briefly collaborated with the military dictatorship only lent credence to the view that they really were the agents of the bourgeoisie. This understanding was especially important in a country like Spain, where the question of communist identity and methods was additionally complicated by the existence of a powerful revolutionary anarchist movement, as well as a socialist alternative. When Manuel Tagüeña Lacorte decided to join the Communist Youth, he explained its attraction as: 'The same utopia as the anarchists, but with a different road, with organisation and discipline that attracted me much more.'[32] The idea of the 'united front from below' also followed logically from this belief that only Bolsheviks understood the real meaning of revolution and knew how to create one. It defined a committed Bolshevik as a kind of revolutionary high priest bringing enlightenment to 'the oppressed masses'. 'Unmasking' anarchist and socialist leaders as false prophets, traitors to the cause and the tools of the capitalist oppressors, not only made sense, but was also necessary in defining what communists themselves stood for. Whatever later feelings were about the formulations of the Third Period, there were good reasons why they were widely welcomed within communist movements as giving a clear direction for their activities. And far from being divisive in themselves, they united communists around the renewal of their special revolutionary mission and helped define their political identity. However, this is not to suggest that the adoption of the Third Period analysis by the Comintern, and the political strategies that accompanied it, had no impact on the PCE.

Perhaps the most significant change after 1928 was a rise in the Comintern's level of interest and involvement with its Spanish section. It is sometimes suggested that small parties were able to pursue a more independent line outside the glare of Moscow's direct gaze; and the PCE had seemed to fit into this pattern. However, this situation was reversed by the internal reorganisation of the Comintern apparatus placed in train by the sixth congress. Its aim was to increase oversight of the national sections by introducing the enhanced system of Land Secretariats which each had responsibility for a group of parties. These bodies had the time and remit to intervene more directly in the affairs of individual parties, and did so even when the central bodies of the ECCI were not that engaged. This brought the PCE within the scope of the Roman Land Secretariat (RLS), whose committee included such powerful figure as Dmitri Manuilsky (quickly nicknamed 'Manu' by the Spaniards), Stoin Minev ('Stepanov' or 'Moreno') and Vassiliev. The level of requests for information and of instructions concerning a range of matters gradually increased as the secretariat became established, including detailed 'advice' on preparations for the PCE's third congress in Paris and Pamplona conference. The RLS also intervened more directly to increase its control over the party to try and remedy its perceived deficiencies of organisation and activity. This included funds for a new central party newspaper, *Mundo Obrero*, which made a brief appearance in December 1930, and then intermittently until July 1931, before becoming properly established as a weekly and then a daily.[33] There was also money to pay the salaries of party officials, all of who (with the exception of Vicente Arroyo who effectively acted as secretary of the executive committee) remained imprisoned, and for the electoral campaign of June 1931.

It was this vacuum of hands-on leadership, lack of membership and the continuing internal crisis within the PCE that led the RLS to send the first permanent delegation to Spain in January 1930. Jacques Duclos, a leading figure in the PCF, initially headed the group of five representatives but, after his early departure, it was the veteran Jules Humbert-Droz who took the leading role during what he saw as a period of 'exile' brought on by his support for Bukharin. Along with Claude Rabaté (representing the Red International of Labour Unions; RILU), the mysterious 'Pierre' from the Communist Youth International, and Edgar Woog ('Stirner', representing the organisational department), it was their task to reorganise and reconstruct the party. An attempt to introduce the ECCI's new predilection for factory cells (Células de Fábrica) and district committees (Comites de Radio) was part of their activities.[34] They also forced a shift of the party headquarters from Madrid to Barcelona in a vain attempt to undermine the influence of the FCC-B. After the departure of Duclos, followed by those of Woog (deported by the police) and 'Pierre', a rump delegation was left with little real authority.[35] But no matter how limited, for the first time 'La Casa' ('home' as the Comintern was named by the Spaniards) had its own independent sources of information and influence in Spain.

Greater intervention in the affairs of the PCE was also prompted by the central bodies of the Comintern – to which the RLS reported – which lost some of their disinterest in developments in Spain as the dictatorship entered into a period of crisis and eventually fell in April 1931. Between March 1930 and March 1931, for example, either the ECCI political commission or political secretariat discussed Spain and the position of the PCE thirteen times, including the sessions that finally ratified the expulsion of Maurín, but which also dealt with reports from the RLS, the issuing of instructions to the party, and with regard to its finances.[36] The Western European Bureau (WEB) established as a means of contact between Comintern and its sections was also mandated to deal with the PCE. So, following the Pamplona conference, Bullejos and Arroyo travelled to Berlin for discussions with Dimitrov, then its director.[37] In line with Third Period analysis, the substance of all this interest was, of course, the prospect for Bolshevik-style revolution in Spain. Perhaps not surprisingly, the temptation to see parallels with Russia in 1917 was overwhelming, with an unpopular monarchy, widespread social unrest, and a tradition of working class and peasant protest. Nor did the fact that by late 1930 an alliance of middle class republicans and socialists formed the main opposition to the regime cause any disturbance to this perspective – again the similarities to February 1917 seemed all too clear. Such forces could not, after all, represent a real alternative to the monarchist regime – merely an alternative form of the same bourgeois domination – and therefore they needed to be combated just as much, if not more so, in order to prevent them from derailing the workers and peasants from a real revolutionary outcome. Given the opportunities that the Comintern perceived, the real danger, therefore, was that the PCE would not be ambitious enough; not be a 'true Bolshevik party'. Accordingly, Moscow constantly urged the PCE to adopt a 'truly revolutionary position', to give 'a class character to the struggle', to 'dispel the democratic illusions of the masses', to create 'a truly mass party' and, naturally, to aim for 'a proletarian regime'. At the ECCI's eleventh plenum, meeting just before the fall of the monarchy in Spain, Manuilsky made clear during his speech on the 'capitalist crisis and the tasks of the national sections', that a revolutionary situation existed in Spain and that the PCE needed to realise this.[38]

These pressures from the Comintern heightened existing tensions over control of the PCE and fed directly into the factional disputes within the party, which now focussed on how to translate revolutionary strategy into appropriate practical tactics. And, once again, this was by no means a two-sided affair, with the official party leadership as much in disagreement with the ECCI over these questions as it was with the 'opposition'. Accusations were couched in the prevailing linguistic fashions of communist abuse – 'Trotskyism', 'Bukharinism', 'rightism' and 'deviationism' – but two central issues really predominated.

The first was the question of how the party should represent its programme, a debate that came down to a choice of slogans. At the third party congress, representatives of the FCC-B had proposed that the PCE propose a 'Democratic Federal Republic' as means to maximise its appeal. This was denounced by the Comintern representative, 'Garlandi' (Ruggiero

Grieco), as 'rightist' and 'reactionary' for playing into the hands of other opponents of the dictatorship – charges that were heavily denied. In this the PCE executive (represented by Vicente Arroyo) joined, suggesting that a 'Workers and Peasants Democratic Dictatorship' should be the proclaimed aim. Of course, this coincidence of view also served to isolate the FCC-B, as Maurín's immediate acceptance of this definition of the party programme showed he realised. This time, however, it was too late, beginning the process by which Maurín was finally placed beyond the pale. Simultaneously, Arroyo, during the preparation of the congress' theses, criticised the interference of the Comintern in the preparation and conduct of the meetings, and complained about its continued toleration of Maurín. Nor was this the end of tensions with the Comintern over this issue. Before and during the Pamplona conference, the party leadership was criticised by the ECCI for continuing to use the word 'democratic' to describe a future regime. It was following this that Bullejos travelled to Berlin to reach a compromise that ushered in the phrase 'Workers and Peasants Government' as a replacement. Even then, there was a further dispute about whether the PCE should participate in the municipal elections of April 1931 and the parliamentary elections of June 1931.

The second related issue concerned syndical activity, where the Comintern favoured the creation of independent communist unions that would supplant those of the socialist UGT and the CNT. Accordingly, Manuel Adame's suggestions that the PCE should infiltrate the collective bargaining committees (comités paritarios) of the dictatorship or seek to unify the two existing union federations into single body it could influence were rejected by the RLS in May 1929.[39] At the third party congress, FCC-B delegates criticised the notion of creating 'red' unions affiliated to the RILU as impossible to achieve given the weakness of the party and a dangerous division of the working class, thereby placing a further nail into their political coffin. While the party leadership never rejected the Comintern's aims, a continuing dispute bubbled away over what approach should be taken. This centred on the CNT as the body containing the most obviously revolutionary section of the organised working class. The proposal was to create a Comité Nacional de Reconstrucción del CNT (National Committee for the Reconstruction of the CNT), as a means to take over its unions and then use this new base to do the same to the UGT. Its feasibility was debated with both the Comintern and RLS delegation. Once again, it was the Comintern view that was finally accepted.

What all of this came down to was how much could realistically be done. The arguments of the leadership were based essentially on a more pessimistic view of the immediate possibilities in Spain rather than any dispute over ideals. At no time were the ultimate objectives in question. But in their dealings with the Comintern, Bullejos and Trilla both emphasised the 'feudal residues' in an underdeveloped country like Spain that, in their view, made the task of proletarian revolution intrinsically more difficult than elsewhere.[40] Such views were swept aside as mere excuses and of no value given the nature of Russia in 1917. In February 1931, at a meeting of the RLS to discuss the situation in Spain, and in the face of repeated demands for action by the PCE from committee members, Trilla – who had returned as party representative after his release from prison – presciently argued that little could really be expected given the current state of the party.[41]

The real actions of the PCE during the fall of the monarchy and the declaration of the Spanish Republic on 14 April 1931 were best summed up by a story often recounted about the events of that day. As the crowds thronged the streets of the capital to celebrate the arrival of the new regime, a small group of communists rode in a truck to the Plaza de Oriente, in front of the royal residence, seeking to recreate their own version of the storming of the Winter Palace. To their dismay, their cries of 'Down with the Bourgeois Republic!' were greeted by either complete indifference or outright hostility.[42] The marginality of the PCE was further confirmed by its disastrous results in the parliamentary elections of June 1931. A post-election meeting of the party's Madrid district organisation ruminated plaintively on developments. 'From 12 April until today the radicalisation of the masses is a fact ... The masses are pushed towards the party by the revolutionary process, but one must take into account the organic weaknesses and deficiencies of our party. In conclusion, the results of the elections could not be satisfactory for us.'[43]

This disappointment at the inability of the PCE to influence events was understandable and would seem to endorse the position of Maurín and other critics of party policy who pointed out that opposing the tide of opinion in favour of 'bourgeois' democracy was suicidal. However, to accept the Republic would have simply made the party virtually indistinguishable from the PSOE, which had become one of the main driving forces towards the new regime along with the middle class republican parties, and which became part of the coalition government after 1931. Though the PCE was still in direct competition with the CNT in offering a revolutionary alternative to the Republic (not that the party recognised the anarchists as such), its aims and approach were still distinctive. Already squeezed by its rivals for working class support, the PCE faced an uphill task in trying to differentiate itself and increase its political attractiveness. But if it did not try, it was certain that it could never grow. Ultimately, of course, the idea that a change of tactics by the PCE would have made a difference to its fortunes remains simply a supposition; but the cynical though perhaps realistic judgement might be that the party was caught in a vicious circle that it was almost impossible to break out of. It was small and therefore insignificant, and because it was insignificant, it was almost bound to stay small.

Unsurprisingly, the ECCI did not take the benign view that the PCE had done as well as could be expected given the circumstances, beginning a process of confrontation that was to lead to the replacement of the party leadership in late 1932. Though they became victims of the Third Period, and even before Soviet sources confirmed the picture, it was long postulated that the source of this divergence with the Comintern was not overtly ideological, but was performance related and about control of the party.[44] From April 1931, complaints from Moscow about the role of the PCE leadership mounted. Meetings in Moscow during May with a Spanish delegation led by Bullejos were followed by an 'open letter' from the ECCI, written by Manuilsky, in which the PCE was castigated for its failure to understand the 'revolutionary situation' that had arisen. In particular, the leadership was castigated for not having achieved the necessary balancing act of not alienating 'the revolutionary masses' who had been duped into supporting 'the counter-revolutionary regime' by the 'social fascists and agents of the bourgeoisie', while at the same time 'unmasking them of their republican illusions'. Accordingly, the immediate task of the leadership was to place itself at the head of the 'revolutionary movement' and steer it in the direction of a Soviet Spain. The tactics of the 'united front from below' were required to undermine and supplant the 'counter-revolutionary' leaderships of the CNT and socialist movement. So, confusingly, by calling for a workers' state the leaders had been too leftist while, at the same time, they had not been revolutionary enough. The true source of their weakness was clear: they 'had not studied and assimilated the rich experience of the Russian Revolution and so had not become a Bolshevik party'.[45] By January 1932, a further 'open letter' sent from the WEB laid out much the same set of charges and called on the party to set its house in order. 'As true revolutionaries should, the Spanish communists must seek out and lay bare the reason for the party's lagging behind and for the mistakes it has made.'[46]

The Comintern's remarks revealed not just a blinkered view of what was happening in Spain, but also illustrated the institutional understanding of the nature of leadership in communist movements and of their task in the Third Period. In the Comintern's view, leaders played a crucial part in directing revolution. 'The masses' were, of course, revolutionary by their very nature given the contradictions of capitalist society, but they required direction in order to achieve revolution. Correspondingly, any action by workers had the potential to become revolutionary, but they could also be diverted from that path by social fascists acting as the agents of the bourgeoisie, or left unfulfilled by reliance on 'spontaneous action'. The latter was an 'anarchist tendency', something of which the ECCI frequently accused the PCE of possessing. Leadership, therefore, became an act of will on the part of communists who would act as an enlightened and clear-sighted minority to guide the masses. By using the correct slogans and proselytising the cause, 'good Bolsheviks' would make the scales fall from the workers' eyes and they would be drawn irresistibly towards revolution. The wave of strikes and demonstrations that occurred with the Republic was thus all the evidence that the Comintern needed that a revolutionary situation was occurring in Spain. It also followed that it could not be the case that 'the masses' did not, in their heart of hearts, desire revolution. That they were not flocking to the PCE was, therefore, evidence that it was the party leadership that was in error: they must not be 'true Bolsheviks'.

Disputes between the PCE leadership and the Comintern over the direction of the party were not the only source of conflict. The ECCI delegation in Spain was also at odds with the 'Troika'. Humbert-Droz saw Bullejos as a 'cacique' (political boss) who viewed the PCE as a private fiefdom. In turn, Bullejos accused the delegates of deliberately seeking to undermine relations with the Comintern and of complete ignorance about the situation in Spain.[47] During a meeting in October 1931 in Moscow between representatives of the PCE and ECCI officials, Etelvino Vega repeated the accusation that 'the head of the delegation, Comrade Messere, for me has demonstrated in his activity in Spain a total incomprehension of the political situation in Spain and also a total incomprehension of the situation of our party'. By attacking the delegation, Vega made the wider point that outside interference in the affairs of the party was not appreciated. Bullejos' report, given at the same meeting, was also guaranteed to anger the Comintern representatives present, arguing that the revolutionary possibilities of 1930–31 had passed and that the bourgeois regime had consolidated itself. Manuilsky was scathing in his reply, suggesting that Trilla was the real power in the PCE and that he bore the greatest blame for the party's continued failings. He went on to argue explicitly that 'the party needs to be reorganised, beginning with the leadership'.[48]

What gradually unfolded was a classic Comintern coup against the PCE leaders. It was not possible to move immediately against them for the lack of a viable alternative. There was also the fear of a further schism if Bullejos was forced out of the party too precipitately. Accordingly, Manuilsky had to backtrack on the January 1932 letter to the party, taking a more conciliatory stance while Comintern officials adopted the device of cultivating potential substitutes within the party organisation via invitations to attend the International Lenin School (ILS) in Moscow, particularly selecting candidates from a younger generation of Spanish communists. Hopes that the fourth party congress, which took place in Seville in March 1932, would lead to a replacement leadership were dashed when Bullejos, Adame, Trilla and Etelvino Vega were all elected to the newly established PCE political bureau (PB). However, some opponents of Bullejos, particularly Manuel Hurtado, who acted on behalf of Comintern, were also included.

By August, the campaign against the leadership was well underway, with the Comintern's wily new delegate in Spain, Vittorio Codovilla, taking a leading part. The end came in a series of acts during the party leadership's preparations for the twelfth ECCI plenum in Moscow. First, in a series of meetings of the PB, Bullejos and his closest collaborators were accused of having taken the wrong attitude to the attempted military putsch of General Sanjurjo on 10 August 1932 by having defended the Republic. Faced with this pretext on which they could be declared to be acting against the 'line' of the International, the leaders presented their resignations – clearly believing that they were in too strong a position for them to be accepted.[49] They then travelled to Moscow for an extended set of deliberations, during which a meeting on 27 September 1932 of the ECCI secretariat strongly condemned Bullejos, Adame, Vega and Trilla. While they were away, Codovilla and his collaborators consulted with local party members and determined that no split would take place. A further meeting of the PB on 5 October 1932 formally called for the expulsion of the leadership from the party as 'counter-revolutionaries'. Finally given the green light, the Comintern used the report of a Spanish Commission to ratify that decision in a meeting of the ECCI Presidium on 31 October 1932.[50]

The new leadership designated by the ECCI was designed to be a new broom that would sweep through the PCE. Perhaps the most surprising choice was the candidate for the post of general secretary, José Díaz, one of the former anarchists from Seville. Known to all by his diminutive, Pepé, he was likeable but deeply uncharismatic. But above all, he was loyal to the Comintern. Meanwhile, Manuel Hurtado received the post of organisation secretary; not the reward he had hoped for. Graduates of the ILS figured prominently among the occupants of other key positions, including Jesús Hernández, Antonio Mije, Pedro Checa, Vicente Uribe, Manuel Delicado and Dolores Ibarruri. Having been paid back in their own coin, the old leadership was completely isolated. Throughout the process they maintained their fidelity to the Comintern and its 'line', but what they had not provided was results: that, and their resistance to direction, was enough to seal their fate. What had occurred was a crisis in the party, but it was not a crisis of faith.

Keeping the Faith

The main impact of the change of leadership was again more organisational than ideological. Indeed the tightening of control – within the party and by the Comintern over it – was seen in Moscow as a necessary corollary to the better application of the same policies: a logical position from a particular point of view. After all, it was not the strategies of the Third Period that had been at fault in Spain, but the malign and truculent leadership of the 'troika' that had failed to apply them properly. Naturally, the continued attacks on the fallen leaders – now described largely in coded language as 'the sectarian group' or, even more cryptically, by their initials 'b.a.v.t.' – masked this essential continuity by asserting their supposed deviation from orthodoxy. It was not enough that they were bad leaders; their failure must mean that they were active traitors who had consciously held back the revolution.[51] For example, in a pamphlet published in late 1932, which blamed the old leadership for everything wrong with the party and reprinted the ECCI's 'open letter' of May 1931, they were described both as 'Trotskyists' and 'Mensheviks' whose consistent aim was to 'sow confusion in the party'.[52] Accordingly, the new leadership, under the firm direction of Codovilla – who used his plenipotentiary powers from the ECCI to dictatorial effect – embarked on a 'reinforcement' of party organisation and discipline.

Part of this further 'Bolshevisation' of the party involved forcing supporters of the old leadership, or anyone accused of dissent, to either rectify or be expelled. The most prominent near-victim of this purge was Dolores Ibarruri, who was attacked in an open letter by Manuel Hurtado, partly one suspects in order to prove his own loyalty to the new order. She was an easy target, as Bullejos had acted as her mentor in the party and because she was one of the few women in a notoriously *machista* movement. Her successful self-criticism made from prison, where she had been placed on a public order offence, strongly reaffirmed her loyalty and claimed that 'the traitorous group' had largely acted in secret, that her protests had been ignored, and that she fully supported the changes initiated by the Comintern. Only after this was she affirmed in her position within the party hierarchy.[53] Whole sections of the party – in Madrid, Seville and Salamanca – also came under criticism and were brought into line.

The other side of change was a tightening of party structures in which the classic Comintern pattern of substitution operated at all levels. At the top a small secretariat, meeting on a fortnightly basis, effectively subsumed the directive functions of the political bureau and the even larger executive committee. There was also an inner group, meeting on a twice-weekly basis with Codovilla exercising decisive control, composed of the secretaries for political, organisation and syndical activity. At the regional and local levels, similar arrangements were put in place, with leaderships nominated from the centre. Separate Catalan and Basque parties – in reality closely tied to the central PCE – were also created at this time, with the Partit Comunista de Catalunya (PCC) charged in particular with combating the BOC. Meanwhile, at the base of the party, the emphasis was on strengthening the district committees and creating party cells. There was also a new initiative on the trade union front with the formation of an independent union federation, the Confederación General del Trabajo Unitaria (CGTU) in 1933. Although this signalled a change in method from the attempt to 'reconstruct' the CNT towards the development of independent 'factory committees' that would 'struggle at the base', the essential spirit of 'class against class' was fully preserved. Money was made available to increase the circulation of *Mundo Obrero* and to expand the regional party newspapers.[54]

Reorganisation was represented as a new start for the PCE. The underlying analysis, objectives and strategy remained the same: to create a Soviet-type regime in Spain to replace the 'bourgeois' Republic, and to build a 'great mass party of the proletariat' towards this end by 'unmasking' the anarchist, socialist and Trotskyist leaderships and winning over their members to the party.[55] Organisational initiatives were therefore matched by a whirlwind of activity in line with the 'united front from below'. At meetings, in print and through open letters, the PCE's rivals were attacked and their trade unions targeted for recruitment. A mountain of paper was also moved in the form of reports, instructions, editorials and circulars generated within the party and in correspondence – naturally dominated by Codovilla – between the PCE and 'la Casa'.

The clearest results of all this activity were in reassuring an ever-sceptical ECCI that the PCE was finally in reliable hands, and in giving the party a greater sense of discipline and urgency. Not that this meant any diminution in the detailed criticism or advice from Moscow that had become a feature of Comintern's relations with all its sections. Rather, the constant flow of information from Madrid about party actions was reassurance that the PCE had become a willing, rather than reluctant, instrument of Comintern policy. Clearly, the party leaders also felt a reciprocal confidence that they, as Bolsheviks imbued by their backgrounds in Moscow with the ethos and practices of the Comintern, could make things work where others had failed. Not that there were no personal tensions between the leaders and especially between them and Codovilla, whose nickname of 'el gordo' ('fatty') gives a flavour of the regard in which he was held, but rather that at this stage there was a basic willingness to follow the 'line' and to accept the Comintern model of control. Consequently, with a few changes of responsibilities, the Comintern was to keep essentially the same leadership through the uncertain change towards the Popular Front policy until after the Civil War, and to retain Codovilla as delegate until mid-1937. No doubt, this was also made easier by the fact that there was no realistic prospect of finding any more malleable set of figures to lead the party.

Both the Comintern and the party were united in one shared hope: that 'class against class' would now provide positive results. It was this reaffirmation of faith in the Third Period analysis which in turn drove forward the vigorous activity of the party and which was in itself an important reason why the 'line' was upheld as long as it was. All the existing reasons for belief in the policies still applied, particularly the underlying sense of an exclusive communist identity and mission. The notion that the preferred policy had not been seriously tried thus became a justification for renewed efforts. Nor, in fact, was this hope entirely irrational. It was not in the end simply faith alone, or blind obedience to the ECCI, that maintained 'class against class', but also some evidence that it was working. In turn, the new leadership was naturally quick to trumpet any signs of improvement in the position of the party and to claim them as the result of their initiatives.

The most significant single improvement was the growth in party membership and trade union influence, which was presented by the PCE as barometer of the progress of 'the Spanish revolution' in its own right. Though not spectacular, and in many ways limited, this was a relatively significant achievement at a time when most European parties experienced a reversal in recruitment. However, this growth was well underway before the new leadership took control of the PCE, suggesting that they had little to do with producing this trend. Instead, a number of factors seem to have been involved, the most important of which were completely outside the control of the party. Perhaps the most basic was the fact that the despised Republic was an open democracy. Though the party did suffer harassment under the regime's public order legislation, designed in part to combat threats from both the far left and right, becoming a member of the PCE was essentially legal (though the party also continued to work clandestinely).[56]

Of crucial importance was the growing plausibility of the party's principal claim to be a serious revolutionary alternative to its main rivals. In this respect, the positions taken by the socialists and anarchists within the Republic had opened up some political space for the PCE. By collaborating in the government, the socialists effectively tied themselves to the success of the economic and social reforms undertaken by the new regime. Though this initially benefited the PSOE, and the unions in particular, as the early promise of change receded so discontent within socialist ranks grew. The anarchists had different problems. Disorganised attempts at revolutionary insurrections in 1932 and 1933 fed into internal divisions about the direction that the CNT should take and served to discredit the organisation. In this sense, the idea that these organisations had leaderships that did not really know where they were going was one whose time had come. And while the PCE could clearly benefit from the problems of its rivals, it did help increase its own credibility by presenting a more disciplined and organised face to the world.

Details on who the new party members were, and exactly why they joined, are inevitably impressionistic, but the evidence suggests a complex dynamic was at work. In particular, it seems that the prediction of 'class against class', that anarchists and socialists would abandon their organisations for the PCE, was not the only, or even the main, source of increased support. Some new members clearly were former anarchists and socialists, but many – like Manuel Tagüeña Lacorte – were drawn directly to the PCE as their first political choice. This also points to the youth of many new recruits and accounts for the relatively greater growth amongst the Communist Youth compared to the mainstream party.[57] The correspondingly marginal status that many of them had, in terms of the kinds of backgrounds they came from and their economic position, is also clear. The party's greatest growth came in areas and occupations where traditions of working class organisation were at their weakest: among unorganised trades in Andalusian cities like Seville and Córdoba, for example, rather than in Asturias and Catalonia.[58] Many were engaged in insecure occupations, or were unemployed – the latter group being targeted by the party recruitment drive during 1933. Recruitment figures, given that they are a snap shot of the party at a given moment in time, also clearly underplay the inevitable volatility of party membership that resulted from this marginality. A hard-core of committed militants was surrounded by shifting numbers of essentially temporary members who dropped in and out, suggesting that the party actually recruited in greater numbers than the figures suggest. As Tagüeña Lacorte commented on the situation in Madrid, 'there was a great fluctuation in affiliates who constantly arrived only to disappear after a few days'.[59]

Some of the difficulties of recruiting and retaining new members were also due to the PCE not always being as welcoming as it might have been. Its general hostility to dissent and the expulsion of dissenters was, of course, the most identifiable aspect of this. There was also the fact that becoming a communist was quite demanding in terms of time and commitment. In addition, most of its meetings were, as Tagüeña Lacorte frankly described them, 'dull'.[60] But the most significant self-imposed limitations were directly linked to the ethos of the Third Period and the drive to define a communist identity, part of which involved the notion of '*obrerismo*' (workerism) and the preference for recruiting 'genuine' members of the working class as the only 'authentic' communists. It went along with the introduction of 'red' weddings, baptisms and funerals, and the attempt to create a communist culture in Spain. This was, for instance, a strong part of José Díaz's appeal as party leader, deriving from his background in the bread making industry of Seville and the poverty of his upbringing. While the notion of a communist community was welcoming to many, it was also guaranteed to ensure hostility to those whose backgrounds did not fit the required definition.

Balbontín's suspicion, for example, that a visceral antipathy towards middle class 'intellectuals' was used as an excuse to explain his questioning of the party line was absolutely correct – as the discussions about his case within the party and in Moscow bear out.[61] He, in turn, was scathing about José Díaz's inability to write and speak good Castilian, and affected to be shocked at a party in which none of its leaders had read Karl Marx. The PCE was indeed wary of middle class recruits, which it described as 'employees' or 'intellectuals', tending to treat them as innately unsuited to being a good communist. In one report on membership in 1932, it was proudly reported that 'less than one per cent are not workers in the main areas of party strength. Madrid has a higher figure of intellectuals but the non-workers are still less than five percent'.[62] The party also had an ambiguous attitude towards the rural population. Although the PCE spoke rhetorically about its support for 'the peasantry', its agrarian programme made little attempt to address the real interests of the rural labourers and impoverished family farmers who formed one of the largest single social groups in Spain during the 1930s. Equally, the party largely alienated women. Class always came before gender in the thinking of the overwhelmingly male communist leadership. In later years, official propaganda was to portray Dolores Ibarruri and José Díaz as almost equal partners in the direction of the party, but this was far from the truth. Before the Republic, 'La Pasionaria' was the only female party member, and she suffered persistent discrimination even after joining the PB in 1932 and as head of the women's secretariat (*Secretariado Femenino*) following the fall of Bullejos. But no real initiatives were taken to specifically recruit women until August 1934, when the Committee of Women Against War and Fascism, headed by Ibarruri, was formed. Even then, it is clear that women were treated with some antagonism and were marginalised within the party when they joined it.[63]

Whether 'class against class' was actually working as it was supposed to mattered little to a PCE leadership that was desperate for signs of success. At last, the party could answer the insistent demands from the ECCI for evidence that the revolution in Spain was back on track. Ever the hard taskmaster, Moscow's response was to raise expectations even further and to demand yet more from the PCE. However, the increased optimism that accompanied the growth in recruitment in 1933 gave way to mounting concern during 1934 as membership stagnated and then went into reverse with the effects of the government crackdown in the aftermath of the Asturian rising. The first real sign that all was not well came with the general elections of November 1933, which were built up by the PCE as another measure of its improved performance. In a speech to the thirteenth plenum of the ECCI a month afterwards, Jesús Hernández proclaimed that the party had increased its vote from 60,000 in June 1931 to 400,000. The reality was that this was a huge exaggeration and the PCE had polled exactly half that number, though the party did gain its first parliamentary deputy, Cayetano Bolívar. On Spain, the plenum reiterated the same formulas towards producing a re-run of the Russian Revolution: Soviets, factory councils, occupation of the land, and the arming of workers and peasants in order to seize power.[64] But unpalatable truths that could not be wished away in so blatant a manner began to accumulate. By mid-1934, it was clear that not just the party, but also the CGTU, had ground to a halt.

The reasons for this reversal of fortunes again had little to do with anything the PCE itself was doing or not doing. Of specific significance was the impact of a growing radicalisation among the socialist rank-and-file in response to the failures of reform. By the end of 1933, the PSOE had swung towards Largo Caballero's wing of the party, breaking the coalition with the republicans and adopting a more radical stance in favour of the creation of a socialist society. Both the Comintern and the PCE had always identified left-socialists as the most dangerous type of 'social fascist', precisely because they disputed exactly the political territory that the communists wished to occupy. Now the socialists closed the political gap that had opened up between them and the PCE, reducing the appeal of the much smaller communist movement. There was also the more localised rivalry in Catalonia with Maurín's BOC, which continued to overshadow the PCC. The response of the party was to redouble its attacks on the socialist leadership and 'Trotskyists' in a vain attempt to recover lost ground. However, the wider problem that the PCE had to face was the change of government. Although the PCE chose to treat this as insignificant, the reality was that the new administration was intent on eliminating any threat from the left. The forcible removal of republican and socialist local administrations across the country was one indication of this, as was support for an employers' offensive which led to the suppression of the national land workers' strike in the summer of 1934 and the closure of all *casas del pueblo* in the south and centre of Spain in its aftermath. This process finally reached its peak with the government-led repression of opposition that followed the abortive rising of October 1934. As a result, the PCE was once again in a situation where its leaders were arrested or in exile, its press and organisation suppressed, and its supporters driven underground.

While it was such circumstances that gave rise to the shift away from the Third Period analysis in Spain, coinciding with a rethink at the centre in response to similar crises within the broader communist movement, the party was actually very reluctant to reject wholesale the policies of 'class against class'. What is striking about those who dissented from the party's position, as it continued to pursue the 'united front from below' and to attack the rival anarchist and socialist leaderships, is how few they were and how little impact they had. It was precisely the isolation of figures such as Balbontín that made them easy to suppress and ignore, and there was never any threat of serious splits in the ranks of the party. This, in part, was an obvious result of the tighter party discipline that now prevailed. But it also reflected a tension between the strong pragmatic pressures for change, to resist the assault of the right and to maintain the influence of communist organisation, and a continuing attachment to the ideals of the Third Period. After all, compromising with rival organisations on the left signified at the very least a watering down of the unique mission that communists had given themselves. To treat them as equals, even in the cause of anti-fascism, was to caste doubt on the reason for being a communist in the first place. The result was a schizophrenic attitude to change that was, in some ways, a battle between the heart and the head that was never entirely resolved.

Even when the New Line was clearly outliving its usefulness, it was not simply abandoned in its entirety by either the Comintern or the PCE. Instead, there was an attempt to pragmatically modify aspects of it while preserving as much of its essence as possible. The emphasis once again was on making the 'line' work better rather than replacing it in its entirety; in this sense, the 'turn' was not sudden and never complete. A gradual and confusing retreat at all levels took place, with considerable doubt and debate at every stage. So, for example, when after much internal wrangling the ECCI finally authorised the terms upon which the PCE was to take the important step of joining the *Alianzas Obreras* in September 1934, many of the essential aims of the 'united front from below' were retained. The party was to use the opportunity to call for national as well as local alliances, the bodies were to be renamed Workers' and Peasants' Alliances, communists were to dominate them, and they were to be used as the basis for a seizure of power and as organs of government – that is to say, as Soviets.[65] Nor did the PCE cease attacking the socialists and anarchists before the anti-fascist alliance, and then the Popular Front, were announced in 1935. Indeed, in the aftermath of Asturias, the party redoubled its criticisms of its rivals in a renewed attempt to supplant them – a situation deepened by the Socialist International's rejection of co-operation.[66] Even when the Popular Front was in the process of being adopted by the PCE, a debate about the extent to which this should include 'bourgeois parties' and 'Trotskyists' ensued which was only resolved very late in the day.

Similarly, after the victory of the Popular Front alliance in the elections of 1936, and with the new 'line' firmly in place as official Comintern policy, the PCE demonstrated further its reluctance to jettison completely the practices of 'class against class'. As late as May and June 1936, Dimitrov was admonishing the PCE for its failure to abandon sectarianism in meetings of the ECCI secretariat and presidium.[67] The reasons for this were due to the manner in which the JSU and PSUC had come into being, which was effectively through exactly the kind of 'united front from below' tactics that were now prohibited by the Comintern as likely to alienate potential allies. Formed in agreement with sections of the PSOE, these organisations swiftly came under communist domination in internal coups. In fact, the growth in party numbers and influence that resulted far from demonstrating the beneficial effects of the Popular Front 'compromise' showed the continued application, and apparently increased efficacy, of the old tactics. Nor was this to be an isolated instance of the PCE having to be restrained from trying to dominate its rivals as conditions became more favourable to the party with the outbreak of the Civil War. In many ways, the position of the PCE was transformed by the war, and its adherence to the Popular Front was deepened; but throughout the conflict, there were continued complaints from anarchists and, above all, socialists that the party could not fully resist taking the opportunity to advance its organisation and interests at their expense.

Conclusion

The Third Period proved to be a roller-coaster ride for the PCE, with both ups and downs rather than the straightforward plunge to the depths that it is often portrayed as being. Indeed the relative longevity of its analysis and the persistence with which the party applied its tactics can only be explained by the fact that it had its successes as well as its evident failures. Above all, the analysis that underpinned it met a deep need on the part of communists for a sense of identity and mission, which transcended factionalism and leadership changes within the Spanish section of the Comintern. By good or ill means, it was during this time that the PCE became an organised and disciplined party for the first time. In a country with a strong tradition of revolutionary activity and with powerful competitors for working class political allegiance, the PCE had to struggle hard to carve out a distinctive ethos. And it was only reluctantly, and under the pressure of great adversity, that 'class against class' was abandoned. Even then, the 'sectarianism' that was its hallmark remained an enduring subterranean force within the party as the question remained, what does it mean to be a communist? The Popular Front did not really address this, or at least it did so only in very shallow terms. In this sense, for the PCE and Comintern more generally, the end of the Third Period marked an uneven break between two eras in the history of international communism. Many of those recruits who flocked to the PCE just before and during the Civil War – and so turning it into a 'great mass party' – did so for the most utilitarian of reasons. They transformed the nature of the party but, in the process, the sense of special revolutionary mission of the old guard, including the party leadership, was watered down. At the same time, the need for the existence of the Comintern itself came increasingly into doubt. What was the need for a 'general staff of the revolution' if that had ceased to be the central and exclusive purpose of communists? It is no exaggeration to say, therefore, that something distinctive about the meaning and purpose of communism, in Spain as elsewhere, disappeared along with the Third Period.

Notes

1. K. McDermott and J. Agnew, *The Comintern. A History of International Communism from Lenin to Stalin* (Basingstoke, 1996), p. 81. For an even more negative assessment, see F. Claudin, *The Communist Movement: From Comintern to Cominform* (London, 1975), pp. 159–66.

2. For overviews of the PCE during this period see J. Estruch, *Historia del PCE (1920–39)* (Barcelona, 1978); P. Pagès, *Historia del Partido Comunista de España* (Barcelona, 1978); M. T. Meshcheryakov, 'Kommunisticheskaya Partiya Ispanii i Komintern', *Novaya i Noveishaya Istoriya*, No. 5 (1991); R. Cruz, *El Partido Comunista de España en la Segunda República* (Madrid, 1987). Recent work incorporates material from the Soviet archives, especially A. Elorza and M. Bizcarrondo, *Queridos camaradas: La Internacional Comunista y España, 1919–39* (Barcelona, 1999).

3. J. Bullejos, *La Comintern en España: Recuerdos de mi vida* (Mexico, 1972), pp. 26–27.

4. The two movements joined in 1936 to form the Partido Obrero de Unificación Marxista (POUM). See A. Durgan, *B.O.C. 1930–36: El Bloque Obero y Campesino* (Barcelona, 1936) and V. Alba and S. Schwartz, *Spanish Marxism Versus Soviet Communism: A History of the POUM* (New Brunswick, 1988).

5. Compare, for instance, the published party election manifestos for June 1931 and November 1933: *Programa del Partido Comunista de España frente a las próximas elecciones* (Madrid, 1931) and *Programa del Gobierno Obrero y Campesino. Plataforma de Lucha del Partido Comunista de España en las elecciones legislativas de 1933* (Madrid, 1933).

6. E. Castro Delgado, *Hombres made in Moscú* (Barcelona, 1965), p. 174.

7. A. Bronces, *Conquistamos las masas! La acentuación de la crisis revolucionaria en España y las tareas del Partido Comunista* (Barcelona, 1934).

8. M. Tagüeña Lacorte, *Testimonio de dos guerras* (Barcelona, 1978), p. 34; J. A. Balbontín, *La España de mi experiencia* (Mexico, 1952), pp. 262–80

9. *La Lucha* 6 March 1934 (emphasis in the original).

10. Dolores Ibarruri expressed disquiet at Balbontín's expulsion, which José Díaz further justified to the ECCI on the grounds that he had been in contact with one of the ousted former leaders, Gabriel León Trilla. See A. Elorza and M. Bizcarrondo, *Queridos camaradas*, p. 210.

11. Reconstructing party membership with any accuracy is difficult: partly because records survive only on a haphazard basis or are impressionistic reports, but also because of doubts over their basic veracity – the PCE was often accused of massaging its membership figures upwards. The following should, therefore, be treated as a trend rather than a reliable expression of reality:

1927	500
1928	1,500
June 1929	1,300
Dec. 1930	1,500
Mid-1931	7,810
March 1932	9,573
July 1932	16,200
March 1933	19,489 (plus 11,275 in the Communist Youth)
Mid-1934	c. 20,000

'Statistics of the Spanish Communist Party', Rossiiskii Gosudarstvennyi Arkhiv Sotsial'no-politicheskoi Istorii (henceforth RGASPI) 495/25/615; 'Situación de la organización del Partido Comunista en España', Archivo del Partido Comunista de España (henceforth APCE), Carpeta 12; 'Report of the Spanish Delegation' RGASPI 495/32/124a; 'Report of the Spanish Delegation' RGASPI 495/32/144; R. Cruz, *El Partido*, pp. 56–62.

12. 'A la Comisión Ejecutiva del Partido Socialista: A todas las organizaciones y obreros socialistas', *Mundo Obrero*, 23 July 1934. Minutes of meetings with the Roman Land Secretariat are to be found in RGASPI 495/32/144. Resolutions and letters to the party from ECCI are in Protokol No. 394 der Sitzung des Politische Kommission des Sekretariats des EKKI am. (SPKS) 11 August 1934; SPKS 397 27 August 1934; SPKS 398

3 September 1934; SPKS 402 15 September 1934 to be found in RGASPI 495/4. The text of party's announcement is in 'Resolución del Comité Central extraordinario del PCE de España (sección de la IC) sobre la participación en las Alianzas Obreras' APCE Carpeta 15, published in *Mundo Obrero* 17 September 1934.

13. Díaz's speech prefigured the Comintern's adoption of the Popular Front in September 1935. The formal launch of the PCE's Popular Front line came with another speech (in yet another cinema) in November. See J. Díaz, *El VII Congreso de la Internacional Comunista y su repercussion en España* (Barcelona, 1935).

14. J. Bullejos, *La Comintern*, p. 209. See also the comments of J. A. Balbontín, *La España*, pp. 361–62.

15. In general, see R. Cruz, *El Partido*, pp. 236–56. On the formation of the JSU, see R. Viñas, *La formación de las Juventudies Socialistas Unificadas, 1934–36* (Madrid, 1978); M. Moreno, *Abono inagotable. Historia del PCC 1932–36* (Barcelona, 1997); J. L. Martín i Ramos, *Els origins del Partit Socialista Unificat de Catalunya 1930–36* (Barcelona, 1977); J. P. Farràs, *Nosaltres les comunistes Catalans: el PSUC i la Internacional Comunista durant la Guerra Civil* (Barcelona, 2001).

16. S. Carrillo, *Memorias* (Barcelona, 1993), p. 14.

17. See B. Lazitch and M. Drachkovitch, *Biographical Dictionary of the Comintern* (Stanford, 1986), pp. 77–78.

18. The PCE was finally created in November 1921 with the fusion of two communist factions that had split from the PSOE, the Partido Comunista Obrero and the Partido Comunista Español. See J. A. Farré, *La fe que vino de Rusia. La revolución bolchevique y los españoless, 1917–31* (Madrid, 1999), especially pp. 259–67; G. Meaker, *The Revolutionary Left in Spain, 1914–23* (Stanford, 1974).

19. See F. E. Sebares, 'El PCE en Asturias, de los orígenes a la Guerra Civil', in V. Burgos et al. (eds), *Los comunistas en Asturias, 1920–82* (Gijón, 1996), pp. 41–51.

20. See A. Durgan, 'The Catalan Federation and the International Communist Movement', in *Centenaire Jules Humbert-Droz: Colloque sur l'Internationale Communiste: Actes* (Geneva, 1992), pp. 279–82; J. Bullejos, *La Comintern*, pp. 58–59.

21. On the campaign against Maurín, see Y. Riottot, *Joaquín Maurín: de l'anarcho-syndicalisme au communisme, 1919-1936* (Paris, 1997), pp. 104-34.

22 'Resolución del Secretariado Político del CEIC, 18 May 1928', APCE Carpeta 9.

23. A. Durgan, 'The Catalan Federation', pp. 282-3

24. See A. Elorza and M. Bizcarrondo, *Queridos camaradas*, pp. 53–57.

25. It was in the aftermath of these strikes that Bullejos was arrested. See J. Bullejos, *La Comintern*, pp. 87–90; A. Elorza and M. Bizcarrondo, *Queridos camaradas*, pp. 57–58.

26. J. Bullejos, *La Comintern*, p. 63.

27. J. Bullejos, *La Comintern*, p. 79.

28. On the continued factional struggle, see A. Elorza and M. Bizcarrondo, *Queridos camaradas*, pp. 60–78; A. Durgan, 'The Catalan Federation', pp. 283–86. E. Sebares, 'El PCE en Asturias', pp. 51–53, gives an Asturian perspective. Maurín rejected the offer to travel to Moscow for fear that this was a device to detain him.

29. Report to Presidium of ECCI quoted in A. Durgan, 'The Catalan Federation', p. 286. See also A. Durgan, *B.O.C*, pp. 52–53. The only open denunciations of Comintern and its 'line' at this time came from Andreu Nin, who returned to Spain in 1930 after his release from house arrest in Moscow.

30. Quoted in A. Durgan, 'The Catalan Federation', p. 284.

31. J. A. Balbontín, *La España*, p. 273.

32. M. Tagüeña Lacorte, *Testimonio*, p. 33.

33. *Mundo Obrero* replaced *La Antorcha*. In Asturias a regional paper, *El Obrero Astur*, also appeared in January 1930. See R. Cruz, *El Partido*, pp. 67–68; R. Cruz, 'La prensa del PCE en la II República', in M. Tuñon de Lara (Ed.), *La prensa de los siglos XIX y XX* (Bilbao, 1986), pp. 263–77; G. Santallano, 'La prensa comunista en Asturias, 1918–75', V. Burgos et al. *Los Comunistas*, pp. 227–33.

34. On the organisation of the party, see R. Cruz, 'La organización del PCE (1920–36)' *Estudios de Historia Social*, No. 31 (1984) and the guide, written by a former party member for anti-communist purposes: E. Matorras, *El comunismo en España* (Madrid, 1935), pp. 7–13. Factory cells were a non-starter as they required a workplace to have a group of at least three party members present, and this was rarely the case in Spain at this time.

35. A. Elorza and M. Bizcarrondo, *Queridos camaradas*, p. 116 gives a very useful summary. See also J. Humbert Droz, *De Leniné a Staline: Dix ans au service de l'internationale communiste, 1921-1931* Neuchatel, 1971), pp. 403–57 and J. Bullejos, *La Comintern*, pp. 101–3.

36. Reports are in RGASPI 495/3/various

37. J. Bullejos, *La Comintern*, p. 100.

38. 'Theses of the Eleventh ECCI Plenum, March–April 1931' in J. Degras (Ed.), *The Communist International 1919–43: Documents Vol. III* (London, 1971), p. 160.

39. 'Letter to the PCE concerning the syndical question', RGASPI 495/32/43

40. See, for example, Trilla's comments to a meeting of the RLS, 'Reunion of the Secretariat, 2 January 1931', RGASPI 495/32/74.

41. Roman Land Secretariat (RLS), 'Reunion of the Secretariat, 22 February 1931' RGASPI 495/32/74.

42. C. Delgado, *Hombres made in Moscu*, pp. 102–4.

43. Radio de Madrid, 'Acta del 1 July 1931', APCE Carpeta 12.

44. R. Cruz, *El Partido*, pp. 156–57. A. Elorza and M. Bizcarrondo, *Queridos camaradas*, pp. 143–69 provides a detailed analysis.

45. See 'Spanish Question' RGASPI 495/32/76'; 'Protokoll 108: Sitzung des Politsekretariats des EKKI, 19 May 1931' RGASPI 495/3/262: SPKS 44, RGASPI 495/4/179

46. 'Extracts From a Letter From the West European Bureau of the ECCI to the Spanish Communist Party', in J. Degras, *The Communist International*, p. 185 and *passim.*

47. See J. Humbert Droz, *De Leniné a Staline*, pp. 420–21 and J. Bullejos, *La Comintern*, pp. 159–60.

48. 'Protokoll 121: Sitzung des Politsekretariats des EKKI, 21 October 1931' RGASPI 495/3/291

49. 'Reunión del BP del 17 de agosto de 1932', 'Reunión del BP del 18 de agosto de 1932' APCE carpeta 13.

50. 'Reunión del BP del 5-6 de octubre de 1932' APCE; 'Protokoll 53: Sitzung des Präsidium, 31 October 1932' RGASPI 495/2/165; 'Announcement of the ECCI to the Spanish Communists of the Exclusion of Seveal Opportunists' RGASPI 495/32/208. For Bullejos' own account, see J. Bullejos, *La Comintern*, pp. 197-206.

51. 'Extracts From an ECCI Manifesto to the Workers, Peasants, and Communists of Spain' in J. Degras, *The Communist International*, pp. 244–46.

52. *La Lucha por la bolchevización del Partido* (Madrid, 1932). See also A. Elorza and M. Bizcarrondo, *Queridos camaradas*, pp. 169–71.

53. The original reply is at: 'Autocrítica de Dolores Ibarruri, Nov. 1932'APCE Carpeta 13. See also R. Cruz, *El Partido*, pp. 83–84 for other examples.

54. See R. Cruz, 'La organización del PCE (1920–36)'.

55. See, for example, the PCE pamphlet, *Tareas de organización* (Madrid, 1933) setting out the tasks of the party.

56. For some insight into the clandestine side of the party see the study of one of the ECCI's 'illegal' agents: D. Ginard I Féron, *Heriberto Quiñones y el movimiento comunista en España, 1931–42* (Palma, 2000).

57. E. Sebares, 'El PCE en Asturias', p. 58, makes a strong case for this point.

58. There was actually a shift in membership away from the heavy industrial area of the north towards the south. For example, see the figures for regions given in 'Situación de la organización del Partido Comunista en España' APCE Carpeta 12.

59. M. Tagüeña Lacorte, *Testimonio*, p. 34; A. Elorza and M. Bizcarrondo, *Queridos camaradas*, p. 182.

60. M. Tagüeña Lacorte, *Testimonio*, p. 34.

61. See J. A. Balbontín, *La España*, pp. 271–72. The minutes of an ECCI political commission meeting of 15 October 1933 make clear this rejection of Balbontín as 'an intellectual not a worker': RGASPI 495/3/339

62. 'Situación de la organización del Partido Comunista en España' APCE Carpeta 12.

63. R. Cruz, *Pasionaria: Dolores Ibarruri, historia y símbolo* (Madrid, 1999) is excellent on this aspect of her career. For a local example, see F. Erice Sebares, 'Mujeres comunistas. La militancia feminine en el comunismo asturiano, de los orígenes al final del franquismo', in V. Burgos et al., *Los comunistas*, p. 319.

64. J. Degras, *The Communist International*, p. 293 and 'Papers of the Spanish Commission' RGASPI 495/60/232

65. Much of the delay was due to the process of clarification that took place between the Political Secretariat of the ECCI and the Roman Land Secretariat. See Protokoll No. 402 SPKS 15 September 1934 RGASPI 495/4 for the final authorised telegram. This actually arrived too late to influence the PCE's own announcement.

66. For example, see Codovilla's report to the RLS on the state of affairs in Spain after October 1934, in which he attacked the 'sabotage of the socialists' and the 'treason of the anarchists': 'Report to the Roman Land Secretariat', 29 January 1935, RGASPI 495/32/165. The Comintern's proposal for joint action with the Socialist International is reproduced in J. Degras, *The Communist International*, pp. 328–31.

67. See *Outline History of the Communist International* (Moscow, 1971), pp. 415–16; M. T. Meshcheryakov, 'Kommunisticheskaya Partiya Ispanii', pp. 19–20.

A Final Stab at Insurrection: The American Communist Party, 1928–34

JAMES RYAN

The Communist Party of the United States (CPUSA) probably included no more than 90,000 members at any given moment, though several times that number moved through its ranks, as hotel patrons might use a revolving door. The party never elected to Congress anyone willing to admit to the name while in office.[1] In the CPUSA's greatest ballot-box achievement, it placed two members on New York's City Council through a since discarded vote-counting method seldom employed in English-speaking nations.[2] In the labour and cultural fields, communists achieved influence far beyond their numbers before the 1950s. Yet, rising anti-communism, which swept the nation during the early Cold War years, drove them out of both areas.

If American communism seemed an oxymoron to most of the twentieth century public, it has nevertheless fascinated scholars. Two tsunamis of CPUSA historiography have crashed across the nation's intellectual shores since about 1975. The first, produced largely by the so-called 'revisionists', sought to refute an earlier, less-prolific school of 'traditionalists' hostile to communism. Revisionists insisted that the CPUSA had been an indigenous, legitimate and democratic participant on the political left. Fraser Ottanelli, writing in 1991, characterised the party as a 'diverse and adaptable organisation rooted in the social and labor struggles' of its era, 'capable of adjusting to the complexity and historical peculiarity of the nation's society'.[3] When Ottanelli's book appeared, revisionist scholarship dominated the field almost totally through literally hundreds of books, articles and dissertations. However, a second great wave inundated America's literary coast after the Soviet archives opened in 1992. Ever since, sensational stories about CPUSA ties to Russian espionage have flooded stateside bookshops and reading rooms. The National Security Agency (NSA) and the Central Intelligence Agency (CIA) have added to the deluge by releasing decryptions of approximately 2,900 Soviet spy cables, which had been intercepted during the Second World War.[4] Known as the Venona project, they complemented the Moscow material and reinvigorated the outnumbered traditionalists. Given the archival page-count, which runs to the millions, there is every reason to expect additional revelations and continued controversy. In 2002, a new, refereed journal, *American Communist History*, appeared. Because its editorial board is balanced between both groups, and includes scholars of communist history from other lands, CPUSA studies will almost certainly continue to flourish.

Surprisingly, neither revisionists nor traditionalists have focused great attention on the party's Third Period. Many revisionist accounts, seeking to legitimise the CPUSA's legacy, have concentrated disproportionately on the party's Popular Front years, 1935 to 1939. Studies by traditionalists, a group especially interested in communist clandestine activities, have also focused on a later era. As Harvey Klehr, John Earl Haynes and Fridrikh Igorevich Firsov have noted, 'during the 1920s, the party had an underground but, upset by vicious internal battles, it did not systematically maintain its covert apparatus'.[5] Revitalising it would consume much of the 1930s.

The Third Period years, 1928 to 1934, brought neither happiness nor success for the CPUSA, but they were also to be amongst the party's most exciting. They made up a confused, troubled time, when spectacular direct action in the streets came more readily than thoughtful analysis. The party was never so clearly Leninist, proclaiming the need for capitalism's violent overthrow in virtually every publication. Espionage did not yet play a significant role in the CPUSA's tasks. Taken generally, the era saw both the party's near death and resuscitation. Gradual abandonment of Third Period policies led directly to the Popular Front and the CPUSA's greatest impact on American life. A concise inquiry into the Third Period should address several questions. Exactly why did the CPUSA adopt a revolutionary line in 1928? What specifically did Third Period policies entail? How did the party come to abandon the era's militancy? What legacy, if any, did the experience of these years leave for American communists?

The American party's Third Period policies appeared in the wake of a worldwide process known as 'Bolshevisation'. Kevin McDermott and Jeremy Agnew have defined the term as pertaining to the Soviet domination of the Communist International (Comintern) and its member sections, to the 'Russification' of its ideological and organisational structures, and to the 'canonisation of the Leninist principles of party unity, discipline and democratic centralism'.[6] By 1925, the Comintern had issued mandatory regulations for all member parties, based on the structure of that in the USSR. Specifically, 'shop branches' or 'factory cells' were to replace neighbourhood nuclei as the basic organisational unit. Members had to form 'communist fractions' within reformist trade unions and other non-party bodies. In the Soviet Union, Joseph Stalin had begun listing enemies; he would go on to first isolate and later criminalize them. His initial ally (and then president of the Comintern), Grigori Zinoviev, had made clear the price of unity at the Comintern's fifth world congress the previous summer: 'we must root out all the remains and survivals of social democratism [sic], federalism, "autonomy", etc.'[7]

McDermott and Agnew argue persuasively that Stalin feared 'the tendency among certain, generally leftist, European communists to draw a distinction between an orthodox Marxism' applicable to western countries and 'a separate Leninism, rooted in the realities of a backward, peasant Russia'.[8] Bolshevisation won easy support within the Comintern. Rapid socialist construction in the USSR and a leftist line 'appealed to impatient and ambitious communist activists', while Stalin was 'arguably more in tune with significant sections of communist rank-and-file opinion than his opponents'. Within various national parties, Bolshevisation met acceptance (eager or reluctant) because of: the Soviet's successful revolution; the tendency towards bureaucratisation in modern organisations; the expanding role of the state that seemed to confirm the central propensities of Marxism–Leninism; and anti-communist assaults on the working class and its institutions.[9] In the United States, Bolshevisation sought also to 'Americanize' the party by destroying the foreign-language federations to which most communists belonged. Klehr and Haynes show that as a direct result, membership dropped from 16,325 in early 1925 to only 7,213 in October. From here to 1930, and despite recruitment, the party ranks remained thin, averaging only 9,000 to 10,000 members. Even so, this costly change did not alter the movement's social fabric, because of the immigrants' residential patterns. 'In a practical sense', most members remained in neighbourhood clubs, rather than shop branches, and many of the former 'tended to be foreign-language clubs in all but name'.[10]

If Bolshevisation legitimised and facilitated the handing down of a revolutionary agenda from above, it was not the lone factor in setting Third Period priorities. At the Comintern's sixth world congress in 1928, theoreticians announced that capitalism's final crisis was at hand. Long exploited workers were about to break their chains and create a socialist society. In response, communists needed to organise the unorganised into 'revolutionary' industrial unions that would strike for demands that, if met, would fatally weaken capitalism. Where this directive meant competing with social democratic or reformist organisations, a 'dual union' policy was necessary. Around the world, ruling elites would try to divert proletarian energies toward imperialist wars. Foreign intervention against the USSR was deemed a distinct possibility.

For years, many American Marxists had resented the appearance of V. I. Lenin's 1920 pamphlet, *Left-Wing Communism: An Infantile Disorder*. It had brought the first historic change of Comintern direction, turning comrades away from the barricades and toward election campaigns and work within existing 'reactionary' trade unions. For many such members who had not abandoned the movement, the Third Period meant redemption. More important, after the stock market crashed during the autumn of 1929, the Comintern's prophesy seemed accurate. American business greed had brought on the Great Depression; unemployment would soon reach a record level nearing twenty-five per cent. The economy would not return to health until the United States mobilised fully for the Second World War in 1942. As the long relief lines of dreary, jobless workers began to fill sidewalks and stretch around corners, never did Stalin seem so prescient. He would not remain relatively unknown among Americans for long.

And yet, McDermott and Agnew have emphasised a crucial aspect of the Third Period that few communists in the United States ever paused to consider. In the final analysis, the Comintern served Soviet foreign policy: 'peace was the overriding aim of the rapidly industrialising USSR'. The 'revolutionary bombast' of official publications did not necessarily reflect the organisation's 'fundamentally cautious, Russo-centric' goals. Except in China, 'no violent uprisings occurred; none were ever planned'. Stalin relied on Soviet diplomacy to sooth relations with foreign governments and, therefore, he 'and his immediate entourage can be accused of manipulating the Comintern and abusing the loyalty of hundreds of thousands of communists worldwide'. The rank-and-file, it appeared, 'sincerely believed in the Third Period's revolutionary postulates'.[11] Before 1932, certainly, no prominent CPUSA figure displayed public reluctance to march on city halls or to battle with police in the streets.

Loyal Only to the Comintern

Bolshevisation helped rid the party of internecine warfare. For much of the 1920s, factional intrigue had been a major pastime for the CPUSA leadership. It had contributed mightily to the movement's apparent irrelevance. When general secretary Charles Ruthenberg died suddenly in March 1927, two competing groups took their quarrels to Moscow. The winner was the group led by Jay Lovestone, a quick-witted graduate of City College who had abandoned New York University Law School in 1919 to pursue the revolution.[12] Like his chief rivals, Lovestone had been to the Soviet capital many times. Through earlier trips, he had developed a friendship with Nikolai Bukharin, who by 1927 headed the Comintern. But although Lovestone is often associated with 'American exceptionalism' – the doctrine that Marxist principles of history do not apply to the United States – Klehr and Haynes have noted that 'Lovestone, Leninist that he was, never held such a view. He did, however, hold that American capitalism had characteristics that required tactics different from those appropriate to Europe'. Lovestone argued that the US economy faced an 'unavoidable crisis', but he assigned this to an indefinite future decade.[13]

Bukharin shared this view, and both would soon be considered part of world communism's 'right-wing', as the term was then understood. Earlier, Bukharin had helped destroy the careers of Stalin's 'leftist' Russian opponents; Leon Trotsky and former Stalin ally Grigori Zinoviev among them. When the emerging dictator turned on Bukharin in 1928, however,

Lovestone's days were numbered.[14] In early 1929, Moscow ordered that Lovestone be removed from his position as CPUSA general secretary, despite the fact that he had already taken the precaution of denouncing his friend Bukharin. The Comintern assigned Lovestone a post overseas. But although foreign service would later bring great career rewards to both Earl Browder and Eugene Dennis, he spurned the offer. The Executive Committee of the Communist International (ECCI) then mandated that his replacement be William Z. Foster, only for the CPUSA's convention to defy the Russians by choosing Benjamin Gitlow, a 'Lovestoneite', as new leader and packing the party committees with persons of similar outlook. Again, ranking members of left and right wing factions sailed to the USSR seeking vindication. A special commission, attended by Stalin himself, accused Lovestone of responding to national circumstances rather than following the International line. This, of course, constituted a right-wing ideological deviation. In May, Gitlow read aloud a statement rejecting Soviet guidance. Written by the Lovestoneites, it pointed to their overwhelming majority in the CPUSA. In angry response, Stalin declared that when they reached home only their wives and girlfriends would support them.[15]

Lovestone, hedging his bets, cabled friends Robert Minor and Jack Stachel in the US to transfer party assets to private bank accounts.[16] Instead, the two recognised the order as a rebellion against Moscow and the Lovestoneites returned to New York to find their majority had vanished, just as Stalin had predicted. In June, the CPUSA expelled Lovestone and his closest cohorts. About 200 followers joined them to form a short-lived splinter group, the Communist Party (Majority Group), later called the Communist Party (Opposition), and after that the Independent Labor League of America. It toiled in obscurity for about a decade before disbanding. Like James P. Cannon, who was expelled from the CPUSA with others for supporting Trotsky in 1928, the expelled Lovestoneites could never begin to compete with the CPUSA for influence.[17] As Granville Hicks has suggested, American radicals during the depression neither understood nor cared about fine points of doctrine; to them it was enough that 'Marxism was in general right and the communist party was in general Marxist'.[18]

No American had stronger claim to CPUSA leadership than Lovestone's factional rival, William Z. Foster. The latter, who had organised Chicago's packinghouse workers and led 1919's Great Steel Strike, stands among the giants in the history of the American left. Foster, rated by biographer James R. Barrett as a working class genius, 'was every bit as cosmopolitan and sophisticated as the corporate strategists he loved to battle'. Another biographer, Edward P. Johanningsmeier, has described Foster as having 'an obstinate revolutionary temperament, unadorned by complex ideological convictions, and only lightly constrained by legal or political convention'. Indeed, had US communists selected their leader in democratic fashion, clearly they would have chosen Foster, who was 'driven by a deeply held hostility to many of the central assumptions of American politics and economic life'.[19] Foster, however, had dragged his feet on the Third Period's switch to dual unionism. Of even greater significance, Stalin, who had engineered Lovestone's removal, 'had become violently critical of American factional struggles'. Accordingly, he now 'sought to weld together a monolithic party loyal only to the Kremlin'.[20] From 1929 until 1932, a collective leadership headed the CPUSA. Its membership changed on two different occasions, a fact the party took its time in publicising. For all except eight months of the era it included Foster, and it always contained someone from the old Lovestone faction. After October 1929, it also included Earl Russell Browder.

Browder had actually recruited Foster to the CPUSA in 1921, and had then spent the decade as his assistant. Browder's quiet demeanour and modest credentials (though a veteran of numerous left-wing movements, he had never led a strike) caused nearly everyone to underestimate both his talents and ambitions. Once considered the party's best-known playboy, Browder had since married a well-connected Moscow figure, Raissa Berkmann Luganovskaya, and undertaken covert Comintern work in China.[21] Significantly, perhaps, he resented Foster deeply.

Land of the Free, Home of the Breadline

Only months after Lovestone's dismissal, the Wall Street crash made possible the CPUSA's most spectacular mass success: riveting the nation's attention on the plight of the jobless. Arguably, nothing the CPUSA did during the Third Period brought so much favourable publicity. Although the policy was mandated in Moscow, it tapped the talents and courage of party rank-and-filers across urban America.

In February 1930, when few seemed ready to discuss the issue of unemployment, the CPUSA dramatised it boldly. In consecutive weeks, protesters descended on city halls in Cleveland, Philadelphia, Los Angeles and New York, demanding social security and weekly grocery bags. Except in Cleveland, police dispersed them brutally. Then, on 6 March, the communists held an international 'unemployment day', staging demonstrations in major industrial nations. Alarmist accounts in right-wing newspapers aided the efforts unwittingly. Without incident, the event drew thousands of peaceful demonstrators in Chicago and Philadelphia. Elsewhere, mounted lawmen used clubs to disperse parades of 1,500 (Milwaukee), 4,000 (Boston) and 75,000 (Detroit). In New York's Union Square, William Z. Foster, Israel Amter and Sam Darcy told 35,000 unemployed workers to take their demands to Mayor Jimmy Walker en masse. As a result, the city experienced, according to Irving Bernstein, its 'worst street riot in generations'.[22]

Human blood on the pavement made joblessness front-page news. There it remained; Republican President Herbert Hoover's economic dogmas precluded effective relief measures. With great fanfare and on Independence Day that summer, the CPUSA created a National Council for the Unemployed to demand such measures anyway. Local chapters conducted rent strikes and fought evictions; idled workers broke locks and returned victims belongings to their apartments. The communists, seeking lasting influence, created a series of Unemployed Councils. By August, the party had articulated a specific plan to fight the depression. Known as the Workers' Unemployment Insurance Bill, it demanded a direct government payment of $25 per week plus $5 per dependent. Funding would come through taxes on high incomes and accumulated wealth. In a nation that lacked any social security system, the proposal made potent propaganda. National hunger marches on Washington DC in November 1931 and December 1932, as Klehr and Haynes have noted, helped establish 'the communist party as the boldest and most visible' of capitalism's opponents. The authorities' 'exaggerated, often times frenetic rhetoric and responses' enhanced the CPUSA's credibility. 'Some Americans, looking for ways to protest against the deepening misery', regarded the organisation as 'the only or the most effective option.'[23]

For Industrial Democracy

The party's labour activities during the early depression years proved less successful, but equally dramatic. Its record of organising unorganised, or non-union, workers predated the Third Period. Back in 1925, for instance, a dynamic young leader named Albert Weisbord led a strike of 16,000 textile workers at mills in Passaic, New Jersey. His 'united front committee' brought together 'workers largely immigrant and perhaps half female', all of whom were ignored by the crafts-oriented American Federation of Labor (AFL). When 'mill owners and police reacted with violence, brutal harassment and an adamant refusal to negotiate', the strike attracted widespread public sympathy. The Comintern, however, considered the united front committee a dual union, and pushed the CPUSA into surrendering Weisbord's organisation to a weaker AFL rival.[24]

Third Period strategy encouraged dual unionism, however. Domestic communists created the Trade Union Unity League (TUUL) and applied the New Line vigorously. Between 1929 and 1932, they led 10,000 'textile workers off their jobs in Lawrence, Massachusetts'. Their National Miners' Union (NMU), 'under William Z. Foster's personal supervision, directed a western Pennsylvania strike of 40,000'. Other NMU organisers 'stirred up 3,000 in Harlan County, Kentucky, one of the nation's poorest and most repressive areas'. With some hyperbole, the CPUSA told Moscow that it had headed one-third of America's strikes in 1931. But although spectacular, the walkouts were ineffective. 'Only the Needle Trades Industrial Union enjoyed success, but it enrolled a mere fraction' of those organised by competing unions.[25] In 1933, the new Democratic Congress enacted the National Industrial Recovery Act (NIRA). Its Section 7A gave millions of American workers collective bargaining rights. That year a TUUL affiliate, the Cannery and Agricultural Workers' Industrial Union (CAWIU) conducted a series of strikes in California, attracted 10,000 members, and inspired novelist John Steinbeck to write *The Grapes of Wrath* and *In Dubious Battles*. In 1934, four major industrial confrontations spread fear of class warfare across the land. In one, a clandestine communist, Harry Bridges, led a west coast maritime walkout that mushroomed into a brief general strike of 100,000 workers. But although TUUL numbers grew, new independent unions suddenly appeared and quickly surpassed communist labour organisations in size. Even the complacent AFL enjoyed a resurgence at this time. The NIRA had persuaded a whole generation of American workers that unions were not unpatriotic.

Meanwhile, by December 1934, the Comintern had become interested in a united front with other progressive forces. Upon its mere suggestion, the CPUSA disbanded the TUUL and sent members toward AFL unions.[26] In March 1935, the TUUL ceased to exist. Although a failure, it left a heroic legacy. As James R. Green has noted, its 'unions had fought on bravely for four years against the most brutal kind of anti-union violence, and they had kept the banner of militant industrial unionism waving'.[27] They also provided valuable experience for organisers who would build the Congress of Industrial Organizations (CIO) later in the decade.

Protecting the 'Darker Comrade'[28]

During the Third Period, American communists also addressed the nation's most-painful issue: race. More than two decades before the modern civil rights movement, they proudly labelled themselves the 'Negro party', and nominated African-American James W. Ford as CPUSA vice-presidential candidate in 1932. In an age when few progressive organisations in the US were willing to attack segregation, the CPUSA paraded 'southern justice' before a world audience. Members championed the cause of Angelo Herndon, a youthful black organiser sentenced to eighteen years imprisonment by an all-white jury under an antebellum Georgia insurrection law. On 29 June 1932, Herndon had put together a demonstration of nearly a thousand unemployed Atlanta workers. They had descended on the Fulton County Courthouse demanding immediate relief without racial discrimination. The influential journal *New Republic* opined that Herndon's sentence virtually proved communist charges about 'capitalist-ruled courts in the Deep South and elsewhere'. In scholarly tones, Charles H. Martin has expressed similar sentiment. 'The fact that it took five long years to establish what should have been obvious from the beginning – Herndon's innocence

– was hardly a stirring endorsement of the southern and American legal systems.'[29] A case that had begun fifteen months earlier, known simply as 'Scottsboro', brought far more national attention, however. Mark Solomon has noted that it 'reverberated throughout the decade, re-energizing the movement for equality, highlighting the issue of African-Americans and communism, and focusing attention on racial oppression to an extent not seen' since the Civil War.[30]

As egregious as Herndon's plight was, it could not rival an affair revolving around charges of interracial gang rape. On 25 March 1931, nine black hobo youths (only one, Charlie Weems, was no longer in his teens) were arrested at Paint Rock, Alabama. First brought to trial in nearby Scottsboro, they were accused of attacking two white female travellers aboard a moving freight train. Supposedly, the assaults took place in a gondola (a high-sided roofless car) filled to within eighteen inches of the top with chert (a coarse gravel used for ballast). The two women, Victoria Price and Ruby Bates, were unemployed textile mill hands who lived in Huntsville and supplemented their meagre wages through colour-blind prostitution. As Dan Carter has noted, the white trial lawyer who first defended the 'Scottsboro boys' possessed two notable character flaws: lying and drinking. 'In neither case did he seem to be able to stop once he had started.'[31] Abundant physical evidence virtually disproved the prosecution's case. Yet, the defendants appeared before a jury of Caucasian males, in a county where many locals 'agreed with the character in the Irvin Cobb story who thought a Negro rapist hanged and burned by a mob "got off awful light"'. An Alabama newspaper later proclaimed 'the honor of one white woman was more important than the life's blood of a black man'.[32] In the event, all defendants were convicted and sentenced to death in a noisy courtroom shielded by armed national guardsmen from an angry mob of 10,000 outside. The state continued to insist on executing the Scottsboro boys, although one defendant, Olen Montgomery, was virtually blind; another, Willie Roberson, had advanced syphilis and gonorrhoea; and one supposed victim, Ruby Bates, recanted her accusations and testified for the defence in subsequent proceedings.[33]

The CPUSA through its affiliate, International Labor Defense (ILD), indicted the Jim Crow-era legal system before public opinion. The *Daily Worker* denounced the National Association for the Advancement of Colored People (NAACP) for failing to take a militant stance against white Southerners who would sanction the death sentence on the testimony of two 'cut-rate whores'. In so doing, the party exposed the feeling among 'moderate' and 'enlightened' white Alabamians, who considered life imprisonment 'an acceptable compromise'. The ILD and its sister organisation, Red Aid, sent Ada Wright, mother of defendants Roy and Andy Wright, on a speaking tour of Europe. According to the CPUSA's

Louis Engdahl, who accompanied her for much of the trip, she traversed sixteen countries in six months, inspiring nearly two hundred meetings and demonstrations, in which 'nearly half a million people took part'. Even if one discounts possible exaggerations, she attracted a 'groundswell of popular support'. As a transatlantic team of historians recently emphasised, she 'broadcast her message from a social democratic radio station' in the Netherlands; and in Belgium, where 'the former president of the Second International, Emile Vandervelde, joined her on the platform.[34] Communist tactics helped prevent the execution of any of the Scottsboro boys and secured the release of four by 1937.[35]

Vote for the Revolution

In contrast to mobilising the jobless and battling for civil rights, communist electoral politics during the Third Period seemed tame. Indeed, given that the 1932 presidential campaign took place during capitalism's most severe crisis to date, they can only be judged a bitter disappointment. In retrospect, one may attribute the failure to an excess of optimism that, as the economy spun into a vortex after 1929, shaded into an impatient and ultimately offensive arrogance. Party political calculations during the era began with reasonable assumptions, though the organisation could have benefited from a public relations lesson. In 1928, the CPUSA recognised the ruling class's apparent health.[36] The communists did not expect to elect governors, representatives or senators. Their campaign was clearly a mass-education publicity vehicle, and considered an investment in a better tomorrow.

Quickly, however, the CPUSA succumbed to sensationalism. In October 1928, screaming *Daily Worker* headlines announced that Benjamin Gitlow, its candidate for vice-president of the United States, had been kidnapped and abandoned in the Arizona desert. On a nationwide speaking tour, he had been last seen in San Diego, California, and had failed to keep speaking engagements in Phoenix, Arizona on the 11th and in Tucson the following day. Even the prestigious *New York Times,* the closest approximation to an American national newspaper, became caught up in the frenzy. It reported that Gitlow had been met at the Phoenix railroad station by American Legion and Ku Klux Klan members and warned to stay on his eastbound train.[37] He surfaced unharmed in Texas on 14 October, where he told reporters that the party's candidate for governor of Arizona had wired him in San Diego cancelling the speaking dates. The *Daily Worker* offered no clarification whatever. Years later, Gitlow blamed the problem on vigilante threats.[38]

Other party campaign incidents and events in 1928 offered less embarrassment. When authorities suppressed party publications in a brief dispute over second-class postal rates, charges of persecution made political capital in a nation already plagued by junk mail. Later, a rally of the Young Pioneers, the communist youth group, highlighted the persistence of child labour.[39] The CPUSA closed the campaign trying to appeal to US workers, but displaying vividly its preoccupation with Soviet superiority. On 3 November, a Saturday, the party welcomed Gitlow and presidential candidate William Z. Foster back to New York. Six thousand participated in a Park Avenue parade that snaked down 25th Street to 4th Avenue and ended with speeches at Union Square. The next day, 12,000 attended a gathering at the famous sports arena, Madison Square Garden, where CPUSA orators hailed the Bolshevik Revolution's eleventh anniversary. An incredulous *Times* reporter noted that 'not a single American flag was visible'. Just the night before, the Democratic presidential candidate – New York Governor Alfred E. Smith – had spoken there. Although Foster sought the very same office as Smith, someone had removed 'thousands of yards' of 'red, white, and blue bunting'. Soviet banners and revolutionary placards appeared everywhere, and some 1,000 of the participants were Young Pioneers in their white blouses and red scarves. Foster's address predicted that the capitalists would attempt to sustain prosperity through imperialist wars. He promised the CPUSA would follow Lenin's dictum to turn them into communist revolutions. A mere 48,000 Americans voted for the party that year.[40]

By the time of the 1932 presidential contest, a quarter of the American workforce was unemployed. Homeless persons, too numerous and transient to count, lived in cardboard and wood shanties called 'Hoovervilles' after the president who had done so little to relieve mass misery, and ate from municipal garbage dumps in every large city. Several million others roamed the vast countryside on an endless search for greener domestic pastures. A small but nonetheless significant number had migrated to the Soviet Union, where work was available.

The CPUSA, expecting to enter the nation's politics in a major way, again nominated Foster. Gitlow, a Lovestoneite, had been expelled, so the CPUSA chose a new running mate, James W. Ford, the grandson of a black lynching victim. The party convention's keynote address, given by rising star Earl Browder, promised to confiscate the industries, banks and railroads 'from the parasite capitalists' who had proven that they did not 'know how to run them'. The proposal presumably would not have bothered many of the unemployed. That same year, however, Foster's most unabashed book, *Toward Soviet America*, announced CPUSA intentions to liquidate 'all the capitalist parties, Republican, Democratic, Progressive, Socialist, etc.' along with the YMCA and 'such fraternal orders as the Masons, Odd Fellows, Elks, [and] Knights of Columbus'. The latter organisations had played an important social role in nineteenth century America, and few workers, especially in small towns, considered them oppressors. For good measure, Foster promised confiscation of church lands. Unlike in parts of Europe, the issue has never been a concern in US politics, and millions of proletarians were religious. Without conscious irony, the candidate proclaimed 'the best of the skyscrapers' would be 'used to house the new government institutions', including the communist party.[41] Evidently, the CPUSA leaders had forgotten that political campaigns needed to persuade as well as educate. *Toward Soviet America* expressed so brazenly partisan a message that it could only appeal to those already convinced. Authorities unwittingly rushed to the communists' aid by briefly jailing Foster on flimsy charges in Los Angeles, California and Lawrence, Massachusetts. Such actions helped persuade the cream of American intellectuals to endorse the Foster–Ford ticket.[42]

On the road, Foster travelled some 17,000 land miles in three months, spoke at seventy meetings from coast to coast, and addressed 200,000 listeners without benefit of modern mass media. A physician diagnosed angina pectoris and predicted a tragedy unless the nominee reduced his activity. Foster promised to comply, but continued the tour scheduled to address thirty-four more rallies in thirteen states plus the nation's capital. At Zeigler, Illinois, fifty armed coal-company goons chased him from the town. On 8 September, he collapsed at Moline while addressing a rally. He insisted on continuing on to Chicago, where he fell again. Immediately, his personal physician termed any further speeches 'absolute suicide'. Biographers report that in addition to a 'severe heart attack', Foster had 'suffered a fairly serious stroke', compounded by 'emotional and psychological problems'. So calamitous were his afflictions that 'it would be nearly three years before he could make a ten-minute speech'.[43] Inspired by Foster's misfortune, rival Browder routed fellow-rival William W. Weinstone before the Comintern in Moscow. The unduly optimistic Russians turned party leadership over to Browder and the now disabled Foster. The latter would play a largely ceremonial role until 1945.

The CPUSA closed the campaign on 6 November 1932 in perfect Third Period style. At the Garden in New York, a capacity-crowd of 20,000 celebrated under red banners bearing a white hammer-and-sickle. Speeches advertised the impending hunger march to be held on 5 December in Washington DC. Foster addressed the rally briefly via telephone from his sickbed in the Bronx. Outside, 3,000 communists – having been denied seats by fire regulations – rioted against the police who guarded the doors. A rainstorm compounded the pandemonium. Although the party's 102,000 votes more than doubled its 1928 total, they paled before the nearly 900,000 received by the Socialist Party (SP). James R. Barrett has summarised CP political efforts concisely: 'The defeat once again measured the limits of the communists' appeal, even in the midst of severe economic and social crisis.'[44]

Natives Replace the Foreign Born

Below the leadership level, the CPUSA's social composition underwent profound changes during the Third Period. Originally a party of Russian, Lithuanian and Ukrainian immigrants, it had seen Finns from the upper-midwest outnumber Slavs by 1923, but never match their influence. By 1932, Jews in big cities held a commanding presence. The party had only about 8,000 total members, but reached 18,000 the following year. As Klehr and Haynes note, the typical communist was 'a white, foreign-born male', aged between thirty and forty, 'and unemployed'. The proportion of immigrants was declining but, by 1935, the jobless membership had risen to fifty-two per cent of the total.[45] Demographics played a role in the rise of Earl Browder to unquestioned leadership in 1932. Indeed, Herbert Romerstein and Eric Breindel have implied that the youthful, photogenic Browder, whose Welsh ancestors had come to America in the seventeenth century, was chosen largely because he was not Jewish. The inference is only partially correct; Moscow also selected Browder because he was not Russian, Latvian or Hungarian. Ethnic considerations do not tell the full story, however. E. H. Carr, telling of an earlier era, pointed out an essential Bolshevik principle that applied in Browder's case: leaders of respective national parties had to be 'not men irrevocably committed to a policy', whether left or right, but figures 'on whose unquestioning loyalty' Comintern authorities 'could count'.[46] Given such reasoning, Browder scored well. His relationship with Raissa Luganovskaya had enabled him to secure a covert Comintern assignment in China during 1927 and 1928. He genuinely admired Stalin; praising him was not mere lip-service.

Browder's subsequent impact on the domestic party is difficult to understate. Between 1932 and 1945, he would lead it to its greatest size and influence. Almost single-handedly, he would popularise a cult-like campaign to link communists to American revolutionary and abolitionist traditions. Through his lieutenants, he would build an extensive Soviet espionage network in the highest Washington circles. All the while, he caused virtually every opponent to overlook or undervalue his abilities.[47]

Conclusion

By late 1934, any thoughtful observer could recognise that Third Period strategy had failed. Although more than 10,000,000 Americans remained unemployed, CPUSA membership had climbed to only 26,000. The bulk of mainstream American workers, products of a culture born in Calvinism and nurtured on Social Darwinism, still frequently internalised their misery. Few who resisted the depression sought revolution. Instead, most of the jobless looked to new President Franklin D. Roosevelt's panoply of relief programs. Concurrently, record numbers of employed workers (inspired by NIRA's

Section 7A) flooded into the reformist unions. Worst of all, from the CPUSA's viewpoint, those most angry did not seek out the party of Browder and Stalin. Instead, colourful demagogues with catchy notions, fuzzy ideologies and creative ways of counting fascinated literally millions of Americans. For instance, Dr. Francis Townsend proposed a wildly generous pension scheme for the aged; radio priest Father Charles Coughlin, who would ultimately express a rabid anti-Semitism, had a different message virtually every week; and senator Huey Long, the most magnetic of all, likened the two major parties to rival snake-oil peddlers. He promised to inflict on the wealthy taxation so progressive as to guarantee every American a home, a job, an automobile, and a radio.

Communism's Third Period doctrine of 'social fascism' taught that socialists constituted the chief barrier to revolution. In the United States, where no strong anti-capitalist tradition existed, the dogma seemed preposterous. The CPUSA was already co-operating with Socialist Party members and other radicals at the local level through May Day activities, the National Committee to Aid Victims of German Fascism, and in other groups that the socialist leadership refused to join formally.[48] Yet, while the CPUSA violated the international line almost every day, it could not, of course, repudiate it.

McDermott and Agnew have argued that abandoning Third Period policies came as a result of a 'triple interaction' of mass agitation 'from below' in numerous national parties; from 'internal debates and initiatives' among 'the Comintern executive' (frequently led by Georgi Dimitrov); and from the Soviet 'quest for security' after Adolf Hitler consolidated his German dictatorship in 1933. As such, the rise of fascism has been seen to have 'provoked a profound crisis of theory and practice' in the world communist movement. For about eighteen months, 'a short-lived moment' in the Comintern's history, Stalin hesitated. During this interlude, his 'ultimate source of authority' was never in question. His steadfast silence, however, hinted at 'a conditional freedom to pilot a new line'.[49] In the US, Browder's conspicuous absence from street confrontations, noticeable and noticed as early as 1930, may have signalled something more basic than a lack of William Z. Foster's physical bravado. It suggests that Browder, with his Moscow contacts and sources, may have realised the era's revolutionary rhetoric did not further Soviet foreign policy interests.

Did the Third Period leave any legacy for American communists? Ever since the first scholarly history of the movement appeared in 1957, writers have condemned the era in the strongest of terms.[50] These years were not, however, a total loss. They taught the CPUSA to abandon forever the language of insurrection in America and to pursue its goals (however positive or negative) through other means. From 1935 to August 1939, the methods would involve a vigorous advocacy of collective security with

Britain and France against Hitler's Germany. From October 1939 until June 1941, the party supported a *de facto* alliance with the Nazis.[51] On one hand, the subsequent German invasion of the USSR brought renewed and stronger ties to the West. At the same time, however, US communists launched a massive espionage offensive against the American government in preparation for the Cold War. From 1945 until the party's demise as a meaningful presence in American life in 1957, it echoed the Soviet Union's every policy shamelessly, while decrying its own persecution by the federal government. Yet, although new strategies brought new mistakes, the CPUSA's Third Period lessons were never gainsaid.

Notes

1. H. Klehr, *The Heyday of American Communism: The Depression Decade* (New York, 1984). Klehr notes that from 1937 to 1939, Farmer–Labor Party member John Toussaint Bernard sat in the House of Representatives. Bernard, probably the only native-born Corsican ever elected to Congress, had been an iron-ore miner on the Mesabi Iron Range and a city fireman in Eveleth, Minnesota. He never admitted to being a communist until he announced his decision to join the party in 1977 at the age of 85. In office, however, he had hired known, open party members to work for him, and had been given to displaying his opera-calibre voice by bursting into the *Internationale* in restaurants (p. 291). John E. Haynes pointed out that while other members of Congress supported pro-communist policies for a time, only Bernard inserted *Daily Worker* articles into the *Congressional Record* – see, J. E. Haynes, *Dubious Alliance: The Making of Minnesota's DFL Party* (Minneapolis, 1984), p. 29.

2. American communist Simon Gerson notes that it was a type of proportional representation (PR), used from 1937 through 1945. Known as the Hare System – a British barrister, Thomas Hare, devised it in the nineteenth century – the form of PR was a simple method for voters to choose candidates in order of preference by numbering them. S. W. Gerson, *Pete: The Story of Peter V. Cacchione, New York's First Communist Councilman* (New York, 1976), p. 61. Cacchione won in 1941, 1943 and 1945, and died in office. African-American communist, Benjamin J. Davis, joined him on the council in 1943, and was re-elected in 1945. See G. Horne, *Black Liberation/Red Scare: Ben Davis and the Communist Party* (Newark, 1994).

3. F. M. Ottanelli, *The Communist Party of the United States: From the Depression to World War II* (New Brunswick, 1991).

4. H. Romerstein and E. Breindel, *The Venona Secrets: Exposing Soviet Espionage and America's Traitors* (Washington, 2000), p. 10.

5. H. Klehr, J. E. Haynes and F. I. Firsov, *The Secret World of American Communism* (New Haven, 1995), p. 73.

6. K. McDermott and J. Agnew, *The Comintern: A History of International Communism from Lenin to Stalin* (Basingstoke, 1996), p. 42.

7. E. H. Carr, *Socialism In One Country, 1924–26*, Vol. 3 (London, 1972), p. 311

8. K. McDermott and J. Agnew, *The Comintern*, p. 64.

9. Ibid. p. 89 and p. 58.

10. H. Klehr and J. E. Haynes, *The American Communist Movement: Storming Heaven Itself* (New York, 1992), p. 54.

11. K. McDermott and J. Agnew, *The Comintern*, p. 96, p. 98 and p. 90.

12. T. Morgan, *A Covert Life: Jay Lovestone, Communist, Anti-communist, and Spymaster* (New York, 1999) pp. 10–16.

13. H. Klehr and J. E. Haynes, *The American Communist Movement*, p. 45.

14. Ibid. pp. 46–47.

15. Ibid. pp. 48–50 and p. 92.

16. Lovestone ally Bertram D. Wolfe was also in Moscow at the time. To weaken the faction, Comintern figure Ossip Piatnitsky, a vigorous Bolsheviser, offered him an assignment with the GPU, a forerunner to the KGB. When the dumbfounded Wolfe asked what could possibly qualify him for covert work, Piatnitsky replied that 'for almost five months you have been sending letters and cables in code to Lovestone in America'. The GPU had handed them to its best experts, but none could crack it. Accordingly, they had developed 'a high opinion' of Wolfe's talents. Theodore Draper has noted that the 'code' was street slang 'likely to be known only to those born and bred in New York City'. B. D. Wolfe, *A Life in Two Centuries: An Autobiography* (New York, 1981), p. 533; T. Draper, *American Communism and Soviet Russia* (New York, 1960), p. 527.

17. H. Klehr and J. E. Haynes, *The American Communist Movement*, p. 92. In the wake of the Comintern's sixth world congress, one American delegate, James P. Cannon, became convinced that Trotsky was Lenin's legitimate ideological heir. Cannon circulated his views and converted about 100 party members. Once the CPUSA leaders heard of the heresy, they expelled the entire group and sacked Cannon's apartment to obtain additional evidence. The Trotskyists subsequently became the Socialist Workers' Party.

18. G. Hicks, 'Communism and the American Intellectual' in I. D. Talmadge (Ed.), *Whose Revolution?* (New York, 1941).

19. J. R. Barrett, *William Z. Foster and the Tragedy of American Radicalism* (Urbana, 1999), p. ix; E. P. Johanningsmeier, *Forging American Communism: The Life of William Z. Foster* (Princeton, 1994), p. 3.

20. J. G. Ryan, *Earl Browder: The Failure of American Communism* (Tuscaloosa, 1997), p. 37.

21. Luganovskaya spelled her first name in this idiosyncratic manner in Roman-alphabet documents. See, '[State] Department's Advisory Opinion, July 17, 1944' and numerous other documents, file Ind./Browder, Mrs. Raissa (Mrs. Earl), (National Archives) Washington DC.

22. *New York Times*, March 7 1930 (the party's *Daily Worker* gave higher figures); I. Bernstein, *The Lean Years* (Boston, 1966), p. 427

23. H. Klehr and J. E. Haynes, *The American Communist Movement*, p. 63.

24. Ibid. p. 44.

25. J. G. Ryan, *Earl Browder*, pp. 42–43.

26. The Fur Workers' Union, led by Ben Gold, proved a notable exception. It was larger than its AFL counterpart.

27. J. R. Green, *The World of the Worker: Labor in Twentieth Century America* (New York, 1980), p. 147.

28. A. Adoff (Ed.), *I Am the Darker Brother: An Anthology of Modern Poems by African Americans* (New York, 1997, revised edition).

29. *New Republic*, 1 February 1933, pp. 308–9; C. H. Martin, *The Angelo Herndon Case and Southern Justice* (Baton Rouge, 1976), p. 210.

30. M. Solomon, *The Cry Was Unity: Communists and African-Americans, 1917–36* (Jackson, 1998), p. 191.

31. D. Carter, *Scottsboro: A Tragedy of the American South* (Baton Rouge and London, 1979, rev. ed.), p. 268, p. 4, pp. 80–85, and p. 75 (quotation).

32. Ibid. p. 7 and p. 134 (quoting *Birmingham Reporter*, 1 April 1933).

33. Ibid. p. 6, p. 451, and pp. 231–34.

34. *Daily Worker*, 1 June 1931; D. Carter, *Scottsboro*, p. 262; J. A. Miller, S. D. Pennybacker and E. Rosenhaft, 'Mother Ada Wright and the International Campaign to Free the Scottsboro Boys, 1931-1934', *American Historical Review*, Vol. 106, No. 2 (2001), p. 409 and pp. 415–16. Engdahl died of pneumonia after he and Mrs. Wright reached Moscow.

35. Far less successful was the Third Period doctrine of 'the right of self-determination of the Negroes in the Black Belt'. According to Theodore Draper, the Comintern defined the area as the 666 southern and border counties in which African-Americans made up more than forty-four per cent of the population. T. Draper, *The Rediscovery of Black Nationalism* (New York, 1970), pp. 63–64. See also M. Solomon, *The Cry Was Unity*, pp. 68–91. Modelled on the Soviet Union's approach to its many subject nationalities, the idea never appealed to many US blacks, most of whom simply sought equal treatment as Americans.

36. During the 1924 presidential campaign, nominee William Z. Foster, returning to New York from the west coast, publicly indicated his surprise that, during a time of alleged prosperity, so many suffered from frequent unemployment. He termed it the 'curse of the worker's life under capitalism'. See *New York Times*, 20 October 1924.

37. *Daily Worker*, 13 October 1928; *New York Times*, 13 October 1928; T. Draper, *American Communism and Soviet Russia*, p. 378.

38. *New York Times*, October 15, 1928; B. Gitlow, *I Confess: The Truth about American Communism* (New York, 1940), pp. 505–06.

39. *New York Times*, 26 and 29 October 1928; *Daily Worker*, 26 and 29 October 1928.

40. *New York Times*, 4 November and 5 November 1928; *Daily Worker*, 4 November 1928. About half of the party members were immigrants, many of whom were legally ineligible to cast ballots.

41. *New York Times*, 29 May 1932; W. Z. Foster, *Toward Soviet America* (New York, 1932), p. 275 and p. 282.

42. *New York Times*, 29 June, 9 August and 12 September 1932.

43. *New York Times*, 15 September 1932; *Daily Worker*, 15 September 1932; J. R. Barrett, *William Z. Foster*, p. 184; E. P. Johanningsmeier, *Forging American Communism*, p. 267.

44. J. G. Ryan, *Earl Browder*, p. 55; *New York Times*, 7 November 1932; J. R. Barrett, *William Z. Foster*, p. 184.

45. H. Klehr and J. E. Haynes, *The American Communist Movement*, p. 45

46. Romerstein and Breindel, in discussing communist anti-Semitism, write 'the Comintern did not like having Jews in the party leadership and, after the "Bolshevization" of the party in 1929, made every effort to replace them with those whom Moscow considered "Americans"'. To the Soviets, 'only a non-Jew like Browder could understand American thinking'. H. Romerstein and E. Breindel, *The Venona Secrets*, p. 391; E. H. Carr, *Socialism in One Country*, p. 317.

47. J. G. Ryan, *Earl Browder*; J. G. Ryan 'Socialist Triumph as a Family Value: Earl Browder and Soviet Espionage', *American Communist History*, Vol. 1, No. 2 (2002).

48. F. M. Ottanelli, *The Communist Party*, pp. 49–80.

49. K. McDermott and J. Agnew, *The Comintern*, p. 129.

50. I. Howe and L. Coser, *The American Communist Party: A Critical History* (Boston, 1957).

51. See F. M. Ottanelli, *The Communist Party*, pp. 182–94; J. G. Ryan, *Earl Browder*, pp. 159–69.

Red or Yellow? Canadian Communists and the 'Long' Third Period, 1927–36

JOHN MANLEY

The evolution of Canada's Third Period can be delineated through edited highlights. I) Spring 1928: Communist Party of Canada (CPC) delegates return from the ninth plenum of the Executive Committee of the Communist International (ECCI) and the fourth congress of the Red International of Labour Unions (RILU) delightedly reporting that Moscow views the CPC as one of the leaders of the struggle for the CI's recently proclaimed New Line. II) December 1928: Stewart Smith, just back in Toronto from two years at the International Lenin School (ILS), tells his first public meeting that an imperialist war is imminent and that the CPC plans to turn it into a civil war; little did complacent Torontonians 'realize that in a very short time the streets in Toronto will be running with blood'. III) November 1929: The CPC's newly installed 'left' leadership loses the first major strike under its 'independent leadership' but describes it as a 'striking vindication of the militant policy of the communist party and the left wing' and a 'precursor of similar and greater mass struggles'. IV) February 1931: Membership, the CPC central committee reports, has halved (from 2,876 to 1,385) in eighteen months. V) November 1931: A desperate battle against 'police terror' climaxes with CPC general secretary Tim Buck and six other political bureau (PB) members handed five-year sentences for membership of an illegal organisation – the CPC. As remaining party leaders pore over manuals on underground work, the 'social fascist' labour movement utters barely a squeak of protest. VI) December 1934: With party membership now exceeding 6,000 (a record), some 17,000 members and sympathisers pack Maple Leaf Gardens to give a hero's welcome to the recently freed Tim Buck.[1]

If we ended our highlights programme at Christmas 1931, we might reasonably conclude that the Canadian experience supports the generalisation that the Third Period had a 'ruinous' impact on international communism.[2] From the perspective of 1934, however, we might well infer that something positive happened to the CPC between 1931–34. Was this because or in spite of the Third Period? Should the negative consensus be revised? This paper seeks to answer these questions.

Domestic Sources of the New Line?

Canada's political economy in 1928 was developing in line with Bukharin's early version of the Third Period, which emphasised that capitalism was in an expansionist phase of indeterminate duration. After recovering slowly from deep recession in 1920–21, Canadian capitalism, concentrated in the Montreal region and southern Ontario, entered a sustained upswing in 1924. By 1928, Canada's grandest industrial corporations, heavily protected and increasingly American-owned, were now recording record levels of production and sales, and cementing worker loyalty with rising wages and elaborate welfare capitalist schemes. The Liberal government assured their access to fresh supplies of labour power by resuming eastern European immigration in 1923 (just as the United States was imposing immigrant quotas). Thanks also to the state's 1925 Railway Agreement, which facilitated expansive recruitment campaigns by Canada's two trans-continental railway companies, 370,000 European workers entered Canada between 1925–31.[3] Their arrival, however, further fragmented a divided and defensive labour movement. Since the petering-out of the post-war 'Canadian Labour Revolt', the unions had lost over 100,000 of the new members recruited between 1916–20; they were almost entirely confined to skilled 'British' or 'Canadian' workers (the terms were often interchangeable), and they had no presence in mass production plants or, except in coal mining, resource industries. They were also divided into three centres: the American Federation of Labor-Trades and Labour Congress of Canada (AFL–TLC), the nationalist All-Canadian Congress of Labour (ACCL), and the Quebec-based *Confédération des travailleurs catholiques du Canada* (CTCC). Only the newest and smallest centre, the ACCL, was friendly to independent labour politics; the oldest and largest, the AFL–TLC, sought Liberal patronage. Canada had only a handful of Independent Labour representatives in the federal parliament and no national, social democratic party.[4]

The CPC was too weak to exploit labourism's political weakness.[5] Proportionate to population (Canada's was 10.4 million in 1931), its 1925 membership of about 4,000–4,500 (though already down on the 1923 figure of 4,808) compared quite favourably with the 5,000 of the British CP or the 16,000 of the American.[6] The CPC, however, was not disproportionately stronger. Though led by skilled Anglo-Celtic immigrants like Scottish general secretary Jack MacDonald and English industrial secretary Tim Buck, it had shallow roots among Anglo-Celtic and French Canadian workers. Between 80–90 per cent of its members were European immigrants working in non-union mass production plants, lumber camps, and coal and metal mining (Finns, for example, comprised about half its membership and Ukrainians about one-fifth). Most were sidelined by the CPC's exclusive orientation on the AFL's craft unions and its use of the united front tactic to transform them into industrial unions – which would *then* organise the unorganised; only Jewish members in the garment and building trades were consistently active trade unionists. With so few members in a position to implement it, the united front failed. Craft unionists quickly rejected the CPC's calls for trade union amalgamation and greater autonomy for the TLC (supposedly less reactionary than the AFL). By 1925, they were acceding to their American headquarters' appeals for a firmer anti-communist stance, although they remained more reluctant than the Americans actually to carry out expulsions. By 1926, demoralisation and exhaustion had caused the CPC's disintegration in such former strongholds as the Cape Breton and Crow's Nest Pass coalfields.[7]

Against this background, the fifth Comintern congress's 'Bolshevisation' directives, ordering affiliated parties to install democratic centralist structures based on workplace cells and locate 'the centre of gravity of work in the midst of the masses in the place of their employment', made tactical sense. Supporters argued that for the party to become entrenched at the point of production, its federal structure of 'language' sections and branches would have to be dissolved and immigrant members drawn out of their ghettoes in party-aligned ethnic associations, such as the Finnish Organization of Canada (FOC) and Ukrainian Labour Farmer Temple Association (ULFTA), where, some sneered, 'singing songs and eating ice cream' substituted for engagement in real struggle. For a variety of reasons, not least the likelihood that a more aggressive workplace role would increase foreign-born workers' vulnerability to unemployment and deportation, ethnic leaders resisted Bolshevisation, forcing a reluctant MacDonald to impose it 1926. There was an immediate haemorrhaging of some 500 Finnish and 300 Ukrainian members.[8]

Meanwhile, the CPC had been so focused on the workplace that it had neglected all other areas of work. Women's work, Joan Sangster notes, was a 'secondary priority'.[9] Children's work was hardly even that (not least because it was usually a part of women's work). The Young Pioneers (YP), for 5–15 year olds, never became a truly national body. Most children's work took place in the ethnic organisations, such as the ULFTA children's sections and the Jewish Labour League *schules*, which gave a strong emphasis to proletarian education and the preservation of national languages and cultures.[10] Cultural work, negatively identified with ethnic opposition to Bolshevisation, received little attention from the party leadership; the CPC began the Third Period without a journal of discussion or a central educational apparatus.

Industrial failure made the party ready for *a* new line.[11] Canada's Third Period might be said to have begun a year early. The mid-1920s had seen several independent *national* unions emerge out of splits from the AFL. The

CPC initially opposed splits. Alberta members, however, were heavily involved in the rank-and-file breakaway from the United Mine Workers of America (UMWA) District 18 that created the Mine Workers' Union of Canada (MWUC) in 1925. Moreover, the new unions tended to explain their actions as an escape from passivity and class collaboration, and invited communists to consider that the logical outcome of their pro-autonomy position was national independence.[12] With the approval of the RILU, the CPC strengthened its national union orientation. When the ACCL was formed in March 1927, the MWUC and Finnish communist-led Lumber Workers' Industrial Union (LWIU) were two of its founder members. The party urged it to make the task of organising the unorganised its 'GREAT work'.[13]

Canadians saw the first version of the official 'new line' as a continuation of existing policy. The party's relationship with the ACCL sharpened international union hostility but diluted the fear of total isolation from the mainstream that initially caused leading communists in other countries to resist the formation of new unions.[14] In conjunction with the ACCL, that summer the CPC made a strong intervention in a strike at General Motors, created 'red' automobile, garment and textile workers' unions, and tried unsuccessfully to persuade the Nova Scotia miners to leave the UMWA for the MWUC. The LWIU, though hostile to any growth of party control, also endorsed a more aggressive line.[15]

From this juncture, Moscow increasingly shaped *the* New Line. Even as the fourth RILU congress rubber-stamped the CPC's industrial policy, the party was digesting Otto Kuusinen's 'Resolution on the Canadian Question', which underlined the Canadians' inability to understand the world historical importance of the international struggle against Trotskyism. 'The ECCI,' Kuusinen warned, 'places on record that by this attitude towards Trotskyism, the [central committee] of our Canadian brother party has completely isolated itself in the communist international.' Although Trotskyism did not exist in Canada, the CPC was put on notice that it would be expected to act promptly if and when any such ideological deformation emerged. Less than a year later, Canada's first group of 'Trotskyites' was expelled.[16]

ECCI reconstruction of the party leadership began after the sixth Comintern congress. Jack MacDonald was Canada's analogue of Heinrich Brandler or Jay Lovestone. Though widely respected in the labour movement and highly popular with the party rank-and-file, he had displayed an untimely streak of independence in prevaricating over Bolshevisation and pronouncing Trotsky guilty (he had even asserted the CPC's right to examine the evidence). Now, in a long, careful report on the sixth congress, he clung to Bukharin's more cautious reading of the New Line, telling the Central Executive Committee (CEC) that, while the party needed a more aggressive trade union policy, including sharper criticism of the ACCL leadership, organising drives 'could not be drawn from the air, they must have their roots in objective conditions, and be real'.[17]

When MacDonald's likeliest successor, *Worker* editor Maurice Spector, chose to join American communist James P. Cannon in launching North American Trotskyism, an unlikely contender entered the contest.[18] The elevation of Tim Buck, MacDonald's right-hand man, suggests that the Comintern knew it could not impose just *anyone* as general secretary. The new leader had to have some degree of authority. Most of the party's 'old Bolsheviks', however (those who had not drifted away in the mid-1920s), had rallied behind MacDonald against Smith and the other Lenin School tyros, who were hot for the New Line but had little else to commend them. Buck, industrial secretary since 1922, industrial *and* organisational secretary since 1925, and a member of the EC of the RILU since 1924, had a safe pair of hands and a long-recognised ability 'always . . . to appear neutral, and thus [have] the confidence of all sides'.[19] Shedding his past without a blush, this pliable centrist (Thälmann to MacDonald's Brandler) disowned the party's industrial record and demanded an aggressive left turn. With Smith as his ideological mentor, a 'left' faction (based on the Young Communist League (YCL) and former followers of Spector) quickly crystallised around him.

Buck cemented his group's ties to Moscow by asking Lozovsky for substantial financial assistance during 'the forthcoming three or four months, which will be decisive' for independent leadership. Money duly arrived, along with a stream of closed and open ECCI letters showing how the Stalinist version of the New Line had completely supplanted Bukharinist caution.[20] Sims and Murphy carried the fight to Windsor, Canada's main automobile centre, where they infuriated ethnic communists by attempting to force them into the tottering Auto Workers' Industrial Union (AWIU), which was already reeling from a sudden downturn in production and the work of company spies at Ford and Chrysler. MacDonald recalled both men to Toronto, and was blamed by the left for the AWIU's collapse.[21] The widening breach between left and right was encapsulated in the demand of former Spectorite Rebecca Buhay for her brother's removal from the CEC; Michael Buhay was one of several garment union veterans, including Joe Salsberg, secretary of the Industrial Union of Needle Trades Workers (IUNTW), who considered the left's trade union stance fundamentally frivolous.[22] The ECCI's secondment of Sam Carr, another Lenin School *Wunderkind*, to orchestrate the Buck-Smith team's takeover at the June convention, showed that there was to be no turning back.[23] At the convention, MacDonald's undimmed authority among Finns and Ukrainians temporarily denied Buck and Smith (even backed by ECCI reinforcements) their expected coronation. Within weeks, however, some complicated manoeuvring handed them control of the CEC and PB.[24]

The 'High' Third Period, 1929–31

The next six months were an extended audition for the new leaders, now joined in a triumvirate by Buck supporter Tom Ewan, imported from Winnipeg as industrial secretary. They sent the ebullient Murphy to Hamilton, to take control of the walkout at National Steel Car that, even in defeat, convinced the leadership that 'mass radicalisation' was at hand.[25] With the Wall Street crash adding final confirmation of the ECCI's genius, the self-styled 'CI elements' proceeded to ban a united front with the Industrial Workers of the World (IWW) in a pulpwood cutters' strike, ordered members in the 'reactionary' garment unions to join the IUNTW, and mimicked Bukharin's removal from the Comintern presidency by expelling Salsberg and others as 'right deviationists'. Finally, after receiving an ECCI reminder, they fulfilled a pledge to launch a 'red' union centre – the Workers' Unity League (WUL).[26]

If Buck thought that he had passed the audition, he was swiftly disabused. Spending the winter of 1929–30 in Moscow, he was informed by the ECCI that he and Smith had been insufficiently vigorous in purging the 'right'. His sense of personal insecurity surely heightened by the hear-hear of the Lenin School's American-Canadian secretariat, he returned to Toronto and promptly suffered a nervous collapse.[27] With Buck temporarily *hors de combat*, the accommodating Smith 'self-criticised' himself and launched the party on the most 'ultra-left' phase of the Third Period. Such was his ardour for rooting out the 'right danger', however, that he committed a 'left error'. Two special ECCI commissions identified his 'mechanical' (that is, crudely Stalinist) handling of the Ukrainian and Finnish sections as the main obstacle to their *rapprochement* with the PB, and the ECCI recalled him to Moscow for political re-education in the Anglo-American Secretariat![28]

With 'Trotskyites' gone and 'Lovestoneites' going, the party seemed to be turning into a party of 'obedient fools'.[29] Buck (now recovered) and Ewan turned deference into submission, symbolically launching a 'Canadian Workers' Pamphlets' series with *The Triumph of Socialism in the Soviet Union*, which reminded members (though they hardly needed it) that failure to resist the imperialist 'war danger' would mean 'increased oppression and slavery throughout the whole earth for years to come': defence of the only workers' state was their first duty.[30] Ewan launched the WUL into disastrous incursions in the Alberta and Nova Scotia coalfields that almost shattered the two provincial parties. Ukrainian dissidents in Alberta mounted a full-scale rebellion against the line, which called for splitting the 'social fascist' UMWA and MWUC and replacing them with a pristine 'red' industrial union. They flatly refused to follow Toronto's directive to call a strike for which there was no rank-and-file support and which would surely shatter a demoralised and disunited workforce; and they did not understand why they should split the MWUC, since it was on the brink of dropping its ACCL affiliation and entering the WUL, or why it had suddenly become social fascist. New district secretary Harvey Murphy expelled several rebels, including former MWUC vice-president John Stokaluk, only to suffer Smith's fate. 'Here we have just been rapped severely for our mechanical methods in combating the Rights,' Buck wrote him, 'and you adopt methods more mechanical than we ever suggested.' After months of upheaval, the PB sent Murphy to the Lenin School, told the RILU it was pressing ahead with plans for a new 'red' union, and surreptitiously reverted to 'boring from within' the MWUC.[31]

No amount of Bolshevik will or ingenuity could overcome the discipline of soaring unemployment: Canadians with jobs were more concerned with keeping them than with resisting 'speed-up' and wage cuts; 1930 saw the lowest number of strikes and striker-days in non-coal mining industry since the turn of the century, and a small upturn in militancy in 1931–32 restored the level of strike activity only to the depressed level of the late 1920s. All that the WUL gained from its first year was experience. In July 1931, 5,930 of 6,570 WUL members were either in unions it had inherited (MWUC, IUNTW, LWIU) or in 'red' opposition groups inside the reformist unions. The party, meanwhile, had not a single factory unit in southern Ontario.[32]

Ewan encountered a distinct lack of interest in Canadian matters at the fifth RILU congress in August. Perhaps lulled by hints of an RILU retreat from its most extreme positions, he casually remarked to Kuusinen that the WUL suffered from a debilitating lack of 'forces'. 'Old Kuus' stamped hard on this incipient opportunism, insisting that Ewan have faith in 'THE WORKERS', who would always provide the forces.[33] In fact, the congress signalled the start of Moscow's long and not yet irreversible retreat from madness.[34] Its directives to the WUL confusingly interwove an emphasis on concrete economic activity and serious work within the reformist unions with a call for relentless struggle against all rightist tendencies and for hegemony over the entire Canadian workers' movement. Slightly bewildered, Ewan returned to Toronto urging WUL organisers to show 'a certain flexibility' while squeezing out the last residues of 'social democratic' passivity.[35]

By late 1930, he and Buck were performing minor miracles keeping the apparatus and *The Worker* afloat. They were *desperate* for Comintern direction on matters great and small, refusing, for example, to issue discussion material for a delayed central committee plenum until Moscow told them what it should contain. Buck complained privately about protocol: even if 'the decision [were] not up to us', the ECCI should still have officially informed the Canadian PB that Smith would not be allowed to return for the plenum. He also provided Carr, Toronto's conduit to the ECCI, with a detailed rationale for the party's modifications to the RILU line on Canada's mining unions. At the February 1931 plenum, however, he accepted that Moscow's criticisms had been right in every respect, represented the slump in membership as a valuable 'cleansing' of the weakest elements, and re-dedicated the party to the Comintern line that a gusher of class militancy was waiting to be tapped, if only the CPC could find the catalyst.[36] According to Smith, Earl Browder, who represented the ECCI at the plenum, reported to Moscow that the CPC was 'far off track to the left'.[37]

In fact, Buck and Ewan did make a partial turn to the right, precisely in line with ECCI expectations. Local industrial cadres were only too happy to take up Ewan's call for flexibility, often exceeding his boundary of acceptability in 'hiding the face of the party'.[38] The party also terminated its self-imposed isolation from the reformist unions. Although Montreal railway shop craftsman Alex Gauld claimed that craft unionists viewed communists as 'splitters' and 'noisy disrupters', he was one of many communists who never left their craft unions.[39] Others left only briefly. The leading 'dual' union was the IUNTW and, from 1931, it concentrated overwhelmingly on the sectors left unorganised by the reformist unions; all of the 'rightist' garment union activists expelled by the party in 1929 returned in 1931. If a patina of subversion still enveloped the WUL, it was largely due to the high level of state violence directed against WUL strikes; some tragic episodes occurred, notably at Estevan, Saskatchewan, where the Royal Canadian Mounted Police (RCMP) shot dead three immigrant miners.[40] Anxious about the possibility of a Section 98 prosecution (Ewan was a Kingston detainee), in late 1932 the party had the WUL replace its 'organic' membership of the RILU with a 'fraternal' relationship and accepted Gauld's plan for a *strategic* turn towards the reformist unions.[41]

An ECCI sanctioned shift to more moderate tactics by the National Unemployed Workers' Association (NUWA) proved unusually effective. Late in 1930, NUWA branches laid the basis for a surge of activity by shifting from permanent confrontation (a tactic that was bringing diminishing returns) to a more flexible combination of community organising and 'fewer, but better' mass demonstrations. Between January and June 1931, the NUWA gathered almost 100,000 signatures in support of the Workers' Unity League Bill for State Non-Contributory Unemployment Insurance, brought tens of thousands onto the streets in two days of action, and recruited some 20,000 members. While most soon dropped out, hundreds moved into the party, ending its downward spiral. For the first time since 1928, the CPC received Moscow's unreserved congratulations (although the same success prompted the state's decision to outlaw the party).[42]

There was no backtracking on the political front. Police attacks on communist meetings, district offices, radical bookstores and ethnic labour halls continued; individual communists were beaten up with impunity; many cadres, in addition to the 'Kingston Eight' served jail terms, and several were deported, leading the CPC to discuss a joint anti-deportation campaign with the CPGB.[43] The onslaught made it possible to overlook the WUL's failures and the CPC's derisory showing in the 1930 federal election, which had installed R. B. Bennett's Conservatives: it *proved* that the 'fascization' of the state was under way and that the party had become 'a definite power and a challenge'. That being so, the party sharpened its attack on 'social fascism'.[44]

Debate on the Canadian left had become increasingly rancorous in the mid-1920s, but social democrats did not expect communists to label them 'enemies of the working class' and seek to deny them a platform (the Essex Scottish militia had to be called out to quell fighting in Windsor).[45] Communists were especially hostile towards those who had been close allies, like J. S. Woodsworth, leader of the federal parliament's Independent Labour caucus. 'Those bastards,' Ewan privately remarked, 'deserve to be howled out of every working class meeting, not only because they are fakers but because they are the worst type of traitor to the unemployed and employed alike.' Social democratic resistance became proof of social fascism! Left-wing socialists could not understand why the party reserved its most vicious attacks for people who were politically closest to it. For Woodsworth, it had abandoned all 'honour and fair play'. Non-possession of these signifiers of British-ness helped place the party beyond Labour's pale; well before the August 1931 arrests, most socialists believed that it had lost any claim on normal working class solidarity.[46]

Illegality, Internal Transformation and Unity, 1932–34

Illegality necessitated more circumspect tactics. The ECCI returned a chastened Smith to Toronto in December 1931, to be joined in a two-man secretariat by veteran Scots-American communist Jack Johnstone (on temporary secondment from the CPUSA). They had close support from Fred Rose and Stanley Ryerson in Quebec, John Navis in the Ukrainian bureau, and Jim Litterick, Joe Gershman, Alex Gauld and Charles Sims in the WUL. The new leadership rapidly constructed an underground organisation, with tightened discipline and security; Smith's movements were 'known to a select few' (though the latter included the RCMP) and scarcely anyone even knew of Johnstone's presence. It also began a programme of internal transformation that, for the first time, prepared the party for struggle outside the realm of production.[47]

Before 1932, women's work had been 'sadly neglected'.[48] Now, it was ruled unconscionable to exclude half the class from combat: no fight was 'a real fight if only half of those affected are in the front ranks'.[49] Communists helped working class women become aware of their 'own special struggles' (over free healthcare, access to family planning, admission of single unemployed women to the relief rolls, inflated food prices, and free meals, clothing and supplies for schoolchildren) and convinced some of their right to occupy male cultural space.[50] Although the jobs women did in the CPC still tended to be 'women's jobs' – gathering relief and running strike kitchens for the Workers' International Relief (WIR) or staffing the new National Children's Council (NCC) – as the party became more influential, these jobs became more plentiful and women's leadership profile rose. While the CPC did not fulfil its aspiration of placing at least one woman on every district bureau, it did produce a cohort of suitable candidates. Behind Rebecca Buhay and Annie Buller, who retained their standing from the 1920s, stood a much larger group of mainly younger communist women with national, district or local reputations.[51] According to Jack Scott, female *cadres* who were willing to go out and '[take their] licks, same as anybody else' were treated as political equals.[52]

Yet, for all the CPC's egalitarian ideology, the proportion of women in the party remained low, and actually fell from 14 per cent to 12 per cent in 1934–35.[53] Leading male comrades often displayed a lack of comradeship towards the women cadres responsible for women's work. More than twenty years after the event, Alice Cooke recalled how her nervousness as she waited to address the 1933 CEC plenum on women's work was in no way alleviated by 'the general exodus which in those days took place immediately this part of the agenda was reached'. Socialised labour was rarely a feature of the communist household. Few male communists were prepared to make the sacrifices that would make it possible 'for men and women to jointly live communist lives', and the party leadership refused to make this an issue. As late as 1937, a woman comrade called attention to the 'contradictions' between 'the ideas presented at branch meetings' and what she saw 'in the homes'. She felt it was 'time this matter was brought to light'.[54]

Until 1933, children's work was sporadic and largely ineffective (early Third Period headlines about communist infiltration of the public schools, notwithstanding). WIR activity during the lengthy Crow's Nest Pass miners' strike in 1932 showed that children's groups *could* be built, but consolidation rarely ensued. There was a tendency to dump children's work on a single comrade – usually a woman – and leave her to get on with it, with minimal backing from the movement at large.[55] In spring 1933, however, the party accepted that the 'proletarian children's movement [was] at a standstill', clarified the purpose of children's work and, dropping a proposal to re-launch the Young Pioneers as the hegemonic children's organisation, created a new 'united front' body, the National Children's Council, to coordinate and build the movement up from its ethnic base.[56] NCC secretary Minnie Shelley reassured the ethnic sections that there was no intention of dissolving their children's groups; instead, she simply urged them to incorporate into their programmes a core of 'songs, yells and pledges in English'.[57]

Shelley and her (usually female) successors continued to struggle to convince hard-pressed activists in other party sections to attend NCC meetings or make support of the NCC/Young Pioneers' paper *Always Ready* a priority; attracting or retaining 'more matured' cadres, especially males, proved especially unrewarding.[58] Children did, however, become an increasingly familiar presence in party life. 'From every truck [in Winnipeg's May Day parade],' the *Winnipeg Free Press* noted, 'treble voices hurled defiance at capitalism and fascism, demanded the repeal of Section 98, lauded the Soviet Union, [and] condemned all other lands.' The party consciously strived to integrate children of different ethnic backgrounds, and some state officials were disconcerted by the implications of its success.[59]

The party sought similar integration of the adult membership. Even as it urged immigrant members to anglicise their names and become citizens, it made multiculturalism a positive signifier of class and nation. As Harvey Murphy told a meeting in the cosmopolitan Crow's Nest Pass: 'This business of dividing people because of their colour or their religion or what lodge they belonged to was so much rot.' There were 'only two colours, and they were 'red and yellow'. The Windsor party's multi-lingual, multi-national platforms visibly proclaimed that African and French Canadians, Jews, Slavs, Finns and Anglo-Celts were comrades; a frequent speaker was African-Canadian, Ernest Hulett, recruited from an all-black NUWA branch in the impoverished Sandwich West district (locally known as 'Tin Can City'). 'Red' unions, notably in defence of East and South Asians in B.C., fought to persuade 'white British' workers that there should be no caste privilege in the working class.[60]

Anglo-Celtic suspicion of cultural work, still evident in Ewan's 1931 remark that 'our members who have long strummed on a mandolin and sung revolutionary songs are hard to pry loose from these quiet pastimes', may have been softened by respect for cultural diversity.[61] After illegality, a vibrant associational life became a crucial means of party building. A distinct party culture evolved out of house parties, dances, 'socials', concerts, workers' sports, and children's outings and camps. This inclusive culture – entrance was often free – proved increasingly attractive to Anglo-Celts and encouraged some degree of social interaction among different ethnic groups.[62] How far attending a Canadian Labor Defence League (CLDL) 'social' or wearing the red jersey of the Workers' Sports Association (WSA) aided in the politicisation of the periphery is questionable: athletes were often more interested in their sport than in its relationship to the class struggle (a phenomenon one YCL organiser attributed to their internalisation of what today would be called a 'dumb jock' mentality). For its historian, however, the WSA 'provided many immigrants with recreational opportunities they otherwise might not have had, in an environment which not only respected but affirmed their non-British heritage'.[63] One might see the totality of the party's associational activities as a potentially revolutionary alternative to bourgeois consumerist culture.

Creating such an alternative was certainly the aim of the cultural radicals who early in 1932 formed the Toronto Progressive Arts Club (PAC) and its journal *Masses*. The PAC brought together proletarians and a bourgeois bohemian fringe around the University of Toronto. Cadres shared their industrial counterparts' sense of mission. They were 'a few earnest people – earnest in the old puritanical meaning of the word'. They aimed to challenge 'all that is corrupt, all that is reactionary in Canadian bourgeois society generally, and in Canadian cultural life particularly', and to redress the Canadian intelligentsia's failure to 'express the feelings and thoughts of their countrymen'. Additional PAC branches were established only in Montreal, Winnipeg and Vancouver, but by 1933 the national office in Toronto was corresponding with over sixty local cultural groups and other party sections were taking up cultural concerns.[64]

The PAC had sections for writers, artists and photographers, and theatrical workers. Drama, however, was first among equals. Theatrical workers had their own special section, the Workers' Experimental Theatre (later simply Workers' Theatre), which produced original agit-prop plays for performance on the streets or in ill-equipped halls. The Toronto WT's very first performance, in May 1932, took place in the Ukrainian Labour Temple; the subject matter of *Deportation* was very relevant to immigrant workers. Plays like *Deportation, Eviction* and Toronto electrician Frank Love's *Looking Forward* formed part of the repertoire of two 1933 Workers' Theatre tours of southern Ontario, playing mainly to ethnic audiences. 'For many,' PAC founder member Toby Ryan observed, 'our visit was the first experience with a theatre doing English plays that were direct and contemporary.' For some of the bohemians, the process of discovery was mutual. For some of the ruling class, ethnic mingling was portentous. English immigrant Harold Griffin recalled that the Vancouver press 'weren't happy' about 'an unknown group [of Anglos] working with foreign-born, largely despised citizens' in a hugely successful (and eventually national prize-winning) production of Clifford Odets' *Waiting for Lefty*.[65]

Party education at last took shape. 'Self-study' courses proliferated in the late 1920s, and some middle-level cadres were sent to the New York Workers' School or rushed through a rudimentary RILU correspondence course.[66] Leslie Morris, quoting Lenin's dictum that 'without revolutionary theory there can be no revolutionary action', argued in 1931 for the immediate construction of a central educational apparatus. Education, Morris stated, would increase rank-and-file understanding of the party line,

make branch life less 'dry and uninteresting' for new members, and increase
the party's ability to produce its own literature, thereby liberating it from the
whim of hostile customs officials. Granted, there was 'no time for study', but
Bolshevik will and organisation could make the time. Buck, preoccupied by
the 'terror' (and no fan of Morris), took no action.[67]

The great leap forward finally came in 1932, when several districts held
their first provincial training schools, most of the remainder following suit in
1933–34.[68] In autumn 1933, the party claimed to have 'several thousand'
students enrolled in formal and self-educational classes at three levels, from a
gentle introduction to Marxism through articles in the party press, to
'advanced' classes using the standard works of Marx, Engels, Lenin and
Stalin, and 'special' classes on the first volume of *Capital,* the epitome of
Marxist knowledge. Party classes were no place for 'Spittoon Philosophers',
'Hair-splitters' or liberalism. Each subject, its intellectual outcomes tightly
structured by 'study outlines' and 'control questions', was 'handled in relation
to the class struggle' and the needs of the line.[69] Where Irishman Jack Scott
found the process dry, plodding and reverential, his compatriot Pat Lenihan
stressed its beneficial political effects, notably in cadre development: even if
a new wave of state repression had 'taken away three hundred people across
Canada . . . the movement would continue'. Scott also witnessed the
consolidation of a reading culture: 'the homes of hundreds and hundreds of
unemployed people you'd go into, and they'd all have what you called the
Little Lenin Library . . . There was almost a mass circulation'. In 1934, the
first edition of 5,000 copies of *What the Communist Party Stands For* sold out in
a matter of weeks, encouraging the CPC to open several public bookstores
to nourish this appetite (and increase its own visibility).[70]

Internal transformation coincided with a sea change in public sentiment,
clearly evident in the electoral battering the Liberals handed incumbent
Conservative administrations: in August 1933, the Tories were swamped in
Nova Scotia; three months later, not a single Tory survived in British
Columbia, and in June 1934 the Ontario Liberals swept them out by a 4–1
margin. Liberalism did not satisfy everyone. Many members of the 'British'
working class turned to the Co-operative Commonwealth Federation (CCF),
a new – and, significantly, national – social democratic party formed in 1932
(it won 31 per cent of the vote in B.C.). For the first time, the CPC
(necessarily disguised as the 'united front' or 'workers' united front') took
electoral politics seriously and started to win municipal seats in heavily
immigrant locales such as Winnipeg, East Windsor and Blairmore, Alberta.[71]

Since 1932, moreover, the party had been promoting anti-Tory sentiment
through a mass, public 'Fight Against the Bennett Government's Hunger
Program'. This ensemble of campaigns conjoining local and national
unemployed struggles with the repeal of Section 98 and an amnesty for the

imprisoned communist leaders lasted beyond Bennett's ouster in 1935 to Mackenzie King's repeal of Section 98 in July 1936. As the main events in just the 1932 calendar demonstrate, it helped communists maintain an impressive level of public activity:

February	Toronto Repeal Section 98 Conference
	Eastern Canada Repeal Conference
	Repeal Delegation to Prime Minister R. B. Bennett
	British Columbia Hunger March
March	National Unemployment Conference
April	Western Canada Repeal Conference
May	Nationwide May Day demonstrations
August	Workers' Economic Conference (to parallel/lampoon Imperial Economic Conference)
	CLDL National Plenum
October	Manitoba Hunger March
December	Nationwide Amnesty Day demonstrations
	Alberta Hunger March

Extensive grass roots activity preceded each event, and activists raised a range of complementary issues, such as local free speech fights, moratoria on farm evictions, anti-deportation campaigns, the Scottsboro Case, and the success of the Soviet five-year-plans, the underground party's positive vision of the future.

Much of this activity took place through 'front' groups, such as the WSA, PAC, CLDL, Workers' Ex-Servicemen's League (WESL), Organisation for Jewish Colonization in Russia (ICOR) and Friends of the Soviet Union (FSU), which brought together party members with a vital – and expanding – periphery of sympathisers. The FSU, for example, formed in 1931, tapped into growing public interest in and sympathy for the USSR, which for the first time since the early 1920s provided reflected glory for its franchise holders. FSU publications were 'in great demand' and its workers' delegations to the USSR offered numerous propaganda opportunities. One of the 'workers' on the 1932 delegation was J. F. White, editor of Canada's leading organ of left-liberal opinion, *Canadian Forum*, his effusive 'Russian Highlights' appeared in six consecutive issues of the magazine.[72]

While the fronts induced only a few thousand Canadians to join the party, they weaned many thousands more from reflexive anti-communism. None did more than their doyen, the CLDL (formed in 1925). Between August 1932 and June 1933, it gathered 200,000 signatures for an Amnesty petition, issued over two *million* supporting leaflets, and had 50,000 pre-addressed postcards sent to federal Minister of Justice Hugh Guthrie. In mid-1933, it had an individual membership of 17,000 (and an affiliated membership of 26,000).[73] The Repeal Section 98 campaign surged in the spring of 1933 when Buck was put on trial as the main ringleader of two days of rioting at Kingston penitentiary the previous October. Little had leaked out about the riot, and Buck dropped a bombshell by alleging that during it, shots had been fired into his cell, a claim the CLDL immediately referred to as an 'assassination attempt'. Supported by several key sections of the labour movement, the CLDL demanded a public inquiry.[74] The state, however, having eased up on repression during 1933, reverted to type. In December, the Toronto PAC gave the first performance of its original play *Eight Men Speak*. After one performance, the play – in which a 'Workers' jury' convicts 'Guard X' of attempted murder – was banned (this also happened in Winnipeg). Shortly afterwards, Toronto police officers charged CLDL national secretary A. E. Smith (Stewart's father) with subversion, under Section 98, for publicly repeating the assassination charge. Illustrating the national mood, however, Smith's jury acquitted him. 'Mass unity,' the CLDL crowed, 'freed A. E. Smith. Greater mass unity can free the seven in Kingston penitentiary.'[75]

The Smith verdict may even have prompted the release of the Kingston prisoners. Only a few months earlier, Bennett had sworn that they would serve every minute of their sentences. In June 1934, however, Sam Carr and Matt Popovic were released, followed by Malcolm Bruce, Tom Hill and John Boychuk in July, Ewan in September, and Buck in late November. The state's decision to stagger their release dates was surely misguided. Each detainee returned to welcome-home celebrations and a speaking tour. Bruce, the greatest of the party's firebrand orators, spent late July and all August touring central Canada before embarking on a triumphal, five week long trans-Canada procession, speaking in virtually every major centre between Toronto and his home city of Vancouver. These were mere *hors d'oeuvres* for Buck's marathon coast-to-coast tour between January and May 1935. Over 100,000 Canadians flocked to hear his message of anti-fascist unity.[76]

Instances of unity 'from below' multiplied. Trotskyists were pleased to see the party learning how to relate to other sections of the class in a 'more . . . correct Leninist' manner; Maurice Spector, heading the International Left Opposition, shared a Free Speech for Communists platform with CCFer John Buckley, secretary of the Toronto District Labour Council (TDLC).[77] A captivating feature (especially to government watchers) of a strike by the 'red' Furniture Workers' Industrial Union (FWIU) in Stratford, Ontario, was the success enjoyed by Glaswegian communist Fred Collins (whose popularity later inspired rumours that he was Hungarian!) in exploiting the outrage of the town's 'British' railway unions at the presence of a sixty-strong, armoured detachment of the Royal Canadian Regiment; Collins elicited their strong support. Practical unity continued after the strike, which contributed to the class feeling that carried a workers' slate to victory in the municipal elections held shortly after it ended. A year later, Stratford Mayor

O. J. Kerr, a CCF member and an outspoken supporter of CCF-communist unity, led 10,000 local citizens in a demonstration of solidarity with Izzy Minster, the FWIU's Jewish national secretary, who had been beaten up by local 'white' vigilantes.[78]

The ambiguous character of the turn to unity was exposed by the party's failure to achieve unity 'from above' with the CCF. The CPC had enthusiastically endorsed the ECCI's instant ruling that the CCF was classically social fascist, a view that was only strengthened by the new party's rapid ascent.[79] Nevertheless, many CCF rank-and-filers were ready to overlook what communists were saying about their leaders in order to exploit their organisational experience and energy in struggle. In Flin Flon, Manitoba, communist organiser Mitch Sago publicly debated with CCF member Alex Stewart the question: 'Can and does the CCF help the working class?' Stewart stuck to social democracy, but he also stuck to the MWUC (which Sago and other Winnipeg comrades were organising) and was a leading activist in the 1934 strike.[80] Several Ontario CCF clubs were suspended when they ignored a provincial directive to play no part in the A. E. Smith defence campaign 'until Mr. J. S. Woodsworth has given his advice in writing as to the advisability of such action'.[81] Such advice was not forthcoming: Woodsworth rejected any alliance with the CPC.[82] Over time, CPC rhetoric on the CCF favoured analysis over abuse, and the party finally ceased to refer to 'social fascism' in mid-1934. Even then, however, its unity appeal to the Second CCF convention was couched in terms CCF leaders were bound to reject: delegates were invited to choose between the 'road of Lenin' that had led to the triumph of Soviet socialism and the road of the 'Second International, of coalition, of class co-operation, of gradualism, of 'democracy" that had led 'directly to the victory of fascism'. Buck, shortly after his release, accompanied a new appeal for CPC–CCF unity with an announcement that he would contest the Winnipeg North seat in the 1935 federal election, a seat held (and retained) by CCFer A. A. Heaps.[83] Heaps and Woodsworth were not alone in being permanently sceptical of unity with people who still viewed them as 'objectively' counter-revolutionary class traitors.[84]

Trade Union Unity, 1934–35

The return to the united front was obviously influenced by Moscow's growing comprehension of the nature of Nazism and the seriousness of its threat. As in 1927–28, however, the CPC was responding in part to the logic of its own circumstances. Dimitrov's call for parties to root themselves in their national cultures and traditions is generally viewed as a post-seventh congress development. In Canada, however, communists started to embrace and re-work 'British traditions' as early as 1933. Conversely, they were slow to give organisational form to the ECCI sanctioned search for allies among the 'Liberal-minded' or 'progressive' bourgeoisie, forming the Canadian League Against War and Fascism (CLAWF) a year later than its American counterpart.[85]

Workers' unity was advancing most slowly on the trade union front. Canada's trade union unity movement offered a striking example of how national forces could influence, but not determine, the international line. Canadian delegates at an RILU central council meeting in late 1931 saw CPGB general secretary Harry Pollitt boldly face down Lozovsky, winning the right for the CPGB to revert *entirely* to work in the mainstream unions. If some 'red' unionists had had their way, 'red' unionism would certainly have been abandoned in 1932 or 1933. Nova Scotia provincial organiser Bill Matheson, after playing a key role in bringing about the split from the UMWA that produced the independent 'red' Amalgamated Mine Workers early in 1932, became convinced that the party's tinkering with the 'red' union line was dishonest and the line itself fundamentally flawed. Apparently gravitating towards Trotskyism, he called for the party to make an honest appraisal of its relationship to the rest of the labour movement. Trotskyists argued that, whatever the case for 'red' unions in 1930, now that 'the masses [were] turning towards organisation and militant action', it was clearly in the interest of both party and class for the CPC to return to the union mainstream and push the TLC into a more purposeful organising role.[86]

Setting aside the RILU's unchanged opposition to liquidation (and the party's distaste for conceding an argument to its most hated rivals), communists drew different lessons from the rank-and-file upsurge provoked by the mild economic upturn of spring 1933. While reformists prevaricated, the WUL responded with enthusiasm; in 1934, when the 483,000 striker-days in non-coal mining industry marked a return to somewhere near the militancy of the post-war labour revolt, it led well over half of all strikes, mainly in unorganised industries such as auto components, meatpacking, logging and lumber, metal mining, garments, textiles, shoe and leather, furniture, and services, accounting for over 70 per cent of striker-days. With around 30,000–40,000 members, it was comparable in size to the passive ACCL and about a quarter to a third the size of the gently stirring TLC. A hostile source claimed that it had done more in a year to build the CPC than the party itself had achieved 'in any previous three years'.[87]

The party's publication in 1933 of a pamphlet by Lozovsky, in which he disinterred Lenin's *Left-Wing Communism: An Infantile Disorder*, might have encouraged some to think that the 'pure, revolutionary' WUL unions were about to go. Party leaders, however, though open to inter-union co-operation (having rejected a united front with the IWW in 1929, the LWIU made common cause with its rival in a major Ontario–Quebec strike in late

1933), were in no hurry to surrender the WUL's organisational gains. None of the other union centres had shown any real enthusiasm for organising the unorganised, far less for building *class* unions willing to fight for the most vulnerable members of the class, organise the 'war' industries or move beyond the confines of unionism towards workers' power. The party not only rejected 'liquidation', but roughed-up 'red' union members who disagreed.[88]

On the other hand, WUL success in opposition work, notably in the Vancouver street-railway and waterfront unions and more generally among garment, communications, construction and railway workers, suggested that it had nothing to fear from unity. There was also the matter of convergence. Rarely could WUL tactics now be described as 'ultra-left'; a good majority of WUL strikes in 1933–34 produced some kind of material advance, such as the shop committee system gained by Stratford's furniture workers (and still functioning effectively several months later).[89] WUL organisers willingly accepted the role of 'good' trade unionists, some even dismissing the notion of a 'revolutionary' union as a contradiction in terms: a 'good' union was simply one that militantly represented its members. Moreover, when a 'red' union consolidated to any degree, the same workers who had been attracted by its insurgent character now demanded that it operate like a 'real' trade union. The WUL was forced to conform to their expectations: a WUL charter, it huffily protested, was 'just as handsome as any granted by the reformist unions'.[90]

By early 1934, the WUL was in danger of becoming legitimate. Government spokesmen started to use every available forum to attack it, claiming that its intemperate methods threatened national recovery.[91] Instead of using Section 98, the state turned to an old voluntarist tactic: inviting 'responsible' unions to offer themselves to the employers as alternatives to radicalism. Ontario Attorney-General W. H. Price issued the pamphlet *Agents of Revolution* to expose the WUL's links to Moscow and rouse the Ontario people, 'particularly the labour unions', against the WUL with its promotion of 'continuous strife, unrest and destruction of property'.[92] Copies of the pamphlet turned up all over Canada, and it contributed to the defeat of a major metal mining strike at Flin Flon, Manitoba. While some of the more unscrupulous elements in the labour movement took up Price's invitation (which came without the inducement of statutory, New Deal-style recognition) few *bona fide* unions did. When the TDLC discussed raiding the WUL, the business agent of the Boot and Shoe Workers' Union vehemently rejected any such suggestion.[93]

Confident about comparing the WUL's record with anyone else's, the party did precisely that when interpreting the guidance it had started to receive from the ECCI on the need for trade union unity against the rising fascist threat.[94] The CPUSA read this material as a green light for liquidating the Trade Union Unity League.[95] Several ECCI draft directives suggested that the CPC should do likewise, by sending smaller 'red' unions into stronger reformist unions and by dropping the WUL's name. Above all, the party had to widen its 'mass influence' by turning decisively 'towards the REFORMIST TRADE UNIONS'.[96]

The CPC accepted only some of this advice. At a National Miners' conference in Montreal, it called for the MWUC, the independent 'red' Amalgamated Mine Workers of Nova Scotia, and 'our brothers in the UMWA' to form a Canadian Miners' Federation; Fred Collins announced to the inaugural CLAWF congress that the WUL would be happy to send the AWIU into the ACCL or TLC, and the WUL did allow some weaker units to enter the AFL. Wholesale liquidation, however, was not in Canadian workers' interest. The WUL's role was to join – as a discrete entity – the common struggle of all workers to 'organise into the unions of their own choice' and of 'all labour unions' for the right to exist. Ewan and Salsberg, now WUL co-leaders, also signalled their readiness to deal with the bourgeois state by accepting an invitation from Mitchell Hepburn's Department of Labour to discuss what would become the Industrial Standards Act.[97] When the ECCI increased pressure on the Canadians to follow the American option, it was surprised by their continuing insistence that the Canadian and American situations were 'in no way to be compared'. Exploiting Dimitrov's approval of greater national discretion in interpreting the line, the Canadians pleaded for national autonomy for Canadian unions and a continued role for the WUL. The TLC, they pointed out, had not been galvanised by supportive legislation (R. B. Bennett's selective conversion to the New Deal stopped short of endorsing collective bargaining), and the WUL – objectively, a much bigger deal than the TUUL – remained the main vehicle for industrial militancy and the organisation of the unorganised. Most surprising of all, in March – without Moscow's explicit approval – the WUL called for the four Canadian union centres to unite in one 'All-inclusive Federation of Canadian Labour'. That remained its position until November 1935.[98]

Conclusions

Whether the CPC would have done more for the class by dissolving the WUL in 1933 and taking its chances within the reformist unions is un-provable. Beyond question, however, when it concluded Canada's 'long' Third Period by liquidating the WUL (in a six-month period following the ninth CEC plenum in November 1935), it undoubtedly had far greater trade union influence than at any time in the 1920s. On that count alone, 'class against class' was a Canadian success story. Sectarianism, moreover, by promoting an outrageous sense of political and moral superiority, stiffened communists' will to tackle unfavourable circumstances. Six years' of hard experience organising among the unemployed and in the workplace enhanced their capacity for industrial intervention (and undoubtedly laid some of the foundation stones of later Committee of Industrial Organization successes), while their efforts outside the realm of production helped the party come to terms with its own multi-ethnic character, placing it in a generally stronger position to struggle for proletarian hegemony. The Third Period had accelerated rather than caused the CPC's decline, and the party's recovery began *during* the Third Period: membership revived to 3,000 in 1933, a record 5,500 in mid-1934, and 8,000 on the eve of the seventh Comintern congress.

Nevertheless, these achievements justify only a modest revision of the consensus. The adoption of 'class against class' *was* rooted in Canadian conditions, but Moscow had to place in power the men and women who were prepared to lead the CPC into the worst sectarian excesses of the 'high' Third Period – and to illegality.[99] That political defeat forced a grudging return to sanity. Advance came when improving objective conditions – including the belated growth of working class solidarity with the beleaguered CPC – meshed with the re-adopted united front. In the process, however, of becoming bigger, stronger and sufficiently influential to regain its legality, the CPC (though less supine than the CPUSA) lost any hope of future unity with social democracy and the last vestiges of political autonomy from Moscow. Nowhere was its Stalinist future more clearly intimated than in the decision, imposed on a bemused membership without warning or serious debate, to liquidate the WUL:

[Truly] a tragic bit of nonsense that was done in response to a decision made by people that didn't know a goddam thing about conditions in Canada . . . It was just seen as a tactic that was necessary from the point of view of the Soviet Union. They needed it, so it had to happen and so everybody had to follow suit, so we followed suit. All our work went to somebody else.[100]

Notes

1. RILU, *Report of the Fourth Congress of the RILU* (London, 1928), pp. 137–8; Communist Party of Canada (CPC), *Minutes of the Trade Union Department* 17 June 1928, (National Archives of Canada; NA, Communist International Fonds; CF, Reel 45, file 334); *Toronto Daily Star*, 27 December 1928, quoted in I. Angus, *Canadian Bolsheviks: The Early Years of the Communist Party of Canada* (Montreal, 1981), p. 258; L. Betcherman, *The Little Band: The Clashes between the Communists and the Political and Legal Establishment in Canada, 1928–32* (Ottawa, 1982), pp. 17–21; S. Smith, *Comrades and Komsomolkas* (Toronto, 1993); Young Communist League, 'Report on Hamilton Steel Car Strike', 14 November 1929 (Provincial Archives of Ontario; AO, CPC Papers, 10C 2295 ff); Sam Carr to Comrade [Peter]

Vasiliev, 25 March 1931, (AO, 4A 2728); G. van Houten, *Canada's Party of Socialism: History of the Communist Party of Canada, 1922–79* (Toronto, 1982), photograph, p. 80.

2. K. McDermott, 'The History of the Comintern in Light of New Documents', in T. Rees and A. Thorpe (eds), *International Communism and the Communist International, 1919–43* (Manchester, 1998), p. 33. For Canadian endorsement see D. Morton, *Working People: An Illustrated History of the Canadian Labour Movement* (Toronto, 1990), pp. 142–45; I. Angus, *Canadian Bolsheviks*, p. 274; B. Palmer, *Working Class Experience: Rethinking the History of Canadian Labour, 1800–1991* (Toronto, 1992), p. 247.

3. C. Heron, 'The Second Industrial Revolution in Canada, 1890–1930', in D. R. Hopkin and G. S. Kealey (eds), *Class, Community and the Labour Movement: Wales and Canada, 1890–1930* (Llafur/CCLH, 1989), pp. 48–67; J. Manley, 'Communists and Autoworkers: The Struggle for Industrial Unionism in the Canadian Automobile Industry, 1925–36', *Labour/Le Travail*, No. 17 (Spring 1986), pp. 106–11; T. Traves, 'Security Without Regulation' and C. Heron, 'The Crisis of the Craftsman: Hamilton's Metal Workers in the Early Twentieth Century', in M. S. Cross and G. S. Kealey (eds), *Readings in Canadian Social History 4: The Consolidation of Capitalism, 1896–1929* (Toronto, 1990), pp. 19–44 and pp. 77–113; G. Friesen, *The Canadian Prairies: A History* (Toronto, 1987), pp. 247–48.

4. C. Lipton, *The Trade Union Movement of Canada 1827–1959* (Toronto, 1973); J. Fudge and E. Tucker, *Labour Before the Law: The Regulation of Workers' Collective Action in Canada, 1900–48* (Toronto, 2001), pp. 135–38.

5. The CPC was lightly regarded by the Comintern, which tended to view it as an appendage of the CPUSA or as a relatively unimportant player in the British Empire 'question'. *Minutes of the Colonial Commission of the Third International*, 3 December 1922 (NA, W. L. M. King Papers, Vol. 63, file 419).

6. W. Rodney, *Soldiers of the International: A History of the Communist Party of Canada, 1919–29* (Toronto, 1968), pp. 61–76; T. Draper, *American Communism and Soviet Russia* (New York, 1960), p. 187; A. Thorpe, *The British Communist Party and Moscow, 1920–43* (Manchester, 2000), p. 81.

7. W. Rodney, *Soldiers*, pp. 81–87; R. Frager, *Sweatshop Strife: Class, Ethnicity, and Gender in the Jewish Labour Movement of Toronto 1900–39* (Toronto, 1992); J. Manley, '"Does the International Labour Movement Need Salvaging?" Communism, Labourism, and the Canadian Trade Unions, 1921–28', *Labour/Le Travail*, No. 41 (Spring 1998), pp. 147–80; J. Manley, 'Preaching the Red Stuff: J. B. McLachlan, Communism, and the Cape Breton Miners, 1922–35,' *Labour/Le Travail*, No. 30 (Fall 1992), pp. 65–114.

8. 'Theses on the Tactics in the Trade Union Movement', in H. Gruber, *Soviet Russia Masters the Comintern: International Communism in the Era of Stalin's Ascendancy* (New York, 1974), pp. 144–50; T. Ewan to the editor, *The Worker*, 15 August 1925; J. Lakeman to the editor, *The Worker*, 5 September 1925; Reports of A. T. Hill and W. Bosowich, *Proceedings of the Fifth National Convention* (Toronto, 1927), pp. 25–31; E. W. Laine, 'Finnish Canadian Radicalism and Canadian Politics: The First Forty Years', in J. Dahlie and T. Fernando (eds), *Ethnicity, Power and Politics in Canada* (Toronto, 1981), pp. 99–100.

9. J. Sangster, *Dreams of Equality: Women On the Canadian Left, 1920–50* (Toronto, 1989), pp. 26–54.

10. Cortland Starnes to Arthur Meighen, 17 July 1926 (NA, Arthur Meighen Papers, Vol. 147); J. Manley, 'Preaching', pp. 84–88.

11. 'Discussion on Trade Union Report and Resolutions', CPC, *Proceedings*, pp. 80–83.

12. Alex Lyon to the editor, *The Worker*, 5 September 1925 and 2 January 1926; W. T. Burford, 'The Crimes of Chicago', *Communication Worker*, August 1926; Aaron Mosher to the editor, *The Worker*, 13 August and 10 September 1927; correspondence between Florence Custance and W. T. Burford, in *Woman Worker*, October 1927, pp. 13–15.

13. *Thee Worker*, 19 March 1927 (original emphasis); A. Miller, 'Labour Conditions in Western Canada', *Labour Monthly*, March 1927, pp. 175–78. The LWIU was formed from the shell of the One Big Union in 1924–25. See Beckie Buhay, 'Ontario Loggers Win Wage Increase', *The Worker*, 13 November 1926; P. Campbell, 'The Cult of Spontaneity: Finnish–Canadian Bushworkers and the Industrial Workers of the World in Northern Ontario, 1919–1934', *Labour/Le Travail*, No. 41 (Spring 1998), pp. 133–37.

14. E. Johanningsmeier, *Forging American Communism: The Life of William Z. Foster* (Princeton, 1994), pp. 238–45; A. Thorpe, *The British Communist Party*, pp. 135–49.

15. J. Manley, 'Communists', pp. 112–20; J. Manley, 'Preaching', pp. 94–97; *Report of Proceedings of the LWIU Convention*, Port Arthur, 31 March to 3 April 1928 (NA, Department of Labour (DOL) Records, Vol. 3133, file 140).

16. O. W. Kuusinen, 'Resolution on the Canadian Question', 25 April 1928 (NA, CF, Reel 4, file 23); *The Militant*, 1 February 1929 and 17 May 1930.

17. *Minutes of the CPC Enlarged Central Executive Committee*, 20–22 October 1928 (AO, CPC Papers, 8C 0132 ff.). MacDonald was clearly taking his cue from Bukharin's version of the New Line.

18. See the discussions among Canada's Lenin School students, who observed MacDonald and Spector at close hand at the sixth world congress. Lesley [Morris] to Dear John [Weir], 21 July 1928; Morris to Dear Danny, 4 August 1928; 'Porter' [Morris] to Dear John [Weir], 22 September 1928). Charles Sims was perhaps the first to identify Spector as a Trotskyist: 'Porter' to Dear Joe [Farbey?], 24 September 1928 (NA, CF, Reel 7, file 55).

19. RCMP 'O' Division reports, 27 November 1921 and 29 November 1922 (NA, Canadian Security Intelligence Service (CSIS), Tim Buck file, Part 3).

20. Tim Buck to A. S. Lozovsky, 8 January 1929; 'Page' [Buck] to Business Manager, Organization Department, RILU, 25 June 1929 (NA, CF, Reel K-313, file 335).

21. J. Manley, 'Communists', pp. 119–20.

22. Unsigned letter to J. B. Salsberg, 28 February 1929; Salsberg to Buck, 7 March 1929 (AO, CPC Papers.)

23. Carr, 23, had emigrated from Poland only five years earlier. He returned to Moscow for his final year at the Lenin School, returning in 1930 as party organisational secretary. See *Canadian Labor Defender*, December 1931.

24. I. Angus, *Canadian Bolsheviks*, is the best published account of these events.

25. Strikes and Lockouts Files (SLF) (NA, DOL, Vol. 343, file 87).

26. L. Morris, 'The Unemployment Crisis and Our Party', *The Worker*, 19 April 1930; S. Repo, 'Rosvall and Voutilainen: Two Union Men Who Never Died', *Labour/Le Travailleur*, No. 8/9 (Autumn 1981/Spring 1982), pp. 80–83; 'Statement of the Political Committee of the CPC on the Expulsion of Salsberg', undated (AO, CPC Papers, 1A 0741–42); *Minutes of the CPC Political Committee*, 13 December 1929 (AO, CPC Papers, 8C 0210); CPC, *Minutes of the Trade Union Department*, 25 December 1929 (10C 1813–14).

27. Tim Buck to Stewart Smith, 24 January 1930; 'Resolution of the American-Canadian Landersecretariat of the International Lenin School on the Situation in the Communist Party of Canada', 2 April 1930 (NA, CF, Reel 11, file 97).

28. S. Smith, 'Right Wing Mistakes and the Necessity of Correction', *The Worker*, 30 July 1930; T. Ewan, 'Rank Opportunism in Needle Trades Organization Work', *The Worker*, 19 July 1930; I. Angus, *Canadian Bolsheviks*, pp. 308–14.

29. This had been Lenin's warning to Zinoviev and Bukharin, which the latter repeated to Stalin in late 1928. S. Cohen, *Bukharin and the Bolshevik Revolution: A Political Biography, 1888–1938* (Oxford, 1980), p. 294.

30. CPC, *The Triumph of Socialism in the Soviet Union* (Toronto, 1930), pp. 7–8.

31. Files on John Stokaluk and Harvey Murphy (NA, CSIS); Tim Buck to Harvey Murphy, 25 July 1930 (NA, CPC Papers, Vol. 8, file 7); Drafts of RILU 'Resolution on Canadian Mining Industry and Perspective for New Union', September 1930 (AO, CPC Papers, 10C 1862, 10C 1942); J. Sloan, 'District President's Report, Fifth Annual Convention of the Mine Workers' Union of Canada', undated [September 1930] (10C 2062–65). For events in Cape Breton, see J. Manley, 'Preaching', pp. 97–101.

32. Tom Ewan to James Sloan, 30 July 1931; CPC District 3, *Organizational Letter No. 1*, 5 March 1931 (AO, CPC, 3A 2310 and 8C 0048).

33. Tom Ewan to Ben Winter, 30 January 1931(AO, CPC Papers, 3A 1710, original emphasis).

34. J. Hladun, 'They Taught Me Treason', *Maclean's Magazine* (1947). 'Textile Worker' to the editor, *Young Worker*, 2 January 1931; A. Lozovsky, 'The United Front of Employed and Unemployed', *Communist International*, No. 8, 1 March 1931, pp. 122–25; O. Piatnitsky, *Unemployment and the Tasks of the Communists* (London, 1931), pp. 40–45; Tom Ewan to Ben Winter, 7 May 1931; Winter to Ewan, 14 May 1931; Ewan to Winter, 26 May 1931 (AO, CPC Papers, 3A 1847–8, 3A 1853–56 and 3A 1863).

35. 'The Resolution of the Anglo–American Section [AAS] of the Profintern on the Situation and Tasks of the Workers' Unity League of Canada', 28 November 1930; correspondence between Ewan and Joshua Gershman, November–December 1930; Tom Ewan, 'Report to Communist Party of Canada Plenum', February 1931 (AO, CPC Papers, 1A 0244–45, 0282–90 and 8C 0607–12.

36. Jack Davis [Sam Carr] to Tim Buck, 25 July 1930; Tim Buck to Stewart Smith, 4 November 1930 (NA, CPC Papers, Vol. 8, file 7); Tim Buck, Reply to Discussion, CEC Plenum, February 1931 (AO, 8C 0588–66).

37. S. Smith, *Comrades*, p. 143.

38. J. Manley, 'Canadian Communists, Revolutionary Unionism, and the Third Period: The Workers' Unity League, 1930–35', *Journal of the Canadian Historical Association*, No. 5 (1994), pp. 167–94.

39. A. Gauld, 'How We MUST Work in the REFORMIST Unions', *Workers' Unity*, March 1933.

40. The evidence does not sustain the accusation levelled at the party by embittered social democrats that outside organisers Annie Buller, Sam Scarlett and Joe Forkin callously put the Estevan strikers in harm's way. See M. J. Campbell, memo re 'Coal Miners' Strike, Estevan and Bienfait, Saskatchewan'. 2 October 1931 (NA, SLF, Vol. 348, file 70).

41. WUL National Executive Board, 'Resolutions on the Reformist Unions and Tasks of the Workers' Unity League', 2 January 1933 (NA, CF, Reel 18, file 153); DOL, *Annual Report on Labour Organizations in Canada 1932* (Ottawa, 1933), p. 37.

42. J. Manley, '"Starve, Be Damned!" Communists and Canada's Urban Unemployed, 1929–39', *The Canadian Historical Review*, Vol. 79 No. 3 (September 1998); Hugh Guthrie to W. H. Price, 18 March 1931 (University of Toronto; UT, Robert Kenny Collection, Box 2).

43. Tom Ewan to Sidney Elias, 29 May 1931 (AO, CPC Papers, 4A 2752). The 'Kingston Eight' consisted of the seven PB members and Tomo Cacic, a middle-level Croatian cadre who had chosen the wrong time to visit party headquarters.

44. CLDL, *Minutes and Reports of 1ˢᵗ Plenum*, Toronto, 11–12 July 1931; Tim Buck to CPC District and Language Fraction Bureaux, 19 August 1931 (UT Kenny Collection, Box 10);

B. Kashtan, 'Carry On the Struggle for Which Our Leaders Were Jailed', *Young Worker*, 8 March 1932; Harry Binder interview (AO, Multi-Cultural History Society of Ontario Collection).

45. CLDL, 'Eastern Canada Emergency Defence Conference Report', Hamilton, 26–27 April 1930 (NA, J. S. Woodsworth Papers, Vol. 10, file 35); *Minutes of OBU Winnipeg Central Labour Council*, 16 June 1931 (Public Archives of Manitoba (AM), R. B. Russell Papers, box 6, file 28); CLDL press release, '"Labor" MP Proves Himself Social Fascist', 3 July 1931 (New York Public Library (NYPL), International Red Aid Papers, Vol. TD1/n.c. 6); S. Carr, 'Sharpening Struggle in Canada', *Labour Monthly*, February 1932, pp. 105–12.

46. Tom Ewan to Arthur Seal, 8 June 1931 (AO, CPC Papers, 2A 1200–01); Ernest Burns to the editor, *Labor Statesman*, 24 July 1931; J. S. Woodsworth to A. E. Smith, 23 April 1931 (NA, J. S. Woodsworth Papers, Vol. 6, file 8); 'Those Strongly Vocal Persons', *Labor Statesman*, 11 September 1931.

47. *RCMP Security Bulletin No. 679*, 3 November 1933, in R. Whitaker and G. S. Kealey (eds), *RCMP Security Bulletins: The Depression Years, Part I, 1933–34* (St. John's, 1993), pp. 56–57; S. Smith, *Comrades*, p. 157

48. Tom Ewan to Tom Bradley, 30 May 1931 (AO, CPC Papers, 4A 2928–29).

49. E. Thomas, 'Women at War in the Forefront of the Fight for Existence', *Canadian Miner*, 24 April 1933; H. Murphy, 'Some Lessons of the Crow's Nest Pass Strike', *Canadian Miner*, 21 April 1932; WUL, *Workers' Unity League: Policy–Tactics–Structure–Demands* (Toronto, 1932), pp. 31–36.

50. J. Manley, 'Starve' pp. 469–70 and pp. 475–76; R. Frager, 'Politicized Housewives in the Jewish Communist Movement of Toronto, 1923–33', in L. Kealey and J. Sangster (eds)., *Beyond the Vote: Canadian Women and Politics* (Toronto, 1989), pp. 258–75; 'WWL Has Busy Summer in "Peg"', *The Worker*, 29 August 1934; M. Luxton, *More Than A Labour of Love: Three Generations of Women's Work in the Home* (Toronto, 1980), p. 218.

51. For glimpses of leading CPC women, see J. Sangster, *Dreams*, chaps. 3 and 5; R. Frager, *Sweatshop*; A. Levesque, *Scenes de la vie en rouge: L'Epoque de Jeanne Corbin 1906–44* (Montreal, 1999).

52. B. Palmer (Ed.), *A Communist Life: Jack Scott and the Canadian Workers' Movement, 1927–85* (St. John's, 1988), p. 25.

53. J. Warren, 'Towards a Mass Party!' Report to the Seventh Session of the Central Committee, CPC, 8 December 1934, in *The Communists Fight for Working Class Unity* (Montreal, 1935), p. 50; 'The Need for Mass Work Among Women', Ninth Plenum of the CPC CC, November 1935, in *Toward A Canadian People's Front* (1935), p. 139.

54. Alice C[ooke] to Annie Guralnick, 10 October 1955 (UT, Kenny Collection, Box 41); interview with Paul Kirzner (Metro Toronto Public Library); V. Post, 'Suggestions for Work Amongst Women', *Discussion*, No. 3, 1937; author's interview with Stan and Sylvia Lowe, Vancouver, 1978; R. Frager, *Sweatshop*, p. 159.

55. 'Red Propaganda in Queen City Schools', *Hamilton Spectator*, 7 December 1928; L. Betcherman, *The Little Band*, pp. 21–22; J. Johnson, 'Notes from the Strike', *Canadian Miner*, 9 July 1932; O. Kay, 'Children's Clubs in the Class Struggle', *Canadian Miner*, 24 April 1933.

56. 'Resolution on Building a Mass Children's Movement', undated [c. February 1933] (NA, FOC Papers, Vol. 16, file 34); Minnie Shelley to 'All District and Local Children's Councils', 1 November 1933; Report of Comrade Kashtan on Situation in the Pioneer Movement, undated [c. November 1933].

57. Minnie Shelley to Finnish Organization of Canada, 8 March 1933 (NA, FO, Vol. 16, file 34).

58. Finnish Organization of Canada to Mildred Stern, 4 June 1934 (NA, FO, Vol. 16, file 34); George Sundquist to *Always Ready*, 5 July 1934; NCC, *Organizational Bulletin – Suggestions to All Pioneer Leaders and Groups*, undated; *RCMP Security Bulletin No. 730*, 31 October 1934, p. 357.

59. 'May Day Devoid of Trouble in Winnipeg', *Winnipeg Free Press*, 2 May 1934; NCC, 'Report on working class children's camps held during the year 1933 and recommendations for the organisation of such camps during 1934', 20 March 1934 (NA, FO, Vol. 16, file 34); J. Brown to Lt. Col. W. Griesinger, 2 May 1933 (DND, DH, File 161.009, D63).

60. Report re 'Communist Party of Canada, Crow's Nest Pass, Harvey Murphy – Communist Agitator', 22 September 1930 (NA, CSIS, Harvey Murphy File); Arthur Seal, 'Report on NUWA Windsor Section', 12 June 1931; correspondence between Tom Ewan and Arthur Seal, 22, 24 and 27 June 1931(AO, CPC Papers, 2A 1216 and 2A 1227–33); Department of Police, City of Windsor, Reports re 'Communist Meeting at Lanspeary Park', 3 September 1931 and 1 May 1932 (DND, Directorate of History, file 161.009, D63); A. Johnson, 'Shingle Workers of B.C. Show Fight', *Lumber Worker*, September 1932; author's interview with Harold Pritchett, Coquitlam, B.C., August 1978; I. MacMillan, 'Strikes, Bogeys, Spares, and Misses: Pin-boy and Caddy Strikes in the 1930s', *Labour/Le Travail*, No. 44 (Fall 1999), pp. 158–60.

61. Tom Ewan to George Drayton, 18 April 1931 (AO, CPC Papers, 4A 2387–88).

62. R. Liversedge, *Recollections of the On-to-Ottawa Trek* (Toronto, 1973) pp. 17–18. Judging from their team sheet, the Vancouver WSA soccer team comprised 10 Anglo-Celts and a Dane. The *Unemployed Worker*, 27 February 1932, noted how its first draw and win – unlike its earlier defeats – was not reported in the city's bourgeois press.

63. Intelligence, Military District No. 11, 'Monthly Report on Aid to the Civil Power', August 1935 (DND, DH, File 322.009, D 804); B. Kidd, *The Struggle for Canadian Sport* (Toronto, 1996), pp. 146–77; B. Kidd, 'Radical Immigrants and the Workers' Sports Federation of Canada, 1924–37' in G. Eisen and D. K. Wiggins (eds), *Ethnicity and Sport in North American Culture* (Westport, 1994), pp. 201–19; E. Reiter, 'Secular Yiddishkait: Left Culture, Politics and Community', *Labour/Le Travail*, No. 49 (Spring 2002), pp. 121–46.

64. Toronto Progressive Arts' Club *Manifesto* and L. F. Edwards, 'Authorship and Canadiana', *Masses*, April 1932; M.S. [Minnie Shelley], *Information Bulletin* re NCC meeting of 6 May 1933 (NAC, FOC Collection, Vol. 16, file 34).

65. T. G. Ryan, *Stage Left: Canadian Workers' Theatre 1929–40* (Toronto, 1981), pp. 34–36, p. 52, p. 63 and p. 84; R. Wright (Ed.), *Eight Men Speak and Other Plays for the Canadian Workers' Theatre*, (New Hogtown, 1976), p. xxiv.

66. 'Self-Study Materials' 1926–28 (NA, CPC Records, Vol. 1, file 19); A. Levesque, *Scenes*, p. 41; District No. 3, 'List of Candidates for RILU Correspondence Training Course', 15 September 1929 (AO, CPC Papers, 1A 0067); 'Report of Work and Situation in the Border Cities', No. 2, 11 April 1931 (10C 1960 ff. and 2A 1164–65).

67. L. M., 'The Question of Party Education', *The Worker*, 21 March 1931; Sam Carr to Tom Ewan, 8 July 1931; Buck to Morris, undated (AO, CPC Papers, 3A 1940–41 and 3A 1971); Ewan to Carr, 12 July 1931 (UT, Kenny Papers, Box 2).

68. G. Sundquist, 'Report of the Executive Committee of the Finnish Organization of Canada to the Enlarged EC Meeting' 10 July 1934; National Publicity Education Department, CLDL, memo on 'Summer Educational Courses', May 1934 (NA, FOC Collection, Vol. 6. file 12 and Vol. 16. file 27).

69. *Young Worker*, 16 October 1933; 'Stalin Stresses to YCL the Need for Study', *Young Worker*, 30 December 1933; 'Workers' Training School Closes Session', *Unemployed Worker*, 8 October 1932.

70. B. Palmer (Ed.), *Jack Scott*, pp. 49–50; G. Levine (Ed.), *Patrick Lenihan: From Irish Rebel to Founder of Canadian Public Sector Unionism* (St. John's, 1998), p. 124.

71. 'Report of Comrade Clarke (Stewart Smith) to AAS, Communist International', 17 July 1935 (NA, CF, Reel K288, file 169). Smith claimed that the party had between 80–100 elected municipal representatives.

72. R. Liversedge, *Recollections*, p. 18; J. F. White, 'Russian Highlights', *Canadian Forum*, February to July 1933; A. E. Smith, *All My Life* (Toronto, 1977), pp. 152–53; J. Manley, 'Preaching', p. 102. See also H. Srebrnik, 'Red Star Over Birobidzhan: Canadian Jewish Communists and the "Jewish Autonomous Region" in the Soviet Union', *Labour/Le Travail*, No. 44 (Fall 1999), pp. 129–47.

73. CLDL, *Report of the First Representative National Convention*, Toronto, 14–17 July 1933 (UT, RKC, Box 10).

74. J. Manley, '"Audacity, audacity, still more audacity": Tim Buck, the Party, and the People, 1932–39', *Labour/Le Travail*, No. 49 (Spring 2002), pp. 11–15.

75. R. Wright (Ed.), *Eight Men Speak*, pp. 27–89 (Guard X placed 'capitalism' in the dock: 'he's the guy who uses us all'); T. G. Ryan, *Stage Left*, pp. 43–46; A. E. Smith United Defence Conference, 'A CALL to the Working and Liberal Minded People of Toronto', February 1934 (AO, miscellaneous manuscripts collection, Mss. 1934, No. 5); 'Stickers Urging Probe of Buck's Shooting Found', *Winnipeg Free Press*, 16 May 1934. The 'Eight' had become seven with Cacic's release and summary deportation.

76. J. Manley, '"Audacity"', pp. 16–17.

77. 'Notes from the Townships', *October Youth*, April 1933; *October Youth*, August–September 1933.

78. DOL, 'Memo *re:* Strike at Stratford, Ontario', 22 September 1933 (NA, R. B. Bennett Papers, 267758); *Toronto Daily Star*, 14, 15 and 17 August 1934; N. Stunden, 'The Stratford Strikes of 1933' (MA research paper, Carleton University, 1975).

79. ECCI, 'The Concrete Tasks of the CPC', 16 September 1932; ECCI, Draft Letters to CPC, 9, 14 May and 28 September 1934 (NA, CF, Reel 15, file 132 and Reel 18, file 155); G. Poole, 'CCF "Justice" to the Alberta Hunger Marchers', *Canadian Labour Defender*, January–February 1933; 'The Careerists', *Nova Scotia Miner*, 25 February 1933; D. W., 'The Toronto "Star" and the CCF', *The Worker*, 10 June 1933.

80. *Flin Flon Miner*, 28 September, and 9 November 1933.

81. D. M. LeBourdais to E. A. Beder, 20 February 1934 (York University, Ontario, E. A. Beder Papers, Box 8); CCF, *Minutes of the Ontario Provincial Council*, 17 February 1934 (UT, J. S. Woodsworth Papers); 'Open Letter to the CCF Clubs of Ontario', 2 April 1934.

82. See correspondence between Woodsworth and Unemployed Councils' leader Hannes Sula, reprinted in *The Worker*, 22 July 1933.

83. N. Penner, *The Canadian Left: A Critical Analysis* (Toronto, 1977), pp. 25–51; *RCMP Security Bulletin* No. 717, 1 August 1934, pp. 171–73; J. Manley, 'Audacity', p. 17.

84. 'Trades and Labour Council Notes', *Winnipeg Weekly News*, 16 March 1934. For Heaps' longstanding hostility to the party, see '"Labor" MP Proves Himself Social Fascist', 3 July 1931; Canada, *House of Commons Debates*, 1932–33, Vol. II, p. 22.

85. W. Findlay, 'Regarding British Traditions' and J. Houston, 'Tasks of the Unemployed Councils', *The Worker*, 10 June 1933; J. Houston, letter to the editor, *Toronto Daily Star*, 1 August 1933; *Proceedings of the First Canadian Congress Against War and Fascism* (Toronto, 1934); P. Hunter, *Which Side Are You On, Boys? Canadian Life on the Left* (Toronto, 1988), pp. 52–54 and pp. 74–77.

86. *RILU Magazine*, 1 February 1932; B. Matheson, 'Revolutionary Strategy in the Trade Unions: The Balance of 'Third Period' Sectarianism', *The Vanguard*, November–December 1932); 'Strike at Hallman and Sable', *October Youth*, August–September 1933; 'The Dressmakers' Strike', *The Vanguard*, February 1934.

87. 'Detailed List of Strikes and Lockouts, 1933', *Labour Gazette*, February 1934, pp. 122–30; 'Detailed List of Strikes and Lockouts, 1934', Labour Gazette, February 1935, pp. 116–28; 'Communism in Canada', *Toronto Labor Leader*, 22 June 1934.

88. A. S. Lozovsky, *The Workers' Economic Struggles and the Fight for Workers' Rule* (Montreal, 1933), p. 17; C. Sims, 'The Daily Struggles and Socialism', *Workers' Unity*, May 1933; P. Campbell, 'The Cult of Spontaneity', pp. 141–42; 'The Need for Honesty with the Workers', *The Vanguard*, September 1934; 'The Struggle for the United Front and the Immediate Tasks', *Communist Review*, December 1934–January 1935.

89. O. J. Kerr, *House of Commons Special Committee on Price Spreads and Mass Buying, Evidence and Proceedings* (1 March 1934), pp. 173–98. See also J. Manley, 'Communists', pp. 124–26.

90. 'This Question of a Charter', *B.C. Lumber Worker*, 24 November 1934.

91. Canada, *House of Commons Debates*, 14 February 1934, pp. 577–78; 'Harmony in Canadian Industry', *Labor Leader*, 16 February 1934.

92. Ontario Attorney General's Office, *Agents of Revolution: A History of the Workers' Unity League Setting Forth Its Origins and Aims* (Toronto, 1934).

93. J. Manley, 'Canadian Communists', pp. 182–86; E. N. Rhodes Papers, folder 3W00, item No. 71229 (Provincial Archives of Nova Scotia; ANS); 'Shoe and Boot Workers Organizing', *The Vanguard*, February 1934; 'Business Agent Gives Homely Truths', *The Worker*, 22 August 1934.

94. 'Challenge Union Men to "Debate in the Open"', *Toronto Daily Star*, 20 August 1934; J. B. McLachlan, 'On With the Battle and "Public Exposure"', *The Worker*, 5 September 1934.

95. Most TUUL unions were dissolved by January 1935. See, for example, R. Keeran, *The Communist Party and the Auto Workers' Unions* (New York, 1986), pp. 115–17.

96. Various drafts of Trade Union Directive first sent in May 1934 (NA, CF, Reel 18, file 155), original emphasis.

97. J. Manley, 'Communists', p. 128; J. Manley, 'Preaching', p. 109; T. C. Sims, *Strike Strategy and Tactics*, Report to the National Executive Board, WUL, 4–5 September 1934; Louis Fine to J. B. Salsberg, 17 January 1935; Transcript of Meeting between Department of Labour, Ontario, and the Workers' Unity League, 23 January 1935 (AO, Ontario Department of Labour, Industrial Standards Officer Files, Vol. 28).

98. Unsigned letter to 'Dear Friends', 8 March 1935 (NA, CF, Reel 22, file 179); *The Worker*, 26 March 1935; AAS, 'Draft Letter to CPC on Trade Union Work', 31 March 1935 (NA, CF, Reel 22, file 181); RILU American Fraction to CPC, 28 April 1935; ECCI, 'The Lessons of the Workers' Struggle and the Tasks of the Communists in the Trade Unions and the Unemployed Movement', Draft Trade Union Resolution, 11 July 1935 (NA, CF, Reel K289, file 176); *The Worker*, 17 October 1935.

99. The official CPC historians' view that 'red unionism', the emblem of 'class against class', was a purely local response to the AFL unions' expulsion of communist militants and refusal to organise the unorganised, is simply wrong. O. Ryan, *Tim Buck: A Conscience for Canada* (Toronto, 1975), pp. 127–28; G. van Houten, *Canada's Party of Socialism*, pp. 83–85.

100. B. Palmer (Ed.), *Jack Scott*, pp. 26–27. For the (preposterous) official view that the winding-up of the WUL was a model of democracy, see T. McEwen, *The Forge Glows Red: From Blacksmith to Revolutionary* (Toronto, 1974), pp. 149–50.

The New Line in the Antipodes: Australian Communists and Class Against Class

STUART MACINTYRE

The Third Period in communist history was marked by an intensification of the class struggle in an atmosphere of imminent crisis. The Communist International (Comintern) anticipated that the mounting difficulties of world capitalism would increase competition among the imperialist powers, which in turn would redouble their attacks on the Soviet Union. Capitalists would shed labour and reduce wages. Governments would discard the trappings of parliamentary democracy. The social democrats would be forced to shed their disguise as the false friends of the workers and work openly on behalf of the bourgeoisie. Under these circumstances, the task of the communists was to concentrate their struggle against the discredited reformists, to dispel any remaining illusions, and to mobilise the growing discontent into a militant campaign of 'class against class'.

This would require both an extension and an intensification of their activity. Third Period communists worked among the unemployed, women, youth and national minorities; they gave greater emphasis to colonial liberation and anti-war agitation; put art, literature and culture at the service of the militant proletariat. They redirected effort from relatively open areas of activity that had served the united front to new ones with a clear and uncompromising revolutionary identity, and from agitation to confrontation. They installed new leaders, imposed a stricter discipline, demanded greater sacrifice, endured harsher repression and suffered repeated setbacks. The revolutionary expectations of the Third Period were nowhere fulfilled, and it was only after Germany fell to the Nazis in 1933 that the Comintern turned back towards the anti-fascist Popular Front and recovery.

The signal failure of the Third Period strategy has often been treated as an object lesson in political futility. 'Class against class' divided the labour movement as it responded to the economic, political and social crisis of the 'great depression'. The concentration of effort against the social democrats, whom communists now anathemised as 'social fascists', weakened working class resistance to the real threat of fascism as well as the governments of national unity that replaced social democratic ones in Australia as well as Britain. The chiliasm of the Third Period analysis took comfort from the weakening of democratic institutions and erosion of civil liberties, just as the

247

sectarian excesses of its exponents discredited the left. The failure has been attributed to the distorted character of the Comintern, a monolithic party directed from Moscow and subject to the intrigues that accompanied Stalin's usurpation of the Communist Party of the Soviet Union (CPSU).[1]

Recent studies have modified this interpretation of the Third Period. Historians of the Australian as well as other communist parties have suggested a more complex interplay of local factors in the turn to 'class against class'. Many communists had chafed at the lack of progress made during the 1920s. They responded to the mounting economic difficulties with greater militancy and needed little encouragement to denounce the leaders of ineffective trade unions and working class parties. Examinations of the Third Period have also suggested the need to distinguish its different stages: a turn to the left began in the late 1920s, and intensified after the Wall Street crash in October 1929, but as early as 1931 some of its Australian excesses were softened. While Hitler's accession to power in January 1933 brought a call for a united front against fascism, it was not until 1935 that the Comintern finally persuaded the Australians that this could only be pursued by abandoning the sectarian abuse that accompanied the initial call for a 'united front from below'.

It was Stalin who distinguished the Third Period from the two previous phases of communist activity, first the revolutionary wave that had accompanied the Great War and then the temporary stabilisation after 1921. An alternative periodisation might suggest a greater continuity in which the changes of policy were variations on an underlying theme. The communist parties formed in the West under Lenin's direction following the Russian Revolution differed in structure and method from the earlier groupings of revolutionary socialists. At least in the West, those groupings had been fragile associations of doctrinaire oppositionists who refused any accommodation with the capitalist order. These communist parties were highly disciplined organisations that practised a dogmatic pragmatism to subvert that order by capturing control of its labour movement. Under Stalin's control they were turned during the Third Period into a party of pragmatic dogmatism, applying their formidable discipline to supplant the existing forms of the labour movement. While they afterwards reverted to a less confrontational stance, the qualities that characterised these Third Period endeavours − the doctrinaire temper, hierarchical control and tactical flexibility − all operated across the lifespan of the Comintern.

Similar observations apply to the revisionist emphasis on communist history from below. The recent attention to local agency recognises that communism in the non-communist world was a commitment made freely, without the sanctions that Stalin exercised in his own country, and that the application of the Comintern line to particular circumstances could never be exact. At the same time, we need to recognise that every section of the

Communist International fell into line with the resolutions of its congress and the instructions of its executive. All of them responded to the same cues for the New Line, adopted the slogans of 'class against class', and entered into the frenzy of activity it prescribed.

Towards the Third Period

The Communist Party of Australia (CPA) on the eve of the Third Period was a small, weak and demoralised sect. Formed in 1920 by enthusiasts from small socialist groups, it was quickly rebuffed by the Australian Labor Party (ALP), which possessed considerable strength. Before the Great War, the ALP had become the first working class party to achieve an electoral majority and govern in its own right. While out of government in the federal parliament from 1916 to 1929, it held office for at least part of the decade in five of the six State governments, which were responsible for most of the substantial public sector, and cemented its relations with the affiliated trade unions. Communists operated on the fringe of the labour movement in the principal cities (Sydney and Melbourne contained one-third of a population that reached 6.5 million at the end of the decade). The CPA attracted trade union militants, especially in more isolated industrial settings such as the coalfields of New South Wales and the sugar mills and meat processing works of north Queensland; but here they were competing with the industrial syndicalism of the Industrial Workers of the World (IWW), which retained a residual influence in Australia and was generally resistant to Bolshevik methods. Moreover, the seasonal and itinerant nature of the latter occupations imparted an episodic character to such militant activities.[2]

The Party's initial base was in the Trades Hall in Sydney, where a group of left-wing union officials had attached themselves to the CPA in the course of a battle for control of the Labor Party in New South Wales. Their leader was Jock Garden, who had attended the fourth world congress of the Comintern as the secretary of the New South Wales Labor Council and, by 1924, was the party secretary. Garden led an application for communist affiliation to the Labor Party and, when it was rejected, he led a slate of communist parliamentary candidates who attracted derisory support. Thwarted on both fronts, the majority of these 'Trades Hall Reds' opted to rejoin the Labor Party in 1925. Garden himself remained for the time a nominal communist (his support for the Pan-Pacific Trade Union Movement of the Red International of Labour Unions (RILU) remained more important to the Comintern than the fortunes of this tiny and distant section) but yielded the leadership to Jack Kavanagh, who arrived in Australia in 1925 after earlier activity in Communist Party of Canada. He inherited a party with just 250 members.

Kavanagh would remain the leading figure in the CPA — through his position was chairman rather than general secretary – over the next five years as the New Line was imposed. His instincts were those of a left militant and he worked as an organiser for the New South Wales Labor Council in a series of major industrial conflicts as employers responded to a downturn in the Australian economy from 1928 with attacks on wages and working conditions. A self-educated intellectual, he re-established party training and saw to improvement of the weekly newspaper. Women's groups and youth sections were reformed. Kavanagh was also an internationalist, scathing of the insularity of the Australian labour movement: 'one is shocked by the docility manifested by the workers' organisations', he noted in his diary shortly after arrival.[3] Under his leadership, the CPA took up a position to the left of the Comintern's resolutions on the united front with the Labor Party and trade unions.

Kavanagh's reformation of the CPA coincided with a belated attention by the Comintern to its backward character. In the early years, Australian delegates had gone to Moscow – no less than nine attended the Comintern's fourth world congress – and told the Comintern officials what they wanted to hear. Opportunities for the ECCI to see what was happening in Australia were limited: Russians active in the formation of the CPA had been deported, while emissaries from the Soviet Union were intercepted.[4] The work of the Australian party was, therefore, supervised loosely by the ECCI's Anglo-American Secretariat (AAS), and the Australians bridled at any intervention from the Communist Party of Great Britain (CPGB). A CPGB representative, R. W. Robson, attended the Australian party's conference in 1927 as a Comintern delegate and criticised the leftism of the delegates, but Kavanagh forced Robson (who had entered Australia under an assumed name) to leave the conference by drawing attention to his presence.[5]

Not until 1926, did the practice begin of calling Australian representatives to Moscow on an annual basis to discuss their work and provide instructions for the subsequent annual conference (the term 'congress' and its democratic centralist forms would be among the changes of the Third Period). The AAS's first assessment in that year of 'The Australian question' identified some of the difficulties the CPA had to overcome. The Australian trade union movement was exceptionally strong, its level of prosperity high. Partly due to such 'conditions' and partly to the conscious effort of the 'petty-bourgeois minded, craft narrowed elements' who dominated the Labor Party, the Australian proletariat was 'almost completely shut off from the proletariat of other continents'. The tasks of the party were therefore to redouble their efforts to provide a militant lead to organised workers, to combat reformism, to campaign against the ideology of White Australia, to get a foothold among the foreign-speaking immigrants and to combat British imperialism.[6]

When the party conference met at the end of 1926, the question of how communists should deal with the Labor Party caused particular argument. Three alternative resolutions were submitted, some delegates seeing the local peculiarities optimistically, some pessimistically; and the Central Executive Committee's (CEC) resolution affirming the need to work where possible within the Labor Party underwent amendment before adoption. Clear factional differences were also evident in the election of the new executive between those who wished to maintain the existing strategy of a united front and those seeking to harden the line against the Labor Party.

The dissidents took these differences to the Comintern. In August 1927, CPA general secretary Tom Wright met with the AAS to discuss his party's political report. Before drafting its response, the secretariat received a copy of a report from Bert Moxon, the chief critic of the existing united front strategy, which painted a highly optimistic picture of its further possibilities.[7] The eventual 'Australian Resolution' formulated in October was trenchant. The Australians were instructed to initiate a 'big mass campaign' on the basis of a revolutionary platform among the workers and make it clear that the Labor Party could not and would not implement the platform. The CPA was to wage a clearer 'ideological fight against the social chauvinism' that found expression in the White Australia immigration policy.[8]

To remedy its deficiencies and sort out the divisions in the CPA, the ECCI despatched R. W. Robson. He left Moscow just as the Comintern was moving towards the New Line that would become known as 'class against class'; Stalin's speech to the fifteenth congress of the CPSU in December 1927 coincided with the CPA conference. Robson did tell the Australian comrades who met in Sydney that they should expect to 'move into general crisis affecting world imperialism',[9] but gave little indication that he sensed how this change would bring with it an abandonment of the Comintern's united front line. He offered no encouragement to the faction that was most impatient with the limitations of the united front and indeed had closest dealings with those who wished to maintain the existing line. Robson was as much concerned with the weakness of the leadership as he was with its internal divisions: he found the 'political level of the party cadres' to be 'very low indeed', but then 'the political level of the entire working class is very, very low'. He was especially critical of the failure of the CPA executive to give a 'lead' to the congress on the question of the Labor Party and astonished at the expectation of delegates that they were free to determine party policy on that question 'despite the fact that the CI had something to say about it'.[10]

The resolution on the Labor Party moved by Kavanagh's group advanced some way from the united front in its proposition that, 'the ALP is at present an avenue for obtaining influence among the masses ... decidedly inferior to the trade unions'. Kavanagh was signalling a greater emphasis on

communist industrial activity as Australia's economic difficulties mounted
and unions prepared to resist an assault on wages and conditions.[11] An
amendment from the leading moderate, Esmonde Higgins, proposing that
communists should pay equal attention to the ALP and the unions, was
decisively defeated.[12] The heated debate spilled over into the election of the
new executive, in which Moxon (the Queensland organiser) deployed a
parcel of proxy votes derived from branches he had organised there to
remove several of the moderates.

Moxon himself then accompanied Robson back to Moscow, criticised his
role in the dispute, and contested his report to the ECCI. He rehearsed the
factional history of the CPA, ostensibly to expose the minority group of
'right-wing opportunists', inferentially to draw attention to the failures of
Kavanagh's majority group. Citing the particular circumstances in his own
State of Queensland, where a Labor government had been in office for more
than a decade and was in open dispute with the militant unions, Moxon
called for an open break with the ALP: continued support of the reformists,
he suggested, was 'next to criminal' and the lead of the AAS would
determine whether the Australian section of the Comintern went forward to
become a 'mass Bolshevik party' or lapsed into a 'bastard reformist party'.
The ECCI adopted his proposal that the CPA organise election contests
against Labor in Queensland, but hedged its bets by inviting Higgins to
attend the sixth world congress of the International later in that year.[13]
Higgins was a former member of the CPGB and probably owed the
invitation to his friend Harry Pollitt.[14]

These decisions of the ECCI secretariat piqued the CEC of the CPA.
Kavanagh's majority group had not expected the call to oppose Labor
electorally, a task that seemed to them both beyond their capacity and a
diversion from their industrial emphasis. Rather than contest the
instructions, they called for clarification. Should they seek to encourage a
left-wing opposition to the Labor leadership, or would this simply foster
reformist illusions? What should be the basis of the electoral programme of
such a left-wing? Was the party strong enough, with only 350 members, to
maintain control of it?[15] The CPGB served as a convenient scapegoat for
Australians' frustration: 'There has been no effective contact with the CI It
takes three months for a reply to be received to letters; there is no one in
Moscow responsible for seeing that Australian matters are attended to; no
good has come of communications with the British party.'[16]

Higgins achieved little. He did not arrive until the day before the last
session of the congress; in every department of the ECCI he experienced
difficulty in pressing Australian needs; he found 'several important comrades
tired of the problems of the Australian party'. Efforts to establish a
permanent Australian representative in Moscow were unsuccessful, as was
the request that Australia be transferred from the AAS to a new group of

Pacific countries.[17]

Higgins was also unsuccessful in his attempt to soften the new line. He was obliged to take back to the CPA, as it gathered in conference at the end of 1928, the news of a deepening world crisis and the message that 'the ALP is now simply part of the capitalist machinery'. The conference duly endorsed 'the Queensland Resolution'. The outcome of the Queensland elections in May 1929 were sufficiently encouraging – 3,000 votes for three communist candidates, not to mention the defeat of the Labor government in that State – for Moxon to call for the application of the New Line throughout Australia.[18] At a time of mounting economic difficulties, major industrial disputes and growing conflict between both union and Labor leaders and their communist critics, the call was received sympathetically by party members in other States. The announcement of a federal election in September 1929 therefore became a test of strength. On 15 September, the CEC resolved that it would not stand candidates and, on 18 September, Moxon and a New South Wales dissident, Lance Sharkey, telegrammed their protest against this 'right deviation' to Tom Bell, the secretary of the AAS.[19]

The ECCI therefore sent a telegram to the general secretary of the CPA that called on the Australian party to run candidates against the Labor Party. The CEC replied on 27 September, again by telegram, that 'organisational difficulties' in standing candidates for an election now little more than a fortnight away prevented compliance. Comintern reiterated its instruction on 28 September. As if realising for the first time the full implications of defiance, the Australians then sent a substantial explanation of their position to Moscow. Combining pragmatism with principle, this distinguished the particular circumstances in Queensland from those in the rest of Australia to argue that there was no basis for mounting an assault on the Labor Party at a time when 'the Labor Party in the federal sphere has gained enormously in prestige amongst the working class', even if the party was in a position to do so.[20] This argument was extended in the debate that was opened in the party press after the election, Kavanagh even disputing that the Third Period was evident in Australia.[21]

That debate was opened in response to a further telegram from the Political Secretariat of ECCI on 18 October, regretting the election of a Labor government in Australia, castigating the failure of the CPA, calling for extensive discussion of the decisions of the sixth world congress and subsequent tenth plenum of the Comintern, foreshadowing the arrival of an 'open letter' to Australian comrades and demanding wide discussion of it as a basis for essential changes in party work.[22] Even then, the CEC of the CPA was loath to circulate the resolutions of the tenth plenum, which put the new tactics of the Third Period beyond doubt. Nor did the executive respond to the 'open letter' itself until Moxon and Sharkey had circulated it.[23] While the CEC then welcomed the letter 'as a necessary corrective to serious mistakes which the central committee and the entire party has been making', it still drew attention to 'certain defects' in its understanding of past Australian events and present circumstances.[24]

Although these arguments were addressed to the ECCI, they were aimed at Australian members as they prepared for the annual party conference due in the last week of the year. There was a wide-ranging debate in the party press lasting more two months that covered a multitude of sins, but the central issue was the applicability of the Third Period to Australia. Moxon and his supporters linked all their criticisms of the leadership to its failure to break with the past and take up the clear revolutionary lead of 'class against class' in accordance with the declared programme of the Comintern. The ECCI put its position beyond doubt in a further telegram that arrived on the second day of the conference: 'The task of the party convention is to subject the party's policy to the severest criticism ... The criticism and the oppositionist attitude adopted by the minority of the central committee and certain local organisations is perfectly sound and necessary.'[25]

Kavanagh was defiant to the last with his insistence that the 'CI letter in lots of instances is a lot of tripe', but the majority of delegates agreed with Moxon and Sharkey's call for 'a correct Comintern line' and a 'single world leadership'. They rejected the outgoing CEC's report for a highly critical minority report, adopted the policy of 'class against class', and turned all but three members of the old guard off the new central committee.[26]

Directing Class Against Class

The account given here makes it clear that the Australian party determined on the New Line. An obdurate leadership of a small and isolated section of the Comintern seemed remarkably naive – it is telling that Kavanagh himself never attended a meeting in Moscow – in the belief that it was free to determine the applicability of instructions sent by the ECCI. While the dissident supporters of 'class against class' appealed to Moscow for support, and received it, they prevailed long after the Third Period policy had been implemented elsewhere and did so only by an open vote of the Australian membership. Yet, if the adoption of the Third Period was the result of local forces, its implementation was closely supervised. In April 1930, a Comintern representative arrived in Sydney and immediately assumed control. He used the identity of Herbert Moore, though his real name was Harry Wicks, a leading member of the Communist Party of the United States of America (CPUSA) and later revealed as an undercover agent for American security organisations for the whole of his party career.[27]

Moore took charge of a fragmentary organisation that was teetering on collapse. In the early months of 1930, Moxon, the new general secretary, had embarked on a frenzy of industrial agitation centred on the northern coalfield of New South Wales. The miners, who had been locked out since March 1929, were the last of the organised wage earners to resist the employers' offensive and, by this time, detachments of armed police were breaking down their resistance. Moxon despatched all available members to defy the prohibition on meetings, and ordered the former leaders to use force if necessary to prevent a return to work. His repeated exhortations to smash the capitalist offensive culminated in a directive in April 1930 for nothing less than a general strike, which evoked not a single response.[28] By this time his campaign against Kavanagh had removed the party's remaining links with the New South Wales Labor Council, while a similar expulsion of Kavanagh's colleague, Jack Ryan, destroyed the Australian Council of Trade Unions' support of the Pan-Pacific Trade Union organisation.[29]

Moore introduced the practice of self-criticism, whereby the disgraced members were forced to confess their errors. This device, which dissolved old loyalties, turned friends into accusers and removed all grounds of principled dissent, proved remarkably effective since most of the former leaders clung to the party for as long as they could. Kavanagh himself protested that 'a communist party is not an association of Pharisees which excuses its sins by blackening the sins of others, nor is it yet an association of sadists taking pleasure in self-flagellation', but he did penance more than once and each time was prescribed an impossible task of redemption.[30] With the collapse of the last major industrial dispute, the members were directed to direct unemployed demonstrations into violent confrontation, and by November so many were serving gaol sentences that the party congress set down for the end of the year had to be postponed until Easter.[31]

The delayed congress completed organisational changes Moore had begun in the previous year. The former state branches of the CPA were reconstituted as districts, each district divided into sections, and the sections into factory and street units. A central committee, guided by a secretariat and political bureau, replaced the former CEC. Procedures were introduced for supervising the work of subordinate levels in this hierarchical structure, and all communication across it was forbidden. The congress was guided by a letter sent from the ECCI that repeated the postulates of the Third Period but already introduced some caveats against the CPA's recent excesses. Admonitions against trailing behind the workers were balanced with warnings against sectarianism and perpetually calling for strikes without adequate preparation. The Australian party was urged to become a 'broad mass organisation' and not an 'isolated adventurist group'.[32]

Moore would depart Australia at the conclusion of the congress, leaving a new leadership. The ECCI's strictures were clearly directed at the novice general secretary. Moxon had assumed the position almost by default as the leader of the left. His organisational deficiencies, profligacy with the funds sent by the Comintern and inability to exercise discipline except by expulsion were exacerbated by a habit of cabling the ECCI whenever he encountered a setback. Moore found him bereft of judgement – he told the unruly Australian that he had only come upon 'class against class' accidentally 'because being a leftist ... you would inevitably hit upon the right line of the Comintern some time or other' – and replaced him with J. B. Miles.[33] The new general secretary was an artisan Scottish immigrant; his caution, frugality and his attention to detail were qualities the CPA sorely needed. His deputy and editor of the newspaper was Lance Sharkey, an Irish-Australian brought up on a farm in the hinterland of New South Wales, and a driving disciplinarian.[34]

The congress also registered an increase of membership. At the end of the year, there were 486 members, 1,135 by April 1931, and a subsequent drive lifted the total to 2,021 in July, where it hovered for the next eighteen months. These figures were based on the returns of districts, which were anxious to report success, and need to be treated with scepticism. As Moore himself cautioned, 'a good part of the increase exists on paper and on paper only'. The national organiser noted a persistent habit of recruitment and failure to retain recruits; he observed that 'the large percentage of unemployed members and the movement of these members from place to place and their consequent falling into inactivity are difficult to tabulate'. Of the members in the Victorian district reported to the tenth congress, just nine per cent were employed and ten per cent were women; the corresponding proportions for the New South Wales district were thirteen and eight per cent, and these were the two largest districts. This was a party of unemployed men.[35]

Even so, it is clear that during the phase of its most quixotic adventurism the party was growing. During its reconstruction the CPA had established or reformed a range of auxiliary organisations: the women's and youth sections, the Minority Movement and the Unemployed Workers' Movement, the League Against Imperialism, International Class War Prisoners' Aid and Workers' International Relief; there was even a Workers' Defence Corps. Each had its own leadership and offices, published its own literature and convened its own national conference. Turnover was high and they relied on the efforts of the party members who funded and directed them, but some of them began to make headway.

The Minority Movement (MM) adopted a stance of absolute opposition to a trade union leadership that was conducting a rearguard campaign against sackings, work rationing, wage cuts and speed-ups. The movement operated outside the union structure, typically in factory committees that refused any accommodation with 'trade union legalism'. It recruited chiefly from the transport, construction, mining and metal industries, though most recruits were sacked as soon as they were identified. The violent denunciation of union officials estranged even the most sympathetic, and repeated disturbances at meetings of the trades hall councils in Sydney, Melbourne, Brisbane and Adelaide during 1930 and 1931 resulted in the suspension of communist delegates.[36] There was only one instance of dual unionism in the Australian Third Period, a Pastoral Workers' Industrial Union that was formed in 1930 out of discontent with the unpopular Australian Workers' Union. It attracted just a few thousand shearers and survived seven years.[37]

A change of approach was signalled at the end of 1931 by MM national organiser, Bill Orr. A Scots immigrant, Orr had worked as a coalminer and attended the fifth congress of the RILU in 1930. A forthright opponent of 'class against class' during the late 1920s, Orr accepted the decisions of the 1929 party conference and never questioned the New Line, but rather worked to modify its application to the party's industrial work. (He was assisted in this by Esmonde Higgins, who at this time edited the MM's weekly newspaper, *Red Leader*.) At the MM conference held at the end of 1931, Orr cautioned delegates against random abuse. Union officials should be condemned for their policies, not their position. Members should base their campaigns around bread-and-butter issues, and they should attend union meetings.[38] Orr took particular exception to those militants who sought to exclude trade union officials from strike committees, and he persuaded the AAS to support his position on a visit to Moscow in October 1932. The CPA accordingly instructed that 'leading members be assisted to become financial and carry on work in the unions to which they belong'.[39] Applying these tactics to his own union, Orr won election to its national presidency a year later.

For the time being, however, the locus of communist activity remained outside the workforce. The Unemployed Workers' Movement (UWM), established nationally in 1930, at first concentrated on rallies that usually marched on the parliament or government offices in the capital cities of the States and generally ended in violence. (The isolation of the new federal capital in Canberra, more than a hundred miles from the nearest city, made it difficult to use similar tactics against the national government.) Apart from repression, the authorities responded to these demonstrations with municipal relief schemes, which in turn encouraged the formation of suburban and local unemployed groups. These groups turned during 1930 to the tactic of preventing the eviction of unemployed families from their homes. This tactic was more successful, partly because it tapped the communal solidarity of working class neighbourhoods, and partly because it gave little advance notice to the police; but during 1931 there was an escalation of violence as armed police stormed fortified dwellings.[40]

Some of the unemployed gathered in shanty towns on urban wasteland. Some abandoned the cities for the bush hinterland, where they could glean an itinerant livelihood from casual work, handouts or living off the land, and they too gathered seasonally. Both types of gathering were fertile sites for communist recruitment, and both were the targets of violence from the police or local vigilantes. The UWM improvised various forms of protest, from protest against repressive relief provisions to armed resistance. Most confrontations ended in defeat, but as one activist put it, 'we felt we've got to make a stand. Do something. Don't cop it passively'.[41]

Towards the end of 1931, the party's general secretary warned that a 'serious sectarian condition' was impairing the work of the UWM. Too many comrades were concerned to display their revolutionary credentials to the disregard of the 'concrete problems of the unemployed'; their denunciation of the relief provisions administered by State Labor governments, and their violent hostility to the relief organisations established by the unions, had isolated them. The UWM was therefore instructed to 'overcome the sectarian tendency of just howling for revolution'.[42]

The evanescent character and local variations in unemployed protest make it difficult to assess the accuracy of Miles' analysis. At least some evidence suggests that the acts of defiance gave hope and strength to the unemployed. While the authorities prevailed in set-piece engagements, the spectre of violent resistance did bring concessions. The forlorn heroism of the diehards, the acts of quixotic bravery and the very sectarianism that he deplored kept the flame of rebellion burning through the economic depression. But the shift away from such confrontation continued as Miles claimed in 1932 that, 'the workers got the impression that in order to get into the UWM you had to bash and you had to be bashed'.[43] After the general secretary declared that 'the communist party cannot be based on bagmen', organisers began to insist that even the unemployed members must be 'clean and presentable'. An unemployed wharf labourer caught the change when he remarked that henceforth it was 'faces to the factory and arseholes to the unemployed'.[44]

Back in 1930, the CPA had recruited from the outcast. The circumstances of the depression were stamped on those it made into communists. They knew hardship not as a temporary misfortune but a constant condition, and the experience never left them. They turned to the class war out of hatred of a system that imposed hunger and humiliation; to resist and fight was to affirm self-respect and concern for others. The recruits were young and their commitment was not made easily. During this period, new laws were introduced to prevent public gatherings. Special police squads were formed and gained a reputation for brutality. There were raids on the party's headquarters in the principal cities, where literature was seized and presses were confiscated. Spies and *agents provocateurs* increased the incidence of prosecution, conviction and imprisonment. For a brief moment, the new leadership toyed with schemes of industrial sabotage and even armed rebellion. The Australian delegates to the RILU congress in August 1930 boasted of these designs and were chastened to discover that the Comintern disapproved.[45] At this time, also, the CPA formed a Workers' Defence Corps to provide protection to the pickets, eviction resisters, public speakers and demonstrators so sorely need in such of assistance. This also flirted initially with more extreme measures: arms were obtained from a police arsenal and explosives stolen from mining stores before tighter discipline was imposed.[46]

The chief threat to public order during the depression in Australia arose not from the left but the right. Paramilitary organisations had been formed during the 1920s, largely from ex-servicemen, to maintain law and order against the spectre of Bolshevism. The inability of the federal Labor government, elected to office in 1929, to solve the economic crisis, and its reluctance to adopt the measures demanded by foreign lenders, the banks and business leaders, brought a conservative mobilisation to defend the national honour around the slogan 'God, King and Empire'. Detachments of these 'secret armies' took to the streets to break up communist meetings and assault speakers. In rural towns, undesirables were rounded up and made to declare their loyalty. This wave of violence built up until the end of 1931 when the federal Labor government fell to the newly formed United Australia Party. In New South Wales, where a populist premier, Jack Lang, continued to denounce the British bondholders, a proto-fascist New Guard kept up street violence until the premier was dismissed in May 1932.[47]

Lang had formed an alliance with the former 'Trades Hall Reds' to establish control of the ALP in that State. His radical rhetoric enjoyed considerable popularity ('Lang is greater than Lenin', Jock Garden now claimed), and his dismissal occasioned an open-air protest meeting that drew 200,000 supporters. But to the CPA Lang was a 'left social fascist', and party members attended the rally only to denounce him as 'the chief force holding the radicalised workers in check and keeping them from the path of struggle against capitalism'.[48] The party fielded 38 candidates in the subsequent State election, and won just 12,351 votes. In the previous New South Wales election in October 1930, there had been 51 candidates and they won 10,445 votes. These campaigns placed a heavy toll on the CPA's energy and resources. At least on the electoral front, the campaign to unmask the reformists was conspicuously unsuccessful.

The Party's Fortunes

Following the election of the new federal government at the end of 1931, there was an intensification of repression. Importation of communist publications was restricted and the postmaster-general refused transmission of local material. The deportation of a foreign-born CPA member convicted for his part in an unemployed demonstration threatened a wider action and the Crimes Act was amended to make it an offence to assist any body that encouraged violent revolution. The party prepared to go underground and stepped up its own security measures. The use of pseudonyms caused particular discomfort as one comrade protested to his district secretary: 'Oh, don't be so fucking stupid. Everyone knows my name's Cliff Jones. How can I run round this town telling them I'm someone else? You must be bloody stark staring mad down in Brisbane.'[49]

In an 'open letter' at the beginning of 1930, the ECCI had observed that while 'class against class' would require some cleansing of the ranks, the rigours of the Third Period provided a natural check on the quality of the membership. Yet, the Australian party took the task of cleansing with a profligate relish. Following the example of the central control commission, districts and sections demonstrated their rigour by expelling members for any laxity in the performance of duties, any infraction of discipline. The pages of the *Workers' Weekly* carried dozens of brief announcements sent in by local secretaries that recorded the expulsion of this coward or that traitor. The practice became endemic until Sharkey, the editor, announced at a party plenum in December 1932 that it should cease. 'All these small, trivial expulsions do not improve the tone or level of the party organ.' In early 1933 it was made clear that indiscriminate bloodletting was to cease: 'expulsions must only be resorted to in cases where comrades bring discredit to the party or where they persist in carrying on a line in opposition to the party line'.[50]

A similar tendency bedevilled the other technique of party discipline, self-criticism. Under the supervision of Herbert Moore, leading members outbid each other in proclamation of their errors, the better to establish their integrity. 'Discipline presupposes the existence of conscious and voluntary submission,' Comrade Stalin had laid down, 'because only a conscious submission can become a discipline of iron.'[51] 'A communist has only one supreme loyalty and that is to the communist party and the Communist International,' Sharkey insisted at a party plenum in 1932. 'If he is doing something out of loyalty to other comrades, he wants to drop that point of view. We have no personal ties in the communist party.' But excessive self-criticism could be just as debilitating as wholesale expulsions, a danger the party recognised when it warned against 'the penitential form of the confession with its mea culpa, mea culpa'. In the ritualised form it so often took, self-criticism served also as a form of self-aggrandisement, the mock humility merely drawing attention to the refractory materials from which the party was constructed.[52]

The forms of organisation and activity that the party assumed during the period of 'class against class' were shaped by the environment in which it operated. The rigid hierarchical structure, the iron discipline enforced by expulsions and reinforced by self-criticism, afforded some protection against the fierce hostility members encountered. The secrecy reduced the exposure to spies. The prohibition of dissent and ban on factional activity were checks on error or disruption. At the same time, these devices perpetuated the beleaguered condition of the party, holding it in a state of tension where mistakes were repeatedly discovered and dangerous tendencies constantly had to be rooted out.

At the party congress in Easter 1931, a 'right danger' was discovered when several leading members criticised the futile electoral contests against Labor candidates, but there were also warnings against left adventurism.[53] This was particularly apparent in the southern State of Victoria, where the traditional rivalry with New South Wales often spilled into political competition. A young and inexperienced leadership in Victoria embarked during 1931 on a frenzy of militancy, including a raid on Trades Hall ('There'll be Soviet power in Melbourne tomorrow', declared its leader) and an assault on the Labor platform on the Yarra Bank during the May Day march.[54] The Melbourne hotheads went up to a plenum of the central committee in Sydney late in 1932, accusing Miles and Sharkey of opportunism and capitulation to capitalist legality. They were immediately expelled.[55]

In the same year, the communist group at the University of Melbourne published an attack on the party leadership by John Anderson, the professor of philosophy at the University of Sydney. Anderson, a libertarian gadfly, had taken up his post a few years earlier and contributed to the *Workers' Weekly*; Moxon had declared him to be the CPA's 'Theoretical Adviser'. Displaced by Miles and Sharkey, he alleged that they were exhibiting 'a fear of spontaneity' that was a sign 'not of leadership but of bureaucracy'.[56] Anderson became a founder member, in 1933, of a self-styled Workers' Party of Australia (Left Opposition) along with Jack Sylvester, recently expelled from the national organiser's position of the UWM. The Workers' Party established links with Trotskyists in the United States, and served as a refuge for other expelled or disillusioned members of the CPA, though it remained small and even more fissiparous than the party. Trotskyism remained more a term of abuse than a serious challenge to Australian communists during the 1930s.[57]

A challenge from the right came from another intellectual, Fred Paterson. A scholarship student, Paterson had graduated from the University of Queensland and then studied at Oxford as a Rhodes scholar. By 1932, he was practising as a lawyer in the North Queensland town of Townsville, where he enjoyed widespread popularity. On the eve of an election in that State, he suggested that the communist party exchange votes with the Labor Party to defeat the conservatives. This was the heresy of the 'lesser evil', and Paterson was ordered to retract it. He did so but refused the degree of contrition the central committee demanded, persisting with what he deemed 'his usual petty bourgeois, individualist, liberal defence of not being convinced and feeling hypocritical if he spoke against his convictions'. That he was allowed to remain in the party was probably due to a combination of circumstances: local support, distance from Sydney and the fact that he did not propagate his heresy.[58] A decade later, he would become the only communist candidate elected to an Australian parliament.

The CPA had responded to the call of the Comintern in March 1933 with an appeal for unity against the threat of fascism. The party leadership recognised that Moscow was signalling 'a very distinct change from the attitude toward the social democratic parties during the Third Period', and worried that it might cause 'a lot of confusion in the party'.[59] Right opportunists such as Paterson would take comfort from it, the leftists who had so recently disrupted the plenum would seize on it as a vindication of their allegation of a right danger. The CPA's call for unity therefore made few concessions to the Labor Party and trade unions: 'We continue to regard them as social fascists ... and arising from this the task of the party is to expose and isolate them from the working class.'[60] The fourth plenum of the CPA in April 1934 reiterated that the main blow must be directed 'against the Labor Party, which paralyses the working class in the face of the advance of fascism and the approach of war'.[61]

In practice, however, the party moved away from this orientation. In its industrial work, it recognised that 'the trade unions are the key to the whole present situation in Australia'. A leading member of the central committee tried to put a Third Period gloss on the emergent strategy by suggesting that communists should seek to win control of the unions to drive the reformists out of them, but Orr disagreed: the object was to win over the reformists.[62] He spoke from a position of strength as the general secretary of the Miners' Federation and by the end of 1934 was re-elected along with a communist president. Earlier in the year, local communists had led a successful strike of the miners in the rural Victorian town of Wonthaggi, employing the organisational methods Orr advocated. As the turn back to the unions continued, bringing growing influence in the transport and metal unions, the party leadership decided that the MM was too narrow and sectarian. They now rejected the 'absurdity of the name', dissolved the MM, and reorganised the membership in trade union fractions that were meant to provide a 'majority movement'.[63]

A similar shift was apparent in other areas of activity. In 1930, the party had established Militant Women's Groups that emphasised the needs of female wage earners and called for day nurseries, access to birth control and legalisation of abortion; the newspaper *Working Woman* serialised Kollontai's *Communism and the Family*.[64] A change of emphasis was signalled in early 1934, when the organiser of the CPA women's department condemned rank-and-file committees of females in the textile industry for 'their attitude towards the men'.[65] Such organisation of women workers gave way to women's auxiliaries supporting male workers, and *Working Woman* changed in the same year from a newspaper to a magazine that was more domestic in orientation, speaking to women as wives and mothers. Kollantai's emphasis on sexual liberation gave way to Clara Zetkin's interview with Lenin, published by the *Communist Review* in 1935, in which he admonished Kollantai. A party that allowed considerable sexual freedom now condemned 'loose practices'. 'Bolshevism demands a steel-like character,' pronounced Miles who was himself conducting a clandestine affair with a female comrade, 'and that has to apply on sexual questions as well as on other questions.'[66]

During 1931, Workers' Art Clubs had been established in Sydney and Melbourne. Taking Lenin's dictum 'Art is a weapon' as their slogan, these clubs offered literature readings, art and drama classes, film and lecture evenings to a predominantly unemployed audience. The approach was strongly influenced by the experiment in Proletcult conducted in the early years of the Russian Revolution, at once liberating culture from the rarefied forms imposed by the capitalist division of labour, and placing it at the disposal of a revolutionary movement. Hence, club members assisted with the design of factory bulletins and painted banners for street marches.[67] The clubs came under criticism by 1932 for excessive realism. When a leading party member first viewed Noel Counihan's stark depictions of the unemployed as maimed victims of capitalism, he asked: 'Why don't you draw something beautiful?' Another cadre dismissed the members of the Melbourne Club as 'a pack of petit-bourgeois degenerates'.[68] By 1934, the Workers' Art Club gave way to the Writers' League that stressed its 'broad and non-sectarian character'. Challenge softened into portrayal, art as a weapon yielded to art as homily, and there was a turning back to popular national literary traditions.[69]

Third Period communists paid particular attention to the issue of race. Among the catalogue of oppression publicised through the League Against Imperialism (LAI), the party stressed the misdeeds of the Australian colonial administration in the mandated territory of New Guinea. Above all, Australian communists concentrated on their own internal colonialism. The programme entitled 'Struggle Against Slavery' that the party published in 1931 defined the Aborigines as the most exploited Australians, the 'slaves of slaves'. They were the victims of 'mass physical extermination', abused by pastoralists and police, denied the most basic human rights by their official protectors. Previously, the revolutionary movement had overlooked the plight of the indigenous Australians; henceforth, 'no struggle of the white workers must be permitted without demands for the aborigines being championed'.[70] The party itself was not free from racism. In 1934, the *Workers' Weekly* rebuked 'Comrades [who] still use the terms 'Pommie', 'Dago', 'Nigger' and so forth'. But it was a party of increasing ethnic diversity in which such language no longer passed without censure. There were growing links between Australian communists and anti-fascist associations formed by southern European immigrants; Jewish immigrants were increasingly prominent.[71]

The campaign against fascism changed in character. With the fall of Germany to the Nazis and the mounting international tension, the LAI turned itself into a Council Against War. The change was consummated at a National Anti-War Congress in Sydney from 30 September to 2 October 1933. At this point, the opposition to war had a sharp revolutionary edge, indeed the indignant denial by the conference organisers that it was simply a communist front was scarcely assisted by the president's opening call that delegates sing 'The Internationale'.[72] The re-designation in 1934 of the Council Against War as the Movement Against War and Fascism signalled a new orientation. For its second National Anti-War congress in Melbourne in November 1934, the CPA arranged for an international delegate, the Czech publicist Egon Kisch. The Commonwealth government banned his entry to Australia and, after Kisch jumped onto the Melbourne wharf, a series of court cases finally secured his freedom. The government's inept handling of the case attracted far greater publicity than the Movement Against War and Fascism could have expected. Kisch's dramatic entry made front-page news. The draconian use of the law brought widespread consternation and, once the courts had freed Kisch, he addressed large audiences all over the country.[73]

Kisch attracted attention as a colourful and flamboyant publicist who could speak with first-hand knowledge of fascist repression. More than this, the government's attempt to prevent his visit awakened concern about the domestic threat to civil liberties. During 1933 there was a protracted communist campaign against bans on street meetings in Melbourne that ultimately succeeded as it attracted wider support. Organised through a Free Speech League, with active Labor participation, this was a successful example of the 'united front from below'. Kisch also appealed to progressive intellectuals, and in Melbourne the Kisch Reception Committee subsequently turned into a Writers' League as the Australian Section of the Writers' International. The new mood encountered the old when a group of Melbourne University student members of the Movement Against War and Fascism took a stencil down to the working class suburb of South Melbourne to be roneoed by the organiser of the local Unemployed Workers' Movement. 'Why can't the fuckin' Anti-War Movement get a bloody duplicator of their own?' he demanded. 'They've always got plenty of the sons and daughters of the bloody Boss class hanging around their office.'[74]

In 1934, the CPA shifted its national headquarters from the dinghy hall it had occupied close to Sydney's wharves and set up premises in a more modern building near the central railway station. It had created a publishing company in the previous year and opened a string of new bookshops. Several of the districts created their own newspapers, and the national *Workers' Weekly* was redesigned. A lighter typeface and bolder headlines, a less crowded page with more illustrations, set off the new coverage of sport.

The transformation was completed at the eleventh congress of the CPA in December 1935. Lance Sharkey, the leading Australian delegate at the Comintern's seventh world congress four months earlier, brought back the new policy of the United Front: 'We have not to think of it in the manner we thought of it previously,' he explained.[75] The party was to seek affiliation to the Labor Party in a public campaign that Miles would lead as general secretary. For some time, Miles had been underground, now he would come out and conduct a national tour. Yet, his new public prominence contrasted with the more discreet conduct of members as adversarial communism yielded to affirmation, confrontation to the patient cultivation of alliances. In 1930, Moxon had instructed members that when they finished a meeting they should leave together, 'march in closed ranks, sing revolutionary songs, cheer for the revolution'. In 1935, Miles laid it down that members should 'come to a meeting place on time and get right into it, when it is dispersed go away in small numbers and get right away'.[76]

Conclusion

In the course of the Third Period, the CPA was transformed from an isolated and irregular outpost to an orthodox section of the Communist International. It remained a small organisation. There were just 1,929 members at the end of 1,932 and 2,371 in mid-1934. The congress at the end of 1935 reported 2,873 members, though only 1,674 were financial. They were still concentrated in Sydney and Melbourne, and less than half of them were employed; there were just 200 country members and 200 women.[77] The rapid growth at the onset of 'class against class' had stalled, and the movement towards a less intransigent style of party activity brought only slow returns. Nor would the Popular Front establish a popular CPA: by 1939, there were still only 4,421 members.[78] It was the entry of the USSR into the Second World War that brought a substantial influx of recruits, and a peak membership of over 20,000 in 1944.

The campaigns that the CPA had conducted during the Third Period brought minimal success. The depression crisis certainly demonstrated the failure of the Labor Party to maintain living standards, and the inability of the unions to protect jobs, but the Labor government of 1929–31 was replaced by a conservative one that held power until 1941. Labor retained its hold on the working class vote, and 'class against class' left a legacy of mistrust among the Labor politicians who had been reviled as social fascists: both the federal executive and the state branches of the ALP flatly rejected all subsequent appeals for unity.

Yet, the Third Period laid the foundations for a communist party that would exert significance influence in Australia for the next two decades. It brought an influx of young unemployed workers who were schooled in the rigours of 'class against class'. With the economic recovery later in the decade, these militants found their way back into employment. Following the lead of Bill Orr, they concentrated their efforts in the unions and built significant support for their effective industrial campaigns. This generation of activists secured improvement of wages and working conditions, decasualisation of manual labour, a place at the table of industrial relations. At least until the onset of the Cold War, they exercised leadership in key industries and exerted a powerful influence on the labour movement. The initiatives of the CPA fostered an increased international awareness and a peace movement that became a significant factor in Australian foreign policy, as well as a solvent on the mono-cultural prejudices of White Australia.

The Third Period also installed a party leadership that would retain control for the next two decades and beyond. Miles remained general secretary until after the Second World War, when Sharkey replaced him. The recruits of the Third Period became the district secretaries, the organisers and public faces of Australian communism. Some of them would fall away and some would be discarded, but they adapted readily to the subsequent changes in international communism, highly disciplined, hard and driving, prepared by their formative experiences for the hostility they would encounter when shifts of policy would require them to endure it.

The Third Period spawned a range of cultural and social organisations that marked out the communist alternative to capitalism. The autonomous forms of party life both connected members and separated them. They were at once community leaders and yet different from their workmates and neighbours, exemplary workers and atypical enthusiasts. The Leninist model of a unified, disciplined body of revolutionaries acting as organic working class intellectuals produced the figure of the Australian communist who enjoyed respect as a wise, disciplined outsider.[79] The growth of the party, its strong presence in the trade unions and increasing participation in a whole range of public activities made it a part of civil society. It continued to contest exploitation and injustice, to agitate for change and improvement, to counterpose Soviet achievement against capitalist barbarism, but it did so from within, seeking to extend its own disciplined unity to the rest of the working class.

By background and temperament, the Australian communist was a radical and a militant, a naysayer and a troublemaker; by training and conviction, that person was an organiser and improver. The party channelled the spirit of rebellion into obedience, banished transgression, and imposed regularity. Its emphasis on unity, firmness and control, its mistrust of spontaneity and local initiative, gave it a formidable capacity to direct campaigns and to withstand campaigns against it. Those qualities were forged in the Third Period.

Notes

1. See, for example, F. Borkenau, *World Communism* (Michigan, 1962). More recent studies are discussed in K. McDermott and J. Agnew, *The Comintern: A History of International Socialism from Lenin to Stalin* (Basingstoke, 1996), chap. 3.

2. V. Burgmann, *Revolutionary Industrial Unionism: The Industrial Workers of the World in Australia* (Cambridge, 1995). Here and subsequently I draw on S. Macintyre, *The Reds: The Communist Party of Australia from Origins to Illegality* (Sydney, 1998).

3. M. Sampson, 'Intellectual History from Below? The Diary of Jack Kavanagh', unpublished paper (University of Newcastle, 1989).

4. 'The Communist Menace in Australia', intelligence report (Latham papers, National Library of Australia MS 1009/27/120–62).

5. R. W. Robson, *Report to the Political Secretariat of ECCI*, 20 April 1928, Comintern records (Russian Centre for the Preservation and Study of Contemporary Historical Documents (RC) 495/3/63); letter to 'Bob' [Stewart?], January 1928 (RC 495/94/41).

6. *Minutes of the British Secretariat*, 22 April and 20 May 1926 (RC 495/72/114). The text of the 'Resolution on the Australian Question' (RC 495/2/57) appears in the *Report of the Sixth Annual Conference of the CPA*, December 1926 (Communist Archives, Mitchell Library, NSW).

7. RC 495/94/42.

8. *Minutes of the British-American Secretariat*, 4 October 1927(RC 495/72/27); *Minutes of the Political Secretariat*, 10 and 14 October 1927 (RC 495/3/39, 40). The resolution appears in the *Report of the Seventh Annual Conference of the CPA*, December 1927 (Communist Archive) pp. 12–15.

9. *Report of the Seventh Annual Conference*, p. 17.

10. R. W. Robson, 'Report on the Situation of the Australian CP', 19 April 1928 (RC 495/94/41; 495/3/63) p. 18.

11. See S. Macintyre, *The Succeeding Age: The Oxford History of Australia, Volume 4, 1901–42* (Melbourne, 1986), chap. 10.

12. *Report of the Seventh Annual Conference*, pp. 74–78.

13. B. Moxon's 'Report of the Representative of the CC of the CPA on "Party Factions"' was presented on 7 April 1928 (RC 495/94/42) and was disputed by Jeffery and Ryan, who were in Moscow for the RILU congress. The political bureau of ECCI endorsed the decision of secretariat on 27 April 1928 (RC 495/3/64).

14. Dutt to Pollitt, 6 January and 13 February 1928, Dutt Papers (Communist Party Archive, National Museum of Labour History (NMLH), Manchester).

15. CPA Executive to Political Secretary of the ECCI, 20 September 1928 (RC 495/94/44).

16. CPA Executive to Secretary of the ECCI, 2 October 1928 (RC 495/6/16).

17. Higgins to CPA Executive, 20 December 1928, *Minutes of the Central Executive Committee (CEC Mins)* (Communist Archives).

18. *Workers' Weekly*, 9 August 1929.

19. *CEC Mins*, 15, 19 and 23 September 1929, and attached correspondence (Communist Archives).

20. *Minutes of the CEC*, 30 September and correspondence (RC 495/94/53).

21. Notes of discussion at Sydney District, *CEC Mins* (Communist Archives).

22. RC 495/94/52.

23. *CEC Mins*, 21 October 1929 (Communist Archives).

24. CPA General Secretary to Anglo-American Secretariat, 16 December 1929 (RC 495/94/52).

25. *Report of the Ninth Annual Conference*, December 1929 (Communist Archives).

26. *Report of the Ninth Annual Conference* (RC 495/94/53) pp. 17–18 and p. 34.

27. B. K. Johnpoll and H. Klehr (eds), *Biographical Dictionary of the American Left* (New York, 1986), pp. 414–15.

28. *Workers' Weekly*, 14 March and 4 April 1931.

29. Ryan to Lozovsky, 9 March 1930 (RC 534/7/5), and correspondence between Ryan and central committee in Kavanagh Papers (Noel Butlin Archives of Business and Labour, Australian National University ANU P12/3/7). See also B. Curthoys, 'The Comintern, the CPA and the Impact of Harry Wicks', *Australian Journal of Politics and History*, Vol. 39 No. 1 (1993), pp. 23–36.

30. *Workers' Weekly*, 5 December 1930; correspondence between Kavanagh and CPA (Kavanagh Papers P12/3/1–5).

31. *Workers' Weekly*, 3 October and 5 December 1930.

32. *Minutes of the Tenth Congress* (Communist Archives).

33. RC 495/94/20; see B. Penrose, 'Hemert Moxon, a Victim of the "Bolshevisation" of the Communist Party', *Labour History*, No. 70 (May 1996), pp. 92–114.

34. For Miles and Sharkey, see *Australian Dictionary of Biography*, Vol. 15, pp. 367–68 and Vol. 16, pp. 217–18.

35. Moore to ECCI, 10 November 1930 (RC 495/7/5); *Minutes of the Tenth Congress*, p. 76; *Workers' Weekly*, 29 May, 31 July and 27 November 1931; 'Organisation Report', 31 December 1931(Communist Archives).

36. *Report of the 1931 Conference of the Minority Movement* (RC 534/7/7).

37. A. Moore, 'The Pastoral Workers Industrial Union', *Labour History*, No. 49 (November 1985), pp. 61–74.

38. *Red Leader*, 15 and 22 January 1932.

39. 'The Situation and Tasks of the MM in Australia', 15 October 1932 (RC 495/72/148); *Minutes of the Political Bureau of the CPA*, 5 November 1931 (Communist Archives).

40. For literature on unemployed protest, see S. Macintyre, *The Reds*, chap. 8.

41. George Bliss, quoted in W. Lowenstein (Ed.), *Weevils in the Flour: An Oral Record of the 1930s Depression in Australia*, (Newham, 1989, revised edition), pp. 173–77.

42. 'Sectarianism – Our Approach to the Masses is Incorrect', *Workers' Weekly*, 20 November 1931.

43. *Minutes of the Third Plenum*, 25–27 December 1932 (Communist Archives).

44. *Minutes of the Eleventh Congress*, 27–31 December 1935 (Communist Archives); Bob Cram in *Communist Review*, Vol. 2, no. 6 (June 1935), pp. 51–5; W. Lowenstein and T. Hills, *Under the Hook: Melbourne Waterside Workers Remember Working Lives and Class War 1900–80* (Prahran, 1982), pp. 67–82.

45. These plans were discussed at a closed session of the central committee plenum, 2 January 1932 (Communist Archives).

46. Sharkey to Lozovsky, n.d. [June 1930] (RC 534/7/5).

47. A. Moore, *The Secret Army and the Premier: Conservative Paramilitary Organisations in New South Wales 193–32* (Kensington, 1989).

48. *Workers' Weekly*, 10 June 1932; see M. Dixson, *Greater than Lenin? Lang and Labor 1916–32* (Melbourne, 1976).

49. Claude Jones recalling his elder brother, interviewed by Laurie Aarons, June 1980 (Mitchell Library, NSW).

50. *Minutes of the Third Plenary Session of the Central Committee*, 25–27 December 1932 (Communist Archives); *Workers' Weekly*, 5 May 1933.

51. The passage from Stalin's codification of *The Foundations of Leninism* was quoted in *Workers' Weekly*, 10 March 1933.

52. *Minutes of the Third Plenum*, p. 59; *Workers' Weekly*, 3 October 1930.

53. *Minutes of the Tenth Congress*.

54. Quotation from R. Gibson, *The People Stand Up* (Ascot Vale, 1983), p. 53.

55. *Political Statement of No. 4 District to the ECCI and Party Plenum*, 1932 (Communist Archives); *Minutes of the Plenum* (RC 495/94/109).

56. 'The Working Class', *Proletariat*, Vol. 1 No. 1 (April 1932) and 'Freedom and the Class Struggle', ibid. No. 2 (July 1932); B. Kennedy, *A Passion to Oppose: John Anderson, Philosopher* (Melbourne, 1995), chap. 6.

57. H. Greenland, *Red Hot: The Life and Times of Nick Origlass* (Neutral Bay, 1998).

58. 'Statement on the "Lesser Evil Theory" by Paterson. 1932', (National Archives of Australia NA A8911, item 158), quoted in R. Fitzgerald, *The People's Champion: Fred Paterson* (St Lucia, 1997), pp. 63–71; *Workers' Weekly*, 12 August, 2 September 1932.

59. *Minutes of the Political Bureau*, 14 March 1933 (RC 95/94/105).

60. 'For the Correct Application of the Line of the Comintern', and 'Some Mistakes Which Must Be Overcome', *Workers' Weekly*, 28 April 12 May 1933.

61. 'On the Present Situation in Australia and the Tasks of the Party', *Workers' Weekly*, 20 April 1934; *Central Committee Minutes (CC Mins)*, 1 July 1934 (Communist Archives).

62. *CC Mins*, 30 June–1 July 1934, 20–23, October 1934, February 1935 (Communist Archives); ECCI to CPA, 23 November 1934 (RC 495/3/427).

63. Dixon in *Workers' Weekly*, 23 February 1934; 'Problems of Militant Trade Unionism', *Communist Review*, Vol. 1 No. 5 (August 1934).

64. *Working Woman*, January 1932; J. Stevens, *Taking the Revolution Home: Work Among Women in the Communist Party of Australia 1920–45* (Fitzroy, 1976), chap. 1.

65. *Minutes of the Fourth Plenum*, 1–2 April 1934 (Communist Archives).

66. C. Zetkin, 'Lenin on the Woman Question', *Communist Review*, Vol. 2 No. 3 (March 1935); *Central Committee to All Districts*, 27 March 1935 (Communist Archives); Miles in *Minutes of the Eleventh Congress*, p. 182; C. Ferrier (Ed.), *Point of Departure: The Autobiography of Jean Devanny* (St Lucia, 1986).

67. See D. Carter, 'Realism as a Contemporary Response to the Modern: Left Wing Cultural Attitudes and the Concept of Modernity in Australia, 1930–65' (MA thesis, University of Melbourne, 1982), chap. 1; B. Smith, *Noel Counihan: Artist and Revolutionary* (Melbourne, 1993), chap. 4.

68. B. Smith, *Noel Counihan*, p. 80.

69. *Workers' Weekly*, 7 September 1934 and 19 April 1935; *CC Mins*, 20–23 October 1934, (Communist Archives).

70. *Workers' Weekly*, 25 September 1931.

71. See G. Cresciani, *Fascism, Anti-Fascism and Italians in Australia, 1922–45* (Canberra, 1980), chaps 5–6; S. Kourbetis, 'Ethnicity versus Class? A Study of Greek Radicals in Australia 1920–89' (MA thesis, La Trobe University, 1990), chap. 3; D. Rechter, 'Beyond the Pale: Jewish Communism in Melbourne' (MA thesis, University of Melbourne, 1986).

72. *Red Leader*, 4 and 11 October 1933.

73. *Workers' Weekly*, 19 October 1934 – 1 March 1935; *Workers Voice*, 5 October 1934. L. J. Louis, 'Victorian Council Against War and Fascism: A Rejoinder', *Labour History*, No. 44 (May 1983), pp. 39–54 is the fullest account and employs the Investigation Branch records; see also E. Kisch, *Australian Landfall* (London, 1937).

74. A. F. Howells, *Against the Stream: The Memories of a Philosophical Anarchist 1927–39* (Melbourne, 1983), p. 76.

75. *Minutes of the Eleventh Congress*, p. 5.

76. *Workers' Weekly*, 21 November 1931, quoted in L. J. Louis, *Trade Unions and the Depression: A Study of Victoria 1930–32* (Canberra, 1968), p. 35; *CC Mins*, 21–22 September 1935 (Communist Archives).

77. L. Donald, 'Forward to a Mass Bolshevik Party', *Communist Review*, Vol. 2 No. 4 (April 1935); *Minutes of the Eleventh Congress*, p. 196.

78. *CC Mins*, June 1939 (Communist Archives).

79. A phrase I owe to Sean Scalmer, 'The Career of Class: Intellectuals and the Labour Movement in Australia, 1942–56' (Ph.D. thesis, University of Sydney, 1996), p. 69.

The Communist Party of New Zealand and the Third Period, 1928–35

KERRY TAYLOR

Early in 1928, the Communist Party of New Zealand (CPNZ) received a cable requesting that a delegate be sent to the sixth congress of the Communist International (Comintern) which was to be held later that year.[1] Dick Griffin, a leading figure in the Wellington group, was selected to represent the party. Griffin, a 28 year old of Irish heritage, left New Zealand carrying with him credentials from the local Seamen's Union which he used to facilitate his travel on the long journey by sea, first to Australia, then to Britain via the Suez Canal and finally overland across Europe. British police were alert to his impending arrival and he was detained and interrogated. While some papers were seized, Griffin was not delayed unduly and he made it to Moscow in time for the congress.[2]

Griffin's journey may seem little more than a footnote in the history of the CPNZ. However, he was the first New Zealander to officially attend a Comintern gathering. More importantly, he was charged with securing the affiliation of the CPNZ to the Comintern as a national section in its own right. Prior to 1928, the New Zealand party had been represented by the Communist Party of Australia (CPA). The congress, held from 17 July to 1 September, accepted the application. New Zealand was in auspicious company; parties from Korea, Cuba, Ireland, Paraguay, Ecuador and Colombia were also admitted.[3]

The timing of the visit may have been less auspicious. New Zealand's affiliation coincided with the Comintern's much discussed 'left turn' and the enunciation of the so-called Third Period policy. The theses of the sixth congress put forward a new analysis of the international situation, suggesting that the world system was entering a period where the contradictions of capitalism would intensify and lead to a new phase of imperialist wars, a general capitalist crisis and unprecedented opportunity for revolutionary change. The new analysis suggested that the role of social democracy in this period would be as a bulwark of capitalism and a check on revolution, it was to become a primary target for communist agitation. According to the analysis, communists in developed countries, such as New Zealand, should focus their energies on the formation of a 'united front from below' instead of the previous tactic of building it 'from above'. The independent and revolutionary leadership of the communist movement needed to be brought more to the fore and the class war intensified.[4]

This period is one of the most contentious in the history of communism. However, analysis has been framed within a very predictable and limited paradigm. For a considerable time there was a 'near universal consensus' on the Third Period – put simply, the ultra-left tactics were a disaster.[5] This paradigm has been unequivocally critical and remarkably consistent in the nature of its critique, regardless of the particular party being examined.[6] This, we are told, was a period where the Comintern, increasingly dominated by Stalin, imposed a tight control on the international movement. In the process, it forced new leaders on reluctant national sections and stifled inner-party democracy by ensuring the establishment of a centralised and increasingly bureaucratic leadership model. The ultra-left tactics led communist movements into sectarianism and isolation; they lost influence in the organisations of the working class and in the process lost much of their own membership.

The dominant international paradigm is reflected in analysis of the New Zealand experience. The history of the CPNZ after 1928 is frequently explained by reference to the Comintern, decisions of its leading organs are assumed to have speedily manifested themselves in the actions of the party. The affiliation to the Comintern, and the timing of this connection, has been portrayed as a significant turning point in the CPNZ's history. Sid Scott argues that it marked the end of an era and suggests that the connection fundamentally transformed the party, moving it away from a New Zealand radical tradition and down a path of sectarianism and dogmatism.[7] Scott's view is extensively cited and uncritically perpetuated by several subsequent commentators.[8] Bert Roth, a far less hostile commentator, also argues that 'the establishment of direct contact with Moscow led to the speedy implementation of the new policy initiated by Stalin'.[9] The Socialist Unity Party's history of communism in New Zealand more pointedly suggests that the linkage catapulted the party into an unprecedented period of 'barren sectarianism' and doomed it to a 'wilderness' for another half decade.[10] Other accounts maintain this characterisation; Graeme Dunstall suggests that Griffin's visit marked the beginning of a more 'doctrinaire and inflexible approach' in conformity with the new international line.[11] In keeping with the dominant international paradigm, the CPNZ after 1928 is frequently portrayed as uncritically 'toeing the Comintern line' with disastrous effects.[12]

Such views, both in New Zealand and overseas, tend to assume that the world communist movement was homogeneous, uniformly subject to the dictates of Moscow, and that in this period the policy of the Comintern was nothing short of a political disaster. There have been, however, dissenting voices and internationally there is a growing move to re-evaluate the relationship between national sections and the Comintern generally, and the

Third Period in particular. This new assessment was, in part, precipitated by the opening up of the Comintern archives following the collapse of the Soviet Union. New sources have facilitated new interpretations.[13]

This so-called revisionism has suggested a number of correctives to the dominant paradigm. The central role of the Communist International has been questioned. Instead of Comintern determinism, revisionists emphasise the relative autonomy from, and resistance to, the Comintern by national sections. National differences and particular histories are highlighted, distinctive rather than homogenous political trajectories are emphasised. Within this broad frame, key periods are being reassessed; the paradigm that sees the Third Period as a sectarian disaster – plain and simple – has been challenged.[14]

There is, however, no new 'near universal consensus'; rather, old debates are being rekindled with the aid of new material from the Comintern archives. For some historians the vast array of new sources has simply led to a reassertion of old arguments, admittedly with new footnotes or in some instances whole documents reproduced.[15] The counter to contemporary revisionism is not simply coming from a perspective seemingly in sympathy with the values of the cold war. The debate is increasingly being driven by a left-wing critique of Stalinism and of those historians who, from this perspective, are unjustifiably rejecting a Stalin/Comintern centred analysis.[16]

This chapter tests the dominant paradigm of the Third Period by exploring the New Zealand experience. Do its assumptions stand or was there a distinctive New Zealand experience of the Third Period? What were the main determinants on the CPNZ's policy? What were the consequences and implications of that policy?

The CPNZ and the Comintern

Clearly, the link with the Comintern was important. The prevailing New Zealand literature assumes a particular type of relationship but does not delve deeply into the available evidence. What was the nature and extent of the relationship between the CPNZ and the Comintern? Were there other factors that shaped CPNZ policy in this crucial period? On the basis of a close examination of the Comintern archives relating to New Zealand, it is argued here that previous commentators have failed to understand the complexities of the relationship. The portrayal of a dutiful and obedient organisation submitting to the dictates of the Comintern holds relatively little weight when more closely examined. A number of factors circumscribed the influence of the Comintern.

The first was difficulties in communication. It took at least six weeks, often several months, for any correspondence to get through.[17] Communication was generally channelled via the CPA and the Communist

Party of Great Britain (CPGB), either by mail to a safe address or by using sympathetic seamen as couriers. The system was unreliable; letters were sometimes intercepted *en route* or arrived after events had overtaken the analysis they contained. The CPNZ frequently complained about the difficulties of communication. At the 1928 Comintern congress, the New Zealand and Australian delegates made a joint request that a more sophisticated courier system be established. This was rejected on the grounds that the amount of mail was insufficient to warrant the cost. All the Comintern could suggest was to find some trustworthy British seamen to carry messages.[18]

This response points to a second factor reducing the Comintern's impact on the CPNZ: the reality that New Zealand was not a priority for the Moscow functionaries. From the outset, the CPNZ thought that the Comintern neglected and marginalised New Zealand. When giving oral testimony to the ECCI political secretariat, Griffin complained that he was reporting on a topic that nobody was interested in; he found nobody who had read the written reports he provided.[19] Such dissatisfaction lingered and the CPNZ continued to let its feelings be known. Comintern neglect, even to acknowledge receipt of communications, had a detrimental effect on the morale of the party, as Fred Freeman (CPNZ leader in 1934), clearly outlined in that year.

> To say the least such silence on your part is very discouraging. We have no exaggerated [sense] of the importance of New Zealand in the World Revolutionary Movement but never-the-less [sic] we think that we are entitled to at least comradely recognition. Your silence gives the impression that no one in the A. A. [Anglo-American] section is the least interested in us.[20]

A number of potential solutions to the difficulties of communication and the relative neglect of the antipodes were canvassed, usually at the instigation of the antipodeans.

In practice, the only thing that significantly raised the level of understanding of New Zealand within the Comintern was the attendance of New Zealanders at the Lenin School for party cadres in Moscow. Between 1928 and 1935, four CPNZ members attended the school.[21] In addition to their studies, the New Zealanders did political work with the Anglo-American Secretariat (AAS) of the ECCI. On arrival, each gave detailed reports on the current state of the party, supplementing and often interpreting the large quantity of information regularly sent by the CPNZ to Moscow.

The work of the New Zealanders within the Comintern apparatus served as another mitigating factor on Comintern influence, not only did the Comintern rely on the CPNZ to provide the material upon which their analysis was based, it also relied on New Zealanders in Moscow to do much of the interpreting. Most of the major communications from the ECCI to the CPNZ were drafted by members of the party.[22] Clearly, the New Zealanders worked broadly within the parameters of the prevailing ideology, and their drafts were subjected to scrutiny and criticism by other functionaries within the Comintern, particularly the AAS.[23] Yet, the whole process of production weakens the traditional 'orders from Moscow' analysis. Those on the receiving end of the 'orders' played a major part in shaping their own destiny.

Even if allowance is made for the mitigating factors suggested above, it is still conceivable that the CPNZ was pushed down a path of 'barren sectarianism' by linking up with the Communist International. Certainly, the coincidence of the CPNZ's affiliation with the adoption of the Third Period policy suggests that the party was liable to be influenced in a particular direction. However, an examination of the ECCI's 'Resolution on the Tasks of the Communist Party of New Zealand' brought back to New Zealand by Dick Griffin suggests no rapid or fundamental shift in party policy at this juncture.[24]

Griffin returned just before the CPNZ's December 1928 conference that discussed the ECCI's resolution, much of which was drawn verbatim from his background papers. Contrary to the suggestion of several commentators, the ECCI's resolution did not encapsulate the New Line. Rather than suggesting that New Zealand was heading towards a more revolutionary situation, the resolution held that 'the steady upward swing of capitalist development, combined with relatively good conditions for the workers, prevent the possibility of a general revolutionary situation in New Zealand and make the main task of the party that of agitation and propaganda'.[25] It still advocated a united front from above, including a campaign for affiliation with the Labour Party.

It was not until a letter dated March 1930 that an ECCI communication to the CPNZ reflected the New Line. It suggested that the previous analysis on New Zealand was now incorrect; the internal contradictions of New Zealand capitalism had intensified, giving the opportunity for the CPNZ to takeover the leadership of the working class. This could only be done by working to 'expose and destroy all the Labourite, pacifist, social democratic illusions about the possibility of solving social problems ... under the existing political and economic regime'.[26] Subsequent communications from the ECCI continued to put forward this general analysis.[27]

Establishing that the Comintern communications did advocate a Third Period policy lends some support to an analysis of Comintern inspired sectarianism, but suggests that such advice came later than previously assumed. The CPNZ accepted that it was bound by the decisions of the ECCI as set down in the 'Conditions of Admission to the Communist

International' (1920), and generally sought to act within the broad parameters of the Comintern analysis. The December 1929 CPNZ conference had in fact discussed and affirmed its commitment to the New Line independent of any prompting from the International.[28] However, two additional factors undermine the conventional analysis.

First, the Comintern's analysis and instructions were not accepted uncritically. On the contrary, they received considerable scrutiny by members of the CPNZ at both national and local level. In June 1929, the CPNZ central executive resolved to categorically reject a letter from the AAS.[29] The following year, the central executive sent copies of the March 1930 ECCI letter to branches for 'study and criticism'. The accompanying note asked branches whether they thought the analysis in each paragraph was correct and stated that the executive had already decided to issue a statement disagreeing with some points in the letter.[30] This critical engagement with Comintern communications continued over time. Such responses coupled with the CPNZ's frequent criticism of Comintern's processes, as opposed to ideas, indicate the party was anything but an uncritical 'slave' of Moscow.

Even in circumstances when there was broad agreement with the Comintern's 'instructions', it is problematic to assume they were diligently put into practice. It took a full year for the CPNZ to even attempt to implement the instructions of the ECCI's 1930 letter. By the end of 1931, Dick Griffin was still lamenting the lack of progress, something the central executive was still admitting at the December 1932 party conference.[31] As late as March 1933, the Comintern sternly warned the CPNZ that they had yet to grasp the tactics of the 'united front from below'.[32] So much for a rapid transformation.

The Domestic Basis of 'Sectarianism'

The CPNZ did move down a more explicitly left-wing path from the late 1920s, however the explanation lies more in the contours of the New Zealand labour movement than the dark corridors of the Comintern. The 'left turn' preceded any instructions from Moscow. The relationship between the Labour Party and the CPNZ, increasingly problematic since the mid-1920s when the Labour Party expelled all known communists, continued to deteriorate. Increasingly, the parties set each other up as the primary negative reference point. For Labour this was partly as a defence against attacks by groups that equated their party with Bolshevism.[33] It also reflected Labour's move towards a more centrist political platform, the party abandoned the long held policy of nationalising land in 1927.[34]

This change by Labour provided space for an unequivocal party of the left, the CPNZ sought to occupy this space and attacks on Labour leaders became more acute. In part, this was driven by rank-and-file party members, the Wellington group in particular targeted workers loyal to the Labour Party.[35] The CPNZ leadership was also increasingly critical of Labour. In 1928, Alan Eaglesham, the secretary of the CPNZ, suggested that:

> [In] every field of political activity, in every industrial dispute, the present policy of the Labour Party leadership and the line of action advocated by the Communist Party are fundamentally antagonistic. This antagonism arises from the fact that the LP is, in its final analysis, a surrender to the forces of capitalism.[36]

Ironically, the link-up with the Comintern may have slowed the CPNZ moving more decisively against the Labour Party. At the behest of the Comintern, the CPNZ, clearly with less and less conviction, sought the removal of Labour's anti-communist pledge and applied for affiliation to the Labour Party.[37] A remit at the 1928 CPNZ conference sought the abandonment of this activity,[38] however the Comintern resolution brought back by Griffin unequivocally insisted that the strategy be continued. Without the link with the Comintern, the CPNZ would undoubtedly have pursued a more militant policy from the end of 1928. Any attempt to affiliate with the Labour Party, and critical support for the party in elections, was finally abandoned at the December 1929 party conference. Again, it is significant that the change occurred prior to the ECCI letter of March 1930, which explicitly advocated the Third Period line.[39]

Attitudes in the industrial arena also hardened ahead of any change in line from the Comintern. Mainstream trade union leaders were increasingly aggressive in their attacks on the CPNZ, who reciprocated in kind. One focus of attention was the CPNZ's paper the *Worker's Vanguard*, about which there was considerable disquiet in the union movement. Early in 1928, the Wellington Trades Council banned its sale in the Trades Hall, while the New Zealand Workers' Union sued the paper for alleging they were involved in strike breaking activity, others did likewise.[40]

At one point, the Wellington Trades Council refused to accept communist delegates to its meetings, one of whom was removed by the police, while the Wellington Labourers' Union banned communists holding official positions in that union.[41] Considerable bitterness persisted over what was perceived to be a communist attempt to take over the Labour paper the *New Zealand Worker*.[42] At the 1928 annual conference of the Alliance of Labour, its secretary Jim Roberts reflected the views of many when he suggested that communists 'lied fluently and poetically against every official of Labour in this country'.[43]

In such a context, the immediate impact of the New Line advocated by the Comintern from the early 1930s did little more than add minor technical changes to a communist battle plan that was already very much in action. The most noticeable change was that of language. Opponents were transformed in communist propaganda from 'yellow fakirs' into 'social fascists'. In general terms, the Comintern's change in line brought international policy into step with the dominant sentiment within the CPNZ, amongst both the rank-and-file and the party leadership. The New Zealand labour movement had been increasingly polarised for several years, communist theory now reflected more closely the prevailing practice on the ground. Party members were now free to follow their instincts into a more open and uncompromising struggle for the leadership of the New Zealand working class, not always with positive results.

Building a Party to Lead the Class Struggle

By the end of the 1920s, the CPNZ believed its organisational basis needed to be strengthened; this was also a consistent theme in Comintern communications from 1928. Indeed, better organisation was frequently defined as the chief task of the party.[44] The 1928 CPNZ conference began the task; the party headquarters was moved from Blackball back to Wellington. A new central executive was elected and a series of committees established to co-ordinate work in industry, on international issues, and among women.[45] In May 1929, the party employed Dick Griffin as its first full-time organiser; in August, he also assumed the position of general secretary.[46]

Despite the dominant international paradigm, there is no suggestion that the Comintern imposed Griffin on the CPNZ. He did not return from Moscow the anointed leader, quite the contrary, several leaders were appointed after Griffin's return, but they were all found wanting. Ultimately, it was a case of Griffin having to take on the job, it helped that he was capable, energetic and wanted to do it.

While a strong centre was the ideal for both the CPNZ and the Comintern, in Griffin's time as leader it was never realised in practice. Despite enormous efforts at reorganisation, the party continued to suffer chronic leadership instability and weakness. Some members were reluctant to commit themselves to leadership positions if it meant moving to Wellington. Others were reluctant to stay once they had arrived and realised the challenge and burden they faced in the job.[47] The Comintern criticised party members for a lack of loyalty to the cause, suggesting they should be more willing to makes sacrifices.[48] This was a harsh criticism given that except for Griffin they were unwaged 'professional' revolutionaries living on the breadline and relying on party supporters for sustenance and sometimes shelter.[49]

In appointing Griffin, the party did not solve the issue of leadership. Personal and political antagonisms within the leadership exacerbated problems of instability. So too did a lack of confidence from rank-and-file members. Griffin was frequently accused of operating a personal dictatorship. Delegates at the January 1932 party conference noted that his leadership style led rank-and-file members to treat instructions from the central executive with contempt; others simply left the party.[50] The conference expressed alarm at the high turnover of membership and the leadership was accused of alienating members and scaring off potential recruits. The gathering was understandably perturbed when it was revealed that the control commission, responsible for internal party security and discipline, had expelled 21 members at a single meeting. J. B. Power, a disgruntled former member of the Wellington branch, suggested that during a period of several months in 1932 some two hundred people had joined the branch, most of who quickly left. Power's figures are undoubtedly exaggerated to score political points, but images of a revolving door appear close to the truth.[51] During 1931, membership in Wellington fluctuated dramatically: during March there were 51 members, by May 80, in August 40, and by January 1932 only 25.[52]

Both at the local and national level, the pool of experienced members was very low indeed; consequently, some party members experienced a meteoric rise to high office. In October 1932, only one member of the central executive had been in the party longer than a year, while several had been members for as little as two months.[53] A relative scarcity of financial resources was also a problem in establishing a better organisational base. Finances continued to be stretched beyond capacity. The cost of running a printery was a major burden but the paper was central to party life, providing both a crucial medium for propaganda and a focus of activity for members.[54] The financial crisis was exacerbated by the success of a series of libel actions brought against the party press.[55] The importation of literature was both a considerable financial burden and security risk, as most was still banned. A certain impropriety and dishonesty on the part of some members did not help the party's financial situation; on several occasions, individuals were accused of dipping into the party coffers for their own benefit.[56]

Adding to this internal instability were increasing attacks on the party by the state. The movement of the headquarters back to Wellington left the leadership more exposed than they had been on the West Coast, and the consequences were soon apparent. A police raid in July 1929, initiated by an undercover detective who had joined the Wellington branch, seized party records and a considerable quantity of literature. The result was the prosecution of five members of the central executive for the possession and sale of seditious literature, each receiving a fine of £50 or three months in prison.[57] In the wake of the case, both the central executive and the Wellington branch effectively ceased to operate.

While the party was never declared illegal, the 1929 raid signalled a more explicit targeting of the CPNZ by the police.[58] Three more members of the party central committee were arrested in 1930, four in 1931, four in 1932, and all seven members of the central committee were imprisoned in 1933. In addition, large numbers of rank-and-file members were arrested over the same period.[59] Some incidents amounted to petty harassment by the police, including charges for obscene language, posting bills, selling papers on a Sunday, and dispersing typed papers without the name of a printer. But more serious charges were also laid: two issues of the *Red Worker* and a pamphlet were declared seditious in 1932, and those responsible for its publication were gaoled for more than twelve months. The definition of sedition was broad and included promotion of 'ill will and hostility between different classes'.[60]

Police infiltration was a significant threat and members were urged to take a greater interest in security, not always with success. To the embarrassment of the party, a police agent succeeded in becoming secretary of the Christchurch branch.[61] In 1932, new Immigration Restriction Regulations were gazetted which barred from entry into the country individuals who supported or were affiliated to the Third International, who espoused the doctrines of communism, or who had been in a country under the control of communism.[62] Older measures were still employed such as the Undesirable Immigrants Exclusion Act, under which the government tried to deport Ivan Tomasevic, an Auckland party member of Croatian origin.[63]

The Limits of Bolshevisation

Just as practice did not match theory in relations between the Comintern and the CPNZ, nor did it in the interaction between the central executive and local committees, branches and individuals. There were limits to which the higher organs could compel lower organs to act on instructions. Indeed, the authority of the centre relied to a considerable extent on the consent of the lower organs. If there was a general agreement with the 'instructions' or 'directives', there was a greater chance that they would be put into effect. However, even this makes the process appear more straightforward than it was in practice. Frequently, branches that were earnestly putting the instructions of the central executive into practice found themselves accused of 'right deviationism' or 'left sectarianism'. At the January 1932 party conference, some members were criticised for their extreme platform style and acting as if they belonged to a secret society, while during 1933 the Dunedin branch was criticised for right deviation on the grounds of an insufficiently critical stance towards the Labour Party during the local body elections.[64] In both instances, the groups were doing what they thought party policy required.

There was always scope for instructions to be interpreted, and implemented in a multiplicity of ways, both wilfully and in innocence. Party records regularly record discussions of the inability or unwillingness of branches and individuals to meet the standards set by the central party organisation.[65] Yet, the criticism could flow both ways. A Dunedin member, exasperated at the demand on the branches from the party leadership, described the central committee as 'chock full of subjective idealism'. He was not alone in his criticism.[66]

Certainly, the party leadership wanted to make the CPNZ more like a Bolshevik party – disciplined and highly organised[67] – but did not come close to creating their ideal organisation. The same handicaps which afflicted the central executive confronted local committees and branches. Local committees were continually frustrated at being unable to impose their will on branches and individuals, and like the national organisation were subject to their own internal divisions. The January 1932 party conference spent a good deal of time discussing the failings of local party committees, and the debate continued at another gathering in December at which party leaders lambasted members for their extreme individualism.[68]

The various levels of the structure did not work well in themselves, nor did they interact in a manner that equated with communist theory or the dominant historical paradigm. Local groups continually refused to accept their subordinate status and tended to question, reject, deliberately misconstrue or simply ignore policies that they found problematic. Even mundane matters such as ensuring the payment of dues or selling the party newspaper became the basis of controversy. As much as half the membership of some party branches were considered 'inactive' by the party leadership, others simply went 'missing' having failed to inform the central committee that they had moved cities.[69] This was partly a reflection of poor organisation at the local level and, in some instances, a lack of will, but it could also be a form of resistance by rank-and-file members in situations where there were more serious differences between the centre and locality over policy matters.[70] Late in 1933, the Comintern noted the lack of progress including the 'absence of Bolshevik discipline'. It urged the party leadership to 'carry on a merciless fight against this evil' although, perhaps sensing a tendency for over reaction, cautioned against 'mechanical expulsion'.[71]

Just as there could be controversy between branches and the centre, so too could there be conflict within branches and local committees. The distressing tendency to turn inward and blame each other for problems caused the party considerable problems, not least the tendency for the loser in power struggles to end up either resigning or, more frequently, being expelled from the party. In 1931, Sid Fournier was expelled from the Christchurch branch in part for his refusal to accept the 'new line of the Communist International', but also for 'the basest treachery', including calling the police to discipline a branch member.[72] J. B. Power wrote a lengthy critique of what to his mind was the 'baneful influence of a sabotaging force' in the Wellington branch, namely party leader Dick Griffin, whom he accused of a range of 'atrocities' against the branch.[73] Sectarianism was the dominant political style during this period, but it owed less to the Comintern than it did to the stroppy, agitational personalities of party members and the party leader himself.

Yet, this style of interaction was by no means universal. Some branches were always more inclined to co-operate with each and other elements in the labour movement. Rather than reflecting any new Third Period sectarianism, much of the explanation for the variation lies in the particular history of the labour movements in different centres and the frequently on-going personal conflicts between individuals. In Christchurch, Sid Fournier and Charlie Saunders had long been thorns in the side of leading figures in the trades and labour council, and were dealt with on the basis of their past actions as much as their current activity.[74] The same applied to the hostility directed at Dick Griffin by some leading Labour Party figures in Wellington. Griffin had been offside with many local labour figures since they had been adversaries in the Wellington Labour Social Club early in 1920s.[75]

The opposite could, of course, be the case. In Dunedin during the early 1930s, there was more co-operation between the CPNZ and the broader labour movement, not least because one of the leading communists – Harold Silverstone – was the son of Mark Silverstone, a high profile Labour figure.[76] The older Silverstone had been one of the few supporting an inclusive policy during the conflict over communist membership of the Labour Party during the mid 1920s.

Taking the Revolution to the Workplace

Expanding the party's influence amongst employed workers was a persistent theme in communications from the Comintern and in the party's self-assessment.[77] The Red International of Labour Unions (RILU) also stressed this as a primary objective; it encouraged a more radical policy for the CPNZ in its communication somewhat earlier than did the Comintern. The RILU set the party very ambitious goal of establishing a 'revolutionary opposition which shall co-ordinate the work of militant sections' to act as a counter to reformist trade unionism.[78] The party had made unsuccessful attempts to establish such movements since the mid-1920s[79], and the new campaign made a poor start; Dick Griffin failed to circulate the RILU's first resolution, for which he was sternly admonished.[80]

There were, however, some initial successes, especially in the Freezing Workers' Union, where a very active rank-and-file movement associated with the CPNZ operated from 1928, and to a lesser extent in the Watersiders' Union.[81] Both petered out with the onset of the economic depression. The party also had for a time considerable influence amongst seamen and miners, although this was through influence in the union hierarchy more than a rank-and-file movement. The RILU considered these two 'revolutionary unions' to be crucial in building a broader revolutionary industrial movement. However, as Bert Roth suggests, the RILU's ambition was 'entirely beyond the resources' of the CPNZ.[82] Worse still, CPNZ influence in the two unions was destroyed by advocacy of a policy in advance of the workers' level of political understanding. The dominant historical paradigm has some weight in this aspect of CPNZ history, although there are two important caveats. Firstly, the sectarianism was as much domestically derived as externally generated by the RILU or the Comintern. Secondly, the first sectarian 'error' predates the 'left turn' in Comintern instructions to New Zealand.

During 1929, the party lost all influence in the Miners' Union and almost its entire membership on the West Coast when it called for a strike in solidarity with striking miners and timber workers in Australia. The central executive's policy of 'Neither Timber Nor Coal' was tersely rejected by communist union officials. However, the party executive insisted that Angus McLagan, a former CPNZ secretary and leader of the Miners' Union, implement party policy. He refused and resigned from the party, prompting the resignations of his West Coast supporters and the decimation of party strength in the region.[83]

Communist influence within the Seamen's Union was similarly lost by insisting on a policy that union members and officials would not support. In 1931, the union declared a Japanese ship 'black' because its 'slave rates of pay' were a threat to the wages and conditions of New Zealand workers. The CPNZ urged the union to take further action and strike in solidarity with the exploited Japanese seamen. Union officials were furious and attacked the party for its 'unrealistic schemes'. The party replied that F. P. Walsh, a former party member and leader of the Seamen's Union, was adopting an anti-working class attitude.[84] The result was alienation from their last contact in the high politics of New Zealand unionism. From this point on, Walsh became a fierce critic of the CPNZ and went out of his way to attack the party.[85] The party attempted to maintain an influence in the Seamen's Union at a rank-and-file level, but this was difficult in the face of such vehement opposition from a union hierarchy that did not hesitate to expel members for essentially political reasons.[86]

The CPNZ's attempts to establish such rank-and-file movements largely failed. The degree to which this was the responsibility of a Comintern inspired ultra-militancy and sectarianism is questionable; the domestic sources of political, and often personal, conflict were deeply rooted. Several factors weakened the party's work amongst paid workers.

First, the leadership of the trade union movement was quick to act against communist activity in unions and the workplace. This was especially so of leaders of the Alliance of Labour such as Jim Roberts, of whom the party had become increasingly critical. Angry at attacks on him, Roberts turned on his critics, frequently attacking the CPNZ at Alliance of Labour conferences.[87] Roberts was not alone in expressing his views.

Second, because the membership for much of this period was overwhelmingly unemployed, the CPNZ had little contact with employed workers. Almost all the membership was unemployed during 1930; in 1932, the figure was about 60 per cent unemployed and remained at that level into 1934.[88] Not only was the party isolated from those in employment, its members faced the personal disruption of either transience in search for permanent employment, seasonal work or relief work, all of which tended to weaken the ties that party members had built in their previous places of employment.[89]

Third, the party's propaganda, by their own admission, was not well directed to ordinary workers. Even some party members considered that it was frequently too theoretical. Rank-and-file newspapers, produced for a short time by seamen, watersiders and some area groups, were criticised within the party as too sectarian and not addressing issues of interest to the workers at whom they were supposedly aimed.[90]

Undeterred, in 1931 the party ambitiously re-organised itself along the lines of 'factory cells' as opposed to area branches. The system was a projection of desire rather than a reflection of actual party strength.[91] Not surprisingly, the following two years saw frequent self-critical reflection for failing to actually put this plan into practice. The bulk of the party remained in area groups rather than factory cells quite simply because they had little or no presence in factories. The objectives of the party continued to be easier to identify than achieve.

Depression – The Making of the Communist Party?

Joseph Powell in his influential thesis on the CPNZ portrays the depression years of the 1930s as a period of considerable progress for the party. Amongst the unemployed, he suggests, the party found a launching pad for a new era.[92] The CPNZ did play the central role in the formation of the Unemployed Workers Movement (UWM) early in 1931, building on its previous activity amongst the unemployed.[93] Suggestions of communists cynically jumping on the bandwagon in the 1930s, principally at the behest of the Comintern, are unfounded.[94] It was the mainstream labour movement that came late to the struggle against unemployment, and then as an attempt to undermine the efforts of the CPNZ.

The UWM sought 'to unify the struggle of the unemployed throughout the country, and to develop the solidarity between employed and unemployed workers'.[95] Yet, the focus of the CPNZ on the unemployed struggle in the early 1930s was by default rather than by design; its preference was to expand its influence amongst paid workers, the social reality of a party composed almost entirely of unemployed people drove the activism as much as any grand political plan, whether hatched in Wellington or Moscow. Even so, commentators have seen this movement as Third Period sectarianism *par excellence*.[96]

The oral tradition of the left also highlights the 1930s unemployed struggles.[97] Here the period is characterised as a triumph of grassroots organising and collective action over the individualising effects of capitalism.[98] But there is more to it than that. I am not suggesting that such memories are inaccurate or without merit, rather that the degree to which the CPNZ as an organisation benefited from the depression experience deserves closer scrutiny. It is assumed that the UWM was a happy recruiting ground for new members, yet CPNZ membership figures qualify this assumption. As Table 1 indicates, party membership did increase between 1930 and 1935, however the base figure was at an all time low, reflecting in part the defection of the miners in 1929. From here, the only way was up.

Table 1:
CPNZ, Official Membership Figures 1926–35

Year	No.
1926	120
1927	105
1928	79
1930	62
1932 (Jan)	81
1932 (Dec)	129
1934 (Dec)	246
1935 (June)	280
1935 (Dec)	353

Membership numbers are not in themselves an accurate reflection of influence. The CPNZ's reach extended far beyond formal membership, and some individuals joined the party later in the 1930s, rather than when they were first associated with the party and active in militant protest. Johnny Mitchell, who became one of New Zealand's leading communist trade unionists, did not join the party until 1937, long after he had become prominent in the UWM and been very closely associated with the CPNZ for most of the decade.[99]

The UWM did bring the CPNZ into closer contact with the 'working class' than at any previous time in its history. Sharing as they did the day-to-day material struggles of ordinary people, both materially and politically, gave party members a solid base upon which to build support in certain communities and suburbs. This was especially so in inner city Wellington, Auckland and Christchurch, but also provincial centres such as Gisborne and Palmerston North, which had not previously had a CPNZ presence.[100] The groundwork for later increases in party membership and influence in trade unions can be traced back to the experiences of the depression. Many prominent activists served their political apprenticeships in the UWM, in the process learning valuable skills put into use later in trade union work.[101]

For many people, the CPNZ's close association with the UWM gave it positive kudos rather than the more negative characteristics one may expect from reading some historical accounts. Party members who put their bodies on the line to prevent evictions, demonstrated over conditions for relief workers, or engaged in less dramatic day-to-day activities, made an impact that was long lasting, if not always appreciated by the government or newspaper editors. Showpiece events, like the 1934 Gisborne Hunger March, left a long lasting impression, not least on those who were participants.[102]

To some extent, the UWM was a proving ground where the party tested more direct actionist tactics and agitational style politics. The anti-eviction struggles, in which party members and other UWM activists boarded themselves into houses to prevent the repossession of furniture and physical eviction of inhabitants, are an example.[103] Such tactics were more self-consciously confrontational of authority than most previous activity. In some respects, they were a two-edged sword. On the one hand, some evictions were prevented and the events were a dramatic means of highlighting issues. On the other, the forces of the state usually prevailed and the financial burden of frequent prosecutions stretched the resources of the UWM and the CPNZ.[104]

Nor was striking the correct political line always easy. The CPNZ leadership was concerned that a number of its members were in danger of 'killing the UWM through sectarianism', by which they meant — among other things — reckless disregard for their own self-preservation.[105] Nor were such militant tactics necessarily the best means to build a mass movement; the expectations of mass militant activity by the unemployed proved to be unduly inflated. Support for strike action and other activity disappointed the UWM and the CPNZ.[106] In such instances where there was spontaneous activity by the unemployed, such as the 'riots' of 1932, the CPNZ found itself in a double bind – unprepared and unable to take a lead, yet the first to be targeted by the police for fomenting violence.[107]

That the CPNZ sought to use the UWM for its own ends is without question. That it was reasonably open about this is perhaps a surprise only to those with a predisposition to characterise all communist activity as secretive and conspiratorial. In fact, the party leadership occasionally had to urge greater discretion on the part of some of its members whose propensity to shout revolutionary slogans and call for strikes at the drop of a hat were endangering the movement.[108] This comes to the heart of the matter in considering the place of the UWM, and similar movements, in the CPNZ's history. Party planning may have been elaborate but the execution was frequently flawed. There are a number of reasons for this.

The inability to put centralised plans into practice due to the frequent unwillingness of the party's own members to act on them. At the December 1933 party conference, the party leadership reported their dissatisfaction with work amongst the unemployed. Some were criticised for general laxity and not treating such work as politically significant. Several groups were accused of not even reading central executive reports on the issue. Others were so engrossed in the UWM that they were in danger of totally submerging the party's identity.[109]

It was more than just a matter of variable enthusiasm for the type of work. There were also political differences over the best tactics to employ. Charlie Saunders, one of the key CPNZ and UWM activists in Christchurch, was accused of extreme rightist activity for opposing a proposal for a relief worker strike during 1933.[110] At the other extreme were those in a permanent barricade mentality, who endangered the party and the UWM with reckless militancy.[111] Given such diversity, it is hardly surprising that party members had been observed speaking in favour of several different policies at UWM conferences.[112]

These factors all impacted on the ability of the party to turn its contacts with the unemployed into rising membership. Some potential members would have been deterred by the apparent militancy and 'bombastic delivery' of certain party members. While some party members were so engrossed in UWM work that they did not consider recruiting.[113] That these outcomes had little to do with what the Comintern wished or instructed is more clear-cut.

Broadening the Movement

During the early 1930s, the CPNZ sought to establish other organisations with which to broaden its base and develop a radical political culture. The Friends of the Soviet Union (FSU), established in Auckland late in 1931, was the most prominent and successful.[114] At its peak, the FSU had branches in most towns. The organisation was not free of controversy. Sid Scott, its leader in Auckland, was condemned as a petty-bourgeois intellectual by some delegates at the January 1932 CPNZ conference, so too was his organisation. Scott defended himself, suggesting the FSU was a means by which the party would be able to establish links with workers in industry.[115] There is some merit in both positions. Certainly, many workers did join the FSU, which blossomed quite quickly, achieving a membership of over 200 in Auckland alone by early 1933. There were industrial branches in most main centres.[116]

Yet, it was amongst the middle class that a significant breakthrough was made. The FSU was the principal vehicle by which a steady trickle of middle class people came into the CPNZ. The most celebrated was Gordon Watson, a Wellington university student who joined the FSU in 1933, quickly rising to the position of national secretary. Watson and a small but significant group of his generation were radicalised in the context of the depression.[117] They established a longstanding 'red' student culture on campuses throughout New Zealand.[118] The broadening of the social base was not without its critics, some party members were worried about the dilution of the working class character of the party.[119] At its best, the FSU provided a meeting ground for people of different classes and to some extent political backgrounds to learn more about the Soviet Union and socialism. At its worst, it was simply another meeting of the local communist party branch. The norm was somewhere between these two extremes.

The fortunes of the FSU, and similar organisations, were shaped by many of the same factors qualifying the success of the UWM. Work by party members was often very poorly co-ordinated; in theory a fraction system operated whereby they worked in co-ordination, in practice this was seldom the case. Party policy was not always promoted and attention to recruiting frequently neglected.[120] In some instances, the political and theoretical level of the non-party members outshone that of party members and led to political defeats. By 1933, the Comintern was concerned that the FSU was out of control of party members and urged the party to sharpen up its act.[121] This suggestion prompted a terse response that the CPNZ had no fraction of the national committee of the FSU and that:

> It was all very well to instruct comrades to form fractions in this or that organisation, but when there is only so few, and those to whom you give the task ... are less politically developed than the leadership of the FSU and this

(individual) cannot command the respect of the non-party members of the organisation, then the task is indeed hard.[122]

Freemanisation

In mid 1933, Fred Freeman, a New Zealander who had spent four years in Moscow at the Comintern, returned to New Zealand and took up the position of general secretary. Freeman was thoroughly imbued with the culture of the Comintern and the policies of the Third Period. Does this moment confirm the dominant paradigm of Comintern initiated leadership change and the imposition of a much more tightly controlling party centre? Perhaps, but the situation was decidedly more opaque.

Freeman had in fact returned reluctantly at the specific request of the CPNZ leadership, who had been begging for his return for nearly a year.[123] The party stressed that the request was urgent; as a young and inexperienced organisation, it was very much in need of a strong directive central executive. It hoped that the return of Freeman would provide this strength and direction.[124] When he finally arrived, in June 1933, the CPNZ was in acute crisis; its entire central committee was in prison having been arrested for the production of a pamphlet, *Karl Marx and the Struggle of the Masses*, which police considered subversive. An emergency executive was struggling to pick up the pieces; Freeman assumed *de facto* leadership of the party on his arrival, which was formalised by the 1933 party conference.[125]

Freeman brought to the leadership qualities that had been lacking in previous years, including political experience, considerable organisational skill, a sound knowledge of communist theory, and a desire to organise the party along democratic centralist lines. Earlier attempts by Griffin to apply this theory were largely unsuccessful. While Freeman had a strong directive style, he generally used it more sensitively than Griffin; expulsion was now no longer the first instinct when there were political differences. As a consequence, the turnover rate of membership declined.[126]

Another skill Freeman brought to the task of leadership was the ability to identify and foster talented young leaders. He was responsible for cultivating Gordon Watson and Elsie Farrelly, two young university graduates who, along with Freeman and the experienced Ernie Brooks, dominated the party leadership from late 1933 to the end 1935. Freeman and Farrelly, who became office manager, did most of the administrative work in the national office.[127] Together they made the work of the central committee more systematic and, for the first time, there were regular circulars, bulletins and directives from the central committee to local party committees and branches. There were also visits from central committee members to party groups.[128] Branches were expected to do their bit. Among other things, they were expected to complete regular census sheets giving details of their membership and the activities they undertook. However, the establishment of a more stable leadership did nothing to ensure that the rank-and-file of the party took seriously central committee instructions; such administrative tasks were frequently ignored.[129]

Another key component of the centralisation process was heightened attention to internal security. Freeman regularly stressed to his colleagues the necessity of combining legal and illegal work.[130] Sometimes, however, this necessity for security could be taken to excess. Freeman used a number of pseudonyms, most frequently 'Steve Dunne', on his return from Moscow. In part, this was an attempt to avoid deportation, as he was in breach of the Immigration Restriction Regulations of 1932, but it was also something of a stylistic preference. He enjoyed being a shadowy figure in the background and the mystique of his years in Moscow added to the aura.[131] He seldom appeared in public on his return to New Zealand, those who had known him before his departure for Moscow were bemused by his obsessive demand that they call him by his new pseudonym.[132]

Some of Freeman's undoubted qualities, when taken to excess, could present their own problems. Some party members found his style of leadership just as dictatorial and frustrating as that of Dick Griffin, and resisted accordingly. In 1935, workers in the party printery went on strike against their own leader. Ironically, the party did not pay its own workers union rates despite such practice being a key part of their own platform. However, this was also a protest at the intrusive style of leadership practiced by Freeman.[133] Despite such hiccups, the immediate benefits of Freeman's leadership outweighed the drawbacks; the bulk of the party membership preferred a strong directive leadership to none at all. In this they were in keeping with the wishes of the Comintern.

Prolonging the Third Period in New Zealand

Comintern policy came under revision from 1933, precipitated by the unexpected and continued success of fascism in Germany. The eventual outcome was to re-emphasise the notion of the united front, which was re-conceptualised as the principal means by which to combat fascism. While a certain ambiguity existed until the seventh Comintern congress held in 1935, it was increasingly accepted that the formation of a united front should be achieved by whatever means possible, whether by agreement from above or agitation from below.[134]

At the end of 1933, the CPNZ, influenced by this 'new thinking', approached the national executive of the Labour Party with a view to joining them in a campaign against fascism. The Labour Party did not respond. Similar approaches were made to the Alliance of Labour and several key unions, including the Miners, Seamen, and Watersiders. All except the

Miners' Union failed to reply.[135] The rebuff was taken by the CPNZ leadership as a signal to step up its campaign for the 'united front from below'. The party considered there was a genuine chance to drive a wedge between leaders of the labour movement and its membership.[136] This response was consistent with a letter the party had received from the Comintern at the end of 1933, which, like its recent predecessors, emphatically promoted the 'class against class' approach, urging the CPNZ to undeviatingly apply the tactic of the 'united front from below'.[137]

The party leadership continued to accept this formulation, and the 1934 central committee plenum recommitted the party to the pursuit of the 'united front from below' and the building of 'Soviet Power' in New Zealand. The leadership targeted right opportunism – in this context interpreted as passivity, sinking the identity of the party, and co-operating with reformism – rather than sectarianism as the party's major internal political problem.[138] This was also a concern of the Comintern, which was disturbed that elements of the CPNZ were too willing to co-operate with the Labour Party.[139]

Crucial to the CPNZ's political assessment was a belief that working class support for the Labour Party and reformist trade unionism was declining. In such conditions, the CPNZ leadership believed a sharper assault, rather than a more conciliatory approach, was required. Fred Freeman told his former comrades in Moscow that the Labour Party was 'ideologically moribund'. In his opinion the Social Credit movement, which was to his mind potentially fascist, was more vital to New Zealand's political life than the Labour Party.[140] Such views were not simply held by Freeman, rather they were widely held by both the leadership and the party more generally. There were, for example, no dissenting voices when such political formulations were discussed at the 1934 central committee plenum, which was attended by sixteen delegates from nine centres. Even Leo Sim, later a champion of the new Comintern line, accepted this critical view of Labour. The December 1934 CPNZ conference also supported the slogan and programme 'For a Soviet New Zealand'.[141]

CPNZ policy was contradictory. At face value, it appeared to be taking on some of the rethinking being undertaken abroad. Several additional approaches were made to the national leadership of the Labour Party in an effort to gain a united front; most importantly there was a request for a joint approach to the 1935 general election, which was firmly rejected by the Labour Party.[142] At the national level, however, relations between the Labour Party and the CPNZ continued to be erratic and characterised by considerable bitterness and mistrust on both sides. Much of this can be attributed to a longstanding personal antagonism between the leaders such as Peter Fraser and Bob Semple for Labour, and Griffin, Freeman and Alex

Galbraith for the CPNZ. Such individuals had behind them a decade of direct personal and political conflict. The sectarian nature of CPNZ approaches further ensured a likely rebuff; the party consistently expected the Labour Party to accept large parts of the CPNZ programme as a basis of unity, rather than a less tangible unity based on defeating the conservative government.[143]

From time to time co-operation between the CPNZ and the Labour Party was achieved at the local and district level. This was partly because some rank-and-file communists considered that local reformist leaders were less 'corrupt' than the national leaders. It was also the result of identifying local issues upon which party political coalitions could be built. A 1934 Auckland Free Speech Campaign illustrates this practice; this saw communists, unionists, labour activists and pacifists combine in a direct challenge to city council restrictions on public speaking.[144]

Yet, such local co-operation was seldom welcomed by either the communist or Labour Party national leadership. The Labour executive warned its local groups to be wary of communist Trojan horse tactics.[145] And the CPNZ executive warned that close co-operation between CPNZ and Labour members, for example during the 1935 Auckland municipal elections, simply brought about the 'sinking of the party'.[146] On certain issues, there was wilful contravention of party policy by some CPNZ members in the districts, most consistently in Auckland. At one level, such groups accepted the notion of democratic centralism, but in practice applied it only when it suited them. The willingness of party members to reject or disregard policy which contravened 'local knowledge', or which would upset the delicate local working arrangements, continued to upset a national leadership of the party that was relatively powerless to do anything about it.[147]

The contradictions of CPNZ policy were further demonstrated by Leo Sim, New Zealand delegate to the Comintern's seventh congress. Sim acknowledged that the CPNZ had pursued a sectarian policy, which he suggested had hampered the creation of a united front with Labour. Yet, he continued to suggest that a distinction be made between Labour leaders and workers. He argued that the CPNZ needed to more successfully expose the 'reactionary Labour leaders'.[148] Despite occasional local level practices to the contrary, official CPNZ policy continued to define the Labour Party as an obstruction rather than an ally. This was most clearly demonstrated by the CPNZ policy at the 1935 general election where the party stood four candidates on a 'class against class' platform and advised members and supporters to oppose Labour and invalidate their ballot papers if there was no communist candidate. The party suggested that any government not comprised of communists would serve the interests of the bosses.[149]

The watershed victory of Labour in the election, and the very poor showing of the CPNZ candidates – all four failed to recover their deposits – brought a quick public admission of error from the CPNZ leadership; they acknowledged that the party had underestimated the hatred that New Zealand working people had for the previous government. The party admitted that seeking a united front based on defeating the government, rather than the party programme, would have been a better approach.[150]

Leo Sim's experience at the Comintern conference and studying in Moscow helped clarify his views and cement his support for the new policy of the Comintern, although it has been suggested that even on his return he did not have a good grasp of the new ideas.[151] As early as October 1935 he had advised the central committee that a 'sharp turn in policy' was necessary in relation to the Labour Party. The response to this call was initially quite positive and a decision was made to encourage party members to discuss the new International line. In addition, as part of the lead up to the party conference in December, the pages of the *Worker's Weekly* were opened for discussion.[152]

The results of this, and reflection upon the unexpected victory of Labour in the general election, were manifest at the 1935 party conference, where delegates voted for a change of leadership. Fred Freeman was voted out as general secretary in favour of Leo Sim. More significantly, the conference revealed that a considerable gulf had emerged between the national leadership and the bulk of the party membership. The former favoured retention of the incumbent leadership, while the later supported a change. It was apparent that party leaders and members favoured a different style of politics, and this was the basis of on-going tension in the subsequent year.[153]

The apparent resolution to the conflict over policy achieved by the 1935 conference was, however, weakened by several factors that combined to ensure the continuance of a relatively sectarian policy well into the 1936. First, Leo Sim was faced with a central committee that was little changed in its composition. Most of the old protagonists were still there, including Fred Freeman who continued to run the national office in his capacity as organisational secretary.[154] Second, there was a legacy of personal bitterness between Freeman and Sim, who both wrote to contacts in Moscow criticising the other. Almost from day one, Sim believed that he did not have the support of the rest of the committee. He described Freeman as 'a clever crook' and characterised Elsie Freeman (nee Farrelly) as a 'good tea party artist'. Putting on a brave face, he declared his intention to 'try and do [his] best to get rid of this counter revolutionary scum and cowardly revolutionary fleas', by which he meant almost the whole central committee.[155] Freeman was more diplomatic in his language but conveyed clearly his dislike for Sim, suggesting accurately that there was a 'certain lack of confidence in Sim'.[156]

Aspects of Sim's personal life were a third factor handicapping his leadership. In the first instance, he did not and would not live in Wellington, so was away from the party centre more often than desirable. His absence was prolonged by the illness of his wife May during a large part of 1936, while he also had on-going health problems.[157]

That only a partial change had been achieved by the 1935 conference was clearly highlighted by the central committee discussion of affiliation to the Labour Party, a step considered by the Comintern to be fundamental to building the united front against fascism. Early in 1936, the central committee was divided into three camps on the issue. The first comprising Connie Birchfield and Miles Ormerod, the former a party candidate in the 1935 general election, the later a one time organiser for the UWM. Both were opposed to any attempt to affiliate to Labour. The second group, by far the largest, comprised Fred and Elsie Freeman, Gordon Watson and Ernie Brooks. They considered that affiliation should be delayed until there had been considerably more groundwork conducted at a rank-and-file level. In effect, they were still conceiving of the approach in terms of a 'united front from below'. The third comprised Sim alone, who stressed the urgency of applying immediately.[158]

Sim stressed to his colleagues that he had been instructed, while in Moscow, to immediately seek affiliation to the Labour Party. Their reply was unsympathetic. The remainder of the committee was adamant that the CPNZ needed to take care and avoid mechanically applying formulations constructed elsewhere.[159] This position further emphasises the limitations of the paradigm that suggests national sections of the Comintern were essentially subservient. The political line was frequently discussed amongst the leadership during the subsequent twelve months, and as the year passed support for the new line grew to a point that by the end of 1936 Freeman was in a minority of one. He alone amongst the central committee wished to remain aloof from Labour. A number of factors brought about this change. The first was a growing hostility to Freeman's personal style. In particular, there was concern that he was still reluctant to take a visible public role. He was considered aloof, and even cowardly, in putting his own safety before that of the cause. Most importantly, his wife and fellow central committee member Elsie Freeman was increasingly at odds with him on both personal and political grounds, in this he lost a key political ally.[160]

Secondly, there was a continued demand from the rank-and-file of the party for a less sectarian policy. In some areas, the prospect of applying for affiliation was so attractive that some individuals joined the Labour Party as individuals. Many of the rank-and-file wished party policy would catch up to their own practice. The Auckland district, in particular, wanted a showdown with Freeman, who they considered was the principal reason for the party not fully adopting the new line.[161]

The final factor in Freeman's demise was the intervention of the CPA, acting on behalf of the Comintern. This took the form of regular communication between the two parties by mail and, from mid 1936, extended visits by leading members of the CPA. The first was Ted Docker, a member of the CPA central executive who attended the CPNZ central committee plenum in July 1936. All the visitors attended meetings of the CPNZ central committee and, frequently, the party's national conference. Most also toured the country for discussions with local groups.[162] There can be no doubt that the presence of CPA leader Lance Sharkey at the CPNZ conference at the end of 1936 ensured that Freeman was finally removed from the party leadership and subsequently suspended from the party for not accepting his fate. Freeman's suspension came after a period where he was sent 'to industry' to overcome his weaknesses. The central committee considered this experiment unsuccessful and he was expelled at the end of 1937.[163] This was, in effect, the last act of the Third Period in New Zealand; it is ironic that despite the dominant paradigm the closest New Zealand came to a Comintern initiated leadership change was to remove the final legacy of the policy they were supposed to have imposed.

McDermott and Agnew suggest that revisionists have highlighted the fact that the Third Period was both 'complex and contradictory'.[164] The New Zealand experience suggests that revisionist historians are correct in shifting the focus from the Comintern to the national and local level, and on the interaction between all three. Relationships within the communist movement were not 'directive', as the dominant paradigm suggests. National sections, local groups and individuals could and did resist unpalatable policy. That the CPNZ took a 'left turn' from 1928 is undeniable. However, the explanation for this, including the on-going influence of sectarianism after the International line changed, lies more in the contours of the New Zealand political scene than it does in the corridors of the Comintern; it comes from particular and specific historical circumstances.

Notes

1. R. F. Griffin, 'Letter to the Sixth Congress Communist International', 21 August 1928, Comintern records (Russian Centre for the Preservation and Study of Contemporary Historical Documents (RC), 495/63/9).

2. R. F. Griffin, *Report to the Political Secretariat of the Executive Committee of the Communist International (ECCI)*, 28 September 1928 (RC 495/3/81).

3. *International Press Correspondence (Inprecorr)* 23 November 1928.

4. J. Degras (Ed.), *The Communist International 1919–43: Documents Vol. II* (London, 1960), pp. 455–526; K. McDermott and J. Agnew, *The Comintern: A History of International Communism from Lenin to Stalin* (Basingstoke, 1996), pp. 81–119.

5. For a succinct summary, see Ibid. p. 81.

6. Classic English language examples include T. Draper, *The Roots of American Communism* (Chicago, 1957) and *American Communism and Soviet Russia* (New York, 1960); H. Pelling, *The British Communist Party: A Historical Profile* (London, 1958).

7. S. Scott, *Rebel in a Wrong Cause* (Auckland 1960), pp. 51–52 and pp. 54–56.

8. For example, P. Warren, 'The Power of Myth: Aspects of Marxist-Leninist Strategical and Ideological Divergence in New Zealand' (BA. Hons Research Essay, University of Otago, 1978), pp. 5–6; D. Carter, 'The Attitude of the NZ Communist Party to Foreign Affairs' (MA Research Essay, University of Auckland, 1981), p. 3; J. Grady, 'The Reds Who Made the Beds: The attitude of the CPNZ towards women and its work amongst women' (MA Research Essay, University of Auckland, 1983), p. 6.

9. B. Roth, 'The Communist Vote in New Zealand', *Political Science*, 17 (1965), p. 26.

10. Socialist Unity Party, *Communism in New Zealand: An Illustrated History* (Auckland, 1986), p. 17 and p. 19. The SUP was an important New Zealand communist group, established in 1966 in the wake of the Sino-Soviet dispute.

11. G. Dunstall, *A Policeman's Paradise? Policing a Stable Society, 1918–45* (Palmerston North, 1999), p. 447.

12. R. T. Robertson, 'Isolation, Ideology and Impotence: Organisations for the Unemployed During the Great Depression, 1930–35', *New Zealand Journal of History*, 12 (1979), p. 151 and p. 156; P. Harris, 'The New Zealand Unemployed Workers Movement, 1931–39: Gisborne and the Relief Workers Strike', *New Zealand Journal of History*, 10 (1976), p. 138.

13. For an assessment of debates in light of the new documents, see K. McDermott, 'The History of the Comintern in Light of New Documents', in T. Rees and A. Thorpe (eds), *International Communism and the Communist International 1919–43* (Manchester 1998), pp. 31–40. However, arguments countering the dominant paradigm were developing before, and independent of, the new sources becoming available. See M. Isserman, *Which Side Are You On? The American Communist Party during the Second World War* (Middletown, 1982).

14. For two excellent examples, see A. Thorpe, *The British Communist Party and Moscow 1920–43* (Manchester, 2000) and M. Worley, *Class Against Class: The Communist Party in Britain between the Wars* (London, 2002).

15. H. Klehr, J. Haynes and F. Firsov, *The Secret World of American Communism* (New Haven, 1995); H. Klehr, J. Haynes and K. Anderson, *The Soviet World of American Communism* (New Haven, 1998).

16. J. McIlroy and A. Campbell, 'Nina Ponomareva's Hats: The New Revisionism, the Communist International and the Communist Party of Great Britain', *Labour/Le Travail* (Spring 2002), pp. 147–87.

17. R. F. Griffin to Anglo-American Secretariat, 4 March 1931 (RC 495/63/30).

18. 'Report of E. M. Higgins the Central Executive Communist Party of Australia on attendance at 6th Congress', 20 December 1928 (J. N. Rawling Collection, N57/571, Noel Butlin Archive, Canberra). For the Comintern reply, see 'Communist International to General Secretary CPNZ', 3 January 1929 (RC 495/63/15).

19. *Minutes of the Political Commission of the Political Secretariat ECCI*, 28 September 1928; R. F. Griffin to Political Secretariat, 28 September 1928 (RC 495/3/81).

20. 'Newlands' to Anglo-American Secretariat, 3 April 1934 (RC 495/63/64.) 'Newlands' was the pseudonym used by Freeman while in Moscow, 1929–33.

21. Fred Freeman, 1929–33, Nellie Scott 1930–31, 'Atheist' (real name unknown) 1933–34, and Leo Sim 1934–35. The only other New Zealanders to travel to Moscow on official business in this period were Dick Griffin, delegate to the 1928 Comintern congress, and Alex Galbraith, delegate to the 1930 conference of the RILU.

22. 'Draft Letter to Communist Party of New Zealand', 20 November 1929 (RC 533/8/8); *Minutes of the Anglo-American Secretariat (AAS Mins)*, 21 November 1929 (RC 495/72/52); *AAS Mins*, 11 November 1932 (RC 495/72/148).

23. *AAS Mins*, 21 November and 11 December 1929 (RC 495/72/52).

24. *Resolution on the Tasks of the Communist Party of New Zealand* (RC 495/20/430).

25. Ibid.

26. Political Secretariat ECCI to CPNZ, 4 March 1930 (RC 495/20/430).

27. Letter to New Zealand, 10 March 1933 and Political Commission to CPNZ, 16 November 1934 (RC 495/20/430).

28. 'Report, CPNZ Conference', December 1929 (RC 495/63/16). The party would have been aware of the Comintern policy from publications such as *The Communist International* and *Inprecorr*, which contained details of the decisions of ECCI plenums.

29. The contents of the letter in question remain obscure, *Minutes of the CPNZ Central Executive (CE Mins)* 25 June 1929 (RC 495/63/17).

30. To Party Members from the General Secretary, July 1930 (Gerald Griffin Papers (GG), Alexander Turnbull Library, Wellington, 86-43-3/02).

31. *Red Worker*, October 1931; *CPNZ Conference Minutes*, December 1932 (RC 495/63/36).

32. Letter to New Zealand, 10 March 1933 (RC 495/20/430).

33. *New Zealand Worker*, 2 November 1927.

34. B. Brown, *The Rise of Labour: A History of the New Zealand Labour Party from 1916 to 1940* (Wellington, 1962), pp. 87–94.

35. *Workers Vanguard*, February 1928; 'An Open Letter to the Workers of the NZ Labor [sic] Party', 1927 (BRP, 94-106-01/1).

36. *Grey River Argus*, 10 October 1928.

37. On the pledge, see *Workers Vanguard*, February 1928; *Notes for Party Speakers Against Anti-Communist Pledge*, undated (1928); Wellington Group, CPNZ to Secretary Wellington LRC, 25 January 1928 (RC 495/63/9); CPNZ Executive to Secretary NZLP, 23 March 1929 (Patrick O'Farrell Papers, Alexander Turnbull Library, Wellington, 1501/8). On the affiliation issue, see *Minutes of the NZLP National Executive*, 13 February 1928 and 31 March 1929, and *Reports of NZLP Annual Conference*, 1928 and 1929 (New Zealand Labour Party Records (NZLPR), Wellington).

38. 'Agenda and Remits', CPNZ Conference 1928 (GG, 86-43-4/19).

39. *Report of the CPNZ Conference* 1929 (RC 495/63/16).

40. *Workers Vanguard*, February 1928. See *New Zealand Worker*, 13 June 1928 and *Workers Vanguard*, May 1928.

41. *New Zealand Worker*, 8 and 29 February, and 14 March 1928; *Workers Vanguard*, February 1928; R. F. Griffin, *The Trade Union Movement in New Zealand*, undated [1928] (RC 495/63/10).

42. *Grey River Argus*, 30 September 1927; *New Zealand Worker*, 24 April 1928.

43. *Minutes of the Annual Meeting, Alliance of Labour*, February 1928 (BRP, 94-106-30/05).

44. *CPNZ Conference Minutes*, December 1928 (RC 495/63/8); *Resolution on the Tasks of the Communist Party of New Zealand* (RC 495/20/430); 'Report on Party Organisation', CPNZ Conference, January 1932 (RC 495/63/35); ECCI to CPNZ, 10 March 1933 (RC 495/20/430).

45. *CPNZ Conference Minutes*, December 1928 (RC 495/63/8); *CE Mins*, 3 January 1929 (RC 495/63/17).

46. *CE Mins*, 20 May and 8 August 1929 (RC 495/63/17).

47. *CE Mins*, 17 August 1929 and 1 January 1930 (RC 495/63/17 and 27*);* 'Report on Party Organisation', January 1932 (RC 495/63/35); *CPNZ Conference Minutes*, December 1932 (RC 495/63/36).

48. ECCI to CPNZ, 10 March 1933 (RC 495/20/430).

49. Interview with Connie Birchfield, 23 March 1988.

50. *CPNZ Conference Minutes*, January 1932 (RC 495/63/35).

51. J. B. Power, 'Open Letter to CP Members and Sympathisers', undated [1932] (BRP, 94-106-01/1).

52. 'Report on Party Organisation', CPNZ Conference January 1932 (RC 495/63/35).

53. 'Organisational Report, CPNZ', October 1932 (RC 495/63/37); *CPNZ Conference Minutes*, December 1932 (RC 495/63/36); interview with Selwyn Devereux, 13 April 1988.

54. *CE Mins*, 17 February 1929 (RC 495/63/17).

55. *Grey River Argus*, 5 February 1930; *Red Worker*, March 1933; *New Zealand Worker*, 15 March 1933.

56. 'Report of CPNZ Conference', December 1929 (RC 495/63/16); *CPNZ Conference Minutes*, December 1932 (RC 495/63/36).

57. *Evening Post*, 25 October 1929; *Grey River Argus*, 22 November 1929; *Red Worker*, October 1929.

58. G. Dunstall, *A Policeman's Paradise*, p. 261.

59. Report by 'Andrews' [Leo Sim], 4 June 1935 (RC 495/63/75).

60. Press Report, CPNZ CE, 1 January to 28 September 1932 (RC 495/63/37); *Red Worker*, October 1932; G. Dunstall, *A Policeman's Paradise*, p. 259.

61. *CPNZ Conference Minutes*, January 1932 (RC 495/63/35).

62. Additional Immigration Restriction Regulations, C. no. 89, 14 March 1932, *New Zealand Gazette*, 1932, p. 541–42.

63. Tomasevic Defence Committee, *The Tomasevic Case* (Auckland, 1933).

64. *CPNZ Conference Minutes*, January 1932 (RC 495/63/35); *Red Worker*, May 1933.

65. 'Report on Organisation', January 1932 (RC 495/63/35); 'Report', December 1933 (RC 495/63/46).

66. *Minutes of the Dunedin Local Party Committee (LPC)*, 21 October 1934 (CPNZ Otago Branch Papers (OBP), Hocken Library, Dunedin, MS 675/1).

67. 'Report on Party Organisation', January 1932 (RC 495/63/35).

68. *CPNZ Conference Minutes*, January 1932 (RC 495/63/35).

69. On refusal to sell newspapers see *Minutes of the Aggregate Meeting of Dunedin CPNZ*, 23 March and 7 June 1934 (OBP, MS 675/1); on dues paying, inactivity and missing members see 'Report on Party Organisation', January 1932 (RC 495/63/35).

70. *Minutes of the Dunedin LPC*, 21 October 1934 (OBP, MS 675/1).

71. 'Special Letter to New Zealand Comrades', *New Zealand Labour Monthly*, March 1934.

72. 'What is the Difference Between Fournier and the Communist Party', Central Executive Statement, undated [1931] (Jack Locke Papers, University of Canterbury Library).

73. J. B. Power, 'Open Letter to CP Members and Sympathisers' undated [1932] (BRP, 94-106-01/1).

74. *Minutes of the Canterbury Trades and Labour Council*, 28 August 1920; *Minutes of Canterbury General Labourers' Union*, 19 June 1928 (University of Canterbury Library; UCL).

75. *Minutes of Wellington Labour Social Club*, 3 October 1923 (John Roberts Papers, Victoria University of Wellington).

76. B. Gustafson, *Labour's Path to Political Independence* (Auckland 1986), p. 167.

77. Political Secretariat ECCI to CPNZ, 4 March 1930 (RC 495/20/430); Letter to New Zealand, 10 March 1933, and ECCI Political Commission to CPNZ, 16 November 1934 RC 495/20/430); 'Report on Party Organisation', January 1932 (RC 495/63/35); 'Organisational Resolution', Communist Party Conference, 1933, *New Zealand Labour Monthly*, May 1934, pp. 6–11.

78. Secretary, RILU to Central Committee, CPNZ, 25 October 1929, (RC 534/6/108).

79. *Minutes of New Zealand Section CPA Conference*, December 1925 (BRP, 94-106-01/1); 'Report, New Zealand Section CPA, Conference', December 1926 (GG, 86-43-3/02). From 1924 to 1926, the CPNZ operated as a section of the Communist Party of Australia.

80. Secretary RILU to Central Committee, 25 October 1929 (RC 534/6/108).

81. *Workers Vanguard*, April 1929; *Red Worker*, July 1929; *The Trade Union Movement in New Zealand*, undated [1929] (RC 495/63/10).

82. B. Roth, *Trade Unions in New Zealand: Past and Present* (Wellington 1973), p. 159.

83. *Workers Vanguard*, June 1929; *CE Mins*, 25 June 1929 (RC 495/63/17).

84. C. Bollinger, *Against the Wind* (Wellington, 1968), pp. 179–80.

85. *Red Worker*, August, September and October 1931.

86. *Communist Review*, August 1934, pp. 12 and October 1934, pp. 7–9. Interview with Johnny Mitchell, 17 May 1988.

87. *Minutes of the Alliance of Labour Annual Meeting*, February 1928 (BRP, 94-106-01/1).

88. 'Andrews', 'Report on New Zealand', 4 June 1935 (RC 495/63/75); Report, January 1932 (RC 495/63/35).

89. Interviews with Jack Locke, 30 July 1988; Johnny Mitchell, 17 May 1988; Selwyn Devereux, 13 April 1988.

90. *CPNZ Conference Minutes*, December 1932 (RC 495/63/35).

91. 'Report', January 1932 (RC 495/63/35).

92. J. R. Powell, 'The History of a Working Class Party' (MA Thesis, Victoria University College, 1949), p. 35.

93. *Minutes of the Wellington Branch, CPNZ*, 1 April 1922 (GG, 86-43-3/01); *Evening Post*, 18 and 21 May and 12 June 1926.

94. R. T. Robertson, 'Isolation, Ideology and Impotence', op., cit.

95. NUWM, 'Policy and Constitution 1933' (BRP, 94-106-01/2).

96. R. T. Robertson, 'Isolation, Ideology and Impotence' and P Harris, 'The New Zealand Unemployed Workers Movement', op., cit.

97. I have conducted more 25 interviews with CPNZ activists from the 1930s.

98. C. Locke, 'Demanding Jobs With Justice: The Organisation of Maori and Pakeha Unemployed in Aotearoa/New Zealand During the 1930s and 1980s' (PhD Thesis, University of Aucklnad, 2000).

99. Interview with Johnny Mitchell, 17 May 1988. Mitchell himself was at a loss to explain this fact.

100. *CPNZ Conference Minutes*, January 1932 (RC 495/63/35).

101. For a classic example, see D. Verran, 'Alexander Drennan', *Dictionary of New Zealand Biography*, Vol. V (Auckland, 2000), pp. 153–54.

102. O. B. Y. Gregory, 'Notes on Hunger March' (BRP, 94-106-01/2).

103. S. Scott, *Rebel in A Wrong Cause*, pp. 62–63.

104. *New Zealand Herald*, 17 October 1931; *Red Worker*, November 1931.

105. *Red Worker*, August 1932.

106. 'Resolution on July Unemployed Struggles', CPNZ CE, 21 July 1933 (RC 495/63/48).

107. *Red Worker*, April 1932.

108. 'Resolution on Unemployment', 1933 (RC 495/63/50).

109. Ibid.

110. 'Resolution on July Unemployed Struggles', 21 July 1933 (RC 495/63/48).

111. Resolution on Unemployment, 1933 (RC 495/63/50).

112. Ibid.

113. *CPNZ Conference Minutes*, January 1932 (RC 495/63/35); 'Report of CPNZ Conference', December 1932 (RC 495/63/36).

114. 'Report of CPNZ Conference', January 1932 (RC 495/63/35).

115. Ibid.

116. 'Newlands' to Communist International, 19 June 1933 (RC 495/63/48).

117. Interview with Doug Edwards, 15 April 1988.

118. E. Locke, *Student at the Gates* (Christchurch 1981), pp. 158–68.

119. 'Report of CPNZ Conference', January 1932 (RC 495/63/35).

120. 'Newlands' to Communist International, 19 June 1933 (RC 495/63/48).

121. Comintern to CPNZ, 10 March 1933 (RC 495/63/430).

122. 'F. Stevens' [Fred Freeman] to unnamed [at Comintern], 8 August 1933 (RC 495/63/48).

123. 'CPNZ Central Executive to Communist International', 9 and 16 September 1932 (RC 495/63/37).

124. Ibid.

125. 'Newlands' to Comintern, 19 June 1933 (RC 495/63/48); 'F. Stevens' to unnamed [at Comintern], 8 August 1933 (RC 495/63/48).

126. Interview with Doug Galbraith, 24 March, 1988.

127. Interviews with Elsie Locke, July 1988 and Doug Galbraith, 24 March 1988.

128. *Minutes of Dunedin LPC*, 21 October 1934 (OBP MS 675/1).

129. *Minutes of CPNZ Central Committee* (*CC Mins*), 12 August 1934 (RC 495/63/63); *Minutes of Dunedin LPC*, 21 October 1934 (OBP MS 675/1); *Minutes of the Gisborne Branch CPNZ*, 4 August 1938 (McAra Papers, University of Auckland, A9, Box 17).

130. *CE Mins*, 8 November and 6 December 1934, and 26 January 1935 (RC 495/63/63).

131. Interview with Doug Edwards, 15 April 1988.

132. Interview with Doug Galbraith, 24 March 1988.

133. Interview with Doug Galbraith, 24 March 1988. Also *CC Mins*, 12 November 1935 and 15 February 1936 (RC 495/63/73 and 495/14/317).

134. J. Degras (Ed.), *The Communist International 1919–43: Documents Vol. III*, (London, 1960), pp. 285–306.

135. 'Andrews', 'Report to Anglo-American Secretariat Bureau', 17 October 1934 (RC 495/72/261).

136. *Minutes of the NZLP National Executive*, 11 December 1933 (NZLPR); *Minutes of CPNZ National Executive*, 7 January 1934 (RC 495/63/63).

137. Letter to New Zealand, 10 March 1933 (RC 495/20/430).

138. *Minutes of the Central Committee Plenum*, 30 June–1 July 1934 (RC 495/63/62).

139. Letter to New Zealand, 10 March 1933 (RC 495/20/430).

140. 'Newlands' to unnamed [at Comintern], 19 June 1933 (RC495/63/48).

141. *Minutes of the Central Committee Plenum*, 30 June–1 July 1934 (RC 495/63/62); *Workers Weekly*, 12 January 1935.

142. *CC Mins*, 27 July 1935 (RC 495/63/67); *Minutes of the NZLP National Executive*, 9 August 1935 (NZLPR); *Workers Weekly*, 10 and 24 August 1935.

143. *Workers Weekly*, 20 April 1935.

144. For a discussion from a major participant, see S. Scott, *Rebel in a Wrong Cause*, pp. 76–80.

145. *Minutes of the NZLP National Executive*, 10 October 1934 (NZLPR).

146. *CC Mins*, 2 March 1935 (RC 495/63/67).

147. *CC Mins*, 18 February 1935 (RC 495/63/63).

148. Leo Sim, 'Speech to Seventh Congress Communist International', 11 August 1935 (RC 494/1/330).

149. *Workers Weekly*, 10 August and 16 November 1935.

150. *Workers Weekly*, 7 December 1935.

151. Interview with Elsie Locke, 30 July 1988; J. Billett to unnamed, 17 August 1936 (RC 495/14/318).

152. *CC Mins*, 26 October 1935 (RC 495/63/73).

153. J. Billett to unnamed, 17 August 1936 (RC 495/14/318).

154. Ibid; 'Report of CPNZ Conference', December 1935 (BRP, 94-106-01/2).

155. Sim to unnamed Friends (Moscow), 23 February 1935 (RC 495/14/318).

156. Freeman to unnamed (Moscow), 3 April 1936 (495/14/318).

157. *CE Mins*, 8 February 1936 (RC 495/14/317).

158. Gordon Watson, 'Report to A. A. Section, Communist International', 8 July 1937 (RC 494/1/330); *CC Mins*, 8 February 1936 (RC 495/63/317).

159. *CC Mins*, 8 February 1936 (RC 495/63/317).

160. J. Billett to unnamed, 17 August 1936 (RC 495/14/318); Interview with Elsie Locke, 30 July 1988.

161. *CC Mins*, 10 April 1936 (RC 495/63/317); J. Billett to unnamed, 17 August 1936 (RC 495/14/318).

162. *CC Mins*, 15 March and 18 April 1936 (RC 495/14/321); *Minutes of CPNZ Central Committee Plenum*, July 1936 (BRP, 94-106-01/3); Secretary Central Committee CPNZ to Secretary, Gisborne Branch CPNZ, 4 August 1936 (McAra Papers, University of Auckland, A9, Box 17, Folder 2).

163. *CPNZ Conference Minutes*, 1936 (BRP, 94-106-01/3); *CC Mins*, 21 December 1937 (RC 495/14/321).

164. K. McDermott and J. Agnew, *The Comintern*, p. 118.

The Chinese Communist Party During the Third Period, 1927–34

Patricia Stranahan

At 4:00 AM on 12 April 1927, the forces of Chiang Kai-shek's Guomindang army, assisted by foreign authorities and anti-union elements, attacked the communist party-led revolutionaries who had taken control of Shanghai – China's largest city – and crushed them. The bloodbath that followed, not only in Shanghai but elsewhere in China, devastated the Chinese Communist Party (CCP) and ended its alliance with the Guomindang (Nationalist Party). Reduced in numbers, abandoned by those believed to be its allies, blamed by Stalin for the failure of his China policy, and facing an uncertain future, the decimated party organisation broke into local and regional units.

The years between 1927 and 1934 were dark ones for the CCP. What began as an urban revolution spread to China's countryside as many party members, including the top leadership, fled increasingly dangerous cities – where Guomindang and foreign powers had joined forces to suppress communists – to the relative safety of rural areas. The CCP hierarchy found itself in remote locations, cut off from each other and unsure of how to implement conflicting – and frequently misunderstood – directives from Moscow. With no cohesive leadership and no concrete plan, the revolution became many revolutions, all united in the goal of seizing power but divided on exactly how to do it. It would be several years before CCP leaders realised the potential value of alliances with other discontents, be they peasants in the countryside or patriotic elites in the cities, and modified their radical policies to accommodate local environments. Only then did the revolutions in China gain a foothold that led to eventual victory.

These were also years of international crisis. Following skirmishes with Chinese troops outside of Mukden on the night of 18 September 1931, Japanese forces invaded the three provinces making up Manchuria. Patriotic people throughout China called for the Chiang Kai-shek government to retaliate but nothing happened. In Shanghai, a city with nearly 30,000 Japanese residents, the situation became so tense that on 28 January 1932 fighting broke out between Japanese marines and Guomindang soldiers in the residential area of Zhabei. For the next thirty-three days, the two sides fought a brutal war – which included the first aerial bombings of civilians – in the midst of China's most populated city. On 5 March, Chinese troops withdrew but it was not until May that a peace agreement was concluded. It humiliated the Chinese by creating a neutral zone around the city.

In August 1932, the government of Japan recognised Manchuria as the independent country 'Manchukuo' and expressed hope that China would join Japan and its ally to advance peace and prosperity in the region. From the staging ground of the former Manchuria, the Japanese army moved south until it reached the Bai River near Tianjin, one of China's largest cities. The Guomindang government entered into negotiations with the Japanese and, in May 1933, the Tanggu Truce created a demilitarised zone in the northeast Hebei province not far from the old capital of Beijing. Government passivism in the face of Japanese aggression gave rise to angry outbursts among patriotic citizens throughout China and created fertile ground for CCP organising.

The Li Lisan Years

In the late 1920s and early 1930s, having instituted the closest thing China had seen to a national government in years, Chiang Kai-shek and the Guomindang were at the height of power. Nevertheless, while Chiang Kai-shek had succeeded in mobilising nationalism, he had never fulfilled its demands. In urban areas, he alienated the bourgeoisie with his monetary extortions and economic policies, while in rural areas the Guomindang's administrative structure left too many problems unsolved and did little to alleviate the dire poverty of the peasants. It would have been advantageous for the CCP to build upon the failures of the Guomindang government by moderating its policies and becoming more attractive to a broader range of people, but the party never took advantage of the opportunity. Instead, it became more radical and, therefore, less appealing during these years.

Through 1927, CCP attempts to implement Stalin's ever-changing policies for China had been futile. Its string of failures, which included the Autumn Harvest Uprising, the Nanchang Uprising, and the Guangzhou Insurrection, had produced contending groups within the party, all confident they had the answer to China's problems and all ready to take control. Pressure increased both inside and outside of the party with factionalism generating as great a threat to the CCP's survival as did the Guomindang. Adhering to the Comintern's view that revolution was just around the corner, CCP leaders put forth nebulous calls for mass organising in urban and rural areas while awaiting revolutionary opportunities. It proved to be a foolish exercise that only exposed cadres to undue danger and created conflict within the party organisation itself.

To understand the factionalism that came to divide the party, it is important to look at CCP policies both before and after the party's sixth congress. Held during the summer of 1928 in a village outside Moscow, the congress was the Comintern's show. General secretary Qu Qiubai's extreme leftist position of permanent revolution lost out to supporters of Stalin's new 'moderate' position as interpreted by his China expert, Pavel Mif. According to the revised view, the party was to recapture working class support in urban areas so the proletariat could lead the peasantry in revolutionary insurrection.[1] The primary tasks of the CCP were to abolish the system of private landowning and to unify China by driving out the imperialists. It was considered the opportune time to establish soviets, confiscate foreign enterprises, achieve better working conditions for urban workers, give land to peasants and soldiers, and unite with the world proletariat.[2]

Implementing these policies would be difficult because it was also decided at the congress that no revolutionary tide presently existed in China even though the prospect was there. Nevertheless, the *potential* for revolution required the party to undertake intense organisational work with the masses. To accommodate the new situation and the changes in policy resulting from the congress, the leadership of the CCP was realigned. Xiang Zhongfa, a forty year-old labourer from Hubei, whose chief asset was that he had a proletarian class background, was named general secretary, but real power lay in the hands of Li Lisan, a stubborn and arrogant labour leader from Hunan. Given Li's background, it is not surprising that at a time when the emphasis had switched to rural areas, he remained convinced that the revolution must be led by the proletariat.

What were urban party branches supposed to do in light of the new emphasis on the land revolution? The Jiangsu provincial committee, which led the Shanghai party and was the home base of most of the Central Committee (CC), decreed that under the new line the party was to organise the masses and use their strength to lead what it termed 'daily struggle'. That meant expanding work among labour associations in order to gain the support of the proletariat. It was an activity that had failed all too often in the past and one for which cadres were no better prepared to implement this time around.[3]

The CCP CC's second plenum, held in June 1929, announced that the party had made good strides forward in penetrating the proletariat, establishing party branches in factories and revitalising the link between the party and mass organisations.[4] There is no statistical or anecdotal evidence that any of these advances actually occurred. The CC, out of touch with the realities of lower-level work and determined to follow Moscow, made demands on cadres that they could not meet given unsafe conditions and an alienated working class in China's cities. Proletarian disaffection stemmed from several sources. One source was the CCP's focus on political issues not concrete economic ones. The concept of relying upon the working class to implement a policy that failed to tangibly better their lives was foolish. Another source of disaffection was the party's insistence on organising workers to participate in public and highly dangerous strikes and demonstrations, many of which took place on well-known commemorative days. In the repressive environment of China's cities, particularly Shanghai where the bulk of the proletariat lived, public displays of dissent were suicidal. In that city, the party organisation paid a heavy price for such actions. Between May 1930 and December 1931, membership in the Shanghai party dropped from more than 2,000 to around 700. Much of that decline can be attributed to arrests and executions.[5]

The party did not fare much better in the countryside, where the CCP had also been active. The young Hunan revolutionary Mao Zedong, an early advocate of the revolutionary potential of the peasantry, had, during 1927, led several unsuccessful uprisings in his home province. Blamed by the CC for these aborted attempts and labelled a 'rightist', Mao was dismissed from the CC and the Hunan provincial committee. Gathering the ragged remnants of the forces that had fought with him in the failed Autumn Harvest Uprising, Mao fled to the Jinggang Mountains on the border between Jiangxi and Hunan provinces in late 1927.

Well before the party's sixth congress of June 1928 had bestowed its blessing, Mao had advocated land redistribution and the formation of soviets. Always a pragmatist, he argued that revolution in China's rural areas would only succeed if peasants practiced mass democracy and controlled their own land in soviets. Because he faced stiff resistance among rich peasants and local lineage organisations, Mao never achieved his dream while in the Jinggang Mountains. Consequently, instead of building a soviet, he created a military base by allying with local bandits – members of the Triad secret societies. He was joined in his work by the brilliant military strategist, Zhu De, and together they created the Red Army. Constantly under attack by the Guomindang, Mao abandoned the Jinggang Mountains in late 1928 and moved the Red Army eastward where he finally settled in the mountainous area between Jiangxi and Fujian provinces and established the Jiangxi Soviet. He remained there until 1934.[6]

Although certainly the most famous, Mao Zedong and Zhu De were not the only revolutionaries to establish CCP-controlled bases in the countryside. There were at least a dozen other areas, including ones on the borders of Jiangxi-Fujian-Zhejiang, Hunan-Hubei-Jiangxi, Henan-Anhui-Hubei, Hunan-Hubei, and Shaanxi-Gansu. Mountainous border areas, where the juncture of different administrative zones often meant confusion about who had governmental authority, had long been a popular safe haven for bandits. In the mind of the Guomindang and the many warlords who controlled vast sections of the country, the CCP were bandits.[7] Nevertheless, not all areas of rural China could sustain a soviet. It was in regions that had primitive economic, commercial and communications systems and that had been exposed only minimally to western influence that the party most successfully transformed peasant fiscal discontent into class warfare.[8]

Despite the primacy of the land revolution in Comintern directives, and despite small but active rural revolutions, the Shanghai-based CCP leadership continued to emphasise the urban revolution. Under Li Lisan, the party's organisation bureau spent more than two-thirds of its time mobilising workers in Shanghai and the remaining one-third on all the rest of China.[9] Li believed that what would begin as a revolutionary upsurge in China's rural regions would rapidly become a proletarian-led urban revolution, hence the need to concentrate on urban areas. For the first time since late 1927, there was talk of using the Red Army to take China's largest cities. Li believed so strongly in forthcoming events and their implication for worldwide revolution that he demanded the USSR send troops through Manchuria and Mongolia to foment the Chinese revolution.

Li's theories on the forthcoming revolution were developed during a period when the Comintern was revising its worldview. It was a time of great change: the onset of the world depression and unrest in capitalist countries, renewed fighting between Chiang Kai-shek and various warlords, the Soviet intervention in Manchuria to protect its interests in the Chinese Eastern Railway, and the challenges to Stalin's power by Trotsky and Bukharin. Because Bukharin had been instrumental in creating the CCP's new politburo, Stalin's attacks on him as a rightist could not help but have an impact on the party in China. In February 1929, the Executive Committee of the Communist International (ECCI) wrote to the CCP CC informing it that while signs of a revolutionary high tide were now visible in China, there was currently a dangerous rightist trend in the party. In October, it sent a second letter that called for greater radicalism. Heeding Moscow, the CC issued resolutions on 20 December and 11 January condemning rightism and calling for increased revolutionary activities in both urban and rural areas. These statements were the beginning of what would later be known as the 'Li Lisan line' and were based, in part, upon a revolutionary tide that did not exist. A directive dated 26 February 1930 clarified the new focus when it ordered the party 'to concentrate its forces and attack'. CCP leaders decided to use the revolutionary movement in rural areas to recapture its positions in the cities.[10]

In a desperate attempt to follow the ECCI directives, Li planned simultaneous armed assaults on Changsha, Wuhan and Nanchang. Peng Dehuai's Third Army Corps took Changsha on 27 July 1930, but was able to hold it for only a week before it was forced to retreat. Similarly, Mao and Zhu De's attack on Nanchang failed but, instead of following orders and going to the aid of Peng, they retreated to Jiangxi where they rebuilt their diminished forces. The expected attack on Wuhan never occurred and, for all intents and purposes, Li Lisan was discredited.

The Li Lisan line was also a disaster for Shanghai. A faction of the city's party organisation led by He Mengxiong opposed Li's unrealistic policies, arguing that they were not feasible in a city as dangerous as Shanghai. Li

Lisan and his followers ignored He's faction, moving instead to eradicate anyone who stood in their way and to further 'Bolshevise' the party. Their tactics created a strong response from those who had a more realistic picture of the situation than did they did.

The Rise of the Internationalists

Li Lisan's inability to incite the expected revolution convinced the Comintern that it was, once again, time to revise its China policy. Japanese aggression in northeast Asia was higher on the Comintern's list of priorities than was revolution in China, so when Li Lisan demand that Soviet troops be sent to aid the revolution it became clear to many in Moscow just who the scapegoat would be. The continued defeats and failed uprisings of the summer of 1930 proved to be too much for the Comintern, and by late summer it was attacking the Li Lisan line. At an August politburo meeting and later at the third plenum, CCP leaders accused Li of tactical errors and halted his policies temporarily. Li Lisan may have been down but he was definitely not out; he retained enough strength to mount a powerful counterattack, particularly against his nemesis Shanghai labour leader He Mengxiong.

He Mengxiong was not without allies. Joining him in opposing Li Lisan were the Internationalists (also known as the 28 Bolsheviks), a group of young Stalin supporters who had studied at Sun Yat-sen University in Moscow, some of whom had recently arrived in Shanghai under the supervision of the Comintern's delegate to China, Pavel Mif. Charged with correcting Li's errors, Mif quickly immersed his faction in the struggle against Li. The match between the Shanghai dissidents led by He and the Internationalists led by Wang Ming was, in many ways, a good partnership. He Mengxiong had experience in practical matters, while Wang Ming was well versed in theory.[11]

Mao Zedong's dissatisfaction with Li Lisan did not carry the weight within the party hierarchy that the Shanghai-based coalition of He Mengxiong and Wang Ming did. Mao agreed with Li Lisan on many principles and had co-operated with him militarily, but he disagreed with him on emphasis. One source of disagreement was Li's insistence on proletarian leadership. The success of the Red Army in the countryside and the violent suppression of the CCP in the cities had created an imbalance in party membership, with peasants outnumbering workers seven to one. Li Lisan feared that this turn of events meant the CCP was no longer following correct communist ideology, one that demanded proletarian leadership. Mao, always a realist, argued that correct proletarian leadership was a matter of education, not location, and could be achieved even if the party was cut off for long periods of time from the origin of its ideology. Two other sources of friction were Mao's gradualist approach to territorial expansion and his moderate land policies. Both conflicted with Li's haste to take advantage of the 'new' revolutionary upsurge. The two men came into real conflict when Li directed all Red Army troops to centralise under one leadership organisation in order to mount a concentrated attack on large cities. Mao supported the first decision but opposed the plan to attack. Being good party members, Mao and Zhu De did attack Nanchang but they retreated within twenty-four hours, an action for which Mao was harshly criticised by the CCP leadership. Nevertheless, despite his failure in the eyes of his fellow party members, Mao continued his rise through the ranks of the military command structure. When he assumed control of the First Front Army in mid-1930, Mao Zedong ended his three-year exile from the party's top ranks.[12]

At the third plenum in September 1930, Li Lisan and former general secretary Qu Qiubai, the dominating forces in the CCP's CC, accused He Mengxiong and Wang Ming of being rightists and anti-party. Realising that ridding the CCP of Li Lisan was going to be more difficult than it had previously thought, the Comintern called Li back to Moscow to prepare for a new plenum where it planned to orchestrate a reorganisation of the CCP and the removal of Li. Meanwhile, the Wang Ming–Mif alliance with He Mengxiong was crumbling when Mif moved to ensure that his protégés had positions of power within the party hierarchy. In October, Wang Ming attacked He in a letter to the CC, and that same month Mif convinced the central committee to dilute the power of the He faction by reorganising the Jiangsu provincial committee (a He stronghold) into a broad-based committee for the Lower Yangzi provinces.

By the middle of November, divisions in the CCP were clearly apparent. Wang Ming and the Internationalists were especially vocal in demanding a thorough reform of the CC and of the 'confused thinking' that pervaded the party. A month later, without prior authorisation from the CC, Mif arranged for a convoluted transfer of power in which Wang Ming – Moscow's choice but a man without real support within the CCP – became acting secretary of the Lower Yangzi committee. It was Mif's plan that once in power Wang Ming would become the leading representative of the 'correct line'. Mif's actions infuriated He Mengxing who had fully expected to take control of the committee. The Comintern representative's duplicity was made worse because at the same time that he was masterminding the CC's attempt to win over the Internationalists in the struggle against He Mengxiong and his supporters, he was also masterminding the takeover of the CC by the Internationalists.

At the Pavel Mif-dominated fourth plenum of January 1931, Li Lisan's mistakes were re-evaluated not as tactical errors as previously claimed but as ideological ones, a much more serious charge. Li was removed from office and Wang Ming was elected to the CC and the politburo. Once Wang Ming was assured of these top-level positions, the Lower Yangzi committee was dissolved and instantly reorganised as the Jiangsu provincial committee. Wang was named secretary of the 'new' provincial committee, a position of power from which he could attack his enemies. With great speed, Mif had achieved his takeover of the CCP leadership with Wang Ming and other members of the Internationalists assuming leadership positions. Every effort was made to thwart He Mengxiong and the other dissidents who were told of the plenum only a few hours before it began and who found, upon their arrival, that there were no seats left for them. Days later, the dissidents were expelled from the party under the pretext that those who opposed the Comintern's representative opposed the party, and that those who opposed the party should be expelled. Within twenty-four hours, He Mengxiong and other 'dissidents' had been arrested by Guomindang agents, who were tipped off by a turncoat, jailed and, in early February, He was executed. In a brilliant set of moves, Mif had established his protégés as the major power brokers within the CCP.[13]

Although Xiang Zhongfa remained general secretary, real power lay in the hands of Wang Ming. After the arrest and execution of Xiang in 1931, the power of the Internationalists was further consolidated when one of its members, Qin Bangxian, became provisional party secretary. Under the new leadership, the strategy of armed insurrections took second place to an emphasis on the expansion of soviet bases and the Red Army. The bases were given great autonomy in managing their own affairs.

During the plenum, Pavel Mif, fearing the growing danger in urban areas and realising the increased importance of the countryside, directed veteran cadres, among them Zhou Enlai, to go to rural soviets. Zhou was named secretary of the central soviet bureau located in the Jiangxi Soviet but, because he was currently occupied in Shanghai, did not immediately assume the position. Another party leader, Xiang Ying, became acting secretary, but real power in Jiangxi lay in the hands of Mao. In April 1931, a delegation from the CC arrived in the Jiangxi Soviet to attend the first meeting of the bureau. There, party members in the soviet first heard the directives of the fourth plenum. Following the meeting, three of the delegates from Shanghai remained behind in Ruijin, the capital of the soviet, and began to consolidate CC power. Assuming that Xiang Ying was their principal opponent, they replaced him with Mao only to realise quickly that it was Mao, not Xiang, who challenged them.

In November, the first all-China soviet congress convened in Ruijin. The congress founded the Chinese Soviet Republic as a national government and created the necessary military and government structures. It also adopted a constitution that designated the Soviet Republic a democratic dictatorship of peasants and proletariat. Although there was no illusion that a proletariat, outside of artisans and handicraftsmen, existed in such a remote area, the constitution explicitly endorsed proletarian leadership of the masses and allocated extra representation for them in the soviet. A new, more moderate, land law was also passed. It called for confiscation of land belonging to landlords, militarists, gentry and village bosses, but made no mention of collectivisation.

The situation in Shanghai was becoming far too dangerous and the CCP leadership was transferring in increased numbers to the safe haven of the Jiangxi Soviet. It was imperative for the new arrivals to cement their leadership and, for many of the new arrivals from Shanghai, Mao's arrogant attitude and independent ways presented too great a threat. At the Gannan conference in November, Mao was harshly criticized for his handling of the Futian Incident and was stripped of his dominant positions in the army and party, retaining only the chairmanship of the soviet government. When Zhou Enlai arrived in December to assume the position of bureau secretary, he recognised Mao's value to the party in Jiangxi and, though he did not restore Mao to his previous eminence, he refrained from destroying him completely.[14] Mao fell in and out of favour for the next several years and was not fully rehabilitated until the fifth plenum in January 1934, when he was again elected to the politburo.

The Search for Allies

In China's urban areas, times were bleak. In addition to internal conflict, party operatives were faced with the combined wrath of the Guomindang and foreign authorities. In Shanghai, where many members of the CC remained, there was the additional threat of the city's powerful gangster element. The ranks of the city's party organisation diminished rapidly with killings, arrests and lost contacts. Many party members simply vanished because they were too afraid or too tired to continue the fight. In December 1931, for example, there were only an estimated 700 CCP members left in the city as compared to 1,799 in December 1927.[15]

It is easy in the safety of historical hindsight to say that the great mistake that the city's party organisation made was to follow directives and concentrate its attention on the working class. But it is important to remember that these were dedicated communist revolutionaries who, while they might not agree with the road chosen by party leaders, were bound through the principles of Leninist discipline to uphold CCP policy. The party's failure to attract members of the working class can be attributed not only to the party's esoteric message but also to the city's repressive and uncertain atmosphere. Workers were well aware that the danger inherent in participating in party-sponsored strikes, demonstrations and assemblies far outweighed the gains produced by them.

The proletariat was not the only potential ally for party urban organising; others existed as well. One promising partner were students who had played pivotal roles during previous social and political upheavals such as the May Fourth Movement. Yet, urban party organisations had little success in mobilising students. Like labour, students were highly fragmented and under close governmental scrutiny. One of the Guomindang's top priorities was to eliminate all vestiges of communist influence in schools and to prevent students from participating in political activities. Any student or teacher suspected of being a communist was dismissed or executed. Nevertheless, CCP failure with this group stemmed not from government repression or lack of interest among students (although both did exist) but, rather, from an inability on the part of party activists to see the value of student allies.[16] The party recognised that it was losing support among intellectuals and needed to reform its work methods in order to recruit more students to the cause, but given the highly volatile and dangerous situation in Shanghai in the late 1920s and early 1930s most party activists were understandably nervous about political work among non-party people.

This was a problem experienced with all potential supporters in China's cities at this time. Years of terror and suppression had left only the most hardcore and committed cadres. They had seen too many close comrades arrested or killed to tolerate the inclusion in their ranks of any but the most dedicated converts. Rather than proselytising new party members, what urban operatives chose to do was to infiltrate and covertly control sympathetic organisations. One popular 'target' were left-leaning literary organisations. The free-wheeling world of Shanghai was a magnet for writers who sought an environment where they would write openly about China's ills. Literary societies, espousing various theories and trends, sprang up as writers searched for a framework in which to relay their message. Many of these young intellectuals were leftists, and while some eventually joined the communist party, others were just 'fellow travellers'. In January 1930, the party capitalised on the common anti-Guomindang and anti-imperialist sentiments of the writers by forming the Shanghai Research Association of Literature and Art (later known as the League of Left-Wing Writers) to discuss how to organise sympathetic writers.[17]

The Chinese Association to Relieve Distress (later known as the Revolutionary Mutual Aid Society) was another important group infiltrated by the CCP. Although not part of the party organisation, the association's core members were party and Youth League operatives who masqueraded as social and economic elites in order to facilitate fund raising among the upper classes. Headquartered in Shanghai, the association had branches all over China and was linked internationally with the Comintern-sponsored Red Aid Society.[18]

The CCP fared much better in attracting supporters in China's countryside. The combination of constant warfare, economic depression, high tenancy rates and government abuse had created an alienated and poverty-stricken population who were ready targets for party organising. Although during the Jiangxi years, the party's policies were less radical than previously – and so more appealing to the peasantry – they had a long way to go before they achieved the workable mix of moderation and practicality that was so successful during the Yanan years (1935–47). Nevertheless, in the Jiangxi and other soviets, party leaders began to develop a systematic way to organise the masses and to cultivate converts from among them. Called the 'mass line', it defined a process through which cadres fostered relationships with different social groups in an attempt to build the infrastructure of organisation necessary to implement effective social, political and economic change. The idea was to see what issues, particularly those regarding land redistribution, education and production, could mobilise the peasants and then to manage those issues to suit party purposes.

The technique for mobilisation varied with location but most commonly a cadre team went into an area to determine the likelihood of successful organising. After listening to people's grievances and assessing the viability of the area against Guomindang and warlord attack, cadres would begin organising among the most progressive elements of society. In some of the rural areas controlled by the CCP, as many as 80 per cent of the eligible young people joined communist-sponsored organisations. Eventually, cadres organised most of the population into one or another mass organisation such as the red guard (ages 16–40), youth vanguards (ages 15–21), children corps, women's corps, poor peasant associations and labour unions. An estimated 60 per cent of the children in the Jiangxi Soviet went to party-sponsored schools, while adults attended reading groups, discussions groups, sewing circles and other group activities all designed to educate the masses and improve their lives while, at the same time, providing cadres with the opportunity to promulgate the party's message.

Financially burdened peasants found economic relief under new laws. It was estimated that in Jiangxi, landlords and rich peasants, who made up ten per cent of the population, controlled 70 per cent of the land, while middle peasants controlled fifteen per cent and poor peasants ten to fifteen per cent. Land rents ran between 50 and 80 per cent of the crop, with interest rates 30 to 40 per cent a year.[19] The new laws cancelled debts and fixed the interest rate ceiling at one per cent per month. They also instituted a system of unified progressive taxes with rates from three per cent to 22 per cent (and later of six to 42 per cent). The radical land policies of the late 1920s that confiscated and redistributed all land, including that owned by middle peasants, were revised and, under the new land law, only the land of landlords and other exploiters of the masses was confiscated. The minimum share of land given to poor peasants varied from three *mou* (about five acres) to five *mou* for adults and two-and-a-half to three *mou* for children. In addition, in each district, land was set aside for the Red Army.[20]

In a region with severe agrarian problems, land redistribution was extremely attractive to the vast majority of people. Cadres organised progressive members of a village or township into land committees who, assisted by poor peasant associations, tenant farmer unions and, of course, the Red Army, carried out the land redistribution. Essential ingredients of the redistribution process were meetings where peasants confronted landlords and rich peasants, and meetings where class status was determined. Both of these were emotional events. The meetings, often referred to as 'trials', where peasants confronted their exploiters allowed them to express pent up anger, a necessary step to accepting the need for change and embracing the revolution. Meetings to establish class status could also be emotional because, in the new society where a low class status was highly desirable, people presented themselves as humbly as possible. It was not unusual for people to retaliate against those they disliked by arguing for a higher class status. The process did not always go smoothly and there were reported cases of harsh and dictatorial actions that unnecessarily alienated middle and rich peasants.

In addition to economic reforms, the party in rural soviets also implemented social reforms. One of the principal areas for change in Jiangxi was marriage. Traditionally, Chinese marriages were arranged with no input from the intended bride and groom. Brides were bought and sold like cattle or goats. Once married, women entered into their husband's families and, for all intents and purposes, had no further contact with their own. Until they produced a son, women had no standing, often simply serving as slaves to members of the husband's family. Even though many women worked as hard in the fields as men (in addition to caring for the home and children), they lacked any kind of legal or economic protection and were denied the right to divorce – a privilege granted only to men.

During the May Fourth Movement, a social reform movement of the previous decade, many Chinese youth, including Mao Zedong, had called for equality of the sexes. Specifically, they called for the reform of the marriage system and demanded that young people have a say in who they married. When they established the Jiangxi Soviet, Mao and like-minded comrades carried these ideas with them. They implemented the Marriage Law of the Jiangxi Soviet that prohibited arranged marriages and the purchase of brides, and encouraged young people to choose their own partners. The law also granted women the right to divorce (unless their husbands were away on active military service), and set the minimum marriage age at twenty for men and eighteen for women.

The implementation of a new marriage law and the demand for equality of the sexes was better in theory than in practice. One of the things that the Jiangxi party leadership failed to consider was what to do with women who divorced. Divorced women became pariahs unwanted by their own families who were often too poor to support them. They were unable to survive economically on their own because they lacked suitable skills and the family economic infrastructure necessary to cope in a difficult environment; and, in some areas, they were unsuitable for remarriage because they were seen as 'used' goods. It was not until the party relocated to northwest China and established the Shaan-Gan-Ning border region in the late 1930s that it modified its position towards marriage and divorce by passing legislation making it more difficult to get a divorce. At the same time, it undertook programs that educated women and got them involved in production so they had the skills to survive on their own.

There was the additional problem of party members themselves. Many mid -and-top level cadres were as unenlightened as the peasants with whom they worked. Wielding enormous power, male cadres often coerced women into marriage or sexual relations against their will. In some areas, widows reported that they were pressured into remarriage within days of their husbands' deaths. Women were recruited as 'teams of laundresses – i.e. prostitutes – to minister to the sexual needs of the army. Even among the top leadership, there was enormous promiscuity as many leaders abandoned traditional wives and children and 'married' revolutionary women. Mao Zedong, for example, lived openly with He Zizhen in the Jiangxi Soviet despite the fact he had a wife and two children elsewhere.[21]

The Dark Days

The years 1931–34 were years of 'white terror' when enemies of the party stopped at nothing to ferret out anyone even suspected of being a communist. No one was immune from suspicion as neighbour betrayed neighbour, friends betrayed friends, and family members betrayed family members. The foreign concessions that had once been a safe haven for radicals of all kinds no longer provided protection, as foreign authorities joined the Guomindang in a communist witch-hunt. Party leaders fled to Mao Zedong's rural stronghold in Jiangxi and, by January 1933, none of the leaders of the national CCP remained in Shanghai. It was not much safer in the countryside because, in October 1930, the Guomindang initiated the first of five anti-communist suppression campaigns.

In Shanghai and other cities, the Guomindang implemented a 'confess one's crimes' policy that promised pardons for party members who provided information on the activities of their comrades. By the mid-1930s, the Guomindang claimed that about a third of the 300 or so CCP members remaining in Shanghai had betrayed the party and were now working for them.[22] Terrified party members found little comfort from their own organisation when they sought guidance and protection in their efforts to survive. Infiltration and betrayal were rampant. Therefore, in order to protect themselves and the organisation, party leaders retaliated with their own 'red terror', an equally brutal suppression of anyone believed to be a traitor to the CCP. Fearing for their lives from all sides, many party members simply broke their connections and disappeared into the urban crowds. Others fled to rural party bases. In Shanghai, the repression was so intense between May 1933 and July 1935, and betrayal inside the party so pervasive, that the provincial committee as well as all the city's district committees ceased to function at one time or another.

There were few options open to CCP members arrested by the Guomindang. Subjected to torture and round-the-clock interrogation, and fearing for their own and their families' safety, many loyal party people 'submitted' and gave information to Nationalist agents in order to save themselves and their loved ones. For others, collaboration occurred not only because of fear but also because of alienation and anger at the CCP hierarchy. Inner-party struggles had left many scars and, among the lower ranks of the Shanghai party, many with little loyalty to the party hierarchy. Not all captured party members collaborated, however; there were those who held out under interrogation and torture and revealed nothing. Nevertheless, decimated both by party policies that overexposed cadres and by the Guomindang and foreign authorities' witch-hunts, the ranks of the urban organisations dwindled and in many cases disappeared.

The CC's evacuation to Jiangxi in 1933 ended direct contact between the Shanghai party organisation and CCP leaders. With the ties to the CC broken, the 300 or so party members left in the city were on their own. The formal party hierarchy had disappeared but pockets of CCP activity remained in peripheral organisations known as Red Mass Leagues. There were two kinds of leagues: proletarian groups concerned with political rights, and intellectual groups concerned with culture. Although members of the Shanghai party infiltrated them, none of the leagues had formal contact with the CCP CC, nor any horizontal relationship between themselves. They were left-leaning public organisations exercising their right to protest through legally sanctioned means such as strikes and demonstrations.[23] Through the leagues, the decimated party organisation became increasingly involved in the burgeoning anti-Japanese movement and strengthened its links to progressives throughout Shanghai. Association with the Red Mass Leagues signalled the transformation of the Shanghai party organisation from the radicalism of the 1920s to the life-saving moderate pragmatism of the late 1930s and 1940s. This was the principal reason why the party organisation survived in this city when it disappeared in most others.

The 'white terror' was not limited to urban areas; the Jiangxi Soviet was undergoing a 'white terror' of its own. Chiang Kai-shek was determined to eradicate the communists, whom he considered more of a threat to his government than the encroaching Japanese. In December 1930, his forces attacked CCP armies in the first of five suppression campaigns. Using a strategy of mobile warfare that lured the enemy deep into the base area where the Red Army was familiar with the terrain and enjoyed the support of the people, Mao Zedong successfully destroyed one-and-a-half Guomindang divisions before Chiang withdrew his troops. In May 1931, Chiang launched a second campaign that also ended in defeat and the destruction of two Guomindang divisions. His third campaign was called off when the Japanese invaded Manchuria. These victories, which resulted in captured weapons, prisoners and territory, did much to raise Mao's status and pre-eminent position within the Red Army.

In the summer of 1932, Chiang's Guomindang army undertook the fourth suppression campaign. Setting up headquarters in Wuhan and amassing half-a-million troops, Chiang planned to first attack the E-Yu-Wan Soviet on the Hubei-Henan-Anhui borders and the Xiang-Exi Soviet on the borders of western Hunan and Hubei before moving onto the Jiangxi Soviet. After bloody fighting, he succeeded in routing the Fourth Front Army of the E-Yu-Wan Soviet which was forced to flee to Sichuan Province. Guomindang forces also attacked the Third Front Army defending the Xiang-Exi Soviet, and after months of fighting forced the communists to evacuate to northeast Guizhou Province. In January 1933, the campaign reached Jiangxi just as the last of the party leadership was arriving from Shanghai. Taking control, Qin Bangxian, the acting secretary of the CCP and an Internationalist, employed a strategy of conventional warfare. After several skirmishes on the perimeters of the soviet, the Red Army retreated to the Lichuan area where it engaged and defeated two Guomindang divisions, forcing Chiang to call off the campaign. The CC proclaimed a victory and declared that it was not necessary for the Red Army to use a strategy of mobile warfare against the Guomindang when conventional military tactics would work.

The fourth suppression campaign might have been a victory for the CC, but it was a significant defeat for Mao Zedong and Zhu De. As described earlier, both men were in conflict with the newly arrived party leadership and their power had been so curtailed that they no longer determined military strategy. In late 1933, Chiang launched the fifth and final campaign, one that differed significantly from the others. At the suggestion of his German advisers, Chiang surrounded the heart of the soviet in a tight blockade and then slowly moved in by building constricting circles of fortifications. Using a strategy of swift thrusts at the enemy, the Red Army suffered one defeat after another and it eventually became apparent that Chiang was going to realise his goal of destroying the CCP army.[24]

Faced with certain defeat, party leaders made the decision in late summer 1934 to evacuate the Jiangxi Soviet. Some 30,000 troops remained behind while the major force of the Red Army – approximately 86,000 men and women – fled to the west. They left with no clear destination in mind, but the undaunted pursuit of the Guomindang limited their possibilities. The Long March, as it became known, ended over a year later in Shaanxi province in northwest China where the party had a small, but still active, base. During that year, marchers walked 6,000 miles over some of the most difficult terrain in China and under constant attack by Guomindang and local forces. With many of the marchers dying and others left along the way, only about 8,000–9,000 soldiers arrived at their destination.

In January 1935, at the Zunyi in Guizhou province, top CCP leaders met to assess what had gone wrong in Jiangxi and what lay ahead. Resolutions issued after the conference supported the view of Mao Zedong that the defeat during the fifth suppression campaign occurred because positional warfare had been used instead of mobile warfare. Not only was he named a full member of the standing committee of the politburo, but he assumed military leadership. It was the beginning of Mao's rise to the unchallenged leadership of the CCP.

Conclusion

At its sixth world congress, the Comintern called for national communist parties to incite the proletariat to lead the rising tide of revolution. For China, it was another in a series of disastrous edicts from Moscow that demanded adherence to policies that were not practical in a country with a small and politically repressed working class, a young and fragmented communist party, and an increasingly powerful national government. Nevertheless, CCP leaders endeavoured to implement the new line, just as they had implemented previous ones. Like the others, this one failed. And like the others, this one had a scapegoat – Li Lisan. As Stalin consolidated his power over the international communist movement in the late 1920s and early 1930s, he blamed others for his lack of success and purged those he claimed had deviated from the correct line. Rather than allowing the CCP to determine its own leadership structure, Stalin sent Pavel Mif to China where he orchestrated a coup that placed his protégés into top positions. Unfortunately, under the Internationalists, the communist movement in China fared no better. By 1933, the urban revolution was dead everywhere except Shanghai, and there it only barely survived. What remained of the revolutionary hierarchy retreated to the countryside where isolated Red Army units were expanding party-controlled territories and promulgating social and economic reforms. Within a year, however, rural base areas were evacuated as the Red Army fled the Guomindang.

Were the dark years of 1927–34 solely the fault of policies fomented by the Comintern? The answer is no. On the one hand, there is no question that communist leaders in Moscow never understood conditions in China and, therefore, initiated policies that were doomed from the outset. Nevertheless, on the other hand, it was also a period when the economic, social and political conditions in China were so unfavourable that even the best led revolutionary movement would have had a difficult time succeeding. Yet, it cannot be concluded that these were years of complete failure. Although the CCP suffered setbacks, it was a critical era in which party leaders stopped blindly accepting Moscow's line and began adapting to local environments and embracing issues that mattered to local populations. It was during these years that the CCP began to develop the pragmatic ideology that would serve it so well in the decade to come.

Notes

1. T. Saich, *The Rise to Power of the Chinese Communist Party* (New York, 1996), p. 282.

2. J. P. Harrison, *The Long March to Power* (New York, 1974), pp. 156–58.

3. 'Jiangsu shengwei guanyu Zhongyang liuci dahui de baogao dagang' [The Jiangsu Provincial Committee's outline report on the CC's sixth congress], in *Jiangsu geming lishi wenjian huiji* [A collection of documents on the revolutionary history of Jiangsu], Vol. 3 (n.p., 1985), p. 177.

4. 'Erzhong quanhui tuanyu Zhongyang zhengzhiju gongzuo baogao de jueyi' [The second plenum's decision regarding the CC politburo's work report] (June 1929), in Zhonggong zhongyang shujichu, *Liuda yilai: danghei mimi wenjian* [Since the sixth congress: inner-party secret documents], Vol. 1 (Beijing, 1980), pp. 74–75.

5. *Zhongguo gongchandang Shanghaishi zuzhishi ziliao (1920.8–1987.10)*[Materials on the CCP's Shanghai organisational history (August 1920–October 1987)], (Shanghai, 1991), p. 85.

6. T. Saich, *The Rise to Power*, pp. 280–82.

7. T. Saich, *The Rise to Power*, p. 282; M. Selden, *The Yenan Way in Revolutionary China* (Cambridge, 1972), p. 31; J. Spence, *The Search for Modern China* (New York, 1990), pp. 370–72.

8. M. Selden, *The Yenan Way*, p. 36.

9. Wang Fang-hsi (Wang Fangxi), *Chinese Revolutionary: Memoirs, 1919–49*, (Oxford, 1980 translated by Gregor Benton), p. 113.

10. T. Saich, *The Rise to Power*, p. 283.

11. P. Stranahan, *Underground: The Shanghai Communist Party and the Politics of Survival, 1927–37* (Lanham, 1998), p. 79.

12. J. P. Harrison, *The Long March*, pp. 170–71; T. Saich, *The Rise to Power*, p. 289.

13. Zhang Yiyu and You Liang, 'He Mengxiong', in *Shanghai Yingliezhuan* [Biographies of Shanghai's heroic martyrs], (Shanghai, 1989), pp. 72–87.

14. T. Saich, *The Rise to Power*, pp. 512–13; T. Kampen, *Mao Zedong, Zhou Enlai and the Evolution of the Chinese Communist Leadership* (Copenhagen, 2000), pp. 52–58.

15. *Zhongguo gongchandang Shanghaishi zuzhishi ziliao*, p. 85.

16. J. Wasserstrom, *Student Protests in Twentieth Century China: The View from Shanghai* (Stanford, 1991), pp. 155–64.

17. P. Stranahan, *Underground*, pp. 158–60.

18. *Zhongguo jinanhui geming hujihui zai Shanghai* [The Chinese Association to Relieve Distress and the Revolutionary Mutual Aid Society in Shanghai] (Shanghai, 1992), pp. 1,7, 24–26, 82–86; *Shanghai Municipal Police Files*, Box 10, Doc. 80.

19. J. P. Harrison, *The Long March*, pp. 211–12.

20. Ibid. pp. 210–11.

21. J. Spence, *The Search for Modern China*, p. 376.

22. J. P. Harrison, *The Long March*, p. 220.

23. Zhang Chengzong, 'KangRi banian de Shanghai dixia douzheng' [The Shanghai underground's eight years in anti-Japanese struggle], in *KangRi fengyun lu* [A record of anti-Japanese unstable conditions], Vol. 1 (Shanghai, 1985), p. 10.

24. T. Saich, *The Rise to Power*, pp. 510–22.

Blowing Up India: The Comintern and India, 1928–35

JOHN CALLAGHAN

The Indian National Congress was little more than a debating society when it was established in 1885. Political India began to change, however, in the early years of the twentieth century. The succession of famines after 1865 did much to support the argument – put forcefully by Romesh Chandra Dutt in his *Economic History of India* (1901) – that the impact of British imperialism had been to weaken the economy of the subcontinent.[1] By 1900, two main tendencies had emerged. The Moderates, led by Gopal Krishna Gokhale, who began to demand a greater degree of representation within the British system of rule, and the so-called Extremists, led by Bal Gangadhar Tilak, who turned away from westernising influences and sought a future in Hindu traditionalism – an emphasis which alarmed a section of Muslim opinion. A terrorist element emerged from the Extremists before 1914, especially after the deeply resented partition of Bengal in 1905. During the Great War, Congress supported the British military effort and was buoyed up by warm talk of political reform on the subcontinent when the conflict ended. However, Tilak, its president in 1916, gave evidence of an increasingly important fissure in the nationalist ranks when he struck a deal with the Muslim League which recognised the latter's demand for separate Muslim constituencies in any future constitutional reform.

It was the disillusioned aftermath of the Great War, when hopes of political reform were dashed and the repressive Rowlatt Bills were passed into law, which allowed Gandhi to turn the national cause into a mass movement involving the rural poor. Mass unrest, strikes and civil disobedience continued throughout 1919–21, and Congress became committed to the achievement of self-government for India in December 1920. By January 1922, as many as 30,000 nationalists had been jailed, but Gandhi demobilised the protest after spontaneous violence erupted the following February at Chauri Chaura. The Muslim League separated from Congress at the moment of anti-climax, and communal disorders increased. C. R. Das formed the Swaraj Party in 1923 in a vain attempt to restore the lost momentum, but the next few years saw little nationalist action. Revival only came in 1927, when the British decided to set up the Simon Commission, without Indian participation, to investigate constitutional reform on the subcontinent. In 1928, Congress still defined its goal as

Dominion status, a decision that led Nehru and Subhas Bose to form the Independence for India League to lobby within Congress for complete independence. Gandhi's conversion to this position was completed by the time he launched the second great campaign of civil disobedience in January 1930. It fizzled out by the end of 1932 after as many as 90,000 nationalists had been imprisoned. While Gandhi participated in talks with the British and then dropped out of overt political activity, the radicals like Nehru moved to the left culminating in the formation of the Congress Socialist Party in 1934.

But what was Congress? For the communists this meant what class interests did Congress represent? Was it the representative of Indian capital or the feudal landowners or both? Did it act as an agent of such class interests or with a degree of relative autonomy? Were the dominant class interests within Congress engaged in forging a partnership with British imperialism or concerned to throw it off altogether? Was capitalism growing, declining or stagnant in India? Was it British capitalism that dominated on the subcontinent, or was an independent Indian capitalism arising? What were the relations between the two? How did the class interests of the dominant economic interests within India relate to the petty-bourgeois, peasant and urban masses? On all these questions there was a diversity of opinion within the Communist International (Comintern), as well as a changing general line that all communists were required to support (until the position was reached in 1928 when the Moscow line tolerated no critics). Gandhi, for example, was variously identified as the key to the political mobilisation of the peasantry, the leader who had made the mass movement possible in 1918; but also the arch-betrayer of the national movement, the obscurantist and social reactionary, the pacifist who yet employed an effective form of coercion on the British Raj. Indian capital was variously seen as rapidly expanding under British patronage; in fierce competition with it; stagnant and retarded; a junior partner; politically removed from/integrated in Congress; fearful of leftism, but an enemy of feudalism. Clearly, the changing tactics of Congress and the unfolding of events influenced communist judgements. So too did the various influences on Comintern policy. But matters were made even more complex by the Comintern's adoption of a general line – favouring tactical orientations towards Congress at one moment only to complete a *volte-face* at another moment – that was negligent of local political opportunities and developments. Thus, for example, the policy of nurturing the Congress left was dropped in 1928–29 at the very moment when its leaders expressed publicly their commitment to socialism and even Marxism.[2]

The communists had to compete against the power of old identities based on religion. Communalism – the belief that a shared religion encompassed shared political and socio-economic interests – was encouraged by certain British policies such as the partition of Bengal, which the viceroy, Lord

Curzon, hoped would 'invest the Mohemmedans ... with a unity they have not enjoyed since the days of the old Musselman viceroys and kings'.[3] It was continued through such devices as the creation of communalist constituencies by the Constitutional Act of 1909 and the Communal Award of 1932, which created reservations for Muslims in the central legislature (which came into force in 1935). But it was obviously not invented by British policy; it succeeded because it reinforced those aspects of Indian society that were fertile ground for communalism. Trotsky expressed the representative communist view when he said in 1924 that 'the old Eastern creeds have lost their power and ... in the imminent historic movement of the revolutionary working masses, these creeds will not be a serious obstacle'.[4] But they were. M. N. Roy observed in 1924 that communal violence in the northern provinces had escalated to 'a veritable civil war'.[5] The formation of Hindu Sabha and the rise of Muslim fears that independence would only mean Hindu supremacy already spoke of deep divisions among those who might line up against British rule. The recession of 1929–41 was another reinforcing factor, and one that is particularly relevant here. It exacerbated the economic insecurity of the middle class, led to status anxieties, intense competition for public sector jobs, and the spread of nepotism and corruption. Arguments for the protection and reservation of jobs on a communalist basis – especially in government (existing or prospective) – flourished in these straitened circumstances. Any concessions to one group aggravated the communalist demands of another. But the neglect of communal opinion could also be damaging, as Congress discovered in 1926 (a year of communal riots all over the country) when it lost Central Legislative Assembly seats in the Punjab and Bengal. The problem was complicated by the fact that communal divisions sometimes coincided with social and class distinctions, as in western Punjab and Sind where the tenants and debtors were mostly Muslim and the propertied tended to be upper caste Hindus. Communists acknowledged some of these facts but tended to dismiss communalist organisations as 'small ultra-reactionary groups dominated by large landlord and banker interests playing for the support of the British government against the popular movement'.[6]

The Comintern was certainly faced with profound problems in India, as well as those of its own making. Whereas in 1892 about a quarter of a million industrial workers existed in India, the number had only risen by 1.1 million as late as 1931 in a population which had grown from 236 to 275 million. Illiteracy rates were as high as 90 per cent. The population was overwhelmingly composed of peasants dispersed in around half a million villages. The country was on a continental scale and regional cultural and socio-economic variations were correspondingly impressive, including numerous languages and, though it was not always recognised, plenty of potential for more than one national movement. Communists struggled to understand the subcontinent and what was happening within it. They exaggerated the strength of the working class, claiming as many as 20 million industrial workers in 1922.[7] In the same year, Roy and his partner Evelyn perceived 'the rapid industrialisation of the country' and 'an industrial proletariat numbering about nine million'.[8] Britain's policy, according to an article attributed to the Communist Party of India in 1925, was 'to transform India into a centre of production'.[9] Rajani Palme Dutt agreed and wrote about the 'lightning development of modern industry in India' in 1926. He identified most of the investment as British.[10] Yet in 1940 – by now corrected, after the Comintern's ruling on this subject in 1928 – Dutt dismissed all talk of India's industrial development as 'modern imperialist propaganda', claiming that the number of industrial workers had actually fallen by over two million between 1911 and 1931, while the population increased by twelve per cent.[11]

The communist analysis of India became truly complex when it drew tactical conclusions from its understanding of the country's political economy. Saklatvala wrote of 'a mutual understanding between the foreign and Indian exploiters who jointly decided to speed up industrialisation'.[12] In 1924, Roy believed that 'Indian capitalism is so much inter-linked with and dependent upon British imperialism, that a serious political conflict leading up to a revolutionary situation has become practically impossible'.[13] The Swaraj Party was accordingly 'ephemeral and lifeless ... garrulous, boasting, self-satisfied, narrow-minded and cowardly'. Dutt also perceived the 'Indian upper classes, the ruling princes, landlords and bourgeoisie exist[ing] under the protection of the British bourgeoisie as subordinate sharers in the spoil'. 'The Indian bourgeoisie is today a counter-revolutionary force', he concluded in 1926. But he acknowledged that Congress 'is and has been the only approach to a mass organisation throughout the Indian people'.[14] What was the relationship of the Indian bourgeoisie to Congress? Roy pronounced Congress to be under the control of 'the upper middle class'. It had, he said, in 1924, become 'a purely middle class affair'.[15] Evelyn Roy announced in 1923 that 'Congress finances largely derive from Indian capitalists'.[16] But Dutt denied that Gandhi's leadership represented the direct control of the big bourgeoisie acting through Congress. The bourgeoisie, he said, remained 'outside the whole campaign of non-co-operation'.[17]

In 1928, when the Comintern insisted that British imperialism retarded Indian capitalism, the way was logically clear to reinstate the Indian bourgeoisie as an active element in the struggle for independence. But it was not to be. While Dutt and his co-thinkers favoured the tactic of the left elements grouping within Congress and the Swaraj Party in 1926 'to carry on a battle of clarification within the existing movement and organisations', the decisions of 1928 led to a communist withdrawal. Roy now saw Gandhi as 'the hero of the petty-bourgeois nationalist masses' – no bad thing since these were moving closer to socialism and the working class in his view and threatening to split from Congress.[18] But Dutt and the Comintern now denounced Gandhi – even on the eve of fresh mass campaigning – as a bourgeois nationalist who would betray the movement that he led.[19] Gandhism was pronounced exhausted in 1931, much as Evelyn Roy had found it nine years earlier.[20] Such talk was dominant after 1928 and continued until the seventh congress of the Comintern in 1935, when Congress once more became 'the National Front uniting all forces in India who struggle for national liberation'.[21] At one level, however, all of this was purely abstract; the Communist Party of India did not exist.

Finding a Communist Party

It was not until 1930 that the Comintern officially recognised the existence of the Communist Party of India (CPI). During the previous decade a number of groups had struggled to lay the basis for its creation, revealing as they did so the many problems attendant on this complex project. Nationalism as a mass movement in India was only as old as the Comintern, and only a handful of nationalist agitators were persuaded of its limitations in 1919. The most prominent of these was M. N. Roy, an exiled Bengali terrorist who turned to Bolshevism as a member of the Mexican Socialist Party. It was Roy who proposed the successful resolution that turned the Socialist Party into the first communist party operating outside Soviet Russia.[22] As outlined above, he made a significant contribution to the debate on the colonial question at the Comintern's second congress in 1920, and generally associated himself with the 'left communists' in the Comintern such as Sneevliet, Brandler and Thalheimer. His disdain for the nationalists was unconcealed – 'derelicts of German intrigue' was how he dismissed the members of the nationalist Indian Revolutionary Committee established in Berlin in 1914. But he also found it difficult to work with other 'experts' on India, even if they belonged to the Comintern. Such was the case with Virendranath Chattopadhya – another former terrorist turned Marxist who had been associated with the Berlin exiles since August 1914 and remained active in the city in the 1920s as a leading figure in the Comintern's 'foreign bureau' of the Communist Party of India.[23] When Roy was co-opted to the 'small bureau' of the Comintern in 1920, Berlin and Moscow became just two of the competing centres for communist influence on the subcontinent.[24] A third was the Communist Party of Great Britain (CPGB), which was expected to take responsibility for nurturing revolutionary organisations in the British colonies. Rajani Palme Dutt, his brother Clemens, and Shapurji Saklatvala were among those who played a leading role in this work.[25] The CPGB was constantly criticised for not doing enough both before and after this devolution of responsibility finally took shape; and Roy, who objected to direct contact between the Comintern and the Indian National Congress when this was decided at the fifth congress in June 1924, often took the lead in heaping criticism upon it.

Roy was also involved in the creation of a Central Asiatic Bureau of the Comintern at Tashkent in December 1920, with Muhammed Shafiq as its first general secretary. A short-lived Indian military school was established there with the intention of harnessing pan-Islamic sentiment for the construction of a revolutionary army in Afghanistan, using Indian army deserters and supporters of the Khilafat movement who were crossing the country to join up with the forces of Mustafa Kemal Pasha in Turkey. Roy and at most 50 of these pilgrims declared that the Communist Party of India had been born at Tashkent in 1920 – much to the annoyance and disbelief of 'Chatto' and virtually everyone who knew anything about India within the Comintern. Chatto's group demanded the dissolution of Roy's 'party' but a group set up in Moscow by the Executive Committee of the Communist International (ECCI) in early 1921 to investigate – headed by Roy's close associates August Thalheimer and Borodin – found in his favour. The Tashkent intrigues are instructive for several reasons. Apart from exposing divisions within the Comintern and pointing to Roy's egoism and adventurism, they illustrate something of the primitive and provisional nature of the early attempts to intervene in India. Within months, the military school was disbanded (May 1921) as part of a Bolshevik rapprochement with Britain; the idea of encouraging pan-Islamic sentiment was dropped; and Afghanistan lost its attraction as a theatre of operations when the Kabul government attempted to find better diplomatic relations with New Delhi. In 1921, the Comintern's central Asian base was disbanded altogether and reappeared in Moscow as its Eastern Section, while students from the Tashkent military school were relocated to the Communist University of the Toilers of the East. Roy nevertheless continued to act as the main channel for Comintern activities in India, shifting his centre of operations to Berlin, which enjoyed better communications with the subcontinent than Moscow. Using Comintern money, he was keen to convert Indian terrorists to Bolshevism. His election in 1922 to candidate member of the ECCI, and his elevation to its Presidium in June 1923, indicate the esteem in which he was then held.

While Roy was inclined to see the struggle between Leninism and Gandhism as a zero-sum conflict, the other members of the Berlin committee were more receptive to the idea of working with the nationalists. But, as we saw, Roy's position as the acknowledged leader on Indian affairs was upheld when it was first called into doubt in early 1921.[26] It was Roy who led the attempt, in the wake of the third congress of the Comintern in the summer of 1921, to forge a communist party from the scattered propaganda groups that existed in Bombay, Calcutta, Madras, Lahore and Kanpur (Cawnpore). By 1922, Roy had established contact with correspondents in these cities, and pro-Soviet newspapers such as *Socialist* (Bombay) and *Langal* (Calcutta) had come into existence. The basic plan was to establish open workers' and peasants' parties that were guided by a clandestine communist party. The Cawnpore Conspiracy Case of April 1924 led to the imprisonment of four activists who had been involved in this project, including Shaukat Usmani and S. A. Dange – two of the most prominent Indian communists of the interwar years. But it was still possible for a British communist to report on the complete absence of communist groups a year after the conspiracy trial – a reconnoitre which sparked off another internecine row within the Comintern and one in which Roy now accused the CPGB of 'imperialism' in its attempts to arrogate responsibility for directing Bolshevik activities in India.[27] In fact, the CPGB was required to take such responsibility, as we have seen, and the fifth congress of the Comintern was the occasion for a reprimand aimed at Roy when Manuilsky said that he had 'exaggerated the social movement in the colonies to the detriment of the nationalist movement'.[28] Clemens Dutt, one of the CPGB's luminaries on India, was reportedly torn between suspicion and amusement when it was announced that a CPI had been formed at Kanpur in 1925. S. V. Ghate later emerged as its general secretary.[29]

A communist party must have seemed implausible in the light of Percy Glading's inability just months earlier to locate any communist groups in India. But the CPI that was now claimed to exist at least showed a measure of realism by instructing its members to work within Congress with the intention of building up a left-wing and a campaigning organisation. The CPGB sent George Allison to Bombay in April 1926 to begin similar work within the Indian TUC. He was arrested in January 1927, sentenced to eighteen months and deported. The next to arrive was Philip Spratt, a twenty-four year old graduate of Downing College Cambridge and sometime worker in the Labour Research Department. His chief qualification for the Indian posting was that he was unknown to the police. Spratt's journey began in December 1926, when he left for Paris in the company of Clemens Dutt. When he arrived in India, he found that the 'party' had between 15 and 20 members nationally.[30] Communists were like the proverbial needles in a haystack. If they had any room for optimism, it was the sympathy for Soviet Russia that existed among the educated urban population. Lajpat Rai, one of the so-called Extremist leaders of Indian nationalism and the first president of the All-India Trade Union Congress, told its first meeting in 1920 that 'socialistic, even Bolshevik, truth is any day better, more reliable and more humane than capitalist and imperialist truth'.[31] Jawaharlal Nehru was enthusiastic to the point of being thought a fellow-traveller by the late 1920s, and even Gandhi praised the 'purest sacrifice' of the Bolsheviks led by 'such master spirits as Lenin'.[32] The enthusiastic response which Shapurji Saklatvala's speaking tour generated from February 1927 helped to give communism a bigger public profile in the Indian cities, as he pressed Congress to adopt demands specifically related to the economic and social condition of the workers and peasants. But few accepted his message that Gandhism was a 'moral plague' on India.[33]

Political India learned something about the Comintern's machinations on the subcontinent, however, when Roy's letter to the Indian communists was read before the Indian Legislative Assembly on 30 December; it talked of hiding an illegal communist party behind legal workers' and peasants' parties and warned against following advice emanating from the CPGB unless it was clearly acting on Comintern instructions.[34] Roy also declared that the workers' and peasants' parties 'magnificently reflected the revolutionary atmosphere prevailing in the country', and warmly recommended the newly-formed League Against Imperialism (LAI) created at the Congress of Oppressed Nationalities in Brussels earlier in the year.[35] Jawaharlal Nehru was one of its sponsors, and the viceroy was becoming uneasy about his association with the communists. Roy still imagined that the communists could detach all that was worthwhile from the nationalist movement and lead the struggle for independence themselves. The Comintern, by contrast, was working on the assumption that the Indian National Congress could develop after the fashion of the Guomindang – that is as a broad-based radical movement with the communists inside its structures.[36]

Ben Bradley joined Spratt in Bombay in December 1927, when the British communist engineer arrived under cover of his brother's firm – which bore the unlikely name of the Crab Patent Underdrain Tile Company. In conjunction with perhaps a score of Indian communists, these two now set about building a left faction in the unions and creating workers' and peasants' parties as legal cover for the CPI. The first Workers' and Peasants' Party (WPP) had been launched by communists such as Muzafar Ahmed in Bengal on 1 November 1925 as the Labour Swaraj Party. It convened a peasants conference at Krishnajar on 6 February 1926, and there renamed itself the Workers' and Peasants' Party of Bengal. A year later, it still had only 40 members – rising to 125 in March 1928 – but claimed 10,000 affiliated members. WPPs were established in Bombay in February 1927 and the Punjab in late 1926. In October, another was established at Meerut in Uttar Pradesh. By 1928, all these groups were brought together as an all-Indian party, and new outposts were established in other parts of the country. They began to function as a left-wing inside the Indian National Congress, especially in Bombay, with the encouragement of nationalists like Nehru.[37] Bombay also became a centre of communist trade union strength in the course of 1928.

Communist progress in the unions was facilitated by the WPP, which gave

Bradley and Spratt, as well as the local communists, a way in to the All-India Trade Union Congress. The latter had maintained such close links with the Indian National Congress that Nehru, his father Motilal, Subhas Bose and C. R. Das all presided over it at one time or another in the interwar years. At the seventh session in March 1927, G. V. Ghate was elected to the position of assistant secretary. At the eighth session later that year in Kanpur, several more offices were taken by communists and Spratt was put in charge of a sub-committee responsible for drafting a charter of labour rights to be implemented by a future Congress government. At the ninth session in Jharia in 1928, Nehru narrowly beat the communist candidate for the presidency, but seven party members were elected to various offices of the union, including the vice-presidencies, assistant secretaryships and the executive. Nehru had in any case moved very close to the communist position, successfully encouraging the Indian National Congress to affiliate to the LAI. These organisational advances were complemented by progress in the Bombay textile mills, where discontent was generated by redundancies. On 16 April 1928, 3,000 workers struck at the Mahomedbhoy Currimbhoy Mill. Communist intervention led to a fusion of the Bombay Millworkers' Union and a break away group of the Girni Kamgar Mahamandal to form the communist-led GKU. The dispute itself escalated into a general strike of the textile industry – all the more remarkable in view of the complete absence of effective trade unionism among Bombay textile workers as recently as 1926. Now a communist – K. N. Joglekar – became secretary of the GKU, Bradley was one of its four vice-presidents and chair of the strike committee, and the membership grew from around 400 to 54,000 by the end of 1928.[38] In total, around 150,000 workers were involved in the strike that lasted six months.

Not content with this, Bradley was involved as vice-president of the railway workers' union, the Great Indian Peninsular (GIP), which took sympathetic strike action during the textile dispute. Over 200 strikes were recorded in the course of 1928 – 111 in Bombay alone. The government of India quickly came to the conclusion that the communists had taken over. Roy's intercepted 'Congress Letter' was produced as evidence in a context of growing anxiety, much of it connected with mounting nationalist discontent. The Indian National Congress – angry about the Westminster government's appointment of the Simon Commission in 1927 – and the communists were beginning to overlap at the margin, especially when Nehru and Subhas Bose set up the left-leaning Independence for India League in 1928. The League was led by men who found much to admire in Bolshevism; it was created to fight for complete independence at a time when it looked as if Gandhi might settle for Dominion status. Even within the Indian National Congress, sympathy for and interest in the Soviet Union had never been higher. A wedge thus had to be driven between the increasingly successful communists and the Congress left, and the method alighted upon was a general exposé of the communists' true aims. Though a jury had already acquitted Spratt of sedition in August 1927, it was decided that legal action would be taken, though not – after due consideration – against Nehru and Bose themselves. Instead, a conspiracy case was prepared against Spratt, Bradley and a third Briton – the fellow travelling Lester Hutchinson – together with Dange, Ahmed, Joglekar and twenty-five others. A Deportation Bill was prepared as a fallback position. British intelligence identified Muzaffar Ahmed and Spratt as the source of the communists' success, reporting that 'Spratt in particular was ubiquitous. He worked in 1927 mainly with the Bombay group, in 1928 with the Bengal party. He played a large part in uniting the Punjab groups into one party and in the formation of those in the United Provinces into another. And all the time he was carrying on correspondence with the conspirators on the Continent and in England, informing them of the progress of the work, discussing difficulties, receiving instructions ...'[39]

Most of the 31 detainees – arrested during March 1929 – were trade unionists, including the majority of the GKU's officials. Nehru volunteered to defend the accused, who were taken to the remote town of Meerut in the United Provinces, far from centres of potential unrest but plausibly connected to the case by its possession of a branch of the WPP. There was no jury. Nehru appealed for support to the British TUC, claiming the trial was an attempt to suppress trade unionism in India, but its general secretary Walter Citrine accepted the official position – it was a political trial, the accused having been charged with attempting to deprive the King-Emperor of his sovereignty over India. Preliminary proceedings opened in April 1929 and lasted eight months. The trial began on 31 January 1930 and dragged on until August 1932, transforming the defendants into national celebrities. Judgement was returned in January 1933. Muzaffar Ahmed was sentenced to transportation for life; five defendants received twelve years; three were sentenced to ten years; and all but four of the rest received four years each.

One of the effects of the trial was to publicise the work of the communists in India. There were still only 1,000 members of the party by the time the trial ended, but it had many more admirers.[40] The prosecution drew attention to the clandestine work of Roy and Dutt, the role of the CPGB, and the work of the four workers' and peasants' parties.[41] Roy, Dange and Ahmed became heroes in nationalist circles.

Sixth Congress of the Comintern

The leadership of the CPI was thus imprisoned when the repercussions of the sixth world congress of the Comintern began to be felt in India. However, preparations for the congress had been publicly set in motion, so far as India was concerned, as early as March 1928, when the loyal Stalinist economist Eugene Varga published 'Economics and Economic Policy in the Fourth Quarter of 1927' in *Inprecorr* and repeated an argument denouncing the Roy–Dutt thesis of rapid industrialisation which had surfaced at the ninth plenum of the ECCI during the previous February. Dutt responded with a defence of his arguments in *Labour Monthly* in June 1928, and the debate was taken into the Comintern's Indian Commission. Well before the congress met, it was already clear that a doctrinal revision was being prepared that would transform tactics on the subcontinent by anathematising the bourgeoisie and the petty-bourgeoisie. The sixth congress laid it down as an axiom that 'the bourgeois-democratic revolution, consistently pursued, will be transformed into the proletarian revolution in those colonies where the proletariat exercises hegemony over the movement'. Even in colonies without a proletariat – and the Comintern admitted that there were some – it looked forward to the establishment of a Soviet regime as a necessary accompaniment of the overthrow of imperialist power.[42] It added that as centres of socialism developed, the colonies that had broken away from imperialism would be drawn into their orbit and thus enabled to by-pass capitalism altogether.

The main point of contention concerning India at the congress maintained the focus on its economic development that Varga had begun in March. But it must be pointed out that all parties to this dispute made infantile errors of logic in their deductions of different tactical position from what were, in the first place, crude enough class and economic analyses of India. As mentioned earlier, throughout the decade Roy, Saklatvala, Rajani Palme Dutt and other members of the CPGB had detected an industrialisation policy on the subcontinent that they traced back to the crisis in Britain caused by the Great War. This policy of rapid industrialisation, they believed, had survived the war and was creating a growing working class in India. We have seen that Roy deduced exaggerated claims for communist leadership in the national struggle from this starting point; or, rather, the theory of rapid industrialisation was used to rationalise his predilections for such a policy. Dutt and his co-thinkers in the CPGB, on the other hand, were content to justify the anti-imperialist united front orthodoxy adopted in 1921. Prior to the sixth congress, it was obvious that Roy's star was waning in the Comintern when he came under criticism in its press for subscribing to a 'decolonisation thesis'. Dutt was also criticised for holding the same heresy – namely that Britain was industrialising the subcontinent and thus paving the way for its future independence. It is difficult to know if any of this was said in good faith, but much of it was certainly tendentious. Roy was in trouble for reasons that had nothing to do with Leninist ideology: his judgement about India had already been revealed as unreliable and there was suspicion that he had misappropriated funds.[43] He knew too much about the Comintern's policy in China and was too closely associated with 'right opportunists' such as Brandler and Thalheimer who opposed the Comintern's lurch to the left. He did not attend the sixth congress on health grounds.

What is remarkable is that the British delegation to the congress – with the exception of J. T. Murphy – defended its distinctive analysis of India and pointed to the absurdities contained in Kuusinen's 'Theses on the Revolutionary Movement in the Colonial and Semi-Colonial Countries'. Kuusinen admitted that most colonial and semi-colonial countries did not have communist parties – a point endorsed for India by Shaukat Usmani and another Indian delegate Razur, while the Japanese delegate Katayama, looking for someone to blame, referred to the CPGB's 'criminal neglect' of its responsibilities.[44] Kuusinen insisted that industrialisation was actually retarded by British imperialism, as Leninist theory predicted. And yet, the main burden of his speech was to demonstrate the necessity for the communist party, based on the working class, to exercise hegemony over the peasantry and take the lead in the national struggle at the expense of a perfidious national bourgeoisie. Andrew Rothstein was one of the British delegates who pointed out the logical contradictions in this position; the working class ought to be shrinking according to Kuusinen's logic and yet more was now expected of it than ever before. Twelve of the British delegation's thirteen votes were cast against Kuusinen's theses, which were of course passed anyway, but not before a formal complaint had been registered about the polemical and misleading character of the ECCI's argument. Murphy and Usmani were rewarded for their compliance with elevation to the ECCI Presidium.

The suspicion that the sixth congress displayed against the national bourgeoisie turned to deep hostility in the course of 1929. By March, it was clear that the national bourgeoisie was to be regarded as the colonial equivalent of the social democratic parties in Europe. The Indian national bourgeoisie was now said to be so afraid of the social revolution that it had abandoned the struggle against British imperialism. On the grounds that the multi-class workers' and peasants' parties were too much dominated by the petty bourgeoisie, it was now decided to liquidate them. The WPP had obtained 12,500 votes in the Bombay municipal elections as recently as January; in March, the Indian communists were required to wind it up, but they were arrested before the decision could be taken. Roy, meanwhile, openly accused the Comintern of adopting the new ultra-leftism as a way of covering up its own errors in China. Comintern and Soviet publications for their part insisted that the Indian National Congress was determined to reach a rapprochement with British imperialism and that Nehru's left-wing – the Independence for India League – was simply a device to derail the growing revolutionary movement of the workers and peasants. On such logic, the communists were told to dissuade activists from joining the nationalist organisations. At the July plenum of the ECCI, Roy was denounced as a Menshevik.[45] He was so out of step with the drift of thinking within the Comintern that he declared – in an article published by *Inprecorr* in February 1929 – that the first conference of the WPP had 'magnificently reflected the revolutionary atmosphere prevailing in the country'.[46]

After the Sixth Congress

After the sixth world congress, it became increasingly obvious that the real meaning of Kuusinen's convoluted class analysis of the colonial revolution was deep hostility to the national bourgeoisie. Indian communists became aware of the left turn taken by the sixth congress from December 1928, but it took time before its full implications were worked out – not least because the Comintern itself sharpened the policy in the course of 1929. By the summer of 1929, it was clear that just as the New Line prescribed a sectarian self-sufficiency of the communists in the metropolitan countries, so it insisted on the dangers of ideological contamination deriving from all sources not directly under communist control in the colonies. The workers' and peasants' parties were a casualty of this logic even though their defenders within the Comintern – like the British delegation to the sixth congress – advocated them, at least in part, as a cover for an illegal communist party that could dictate their policy. The first conference of the All-India WPP met on 21–24 December 1928 in Calcutta, that is nearly four months after the sixth congress of the Comintern. Its behaviour suggested that aspects of the Comintern's left turn had already filtered through. An executive was elected dominated by communists, and the membership was exhorted to split the left-wing away from the Indian National Congress and the Independence for India League, which was denounced as an obstacle to the national struggle.

And yet, the WPPs survived and the Indian communists (and the British) had to be criticised for not observing the sixth congress positions. Mixed signals on this issue continued to flow from London after September 1928. Palme Dutt and Robin Page Arnot both wrote in favour of WPPs in the spring of 1929, as did Roy.[47] It took the tenth plenum of the ECCI, which met six months after the foundation conference of the All-India WPP, in July 1929, to clarify matters – possibly because Stalin had taken the intervening time to consolidate his ultra-leftist line within the Communist Party of the Soviet Union. In any case, the tenth plenum – which denounced the CPGB for its uncorrected errors ('a society of great friends', Manuilsky sneered) – repeated the instruction to disband the WPP and cut all association with the Indian National Congress. Clemens Dutt made the same argument in *Labour Monthly*, the journal run by his brother from London.[48]

Meerut and the strike wave preceding it were now said to signify 'the emergence of the proletariat as an independent political force' in India. Congress, according to Dutt, was torn between bourgeois and proletarian-peasant interests but, 'taken as a whole, the bourgeois nationalist movement is on the decline because it can no longer lead the struggle of the whole nation and it is adopting a more definitely class-conscious hostile attitude towards the proletarian struggle'. As for the WPP, Dutt argued that the 'campaign of terrorism' waged by imperialism had already weakened it prior to the Meerut arrests. It had, in any case, showed 'signs of weakness owing to the variety of class interests it attempted to represent and the mixture of semi-reformist and class-conscious elements within it'. It was not a mass party, he concluded, and it did not fulfil the needs of the workers. It was inevitable that a revolutionary communist party would arise to do this.[49]

In December, he returned to the same theme, demanding an independent communist party in India and predicting that Gandhi's most recent ultimatum to the British would lead to nothing.[50] In fact, of course, the communists had decided that the Indian National Congress had no interest in confronting British rule at the precise moment when the stage was set for a major collision. Gandhi had given the viceroy until 1 January 1930 to produce a timetable for complete independence – a demand that effectively rendered Nehru's Independence for India League obsolete – and restored the INC's hegemony among the young militants. Gandhi had also made clear his intention to launch another great disobedience campaign on 1 January if his demand was not met. But communists who had always maintained close links with the national leaders – such as Chattopadhya and his Berlin-based associates – were told to sever them just when such connections could prove to be very useful.[51] To underline the point, Congress adopted the so-called Karachi resolution in 1931, which produced the policy on labour – hours, conditions, arbitration, unemployment, sickness and pensions – which the communists had always said it needed. None of this now mattered, because Stalin himself declared, at the sixteenth congress of the CPSU (June–July 1930), that Gandhi was the tool of imperialism and in deadly fear of the national revolution.

When the mass campaign against British rule was launched on schedule, the Comintern denounced it as 'an anti-imperialist sham fight' designed to secure bourgeois hegemony of the national movement. Congress, according to Kuusinen, was 'at bottom, nothing else but the counter-revolutionary strategy of Ghandi [sic]', and this applied whoever actually led Congress – Nehru and the left included.[52] The imprisonment of Gandhi was not allowed to disturb this reasoning. The Comintern was determined to pronounce bourgeois nationalism a spent force, just as it was determined to deny any significant industrialisation of India while insisting that an independent communist party could be built. The bizarre logic of the Comintern's colonial policy was given further exposure at the meeting of the ECCI Presidium in February 1930, where Manuilsky concluded the session by demanding working class (that is, communist party) hegemony over the peasantry in India and Indonesia while admitting that there was no properly functioning communist party in either country. India, he said, had cells but no central committee, while Indonesia had a central committee but no cells. The problem in India was treated as a function of the bourgeoisie's success in isolating the communists – a problem to be overcome by repeated denunciations of Gandhi as an agent of British imperialism.

The New Line divided the Indian communists as it divided communists everywhere. But the Indian communists were divided in any case by the fact that most of the leaders were imprisoned and communication with those outside was extremely difficult. Spratt recalled in his memoirs that his instinctive response, on hearing about the sixth congress resolutions, was to trust in the collective wisdom of the Comintern. No doubt, others did too. But he also tells us that it was only after two more years elapsed – years he spent in jail – that the sixth congress line truly sank in.[53] The prisoners used their time converting members of terrorist organisations such as the Anushilan Party and Juganter Party to communism.[54] Some of the Meerut defendants appear to have been opposed to the new ultra-leftism; others blamed the growing isolation of the communists on the acting leadership beyond the prison walls. Some of these, like P. C. Joshi, were also critical of the New Line.[55] They were, in any case, few and far between. Palme Dutt wrote at the end of 1930 that the Indian revolutionary movement 'remained at the level of primitive and sporadic class struggle' in the absence of a proper communist party.[56] The Comintern's theoretical journal complained that the Indian communists did not accept the truth – namely that the Congress was acting in the interests of British imperialism.[57] This may well explain why despite splitting the All-India TUC in 1929 – which left the communists in control – they continued to work with the nationalists until 1931, when a message from Saklatvala was read to the unions denouncing 'the treacherous role of Gandhi'. Only then did the communists establish their own All-India Red TUC. The Comintern was still rebuking the Indian communists in June 1932, when an 'Open Letter to the Indian Communists' was published in *Communist International.*

All shades of communist opinion came under the guidance of both the CPGB and a secretariat in Berlin – which moved to Paris after Hitler came to power – headed by Clemens Dutt and Chattopadhya. But in the light of Spratt's remarks about the inevitable time lags that slowed communication and the paucity and disorganisation of active communists, it is not clear how effective they could be. The Indian Communist Party itself, officially recognised by the Comintern in 1930, still did not exist in June 1932 according to an 'open letter' from the communists of China, Britain and

Germany published in the Comintern journal.[58] Whether it did or did not, it is obvious that a number of weak and dispersed groups existed incapable of central, co-ordinated action around the line advocated by the Comintern. Roy's return to India, preaching co-operation with Congress, had no discernible effect because he was now on his own and, after his arrest in July 1931, out of circulation. But this did not prevent the Comintern condemning him as an agent of British imperialism and the 'worst enemy of the CPI'. An article in *Communist International* told how Roy had passed from 'left-wing communism' – denying the independent role of the peasantry – to 'putting all his hopes in ... the Guomindang road' after the fourth congress of Comintern, so distorting the Comintern line in China; and finally to the theory of decolonisation.[59]

The CPI, such as it was, was banned in July 1934 and still only amounted to around 1,000 members.[60] If all was not lost, it was because, as even unsympathetic observers have noted, the prestige of the Bolshevik Revolution ran high among nationalists and Marxism had spread within their ranks. When the Congress Socialist Party was formed in 1934, the socialists 'passionately wooed the communists', despite the 'social fascist' label that Comintern publications tried to pin on them. Even before the seventh congress of the Comintern called for unity in anti-fascist struggle in 1935, the socialists wanted agreement with the communists and they were able to coexist, some even within the new organisation.[61]

Notes

1. B. Chandra, *The Rise and Growth of Economic Nationalism in India: Economic Policies of the Indian National Leadership, 1880–1905* (New Delhi, 1966), pp. 13–14.

2. B. Chandra, *Nationalism and Colonialism in Modern India* (New Delhi, 1979). See the essay on Nehru, pp. 171–98.

3. Quoted in B. Chandra, *Communalism in Modern India* (New Delhi, 1986), pp. 264–65.

4. L. Trotsky, 'Prospects and Tasks in the East', *International Press Correspondence (Inprecorr)*, 29 May 1924, p. 307.

5. M. N. Roy, 'The New Trend of Indian Nationalism', *Labour Monthly*, January 1924, p. 23.

6. R. P. Dutt, *India To-Day* (London, 1940), p. 413.

7. S. Karsan, 'The Revolt of Labour in India', *Inprecorr*, 14 February 1922, p. 86.

8. E. Roy, 'The Awakening of India', *Inprecorr*, 5 May 1922, p. 247.

9. 'Imperialism and Labour', *Inprecorr*, 27 August 1925, p. 976.

10. R. P. Dutt, *Modern India* (London, 1927), p. 58. The Indian edition was published in spring 1926.

11. R. P. Dutt, *India To-Day*, p. 150 and p. 165.

12. S. Saklatvala, 'India in the Labour World', *Labour Monthly*, November 1921.

13. M. N. Roy, 'Who Will Lead?' *Communist International*, No. 11, 1924, p. 64.

14. R. P. Dutt, *Modern India*, p. 13, p. 17 and p. 81.

15. M. N. Roy, 'The New Trend of Indian Nationalism', *Labour Monthly*, February 1924, pp. 97–98.

16. E. Roy, 'Mahatma Gandhi: Revolutionary or Counter-revolutionary', *Labour Monthly*, September 1923, p. 161.

17. R. P. Dutt, *Modern India*, p. 81.

18. M. N. Roy, 'The Ways of the Indian Revolution' *Inprecorr*, 18 January 1929, p. 64; 'The Conference of the Workers' and Peasants Party in India', *Inprecorr*, 1 February 1929, p. 93.

19. *Daily Worker*, 11 January 1930.

20. R. P. Dutt 'India', *Labour Monthly*, May 1931, p. 263; E. Roy, 'The Debacle of Gandhism', *Labour Monthly*, July 1922, pp. 32–43.

21. R. P. Dutt, B. Bradley and H. Pollitt, 'On the Eve of the Indian National Congress', *Labour Monthly*, March 1938, p. 184.

22. Narendra Nath Bhattacharya, aka M. N. Roy, was born near Calcutta in 1893. He became a member of the Juguntar terrorist group before moving to San Francisco in June 1916. He became a Marxist in New York the following year and moved to Mexico to avoid arrest in June 1917. There he joined the Mexican Socialist Party, before meeting the Comintern agent Borodin in Mexico City. The Partido Comunista Mexicano affiliated to the Comintern in 1920. M. N. Roy, *M. N. Roy's Memoirs* (Bombay, 1964), pp. 204–05.

23. G. Adhikari (Ed.), *Documents of the History of the Communist Party of India, Vol. 2, 1923–25* (New Delhi, 1974), pp. 498–99.

24. From Berlin, Roy published *Vanguard of Indian Independence* from May 1922; it became *Masses of India* in January 1925.

25. Clemens Dutt collaborated with Roy in publishing *Masses of India* and was active in Berlin, acting as a member of the Communist Party of India in exile and, among many other activities, serving as international secretary of the League Against Imperialism in 1931–33. Saklatvala, born in Bombay of Parsee parents of the Zoroastrian faith, emigrated to Britain in 1905. Elected Labour MP for Battersea North in October 1922, though a communist, he lost the seat in November 1923 but retook it as an open party member in October 1924 with the support of the local Labour Party. His London-based Workers' Welfare League of India acted as agent for the All-India Trade Union Congress. Rajani Palme Dutt established himself as an authority on India through his writings such as *Modern India*.

26. S. R. Chowdhuri, *Leftist Movements in India, 1917–47* (Calcutta, 1976), p. 65.

27. This was Percy Glading. See *Communist Papers* (London, 1926).

28. See J. P. Haithcox, *Communism and Nationalism in India* (Princeton, 1971), p. 39.

29. P. Spratt, *Blowing Up India: Reminiscences and Reflections of a Former Comintern Emissary* (Calcutta, 1955), p. 35.

30. Ibid, p. 35.

31. Quoted in S. Ghose, *Socialism and Communism in India* (Bombay, 1971), p. 14.

32. Ibid. p. 123.

33. S. Saklatvala, *Is India Different?* (London, 1927), p. 27.

34. S. R. Chowdhuri, pp. 78–79.

35. M. N. Roy, 'The Conference of the Workers' and Peasants' Party in India', *Inprecorr*, 1 February 1929.

36. *Inprecorr*, 25 February 1927, report on the Congress of Oppressed Nationalities.

37. B. Chandra et. al., *India's Struggle for Independence* (London, 1989), p. 301.

38. R. Newman, *Workers and unions in Bombay 1918–29* (Canberra, 1981), p. 216; J. Jones, *Ben Bradley: Fighter for India's Freedom* (London, undated), pp. 8–9.

39. Quoted in J. P. Haithcox, *Communism and Nationalism*, p. 107.

40. S. Ghose, *Socialism and Communism*, p. 312.

41. S. Roy (Ed.), *Communism in India: Unpublished Documents, 1925–34* (Calcutta, 1972), p. 107.

42. 'Programme of the Communist International', adopted 1 September 1928, J. Degras (Ed.), *The Communist International 1919–43: Documents Vol. II*, (Oxford, 1971), p. 507.

43. Roy's exaggerations about the size of the Indian working class and the number of communists on the subcontinent probably led the Comintern to spend far more money on the Indian revolutionaries than the tiny groups of militants warranted – £120,000 by 1922 according to one account. When he returned to Moscow from China in September, the moment was opportune for invoking charges of misappropriation that Ossip Piatnitsky levelled against him. See S. Ghose, *Socialism and Communism*, p. 156; J. P. Haithcox, *Communism and Nationalism in India*, p. 15, p. 29, and p. 80; M. Ahmed, *Myself and the Communist Party of India* (Calcutta, 1970), p. 478 and pp. 479–80.

44. None of the six Indians present at the congress had a mandate to speak for the Indian communists.

45. After the sixth congress of the Comintern, Roy worked for another year in Berlin. He blamed his expulsion at the tenth plenum of the ECCI on 'internal intrigue' and said that 'the desire of the Communist Party of Great Britain to establish its protectorate over the Indian communist movement had a good deal to do with it'. Quoted in S. Ghose *Socialism and Communism*, p. 160. He returned to India in December 1930 and was arrested and imprisoned until 1936 on charges arising from the Cawnpore Conspiracy Case of 1924.

46. M. N. Roy, 'The Conference of the Workers' and Peasants' Party in India' *Inprecorr*, 1 February 1929, p. 94.

47. G. D. Overstreet and M. Windmiller, *Communism in India* (Berkeley, 1959), pp. 128–30.

48. C. Dutt, 'The Class Struggle in India', *Labour Monthly*, July 1929, pp. 405–16.

49. Ibid. p. 416.

50. C. Dutt, 'The Role and leadership of the Indian Working Class', *Labour Monthly*, December 1929.

51. Chatto wrote to Nehru accusing him of betrayal in December 1929. See J. P. Haithcox, *Communism and Nationalism*, p. 740.

52. O. Kuusinen, 'The Indian Revolution and Ghandi's Manoeuvre', *Inprecorr*, 20 March 1930.

53. P. Spratt, *Blowing-Up India*, p. 44 and p. 53.

54. B. Chandra, 'The Ideological Development of the Revolutionary Terrorists in Northern India', in his *Nationalism and Colonialism in Modern India*, pp. 223–51. Chandra points out that the Bolshevik Revolution had a major impact on these groups.

55. P. Spratt, *Blowing-Up India*, pp. 53–54.

56. Quoted by J. Degras, *The Communist International 1919–43: Documents Vol. III* (Oxford, 1971) p. 156.

57. Ibid. p. 156.

58. J. Degras, *The Communist International, Vol. III*, p. 220.

59. G. Safarov, 'The End of Mr. Roy', *Communist International*, 1 January 1930.

60. S. Ghose, *Stalinism and Communism*, p. 312.

61. M. R. Masani, *The Communist Party of India* (London, 1954) p. 54.

The New Line in South Africa: Ideology and Perception in a Very Small Communist Party

ALLISON DREW

Consideration of the New Line in South Africa raises two questions: firstly, why did South African communists go along with the New Line, and, secondly, what happened once it was adopted? As was the case with communist parties around the world, South African communists followed the New Line because they accepted the Comintern's legitimacy as the guiding element in the international communist network. Moreover, as was also the case elsewhere, this new orientation seemed to offer a plausible response to South African political conditions at the close of the 1920s. The New Line accentuated an ideological framework that interpreted both collective and individual political behaviour in polarised terms. This was accomplished through the use of a strident political discourse that rejected the tolerance of difference and that vilified those constructed as opponents or, even worse, as renegades. The accentuation of this framework in the late 1920s and early 1930s, years of increasing state repression, had a destructive effect on a party that was extremely small, both in national terms and in comparison with other communist parties. The Union of South Africa established in 1910 was premised on the intolerance and exclusion of those who differed from the racialized and gendered 'norm' on which citizenship was based. Despite communists' opposition to racism, the New Line introduced analogous notions of intolerance and exclusion into the small and marginal left.[1]

The Early Years of South African Communism

The Communist Party of South Africa (CPSA) (Section of the Communist International) was founded on 30 July 1921, after almost a year of discussion and planning involving more than ten groups. Compared to industrialised countries in Europe, the socialist movement in South Africa was very young. Socialist currents opposed to capitalism had begun to filter into South Africa around the turn of the century, chiefly through Eastern European and British immigrants. By the early 1910s a number of tiny socialist and syndicalist groups had been formed, generally modelled on Russian, British or American organisations. Given the eclectic nature of the South African socialist movement, acceptance of the Comintern's 21 points was a large leap, and one which not all socialist groups endorsed – some already feared the Comintern's centralising power and anti-democratic tendencies. But awe of the October 1917 Russian revolution made the Russian model compelling for the majority of these early socialists. Significantly, the absence of a social democratic movement and the fragility of the diverse currents comprising the CPSA meant that in South Africa there was no credible left alternative to the Bolshevik exemplar.

Communist politics was at the very margin of South African society. The delegates at the CPSA's launch represented no more than 175 members – virtually all white and mostly male – out of a country of seven million. Trade union organisation dated from the late nineteenth century as white workers from overseas, lured by the diamond and gold mining industries, brought their craft union traditions with them. But within the context of a colonial conquest society, craft-based exclusion became transformed into racial exclusion, a practice that continued into the industrial era. Within six months of its formation, the CPSA was jolted by the realities of South Africa's racial politics. The 1922 Rand Revolt, an uprising of white working class people that began as a strike of white mineworkers, starkly exposed the racial divisions of South Africa's labour force. A now notorious banner held aloft by white male workers and their wives proclaimed 'Workers of the World Fight and Unite for a White S.A.'[2]

A handful of communists had heretofore recognised the imperative of approaching black workers. Although the black population was overwhelmingly rural, an urban black working class was developing rapidly. The year 1912 had seen the formation of the African National Congress (ANC), which upheld the rights of black people and supported anti-pass protests by African workers; January 1919 saw the formation of the Industrial and Commercial Workers' Union (ICU), initially a trade union of black dockworkers. In February 1920, a massive strike of black mineworkers brought many mines to a standstill. On the eve of the CPSA's launch, Sam Barlin and David Ivon Jones, the two South African delegates to the Comintern's third congress in 1921, were keenly aware of the limitations imposed by the party's social composition. They appealed to the Comintern to send a representative to South Africa to study the 'Negro question and its relation to the communist party' and to provide financial assistance. 'What is required,' they argued, 'is to assure economic sustenance to a few native workers as agitators and organisers ... to organise their brothers. This primitive mass is waiting to be stirred.'[3]

Following the Rand Revolt, a few idealists – notably Sidney Bunting, an Oxford graduate who had emigrated to South Africa at the time of the Anglo-Boer War and who later helped found the CPSA – hoped that the state's brutal crushing of the white labour movement would inspire white workers to reconsider their attitudes towards black labour. These hopes were soon dashed. The aftermath of the revolt saw an increase in white racism. In June 1924, white workers used their franchise to elect the 'Pact government' formed by the Labour and National parties. The ensuing implementation of white – or 'civilised' – labour policies represented the state's co-optation of white labour representatives following their industrial defeat.[4]

Comintern Intervention in the CPSA before the New Line

South Africa's geographic distance from the Comintern's headquarters in Moscow and its relative lack of importance in international communist politics meant that sustained Comintern intervention in its South African affiliate began later than in other countries. However, between the Comintern's formation in 1919 and its second congress in July 1920, it had begun to re-examine its position on the 'national and colonial question'. As the prospects of revolution in Europe waned, anti-colonial and national liberation struggles were seen as means to weaken imperialism. At the second congress, the main issue concerned the significance of national liberation movements for socialism. Two years later, with international socialism clearly in retreat, the main issues at the fourth congress were 'immediate demands' and 'united fronts'. The Comintern also introduced theses on the 'Negro question', which argued that the exploitation of black people was a result of imperialism.[5]

Sidney and Rebecca Bunting attended the fourth congress on the CPSA's behalf. On their return to South Africa, Sidney Bunting attempted to combine the Comintern's prescriptions on united fronts with his own agenda to orient the CPSA towards black workers. Over the next two years, Bunting, along with members of the Young Communist League and activists from the party's Cape Town branch, promoted this agenda. The CPSA's third congress in December 1924 put the 'native question' firmly on the party's agenda. White members drifted away. Nonetheless, the party thrived, recruiting black members and developing links with popular organisations. By 1926, black communists were playing leading roles in the ICU. The CPSA also found a sympathiser in the ANC's president-general, J. T. Gumede, who in 1927 attended the League Against Imperialism conference in Brussels and visited the Soviet Union. By 1928, the CPSA claimed about 1,600 African members out of approximately 1,750.[6]

The first significant Comintern intervention in the CPSA's affairs began in September 1927 with the introduction of a thesis on an 'independent Native Republic'. The Native Republic thesis, which the Comintern promoted both in South Africa and in the United States, was one example of Comintern efforts to promote national liberation struggles. It reflected the thinking of Nikolai Bukharin, the central figure on the Comintern in 1926 and 1927.

South African communist Jimmy La Guma visited Moscow in 1927, met with Comintern officials and helped to transplant the thesis to South Africa. The proposed thesis called for 'an independent native South African republic, as a stage towards a workers' and peasants' republic, with full equal rights for all races, black, coloured and white'.[7] Yet, the thesis's peasant-based model differed in crucial respects from late 1920s South Africa. Most Africans lived in restricted areas called reserves where they had access to small plots of land. They could not be neatly categorised as self-sufficient peasants. Typically, by the 1930s, a third of the male population were contract or migrant workers on farms or mines, and in some areas, this reached close to 100 per cent, meaning that the burden of cultivation fell increasingly on women. Other rural Africans were squatters or labour-tenants on white farms.

The Comintern's efforts to promote the Native Republic thesis sparked a controversy amongst South African communists. Sidney Bunting argued forcefully against the thesis on behalf of the CPSA majority at the sixth Comintern congress in 1928. Some communists were concerned about the thesis's rural bias and its assumption of a homogenous peasantry. Many, especially those involved in trade union work, feared that the call for a black republic would alienate white workers and undermine the party's ability to organise on class lines. Nonetheless, after much argument, at its seventh annual conference on 29 December 1928–2 January 1929, the party finally adopted a version of the thesis that '[guaranteed] protection and complete equality to all national minorities'.[8] Loyal to the Comintern, Bunting had eventually supported the thesis, explaining that 'we agreed on interpreting the slogan as meaning much the same as a (predominantly & characteristically native) Workers & Peasants republic, and not meaning a black dictatorship'.[9]

The Introduction of the New Line in South Africa

If the Native Republic thesis subordinated the struggle for socialism to the prior achievement of national liberation and bourgeois democracy, the implementation of the Comintern's New Line in South Africa began to swing the pendulum back. With fascism seemingly secure in Italy and the left in retreat elsewhere in Europe, the Comintern now argued that the crisis of capitalism had reached its 'third period', one in which the contradictions of the capitalist system were rapidly leading to its collapse. Working class immiseration, it was assumed, would lay the conditions for revolutionary proletarian class-consciousness. With worldwide revolution imminent, social democratic and reformist policies were seen as counter-revolutionary attempts to divert the working class from the struggle against capitalism. Hence, the Comintern's repudiation of united fronts from above and its introduction of the New Line of independent leadership and of 'class against class'.

The New Line's development can certainly be related to power struggles within the Communist Party of the Soviet Union. Trotsky and Zinoviev were expelled from the Russian Communist Party in December 1927, and Stalin won his battle against Bukharin in autumn 1928. As the New Line became law, the old and allegedly 'social democratic' and 'right deviationist' leaders were ousted. Political conformity and loyalty to Stalin became paramount; ideological diversity was no longer tolerated. Both the Comintern's central bureaucracy and its national affiliates were rent by denunciations and expulsions. But the New Line's acceptance by Comintern affiliates can also be understood in part as a reaction to the strengthening of right-wing and anti-communist practices within trade unions and social democratic parties. Excluded from united fronts with labour and social democratic organisations, communist parties hoped to pull workers away from those organisations and to form united fronts 'from below'. These conditions gave the New Line certain credibility amongst many communist activists.[10]

In South Africa, similarly, the CPSA was excluded both from the all-white Labour Party and from black organisations. The ICU, which was beginning to fragment, had expelled communists from its National Council in December 1926. At the ANC's second annual convention of Chiefs, held at Bloemfontein in April 1928, mention of the CPSA caused such uproar that the meeting had to be recessed. When it was reconvened, the ICU leaders insisted the ANC renounce its relationship with the CPSA, to which the Chiefs unanimously agreed. In June 1929, General Hertzog's National Party came to power, inaugurating a reign of white terror. By 1930, the South African state had smashed the latest wave of black working class protest. Against this backdrop, in April 1930, the ANC turned to the right. Its president-general, J. T. Gumede, was replaced by Pixley ka Izaka Seme and a conservative slate of officials.[11] The CPSA's political marginalisation from both the ICU and the ANC gave the call for independent leadership credibility.

The New Line meant that alliances with national liberation organisations were shunned in favour of calls for the class struggle of black and white workers. The call for proletarian unity, while seemingly radical, was ill-suited for South Africa's racially divided class structure where democratic reforms were desperately needed. Given the enormity of racial oppression, which stifled the development of even a tiny black bourgeoisie, black political leaders were scarcely in a position to align with the white bourgeoisie. White workers in South Africa derived economic, political and social benefits from their position in the racial hierarchy, meaning that, with rare exceptions, working class unity across the colour line was virtually impossible; white labour organisations would not tolerate demands for black democratic rights. The only feasible organisational possibilities that did not concede to white chauvinism were the direct organisation of black workers and the alliance of all blacks on a common democratic platform.

The imposition of the New Line in South Africa occurred later than in other affiliates, at a time when the CPSA's internal relations were in a state of turmoil, particularly in the Johannesburg headquarters. Political relationships in the CPSA were fraught and complex, characterised by shifting political alignments and complicated by personal rivalries. In part, this reflected the fallout from the Native Republic disputes. Long-time friends and comrades became enemies, ratting on each other, using New Line discourse to settle old scores. The denunciation of Sidney Bunting and 'Buntingism' became the prime test of loyalty. The New Line enabled new personnel to take direction of the party, displacing the older generation of socialists who had founded the CPSA. It gave new recruits – generally Africans – the opportunity to rise rapidly in the party hierarchy through a policy of Africanisation.

Latent Promises and Pressures

At first glance, the CPSA seemed to be in a relatively promising position in 1929. The twenty black and ten white delegates attending the party's seventh conference at the start of the new year claimed to represent nearly 3,000 members.[12] But this seeming success masked serious difficulties. Finances were a major problem. In its first years, the party had relied on contributions from white members and sympathisers. This source dried up with the party's turn to black labour, and it was not able to organise effective fund raising drives or regular payments of dues by its black members. The party's financial woes were a source of simmering tensions on its Central Executive Committee (CEC).[13]

The party's expansion was a source of promise and stress. After the ICU's expulsions of communists, the party had turned its attention to forming black trade unions, organising a Federation of Non-European Trade Unions (FNETU), which grew rapidly. In 1929, the CPSA was growing in a number of key branches, as local militants forged alliances with popular movements. In the Western Cape, the party had links with the militant Western Cape ANC, led by Bransby Ndobe and Elliot Tonjeni. In Natal, Durban's militant environment provided fertile conditions for the party's growth. The ICU *yase* Natal was still a force to be reckoned with. The year 1929 saw a boycott of 'native' beer halls that spread to a number of towns in Natal and lasted several months. This was instigated by African women who brewed beer as their main source of income and saw these beer halls as an economic threat. The CPSA capitalised on this militant mood, due chiefly to the efforts of

Johannes Nkosi, a popular ICU organiser who joined the party in 1926.[14] The party also gained a foothold in the rural town of Potchefstroom, where Edwin Mofutsanyana organised from 1928 to 1931. The party grew rapidly there because it was able to link up with a local struggle against lodgers' permits that lasted several years, and in which women were particularly active. Josie Mpama, a domestic worker who was keen to organise women, became the party's local branch secretary. Similarly, in Bloemfontein, Sam Malkinson, who recruited a large number of Africans, was invaluable in building the local branch.[15] But the rapid influx of new, politically inexperienced members was undercut by the lack of experienced cadre, a problem particularly notable in towns like Potchefstroom and Vereeniging and rural areas like the Transkei.[16]

Early Portents

The first tangible sign of the New Line's implications for South Africa came in October 1929. Cape Africans still had a qualified franchise, and earlier that year the CPSA had put forward two candidates in the parliamentary electoral campaign. Douglas Wolton ran as a candidate in the Cape Flats, and Bunting campaigned under the Native Republic banner in the Transkei. During his campaign, Bunting founded an organisation known as the League of African Rights, which aimed to capture those politically untried but enthusiastic people. It grew rapidly, evidently sparking a chord with local needs. Notwithstanding the earlier communist criticisms of the Native Republic thesis, the slogan captured African aspirations.

But in October 1929, the Comintern ordered the League's disbanding on the grounds of possible fusion with reformist organisations or leadership.[17] The Communist Party of Great Britain (CPGB) firmly endorsed the Comintern's stance. The CPGB's Aitken Ferguson had already complained to the Comintern that '[the] Anti-Bolshevik nature of our C.P.S.A leadership is shown by their founding of the "League for African Rights", (a title which by the way reveals the essentially liberal nature of their outlook) and by the programme of this league'. The British party, he underlined, 'vehemently attacks the whole conception'.[18]

In vain, the CPSA's general secretary, Eddie Roux, tried to convince the Comintern of the League's value. Canvassing for the League's petition for democratic rights entailed mass meetings that threatened the white establishment and from which moderate black leaders generally remained aloof, he argued. The League was a practical way of spreading communist influence in country towns, particularly important in the likely event that the party was banned. But the Comintern was adamant. 'At a time when the natives are proving their revolutionary determination to struggle by openly violating the slave laws,' it remonstrated, 'the party, through the agency of the League, puts forward an extremely mild reformist programme.'[19] This was an assessment that reflected its own ideological imperatives – not South African realities.

The CPSA did not immediately comply but went ahead organising the League's first conference. However, a number of ANC and ICU leader opposed the League. Faced with this opposition and the Comintern's condemnation, the CPSA stopped promoting the League, which soon collapsed.[20] It was clearly a traumatic episode for the South African affiliate. For the next year, the Comintern disparaged the local party for having formed such an organisation and, following this cue, the local communists berated themselves for having done so.[21] However, although the Comintern was definitely letting the South African affiliate feel its boot, the CPSA did not always passively accept this. '[We] would ask you not to be always seeking occasion for vilification of us on the one hand or public laudation of yourselves at our expense on the other', complained Albert Nzula to the Comintern in December 1929. 'It is not impressive nor is it comradely ... we do not only our best but better than, if we may say so, you can teach us to do when it comes to local details.'[22]

The CPSA was squeezed between the pressure of mounting legal repression, on the one hand, and organisational weakness coupled with increasing intervention by the Comintern, on the other. Under those circumstances, it was virtually inevitable that communists would turn on each other as their perceptions of the party's situation increasingly diverged. In 1929, the Johannesburg headquarters was rent by tensions from the apparent rivalry of T. W. Thibedi and Albert Nzula. Thibedi, an invaluable organiser, had been involved in socialist politics since the late 1910s and until 1925 had been the CPSA's only African member. Now FNETU's general secretary, he staunchly opposed the Native Republic thesis. Nzula, drawn to radical ideas in the late 1920s, joined the CPSA in August 1928. A talented speaker and writer, Nzula was groomed by Douglas Wolton and in 1929 briefly became the CPSA's first African general secretary. Such personal rivalries immersed the party's eighth conference at the end of December 1929, when Thibedi was suspended from the party and then hurriedly expelled for allegedly mismanaging trade union funds. The precise circumstances were never clearly explained, and a number of people, including Bunting, had doubts about the fairness of his treatment.[23]

Tensions revolving around Bunting's leadership and accusations of white chauvinism mounted in 1930; the meetings of the CEC and of the Johannesburg branch frequently collapsed into vicious recriminations. Ironically, Bunting had been a key advocate of the turn to black labour. Yet, in personality and style he appeared ponderous and slow to change – particularly in the eyes of the party's more recent African recruits. He also had very high standards – which he applied to himself as well as others – and which he expressed in a moralistic tone. By 1930, more Africans were assuming leadership positions in the party, and Bunting's missionary style irked them. Moreover, Comintern communiqués were critical of Bunting because of his past positions. The relatively new members characterised Bunting as an obstacle to change. Moses Kotane, for instance, was scathing about Bunting, suggesting that if Bunting resigned 'that will desist the Buntingites of their influence in the party as a whole'.[24] A spate of letters found their way to Moscow in late 1930 criticising Bunting's leadership. Some were meant for Comintern officials. Others were sent to Douglas and Molly Wolton, members of the CPSA who were then in Moscow. These latter letters made their way into the Comintern files.[25] The cumulative effect of the correspondence with Moscow was to erode Bunting's credibility in the party. This laid the basis for a change in leadership and in policy.

The Ninth Party Conference

The principal figure responsible for introducing the New Line in South Africa was Douglas Wolton, an Englishman who joined the CPSA in 1925 and rose rapidly up the ranks. In July 1929, Douglas and Molly Wolton left South Africa for England, where Douglas Wolton assisted the CPGB's colonial department. The next year the Woltons made their way to Moscow in the hope of attending the fifth conference of the RILU in August. With the help of the British party, Douglas Wolton was eventually given a consultative vote enabling him to participate in discussions on the South African question at the RILU conference.[26] The Woltons helped the Comintern executive draft two directives on the 'right danger' in South Africa. In September 1930, Douglas Wolton was instructed to return to South Africa 'and had the general political line to be pursued in South Africa laid down'. Molly Wolton stayed in Moscow to study at the Lenin School.

When Douglas Wolton arrived back in November, the CPSA was preparing for the upcoming Dingaan's Day demonstrations. Dingaan's Day was the anniversary of the Battle of Blood River on 16 December 1838, when Zulu chief Dingane and 100,000 Zulu warriors were defeated by Voortrekkers on the banks of the Ncome River in Natal, triggering a civil war in the Zulu kingdom. Wolton remained aloof from the preparations. '[The] party [was] in a very bad state', he recalled several years later in a report to the Comintern. The headquarters were on the verge of being relocated from Johannesburg to Cape Town, membership had plummeted, and 'the white chauvinist Bunting leadership was firmly entrenched in the leading positions. Except for occasional loosely organised mass meetings, no activities whatever were being conducted.'[27] Accordingly, Wolton prepared for the CPSA's upcoming ninth annual conference, scheduled for December 1930, circulating the Comintern resolutions on the 'right danger'. This right-wing, it was alleged, had opposed the Native Republic thesis and was now preventing Africans from playing a leadership role.

The discussion at the party conference centred on two problems. First, was the intense repression faced by party activists, especially Africans, who were subject to various forms of intimidation, including imprisonment, eviction and the loss of their jobs. Secondly, the acute stress that African communists faced inevitably led them to criticise the leadership, personified by Bunting, for allegedly failing to deal adequately with this problem. The leadership was criticised on two grounds: first, in Nzula's words, for its 'disbelief in the native masses having the spirit to fight for their rights', causing the party to lag behind the masses instead of providing guidance; and second, for failing to train African cadre. As John Marks exhorted: 'We must have some of our African leaders educated'. Nzula underlined the point: 'The old leaders have not taught the new members like myself and the native members ... We need a new leadership, without it ... we are going to commit the same mistakes as in the past.' But Fanny Klenerman, who had organised South Africa's first trade union of women workers, would not accept this. 'What constitutes white chauvinism?' she asked. 'If the comrades accept and practice the [Native Republic] slogan, where is white chauvinism?'

The dispute did not simply follow racial lines. Gana Makabeni defended Bunting, claiming that '[there] is no discipline at all in the party, there are natives who are given work to do by the meeting and they do not do it'. Rebecca Bunting insisted that the CPSA had loyally followed the Comintern line. 'When mistakes were pointed out,' she noted, 'those mistakes were corrected ... The leadership is only a reflection of the state in which the whole country is in, politically and economically.'[28]

Organisational restructuring mandated by the Comintern was implemented. Wolton outlined the characteristics of a Bolshevik organisation: democratic centralism; iron discipline (meaning payment of dues); the direct participation of all members; the formation of factory, mine and farm cells; the training of professional revolutionaries; the elimination of fractions; and self-criticism. Wolton's nominations for a Presidium were accepted by the delegates, as were the Presidium's suggestions for four commissions and the panel commission's recommendations for the twenty-four members of the CEC. As Roux recalled, Wolton's request that the list of names he submitted 'be voted for *en bloc*' came 'with a broad hint that anyone who voted against the list was disloyal to the party and the Comintern'.[29] The method posed no problems for the new leadership. Nzula, for one, insisted that if a communist party's policy meant anything, 'it means that everybody has to agree to it, if everybody does not agree to it then it means there is no discipline'.[30] Wolton became the new general secretary, assisted by three whites, Solly Sachs (who despised Bunting),

Charles Baker and Eddie Roux, and by nineteen Africans. The 'right-wing elements' – Bunting and Malkinson – were carefully excluded.[31]

Purifying the Party

Propagating the New Line entailed the centralised control of information. One of Wolton's first acts upon his return had been to take control of the party paper, *South African Worker*. Until 1930, the paper had been published in Johannesburg. However, the branch's political turmoil hampered production, which became irregular. In early 1930, Roux persuaded the executive to let him move the paper to Cape Town. Away from the Johannesburg squabbles, the paper thrived. Roux renamed it *Umsebenzi* (Worker), added a new feature of linocut cartoons, and printed half the paper in English and the remaining articles in a variety of Bantu languages contributed by African comrades. Circulation swelled from 3,000 at the beginning of the year to 5,000 at year's end.[32] But Wolton persuaded Roux to transfer the paper back to Johannesburg under the direct control of the executive. Roux admired Wolton. 'Here was a man with a definite theory of revolution, with a clear-cut doctrine and a programme of action – all beautifully co-ordinated and tabulated. Next to him Bunting appeared a mere empiricist.'[33]

In December 1930, *Umsebenzi* ran a two-part statement from the Comintern detailing the CPSA's 'right opportunist' mistakes. Increasingly dense theoretical statements – 'Imprecor [sic] language' – replaced popular articles on issues of interest to black workers. Within a year after the transfer to Johannesburg, production became irregular and circulation fell. Black workers had to husband their meagre resources carefully and could ill afford needless expenditures. As one Leipke Sender wryly noted about his efforts to sell *Umsebenzi* in Sophiatown: 'I stopped a Blackman and asked him to buy the Umsebenzi. I told him that it was the light, and that he could buy it for a penny. But he replied that for one penny he could buy a candle.'[34]

Heretofore, the CPSA had escaped the complete 'Bolshevisation' that had taken place in other Comintern affiliates. Now, with the paper under their editorial control, the new leadership busied itself with Bolshevising the party and implementing the New Line. Behind the scenes was the triumvirate of Douglas and Molly Wolton and Lazar Bach. Molly Wolton returned in 1931 – a brilliant agitator with an authoritarian personality. To Roux, she was 'easily our most gifted orator, brilliant in repartée'. However, he added, she was inflexible about getting her own way: 'She had to be right, always right'.[35] To Trotskyist Charlie van Gelderen, she was a demagogue – the real boss – of whom they were all terrified.[36] The Woltons were assisted by a Latvian émigré named Lazar Bach, a leather worker in his early twenties and a master of Comintern doctrine, who arrived in late 1930 and joined the

CPSA in 1931. Together the triumvirate acted as the Comintern's interpreters, pointing the finger at all those who had at any time challenged authority. Although Roux naively believed that theoretical mastery was the key to success, obedience, not theory, was the order of the day.

The year 1931 saw a spate of expulsions of those who, over the previous decade, had built the party. Many years later Douglas Wolton told veteran communist Jack Simons that the decision to expel these people came entirely from the CPSA, and not from Moscow. No doubt, he believed this. Nonetheless, the Woltons were precisely the type of local leaders chosen by the Comintern during the New Line years for their loyalty to authority above all else. They had been empowered by the Comintern, and they acted in line with what they believed to be the Comintern's wishes.[37]

The CPSA finally resolved the dilemma posed by Thibedi, even though it entailed the destruction of FNETU. Despite Thibedi's earlier ousting from both the CPSA and FNETU, in September 1930 he had been reinstated in FNETU because 'the trade unionists demanded Thibedi's return' and '[the] workers could not see that Thibedi was a thief'.[38] Thibedi's re-involvement with FNETU was a thorn in the CPSA's side. In January 1931, under Wolton's guidance, Thibedi was expelled from FNETU, which the party reconstituted as the African Federation of Trade Unions (AFTU). 'The communists have crashed', commented William Ballinger, a Scottish trade unionist with roots in the Independent Labour Party, who had been recruited to South Africa to assist the ICU. 'Their industrial wing the S.A. non-European Fed. of Trade Unions is defunct. They are attempting revival under a new name "The African Fed. of Trade Unions".'[39] AFTU aimed to expose the bankruptcy of the official trade union leaders and to provide revolutionary leadership.[40]

AFTU never got off the ground. Nzula ran it as a political movement, its members taking part in rallies and demonstrations for the unemployed. Ballinger sympathised with Nzula, despite the fact that he 'represents no one. He is trying to rebuild on the ruins of the old [FNETU]. But he is a good man and is at the moment probably the only non-self-seeking native agitator.' Nzula was not adept at building bridges across the racial divide, however. In 1931, he addressed the Trades and Labour Council's conference in Durban on behalf of AFTU. The Trades and Labour Council, he claimed, 'has betrayed the masses in general strikes' and was 'sabotaging and betraying joint black and white workers strike struggles in the factories of Johannesburg'; hence the need for AFTU's 'alternative leadership, built and based upon militant class struggle'. Not surprisingly, his speech was not a big hit with his audience: 'The White T. Unionists will not invite him again', noted Ballinger dryly.[41] Over the next year, AFTU lost a number of affiliates.

Following Thibedi's expulsion came the case of Sam Malkinson, who had built up the Bloemfontein branch and who sought an explanation for his having been dropped from the CEC at the party's ninth conference. After several months he received a reply from Wolton that claimed, in Malkinson's words, 'that I did not accept the new line. When I retorted that he knows very well I did ... he said there was some vagueness about it in my mind.' Malkinson responded that he was being victimised on personal grounds.[42] The Political Bureau (PB) expelled Malkinson for factional activities, appealing to the Bloemfontein branch to 'detach itself from the actions of Com. Malkinson', and 'to recant and isolate disruptive elements within the party and to align itself with the Leninist leadership of the party'.[43] The local branch refused to comply, claiming that Malkinson had been unfairly treated, that the branch had 'nothing to recant on', and that it was 'disgusted at the threat ... of the liquidation of the local DPC [District Party Committee]'. It expressed alarm at 'the Mussolini-like attitude adopted by the PB' and insisted on 'the Leninist principle of self criticism'. The PB never replied.[44]

Malkinson explained the dynamics behind his expulsion in terms of a power struggle between the 'Nzula-ites' and the 'Buntingites', claiming that Wolton had removed him from the CEC 'because Nzula was against me, and Wolton had to support him'. Nzula's abuse of alcohol had led to 'complete chaos', he added, urging the CPSA to 'purge itself of such elements, as they are dangerous to the party, particularly as leaders'. But he also pointed to the party's 'criminal neglecting of the livelihood of leaders (Nzula and Baker) who were starving [and] the concentration of the little money that there is in one's hands (Bunting's)'.[45] Not surprisingly, Malkinson's explanations went unheeded, and the Bloemfontein branch declined.[46]

Douglas Wolton assumed the role of high priest at the CEC meetings. In July 1931, he warned against the right danger revealed in Bunting's legal work, cautioning that: 'We must view these questions very seriously as they now border on counter-revolutionary activities.' Yet, although the local communists accepted the authority of the Comintern's directives, they nonetheless questioned some of Douglas Wolton's interpretations. Moses Kotane, for instance, queried whether the Independent ANC was really a reactionary organisation. 'I do not intend to defend these people,' he hastened to add, 'but I want to know whether we are accusing them wrongly.'

African communists familiar with the Transkei questioned Wolton's idealised notions of rural class structure and consciousness. When Gana Makabeni observed that people in the Transkei did 'not wish to be organised into subsidiary organisations like peasant organisations but direct into the party', Wolton replied that the party needed an agrarian programme that distinguished 'between rich, middle and poor native farmers'. But Kotane countered that '[there] are no rich farmers', and Makabeni explained that '[by] agricultural workers I mean those who work in the towns but live on their plots because they cannot subsist on their plots. There are no rich farmers who hire labourers'.[47] The classical Marxist conception of rural class structure did not exist in the Transkei, and the communists who organised in the region were clearly aware of this.

Nonetheless, such recognition of local specificities by activists did not diminish the New Line's impact. The Wolton–Bach leadership counted for support on the Jewish Workers' Club, a cultural club whose members were recent immigrants from Eastern Europe, earnest communists or fellow travellers with little knowledge of South African politics or of the CPSA's inner dynamics. As Roux remarked: 'They were told by Bach that Bunting was a traitor and that was enough for them.'[48] Benny Sachs remembered 'a certain party meeting – a veritable Witches' Sabbath – with everybody shouting Bunting down and calling him 'Lord' Bunting ... An elderly woman, whom Bunting had befriended over years, turned her posterior towards him with her dress lifted high'. Why, Sachs pondered, did this woman behave like this? It was not a question of her own self-advancement in the party, as 'she was only one of our strays'. Yet, the venomous atmosphere infected her. Benny Sachs knew his own departure from the party was fated.[49]

In September 1931, Bill Andrews, C. B. Tyler, Solly Sachs, Fanny Klenerman, Ben Weinbren and Sidney Bunting were ousted from the party. Aside from Bunting, all were experienced trade unionists, expelled on charges of using reformist and social democratic methods and of neglecting AFTU's ostensibly 'red' trade unions. Bunting, it was alleged, had continued to engage in right-wing activities: appealing for leniency while defending unemployed demonstrators arrested at a May Day rally; persuading a fellow communist charged with contempt to apologise to the court; appearing on the same platform as the ICU and ANC; and seeking Thibedi's reinstatement to the party.[50] But as Bunting explained to the Comintern, his expulsion was due to Wolton's 'increasing obsession with him since he gained the ear of powerful allies overseas [sic]'. Bunting never lost his faith in the Comintern – only in its local interpreters.[51]

The purges strengthened a climate of intimidation: the Johannesburg expulsions were emulated in other branches, as long-standing friends and comrades turned on each other, hoping to prove their own ideological purity. The year before, in October 1930 – prior to Douglas Wolton's return – Johnny Gomas and Eddie Roux had heard rumours of an attempt to oust Bunting from the CEC; the Cape Town branch immediately requested an explanation and expressed its sympathies for Bunting. Now, a year later, the Cape Town district party committee, led by Gomas and Roux, took up the gauntlet thrown down by Johannesburg and expelled its own 'right-wing'. Among these was Jimmy La Guma, having only recently been reinstated after apologising for opposing Wolton's parliamentary campaign. La Guma's expulsion order was signed by his long-time friend Johnny Gomas. And in 1932, Roux reported to the PB a putative link between Bunting and Thibedi

– who had written to Trotsky and started a socialist group outside the CPSA. This led to a new round of allegations against 'Buntingism' and Trotskyism in *Umsebenzi*. Only Gana Makabeni defended Bunting – until his own expulsion on charges of 'Buntingism'.[52]

The Durban branch was in disarray in 1931. The 1929 beer hall boycott had led to a clampdown by state authorities that continued into the next year. The 1930 Dingaan's Day demonstration had taken place in an atmosphere of tension and intimidation, culminating in violence. As the police charged the demonstration, Johannes Nkosi, the party's leading local activist, was shot and stabbed. After Nkosi's murder, a succession of party activists were sent down to Durban by the head office, including Gana Makabeni and Edwin Mofutsanyana, only to be arrested and deported. When Roux went to reorganise the branch in March 1931, he found the city in a state of terror and the local party, 'a practical non-entity ... There were no contacts worth speaking of in the factories, docks, etc ... There was no office or rendezvous whatsoever where members could get in touch with the party or obtain Umsebenzi.' In October, the Durban district party committee endorsed the Johannesburg purges. The intense problems experienced by local activists might very well have led them to blame the old-guard leaders; however, the branch's very weakness would likely have precluded it from standing up to the new authority.[53]

Dissenting Voices

The autocratic methods and expulsions did not go unchallenged. Critics were divided between those who believed that the party could be reformed through a change in leadership and those who felt that reform was no longer possible. Some of the latter made links with Trotskyists overseas. Two former white communists, Frank Glass and Manny Lopes, contacted the Communist League of America (Opposition) in 1930. The following year, various Cape Town socialists formed the International Socialist Club. By April 1932, William Thibedi had formed a Johannesburg group called the Communist League of Africa, which made contact with Trotsky and his overseas supporters.[54]

Gana Makabeni tried to reform the party from within. In November 1931, he and other members of the Johannesburg branch convened a meeting to which they invited the PB. The critics lashed out at the leadership for 'having taken a holiday in organising the oppressed, exploited and voiceless masses in South Africa ... while considering who should be expelled in the next issue of Umsebenzi'. In fact, some of those expelled, they continued, were 'not reported in Umsebenzi because of their unimportance and inferiority or because they are mostly Blacks'. A fight broke out. The branch members evicted the PB members and called a conference at Inchcape Hall on 27

December.

This, too, was far from peaceful. A report prepared by the dissident members and signed by Makabeni criticised the autocratic methods of the leadership, particularly Wolton. Those 'who have the machine of the party in their own hands would do anything detrimental to either movement or workers in order to keep their positions regardless of consequences', the report charged. Moreover, racism was rife. 'Native masses are not only neglected and no agitation is carried in their localities, but [they] are abused by the officials of the party of being barbarians "from the long grass"'.... black comrades [are] expelled for daring to hold any views of their own.' As a result, '[the] party has become mainly a white man's affair, almost completely in the hands of the Jewish Workers Club (mostly petty bourgeois)'. Many of the original white members of the CPSA had left the party 'when it adopted the true policy of the communist party to embrace all nationalities of workers' claiming 'that it was not time yet, to combine with natives'. Now, the report continued, we see '[these] whites resuming their old seats in the party because probably "kaffirs" have been swept away'. The conference delegates designated a committee to draw up a report to send to 'Headquarters' in Moscow 'in full confidence in the International', and decided that in the meantime, 'no opposition of any nature must be carried or allowed to prevail in the party'.[55]

These criticisms provoked a harsh response at the CEC's next meeting. Makabeni was the chief target. Joseph Sepeng charged that Makabeni 'has shown himself in his true colour'. Charles Baker criticised the PB's handling of the 'right danger'. Some of those involved in 'the raid on the party hall' had subsequently been expelled but the 'main engineer, Makabeni, was left untouched', he complained. 'To say that because he is a native, he sould [sic] be dealt with leniently is wrong. We are not whites, blacks or coloured, we are communists. Ignorance cannot be pleaded by Makabeni. He is a traitor.' Josie Mpama echoed the sentiment, demanding: 'Anyone who does wrong should be expelled, no matter what his colour is.'[56] These conflicts permeated the Friends of the Soviet Union and *Ikaka labaSebenzi*. Bunting and other purged communists were marginalised and expelled from the Friends of the Soviet Union. Makabeni, who had been elected chair of *Ikaka labaSebenzi*, was stripped of his office without notification and allegedly beaten up by John Marks when he demanded an explanation. In March 1932, Makabeni was expelled from the party.[57]

In November 1932, Makabeni and eight other African delegates met to discuss the state of affairs. Also present were the Buntings and I. Stein. Two of those present, Frans Mopu and Lucas Malupi, had been involved with Thibedi's Communist League of Africa. Despite this, Thibedi's request to attend the meeting was denied on the grounds that 'it was a meeting of those who had always been against forming any opposition organisation, whereas

Thibedi had formed one'. However, the group failed to reach agreement on a future strategy.

Bunting believed that Douglas Wolton's desire to oust him was the root of the party's troubles and asked the group to cut him out and 'to carry on as if he did not exist'. But he also opposed forming a separate organisation outside the party. 'The C.I. and its sections rightly claim a monopolistic position – there can be only one machine, and isolated groups only confuse the masses.' By contrast, one Solundwana argued that, '[we] must have a centre at which branches can meet and give or obtain advice. We can't work with head office. It fights against us.' This view was endorsed by Stein, who stated, 'Bunting's advice will not result in any good but only in justifying the leaders' mistakes. Let us organise separately and see who is right.' Makabeni came down in the middle, '[opposing] the return to the party pending reply from Moscow. We Africans are flouted by the white members of the party. We must organise ourselves as a race ... I am against going back to the party until it is put in order. Rather, let us thrash those who have spoilt it. The natives at head office are not champions of the black man, they are there only for their pay and have to say and do what they are bid.' Hence, the decision as to whether or not to try to work within the party was postponed 'pending reply from the C.I.'[58] Evidently, the Comintern never replied, and the idea of forming a ginger group to reform the party was dropped.

Toeing the New Line

In 1931–32, the party became thoroughly Bolshevised, its few remaining members seemingly secure in their ideological purity. The state clamped down heavily on protest activity and communists paid the price. Many of the party's leading members suffered imprisonment and banishment in the early 1930s. In consequence, the Wolton–Bach leadership stressed secrecy. At one point, most of the party's open work was done by Roux and by Louis Joffe, an ardent disciple of the Comintern line.[59]

For those who toed the line, there was now even less intellectual autonomy in the party, indicated by the response to the Comintern's new interpretation of the Native Republic thesis. At a CEC meeting in December 1931, Joseph Sepeng introduced the new version, which called for 'a Government of the Bechuana, of the Basutos, Zwalis [sic] etc. and all of these will federate in one Union, free from the domination of any one nation, as is the case in the [USSR]'. Washington Nchee's was the sole dissenting voice, arguing that 'there are too many tribes and we would have too many republics ... if German, French, English and other people can live together why cannot we be a contented nation'. He pointed to the ICU, where '[all] the different tribes were combined under the ICU and then Champion tried to form a Zulu republic by forming the ICU Yase Natal'.

But Johnny Gomas countered that whites were not united, adding that the 'Dutch would not have had an official language if the Nationalists had not come into power ... There can be no unity under capitalism'. Ultimately, Nchee's cynical concession only underlined the lack of tolerance in the party: 'We had this discussion in Durban and I was beaten and given to understand there', he stated. 'I only brought this up for discussion and thought I might get support, but I now give up.'[60] This new variant of the Native Republic thesis was even more out of sync with South African conditions than its predecessor – the ANC was striving to unite Africans across tribal lines, not to fragment them. That did not prevent the CEC from endorsing the new version.

Protected by the myth of their own political superiority, the party's leadership even tried to encroach on the personal lives of its members. When Eddie Roux and Winifred Lunt wanted to marry, Roux was instructed that as a revolutionary he should not do so – this despite the presence of a number of married couples in the party hierarchy – while Winifred Lunt, who joined the CPSA in late 1931, was informed that as a 'petty bourgeois intellectual' she was not suited to be a revolutionary's wife. On this occasion, they defied party discipline. They discussed the party's lack of internal democracy between themselves. But both were inclined towards practical work, and the party gave them a political home.[61]

The Comintern now kept a tighter rein on the CPSA. Moscow's hand was felt via the Lenin School and the Eastern Workers' Communist University (KUTVU). In 1931, renewed efforts were made to enable African communists to study in Moscow; they generally had to travel under assumed identities. After some difficulties, Nzula and Kotane arrived in Moscow in August and September 1931, and Edwin Mofutsanyana, John Marks and B. Nikin, thereafter. Gana Makabeni, who had initially been selected to study in Moscow, never went.[62] Several KUTVU graduates subsequently rose up in the party hierarchy, notably Kotane, Mofutsanyana and Marks. In contrast, Albert Nzula spent the last two-and-a-half years of his life in Moscow, working with A. Z. Zusmanovich and I. Z. Potekhin in the KUTVU's Africa Bureau and editing the *Negro Worker*. However, he became increasingly disenchanted with the Soviet regime and was reputedly overtly critical when he was drunk. He died in Moscow in January 1934, evidently of pneumonia.[63]

Two foreign emissaries came to South Africa in 1932 to propagate Comintern policy. The American communist Eugene Dennis, who used the pseudonym 'Russell', oversaw the implementation of the New Line in 1932–33.[64] Polish-born Gina Medem came to discuss Jewish land settlement in Bira Bidjan in the Eastern Soviet Union, while promoting the Comintern line more broadly.[65] But there were indications that the party's leadership was seen as having been overly zealous in its implementation of the New

Line. One report to the Comintern chided the CPSA's leadership for trying to justify the drop in membership as a political cleansing when in fact it represented a divorce from the masses.[66] AFTU had been decimated by the CPSA's attempts to oust former communists from its affiliates; by late 1932, AFTU's numbers had evidently dwindled to about 200.[67] The CPGB's Harry Pollitt criticised the CPSA's 'expulsions from above' and its setting of the 'red' unions against white workers – an indication from a communist leader that the Wolton–Bach triumvirate had gone too far.[68]

The CPSA's depleted membership precluded large-scale activities. Anticipating that the capitalist depression would radicalise white workers, the CPSA now tried to organise unemployed workers across colour lines. The party ran a soup kitchen in Ferreirastown and organised unemployed people to raise funds for it. Yet, aside from a notable demonstration on May Day 1931, the attempts at joint black–white activities were largely unsuccessful; one effort, at least, almost led to a riot. Gideon Botha concentrated on the white unemployed, but the growing poverty of Afrikaner peasants and workers was not reflected in a non-racial consciousness. 'The problem,' Roux noted, 'was always to get white and native unemployed to march together in a demonstration.' Despite the best efforts of the communist organisers to unite black and white in one procession, 'by the time they arrived anywhere ... most of the whites had vanished'.[69]

But as Ballinger saw it, '[the] "CPers" have overexploited the situation and in consequence the poor unemployed blacks are the sufferers'.[70] Makabeni was scathing. He claimed that the CPSA's attempt to organise unemployed blacks had foundered after one week. He also pointed to the absence of May Day celebrations in 1932 and noted that the only time recently that an African comrade appeared on the City Hall steps, on 30 April, those responsible for protecting the white communist speakers failed to protect the African from a trouncing by the police. 'This gave some suspicion even to the "hangers on" of the party that the party had nothing in common with natives', Makabeni noted. A CPSA demonstration, he concluded cynically, 'only means a white people's meeting to be held at City Steps where a "nigger" cannot have his share at the meeting'.[71]

In 1932, Lazar Bach went to Durban to organise black trade unions. Late in the year, he was recalled to Johannesburg, and the Woltons went to Cape Town. Eddie and Winifred Roux seized the opportunity to revive *Umsebenzi*. They aimed the paper at the black intelligentsia, teachers, ministers, clerks, officials and traders whom the CPSA had earlier labelled as reformist – an indication that party activists did, at times, give primacy to local conditions rather than Comintern directives. Their approach worked: *Umsebenzi* soon outsold its rivals, *Umteteli wa Bantu* and *Bantu World*. The Rouxs also started a monthly magazine called *Indlela Yenkululeko* (The Road to Freedom), which they posted to various institutions around the country, including Fort Hare College.[72]

In late 1932, a by-election was held in Germiston. The previous incumbent had been a member of the National Party, which favoured keeping South Africa on the gold standard, while the South African Party, under Jan Smuts, wished to take the country off gold to suit the Chamber of Mines. The CPSA decided to protest against the fact that Africans in the Transvaal lacked the rights to vote or run for parliament, putting forward John Marks as a black 'demonstrative candidate'. This struck a chord with popular aspirations: despite rigid controls on Germiston's African location, the CPSA attracted huge crowds. Not surprisingly, the election authorities did not accept Marks's candidature. The party's top local white activists were banished from the Witwatersrand for a year; Eddie Roux remained and operated clandestinely. The South African party won an overwhelming victory, and subsequent communist attempts to hold meetings in the African location were squashed with violence.

The CPSA's tiny numbers left it with few resources in the face of this repression. This increased the chances of political burnout. In 1933, Molly Wolton had 'a complete physical and mental breakdown'. In order to recuperate, avowed her husband, 'she needed complete removal from the sense of responsibility which was ever present wherever she was in South Africa'. Thus, when Douglas Wolton's brother wrote him in August 1933 about a job on the *Yorkshire Times*, the Woltons left speedily for England. In a subsequent explanation to both the CPGB and the Comintern about their unauthorised departure, Douglas Wolton remained utterly convinced that he and his wife had done their utmost for the party.[73]

Conclusion

A small, marginal party like the CPSA did not have the resources to withstand the New Line's intense polemics, particularly while the state was intensifying its attacks on political opponents. The New Line inevitably led to schisms in the CPSA, as alleged non-conformists either left or were expelled. The party's membership collapsed. From a claimed peak of almost 3,000 in early 1929, membership had plummeted to 100 by April 1931; by January 1932, it had dropped to about 60.[74] The ICU and ANC were already distancing themselves from the CPSA when the New Line was introduced. Hence, while the New Line did not cause the CPSA's isolation from these organisations, it no doubt intensified it. Moreover, the New Line set back the nascent black trade union movement for several years; trade union structures collapsed due to inadequate attention to basic organisational tasks, polemical disputes and the departure of organisers.

From its earliest days, the South African socialist movement had been characterised by sometimes acrimonious debates. Nonetheless, perhaps the New Line's greatest legacy was that it eroded a sense of trust and comradeship amongst South African socialists. New Line discourse promoted the value of exclusion rather than inclusion. The party was wracked by faction fights, and discussion and debate were stifled, replaced by the correct interpretation of dogma, by the use of personal abuse against dissenting voices, and by the expulsion of dissidents. Democratic practices were subordinated to loyalty to authority.

Socialists came to see each other in terms of categories that had been constructed in the context of power struggles in the Soviet Union and Europe. These imported categories were not directly applicable to early 1930s South African conditions; they had little resonance, if any, with local politics. Nonetheless, the repetitive use of such discourse and styles of argumentation by the prestigious authority of the Comintern and by those local communists who gained the Comintern's ear had lasting consequences, providing a framework according to which communists and former communists interpreted each other's political behaviour and actions.

Notes

1. A. Drew, *Discordant Comrades: Identities and Loyalties on the South African Left* (Aldershot, 2000), pp. 112–36; S. Johns, *Raising the Red Flag: The International Socialist League & the Communist Party of South Africa, 1914–32* (Bellville, 1995), pp. 230–94; J. and R. Simons, *Class and Colour in South Africa 1850–1950* (International Defence and Aid Fund, 1983), pp. 438–61. For comparative discussions, see G. Eley, *Forging Democracy: The History of the Left in Europe, 1850–2000* (Oxford, 2002), pp. 249–60; K. McDermott and J. Agnew, *The Comintern: A History of International Communism from Lenin to Stalin* (Basingstoke, 1996), pp. 68–119.

2. A. Drew, *Discordant*, pp. 13–16, pp. 20–57, and pp. 59–64.

3. Memorandum to Small Bureau of the Comintern on the Situation in Africa from D. Ivon Jones and Sam Barlin, 16 July 1921, pp. 2–3 (Communist International Archives, Rossiiskii tsentr khraneniia i izucheniia dokumentov noveishei istorii [Russian Centre for the Conservation and Study of Modern History Records; RC], Moscow, 495/64/25).

4. A. Drew, *Discordant*, pp. 58–59 and pp. 64–68.

5. S. Johns, 'The Comintern, South Africa and the Black Diaspora', *Review of Politics*, Vol. 37 No. 2 (1975), pp. 200–34.

6. E. Roux, *S. P. Bunting: A Political Biography* [1944] (Bellville, 1993), pp. 96–99; A. Drew, *Discordant*, pp. 68–71 and pp. 76–79.

7. 'Resolution on "The South African Question" adopted by the Executive Committee of the Communist International', in B. Bunting (Ed.), *South African Communists Speak: Documents from the History of the South African Communist Party 1915–80* (London, 1981), pp. 91–97.

8. 'Programme of the Communist Party of South Africa adopted at the seventh annual conference of the Party on January 1, 1929', in B. Bunting (Ed.), *South African Communists Speak*, pp. 100–6; A. Drew, *Discordant*, pp. 94–111.

9. S. P. Bunting to E. R. Roux, 9 January 1929, in A. Drew (Ed.), *South Africa's Radical Tradition: A Documentary History, Vol. 1* (Cape Town, 1996), p. 101.

10. R. Martin, *Communism and the British Trade Unions 1924–33* (Oxford, 1969), pp. 102–3 and p. 108; M. Worley, *Class against Class: the Communist Party in Britain Between the Wars* (London, 2002), pp. 311–13; K. McDermott and J. Agnew, *The Comintern*, pp. 71–72 and pp. 83–84.

11. H. Bradford, *A Taste of Freedom: The ICU in Rural South Africa, 1924–30* (New Haven, 1987), pp. 272–78; J. and R. Simons, *Class and Colour*, pp. 427–29; A. Drew, *Discordant*, p. 81 and pp. 98–99.

12. E. Roux, *Time Longer than Rope* (Wisconsin, 1964, 2nd ed), p. 217.

13. Report of Comrade X (ECCI Representative in South Africa), 25 September 1929, p. 6, (RC 495/64/81).

14. H. Bradford, *Taste of Freedom*, pp. 247–52; B. Sachs, *Multitude of Dreams: A Semi-Autobiographical Study* (Johannesburg, 1949), pp. 153–56; E. Roux, *Bunting*, pp. 142–44.

15. L. Callinicos, *Working Life, 1886–1940: Factories, Townships and Popular Culture on the Rand* (Johannesburg, 1987), pp. 190–91; R. Edgar, interview with Edwin Mofutsanyana, Roma, Lesotho, July 1981, pp. 12–20.

16. D. G. Wolton, Report on South Africa, 20 September 1929 (RC 495/64/81); Report of Comrade X, p. 2.

17. E. Roux, *Bunting*, pp. 141–42.

18. Letter from A. Ferguson [date stamped 4 January 1930] (RC 495/64/85).

19. Letter to CPSA from Presidium of ECCI, 7 May 1930 (RC 495/64/89).

20. Correspondence (E. Roux Papers, A 2667, B 2, Historical Papers Library, University of the Witwatersrand).

21. A. Nzula, 'Resolution on South Africa', in *Report on Ninth Annual Conference of the Communist Party (South Africa)*, 26–28 December 1930, p. 10 (RC 495/64/96).

22. A. Nzula to ECCI, 11 December 1929 (RC 495/64/85).

23. Letter to Molly, 26 August 1930, (RC 495/64/99); E. Roux, *Bunting*, p. 145.

24. Moses M. Kotane to Comrade Willy, 22 November 1930 (RC 495/64/99).

25. Report from A. Green, 8 October 1930; Letter from [Solly Sachs?] to Comrades, 24 July 1930 (RC 495/64/100).

26. Letters from [Campbell] to Political Commission, ECCI, 15 and 16 August 1930 (RC 495/64/92).

27. Report of Comrade D. G. Wolton to ECCI, 13 March 1934, p. 1 (RC 495/64/132).

28. *Report on Ninth Annual Conference of the Communist Party*, p. 4, pp. 11–16.

29. E. Roux, *Bunting*, p. 149.

30. *Report on Ninth Annual Conference of the Communist Party*, p. 11.

31. J. and R. Simons, *Class and Colour*, p. 443.

32. E. and W. Roux, *Rebel Pity: The Life of Eddie Roux* (London, 1970), p. 74 and pp. 81–82; J. and R. Simons, *Class and Colour*, p. 442.

33. E. Roux, *Bunting*, p. 149 and p. 153.

34. Quoted in B. Sachs, *Multitude of Dreams*, p. 195.

35. E. and W. Roux, *Rebel Pity*, p. 96.

36. Interview with Charlie van Gelderen, Cottenham, July 1997.

37. Statement of Douglas Wolton, 23 August 1967 (Jack Simons Collection, South African Communist Party, Manuscripts and Archives Department, University of Cape Town); cf. B. Bunting, *Moses Kotane: South African Revolutionary* (London, 1975), p. 56.

38. Letter to Molly, p. 1.

39. Ballinger to Holtby, 25 March 1931 (Winifred Holtby Collection, Kingston upon Hull Local Studies Library).

40. S. Johns, *Raising the Red Flag*, pp. 274–76; A. T. Nzula, I. I. Potekhin and A. Z. Zusmanovich, *Forced Labour in Colonial Africa* (London, 1979), pp. 9–10 and pp. 130–37.

41. Ballinger to Holtby, 14 April 1931; Report on Meeting of South African Trades & Labour Council, Durban, Easter 1931 (Holtby Collection).

42. Letter from S. Malkinson, 10 March 1931 (RC 495/64/109).

43. Moses Kotane to Bloemfontein DPC, 20 March 1931; CPSA Political Bureau to S. Malkinson, 20 March 1931 (both in RC 495/64/109).

44. DPC Bloemfontein to Secretariat, Johannesburg, 26 March 1931 (RC 495/64/109).

45. S. Malkinson, Explanation, 2 June 1931 (RC 495/64/109).

46. E. and W. Roux, *Rebel Pity*, 98; cf. J. and R. Simons, *Class and Colour*, p. 447.

47. *Minutes of Central Committee*, 4 July 1931 (RC 495/64/113).

48. E. and W. Roux, *Rebel Pity*, p. 103 and p. 109.

49. B. Sachs, *Multitude of Dreams*, pp. 164–65.

50. E. Roux, *Bunting*, pp. 157–58; J. and R. Simons, *Class and Colour*, p. 448.

51. S. P. Bunting to Comrades of the Communist Party (draft), September 1931 (RC 495/64/118).

52. E. Roux, *Bunting*, p. 158 and pp. 163–64; J. and R. Simons, *Class and Colour*, p. 449.

53. *Minutes of Central Committee*, 4 July 1931; E. and W. Roux, *Rebel Pity*, p. 99; J. and R. Simons, *Class and Colour*, p. 449.

54. A. Drew, *Discordant*, pp. 137–65.

55. Introductory of the Report and Report to the Second Conference of Party Members Dissatisfied with the Party Position, signed by Garner Makabeni, pp, 12 and p. 2 (RC 495/64/108).

56. Report of Meeting of the Central Committee of the CPSA, 28–30 December 1931, p. 3 and p. 21 (RC 495/64/113).

57. Introductory of the Report, pp. 6–7 and p. 12; E. Roux, Bunting, pp. 163–64.

58. *Minutes of a Meeting of Communist Delegates*, 13 November, 1932 (RC 495/64/122), reprinted in *Comparative Studies of South Asia, Africa and the Middle East*, Vol. 19 No. 1 (1999), pp. 103–5; E. Roux, *Bunting*, p. 168.

59. E. and W. Roux, *Rebel Pity*, pp. 111–13.

60. Report of Meeting of the Central Committee of the CPSA, p. 3 and pp. 13–16; B. Bunting, *Kotane*, p. 41; J. and R. Simons, *Class and Colour*, p. 473.

61. E. and R. Roux, *Rebel Pity*, pp. 131–32 and pp. 127–28.

62. B. Bunting, *Kotane*, p. 44, p. 46, pp. 58–59 and p. 117. Edgar, interview with Mofutsanyana, pp. 26–28.

63. A. T. Nzula et al., *Forced Labour*, pp. 12–15; A. Drew, *Discordant*, pp. 135–36, n. 79.

64. J. and R. Simons, *Class and Colour*, p. 453; E. and W. Roux, *Rebel Pity*, p. 143.

65. Interview with Lilian Dubb, Cape Town, July 1999.

66. Urgent Questions on the Work of the CPSA, 21 June 1932 (RC 495/64/119).

67. J. and R. Simons, *Class and Colour*, p. 457; S. Johns, *Raising the Red Flag*, p. 282; Introductory of the Report, pp. 7–8.

68. B. Bunting, *Kotane*, p. 62; *Letter from Dennis*, 16 July 1932; *Minutes of the Fourth Plenum of the Communist Party (South Africa)*, 6–8 February 1933 (RC 495/64/129).

69. E. and R. Roux, *Rebel Pity*, p. 131; J. and R. Simons, *Class and Colour*, p. 456; *Minutes of the Fourth Plenum of the Communist Party*, p. 41.

70. Ballinger to Holtby, 20 April 1932 (Holtby Collection, file 4.12, item 35).

71. Introductory to the Report, p. 5 and p. 9.

72. E. and R. Roux, *Rebel Pity*, p. 130.

73. Supplementary Report of Comrade D. G. Wolton to ECCI, 13 March 1934 (RC 495/64/132); CPSA to M. Wolton, 7 July 1933; J. W. Macauley to Secretariat, CPGB, 12 September 1933 (RC 495/64/126); E. Roux, *Bunting*, pp. 169–70.

74. Letter from Dennis, 16 July 1932 (RC 495/64/120).

Moscow in the Tropics: The Third Period, Brazilian Style[1]

MARCO SANTANA

Upon officially terminating its activities in 1992, the Partido Comunista do Brasil (PCB) put an end to a 70-year trajectory. Though it was one of the longest living political parties in Brazil, the PCB had enjoyed only brief periods of legalisation. The greater part of the party's history had been played out clandestinely, under constant police repression. This state of affairs not only made life difficult for party activists on many different levels; it has also complicated the task of researchers wishing to bring to light the party's struggle throughout its many political and historical periods.[2] Although a complete and definitive history of the PCB has not yet been written (despite many attempts), the party has been the subject of numerous studies detailing key aspects of the party's experience. Furthermore, as a participant in many a vicious political dispute – both inside and outside of the leftist movement – the party has found itself at the centre of several controversies that have tended to mix both political and academic analysis. Indeed, one question that continues to lay at the heart of many a critique of the PCB regards the party's subservience to the directives of the late Soviet Union. Historians disagree as to the extent of this 'subservience'. Even so, it must be acknowledged that the party did receive directives from Moscow, some of which were inappropriate, and for which the party sometimes paid a high price. An example was the party's so-called 'workers' period', from 1929 to 1934. This epoch was linked directly to the Third Period established by the Comintern from 1928, which passed like a wave through the world's communist parties.

The following chapter examines the ways in which the PCB was affected by this wave. However, it is not intended to portray the party as a passive victim of Moscow's guidance. Rather, it is intended to analyse the particular mechanisms through which the party carried out its directives, and to consider the party's indigenous interpretation of Moscow's instructions.

Preludes (1922–28)

The PCB was established in March 1922. Nine members from the various communist groups then extant in Brazil were present.[3] Many of these were veterans of the anarcho-syndicalist movement, which had been dominant in

Brazil during the first decades of the twentieth century under the leadership of Italian immigrants. Astrojildo Pereira was appointed PCB general secretary.

It is impossible to downplay the influence that the 1917 Russian Revolution had upon a certain group of militants in Brazil. The revolution made explicit the need for greater theoretical depth and emphasised the importance of the political party in the revolutionary process, two things that had been negated and criticised by the anarchists. It must be remembered, however, that interpretations as to what the Russian Revolution 'was' and 'would be' remained diverse among militant Brazilian workers.

In July 1922, shortly after the party's formation, the PCB learnt about the hardships of illegality as it was subjected to the Washington Luis government's 'state of siege' decree, originally directed against a military revolt. The party was to live with this situation until 1925, when the political situation opened up enough to allow the PCB to act above ground. Even so, the party's early difficulties were to extend further than repressive governmental forces; it was also involved in a bitter political and ideological struggle against the anarchists, disputing their hegemony in the Brazilian workers' movement. Moreover, the PCB suffered from a series of internal disputes. In the first year of existence, for example, the party was faced with an internal problem that had international repercussions: the so-called 'Canellas incident'.

In late 1922, the PCB sent representatives to the Comintern's fourth world congress with the objective – among other things – of establishing PCB affiliation to the Third International. Astrojildo Pereira appointed Bernardo Canellas as the PCB delegate, a trade unionist who was already in Europe attending a trade union congress.[4] Canellas' antics in Moscow were frankly absurd. As he had contacts with reformist French intellectuals and still harboured some anarchist ideals, Canellas defended proposals that ran against those supported by the PCB. In one of his pronouncements, he even claimed that the party had Masons, Protestants and Catholics as members, suggesting that it remained neutral on such matters. Complicating things further, the Brazilian delegate then registered the only vote against the organisational proposals presented to the Comintern by Lenin. As a result, Canellas was nicknamed 'the South American phenomenon' by Trotsky and, more significantly, the Comintern denied the PCB's request for affiliation, accepting the party only as a sympathetic organisation and sending an emissary to study the situation in Brazil. Though he defended his acts, Canellas was expelled from the party forthwith. As it was, the PCB was eventually able to affiliate to the Comintern in 1924, after Rodolfo Ghioldi, a member of the Partido Comunista de la Argentina (PCA), had sent a more favourable report to the Executive Committee of the Communist International (ECCI). Despite this, relations between the PCB and the

Comintern remained tenuous prior to 1928. Brazilian communists even complained that the Comintern's South American Secretariat was not giving adequate political guidance to its various constituent parties.[5]

The PCB held its second congress in 1925, at which the party evaluated its organisational work and resolved to base itself on the Soviet 'factory cell' model. In this way, the PCB tried to come to terms with the Comintern's increasingly 'Bolshevised' orientation. Astrojildo Pereira, critically reviewing the party's numerical strength, commented: 'In Rio and Niterói, where half of the PCB's members are located, we have 150 adherents, at most. This is an insignificance that borders on the ridiculous. Rio is the country's densest industrial centre, where the largest mass of workers is concentrated.' In order to redeem the situation, he suggested that 'we take to heart our goal: [to create] a cell in 100 factories by 30 June, next. Six months later at year's end, we will have doubled the number of our members and will thus look like a communist party, the organised detachment of the vanguard of our proletariat.'[6]

The theses approved by the PCB's second congress, though a serious attempt to interpret Brazilian realities through a Marxist lens, made clear the communists' theoretical limitations.[7] According to the PCB, Brazil was undergoing a struggle between semi-feudal agrarian capitalism and the modern industrial variant. This was seen as being the fundamental contradiction in Brazilian society. Based upon this idea, the party inclined towards a two-stage revolution. The first stage was the 'third blow', characterised by petit-bourgeois revolts such as the *tententista* military insurrections of 1922 and 1924.[8] The bourgeoisie would come to power with the aid of the proletariat, which, in the second stage of the revolution, would administer its blow against the now-dominant class. Within such a theory, it is possible to discern an almost mechanical attempt to transfer the revolutionary model of 1917 Russia on to Brazil.

In 1926, the government of Arthur Bernardes came to an end and with it the 'state of siege'. The PCB was greatly aided by this, becoming legal in 1927. With legality, the party could once again openly challenge for control of the Brazilian workers' movement. Aside from this, the party sought to intervene in national political life on a wider scale. It proposed to launch a 'united front' for the upcoming parliamentary elections, which would incorporate 'diverse proletarian organisations and sectors of the petit bourgeoisie, with the object of supporting candidates that are acceptable to both groups. This was the Workers' Bloc, launched ... on 5 January 1927 and later changed to the Workers' and Peasants' Bloc (BOC), even though it never had much support among the rural masses'.[9]

In reality, the BOC was an instrument utilized by the PCB as a legal alternative. It allowed the party to participate in state and municipal elections, and to agitate among the proletarian masses. In the process, the party made contact with progressive politicians who could be supported by the BOC. This attempt to forge a 'united front' led Astrojildo Pereira to travel to Bolivia where he contacted the exiled Luiz Carlos Prestes, the primary exponent of *tenentismo* and commander of the 'Prestes Column'.[10] Without doubt, the BOC formed an important part of the PCB's early history, as 'for the first time, it engaged in an intense propaganda campaign under conditions of legality. Aside from this, it permitted the widening of the party's influence with the installation of the Workers' Bloc's several sections'.[11] However, if the BOC served as a legal facade for the recently illegal party's activities, then this legality itself was already threatened by new government persecution. By providing the party visibility and wider fields of activity, the BOC also set the communists firmly in the government's sights. Furthermore, the BOC created the illusion of a PCB victory in the 1928 election, helping the party elect two politicians to local positions in Rio de Janeiro, as well as a national congressman. With this 'victory', the communists were open to charges of leaning towards what was then called 'electoralism'. Indeed, the BOC had already been criticised by the Comintern's Latin American Secretariat, whose leader, Jules Humbert-Droz, considered the Bloc to be 'like the Brazilian Guomindang, bringing together worker and peasant organisations and running the permanent risk that petit bourgeois elements might incorporate themselves in it'.[12] By advancing their own critiques of the BOC's position, the Brazilian delegates to the Comintern's sixth world congress (1928) soon began to support Humbert-Droz' position.

An evaluation of this period indicates that 'in 1928, the PCB was already a party with a relatively consolidated internal structure, a certain influence in the workers' movement and recognition at the international level. From the handful of militants present at its founding, it had grown to approximately 1,200 members in 1928. In this formative period (1922–28), the PCB, despite its political, theoretical and ideological difficulties, became an effective party, alive and capable of actively intervening at practically all levels, and also capable of elaborating a national–popular political line'.[13]

Preparing the Ground (1928–29)

The PCB's growth was not without its tensions, however. The year 1928 would be marked by the expulsion of one of the party's founders, Joaquim Barbosa, then union secretary of the executive committee. In 1927, Barbosa and other members of the so-called 'syndicalist opposition' had already diverged from and criticised what they considered to be the PCB's 'alliance with the petit bourgeoisie'.[14] Such disagreement developed elsewhere as well, spreading even to the party press. Barbosa called the PCB's leadership 'sectarian' and was accused, in turn, of factionalism and promoting a 'petit bourgeois and anarcho-syndicalist ideology'. In May 1928, this opposition group asked to be dismissed from the party, though some of its members later sought reinstatement.

All this had occurred on the eve of the PCB's third congress, in December 1928 and January 1929. As Segatto has made clear: 'It is apparent that in the resolutions of the third congress of the PCB, many points were already in close approximation with the theses of the sixth congress of the Comintern, held between July and September 1928. These were principally notable for their rejection of [united] front politics. They sought to undermine any possibility of party political alliances with the petit bourgeoisie and other sectors, as well as establishing for themselves the *a priori* direction of the proletariat and the hegemony of the working peoples' movement. These individuals were still somewhat camouflaged and did not yet make their opinions widely and openly known, as they would shortly after the congress.'[15]

It was at the sixth world congress that the Comintern had 'for the first time directed its attention towards Latin America and the strategies that the communist parties in the region were to adopt'.[16] It was significant, therefore, that as soon as the PCB delegation returned to Brazil they published their interventions in the *debate tribune* of the third congress, transmitting to the party leadership the political line defined in Moscow regarding revolution in Latin America and the 'colonial question'.

The line adopted at the PCB's third congress defined the Brazilian economy as 'agrarian, semi-feudal and semi-colonial'. In such a way, it suggested that a struggle was going on between internal forces seeking to advance their own interests, and external forces – representing imperialism – that sought to stymie this development. Similar to its previous analysis, the party foresaw a 'third revolutionary explosion' that would continue the revolts of 1922 and 1924, but which would be much more widespread. According to Astrojildo Pereira, 'all of the communist party's tactics should thus seek to subordinate this mobilisation of the masses in order to conquer, via successive stages, not only the leadership of the proletarian faction, but hegemony within the movement as a whole'.[17] Crucially, however, the third congress' resolution no longer described the Brazilian revolution as being 'democratic-petit-bourgeois' in character (as it had done in 1924). As a result, changes were made to the principal thrust of the party's activities, rejecting an alliance with the (urban) petit bourgeois in an attempt to form links with the peasant masses.[18] Given such analysis, the BOC became the target of harsh criticism. The third congress adopted as its own the positions contained in Jules Humbert-Droz's report to the Comintern congress, which suggested drastic alterations in the Bloc's orientation.

Moscow in the Tropics (1930–34)

By the end of the 1920s, the PCB was engaged in self-criticism of its original political and theoretical conceptions, adopting a more radical discourse in its wake. As we have seen, relations between the party and the Comintern became closer throughout the period, moving the party towards greater subservience to the directives of Moscow. All this was undertaken against a background of internal disagreement at the highest levels of the international communist movement (the polemics involving Trotsky, Zinoviev and Kamenev, for example). Two important developments emerged as a result of this. In 1929, the PCB participated in the first Latin American Communist Party Conference, organised by the Comintern's South American Secretariat under the leadership of the Lithuanian August Guralski. It was here that the resolutions of the sixth world congress were reaffirmed. In this same year, Astrojildo Pereira travelled to Moscow to help formulate the Comintern's analysis of the 'character of the Brazilian revolution'. He returned to Brazil in 1930 carrying documents that outlined the party's new direction, thereby necessitating changes to the party line, some of which had already been evident at the third PCB congress. As Segatto has suggested, two points were most evident: a definitive break with the politics of the united front, and the proletarianisation of the PCB. [19]

Difficulties were soon to emerge. Towards the middle of 1930, the Comintern's South American Secretariat convened a second Latin American Communist Party Conference in Buenos Aires. This was intended to assess the revolutionary potential of the economic crises experienced by capitalism in 1929, and to establish the communists' response. Among the Brazilian delegation were Octavio Brandão and Astrojildo Pereira. During the discussion of the 'Brazilian question' undertaken at the conference, Brandão, an important PCB theoretician up to that point, was harshly criticised and subjected to no less than sixteen speeches condemning his supposed 'erroneous positions'. The two militants – considered to be the PCB's 'guiding nucleus' – were then removed from the party leadership upon their return to Brazil, and obliged to undergo a self-criticism of their 'petit bourgeois ways' in order to avoid expulsion. Immediately prior to the conference, the Comintern, under Dmitri Manuilsky's direction, had made several criticisms not only of Brandão's position – considered to be 'Menshevist, anti-Leninist and anti-Marxist' – but also of the theses adopted at the third PCB congress with regard to the 'Brazilian revolution'. According to the Comintern, the congress' resolutions put the proletariat in the background during a 'petit-bourgeois *tent-entista* revolt', thereby failing to establish the leading role of the party.

Armed with such concepts and undergoing internal purges and struggles, the PCB watched the so-called Brazilian Revolution of October 1930 unfold. Interpreting events as a struggle between national oligarchies and American and English imperialism, the party did not try to influence events through its connections with the progressive and popular sectors involved in the struggle. And this had even been the party's position throughout the presidential elections that preceded the revolution.[20] However, though the PCB was to remain aloof from the struggle, the party suffered from its consequences, enduring intense governmental repression once the movement was under way. The 'revolution' put Getúlio Vargas in power and opened the way for the installation of a corporatist regime in Brazil.

Concurrently, the process of 'radicalising the party' advanced by leaps and bounds, unleashing harsh critiques against 'united front' politics. Because of this, the party became increasingly isolated, pushing itself away from other progressive sectors by advocating the idea that 'the communist party, being the party of the proletariat, is the only party truly free of any connection to the imperialists'.[21] This 'radicalisation' implied changes in the party's internal organisation. The New Line's idea of 'proletarianisation' was understood not as establishing the party as a presence in the midst of the working masses, but as the incorporation of workers within its upper echelons. The leadership and organisational capacity of these people were not taken into consideration; the fact that they were workers was enough to qualify them for the party's highest positions. And things did not stop there. As Leôncio Basbaum recalls, 'the critique of the petit bourgeois position passed from ideology to the party's organisation and from there to the simplification of lifestyles ... *Proletarianisation* thus took on a romantic and erroneous meaning as party members made a point of buying cheap cigarettes, dressing poorly, not using ties, etc ... Even a daily shower could be seen as a petit bourgeois relic which could undermine the party's proletarian ideology.'[22]

Such a perspective led, after a heated debate in the PCB Central Committee (CC), to a reduction in the number of intellectuals included in the party executive. Comrades who had figured prominently in the party's early history began to be removed from their jobs at this point. Octavio Brandão and José Casini, for example, were removed from the leadership. Brandão harshly criticised Astrojildo Pereira, accusing him of linking the PCB's goals to those of a Comintern that was, in his analysis, riddled with 'Trotskyites'. Despite this, Brandão submitted to 'centralism' and remained within the party, while Casini preferred to detach himself from the PCB. Those who stayed were directed to the heaviest tasks in order 'to become proletarians'. Astrojildo Pereira himself was criticised for his supposed opposition to the 'proletarianisation of the party'. In 1931, he asked to be removed from the organisation due to his discontent with the party's current political line, emphasising that even though he no longer wanted to be a part of it, he would still support the PCB

The organisational instability provoked by the 'proletarianisation policy' was also felt in terms of the constantly changing composition of the party leadership. With Astrojildo removed from his position as general secretary, Heitor Ferreira Lima, an intellectual of working class origins and student at the International Lenin School in Moscow from 1927 to 1930, assumed the reins of the PCB. Whether through the recasting of their responsibilities or through their removal from the party hierarchy, almost the entire guiding nucleus of the PCB, which had lead party for several years, was dissolved. The PCB began to fall under the influence of Fernando de Lacerda, one of the leading proponents of the 'workers' period'.

Despite the internal problems brought about by the party's 'proletarianisation' policy, and despite the political isolation that this created, it must be noted that communists continued to intervene in the workers' movement and in national political life. In January 1931, using its influence within the trade union movement, the PCB attempted to organise an immense demonstration in Rio de Janeiro. This was cancelled due to strong police repression. During the same month, and in a climate of suppression, the communists, through the Brazilian General Confederation of Labour (CGT), convoked the population to join the 'march against hunger', a demonstration against the provisional government. Many of the party leaders were arrested in this public act. Government repression against communist activity intensified, with the leaderships of both the PCB and the BOC imprisoned and, in some cases, deported. The Vargas provisional government's preoccupation with the PCB activities led to the creation of a special service for the repression of the communists.

Meanwhile, contact with the Comintern increased. In February of 1931, Inês Guralski, August Guralski's wife, arrived in Brazil, charged with giving political direction to the PCB. Her arrival, following the Comintern's decision to intervene into the affairs of those parties deemed to be demonstrating 'deviant tendencies', further reinforced the PCB's dominant 'workerist' tendency. Guralski's principal objective was 'to avoid the hegemony of petit bourgeois revolutionaries in the revolutionary process now underway'.[23] This, in turn, was intended to undermine the possible attraction that communists might begin to feel towards Luiz Carlos Prestes' position at this time, which was evolving in direction of the left. It may be said that while she was on Brazilian soil, Inês was the true leader of the PCB, with Fernando de Lacerda and his wife, Cina, as her aids.

The attacks against Prestes endeavoured to show that only through the PCB and proletarian hegemony could the revolution be made in Brazil. Throughout this period, the party's relationship with Prestes vacillated between approximation and withdrawal. Prestes had led important movements of armed *tenentista* and military revolt. He had, bit by bit, discarded his original 'progressive' stance to take up a position approximate with those of the left. The last step in this process was characterised by the creation of the League for Revolutionary Action (LAR) in 1930, which animated even the more radical sectors. The LAR, criticising those *tenentistas* that supported Vargas, called for an 'anti-imperialist and agrarian revolution', inviting the PCB, as the leader of the working class, to direct the organisation. In response, the PCB classified Prestes as the party's 'most dangerous adversary'. The LAR was unable to attract many followers, however, and towards the end of 1930, while Vargas' provisional government reigned, Prestes dissolved the League and indicated his interest in joining the PCB, calling upon his old comrades to do the same.

Although Prestes did not immediately become a party member, he nevertheless bolstered his contacts (already begun) with the Comintern's South American Secretariat whilst exiled in Uruguay. Prestes' approaches to the PCB on the international level then became even more significant in March 1931, when he declared himself to be a communist and took on to himself the party's criticisms of 'Prestesism', giving his total support to the PCB. This was not enough to diminish the PCB's misgivings. However, if the PCB did not accept him, Prestes had by now found protectors in the South American Secretariat. He was invited to Moscow where he was received by Manuilsky, studied, and participated in meetings with leading members of communist parties from around the world. Prestes only returned to Brazil in 1935.

But while Prestes involved himself in international affairs, the 'workers' period' continued to cut a swath through the PCB in Brazil. Heitor Ferreira Lima, Astrojildo Pereira's substitute, was the next victim of internal sectarianism. In July 1931, he was removed from his position as general secretary, having been accused of opposing the 'proletarianisation policy' led by Guralski and Lacerda. Sectarianism then reached its apex in 1932. The hamstringing of the party's leading organs continued apace, along with the expulsion from the party of all supposed opposition. Intellectuals continued to be *personas non-gratis*. In January 1932, those members of the PCB leadership who had not been gaoled by the repression or expelled during the party purges met in São Paulo to adopt José Villar (a worker, obviously) as the new general secretary. During the meeting, Lacerda made a proposal, opposed by Leôncio Basbaum, that intellectuals be prohibited from voting in the party's leadership organs. The only exception to this rule would be Lacerda's spouse, Cina, who – though petit bourgeois in origin and educated in Europe – maintained the right to vote as she claimed to 'stitch and patch her husband's clothes'.[24]

Given the chaos and instability apparent in the PCB, yet another Comintern emissary of the South American Secretariat was dispatched to Brazil in April 1932 to assess the situation. This was the Argentinean González Alberti, who undertook separate meetings with Lacerda and Basbaum, and participated in meetings of the CC. While discussing preparations for May Day, Lacerda defended the position that the party did not need to undertake agitation campaigns given that the masses were already revolutionary by nature. Alberti harshly criticised Lacerda's position, considering it clearly to be 'anarchist'. In the event, May Day was a failure and blame for this was placed squarely on Lacerda's doorstep. Consequently, his wife was removed from the CC and he was removed from the party secretariat. José Caetano Machado, a baker from the Northeast of Brazil was elected as the party's new general secretary. He had been one of the members of the opposition who had removed themselves from the party in 1928, though he had later returned. Basbaum also assumed an important position within the secretariat. The party's internal balance of power was evidently shifting.

Though the party's May Day demonstration had been a fiasco, the PCB nevertheless attempted to intervene and lead the spontaneous strike movements that had begun in São Paulo in protest against appalling work conditions. The party worked to widen the movements' goals, attempting to transform them into a general strike. Police repression during this period was unusually harsh and resulted in the arrest of many militants and communist leaders. Thanks to this, the recently elected CC was to experience a somewhat short lifespan. Those few leaders who managed to escape prison and banishment met for a national conference in Rio de Janeiro in November, in order to change the composition of the CC yet again. At this meeting, Duvitiliano Ramos, a textile mill worker, was elected as general secretary. Once again, hostility was shown towards 'intellectuals and militants of petit bourgeois origin'. A good example of this can be found in relation to Basbaum. He had been arrested and only recently released from prison. Nevertheless, his duties and activities within the party were 'frozen' and, afterwards, at a meeting of the CC held at the beginning of 1933, he was accused of exercising a pernicious petit bourgeois influence over the party. Disappointed, Basbaum withdrew from the PCB. He would later be formally expelled, along with Heitor Ferreira and others, under the accusation of being a 'Trotskyite' and an 'agent of imperialism'.

There can be little doubt that the 'policy of proletarianisation' served to isolate and weaken the PCB. However, any objective analysis of this period must recognise that the party also intensified its action and influence among the workers through the trade unions and the strikes that it sought to control. Aside from this, the PCB was able to affect other sectors of society by consolidating cells within the armed forces. Finally, the communists fought against Nazi-fascist influences in *terras brasileiras* through their opposition to Plínio Salgado's Integralista Party. It should be noted, too, ideological considerations aside, that the PCB tried to register their illegal party in order to participate in the 1933 elections. The party's request was denied under the allegation that it was an 'internationalist' political party.

Even so, the PCB was able to run in the elections under the umbrella of the Peasant and Workers' Union. It did so unsuccessfully.

It would not be until the end of 1933 that the PCB began to show some signs of tiring of its 'policy of proletarianisation', indicating that it might rethink the expulsion of certain important erstwhile members. Significantly, between 1932 and 1934, the party had begun to receive old members of the *tenentista* movement among its ranks. The ascension of these people to key positions within the PCB obviously had an impact upon the party's organisation and political orientation. This became even clearer when one of Prestes' old *tenentista* comrades became the party's general secretary in July 1934. The election of Antonio Manoel Bonfim occurred during the first national conference of the PCB. Prestes himself, already a member of the Communist Party of the Soviet Union and the ECCI Presidium, was incorporated into the PCB in this year under Manuilsky's auspices, despite some Brazilian resistance.[25]

The PCB conference also elected delegates to represent Brazil at the seventh world congress of the Comintern. It is worth remembering that by this point, after several reverses and a general decline in the international communist movement, the Comintern had already revised its opposition to united front politics, and was not only accepting alliances but, in fact, encouraging them. Yet, although the PCB had demonstrated some flexibility in its 'policy of proletarianisation', it continued initially to resist the formation of united fronts. For this reason, in the electoral campaign of 1934, the party frustrated attempts at forming 'electoral fronts' such as the so-called 'coalition of the lefts'. In the view of the PCB, any 'political front' should base itself upon the struggles of the working class and the trade union movement, not merely upon electoral expediency. Even so, the PCB was not prepared to abandon its loyalty to Moscow as it prepared to leave the Third Period and enter into a new historical 'phase'. The 1935 organisation of the Aliança Nacional Libertadora (National Liberation Alliance), a 'front' that brought together *tenentistas*, liberals and communists under the leadership of Prestes (now a PCB member), was an example of this new direction in PCB policy.

Conclusion

An analysis of the years stretching from 1929 to 1934 clearly shows the strong influence exerted by the Comintern on the activities of the PCB. This relationship was forged primarily through the South American Secretariat, which, at the height of this period, effectively ran the party through one of its cadres. However, it should be remembered that the frequent visits by Brazilians to Moscow for study, meetings and conferences also contributed to the solidification of the link between the national and international communist movements.

The influence of the Comintern was not to blame for everything. The PCB gave this influence space in which to grow and to make itself manifest. It may even be argued that the party's original, poorly received attempt to affiliate to the Comintern played a role in obliging the PCB to demonstrate that this early error was only an isolated event; that the party would from thereon correctly toe the international line. Clearly, from its foundation until the end of the 1920s, the PCB was a party intent on strengthening its ties to international communism. It was only after 1928, in a new international context, that the Comintern's increased interest in consolidating its relationship with the 'fraternal parties' created a reciprocal attraction. However, we must remember that the 'correct line' dispatched from Moscow provoked a very turbulent period of PCB history, both in political and organisational terms. Directives were accepted by some and criticised by others. Sometimes, even the party's defenders were discharged, labelled as 'poor followers' or 'deviants'. The difficulties faced by those trying to execute the 'correct implementation' of a political line in Brazil are indicated by the fact that despite the presence of native supporters, international cadres were sent overseas to set the party on the 'right track'. The cold of Moscow was forced to come to the tropics in order to prevent its line from melting away. In any case, the isolation that this policy caused for the party, even at its most extreme, did not lead to a total paralysis of party life. This continued apace, though modified, and paved the way for several organisational conquests within the workers' movement.

Notes

1. I dedicate the present article to Adir Maura Otília da Silva, my mother, *in memoriam*. I would like also to thank Thadeus Blanchette who translated it.

2. For more details about different periods of the PCB, see K. Morgan and M. A. Santana, 'A Limit to Everything: Union Activists and "Bolshevik Discipline" in Britain and Brazil', *Scottish Labour History*, No. 34 (1999). Also R. Chilcote, *Communist Party: Conflict and Integration, 1922–72* (Oxford, 1974).

3. They were delegates from organised groups in the cities of Porto Alegre, Recife, São Paulo, Cruzeiro, Niterói and Rio de Janeiro. The delegates from the cities of Santos and Juiz de Fora were not present. According to Segatto, the delegates (and their professional categories) were: Abílio de Nequete (barber), Astrojildo Pereira (journalist), Cristiano Cordeiro (public employee), Hermogêneo Silva (electrician), João da Costa Pimenta (printer), Joaquim Barbosa (tailor), José Elias da Silva (public employee), Luís Peres (broom factory worker) and Manoel Cendon (tailor). See J. A. Segatto, *Breve História do PCB* (Belo Horizonte, 1989).

4. Mario Barrel, a member of the French Communist Party, was also sent as a representative. According to reports, however, Canellas fooled the Frenchman and travelled to Moscow alone

5. M. Zaidan, *O PCB e a Internacional Comunista, 1922–29* (São Paulo, 1988).

6. A. Pereira, *Formação do PCB,1922–28* (Lisbon, 1976), p. 84.

7. E. Pacheco, *O Partido Comunista Brasileiro (1922–64)* (São Paulo, 1984).

8. The so-called 'first republic' in Brazil (1899–1930) was marked by military revolts. The movement of army lieutenants (*tenentes* do exército) rebelled several times in different parts of Brazil in favour of political and social reform. The movement, which gained support even among certain generals, never had a definite political programme. In its first phase, 1922, *tenentismo* expressed a certain degree of liberal ideology. From 1924, the movement incorporated two distinct visions: a radical analysis that defended structural changes in society and the economy, and a liberal variant that only sought political reform. Among the principal names involved in this movement, we find: Joaquim Távora, Juarez Távora, Eduardo Gomes, Miguel Costa (general), Isidoro Lopes (general) and Luis Carlos Prestes.

9. E. Pacheco, *Partido Comunista Brasileiro*, p. 103.

10. The 'Prestes Column' was an armed movement that fought throughout the backlands of Brazil between April 1925 and February 1927. Led by Miguel Costa and Luiz Carlos Prestes, members of the radical faction of *tenentismo*, the 'Prestes Column' travelled some 24,000 kilometres whilst fighting against government troops. In 1929, the Column's leaders exiled themselves in Bolivia. In exile, Prestes criticised himself for letting the Column concentrate overmuch upon the struggle against then president, Arthur Bernardes. He admitted that the movement had lost its meaning, given that the president against which it had fought was no longer in power.

11. E. Pacheco, *O Partido Comunista Brasileiro*, p. 110.

12. M. Zaidan, *O PCB e a Internacional Comunista*, p. 35.

13. J. A. Segatto, *Breve História do PCB*, p. 33.

14. According to E. Pacheco in *O Partido Comunista Brasileiro*, p. 117, '[The] opposition included seven petit bourgeois intellectuals, three small bosses, six artisans, eighteen ex-anarchists, ten of who were workers. They were mainly militants who had recently joined the party, sixteen having affiliated in 1927 and eight in 1926'.

15. J. A. Segatto, *Breve História do PCB*, p. 36.

16. M. Zaidan, *O PCB e a Internacional Comunista*, p. 63.

17. A. Pereira, A. *Formação do PCB*, pp. 133–34.

18. M. Zaidan, *O PCB e a Internacional Comunista*, p. 65.

19. J. A. Segatto, *Breve História do PCB*, p. 39.

20. The presidential election pitted two candidates connected to the dominant oligarchy against each other: Julio Prestes from the government party and Getúlio Vargas from the Liberal Alliance, which represented dissident sectors of the oligarchy but which ended up incorporating other elements, including the urban petit bourgeoisie and sectors of the *tenentista* movement. Júlio Prestes won the election, which like all the others before it, had involved massive fraud on all sides. Though perhaps its leading protagonists might have wished to remain quiet, the participation of popular movements in the elections and the assassination of João Pessoa, Vargas' vice-presidential candidate, ignited a coup de etat.

21. This idea appears frequently in documents of the period. See E. Carone, *O PCB, 1922–43* (São Paulo, 1982), pp. 105–17.

22. Ibid. pp. 234–35. See also D. Pandolfi, *Camaradas e companheiros: história e memória do PCB* (Rio de Janeiro, 1995).

23. See Arquivo de Memória Operária do Rio de Janeiro, *Partido Comunista Brasileiro: Caminhos da Revolução, 1929–35* (São Paulo, 1995), p. 17.

24. Ibid. p. 18.

25. M. Vinhas, *O partidão - a luta por um partido de massas, 1922–74* (São Paulo, 1982), indicates the resistance of Brazilian communists against what they thought to be a top-down intervention.

Index

DATE DUE